T0211231

Lecture Notes in Computer Science 10493

Commenced Publication in 1973
Founding and Former Series Editors:
Gerhard Goos, Juris Hartmanis, and Jan van Leeuwen

More information about this series at http://www.springer.com/series/7410

Simon N. Foley · Dieter Gollmann
Einar Snekkenes (Eds.)

Computer Security – ESORICS 2017

22nd European Symposium on Research in Computer Security
Oslo, Norway, September 11–15, 2017
Proceedings, Part II

Springer

Editors
Simon N. Foley
IMT Atlantique
Rennes
France

Einar Snekkenes
NTNU
Gjøvik
Norway

Dieter Gollmann
Hamburg University of Technology
Hamburg
Germany

ISSN 0302-9743 ISSN 1611-3349 (electronic)
Lecture Notes in Computer Science
ISBN 978-3-319-66398-2 ISBN 978-3-319-66399-9 (eBook)
DOI 10.1007/978-3-319-66399-9

Library of Congress Control Number: 2017949525

LNCS Sublibrary: SL4 – Security and Cryptology

Printed on acid-free paper

This Springer imprint is published by Springer Nature
The registered company is Springer International Publishing AG
The registered company address is: Gewerbestrasse 11, 6330 Cham, Switzerland

Preface

This book contains the papers that were selected for presentation and publication at the 22nd European Symposium on Research in Computer Security, ESORICS 2017, which was held in Oslo, Norway, September 11–15, 2017. The aim of ESORICS is to further the progress of research in computer security by bringing together researchers in the area, by promoting the exchange of ideas with system developers and by encouraging links with researchers in related areas.

The Program Committee accepted 54 papers out of a total of 338 papers that were submitted from 51 different countries, resulting in an acceptance rate of 16%. The accepted papers are drawn from a wide range of topics, including data protection, security protocols, systems, web and network security, privacy, threat modelling and detection, information flow and security in emerging applications such as cryptocurrencies, the Internet of Things, and automotive. The 120-member Program Committee, assisted by a further 334 external reviewers, reviewed and discussed the papers online over a period of 8 weeks, writing a total of 1015 reviews for authors.

ESORICS 2017 would not have been possible without the contributions of the many volunteers who freely gave their time and expertise. We would like to thank the members of the Program Committee and the external reviewers for their substantial work in evaluating the papers. We would also like to thank the ESORICS Steering Committee and its Chair Pierangela Samarati; the Organisation Chair Laura Georg; the Publicity Chair Cristina Alcaraz; the Workshop Chair Sokratis Katsikas and all workshop co-chairs, who organized the workshops co-located with ESORICS. We would like to especially thank the sponsors of this year's ESORICS conference: the Center for Cyber and Information Security, COINS Research School, KPMG, the Norwegian University of Science and Technology NTNU, Oxford University Press, and the Research Council of Norway.

Finally, we would like to express our thanks to the authors who submitted papers to ESORICS. They, more than anyone else, are what makes this conference possible.

July 2017

Simon Foley
Dieter Gollmann
Einar Snekkenes

Organization

Program Committee

Gail-Joon Ahn	Arizona State University, USA
Alessandro Armando	University of Genoa and Fondazione Bruno Kessler, Italy
Frederik Armknecht	Universität Mannheim, Germany
Michael Backes	CISPA, Saarland University, Germany
Giampaolo Bella	Università di Catania, Italy
Zinaida Benenson	University of Erlangen-Nuremberg, Germany
Elisa Bertino	Purdue University, USA
Carlo Blundo	Università degli Studi di Salerno, Italy
Rainer Boehme	University of Innsbruck, Austria
Colin Boyd	Norwegian University of Science and Technology (NTNU), Norway
Stefan Brunthaler	Paderborn University, Germany
Chris Brzuska	TU Hamburg, Germany
Tom Chothia	University of Birmingham, UK
Sherman S.M. Chow	Chinese University of Hong Kong, Hong Kong, China
Mauro Conti	University of Padua, Italy
Cas Cremers	University of Oxford, UK
Frédéric Cuppens	IMT Atlantique, France
Nora Cuppens-Boulahia	IMT Atlantique, France
Mads Dam	KTH, Sweden
Sabrina De Capitani di Vimercati	Università degli Studi di Milano, Italy
Hervé Debar	Télécom SudParis, France
Roberto Di Pietro	Bell Labs, France
Josep Domingo-Ferrer	Universitat Rovira i Virgili, Spain
Wenliang Du	Syracuse University, USA
Pavlos Efraimidis	Democritus University of Thrace, Greece
Hannes Federrath	University of Hamburg, Germany
Simone Fischer-Hübner	Karlstad University, Sweden
Riccardo Focardi	Università Ca' Foscari, Venice, Italy
Simon Foley	IMT Atlantique, France
Sara Foresti	DI - Università degli Studi di Milano, Italy
Felix Freiling	Friedrich-Alexander-Universität Erlangen-Nürnberg (FAU), Germany
Sibylle Froeschle	University of Oldenburg, Germany
Lenzini Gabriele	SnT/University of Luxembourg, Luxembourg
Joaquin Garcia-Alfaro	Télécom SudParis, France
Dieter Gollmann	TU Hamburg, Germany

Jeff Yan	Lancaster University, UK
Meng Yu	University of Texas at San Antonio, USA
Ben Zhao	University of Chicago, USA
Jianying Zhou	Singapore University of Technology and Design, Singapore
Haojin Zhu	Shanghai Jiao Tong University, China

Additional Reviewers

Abdullah, Lamya
Abramova, Svetlana
Agudo, Isaac
Ah-Fat, Patrick
Ahlawat, Amit
Akowuah, Francis
Albanese, Massimiliano
Alimohammadifar, Amir
Alpirez Bock, Estuardo
Alrabaee, Saed
Ambrosin, Moreno
Aminanto, Muhamad Erza
Anand, S Abhishek
Angles-Tafalla, Carles
Aonzo, Simone
Arlitt, Martin
Arriaga, Afonso
Assaf, Mounir
Atzeni, Andrea
Auerbach, Benedikt
Avizheh, Sepideh
Bacis, Enrico
Bag, Samiran
Bajramovic, Edita
Ban Kirigin, Tajana
Barber, Simon
Bardin, Sebastien
Bastys, Iulia
Basu, Hridam
Baumann, Christoph
Belgacem, Boutheyna
Berbecaru, Diana
Besson, Frédéric
Bilzhause, Arne
Biondi, Fabrizio
Bkakria, Anis

Blanc, Gregory
Blanco-Justicia, Alberto
Blochberger, Maximilian
Bogaerts, Jasper
Boschini, Cecilia
Bossen, Jannek Alexander Westerhof
Boureanu, Ioana
Bours, Patrick
Brandt, Markus
Brooks, Tyson
Bruni, Alessandro
Buhov, Damjan
Bullee, Jan-Willem
Burkert, Christian
Bursuc, Sergiu
Busch, Marcel
Butin, Denis
Böhm, Fabian
Calzavara, Stefano
Carmichael, Peter
Ceccato, Mariano
Chen, Jie
Chen, Long
Chen, Rongmao
Cheng, Peng
Cheval, Vincent
Choi, Rakyong
Ciampi, Michele
Clark, Daniel
Cohn-Gordon, Katriel
Costa, Gabriele
Costache, Anamaria
Costantino, Gianpiero
Courtois, Nicolas
Dai, Tianxiang
Dantas, Yuri Gil

Davies, Gareth T.
De Benedictis, Marco
De Gaspari, Fabio
De Meo, Federico
Dehnel-Wild, Martin
Del Pino, Rafaël
Desmet, Lieven
Drogkaris, Prokopios
Drosatos, George
Duman, Onur
Duong, Tuyet
Fan, Xiong
Farràs, Oriol
Fernandez, Carmen
Ferrari, Stefano
Fett, Daniel
Fleischhacker, Nils
Freeman, Kevin
Frey, Sylvain
Gadyatskaya, Olga
Garratt, Luke
Gazeau, Ivan
Genc, Ziya A.
Geneiatakis, Dimitris
Georgiopoulou, Zafeiroula
Gervais, Arthur
Giustolisi, Rosario
Gogioso, Stefano
Gonzalez-Burgueño, Antonio
Gritti, Clémentine
Groll, Sebastian
Grosz, Akos
Guan, Le
Guanciale, Roberto
Gunasinghe, Hasini
Gyftopoulos, Sotirios
Gérard, François
Götzfried, Johannes
Hallgren, Per
Hamann, Tobias
Hammann, Sven
Han, Jinguang
Harborth, David
Hartmann, Lukas
Hassan, Sabri
Hatamian, Majid

Haupert, Vincent
Hausknecht, Daniel
Herrera, Jordi
Hils, Maximilian
Huang, Yi
Hummer, Matthias
Ilia, Panagiotis
Iovino, Vincenzo
Islam, Morshed
Issel, Katharina
Iwaya, Leonardo
Jackson, Dennis
Jansen, Kai
Jansen, Rob
Jhawar, Ravi
Joensen, Ólavur Debes
Johannes, Schickel
Jonker, Hugo
Jourdan, Jacques-Henri
Jäschke, Angela
Kalloniatis, Christos
Kandias, Miltiadis
Katz, Jonathan
Kerstan, Henning
Kersten, Rody
Kintis, Panagiotis
Kohls, Katharina
Kokolakis, Spyros
Kountouras, Athanasios
Kuchta, Veronika
Kälber, Sven
Köstler, Johannes
Labunets, Katsiaryna
Lacoste, Marc
Lagorio, Giovanni
Lai, Russell W.F.
Lain, Daniele
Lal, Chhagan
Laperdrix, Pierre
Laporte, Vincent
Latzo, Tobias
Lazrig, Ibrahim
Learney, Robert
Lehmann, Anja
Leontiadis, Iraklis
Li, Hanyi

Li, Ximeng
Liang, Kaitai
Lin, Fuchun
Liu, Ximeng
Liu, Ximing
Lochbihler, Andreas
Lopez, Jose M.
Lu, Yuan
Lyvas, Christos
Ma, Jack P.K.
Mace, John
Madi, Taous
Magkos, Emmanouil
Mahgoub Yahia Mohamed, Muzamil
Majumdar, Suryadipta
Maragoudakis, Manolis
Marino, Francesco
Marktscheffel, Tobias
Martinez, Sergio
Marx, Matthias
Mateus, Paulo
McEvoy, Richard
Mehnaz, Shagufta
Melicher, William
Mercaldo, Francesco
Meyer, Maxime
Mizera, Andrzej
Momeni, Sadaf
Moore, Nicholas
Muehlberg, Jan Tobias
Müeller, Johannes
Mukherjee, Subhojeet
Mulamba, Dieudonne
Mylonas, Alexios
Navarro-Arribas, Guillermo
Nemati, Hamed
Neupane, Ajaya
Neven, Gregory
Nieto, Ana
Ntouskas, Teo
Nuñez, David
Olesen, Anders Trier
Oqaily, Momen
Ordean, Mihai
Önen, Melek
Palmarini, Francesco

Pang, Jun
Panico, Agostino
Parra-Arnau, Javier
Pasquini, Cecilia
Patachi, Stefan
Pelosi, Gerardo
Petit, Christophe
Petrovic, Slobodan
Pham, Vinh
Pitropakis, Nikolaos
Preuveneers, Davy
Pridöhl, Henning
Puchta, Alexander
Pulls, Tobias
Pérez-Solà, Cristina
Rafnsson, Willard
Rajagopalan, Siva
Rakotondravony, Noelle
Rao, Fang-Yu
Rausch, Daniel
Rekleitis, Evangelos
Reuben, Jenni
Ribes-González, Jordi
Ricci, Sara
Richthammer, Hartmut
Rios, Ruben
Rosa, Marco
Roth, Christian
Roux-Langlois, Adeline
Rupprecht, David
Saracino, Andrea
Satvat, Kiavash
Saxena, Neetesh
Schiffman, Joshua
Schmid, Lara
Schmitz, Christopher
Schmitz, Guido
Schneider, David
Schnitzler, Theodor
Schoepe, Daniel
Schoettle, Pascal
Schroeder, Dominique
Schwarz, Oliver
Sciarretta, Giada
Senf, Daniel
Sgandurra, Daniele

Shah, Ankit
Shahandashti, Siamak
Sheikhalishahi, Mina
Shen, Jian
Shirani, Paria
Shirvanian, Maliheh
Shrestha, Prakash
Shulman, Haya
Simo, Hervais
Siniscalchi, Luisa
Sjösten, Alexander
Skrobot, Marjan
Smith, Geoffrey
Soria-Comas, Jordi
Soska, Kyle
Spolaor, Riccardo
Stamatelatos, Giorgos
Stergiopoulos, George
Strackx, Raoul
Stübs, Marius
Su, Tao
Sy, Erik
Sänger, Johannes
Tai, Raymond K.H.
Tasch, Markus
Tasidou, Aimilia
Taubmann, Benjamin
Taylor, Gareth
Tesfay, Welderufael
Tolomei, Gabriele
Truderung, Tomasz
Trujillo, Rolando
Tsalis, Nikolaos
Tupakula, Uday
Vallini, Marco
Van Acker, Steven
Van Bulck, Jo
van Ginkel, Neline
Van Rompay, Cédric
Vanbrabant, Bart
Vasilopoulos, Dimitrios

Vazquez Sandoval, Itzel
Venkatesan, Sridhar
Venturi, Daniele
Veseli, Fatbardh
Vielberth, Manfred
Virvilis, Nick
Vissers, Thomas
Volkamer, Melanie
Wang, Jiafan
Wang, Minqian
Wang, Qinglong
Wang, Wei
Wang, Xiuhua
Weber, Alexandra
Weber, Michael
Wikström, Douglas
Wolter, Katinka
Wong, Harry W.H.
Woo, Maverick
Xu, Jun
Xu, Ke
Xu, Peng
Yaich, Reda
Yang, S.J.
Yautsiukhin, Artsiom
Yesuf, Ahmed Seid
Ying, Kailiang
Yu, Jiangshan
Yu, Xingjie
Zamyatin, Alexei
Zavatteri, Matteo
Zhang, Liang Feng
Zhang, Mengyuan
Zhang, Yuqing
Zhao, Yongjun
Zhao, Yunwei
Zhou, Lan
Zhu, Fei
Ziener, Daniel
Zimmer, Ephraim

Contents – Part II

Contents – Part I

Automated Analysis of Equivalence Properties for Security Protocols Using Else Branches

Ivan Gazeau[✉] and Steve Kremer[✉]

LORIA, Inria Nancy - Grand-Est, Villers-lès-Nancy, France
{ivan.gazeau,steve.kremer}@inria.fr

Abstract. In this paper we present an extension of the AKISS protocol verification tool which allows to verify equivalence properties for protocols with else branches, i.e., disequality tests. While many protocols are represented as linear sequences or inputs, outputs and equality tests, the reality is often more complex. When verifying equivalence properties one needs to model precisely the error messages sent out when equality tests fail. While ignoring these branches may often be safe when studying trace properties this is not the case for equivalence properties, as for instance witnessed by an attack on the European electronic passport. One appealing feature of our approach is that our extension re-uses the saturation procedure which is at the heart of the verification procedure of AKISS as a black box, without need to modify it. As a result we obtain the first tool that is able verify equivalence properties for protocols that may use xor and else branches. We demonstrate the tool's effectiveness on several case studies, including the AKA protocol deployed in mobile telephony.

1 Introduction

Security protocols are communication protocols that rely on cryptographic primitives, e.g. encryption, or digital signatures to ensure security properties, e.g., confidentiality or authentication. Well-known examples of security protocols include TLS [23], Kerberos [28] and IKE [27]. These protocols are extremely difficult to design as they must ensure the expected security property, even if the network is under control of an attacker: each message sent on the network can be intercepted by the attacker, each received message potentially originates from the attacker, and the attacker may manipulate all received data by applying functions on it. Moreover, as several sessions of the protocol may be executed concurrently, one must consider all possible interleavings, and the attacker may even participate in some of these sessions as a legitimate participant. As a result,

The research leading to these results has received funding from the European Research Council (ERC) under the European Union's Horizon 2020 research and innovation program (grant agreements No. 645865-SPOOC), as well as from the French National Research Agency (ANR) under the project Sequoia.

© Springer International Publishing AG 2017
S.N. Foley et al. (Eds.): ESORICS 2017, Part II, LNCS 10493, pp. 1–20, 2017.
DOI: 10.1007/978-3-319-66399-9_1

a security proof by hand is extremely tricky as it would require to explore all of the possible cases.

A successful approach to discover weaknesses in such protocols, or show their absence is to use dedicated formal verification tools. A variety of tools for analysing protocols exist: ProVerif [14], Scyther [21], Maude-NPA [24], Tamarin [31], AVISPA [7], ... These tools were generally initially developed for verifying trace properties of rather simple protocols. In the last years there has been a large body of works for extending these tools to handle more general properties and more complex protocols.

Most tools were designed for analysing trace properties: a protocol cannot reach a bad state, e.g., a state where the attacker knows a secret value. Many important security properties are however stated in terms of *indistinguishability*: can an attacker distinguish two protocols? For instance *real-or-random* secrecy states the indistinguishability of two protocols, one outputting at the end of the run the "real" secret, used within the protocol, while the other protocol outputs a freshly generated random secret. Similarly, *unlinkability* can be modeled by the adversary's inability to distinguish two sessions run by the same party form two sessions run by two different parties. More generally, strong flavours of secrecy [12], anonymity and unlinkability [5], as well as vote privacy [22], are expressed as indistinguishability. This notion is naturally modelled in formal models through behavioural equivalences in cryptographic process calculi, such as the spi [3] and applied pi calculus [1]. During the last years, several specific tools for checking such equivalences have been developed [15,17,32], or existing tools have been extended to handle these properties [10,13,30].

Similarly, many tools were designed to verify protocols that have a simple, linear execution flow: many protocol specification languages allow several roles in parallel, each consisting of a sequence of input, or output actions with the possibility to check equality between parts of messages. More complex protocols do however require branching, and allow to react differently according to whether an equality test holds or not (rather than just halting if a test fails). As demonstrated by an attack on the European electronic passport [20], taking into account the exact error message in case a test fails may be crucial: the fact that in some versions of the passport output different error messages allowed an attacker to trace a given passport. In this paper we will extend the AKISS tool with the ability to verify protocols that have else branches.

An Overview of the AKISS Tool. The AKISS tool [15] is a verification tool for checking indistinguishability properties. Møre precisely, it verifies trace equivalence in a replication free (i.e., considering a bounded number of sessions) and positive (no else branches) fragment of the applied pi calculus. The tool allows a wide range of cryptographic primitives that are specified by the means of a user defined equational theory. The tool is correct for any equational theory that can be oriented into a convergent rewrite system which has the finite variant property and was shown to guarantee termination on any subterm convergent equational theory. This class of theories include classical cryptographic primitives such as encryption, signatures and hashes, but also non-interactive zero knowledge proofs. Moreover, even though termination is not guaranteed protocols relying on blind signatures or trapdoor commitments have been successfully analysed. In addition, a recent extension of AKISS provides support for protocols that use the exclusive or (xor) operation [8].

In a nutshell, AKISS proceeds as follows. Protocols are translated into first-order Horn clauses. Next, the set of Horn clauses is saturated using a dedicated Horn clause resolution procedure. This saturated set of clauses provides a finite representation of all reachable states of the protocols, of the intruder knowledge and equality tests that hold on the protocol outputs. These equality tests are used by the adversary to distinguish protocols, i.e., its aim is to find a test which holds on one protocol, but not the other. Next, AKISS uses this saturated set of Horn clauses to decide trace equivalence when the processes specifying the protocol are determinate (the precise definition of determinacy will be given in Sect. 2). On general processes, AKISS may over- and under-approximate trace equivalence, as discussed in [15].

Our Contributions. Our main contribution is to extend the AKISS tool to allow more complex protocols which allow non trivial else branches. An interesting point of our approach is that we do not need to modify the saturation procedure of AKISS: we only need to saturate positive processes (in which disequality tests are ignored). The algorithm is based on the following simple observation: whenever a trace is not executable because of the failure of a disequality test $t_1 \neq t_2$, the saturation of the process in which $t_1 \neq t_2$ is replaced by $t_1 = t_2$ computes all the traces that fail to execute on the original process (due to this particular disequality test). This test can then be confronted to the other process that we expect to be trace equivalent.

From a theoretical point, given that the saturation of AKISS was shown to terminate on any subterm convergent rewrite system our algorithm provides, *en passant*, a new decidability result for the class of subterm convergent equational theories for protocols with else branches, generalising the results of [11,19] that do not allow else branches and the result of [16], which only applies to a particular equational theory. Moreover, the result is modular, in the sense that if we generalize the saturation procedure to other equational theories support for else branches comes for "for free". From a more practical point, we have implemented our new procedure in the AKISS tool and demonstrate its effectiveness on several case studies. Hence, we provide the first tool that is able to handle protocols that require both xor and else braches: in addition to previously analysed protocols, such as the private authentication protocol and the BAC protocol implemented in the European passport, this allows us to analyse protocols using xor, such as the AKA protocol [4] used in 3G and 4G mobile telephony, as well as xor-based RFID protocols with key update (which requires an else branch for the modelling). A previous analysis of the AKA protocol with ProVerif replaced the use of xor with encryption [6]. Replacing xor by encryption may however miss attacks as it was shown by Ryan and Schneider in [29].

Related Work. We consider two kinds of tools: those restricted to a bounded number of sessions (as in our work) and those that allow for an unbounded number of sessions. The first kind of tools includes the SPEC and APTE tools. SPEC [32] allows to verify a symbolic bisimulation: it only supports a fixed equational theory (encryption, signature, hash and mac) and has no support for else branches. The APTE tool also supports a fixed equational theory (similar to SPEC), but allows else branches. Both tools are not restricted to determinate processes. Tools that allow protocol verification for an unbounded number of sessions include ProVerif, Maude NPA and Tamarin. Given that the underlying problem is undecidable when the number of sessions is not bounded, termination is not guaranteed. Each of these tools allows for else branches user-defined equational theories, but ProVerif and Tamarin do not include support for xor. While Maude NPA does support xor in principle, termination fails even on simple examples [30]. We may also note that the support for else branches in Maude NPA is very recent [34]. Finally, each of these three tools checks a more fine-grained relation that trace or observational equivalence, called *diff-equivalence*: this equivalence requires both processes to follow the same execution flow and is too fine-grained for some applications.

Full proofs, omitted because of lack of space, are available in [25].

2   A Formal Model for Security Protocols

In this section we introduce our formal language for modelling security protocols. Messages are modelled as *terms* and equipped with an *equational theory*, that models the algebraic properties of cryptographic primitives. The protocols themselves will be modelled in a process calculus similar to the applied pi calculus [1]: protocol participants are modelled as processes and their interaction through message passing.

2.1   Term Algebra

Terms are built over the following atomic messages: the set of *names* $\mathcal{N}$, that is partitioned into *private names* $\mathcal{N}_{\mathsf{prv}}$ and *public names* $\mathcal{N}_{\mathsf{pub}}$; the set of *message variables* $\mathcal{X}$, denoted x, y, ...; the set of parameters $\mathcal{W} = \{\mathsf{w}_1, \mathsf{w}_2, \ldots\}$. Private names are used to model fresh, secret values, such as nonces or cryptographic keys. Public names represent publically known values such as identifier and are available to the attacker. Parameters allow the adversary to refer to messages that were previously output.

We consider a *signature* Σ, i.e., a finite set of function symbols together with their arity. Function symbols of arity 0 are called *constants*. Given a signature Σ and a set of atoms $\mathcal{A}$ we denote by $\mathcal{T}(\Sigma, \mathcal{A})$ the set of *terms*, defined as the smallest set that contains $\mathcal{A}$ and is closed under application of function symbols. We denote by $vars(t)$ the set of *variables* occurring in a term t. A *substitution* is a function from variables to terms, lifted to terms homomorphically. The application of a substitution σ to a term u is written $u\sigma$, and we denote $dom(\sigma)$

its *domain*, i.e. $dom(\sigma) = \{x \mid \sigma(x) \neq x\}$. We denote the identity substitution whose domain is the empty set by $\emptyset$.

We equip the signature Σ with an *equational theory* E: an equational theory is defined by a set of equations $M = N$ with $M, N \in \mathcal{T}(\Sigma, \mathcal{X})$. The equational theory E induces an equivalence relation $=_E$ on terms: $=_E$ is the smallest equivalence on terms, which contains all equations $M = N$ in E, is closed under application of function symbols and substitutions of variables by terms.

Example 1. As an example we model the exclusive-or operator. Let $\Sigma_{\text{xor}} = \{\oplus, 0\}$, and the equational theory E_{xor} defined by the following equations:

$$x \oplus x = 0 \qquad x \oplus (y \oplus z) = (x \oplus y) \oplus z \qquad x \oplus 0 = x \qquad x \oplus y = y \oplus x$$

Additional primitives, e.g. pairs, symmetric and asymmetric encryptions, signatures, hashes, *etc*, can be modelled by extending the signature and equational theory.

Example 2. Let $\Sigma_{\text{xor}}^+ = \Sigma_{\text{xor}} \uplus \{\langle \cdot, \cdot \rangle, \mathsf{proj}_1, \mathsf{proj}_2, \mathsf{h}\}$, and $\mathsf{E}_{\text{xor}}^+$ be defined by extending E_{xor} with the following equations: $\mathsf{proj}_1(\langle x, y \rangle) = x$, and $\mathsf{proj}_2(\langle x, y \rangle) = y$.

The symbol $\langle \cdot, \cdot \rangle$ models pairs and proj_1 and proj_2 projections of the first and second element. The unary symbol h models a cryptographic hash function. Let $AUTN = \langle SQN_N \oplus AK, MAC \rangle$, then we have $\mathsf{proj}_1(AUTN) \oplus AK =_E SQN_N$.

As we build on the AKISS tool [8,15] we suppose in the following that the signature and equational theory are an extension the theory of exclusive or, i.e., Σ is such that $\Sigma_{\text{xor}} \subseteq \Sigma$ and $\mathsf{E} = \mathsf{E}_{\text{xor}} \cup \{M = N \mid M, N \in \mathcal{T}(\Sigma \smallsetminus \Sigma_{\text{xor}}, \mathcal{X})\}$. and that E can be oriented into a convergent rewrite system which has the finite variant property. This allows to model a wide range of cryptographic primitives, including symmetric and asymmetric encryption, digital signatures, hash functions and also zero knowledge proofs or blind signatures. We refer the reader to [15] for the precise technical definitions, which are not crucial for this paper.

2.2   Process Calculus

Syntax. Let $\mathcal{C}h$ be a set of public channel names. A *protocol* is a set of processes and a *process* is generated by the following grammar:

$$
\begin{array}{lll}
P, P', P_1, P_2 :: = & \mathbf{0} & \text{null process} \\
& \mathbf{in}(c, x).P & \text{input} \\
& \mathbf{out}(c, t).P & \text{output} \\
& [s = t].P & \text{test}^= \\
& [s \neq t].P & \text{test}^{\neq}
\end{array}
$$

where $x \in \mathcal{X}, s, t \in \mathcal{T}(\Sigma, \mathcal{N} \cup \mathcal{X})$, and $c \in \mathcal{C}h$.

A receive action $\mathbf{in}(c, x)$ acts as a binding construct for the variable x and *free* and *bound variables* of processes are defined as usual. We also assume that each variable is bound at most once. A process is *ground* if it does not contain any free variables. For sake of conciseness, we sometimes omit the null process at the end of a process.

Following [15], we only consider a minimalistic core calculus. Given that we only consider a bounded number of sessions (i.e., a process calculus without replication) and that we aim at verifying trace equivalence, parallel composition, denoted $P \parallel Q$ can be added as syntactic sugar to denote the set of all interleavings at a cost of an exponential blow-up (see [15]). Similarly, we can encode conditionals: a process

$$\textbf{if } t_1 = t_2 \textbf{ then } P \textbf{ else } Q$$

can be encoded by the set $\{[t_1 = t_2].P, [t_1 \neq t_2].Q\}$. As usual we omit **else** Q when $Q = 0$ and sometimes write **if** $t_1 \neq t_2$ **then** P **else** Q for **if** $t_1 = t_2$ **then** Q **else** P. This will ease the specification of protocols and improve readability. A protocol typically consists of the set of all possible interleavings.

Example 3. As an example consider a simplified version of the AKA protocol, which is vulnerable to replay attacks, depicted in Fig. 1. The network (NS) and mobile station (MS) share a secret key k_{IMSI}. NS generates a nonce r which it sends to MS together with $f(k_{IMSI}, r)$ where f models a message authentication code (MAC). MS verifies the MAC: if successful it sends another MAC based on function f_2 and generates sessions keys from r and k_{IMSI}; otherwise, it sends an error message. NS checks whether the received message is the expected MAC or

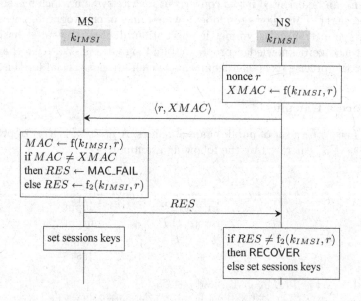

Fig. 1. A simplified version of the AKA protocol

the error message. In case the MAC is received it generates the sessions keys; otherwise it starts a recovery protocol.

Using the additional operators introduced above, we can model the protocol as $MS \parallel NS$ where

$$NS \triangleq \mathbf{out}(c, \langle r, f(k_{IMSI}, r)\rangle).\mathbf{in}(c, x).\mathbf{if}\ x \neq f_2(k_{IMSI}, r)\ \mathbf{then}\ \mathbf{out}(c, \mathsf{RECOVER})$$
$$MS \triangleq \mathbf{in}(c, y).\ \mathbf{if}\ y \neq f(k_{IMSI}, r)\ \mathbf{then}\ \mathbf{out}(c, \mathsf{MAC\_FAIL})\ \mathbf{else}\ \mathbf{out}(c, f_2(k_{IMSI}, r))$$

If we skip the actions $[x \neq f_2(k_{IMSI}, r)].\mathbf{out}(c, \mathsf{RECOVER})$, the protocol corresponds to a set of 12 processes which include, for instance, the 4 following processes.

$\mathbf{out}(c, \langle r, f(k_{IMSI}, r)\rangle).\mathbf{in}(c, y).[y \neq f(k_{IMSI}, r)].\mathbf{out}(c, \mathsf{MAC\_FAIL}).\mathbf{in}(c, x)$
$\mathbf{out}(c, \langle r, f(k_{IMSI}, r)\rangle).\mathbf{in}(c, y).[y = f(k_{IMSI}, r)].\mathbf{out}(c, f_2(k_{IMSI}, r)).\mathbf{in}(c, x)$
$\mathbf{out}(c, \langle r, f(k_{IMSI}, r)\rangle).\mathbf{in}(c, y).\mathbf{in}(c, x).[y \neq f(k_{IMSI}, r)].\mathbf{out}(c, \mathsf{MAC\_FAIL})$
$\mathbf{out}(c, \langle r, f(k_{IMSI}, r)\rangle).\mathbf{in}(c, y).\mathbf{in}(c, x).[y = f(k_{IMSI}, r)].\mathbf{out}(c, f_2(k_{IMSI}, r))$

Note that since a test is an invisible action, there is no need to consider traces where a test does not strictly precede its following action. The correctness of this optimization is proven in [15].

Semantics. In order to define the operational semantics of our process calculus we define the notion of *message deduction*. Intuitively, message deduction models which new messages an intruder can construct from previously learnt messages. The messages output during a protocol execution are presented by a *frame*:

$$\varphi = \{w_1 \mapsto t_1, \ldots, w_\ell \mapsto t_\ell\}$$

A frame is a substitution $dom(\varphi) = \{w_1, \ldots, w_\ell\}$. An intruder may refer to the ith term through the parameter w_i.

Definition 1. *Let φ be a frame, $t \in \mathcal{T}(\Sigma, \mathcal{N})$ and $R \in \mathcal{T}(\Sigma, \mathcal{N}_{\mathsf{pub}} \cup dom(\varphi))$. We say that t is deducible from φ using R, written $\varphi \vdash_R t$, when $R\varphi =_E t$.*

Intuitively, an attacker can deduce new messages by applying function symbols in Σ to public names (in $\mathcal{N}_{\mathsf{pub}}$) and terms he already knows (those in φ). The term R is called a *recipe*.

A *configuration* is a pair (P, φ) where P is a ground process, and φ is a frame. The operational semantics is defined as a labelled transition relation on configurations $\xrightarrow{\ell}$ where ℓ is either an input, an output, or an unobservable action **test** defined as follows:

$$\text{RECV}\ (\mathbf{in}(c, x).P, \varphi) \xrightarrow{\mathsf{in}(c,R)} (P\{x \mapsto t\}, \varphi)\quad \text{if } \varphi \vdash_R t$$
$$\text{SEND}\ (\mathbf{out}(c, t).P, \varphi) \xrightarrow{\mathsf{out}(c)} (P, \varphi \cup \{w_{|\varphi|+1} \mapsto t\})$$
$$\text{TEST}^=\ ([s = t].P, \varphi) \xrightarrow{\mathsf{test}} (P, \varphi)\qquad \text{if } s =_E t$$
$$\text{TEST}^{\neq}\ ([s \neq t].P, \varphi) \xrightarrow{\mathsf{test}} (P, \varphi)\qquad \text{if } s \neq_E t$$

Intuitively, the labels have the following meaning:

- **in**(c, R) represents the input of a message sent by the attacker on channel c and the message is deduced using recipe R;
- **out**(c) represents the output of a message on channel c (adding the message to the frame);
- **test** represents the evaluation of a conditional (in the equational theory).

When $\ell \neq$ **test** we define $\overset{\ell}{\Rightarrow}$ to be $\xrightarrow{\textbf{test}}^{*} \overset{\ell}{\rightarrow} \xrightarrow{\textbf{test}}^{*}$ and we lift $\overset{\ell}{\rightarrow}$ and $\overset{\ell}{\Rightarrow}$ to sequences of actions. Given a protocol $\mathcal{P}$, we write $(\mathcal{P}, \varphi) \xrightarrow{\ell_1, \ldots, \ell_n} (P', \varphi')$ if there exists $P \in \mathcal{P}$ such that $(P, \varphi) \xrightarrow{\ell_1, \ldots, \ell_n} (P', \varphi')$, and similarly for $\overset{\ell}{\Rightarrow}$.

2.3 Trace Equivalence

The fact that an attacker cannot distinguish two protocols will be modelled through *trace equivalence*. We first define the notion of a test which an attacker may apply on a frame to try to distinguish two processes.

Definition 2. *Let φ be a frame and R_1, R_2 be two terms in $\mathcal{T}(\Sigma, \mathcal{N}_{\text{pub}} \cup dom(\varphi))$. The test $R_1 \overset{?}{=} R_2$ holds on frame φ, written $(R_1 = R_2)\varphi$, if $R_1\varphi =_E R_2\varphi$.*

Trace equivalence of processes P and Q states that any test that holds on process P (after some execution) also holds on process Q after the same execution.

Definition 3 [15]. *A protocol $\mathcal{P}$ is trace included in a protocol $\mathcal{Q}$, denoted $\mathcal{P} \sqsubseteq \mathcal{Q}$, if whenever $(\mathcal{P}, \emptyset) \xrightarrow{\ell_1, \ldots, \ell_n} (P, \varphi)$ and $(R_1 = R_2)\varphi$, then there exists a configuration (Q', φ') such that $(\mathcal{Q}, \emptyset) \xrightarrow{\ell_1, \ldots, \ell_n} (Q', \varphi')$ and $(R_1 = R_2)\varphi'$.*
We say that $\mathcal{P}$ and $\mathcal{Q}$ are equivalent, *written $\mathcal{P} \approx \mathcal{Q}$, if $\mathcal{P} \sqsubseteq \mathcal{Q}$ and $\mathcal{Q} \sqsubseteq \mathcal{P}$.*

This notion of equivalence does not coincide with the usual notion of trace equivalence as defined e.g. in [18]. It is actually coarser and is therefore sound for finding attacks. However, it has been shown that the classical and above defined notions coincide for the class of determinate processes [15].

Definition 4 [15]. *We say that a protocol $\mathcal{P}$ is* determinate *if whenever $(\mathcal{P}, \emptyset) \xrightarrow{\ell_1, \ldots, \ell_n} (P, \varphi)$, and $(\mathcal{P}, \emptyset) \xrightarrow{\ell_1, \ldots, \ell_n} (P', \varphi')$, then for any test $R_1 \overset{?}{=} R_2$, we have that:*

$$(R_1 = R_2)\varphi \text{ if, and only if } (R_1 = R_2)\varphi'.$$

Determinacy of a protocol can be achieved through sufficient syntactic conditions, e.g. enforcing action-determinism [9]: all executions of an action determinate process ensure that we cannot reach a process P where the same action may lead to two different processes, e.g. we forbid the set of processes generated by $(\textbf{out}(c, a).P_1) \parallel ((\textbf{out}(c, b).P_2)$ but allow $(\textbf{out}(c_1, a).P_1) \parallel ((\textbf{out}(c_2, b).P_2)$.

Action-determinism is automatically checked by AKISS. Whenever processes are not determinate, the above equivalence can be used to disprove trace equivalence, i.e., find attacks. The capability of AKISS to under approximate trace equivalence consists in finding a one-to-one mapping between each process of $\mathcal{P}$ and $\mathcal{Q}$ such that the pair of processes, which are determinate by construction, are equivalent. Such an approach is still possible with our procedure. In this paper we develop a procedure which checks trace equivalence on determinate processes and may be used for finding attacks on general processes.

3 Modelling Using Horn Clauses

Our decision procedure is based on a fully abstract modelling of a process in first-order Horn clauses which has initially been developed in [15] and adapted to support the Xor operator in [8]. In this section we recall the main definitions and theorems of [8].

3.1 Predicates

We define the set of *symbolic runs*, denoted $u, v, w, \ldots$, as the set of finite sequences of symbolic labels:

$$u, v, w := \epsilon \mid \ell, w$$

with $\ell \in \{\mathbf{in}(c, t), \mathbf{out}(c), \mathbf{test} \mid t \in \mathcal{T}(\Sigma, \mathcal{N} \cup \mathcal{X}), c \in \mathcal{C}h\}$

The empty sequence is denoted by ϵ. Intuitively, a symbolic run stands for a set of possible runs of the protocol. We denote $u \sqsubseteq_E v$ when u is a prefix (modulo E) of v.

We assume a set $\mathcal{Y}$ of *recipe variables* disjoint from $\mathcal{X}$, and we use capital letters X, Y, Z to range over $\mathcal{Y}$. We assume that such variables may only be substituted by terms in $\mathcal{T}(\Sigma, \mathcal{N}_{\mathsf{pub}} \cup \mathcal{W} \cup \mathcal{Y})$.

We consider four kinds of predicates over which we construct the atomic formulas of our logic. Below, w denotes a symbolic run, R, R' are terms in $\mathcal{T}(\Sigma, \mathcal{N}_{\mathsf{pub}} \cup \mathcal{W} \cup \mathcal{Y})$, and t is a term in $\mathcal{T}(\Sigma, \mathcal{N} \cup \mathcal{X})$. Informally, these predicates have the following meaning (see Fig. 2 for the formal semantics).

$(P_0, \varphi_0) \models r_{\ell_1, \ldots, \ell_n}$ if $(P_0, \varphi_0) \xrightarrow{L_1} (P_1, \varphi_1) \ldots \xrightarrow{L_n} (P_n, \varphi_n)$
     such that $\ell_i =_E L_i \varphi_{i-1}$ for all $1 \le i \le n$

$(P_0, \varphi_0) \models k_{\ell_1, \ldots, \ell_n}(R, t)$ if when $(P_0, \varphi_0) \xrightarrow{L_1} (P_1, \varphi_1) \xrightarrow{L_2} \ldots \xrightarrow{L_n} (P_n, \varphi_n)$
     such that $\ell_i =_E L_i \varphi_{i-1}$ for all $1 \le i \le n$, then $\varphi_n \vdash_R t$

$(P_0, \varphi_0) \models i_{\ell_1, \ldots, \ell_n}(R, R')$ if there exists t such that $(P_0, \varphi_0) \models k_{\ell_1, \ldots, \ell_n}(R, t)$
     and $(P_0, \varphi_0) \models k_{\ell_1, \ldots, \ell_n}(R', t)$

$(P_0, \varphi_0) \models ri_{\ell_1, \ldots, \ell_n}(R, R')$ if $(P_0, \varphi_0) \models r_{\ell_1, \ldots, \ell_n}$ and $(P_0, \varphi_0) \models i_{\ell_1, \ldots, \ell_n}(R, R')$

Fig. 2. Semantics of atomic formulas

- r_w holds when the run represented by w is executable;
- $k_w(R, t)$ holds if whenever the run represented by w is executable, the message t can be constructed by the intruder using the recipe R;
- $i_w(R, R')$ holds if whenever the run w is executable, R and R' are recipes for the same term; and
- $ri_w(R, R')$ is a short form for the conjunction of the predicates r_w and $i_w(R, R')$.

A (ground) atomic formula is interpreted over a pair consisting of a process P and a frame φ, and we write $(P, \varphi) \models f$ when the atomic formula f holds for (P, φ) or simply $P \models f$ when φ is the empty frame. We consider first-order formulas built over the above atomic formulas and the usual connectives (conjunction, disjunction, negation, implication, existential and universal quantification). The semantics is defined as expected, but the domain of quantified variables depends on their type: variables in $\mathcal{X}$ may be mapped to any term in $\mathcal{T}(\Sigma, \mathcal{N})$, while recipe variables in $\mathcal{Y}$ are mapped to recipes, i.e. terms in $\mathcal{T}(\Sigma, \mathcal{N}_{\mathsf{pub}} \cup \mathcal{W})$.

3.2   Statements and Saturation

We now identify a subset of the formulas, which we call *statements*. Statements will take the form of Horn clauses, and we shall be mainly concerned with them.

Definition 5 [15]. *A statement is a Horn clause of the form $H \Leftarrow k_{u_1}(X_1, t_1), \ldots, k_{u_n}(X_n, t_n)$ where:*

- $H \in \{r_{u_0}, k_{u_0}(R, t), i_{u_0}(R, R'), ri_{u_0}(R, R')\}$;
- $u_0, u_1, \ldots, u_n$ *are symbolic runs such that $u_i \sqsubseteq_E u_0$ for any $i \in \{1, \ldots, n\}$;*
- $t, t_1, \ldots, t_n \in \mathcal{T}(\Sigma, \mathcal{N} \cup \mathcal{X})$;
- $R, R' \in \mathcal{T}(\Sigma, \mathcal{N}_{\mathsf{pub}} \cup \mathcal{W} \cup \mathcal{Y})$; *and*
- $X_1, \ldots, X_n$ *are distinct variables from $\mathcal{Y}$.*

Lastly, $vars(t) \subseteq vars(t_1, \ldots, t_n)$ when $H = k_{u_0}(R, t)$.

In the definition above, we implicitly assume that all variables are universally quantified, i.e. all statements are ground. By abuse of language we sometimes call σ a grounding substitution for a statement $H \Leftarrow B_1, \ldots, B_n$ when σ is grounding for each of the atomic formulas $H, B_1, \ldots, B_n$.

In [15], the authors present a saturation-based procedure sat that given a ground process P produces a fully abstract set of solved statements $\mathsf{sat}(P)$. The procedure starts by translating P and the equational theory into a finite set of statements. Then this set is saturated by applying Horn clause resolution rules. Finally, if the procedure terminates (which is guaranteed for subterm convergent equational theories), the set of solved statements K produced by the saturation procedure is a sound and complete abstraction of P: any statement that holds on the protocol P is a logical consequence of K. The notion of logical consequence is formalised through the (infinite) set $\mathcal{H}_e(K)$.

Definition 6 [8]. *Given a set K of statements, $\mathcal{H}(K)$ is the smallest set of ground facts that is closed under the rules of Fig. 3. We define $\mathcal{H}_e(K)$ to be the smallest set of ground facts containing $\mathcal{H}(K)$ and that is closed under the rules of Fig. 4.*

CONSEQ
$$\frac{f = \left(H \Leftarrow B_1, \ldots, B_n\right) \in K \qquad \sigma \text{ grounding for } f \qquad B_1\sigma \in \mathcal{H}(K), \ldots, B_n\sigma \in \mathcal{H}(K)}{H\sigma \in \mathcal{H}(K)}$$

EXTEND
$$\frac{\mathsf{k}_u(R,t) \in \mathcal{H}(K)}{\mathsf{k}_{uv}(R,t) \in \mathcal{H}(K)}$$

Fig. 3. Rules of $\mathcal{H}(K)$

REFL $\dfrac{}{\mathsf{i}_w(R,R) \in \mathcal{H}_e(K)}$
CONG $\dfrac{\mathsf{i}_w(R_1,R_1'), \ldots, \mathsf{i}_w(R_n,R_n') \in \mathcal{H}_e(K) \quad \mathsf{f} \in \Sigma}{\mathsf{i}_w(\mathsf{f}(R_1, \ldots R_n), \mathsf{f}(R_1', \ldots R_n')) \in \mathcal{H}_e(K)}$

EXT $\dfrac{\mathsf{i}_u(R,R') \in \mathcal{H}_e(K)}{\mathsf{i}_{uv}(R,R') \in \mathcal{H}_e(K)}$
EQ. CONSEQ. $\dfrac{\mathsf{k}_w(R,t) \in \mathcal{H}(K) \quad \mathsf{i}_w(R,R') \in \mathcal{H}_e(K)}{\mathsf{k}_w(R',t) \in \mathcal{H}_e(K)}$

Fig. 4. Rules of $\mathcal{H}_e(K)$

Theorem 1 [8]. *Let $K = \mathsf{sat}(P)$ for some ground process P. We have that:*

- *$P \models f$ for any $f \in K \cup \mathcal{H}_e(K)$;*
- *If $(P, \emptyset) \xrightarrow{L_1, \ldots, L_n} (Q, \varphi)$ then*
  1. *$\mathsf{r}_{L_1\varphi, \ldots, L_n\varphi} \in_E \mathcal{H}_e(K)$;*
  2. *if $\varphi \vdash_R t$ then $\mathsf{k}_{L_1\varphi, \ldots, L_n\varphi}(R,t) \in_E \mathcal{H}_e(K)$;*
  3. *if $\varphi \vdash_R t$ and $\varphi \vdash_{R'} t$, then $\mathsf{i}_{L_1\varphi, \ldots, L_n\varphi}(R,R') \in_E \mathcal{H}_e(K)$.*

4 Algorithm

We first introduce a few notations and preliminary definitions. We start by introducing the *recipe function*: its goal is to associate a sequence of labels to a symbolic run and a positive process (in the labels we replace the input terms of the symbolic run by the recipes used to deduce them).

Definition 7. *Given a positive process P and a symbolic run $\ell_1, \ldots, \ell_k$ we define a function $\mathsf{rec}_P(\ell_1 \ldots \ell_k) = L_1 \ldots L_k$ where*

$$L_i = \begin{cases} \boldsymbol{in}(c, R) \text{ if } \ell_i = \boldsymbol{in}(c,t) \text{ and } \mathsf{k}_{\ell_1 \ldots \ell_{i-1}}(R,t) \in \mathcal{H}(\mathsf{sat}(P) \cup K) \\ \ell_i \qquad \text{otherwise} \end{cases}$$

and $K = \{\mathsf{k}_\epsilon(X_i, x_i) \mid 1 \le i \le n, vars(\ell_1, \ldots, \ell_k) = \{x_1, \ldots x_n\}, X_1, \ldots X_n \in \mathcal{Y}$ are pairwise distinct and fresh$\}$.

Note that several functions may satisfy the specification of this definition. Here we consider any possible implementation of this specification, e.g., the one presented in [15]. The complicated case is when the symbolic label is an input: in that case we need to retrieve the corresponding recipe in $\mathsf{sat}(P)$. As the symbolic labels may not be closed we simply enhance $\mathsf{sat}(P)$ with a recipe X for each variable x (the set K).

To check equivalence between processes we rely on the notion of *reachable identity test* written $\mathsf{RId}_{L_1,\ldots,L_k}(R, R')$ where $L_1,\ldots,L_k$ are (not necessarily ground) labels and R, R' (not necessarily ground) recipes. For a test t we denote by $\mathsf{lbl}(t)$ its sequence of labels $L_1,\ldots,L_k$. For commodity reason, we also define a reachability test as: $\mathsf{R}_{L_1,\ldots,L_k} \hat{=} \mathsf{RId}_{L_1,\ldots,L_k}(0,0)$.

Given a ground process P and a test t the predicate $\mathsf{Ver}_P(t)$ checks whether t holds in P. We define $\mathsf{Ver}_P(\mathsf{RId}_{L_1,\ldots,L_k})(R, R')$ to hold when $(P, \emptyset) \xrightarrow{L_1\sigma,\ldots,L_k\sigma} (P', \varphi)$ and $(R\sigma = R'\sigma)\varphi$ where σ is a bijection from $vars(L_1,\ldots,L_k,R,R')$ to fresh names $\{c_1,\ldots,c_n\}$. Finally the predicate is lifted to protocols and we write $\mathsf{Ver}_{\mathcal{P}}(t)$ for $\exists P \in \mathcal{P}. \mathsf{Ver}_P(t)$.

We note that when $\mathsf{Ver}_P(t)$ holds and P is positive then $\mathsf{Ver}_P(t\sigma)$ holds for any σ, as equality is stable by substitution. However, a disequality may hold when instantiated by distinct fresh names, while a different instantiation may make the test fail.

Next we define the process $\mathbf{rm}^{\neq}(P)$ which simply removes all inequality tests.

Definition 8. *Let P be a process such that $P = P_1.[t_1 \neq t_1']. P_2.\ldots.[t_m \neq t_m'].P_{m+1}$ and $P_1.P_2.\ldots.P_{m+1}$ is positive. We define the process $\mathbf{rm}^{\neq}(P) \hat{=} P_1.\ldots.P_{m+1}$.*

Given a process P we define the set of reachable identity tests $\mathsf{Test}^{\mathsf{RId}}(P)$.

$\mathsf{Test}^{\mathsf{RId}}(P) = \{\mathsf{RId}_{L_1,\ldots,L_k}(R, R') \mid$
$\quad \mathsf{ri}_{\ell_1,\ldots,\ell_k}(R, R') \Leftarrow \mathsf{k}_{u_1}(X_1, x_1), \ldots, \mathsf{k}_{u_n}(X_n, x_n) \in \mathsf{sat}(\mathbf{rm}^{\neq}(P)),$
$\quad L_1,\ldots,L_k = (\mathsf{rec}_P(\ell_1,\ldots,\ell_k))\sigma$ where $\sigma = \{X_j \mapsto X_{\min\{i \mid x_i = x_j\}} \mid 1 \leq j \leq k\},$
$\quad \mathsf{Ver}_P(\mathsf{RId}_{L_1,\ldots,L_k}(R, R'))\}$

We also define reachability tests $\mathsf{Test}^{\mathsf{R}}(P)$ for a process P:

$$\mathsf{Test}^{\mathsf{R}}(P) = \{t \mid t \in \mathsf{Test}^{\mathsf{RId}}(P), \quad \exists L_1,\ldots,L_k, \ t = \mathsf{R}_{L_1,\ldots,L_k'}\}$$

We note that we can only apply the sat function to positive processes. If P was already a positive process $\mathsf{Ver}_P(t)$ would hold for each of the constructed tests because of the soundness of sat. However, in general, $\mathsf{Ver}_{\mathbf{rm}^{\neq}(P)}(t)$ may hold while $\mathsf{Ver}_P(t)$ does not hold, which is why we explicitly test the validity of t in P.

In [15] it is shown that given a positive ground process P and a positive determinate protocol $\mathcal{Q}$, we have that

$$P \sqsubseteq_t \mathcal{Q} \quad \text{iff} \quad \forall t \in \mathsf{Test}^{\mathsf{RId}}(P). \mathsf{Ver}_{\mathcal{Q}}(t)$$

which can be used to check trace inclusion between protocols (as $\mathcal{P} \sqsubseteq_t \mathcal{Q}$ iff $\forall P \in \mathcal{P}.P \sqsubseteq_t \mathcal{Q}$) and trace equivalence (as $\mathcal{P} \approx_t \mathcal{Q}$ iff $\mathcal{P} \sqsubseteq_t \mathcal{Q}$ and $\mathcal{Q} \sqsubseteq_t \mathcal{P}$). This result does however not hold for processes with disequality tests.

Example 4. Let $P = \mathbf{in}(c,x).\mathbf{out}(c,a)$ and $Q = \mathbf{in}(c,x).[x \neq a].\mathbf{out}(c,a)$. We have that $P \not\approx_t Q$ but all tests that hold on P also hold on Q (and vice-versa). In particular $\mathsf{R}_{\mathbf{in}(c,X).\mathbf{out}(c)} \in \mathsf{Test}^{\mathsf{R}}(P)$ holds in Q, as $(Q, \emptyset) \xrightarrow{\mathbf{in}(c,c_1).\mathbf{out}(c)} (0, \varphi)$ for a fresh name c_1.

Whenever a test holds on $\mathbf{rm}^{\neq}(P)$ but not on P, it must be that a disequality test in P did not hold. We therefore compute the *complement* of a process, which is the set of positive processes which transforms a disequality into an equality and removes remaining disequalities.

Definition 9. *Let P be a process such that*

$$P = P_1.[t_1 \neq t_1'].P_2.\ldots.[t_m \neq t_m'].P_{m+1}$$

and $P_1.P_2.\ldots.P_{m+1}$ is positive. We define the complement of P, $\mathsf{comp}(P)$ to be the set

$$\{P_1.P_2.\ldots.P_{i-1}.[t_i = t_i'].P_i.\ldots.P_m.P_{m+1} \mid 1 \leq i \leq m\}$$

We easily see that we have the following property.

Lemma 1. *Let P be a process and t a test. We have that*

$$\mathsf{Ver}_{\mathbf{rm}^{\neq}(P)}(t) \ \textit{iff either} \ \mathsf{Ver}_P(t) \, \textit{or} \, \mathsf{Ver}_{\mathsf{comp}(P)}(t)$$

Lastly, before explaining our algorithm we need to introduce the *shrink* operator on processes which is used in conjunction with the Inst operators on sequences of labels. Given a process P and a sequence of labels lbl we define a process that only executes instances of lbl (up to test actions which are ignored). In the following we suppose that variables in $\mathcal{Y}, \mathcal{X}$ and names in $\mathcal{N}$ are totally ordered by an order $<_{\mathcal{Y}}, <_{\mathcal{X}}$ resp. $<_{\mathcal{N}}$.

Definition 10. *Let P be a process, lbl a sequence of labels, σ an increasing bijection from $vars(lbl) \cap \mathcal{Y}$ to a set of fresh and pairwise distinct term variable in $\mathcal{X}$, θ an increasing bijection from $vars(lbl) \cap \mathcal{Y}$ to a set of fresh and pairwise distinct names in $\mathcal{N}$, such that $(P, \emptyset) \xrightarrow{L_1\theta, \ldots, L_n\theta} (P', \varphi)$. Let lbl_0 be the subsequence of lbl obtained by removing all **test** labels. We define $\mathsf{shrink}_{lbl}(P)$ as $\mathsf{shr}^{\emptyset}_{lbl_0}(P)$ where*

- $\mathsf{shr}^v_{lbl}([s \sim t].P) = [s \sim t].\mathsf{shr}^v_{lbl}(P) \quad for \sim \in \{=, \neq\}$
- $\mathsf{shr}^v_{\mathbf{out}(c) \cdot lbl}(\mathbf{out}(c,t).P) = \mathbf{out}(c,t).\mathsf{shr}^v_{lbl}(P),$
- $\mathsf{shr}^v_{\mathbf{in}(c,R) \cdot lbl}(\mathbf{in}(c,x).P)$
  $= \mathbf{in}(c_s, X_1\sigma).\ldots.\mathbf{in}(c_s, X_n\sigma).\mathbf{in}(c,x).[x = R\varphi\theta^{-1}\sigma].\mathsf{shr}^{vars(R) \cup v}_{lbl\sigma}(P)$
  where $vars(R) \cap \mathcal{Y} \setminus v = \{X_1, \ldots, X_n\}$ and $X_i < X_{i+1}$,
- 0 *otherwise*

and c_s is a dedicated channel not appearing in P.

Note that the function shrink depends on the chosen bijection but this only changes the process up to alpha renaming. Note that we cannot force an execution to contain an instance of a particular recipe R. The inserted test $[x = R\varphi\sigma]$ only ensures that the input of x is produced by some recipe R' such that $(R\sigma = R')\varphi$. We therefore additionally add inputs $\mathbf{in}(c_s, x_i)$ which will allow us to retrieve instance $R\theta$ of R that yields the same protocol message as R.

Definition 11. *Let lbl, lbl' be sequences of labels. If*

$$\mathbf{in}(lbl) = \mathbf{in}(c_s, R_1^1)\ldots\mathbf{in}(c_s, R_1^{n_1}).\mathbf{in}(c_1, R_1).\ldots.\mathbf{in}(c_s, R_1^k)\ldots\mathbf{in}(c_s, R_k^{n_k}).\mathbf{in}(c_k, R_k);$$

$$\mathbf{in}(lbl') = \mathbf{in}(c_1, R_1').\ldots.\mathbf{in}(c_k, R_k') \text{ and } vars(R_i') \setminus \bigcup_{j<i} vars(R_j') = \{X_i^1, \ldots, X_i^{n_i}\}$$

with $X_i^j < X_i^{j+1}$ then we define $\mathsf{Inst}(lbl, lbl') = \{X_i^j \mapsto R_i^j \mid 1 \le i \le k, 1 \le j \le n_i\}$. Otherwise $\mathsf{Inst}(lbl, lbl') = \bot$.

Example 5. Let $P = \mathbf{in}(c, x).\mathbf{out}(c, 0)$ be a process and $lbl = \mathbf{in}(c, \langle Y, 0\rangle), \mathbf{out}(c)$ a sequence of labels. Consider two bijections $\sigma = \{Y \mapsto y\}$ and $\theta = \{Y \mapsto a\}$. The process $\mathsf{shrink}_{lbl}(P) = \mathbf{in}(c_s, y).\mathbf{in}(c, x).[x = \langle y, 0\rangle].\mathbf{out}(c, 0)$ allows to identify the recipes Y such that $(P, \varphi) \xrightarrow{lbl\sigma} (P', \varphi')$. Indeed, assume $\mathsf{Test}^R(\mathsf{shrink}_{lbl}(P))$ contains $r = \mathsf{R}_{\mathbf{in}(c_s, h(0)).\mathbf{in}(c,\langle h(0),0\rangle.\mathbf{out}(c))}$, then $r\tau = \mathsf{R}_{\mathbf{in}(c,\langle h(0),0\rangle.\mathbf{out}(c))}$ where $\tau = \mathsf{Inst}(lbl, \mathsf{lbl}(r))$ is such that $\mathsf{Ver}_{r\tau}(P)$ and $\mathsf{lbl}(r\tau)$ is an instance of l.

The algorithm $\mathtt{Equiv}$ for verifying trace equivalence on determinate processes is detailed in Algorithm 1.

Theorem 2. *Let $\mathcal{P}$ and $\mathcal{Q}$ be two determinate protocols. Then we have that*

$$\mathcal{P} \approx_t \mathcal{Q} \quad \textit{iff} \quad \mathtt{Equiv}(\mathcal{P} \approx_t \mathcal{Q})$$

The algorithm proceeds as follows. For each $P \in \mathcal{P}$ we check whether all traces of P are included in $\mathcal{Q}$. For this we compute the set Rid_P of reachable identity tests that hold in P and that need to be checked on $\mathcal{Q}$. We next pick a test rid from the set (and remove it from the set, denoted $rid := \mathrm{pop}(Rid_P)$) and check whether this test holds for some process Q in $\mathcal{Q}$. If this is not the case we violate trace equivalence. Otherwise we need to perform additional checks: indeed even if the test rid holds, an instance of rid might not hold on Q but still hold in P. Consider the following simple example:

$$P = \mathbf{in}(c, x).\mathbf{out}(c, a) \qquad Q_1 = \mathbf{in}(c, x).[x \ne a].\mathbf{out}(c, a)$$
$$\mathcal{Q} = \{Q_1, Q_2\} \qquad\qquad Q_2 = \mathbf{in}(c, x).[x = a].\mathbf{out}(c, a)$$

Algorithm 1. Decision procedure for $\mathcal{P} \approx_t \mathcal{Q}$

Function Check$(P, \mathcal{Q})$
   Input: Process P, protocol $\mathcal{Q}$
   Output: Boolean

   $Rid_P := \mathsf{Test}^{\mathsf{Rld}}(P)$;
   while $Rid_P \neq \emptyset$ do
      $rid := \mathrm{pop}(Rid_P)$;
      $S_Q := \{Q \in \mathcal{Q} \mid \mathsf{Ver}_Q(rid)\}$;
      if $S_Q = \emptyset$ then return false;
      $Q := \mathrm{pop}(S_Q)$;
      foreach $\overline{Q} \in \mathsf{comp}(\mathsf{shrink}_{\mathsf{lbl}(rid)}(Q))$ do
         $R_{\overline{Q}} := \{r \in \mathsf{Test}^{\mathsf{R}}(\overline{Q}) \mid |\mathsf{lbl}(r)| = |\overline{Q}|\}$;
         foreach $r \in R_{\overline{Q}}$ do
            $\sigma := \mathsf{Inst}(\mathsf{lbl}(r), \mathsf{lbl}(rid))$;
            if $\mathsf{Ver}_P(\mathsf{R}_{\mathsf{lbl}(rid)}\sigma)$ then $Rid_P := Rid_P \cup \{rid\sigma\}$;
   return true

Function Equiv$(\mathcal{P}, \mathcal{Q})$
   Input: Protocols $\mathcal{P}, \mathcal{Q}$
   Output: Boolean

   return $\bigwedge_{P \in \mathcal{P}}$ Check$(P, \mathcal{Q}) \wedge \bigwedge_{Q \in \mathcal{Q}}$ Check$(Q, \mathcal{P})$

Note that $P \approx_t \mathcal{Q}$. Let $rid = \mathsf{Rld}_{\mathsf{in}(c,X).\mathsf{out}(c)}(a, a)$. This test holds in Q_1. However, the more instantiated test $\mathsf{Rld}_{\mathsf{in}(c,a).\mathsf{out}(c)}(a, a)$ would not hold. (Note that the test may actually only fail because reachability is violated.) We therefore need to identify the instances of rid Q_1 that do not hold on Q_1. The process $\mathsf{shrink}_Q(\mathsf{lbl}(rid))$ defines the process that only verifies instances of rid. Computing its complement defines the processes that verify the instances of rid that are not verified by Q: in our example we would identify the test $r = \mathsf{R}_{\mathsf{in}(c,a).\mathsf{out}(c)}$, as computing the complement transforms $[x \neq a]$ into $[x = a]$. Finally, we check whether r is verified by P. If this is the case, we add the more instantiated test $\mathsf{Rld}_{\mathsf{in}(c,a).\mathsf{out}(c)}(a, a)$ to the set Rid_P of tests to be checked. We note that the fact that Q_1 does not verify r, but P does is not yet a violation of trace equivalence: another trace in $\mathcal{Q}$ may well verify the instantiated test. In our example, indeed the process Q_2 verifies $\mathsf{Rld}_{\mathsf{in}(c,a).\mathsf{out}(c)}(a, a)$.

Theorem 2 above ensures partial correctness, i.e., soundness and completeness. We now state that total correctness only depends on the termination of sat.

Theorem 3. *If procedure* sat *terminates then procedure* Equiv *terminates.*

As it was shown in [15], termination of sat is ensured for a wide class of subterm convergent equational theories. While sat may not terminate in generalon other theories such as xor, or blind signatures, the tool does terminate in practice on a wide range of examples [8,15] (and Theorem 2 ensures the correctness of the result).

5   Implementation and Case Studies

5.1   The AKISS Tool

In addition to parallel composition $P \parallel Q$ and conditionals AKISS also supports non-deterministic choice $P + +Q$, sequences $P :: Q$ and phases $P \gg Q$, which are convenient for defining complex scenarios under which we analyse protocols. A sequence $P :: Q$ contains all sequences of a trace of P followed by a trace of Q while the set of traces for a phase $P \gg Q$ contains all traces made of the beginning of a trace of P followed by a full trace of Q.

We model unlinkability for two sessions in each of the protocols below as follows:

$$P_A^1 \gg P_A^2 \approx P_A^1 \gg P_B^2$$

The attacker first interacts with a first session of protocol P executed by A, denoted P_A^1. Then, in a new phase he interacts with a second session of the protocol, which is either executed by A (process P_A^2) or by B (process P_A^2). The protocol P satisfies unlinkability if the two scenarios cannot be distinguished. Note that the use of the phase operator is preferable to the sequential composition, as an attacker may not be able to finish the first session completely before starting the second session.

The implementation of the tool and the files corresponding to our case studies are freely available at https://github.com/akiss/.

5.2   The AKA Protocol

Unlike the simplified version of AKA described in Fig. 1, the actual AKA protocol [25] provides a mechanism against replay attacks. In addition to the mac value, both the network and the mobile station store a counter SQN used as a timestamps: each time the network station starts a session with a same mobile station, it sends in addition to the random value and the mac an obfuscated message $SQN \oplus k_{IMSI}$ containing the incremented value of the counter. The mobile stores the maximum value which has been received. If the received value is not strictly greater than this maximum, the mobile sends a synchronization error message. Otherwise it updates the stored value.

Unlinkability is modelled as explained above: in a first session a mobile station A interacts with the network station and in a second session either mobile A or mobile B interact with the network station. The AKISS tool does not allow for comparison of integer. Instead we just check that the sent value was not the same as a previous one. Therefore during the first phase, since there was no SQN value sent to the mobile there is no need to perform a check while in the second session of the mobile A (in the first scenario) we check that the new SQN value is distinct from the first time.

Using the AKISS tool we find the (previously known) attack consisting of observing the first phase and sending the network station's message of the first phase in the second one: if the second phase is with the same mobile station then it sends a synchronization error message while if its another mobile station it sends a mac error message. Running our tool on a 30 core Intel(R) Xeon(R) CPU E5-2687W v3 @ 3.10 GHz, the attack is found in 3 min.

5.3   Unlinkability on Some Other Protocols

We also analysed the Basic Access Control (BAC) protocol [26], the Private Authentication Protocol (PAP) [2] and two RFID protocols [33]: LAK and SLK.

All these protocols use else branches to send error messages except for the LAK RFID protocol. However, even though this protocol does not contain branches, the scenarios required for expressing unlinkability does requires the use of an else branch for the key update. Indeed, when a session succeeds, the key is updated for the next session, while the previous key is reused in case of failure. This results into an *if then else* structure. Finally, for the SLK and LAK protocols where both the tag and the reader update their data, the scenarios to consider for two sessions are the following.

$$
\begin{aligned}
Psame \;=\; & ((Tag_{Aa} \parallel Reader_a) \gg (Tag_A \parallel Reader)) \\
& ++ \, ((Tag_A \parallel (Reader_a \gg 0)) :: (Tag_{Au} \parallel Reader)) \\
& ++ \, (((Tag_{Aa} \gg 0) \parallel Reader) :: (Tag_A \parallel Reader_u)) \\
& ++ \, ((Tag_A \parallel Reader) :: (Ttag_{Au} \parallel Reader_u))
\end{aligned}
$$

The roles with index u model the role with a preliminary update **if test then** R **else** R' where R' is R with updated values. As the update test is not defined before all inputs have been received, we introduce R_a for each role R to be the process where the last input and the update test are missing (and moreover the construct $R \gg 0$ allows the adversary to stop that instance of the role even earlier): in this case, the update will not happen anyway. Therefore, our scenario has four cases depending on whether the tag, the reader, both or none have reached the update test or not. The scenario where the instances of the tags corresponds to different tag is similar.

$$
\begin{aligned}
Pdiff \;=\; & ((Tag_A \parallel Reader_a) \gg (Tag_B \parallel Reader)) \\
& ++ \, (((Tag_A \gg 0) \parallel Reader) :: (Tag_B \parallel Reader_u))
\end{aligned}
$$

Note that as we consider a different tag in the second session we do not need to worry whether Tag_A was updated or not.

The AKISS tool establishes the equivalence for PAP in 4s. It finds known attacks on BAC in 1m30, on SLK in 6s and in 7h for LAK. The much longer time for LAK is due to the particular use of xor which leads to complex unifiers.

6   Conclusion

In this paper we present an extension of AKISS which allows automated verification of protocols with else branches. An appealing aspect of our approach is that we do not modify the saturation procedure underlying the AKISS tool. As a result we obtain a new decidability result for the class of subterm convergent equational theories and an effective automated analysis tool. We have been able to analyse several protocols including the AKA protocol, and RFID protocols which require both support for xor and else branches.

References

1. Abadi, M., Fournet, C.: Mobile values, new names, and secure communication. In: 28th Symposium on Principles of Programming Languages (POPL 2001), pp. 104–115. ACM (2001)
2. Abadi, M., Fournet, C.: Private authentication. Theoret. Comput. Sci. **322**(3), 427–476 (2004)
3. Abadi, M., Gordon, A.D.: A calculus for cryptographic protocols: the spi calculus. Inf. Comput. **148**(1), 1–70 (1999)
4. 3GPP: Technical specification group services and system aspects; 3G security; security architecture (release 9). Technical report, Technical Report TS 33.102 V9.3.0, 3rd Generation Partnership Project (2010)
5. Arapinis, M., Chothia, T., Ritter, E., Ryan, M.D.: Analysing unlinkability and anonymity using the applied pi calculus. In: 23rd Computer Security Foundations Symposium (CSF 2010), pp. 107–121. IEEE Computer Society (2010)
6. Arapinis, M., Mancini, L.I., Ritter, E., Ryan, M., Golde, N., Redon, K., Borgaonkar, R.: New privacy issues in mobile telephony: fix and verification. In: 19th Conference on Computer and Communications Security (CCS 2012), pp. 205–216. ACM (2012)
7. Armando, A., et al.: The AVISPA tool for the automated validation of internet security protocols and applications. In: Etessami, K., Rajamani, S.K. (eds.) CAV 2005. LNCS, vol. 3576, pp. 281–285. Springer, Heidelberg (2005). doi:10.1007/11513988_27
8. Baelde, D., Delaune, S., Gazeau, I., Kremer, S.: Symbolic verification of privacy-type properties for security protocols with XOR. In: 30th Computer Security Foundations Symposium (CSF 2017). IEEE Computer Society (2017, to appear)
9. Baelde, D., Delaune, S., Hirschi, L.: Partial order reduction for security protocols. In: 26th International Conference on Concurrency Theory (CONCUR 2015). LIPICS, vol. 42, pp. 497–510. Leibniz-Zentrum für Informatik (2015)
10. Basin, D.A., Dreier, J., Sasse, R.: Automated symbolic proofs of observational equivalence. In: 22nd Conference on Computer and Communications Security (CCS 2015), pp. 1144–1155. ACM (2015)
11. Baudet, M.: Deciding security of protocols against off-line guessing attacks. In: 12th Conference on Computer and Communications Security (CCS 2005), pp. 16–25. ACM (2005)
12. Blanchet, B.: Automatic proof of strong secrecy for security protocols. In: Symposium on Security and Privacy (S&P 2004), pp. 86–100. IEEE Computer Society (2004)

13. Blanchet, B., Abadi, M., Fournet, C.: Automated verification of selected equivalences for security protocols. J. Log. Algebr. Program. **75**(1), 3–51 (2008)
14. Blanchet, B., Smyth, B., Cheval, V.: Automatic Cryptographic Protocol Verifier, User Manual and Tutorial (2016)
15. Chadha, R., Cheval, V., Ciobâcă, Ş., Kremer, S.: Automated verification of equivalence properties of cryptographic protocol. ACM Trans. Comput. Logic **17**(4), 23:1–23:32 (2016). Article no. 23
16. Cheval, V., Comon-Lundh, H., Delaune, S.: Automating security analysis: symbolic equivalence of constraint systems. In: Giesl, J., Hähnle, R. (eds.) IJCAR 2010. LNCS, vol. 6173, pp. 412–426. Springer, Heidelberg (2010). doi:10.1007/978-3-642-14203-1_35
17. Cheval, V., Comon-Lundh, H., Delaune, S.: Trace equivalence decision: negative tests and non-determinism. In: 18th Conference on Computer and Communications Security (CCS 2011), pp. 321–330. ACM (2011)
18. Cheval, V., Cortier, V., Delaune, S.: Deciding equivalence-based properties using constraint solving. Theoret. Comput. Sci. **492**, 1–39 (2013)
19. Chevalier, Y., Rusinowitch, M.: Decidability of equivalence of symbolic derivations. J. Autom. Reason. (2010, to appear)
20. Chothia, T., Smirnov, V.: A traceability attack against e-passports. In: Sion, R. (ed.) FC 2010. LNCS, vol. 6052, pp. 20–34. Springer, Heidelberg (2010). doi:10.1007/978-3-642-14577-3_5
21. Cremers, C.J.F.: The scyther tool: verification, falsification, and analysis of security protocols. In: Gupta, A., Malik, S. (eds.) CAV 2008. LNCS, vol. 5123, pp. 414–418. Springer, Heidelberg (2008). doi:10.1007/978-3-540-70545-1_38
22. Delaune, S., Kremer, S., Ryan, M.D.: Verifying privacy-type properties of electronic voting protocols. J. Comput. Secur. **17**(4), 435–487 (2009)
23. Dierks, T., Rescorla, E.: The transport layer security (TLS) protocol version 1.1. RFC 4346, Internet Engineering Task Force (2008)
24. Escobar, S., Meadows, C., Meseguer, J.: Maude-NPA: cryptographic protocol analysis modulo equational properties. In: Aldini, A., Barthe, G., Gorrieri, R. (eds.) FOSAD 2007-2009. LNCS, vol. 5705, pp. 1–50. Springer, Heidelberg (2009). doi:10.1007/978-3-642-03829-7_1
25. Gazeau, I., Kremer, S.: Automated analysis of equivalence properties for security protocols using else branches (extended version). Research report, Inria Nancy - Grand Est (2017). https://hal.inria.fr/hal-01547017
26. Machine readable travel documents. Doc 9303, International Civil Aviation Organization (ICAO) (2008)
27. Kaufman, C., Hoffman, P., Nir, Y., Eronen, P.: Internet key exchange protocol version 2 (ikev2). RFC 7296, Internet Engineering Task Force (2014)
28. Neuman, C., Hartman, S., Raeburn, K.: The kerberos network authentication service (v5). RFC 4120, Internet Engineering Task Force (2005)
29. Ryan, P.Y.A., Schneider, S.A.: An attack on a recursive authentication protocol. A cautionary tale. Inf. Process. Lett. **65**(1), 7–10 (1998)
30. Santiago, S., Escobar, S., Meadows, C., Meseguer, J.: A formal definition of protocol indistinguishability and its verification using maude-NPA. In: Mauw, S., Jensen, C.D. (eds.) STM 2014. LNCS, vol. 8743, pp. 162–177. Springer, Cham (2014). doi:10.1007/978-3-319-11851-2_11
31. Meier, S., Schmidt, B., Cremers, C., Basin, D.: The TAMARIN prover for the symbolic analysis of security protocols. In: Sharygina, N., Veith, H. (eds.) CAV 2013. LNCS, vol. 8044, pp. 696–701. Springer, Heidelberg (2013). doi:10.1007/978-3-642-39799-8_48

32. Tiu, A., Dawson, J.: Automating open bisimulation checking for the spi-calculus. In: 23rd Computer Security Foundations Symposium (CSF 2010), pp. 307–321. IEEE Computer Society (2010)
33. van Deursen, T., Radomirovic, S.: Attacks on RFID protocols. IACR Cryptology ePrint Archive, 2008:310 (2008)
34. Yang, F., Escobar, S., Meadows, C.A., Meseguer, J., Santiago, S.: Strand spaces with choice via a process algebra semantics. In: 18th International Symposium on Principles and Practice of Declarative Programming (PPDP 2016), pp. 76–89. ACM (2016)

Quantifying Web Adblocker Privacy

Arthur Gervais[1]([⊠]), Alexandros Filios[1], Vincent Lenders[2], and Srdjan Capkun[1]

[1] ETH Zurich, Zurich, Switzerland
arthur.gervais@inf.ethz.ch
[2] Armasuisse, Thun, Switzerland

Abstract. Web advertisements, an integral part of today's web browsing experience, financially support countless websites. Meaningful advertisements, however, require behavioral targeting, user tracking and profile fingerprinting that raise serious privacy concerns. To counter privacy issues and enhance usability, adblockers emerged as a popular way to filter web requests that do not serve the website's main content. Despite their popularity, little work has focused on quantifying the privacy provisions of adblockers.

In this paper, we develop a quantitative framework to compare the privacy provisions of adblockers objectively. For our methodology, we introduce several privacy metrics that capture not only the technical web architecture but also the underlying corporate institutions of the problem across time and geography.

Using our framework, we quantify the web privacy implications of 12 ad-blocking software combinations and browser settings on 1000 websites on a daily basis over a timespan of three weeks (a total of 252'000 crawls). Our results highlight a significant difference among adblockers regarding filtering performance, in particular, affected by the applied configurations. Our experimental results confirm that our framework provides consistent results and hence can be used as a quantitative methodology to assess other configurations and adblockers further.

1 Introduction

Online advertising provides a viable way to support online businesses that offer content free of charge to their users, such as news, blogs and social networks. To achieve targeted and hence more effective advertising however, advertisers and tracking companies record user browsing behavior, e.g. pages viewed, searches conducted, products purchased [8,14,20,25,33]. Such techniques are known as *online profiling* and have raised significant privacy concerns because online user profiles can be used to infer private sensitive information and user interests [10, 11,23,27].

Adblockers aim to improve the user experience and privacy by eliminating undesired advertising content, as well as preventing the leakage of sensitive user information towards third-party servers. The most well-known adblocker solutions are browser extensions such as *Ghostery* or *Adblock Plus* which suppress unnecessary requests to third-party advertisements and tracking servers, thereby

© Springer International Publishing AG 2017
S.N. Foley et al. (Eds.): ESORICS 2017, Part II, LNCS 10493, pp. 21–42, 2017.
DOI: 10.1007/978-3-319-66399-9_2

limiting the risk of data leakage towards these servers. Recently, we have experienced a proliferation of adblocker browser extensions in the wild which might be due to users' privacy concerns and awareness about online profiling as well as due to the increasingly intrusive advertisements. According to Mozilla and Google usage statistics [2,4], already more than thirty million surfers are actively using a browser with the Adblock Plus extension enabled. In a recent measurement study [29], researchers show that 22% of the most active users are using the Adblock Plus adblocker while surfing the Web.

Despite the popularity of adblocking tools, surprisingly little research has been performed to understand how well adblocking actually improves the privacy of its users. While the methods employed in advertisement and tracking and their privacy implications have been well researched in the literature [13,19,21,28], the protection that adblockers offer, has not been investigated that much in the literature. Works such as [9,18,29,32] analyze ablockers's performance, however the impact of user privacy is not in the main scope of these studies, as they focus on the effectiveness of the adblocker's implementations and the usage in the wild. Understanding how adblockers affect user privacy is fundamental to their use, because it not only provides feedback to the users, but also helps at correctly using and configuring those systems. Adblockers rely on complex filter configurations in the form of blacklisted URLs and regular expressions, and as we show in this paper, existing adblockers are not necessarily configured by default to provide the best privacy protection to their users.

Our goal in this work is to define a framework and associated metrics to assess the web privacy level that web adblockers provide. We address this problem by developing a quantitative model to compare adblocker filtering performance across various privacy dimensions. Our model includes simple count metrics to third-parties, but also considers more advanced metrics on the level of organizations (legal entities) and countries as well as their relationships. Our primary aim is to provide a methodology, not to conduct a large-scale analysis. While related work with large-scale analysis has focused on one time instant, we provide a daily analysis over several weeks to understand the temporal dynamics of the web.

We have developed a testbed system which allows us to repetitively browse the same Web sites in a systematic way and classify the number of HTTP requests that go to first and third parties without any classification errors. We evaluate 12 different browser profile configurations in our testbed, capturing different adblocker instances and combinations of desktop/mobile user client agents. During three weeks, we surfed on a daily basis the Alexa's top 500 global sites and 500 randomly selected sites and analyzed how different configurations influence these privacy metrics. Because our primary goal is to define the framework to assess the privacy level, we do not attempt to test all extensions, nor to distinguish among anti-tracking tools and adblockers. Our configurations confirm that the metrics provided consistent results and hence can be used to assess other configurations and adblockers further.

Our results show that the usage of adblockers provides a significant improvement in terms of user privacy. However, the degree of protection is highly depending on the configuration. For example, by default Ghostery does not block any third-party requests and Adblock Plus still allows a significant amount of requests to third parties. These results are consistent for the desktop and the mobile user agents. When increasing the level of protection in Ghostery and Adblock Plus however, these tools manage to effectively suppress requests to third-parties and thus improve the privacy. Except for Google Inc. which still receives around 50% of third-party requests because it hosts relevant content not related to advertisement and tracking, the amount of third-party requests towards the other top ten companies in our experiments is only 2.6% of the total amount that would result when surfing without an adblocker.

Our contributions in this paper can be summarized as follows:

- We provide a quantitative methodology to objectively compare the filtering performance of web adblockers.
- We capture the temporal evolution of adblocker filtering performances and study the differences between mobile and desktop devices, as well as the impact of the *do not track* header. Our methodology further allows to measure the influence of other parameters (e.g. third-party cookies) on adblocker filtering performance.
- Beyond the domain of the third parties, our model takes into account the underlying legal entities, their corresponding geographical locations as well as their relationships.
- Using our model, we quantify the privacy of 12 different adblocker browser profile configurations over 1000 different Web sites for repetitive daily measurements over the duration of 3 weeks and discuss the implications in terms of user protection.

The remainder of the paper is organized as follows. In Sect. 2 we illustrate the objective and functionality of adblockers, while in Sect. 3 we outline our privacy metrics. Section 4 outlines our methodology, Sect. 5 discusses the experimental setup and the results. Section 6 presents the related work and Sect. 7 summarizes our work.

2 Web Tracking and Adblockers Background

This section provides relevant background on third-party tracking in the web and how adblocker browser extensions aim at improving user experience and privacy.

2.1 Third-Party Tracking

When visiting an HTTP-based website on a domain (commonly referred to as first party), the web browser sends an HTTP request to the first-party server that hosts the website and loads the content of the first-party domain. The HTML code of the first party is then able to trigger (without the awareness of the user) further HTTP requests to remote servers (commonly referred to as third parties) in order to load further resources that they host. External resources vary in their format and are applied with different objectives, such as the inclusion of external libraries—e.g. jQuery—that are indispensable for the functionality of the website itself. Further reasons include the promotion of advertising content that can be externally loaded and placed at a pre-allocated space on the website.

This third-party content loading mechanism clearly facilitates the development and deployment of dynamic websites because it allows to use different content providers to load resources that do not need to be served from the first party. However, as shown in previous works [8,20,25,33], HTTP requests to third-parties lead to severe privacy implications because third parties can follow the activity of the users and reveal the pages they are looking at while surfing the web. For example, it has been shown in [14] that dominant players in the market such as Google Inc. are embedded as third-parties in so many web sites that they can follow 80% percent of all web activities. Since the web page content and thus user interests can be inferred by the uploaded requests to the third parties, personal profiles of users can easily be derived and potentially used to discriminate people or spy on their interests and habits without getting noticed by the users.

2.2   Adblocker Browser Extensions

To address the aforementioned implications and challenges, numerous software and hardware-based solutions—commonly referred to as *adblockers*—have been proposed in order to remove or alter the advertising and third party content in a web page. Although there exist multiple ad-blocking methods (e.g. DNS sinkholing, proxies run by internet providers (externally) or by an application on the same client machine, special hardware) we focus in this work on one of the most popular solutions: browser extensions, such as *Ghostery* and *AdblockPlus*.

Adblocker browser extensions use one or more lists that describe the content that is to be allowed (whitelists) or blocked (blacklists) and update those on a regular basis. There are two principal methods how adblockers apply these lists to remove ads/third parties from a web page: One is filtering the resource according to the result of an URL-pattern matching, before this resource is loaded by the web browser. The second consists in hiding loaded content with the use of CSS rules (*element hiding*) within the HTML content. In terms of privacy, filtering the resources before they are requested by the browser is the only effective method because these requests are the ones revealing the activity of the users.

Adblocker browser extensions are very popular by users today and their popularity is continuously on the rise [2,4,29]. However, content providers and advertisers see this trend as a risk to their own business models because they regard the application of theses tools as a way for the comsumers to evade "paying for the content". Juniper Research estimates that digital publishers are going to lose over 27 billion dollars by 2020 due to the use of ad blocking services [3]. There is therefore high pressure by these industries on the developers of adblockers to not blacklist their services. For example, Adblock Plus has introduced in 2011 the concept of "non-intrusive advertising", which basically allows third-party advertisements for ads which do not *disrupt the user's natural reading flow* [1]. However, these practices raise concern in terms of privacy because non-intrusive advertisement services may well perform intensive tracking without falling in this category. We therefore argue that it is important to quantify independently the privacy of these tools as we do in this work.

3   Privacy Model and Metrics

In this section, we introduce our privacy model and the metrics we use in order to quantify the privacy provisions of adblockers.

3.1   Threat Definition

A key issue for a threat model in adblocking is to define which third-parties should be considered as a privacy threat to users. In this work, we consider all third-parties as potential threats irrespective of the type and content of the queries towards these third parties. This approach may arguably seem conservative, but it is practically impossible to exclude for sure any third-party from performing tracking and/or profiling given the multitude of possible mechanisms that are available and continuously invented for fingerprinting and tracking user behavior in the web.

In our notion, the privacy objective of the abblocker is therefore to reduce as many requests as possible towards third parties. Notice here the difference of our threat model definition to the slightly different objective that adblockers such as Adblock Plus have. By default, Adblock Plus aims at improving user satisfaction by minimizing the display of intrusive advertisements which annoy the users while third-party requests to non-disturbing advertisements and tracking services for commercial purposes are considered to be acceptable [1].

3.2   User Tracking Model

We model the tracking of a user U through third parties as undirected graph $G = (E, V)$, where E are edges, and V vertices. A vertex V_S represents a web domain and is connected to another vertex V_T through an edge E, if and only if at least one request has been sent from V_S to V_T. In that case, V_S is the *source* of the request and V_T the *target* of the request.

In the following, we use the term *third-party request* (TPR) to denote the requests that are sent to a target domain T that differs from the source domain S and corresponds to a graph edge E between the nodes V_S and V_T. On the contrary, the requests whose source and target coincide are designated as *first-party requests* (FPR) and are not taken into consideration for the construction of G, since no information leaks to third parties and hence they do not bring about further risks for user's privacy[1]. The source and the target domain are referred to as *first-party domain* (FPD) and *third-party domain* (TPD) and correspond to FPD and TPD graph nodes, V_S and V_T, respectively.

Compared to previous works on third-party traffic characterization [9,13], we augment G by incorporating the ownership of third party domains to their corresponding legal entities, i.e. the organizations who own the different TPDs. Two TPD, belong to the same legal entity if they are registered to the same organization (e.g., doubleclick.net and google-analytics.com both belong to Google Inc.) and are thus combined into one vertex, resulting in a hierarchical graph (cf. Fig. 1). Considering the information flow of third-party requests towards legal entities is particularly important for the scope of privacy because legal entities which own multiple domains can fuse the information they collect from their different domains in order to increase their tracking and profiling coverage, thus resulting in a higher privacy threat to the users.

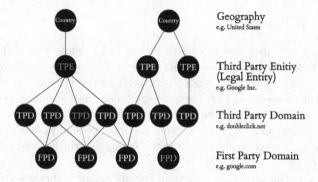

Fig. 1. Graphical representation of our user tracking model. The colored third-party domain (TPD) has a node degree of 3, the colored first-party domain (FPD) has a node degree of 2. The colored third-party entity (TPE) spans all its child TPD nodes and hence has a degree of 3. (Color figure online)

Finally, we further attribute each legal entity to a geographical location (the country where the headquarter of the legal entity is situated) in order to model which countries govern the regulations over which legal entities. This geographical perspective is also of special importance to privacy, because most data privacy laws are specific to local laws of the countries, thus affecting the regulations that apply to the user data that is collected by the legal entities.

3.3   Privacy Metrics

Given the graph representation G of our user tracking model, we evaluate the respective privacy provisions based on the following metrics.

---

[1] Arguably, users also leak private information to first party domains when they visit and interact with those sites, however, since users are visiting these first parties deliberately, the privacy risks are known to the users and controllable without an adblocker.

Degree of First Party Domain. The degree of a FPD node of graph G refers to the number of TPDs that it has sent at least one third-party request to when loading the web page from the FPD. That is, the more edges a FPD node has—or, equivalently, the more third parties loaded by a first-party—the more third parties are able to track the web-browsing history of a user. The FPD node degree is a metric that is commonly used to evaluate the adblocker's performance [32]. However, it is alone not a sufficient metric to capture the impact on user privacy, as it does not represent the structure behind the relationships between FPD and TPD. The following metrics therefore aim at capturing these relationships.

Degree of Third Party Domain. The degree of a TPD node can be directly translated to the number of first-party websites that a particular third party exchanges information with and potentially tracks. Clearly, the more often a third party is accessed over the user's series of websites S_U, the less privacy the user experiences from this particular third party. To exemplify this statement, let's assume that a third party is requested by only one of the first-party websites S_U visited by U. This third party will in this case learn that the user has accessed the respective first party, but has a limited view of their browsing behavior. If the third party, however, is requested by over 80% of the user's visited websites, S_U, the third party will likely be able to recover up to 80% of the web behavior of U.

Degree of Legal Entity. Instead of focusing on domain degrees, the degree of a legal entity reflects the number of third-party domains that belong to a legal entity. Third-party domains such as doubleclick.net and google.com for example are both owned by the same entity Google Inc. Their collusion therefore seems more likely, and affects the privacy of a web user U more significantly, than if both were belonging to two different legal entities. By incorporating the legal relation among third party domains, we therefore capture a more realistic privacy leakage through user web surf activity.

Geographical Location. After having mapped the TPD's to legal entities, we further assign a geographical location to the TPD. This allows our model to capture the geographical distribution of the TPDs and thus infer which geographical countries have for instance the most TPD. The geographical location of a legal entity is defined by the country in which its headquarter resides. Alternatively, we could consider the particular location of the servers as derived from the IP address, but content retrieved from web services is often hosted on distributed caches and content distribution networks and hence the server IP address does not necessarily reflect the country to which the user data is finally sent to. By choosing the headquarter's location, we thus aim at modelling the country in which the privacy laws and regulations will apply to the user data as collected by the third-party.

Graph Density. In addition to the degree metrics outlined above, we consider a metric based on the graph density of G. Since an edge on the graph G represents a partial tracking relationship between a third and a first party, we expect that the denser the graph G, the more information can be retrieved by third parties/can leak to third parties with respect to the browsing behavior of the user. We observe that the more dense G is, the more third parties are likely able to track the user U. The graph density therefore allows to reason about the possible privacy improvements by the respective ad-blocking software. We rely on a common definition of the graph density as:

$$D = \frac{2|E|}{|V|(|V| - 1)} \tag{1}$$

Note however that we cannot achieve the maximum density of 1, because the first parties in G are not directly connected (cf. Definition in Sect. 3.2).

4   Evaluation Methodology

In order to compare the privacy of different adblockers, as well as the influence of different browser settings on their adblocking efficiency, we create different browsing configurations without adblockers, with the Ghostery, and with the Adblock Plus browser extenstions installed in the Firefox browser.

4.1   Considered Browser Profiles

All our experiments are performed on "Linux (Release: Ubuntu 14.04.4 LTS, Version: 4.2.0-35-generic GNU/Linux)" with the version 45.0.1 of the Firefox browser. For Ghostery, we use the browser plugin version 6.1.0 and for Adblock Plus the plugin version 2.7.2. The different protection levels, *Default* or *Max-Protection*, for the two adblockers *AdblockPlus* and *Ghostery* respectively, are achieved through the use of a different combination of blacklists. AdblockPlus and Ghostery store their respective blacklists in the form of URL and CSS regular expressions. The blocking options of AdblockPlus are set through the direct inclusion of blacklists to be applied, while Ghostery's blacklist configuration consists in the selection among a multitude of tracker categories to be blocked. An overview of these configurations is presented in Table 1.

Table 1. AdblockPlus blacklist combination for default and maximal protection level. Ghostery's default and maximal protection correspond to the selection of none and all tracker categories, respectively.

Protection level	Lists			
	AdServers	EasyList	EasyListChina	EasyPrivacy
Default		✓		
Maximal	✓	✓	✓	✓

Modern web browsers such as Firefox further allow to set the *do not track* HTTP header option, to express their personal preference regarding tracking to each server they request content from, thereby allowing recipients of that preference to adjust tracking behavior, accordingly [31]. It remains the sole responsibility of the web server to respect the request of its clients. Almost 10% of the Firefox users have enabled this option on their desktop browsers in 2014 [5]. In order to evaluate to which extend the DNT header has an influence on our proposed metrics we as well include the DNT option in our evaluation.

The usage of mobile devices for web browsing has recently witnessed a steady growth [6]. As a consequence, an ever increasing number of websites has been adapting to the demands of the mobile user agents. Because of the dimensions and the reduced-bandwidth requirements of the mobile devices, the structure and content of the web pages has to be adjusted accordingly and the advertising content could not remain unaffected by these limitations. To investigate the effects of user agents from a privacy-related perspective, we consider this parameter in the design of the experimental evaluation and evaluate several mobile-device instances by setting the HTTP header *User-Agent* accordingly.

Faking a user agent is trivially detectable. Even if some hosts, however, recognized this fact, our results indicate a clear difference between the privacy levels for desktop and mobile user agents and confirm the validity of our metrics, which is the primary goal of our study.

Based on above mentioned criteria, we create 12 browser profiles, U as described in Table 2. Each configuration is defined as a combination of the following parameters:

- Adblocker: No adblocker, Ghostery, or Adblock Plus
- Block policy: maximum or default protection

Table 2. Overview of browser profiles examined

Browser profile	Adblocker	Block policy	DNT	User agent	Legend
Ghostery_Default	Ghostery	Default	No	Desktop	——
Ghostery_MaxProtection	Ghostery	Max	No	Desktop	▬▬
Adblockplus_Default	AdblockPlus	Default	No	Desktop	——
Adblockplus_MaxProtection	AdblockPlus	Max	No	Desktop	▬▬
NoAdblocker	None	-	No	Desktop	——
NoAdblocker_DNT	None	-	Yes	Desktop	▬▬
Ghostery_Default_MUA	Ghostery	Default	No	Mobile	- - -
Ghostery_MaxProtection_MUA	Ghostery	Max	No	Mobile	▪▪▪
Adblockplus_Default_MUA	AdblockPlus	Default	No	Mobile	- - -
Adblockplus_MaxProtection_MUA	AdblockPlus	Max	No	Mobile	▪▪▪
NoAdblocker_MUA	None	-	No	Mobile	- - -
NoAdblocker_DNT_MUA	None	-	Yes	Mobile	▪▪▪

– User agent: mobile or desktop
– Do Not Track (DNT): header enabled or disabled

Throughout the remaining of the paper, we use the following conventions for each browser profile U (cf. Table 2):

– The *color* denotes the adblocker installed.
– The *line width* indicates the protection degree—i.e. default, maximum protection or DNT header.
– Profiles with Mobile User Agent are plotted in *dashed lines*.

4.2 Experimental Setup

The distinction between FPRs and TPRs is crucial in our attempt to precisely quantify the filtering capability for each browser profile, since they define the exact topology of the derived graph G. Passive classification of HTTP requests into first-party and third party requests is not a trivial task given the complex and dynamic structure of Web pages [29]. For this reason, we rely in this work on an active approach in which we collect our own synthetic web surfing traffic with automated web surfing agents. To create a realistic and representative dataset, the agents visits Alexa's top 500 web sites (the 500 domains with the highest incoming traffic in the web) and 500 web sites which are sampled uniformly among Alexa's top 1 million most-visited domains. The motivation for including less popular web sites is to avoid the risk of favoring an adblocker optimized to perform best for the most popular web sites, eventually biasing the experimental results. The overall sample set S of 1000 URLs is retrieved once and kept unchanged throughout the evaluation period, so as to de-correlate any variations of the results between different days.

Since nowadays most web applications are based on asynchronous calls to fetch data, it is insufficient to wait for the DOM to finish rendering to record all resource requests sent from the website to any first or third parties. To collect the complete data and better evaluate the common user browsing behavior, our agent therefore waits 20 s on each website of our sample set S and records any requests sent, before closing and proceeding to the next domain. We visit the same set of web sites every day during three weeks from 28/04/2016 until 19/05/2016. To decouple the experimental conditions from the influence of any time- or location-related effects—i.e. variations of the served content, locale-based personalization—all browser profiles U execute the same crawling routine simultaneously, whilst running on the same machine, thus behind the same IP address, browser and operating system. However, some of the instances are configured to send their requests with a User-Agent HTTP header that corresponds to a mobile device (iPhone with iOS 6[2]), in order to extend our observations for mobile users.

---

[2] User Agent: Mozilla/5.0 (iPhone; CPU iPhone OS 6_0 like Mac OS X) AppleWebKit/ 536.26 (KHTML, like Gecko) Version/6.0 Mobile/10A5376e Safari/8536.25.

In order to record all HTTP requests, we rely on the *Lightbeam* plugin. However in contrast to [32], we do not use Lightbeam to determine the source domain that a request is initiated from and to classify it accordingly as a FPR or a TPR because Lightbeam relies on heuristics that are too error-prone for our purpose. More precisely, the classification of Lightbeam is not always in accordance with our definitions of FPR and TPR, as introduced in Sect. 3. By examining the request logs after a complete crawl cycle and comparing the estimated source to the actual visited domain, two types of false-positive cases (cf. Table 3) arise in Lightbeam:

- **Unrecognized TPRs:** The request is mistakenly considered to be a FPR according to the Lightbeam heuristics, this way "hiding" a TPR edge from the graph.
- **Misclassified TPRs:** The request is correctly found to be a TPR, but not for the correct FPD node, i.e. the one corresponding to the actually crawled domain. The inaccuracy introduced to the graph results from the potential introduction of a bogus FPD node, as well as the false number of TPR edges starting from the correct and the bogus FPD nodes.

As results from the experimental evaluation on the data of one full crawl cycle (1000 visited first parties) and 12 different browser profiles, the misclassified and unrecognized TPRs make up for 2.0%–12.0% and 4.0%–11.0% of the total requests, depending on the respective browser profiles that we define in the following.

Table 3. Examples of misclassified and unrecognized TPRs

	Visited domain	Estimated source	Target
Recognized	wp.pl	wp.pl	facebook.com
Misclassified	wp.pl	facebook.com	fbcdn.net
Unrecognized	wp.pl	facebook.com	facebook.com

We thus modify Lightbeam to account for the currently visited first-party as a priori known by the agent which triggers page visits.

Note that we do not simulate an interaction with the website, e.g., mouse mouvements, scrolling or keystrokes and leave this for future work.

4.3   Classification of Domains to Legal Entities and Locations

We infer the legal entities' domains and locations by inspecting the WHOIS database. The WHOIS database provides information about the holders of Web domains. For each domain, we look up the legal entity that is registered as holder and the country of the holder's address. Note that only a part of the considered domains—accounting for about 60%—could be assigned to a legal entity and followingly to a country. One reason is that WHOIS does not provide sufficient information for all of the domains loaded. Moreover, our parser that allowed for the automated extraction of the entity information depends on a relatively uniform format of the WHOIS documents and as a result, deviations from this format causes information loss.

5   Evaluation

We examine the impact of the configuration parameters on the achieved privacy level using our privacy metrics from Sect. 3.

5.1   Effectiveness of Adblockers at Suppressing Third-Party Requests

Baseline Without Adblocking. Before investigating the effect of the different adblockers, we characterize the FPD node degree with the *NoAdblocker* and *NoAdblocker_MUA* browser profiles as a baseline. Figure 2 shows the cumulative distribution function (CDF) of the FPD node degree of both profiles on a single day (28/04/2016) for the top-ranked 500 domains and the 500 uniformly-selected ones. As can be seen, in both the top 500 and the uniformly selected domains, almost 20% of the websites did not load any third-parties at all. These domains do therefore not impose a privacy risks to the users. On the other hand, more than 80% of the visited domains generate requests to third parties. In general, we can say that the top 500 domains tend to generate more requests to third-parties than the uniformly selected domains, indicating that advertisement and tracking is more likely to happen on popular domains. However, even the randomly selected domains have a quite significant number of third-party requests. While the mean FPD node degree for the top 500 domains and uniformly selected domains are around 17 and 12 respectively, both FPD node degree distributions has a quite long tail. We observe a significant number of FPD node degrees above 100 with one domain in the top 500 exhibiting a degree of 180. These sites raise serious concerns in terms of privacy since each individual third-party request could potentially leak personal information of the visiting users to these third parties.

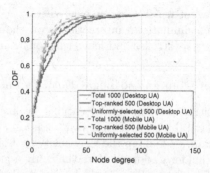

Fig. 2. FPD node degree for the browser profiles *NoAdblocker* (solid line) and *NoAdblocker_MUA* (dotted line) on 28/04/2016.

Comparison of the Different Browser Profiles. To understand the effectiveness of the different adblockers and browser profiles at suppressing requests to third-parties, we plot in Fig. 3 the FPD node degree distribution for all domains as a CDF. Figure 3a shows the node degree distribution averaged over the different days while Fig. 3b represents the standard deviation of the node degree over the same days. Our results indicate the following findings.

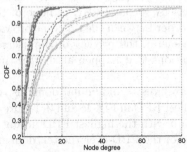
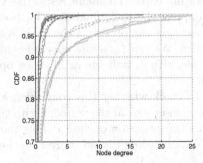

(a) CDF of the average node degree over 3 weeks.

(b) CDF of the standard deviation of the node degree over 3 weeks.

Fig. 3. FPD node degree distribution for all browser profiles. Legend is provided in Table 2.

The worst filtering performance is achieved with the *do not track* HTTP header options (*NoAdblocker_DNT* and *NoAdblocker_DNT_MUA*) and Ghostery in default mode (*Ghostery_Default* and *Ghostery_Default_MUA*). With these browser profile configurations, almost none of the third-party requests are blocked. AdblockPlus (*Adblockplus_Default* and *Adblockplus_Default_MUA* with its default settings has a FPD node degree that is significantly lower than the aforementioned cases, i.e., the browser profiles with the DNT header enabled and Ghostery in its default configuration. Unsurprisingly, the browser profiles that filter the most third parties are those with adblockers configured to a maximum protection level. We observe that *Ghostery_MaxProtection* decreases the mean FPD node degree by approximately 80% compared to *NoAdblocker*. On the other hand, the FDP node degree of Adblock Plus (*AdblockPlus_MaxProtection*) is reduced by almost 75% which is slightly behind the performance of Ghostery, but still significantly better than the default configuration option.

Interesting to note here is the large difference in blocking performance between the different configurations of the same adblockers. This result suggests that the privacy of the users is highly affected by a good configuration of the tools and that by default, these tools still permit a significant portion of the third-party requests.

The standard deviation of the FPD node degree over all domains is shown in Fig. 3b. As we can see, the profiles which have a large FPD node degree tail such as *NoAdblocker*, *NoAdblocker_MUA*, *NoAdblocker_DNT*, *NoAdblocker_DNT_MUA*, and *Ghostery_Default* also exhibit this tail in the standard deviation. However, the profiles which tend to have a small FDP node degree feature a small standard deviation as well.

Temporal Dynamics. To capture the temporal dynamics of third-party requests, we plot in Fig. 4 the FPD over time in the considered period of 3 weeks. Figure 4a and b show the mean FPD for the top 500 domains and the uniformly selected domains respectively. We observe a quite stable temporal evolution over the individual days for both datasets. In particular, in none of the datasets, we can observe a change in relative order between the different browser profiles. We can therefore conclude that in general, the privacy of the users is not sensitive to web site or blacklist optimizations that happen at shorter time scales.

To check whether this conclusion also translates to individual domains, we take a closer look at the domains with the highest FPD in Fig. 4c and d. Figure 4c shows the evolution of the FPD for the domain with the highest FPD in any of the dataset while Fig. 4d represents the mean of the FPD over the ten domains

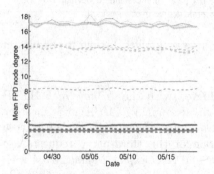

(a) Mean FPD over the top 500 domains.

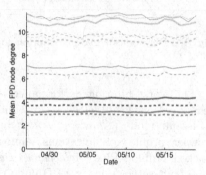

(b) Mean FPD over the 500 uniformly-selected domains.

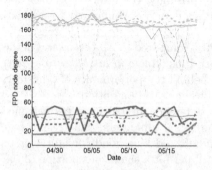

(c) Maximum FPD over all visited domains.

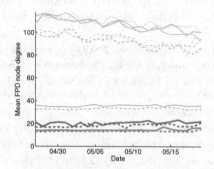

(d) Mean FPD over the 10 domains with the highest FPD from all visited domains.

Fig. 4. Evolution over time of the first party node degree (FPD). Legend is provided in Table 2.

with the highest FPD. We make two interesting observations here. First, the domains with the largest FPDs tend to exhibit a higher variation over different days. In particular, for *Ghostery_Default* and *Ghostery_Default_MUA* in Fig. 4c, the filtering of third-party requests shows a larger fluctuation over time. Also, *AdblockPlus_MaxProtection* and *AdblockPlus_MaxProtection_MUA* has a significantly higher fluctuation for the top domain than on average. Second, the filtering performance of the different browser profiles is more clustered than it is was on average for all the domains. For example, on most days, the performance of *Ghostery_Default* and *Ghostery_Default_MUA* is almost identical to *NoAdblocker*, while those two profiles where significantly outperforming the *NoAdblocker* profile in Fig. 4a and b. These two observations indicate that these domains with a high FPD score could be more active at circumventing blocking strategies by adblockers.

5.2 How do Adblockers Reduce the Tracking Range of Third-Party Domains?

In order to understand the extend to which individual third-parties are able to track users while surfing across different domains, we look next at the degree of third-party domains (TPD). The TPD degree reflects how many visits to different first-party domains an individual third-party can observe. We observe, that the TPD is highly skewed. Only 10% of the third-parties have a TPD of more than 10 for the *NoAdblocker* profile while the largest TPD degree we observe is 486 (*None* column of Table 4). In general, we can therefore say that a small number of third-party domains are able to capture the vast majority of the visits to first parties.

Table 4. Top-loaded TPDs for browser profile *NoAdblocker* and the corresponding values for Ghostery and AdblockPlus with maximum-protection settings (browser profiles *Ghostery_MaxProtection* and *AdblockPlus_MaxProtection*) on 28/04/2016

Third-party domain	Legal entity	TPD degree		
		None	Ghostery	AdblockPlus
doubleclick.net	Google Inc.	486	0	1
google-analytics.com	Google Inc.	476	4	0
google.com	Google Inc.	383	93	144
facebook.com	Facebook Inc.	318	5	164
gstatic.com	Google Inc.	308	226	235
googlesyndication.com	Google Inc.	204	0	0
google.ch	Google Inc.	189	0	0
fonts.googleapis.com	Google Inc.	185	145	141
adnxs.com	AppNexus Inc.	159	0	0
facebook.net	Facebook Inc.	157	0	140

Considering the effect of the different browser profiles, we observe a similar trend as for the FPD degree. The *Ghostery_MaxProtection* and *Adblock-Plus_MaxProtection* profiles manage to effectively reduce the TPD node degree of all domains. However, in their default settings, AdblockPlus and Ghostery have only a noticeable effect on the domains with a small TPD degree, while these profiles have almost no impact on the filtering performance of domains with a large TPD node degree. Again, the browser profiles with the Do Not Track option enabled result in similar TPD node degrees as without the option.

In Table 4, we list the 10 domains with the highest TPD node degree (when no adblocker is applied) and compare how these numbers decrease with the *Ghostery_MaxProtection* and *AdblockPlus _MaxProtection* browser profiles. Ghostery achieves generally better performance, although AdblockPlus outperforms Ghostery slightly for two domains. Interesting to notice here is that some third-party domains from this list still exhibit a high TPD node degree with any of the adblockers enabled. These are the domains google.com, gstatic.com, and fonts.googleapis.com. These domains provide important content to render the web pages of the first parties and can therefore not be blocked. The other domains relate to advertisements, tracking, and social media and their TPD degrees are effectively reduced by Ghostery. AdblockPlus is not so effective at reducing the TPD degree of domains such as facebook.com and facebook.net.

5.3 How do Adblockers Reduce the Tracking Range of Legal Entities?

As we have seen in Table 4, the TPD degree of many domains was effectively reduced with adblockers, but some domains still remain with a high TPD node degree, mostly in order to provide useful content when rendering the page of the FPD. As a next step, we aim to understand how adblockers reduce the tracking range at the level of legal entities. A legal entity may acquire multiple domains and therefore still receive a lot of third-party requests despite some of its domains being blocked by the adblockers.

Table 5 summarizes the 10 legal entities with the highest TPD node degree, i.e. that were present on most of the visited URLs when the default Browser settings were applied (*NoAdblocker*). As the data suggests, domains owned by *Google Inc.* are loaded by 674 out of the 1000 URLs visited, thus having the most frequent presence among the rest of the third-party entities. Followed by Google Inc. are Facebook Inc., AppNexus Inc., and TMRG Inc. with node degrees of 328, 159, and 143 respectively. The degree of the following domains then quickly drops below 100.

Also presented in Table 5 is the node degree of the top 10 legal entites with the *Ghostery_MaxProtection* and *AdblockPlus_MaxProtection* browser profiles enabled. Except for Google Inc., Ghostery is able to suppress the node degree of all top 10 legal entities below 10. Google Inc. however remains with a node degree of 328, meaning that despite using Ghostery, Google Inc. is able to track more than 30% of the page visits to the FPDs. AdblockPlus is significantly less

Table 5. Legal entities with the highest TPE node degree for browser profile *NoAdblocker* and the corresponding values for Ghostery and AdblockPlus with maximum-protection settings (browser profiles *Ghostery_MaxProtection* and *Adblock-Plus_MaxProtection*) on 28/04/2016.

Legal entity	Degree		
	None	Ghostery	AdblockPlus
Google Inc.	666	328	354
Facebook Inc.	328	6	211
AppNexus Inc.	159	0	0
TMRG Inc.	143	0	4
Twitter Inc.	137	9	87
Oracle corporation	123	2	39
Adobe systems	107	6	32
Yahoo! Inc.	99	7	5
AOL Inc.	88	3	3
OpenX technologies	88	0	0

effective than Ghostery even in the maximum protection mode. Still, it reduces significantly the TPD node degree for most TPDs.

5.4 Geographical Considerations

Another key privacy dimension is the geographical location to which third-party requests are transferred to since local regulations govern what legal entities may do with the personal data that they collect about users. Table 6 lists the 10 countries with the highest number of legal entities acting as first party in our

Table 6. Countries hosting the highest percentage first-party entities

Country	First-party entities
United States	35.7%
Canada	7.4%
Japan	4.8%
Switzerland	4.0%
Germany	3.8%
India	3.5%
Great Britain	3.0%
Russia	2.6%
France	2.6%
Panama	2.0%

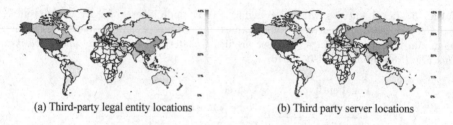

(a) Third-party legal entity locations   (b) Third party server locations

Fig. 5. World map depicting the locations of the legal entities and the servers for the third parties loaded during our experiments. (Color figure online)

traces. The country with the most first parties is the United States (35.7%) followed by Canada (7.4%) and Japan (4.8%). Figure 5a visualizes the relative number of legal entities acting as third parties in each country. The darkest regions (red) are the countries with the most TPEs loaded, while the white ones host none of the TPEs found in our graphs. As we would expect, the USA hosts most of the first and third-party domains, while regions such as Africa or Latin America contain very few TPEs.

A more detailed view of the number of TPEs hosted by the top 10 countries is presented in Table 7. For each row, the absolute numbers refer to the TPDs that were recognized and assigned to a TPE for the specific country, while the percentages refer to the ratio of these TPEs over the total number of TPEs that

Table 7. Countries hosting the highest percentage TPEs when no adblocker is used (browser profile *NoAdblocker*), and the corresponding percentages when Ghostery and AdblockPlus are used under maximum protection settings (browser profiles *Ghostery_MaxProtection* and *Adblockplus_MaxProtection*) on 28/04/2016.

Country	Third-party entities		
	None	Ghostery	AdblockPlus
United States	784 (45%)	483 (42%)	500 (45%)
Germany	106 (6%)	40 (4%)	34 (3%)
China	82 (5%)	70 (6%)	67 (6%)
Japan	80 (5%)	62 (5%)	61 (6%)
Great Britain	77 (4%)	43 (4%)	44 (4%)
France	69 (4%)	33 (3%)	31 (3%)
Canada	49 (3%)	33 (3%)	28 (3%)
India	46 (3%)	38 (3%)	38 (3%)
Panama	41 (2%)	32 (3%)	25 (2%)
Turkey	32 (2%)	27 (2%)	27 (2%)
Total	2908	1866	1812
Found	1748 (60.1%)	1140 (61.1%)	1097 (60.5%)

were recognized by our automated script. In this table, we compare the TPEs hosted by each of these countries (column *None*) to the number of TPEs loaded when the adblockers Ghostery and AdblockPlus are deployed under maximum-protection settings (columns *Ghostery* and *AdblockPlus*).

Interesting to note here is the difference in rank between countries in terms of legal entities that act as first and third parties. For example, China does not appear in the top ten list of countries for first parties, but ranks third in the ranking for legal entities that act as third-parties. This indicates that China hosts in relation to the other countries more third-party domains than first-party domains. The opposite is true for Switzerland and Russia which rank 4th and 7th in the ranking for first-party entities but don't appear in the top ten of third-party entities. Regarding the effect of the Ghostery and AdblockPlus, we can see that these adblockers do not significantly affect the overall distribution and ranking of the third-party legal entities. All countries experience a diminishing number of third-party legal entities that is in proportion relatively equal.

5.5 Graph Density

When grouping the TPD nodes according to the legal entities they belong to, we observe a considerable reduction of the mean FDP node degree, asserting that the number of legal entities potentially collecting information about the user is indeed less than that of the actual third-party domains tracking them.

On the contrary, the mean TPD node degree, as well as the graph density do not present any significant variation, which leads us to the conclusion that the various legal entities have on average access to roughly the same first parties, although controlling multiple third-party domains.

6 Related Work

Privacy Concerns: Many works in the literature have been dedicated to the privacy concerns as a consequence of tracking and fingerprinting by third-party domains [8,13,20,23,28,33]. Castelluccia *et al.* [10] showed that the user's interests can be inferred by the ads they receive and their whole profile can be reconstructed. This can lead to discriminations of the users according to their profile details and configurations, as shown in [11,27].

Countermeasures: As a result, several methods have been proposed that enable targeted advertisements without compromising user privacy [16,17,22, 34]. Additionally, there have been a lot of attempts for the detection of tracking behavior and ad-blocking blacklist ehnancements [15,24,35], while some studies have proposed further mitigation techniques [18,30].

Comparison of Mitigation-Techniques: Balebako *et al.* [7] propose a method to measure behavioral targeting and the effect of privacy-protection techniques—e.g. disabling of third-party cookies, Do-Not-Track header, ad-blocking tools—in the limitation of the behavioral-targeted character of the advertising content, while Krishnamurthy *et al.* [19] compare different privacy-protection techniques against the trade-offs between privacy and page quality. Leon *et al.* [21] investigate and compare the usability of some existing tools designed to limit advertising. Pujol *et al.* [29] aim to infer the use or no use of an adblocker by examining the HTTP(S) requests sent by a browser, using the ratio of the ad requests and the downloads of filter lists as indicators. Ruffell *et al.* [32] analyze the effectiveness of various browser add-ons in mitigating and protecting users from third-party tracking networks. However, the time evolution of these metrics is not examined and no legal-entity details are taken into consideration for the graph creation. Mayer and Mitchell [25] implemented the tool FourthParty—an open-source platform for measuring dynamic web content—as an extension to Mozilla Firefox. Englehardt and Narayanan [13] use OpenWPM [12], a web privacy measurement platform that can simulate users, collect data and record observations, e.g. response metadata, cookies and behavior of scripts. Although their study spans across 1 million sites, their measurement provide insights on one time instant, while we provide insights on the daily temporal evolution of web privacy. Recently, Merzdovnik *et al.* [26] performed a large scale study on more than 100,000 popular websites. Unlike our study, their work does not perform an observation of the temporal evolution.

7   Conclusions

The emerging trend of web advertising as well as the earning potential that it has to offer have turned it into the driving force for the development of a broad spectrum of websites and businesses. However, this practice is in direct conflict with privacy matters of the end-user, since the protection of their personal information is at stake through fingerprinting and online-profiling techniques whose objective is to optimize the efficiency of the web advertisements. Adblockers aim to counter these risks by removing advertising content and preventing third-party tracking.

Our analysis provides a quantitative methodology to compare the filtering performance of different adblockers. After the inspection of multiple browser profiles—i.e. combinations of ad-blocking software and configurations—for desktop and mobile devices, we show that the usage of an adblocker can indeed increase the privacy level and restrain the leakage of information concerning the browsing behavior of the user towards third-party trackers. The most important factor that can determine the achieved privacy level is according to our experiments the selection of blacklists, whilst the activation of the *do not track* HTTP header only has a minor effect. Our findings indicate that the best-performing adblockers are Ghostery and then AdblockPlus, when both are set to a maximal-protection level, whilst the highest privacy risks exist when no adblocker or Ghostery with its default blacklist settings is used.

References

1. Allowing acceptable ads in adblock plus. https://adblockplus.org/en/acceptable-ads
2. Google chrome adblock plus. https://chrome.google.com/webstore/detail/adblock-plus/cfhdojbkjhnklbpkdaibdccddilifddb/support?hl=en-GB
3. Juniper research. http://www.juniperresearch.com/press/press-releases/ad-blocking-to-cost-publishers-$27bn-in-lost-reven
4. Mozilla statistics for adblock plus. https://addons.mozilla.org/en-US/firefox/addon/adblock-plus/statistics/?last=30
5. The state of do not track in firefox. https://dnt-dashboard.mozilla.org/
6. Number of mobile-only internet users now exceeds desktop-only in the U.S, April 2015. http://www.comscore.com/Insights/Blog/Number-of-Mobile-Only-Internet-Users-Now-Exceeds-Desktop-Only-in-the-U.S
7. Balebako, R., Leon, P., Shay, R., Ur, B., Wang, Y., Cranor, L.: Measuring the effectiveness of privacy tools for limiting behavioral advertising. Web (2012)
8. Barford, P., Canadi, I., Krushevskaja, D., Ma, O., Muthukrishnan, S.: Adscape: harvesting and analyzing online display ads. In: Proceedings of the 23rd International Conference on World Wide Web, pp. 597–608. ACM (2014)
9. Butkiewicz, M., Madhyastha, H.V., Sekar, V.: Understanding website complexity: measurements, metrics, and implications. In: Proceedings of the 2011 ACM SIGCOMM Conference on Internet Measurement Conference, pp. 313–328. ACM (2011)
10. Castelluccia, C., Kaafar, M.-A., Tran, M.-D.: Betrayed by your ads!. In: Fischer-Hübner, S., Wright, M. (eds.) PETS 2012. LNCS, vol. 7384, pp. 1–17. Springer, Heidelberg (2012). doi:10.1007/978-3-642-31680-7_1
11. Datta, A., Tschantz, M.C., Datta, A.: Automated experiments on ad privacy settings. Proc. Priv. Enhanc. Technol. **2015**(1), 92–112 (2015)
12. Englehardt, S., Eubank, C., Zimmerman, P., Reisman, D., Narayanan, A.: Web privacy measurement: scientific principles, engineering platform, and new results (2014). http://randomwalker.info/publications/WebPrivacyMeasurement.pdf
13. Englehardt, S., Narayanan, A.: Online tracking: a 1-million-site measurement and analysis. In: Proceedings of the 2016 ACM SIGSAC Conference on Computer and Communications Security, pp. 1388–1401. ACM (2016)
14. Gill, P., Erramilli, V., Chaintreau, A., Krishnamurthy, B., Papagiannaki, K., Rodriguez, P.: Best paper - follow the money: understanding economics of online aggregation and advertising. In: Proceedings of the 2013 Conference on Internet Measurement Conference, IMC 2013, pp. 141–148. ACM, New York (2013)
15. Gugelmann, D., Happe, M., Ager, B., Lenders, V.: An automated approach for complementing ad blockers' blacklists. Proc. Priv. Enhanc. Technol. **2015**(2), 282–298 (2015)
16. Guha, S., Cheng, B., Francis, P.: Privad: practical privacy in online advertising. In: USENIX Conference on Networked Systems Design and Implementation, pp. 169–182 (2011)
17. Haddadi, H., Guha, S., Francis, P.: Not all adware is badware: towards privacy-aware advertising. In: Godart, C., Gronau, N., Sharma, S., Canals, G. (eds.) I3E 2009. IAICT, vol. 305, pp. 161–172. Springer, Heidelberg (2009). doi:10.1007/978-3-642-04280-5_14
18. Kontaxis, G., Chew, M.: Tracking protection in firefox for privacy and performance. arXiv preprint arXiv:1506.04104 (2015)

19. Krishnamurthy, B., Malandrino, D., Wills, C.E.: Measuring privacy loss and the impact of privacy protection in web browsing. In: Proceedings of the 3rd Symposium on Usable Privacy and Security, pp. 52–63. ACM (2007)

20. Krishnamurthy, B., Wills, C.: Privacy diffusion on the web: a longitudinal perspective. In: Proceedings of the 18th International Conference on World Wide Web, pp. 541–550. ACM (2009)

21. Leon, P., Ur, B., Shay, R., Wang, Y., Balebako, R., Cranor, L.: Why johnny can't opt out: a usability evaluation of tools to limit online behavioral advertising. In: Proceedings of the SIGCHI Conference on Human Factors in Computing Systems, pp. 589–598. ACM (2012)

22. Levin, D., Bhattacharjee, B., Douceur, J.R., Lorch, J.R., Mickens, J., Moscibroda, T.: Nurikabe: private yet accountable targeted advertising (2009, under submission). johndo@microsoft.com

23. Libert, T.: Exposing the invisible web: an analysis of third-party http requests on 1 million websites. Int. J. Commun. 9, 18 (2015)

24. Ma, J., Saul, L.K., Savage, S., Voelker, G.M.: Beyond blacklists: learning to detect malicious web sites from suspicious URLs. In: Proceedings of the 15th ACM SIGKDD International Conference on Knowledge Discovery and Data Mining, pp. 1245–1254. ACM (2009)

25. Mayer, J.R., Mitchell, J.C.: Third-party web tracking: policy and technology. In: 2012 IEEE Symposium on Security and Privacy (SP), pp. 413–427. IEEE (2012)

26. Merzdovnik, G., Huber, M., Buhov, D., Nikiforakis, N., Neuner, S., Schmiedecker, M., Weippl, E.: Block me if you can: a large-scale study of tracker-blocking tools. In: 2nd IEEE European Symposium on Security and Privacy, Paris, France (2017)

27. Mikians, J., Gyarmati, L., Erramilli, V., Laoutaris, N.: Detecting price and search discrimination on the internet. In: Proceedings of the 11th ACM Workshop on Hot Topics in Networks, pp. 79–84. ACM (2012)

28. Nikiforakis, N., Acar, G.: Browse at your own risk. IEEE Spectr. 51(8), 30–35 (2014)

29. Pujol, E., Hohlfeld, O., Feldmann, A.: Annoyed users: ads and ad-block usage in the wild. In: Proceedings of the 2015 ACM Conference on Internet Measurement Conference, pp. 93–106. ACM (2015)

30. Roesner, F., Kohno, T., Wetherall, D.: Detecting and defending against third-party tracking on the web. In: Proceedings of the 9th USENIX conference on Networked Systems Design and Implementation, pp. 12–12. USENIX Association (2012)

31. Singer, D., Fielding, R.T.: Tracking preference expression (DNT). Technical report, May 2015

32. Ruffell, M., Hong, J.B., Kim, D.S.: Analyzing the effectiveness of privacy related add-ons employed to thwart web based tracking. In: 2015 IEEE 21st Pacific Rim International Symposium on Dependable Computing (PRDC), pp. 264–272. IEEE (2015)

33. Soltani, A., Canty, S., Mayo, Q., Thomas, L., Hoofnagle, C.J.: Flash cookies and privacy. In: AAAI Spring Symposium: Intelligent Information Privacy Management, vol. 2010, pp. 158–163 (2010)

34. Toubiana, V., Narayanan, A., Boneh, D., Nissenbaum, H., Barocas, S.: Adnostic: privacy preserving targeted advertising. In: Proceedings Network and Distributed System Symposium (2010)

35. Tran, M., Dong, X., Liang, Z., Jiang, X.: Tracking the trackers: fast and scalable dynamic analysis of web content for privacy violations. In: Bao, F., Samarati, P., Zhou, J. (eds.) ACNS 2012. LNCS, vol. 7341, pp. 418–435. Springer, Heidelberg (2012). doi:10.1007/978-3-642-31284-7_25

More Efficient Structure-Preserving Signatures - Or: Bypassing the Type-III Lower Bounds

Essam Ghadafi[✉]

University of the West of England, Bristol, UK
essam.ghadafi@uwe.ac.uk

Abstract. Structure-Preserving Signatures (SPSs) are an important cryptographic primitive that is useful for the design of modular cryptographic protocols. It has be shown that in the most efficient Type-III bilinear group setting such schemes have a lower bound of 3-element signatures, which must include elements from both base groups, and a verification overhead of at least 2 Pairing-Product Equations (PPEs). In this work we show how to circumvent these lower bounds by constructing more efficient schemes than existing optimal schemes. Towards this end, we first formally define the notion of Unilateral Structure-Preserving Signatures on Diffie-Hellman pairs (USPSDH) as Type-III SPS schemes with messages being Diffie-Hellman pairs and signatures being elements of one of the base groups, i.e. unilateral. We construct a number of new fully randomizable SPS schemes that are existentially unforgeable against adaptive chosen-message attacks, and which yield signatures consisting of only 2 elements from the shorter base group, and which require only a single PPE for verification (not counting the cost of verifying the well-formedness of the message). Thus, our signatures are at least half the size of the best existing scheme for unilateral messages. Our first scheme has a feature that permits controlled randomizability which might be of independent interest. We also give various optimal strongly unforgeable one-time schemes with 1-element signatures, including a new scheme for unilateral messages that matches the best existing scheme in every respect. We prove optimality of our constructions by proving different lower bounds and giving some impossibility results. We also show how to extend our schemes to sign a vector of messages. Finally, we highlight how our schemes yield more efficient instantiations of various cryptographic protocols, including variants of attribute-based signatures and direct anonymous attestation, which is a protocol deployed in practice. Our results offer value along two fronts: On the theoretical side, our results serve as a workaround to bypass existing lower bounds. On the practical side, our constructions could lead to more efficient instantiations of various cryptographic protocols.

The research leading to these results has received funding from the European Research Council under the European Union's Seventh Framework Programme (FP/2007-2013)/ERC Grant Agreement no. 307937 and EPSRC grant EP/J009520/1. The work was also sponsored by the Computer Science and Creative Technologies Department at the University of the West of England. Part of the work was done while the author was at University College London.

© Springer International Publishing AG 2017
S.N. Foley et al. (Eds.): ESORICS 2017, Part II, LNCS 10493, pp. 43–61, 2017.
DOI: 10.1007/978-3-319-66399-9_3

1   Introduction

Structure-Preserving Signatures (SPSs) [3] are pairing-based digital signature schemes whose messages, verification key and signatures are all group elements from one or both base groups, and signature verification involves evaluating Pairing-Product Equations (PPEs). Such schemes compose nicely with existing popular tools such as Groth-Sahai proofs [37] and ElGamal encryption [23] and hence they are a useful tool for the design of cryptographic protocols not relying on random oracles [25]. They have numerous applications which include group signatures, e.g. [3,41], blind signatures, e.g. [3,28], attribute-based signatures, e.g. [24,31], tightly secure encryption, e.g. [2,38], malleable signatures, e.g. [10], anonymous credentials, e.g. [17,27], network coding, e.g. [10], oblivious transfer, e.g. [34], direct anonymous attestation, e.g. [13,32], and e-cash, e.g. [11].

Related Work. The term "structure-preserving signature" was coined by Abe et al. [3] but earlier schemes conforming to the definition were given in [34,35]. The notion received a significant amount of attention and many studies regarding lower bounds for the design of such schemes as well as new schemes matching those bounds have been published. Abe et al. [3] constructed schemes based on non-interactive intractability assumptions which work in the different bilinear group settings. Abe et al. [4] showed that signature of such schemes in the Type-III bilinear group setting (cf. Sect. 2.1) must have at least 3 elements, which must come from both base groups, and require at least 2 PPEs for verification which rules out the existence of schemes with unilateral signatures. They gave optimal constructions and proved their security in the generic group model [43,45]. Abe et al. [5] proved that it is impossible to base the security of an optimal Type-III scheme on non-interactive intractability assumptions. Other Type-III constructions were given in [6,21,30,36]. Recently, Ghadafi [32] gave a randomizable scheme with signatures consisting of 3 elements from the shorther base group which can also be regarded as a USPSDH scheme. Verification in his scheme requires, besides checking the well-formedness of the message, the evaluation of 2 PPEs.

Constructions relying on standard assumptions, e.g. DLIN or DDH, were given by [1,2,16,19,39–41]. It is well known that schemes based on standard assumptions are less efficient than their counterparts relying on non-standard assumptions or those proven directly in the generic group model.

Constructions in the Type-II setting (where there is an efficiently computable isomorphism between the base groups in one direction) were given in [7,12,21].

Recently, fully structure-preserving schemes where even the secret key consists of only group elements from the base groups were given in [8,36,46].

Our Techniques. All existing Type-III constructions for unilateral messages have the common feature that one of the signature components involves an exponent that is either the inverse or the square of some random field element chosen as part of the signing. Hence, verification in these schemes relies on a pairing involving two signature components and this is the reason that none of these schemes has unilateral signatures. In fact, as proven by Abe et al. [4], it is impossible to have a Type-III scheme for unilateral messages with unilateral signatures. We adopt a different approach to obtain schemes with short unilateral signatures. First, we require that messages are Diffie-Hellman pairs [3,26] of the form $(G^m, \tilde{H}^m)$ for some $m \in \mathbb{Z}_p$ where $\hat{e} : \mathbb{G} \times \mathbb{H} \longrightarrow \mathbb{T}$ is a bilinear map (cf. Sect. 2.1) and $\mathbb{G} := \langle G \rangle$ and $\mathbb{H} := \langle \tilde{H} \rangle$. Also, unlike existing schemes, none of the signature components in our schemes involves inverses or squares of the randomness used in the signing. Instead, one of the signature components involves the inverse of a field element from the secret key which can be cancelled out in the verification by pairing the concerned signature component with the corresponding public key which belongs to the opposite base group. This way we obtain schemes with optimal unilateral signatures and which require optimal number of verification equations. We remark that there exist Type-III schemes for the same message space as ours yielding unilateral signatures, e.g. [30,32], however, those schemes are not optimal.

Our Contribution. After defining USPSDH schemes in Sect. 2.4, we provide the following contributions:-

- (Sect. 3) Two new fully randomizable SPS schemes that are existentially unforgeable against a chosen-message attack. Our schemes yield unilateral signatures consisting of only 2 elements and hence they are at least half the size of the shortest existing Type-III SPS scheme. Verification in our schemes requires, besides checking the well-formedness of the message, the evaluation of a single PPE. Our first construction has a feature that permits controlled randomizability (combined unforgeability) which might be of independent interest.
- (Sect. 4) New optimal strongly EUF-CMA secure one-time schemes for a vector of messages with 1 element signatures, including a scheme for unilateral messages matching the best existing scheme [6] in every measure.
- (Sect. 5) An optimal CMA-secure partially structure-preserving scheme that simultaneously signs a Diffie-Hellman pair and a vector in $\mathbb{Z}_p^k$.
- We highlight (in Sect. 6) some applications of our schemes which include efficient instantiations of Direct Anonymous Attestation (DAA) [15] and variants of attribute-based signatures [24,31,42] which outperform existing constructions not relying on random oracles.
- We prove (in Sect. 7) the following lower bound/impossibility results:
  (i) A lower bound of 2 elements for signatures of schemes secure against a random-message attack for more than 1 signing query.
  (ii) A lower bound of 2 elements for the verification key of optimal schemes. This holds even when the adversary is restricted to 1 random-message signing query.
  (iii) The impossibility of strongly existentially-unforgeable schemes secure against more than 1 chosen-message signing query.

Why are USPSDH Schemes Interesting? From our results, it is clear that USPSDH signature schemes yield the shortest SPS signatures since they allow one to circumvent the lower bounds in the Type-III setting. It is particularly interesting when the signatures are from the first base group as the bit size of the elements of that group is at least half the size of those of the second group.

While traditional Type-III SPS schemes have shorter messages since message components of those schemes lie in one of the base groups and not both, this is a small price to pay to get smaller signatures and more efficient verification. Even though the restriction that messages are Diffie-Hellman pairs imposed by USPSDH schemes might give the false impression that these variants are less general than traditional SPS schemes, we stress that such a restriction is not a too strong one and USPSDH schemes suffice for many practical applications of traditional SPS schemes. So besides serving as a workaround to circumvent the lower bounds, such variants are useful in practice.

Being in the Type-III setting, (optimal) USPSDH schemes enjoy much better efficiency (including shorter message sizes) than existing Type-II schemes since the Type-III setting yields shorter group representations and better efficiency. Note that verifying the well-formedness of the message only needs to be performed once when verifying multiple signatures on the same message. Consider, for example, attribute-based signatures [42] where the signer needs to prove she has multiple attributes from (possibly different) attribute authorities. The same applies to applications requiring a user to prove that she has multiple tokens/credentials/certificates from an authority or possibly different authorities. Even when considering a single signature on the message, ours still compare favorably to existing ones in many aspects as shown in Table 1, where numbers superscripted with † are the number of pairings that can be precomputed, whereas numbers superscripted with * are the cost needed to verify well-formedness of the Diffie-Hellman message. The latter cost is constant when verifying multiple signatures on the same message. For all schemes listed, public parameters do not include the default group generators. Note that the security of all schemes in the table except for [3,26] which rely on non-interactive q-type assumptions and [30] which relies on an interactive assumption is proven in the generic group model.

Our schemes compare favorably even to some widely-used non-structure-preserving schemes. For instance, ours are more efficient than the Camenisch-Lysyanskaya scheme [18] and Waters' scheme [20,47]. Also, the size of our signatures and the verification key are the same as those of the recent scheme by Pointcheval and Sanders [44]. Moreover, the (interactive) intractability assumptions underlying our schemes are comparable to those underlying [18,44].

Notation. We write $y \coloneqq A(x; r)$ when algorithm A on input x and randomness r outputs y. We write $y \leftarrow A(x)$ for the process of setting $y = A(x; r)$ where r is sampled at random. We also write $y \leftarrow S$ for sampling y uniformly at random from a set S. A function $\nu(.) : \mathbb{N} \to \mathbb{R}^+$ is negligible (in n) if for every polynomial $p(.)$ and all sufficiently large values of n, it holds that $\nu(n) < \frac{1}{p(n)}$. By PPT we mean running in probabilistic polynomial time in the relevant security parameter. By $[k]$, we denote the set $\{1, \ldots, k\}$. We will use capital letters for group elements and small letters for field elements.

Table 1. Efficiency comparison between our schemes and existing Type-III schemes

Work	σ		vk		PP		$\mathcal{M}$	Randomizable	#PPE	#Pairings
	G	H	G	H	G	H				
[26]	3	2	1	1	3	1	$\widehat{\mathbb{GH}}$	No	$3+1^*$	$7+2^*$
[3] 1	5	2	10	4	-	-	$\mathbb{G}$	Partially	2	$8+4^\dagger$
[3] 2	2	5	10	4	-	-	$\mathbb{H}$	Partially	2	$8+4^\dagger$
[4] 1	2	1	1	3	-	-	$\mathbb{G} \times \mathbb{H}$	No	2	$5+2^\dagger$
[4] 2	2	1	1	1	-	-	$\mathbb{H}$	Yes	2	$4+1^\dagger$
[30]	4	-	-	2	-	-	$\widehat{\mathbb{GH}}$	Yes	$3+1^*$	$6+2^*$
[21] 1	1	2	2	-	-	-	$\mathbb{H}$	No	2	$4+1^\dagger$
[21] 2	1	2	2	-	-	-	$\mathbb{H}$	Yes	2	$5+1^\dagger$
[21] 3	2	1	-	2	-	-	$\mathbb{G}$	Yes	2	$5+1^\dagger$
[6] 1	3	1	-	1	1	-	$\mathbb{G}$	Yes	2	$4+2^\dagger$
[6] 2	2	1	-	1	1	-	$\mathbb{G}$	No	2	$4+2^\dagger$
[12]	1	2	2	-	-	-	$\mathbb{H}$	Yes	2	$3+2^\dagger$
[36] 1	1	2	1	-	-	1	$\mathbb{H}$	Yes	2	$3+3^\dagger$
[36] 2	1	2	1	-	-	1	$\mathbb{H}$	No	2	$4+3^\dagger$
[32]	3	-	-	2	-	-	$\widehat{\mathbb{GH}}$	Yes	$2+1^*$	$5+2^*$
Ours I	2	-	-	2	-	-	$\widehat{\mathbb{GH}}$	Yes[1]	$1+1^*$	$2+1^\dagger+2^*$
Ours II	2	-	-	2	-	-	$\widehat{\mathbb{GH}}$	Yes	$1+1^*$	$2+2^*$

[1] Randomization requires possession of at least 2 distinct signatures on the message.

2   Preliminaries

In this section we provide some preliminary definitions.

2.1   Bilinear Groups

A bilinear group is a tuple $\mathcal{P} := (\mathbb{G}, \mathbb{H}, \mathbb{T}, p, G, \tilde{H}, \hat{e})$ where $\mathbb{G}$, $\mathbb{H}$ and $\mathbb{T}$ are groups of a prime order p, and G and $\tilde{H}$ generate $\mathbb{G}$ and $\mathbb{H}$, respectively. The function $\hat{e}$ is a non-degenerate bilinear map $\hat{e} : \mathbb{G} \times \mathbb{H} \longrightarrow \mathbb{T}$. For clarity, elements of $\mathbb{H}$ will be accented with $\tilde{\ }$. We use multiplicative notation for all the groups. We let $\mathbb{G}^\times := \mathbb{G} \setminus \{1_\mathbb{G}\}$ and $\mathbb{H}^\times := \mathbb{H} \setminus \{1_\mathbb{H}\}$. In this paper, we work in the efficient Type-III setting [29], where $\mathbb{G} \neq \mathbb{H}$ and there is no efficiently computable isomorphism between the groups in either direction. We assume there is an algorithm $\mathcal{BG}$ that on input a security parameter κ, outputs a description of bilinear groups.

The message space of the schemes we consider is the set of elements of the subgroup $\widehat{\mathbb{GH}}$ of $\mathbb{G} \times \mathbb{H}$ defined as the image of the map $\psi : x \longmapsto (G^x, \tilde{H}^x)$ for $x \in \mathbb{Z}_p$. One can efficiently test whether $(M, \tilde{N}) \in \widehat{\mathbb{GH}}$ by checking $\hat{e}(M, \tilde{H}) = \hat{e}(G, \tilde{N})$. Such pairs were called Diffie-Hellman pairs in [3,26].

2.2 Digital Signatures

A digital signature scheme $\mathcal{DS}$ over a bilinear group $\mathcal{P}$ generated by $\mathcal{BG}$ for a message space $\mathcal{M}$ consists of the following algorithms:

KeyGen($\mathcal{P}$) on input $\mathcal{P}$, it outputs a pair of secret/verification keys (sk, vk).
Sign(sk, m) on input sk and a message $m \in \mathcal{M}$, it outputs a signature σ.
Verify(vk, m, σ) outputs 1 if σ is a valid signature on m w.r.t. vk and 0 otherwise.

Besides the usual correctness requirement, we require existential unforgeability.

Definition 1 (Existential Unforgeability). *A signature scheme $\mathcal{DS}$ over a bilinear group generator $\mathcal{BG}$ is* Existentially-Unforgeable against adaptive Chosen-Message Attack (EUF-CMA) *if for all $\kappa \in \mathbb{N}$ for all PPT adversaries $\mathcal{A}$, the following is negligible (in κ)*

$$\Pr\left[\begin{array}{c} \mathcal{P} \leftarrow \mathcal{BG}(1^{\kappa}); (\text{sk}, \text{vk}) \leftarrow \text{KeyGen}(\mathcal{P}); (\sigma^*, m^*) \leftarrow \mathcal{A}^{\text{Sign}(\text{sk}, \cdot)}(\mathcal{P}, \text{vk}) \\ : \text{Verify}(\text{vk}, m^*, \sigma^*) = 1 \ \wedge \ m^* \notin Q_{\text{Sign}} \end{array}\right],$$

where Q_{Sign} is the set of messages queried to Sign.

Strong Existential Unforgeability against adaptive Chosen-Message Attack (sEUF-CMA) requires that the adversary cannot even output a new signature on a message that was queried to the sign oracle.

A weaker variant of EUF-CMA is *Existential Unforgeability against a Random-Message Attack (EUF-RMA)* in which the sign oracle samples a message uniformly from the message space and returns the message and a signature on it. In one-time signatures, the adversary is restricted to a single signing query.

We consider schemes which are publicly re-randomizable where there is an algorithm Randomize that on input (vk, m, σ) outputs a new signature σ' on m. A desirable property for such class of schemes is that randomized signatures are indistinguishable from fresh signatures.

Definition 2 (Randomizability). *A signature scheme $\mathcal{DS}$ over a bilinear group generator $\mathcal{BG}$ is* randomizable *if for all $\kappa \in \mathbb{N}$ for all stateful adversaries $\mathcal{A}$ the following probability is negligibly close to $\frac{1}{2}$.*

$$\Pr\left[\begin{array}{c} \mathcal{P} \leftarrow \mathcal{BG}(1^{\kappa}); (\text{sk}, \text{vk}) \leftarrow \text{KeyGen}(\mathcal{P}); (\sigma^*, m^*) \leftarrow \mathcal{A}(\mathcal{P}, \text{sk}, \text{vk}); \sigma_0 \leftarrow \text{Sign}(\text{sk}, m^*); \\ \sigma_1 \leftarrow \text{Randomize}(\text{vk}, m^*, \sigma^*); b \leftarrow \{0, 1\} : \text{Verify}(\text{vk}, m^*, \sigma^*) = 1 \ \wedge \ \mathcal{A}(\sigma_b) = b \end{array}\right]$$

When the above is exactly $\frac{1}{2}$, we say the scheme has *Perfect Randomizability*.

2.3 Structure-Preserving Signatures

Structure-preserving signatures [3] are signature schemes defined over bilinear groups where the messages, the verification key and signatures are all group elements from either or both base groups, and verifying signatures only involves deciding group membership of the signature components and evaluating PPEs of the form of Eq. (1).

$$\prod_i \prod_j \hat{e}(A_i, \tilde{B}_j)^{c_{i,j}} = 1_{\mathbb{T}}, \tag{1}$$

where $A_i \in \mathbb{G}$ and $\tilde{B}_j \in \mathbb{H}$ are group elements appearing in $\mathcal{P}, m, \mathsf{vk}, \sigma$, whereas $c_{i,j} \in \mathbb{Z}_p$ are constants.

Generic Signer. We refer to a signer that can only decide group membership, evaluate the bilinear map $\hat{e}$, compute the group operations in groups $\mathbb{G}, \mathbb{H}$ and $\mathbb{T}$, and compare group elements as a *generic signer*.

2.4 Unilateral Structure-Preserving Signatures on Diffie-Hellman Pairs

We define Unilateral Structure-Preserving Signatures on Diffie-Hellman Pairs (USPSDH) as Type-III SPS schemes with the following additional requirements:

(i) Messages are of the form $(M, \tilde{N}) \in \widehat{\mathbb{GH}} \subset \mathbb{G} \times \mathbb{H}$.
(ii) Either signatures are of the form $\sigma = (S_1, \dots, S_k) \in \mathbb{G}^k$ and the verification key is $\mathsf{vk} = (\tilde{Y}_1, \dots, \tilde{Y}_n) \in \mathbb{H}^n$ or signatures are of the form $\sigma = (\tilde{S}_1, \dots, \tilde{S}_k) \in \mathbb{H}^k$ and the verification key is $\mathsf{vk} = (Y_1, \dots, Y_n) \in \mathbb{G}^n$.

We remark that there exist schemes, e.g. [30,32], which conform to the above requirements. Also, there are schemes, e.g. [3,26], which satisfy the first requirement but not the second.

3 Optimal EUF-CMA Secure Constructions

In this section, we give two new optimal constructions of USPSDH schemes.

3.1 Construction I

Here we give our first EUF-CMA secure construction. Given the description of Type-III bilinear groups $\mathcal{P}$ output by $\mathcal{BG}(1^\kappa)$, the scheme is as follows:

- KeyGen($\mathcal{P}$): Select $x, y \leftarrow \mathbb{Z}_p^\times$. Set $\mathsf{sk} := (x, y)$, $\mathsf{vk} := (\tilde{X}, \tilde{Y}) = (\tilde{H}^x, \tilde{H}^y) \in \mathbb{H}^2$.
- Sign($\mathsf{sk}, (M, \tilde{N})$): To sign $(M, \tilde{N}) \in \widehat{\mathbb{GH}}$, select $r \leftarrow \mathbb{Z}_p$, and set $R := G^r$, $S := ((G^x \cdot M)^r \cdot G)^{\frac{1}{y}}$. Return $\sigma := (R, S) \in \mathbb{G}^2$.
- Verify($\mathsf{vk}, (M, \tilde{N}), \sigma = (R, S)$): Return 1 iff $R, S \in \mathbb{G}$, $(M, \tilde{N}) \in \widehat{\mathbb{GH}}$, and $\hat{e}(S, \tilde{Y}) = \hat{e}(R, \tilde{X} \cdot \tilde{N})\hat{e}(G, \tilde{H})$.

Correctness of the scheme follows by inspection and is straightforward to verify. The scheme is not strongly unforgeable since for instance given two distinct signatures $\sigma_1 = (R_1, S_1)$ and $\sigma_2 = (R_2, S_2)$ on a message $(M, \tilde{N})$, one can without knowledge of the signing key compute a new signature $\sigma' = (R', S')$ on the same message by computing e.g. $(R' := R_1^2 \cdot R_2^{-1}, S' := S_1^2 \cdot S_2^{-1})$.

Theorem 1. *The scheme is EUF-CMA secure in the generic group model.*[1]

Proof. We prove that no linear combinations (which represent Laurent polynomials in the discrete logarithms) of the group elements the adversary sees in the game correspond to a forgery on a new message.

At the start of the game, the only elements in $\mathbb{H}$ the adversary sees are $\tilde{H}$, $\tilde{X}, \tilde{Y}$ which correspond to the discrete logarithms 1, x and y, respectively. Note the signing oracle produces no new elements in $\mathbb{H}$. Thus, at the i-th sign query on $(M_i, \tilde{N}_i)$, $\tilde{N}_i$ can only be a linear combination of $\tilde{H}$, $\tilde{X}$, and $\tilde{Y}$. Similarly, M_i can only be a linear combination of $G, \{R_j\}_{j=1}^{i-1}, \{S_j\}_{j=1}^{i-1}$. Thus, we have

$$n_i = a_{n_i} + b_{n_i}x + c_{n_i}y \qquad m_i = a_{m_i} + \sum_{j=1}^{i-1} b_{m_{i,j}}r_j + \sum_{j=1}^{i-1} c_{m_{i,j}}\left(\frac{r_jx + r_jm_j + 1}{y}\right)$$

Since we must have $n_i = m_i$ to have $(M_i, \tilde{N}_i) \in \widehat{\mathbb{G}\mathbb{H}}$, we must have $a_{m_i} = a_{n_i}$, $b_{n_i} = c_{n_i} = 0$, $b_{m_{i,j}} = c_{m_{i,j}} = 0$ for all j, i.e. messages correspond to constant polynomials. Similarly, at the end of the game, (m^*, n^*) which is the discrete logarithm of the forged message $(M^*, \tilde{N}^*)$ must be of the form $m^* = n^* = a_m$.

The forgery (R^*, S^*) can only be a linear combination of the group elements from $\mathbb{G}$, i.e. a linear combination of $G, \{R_i\}_{i=1}^q$ and $\{S_i\}_{i=1}^q$. Thus, we have

$$r^* = a_r + \sum_{i=1}^q b_{r,i}r_i + \sum_{i=1}^q c_{r,i}\left(\frac{r_ix + r_im_i + 1}{y}\right)$$

$$s^* = a_s + \sum_{i=1}^q b_{s,i}r_i + \sum_{i=1}^q c_{s,i}\left(\frac{r_ix + r_im_i + 1}{y}\right)$$

For the forgery to be accepted, r^* and s^* must satisfy $s^*y = r^*x + r^*m^* + 1$. Therefore, we must have

$$a_sy + \sum_{i=1}^q b_{s,i}r_iy + \sum_{i=1}^q c_{s,i}(r_ix + r_im_i + 1) = a_rx + \sum_{i=1}^q b_{r,i}r_ix + \sum_{i=1}^q c_{r,i}\left(\frac{r_ix^2}{y} + \frac{r_im_ix}{y} + \frac{x}{y}\right)$$

$$+ \left(a_r + \sum_{i=1}^q b_{r,i}r_i + \sum_{i=1}^q c_{r,i}\left(\frac{r_ix}{y} + \frac{r_im_i}{y} + \frac{1}{y}\right)\right)m^* + 1$$

There is no term in y or r_iy on the right-hand side so we must have $a_s = 0$, and $b_{s,i} = 0$ for all i. Also, there is no term in $\frac{r_ix^2}{y}$ or x on the left-hand side so we must have $a_r = 0$ and $c_{r,i} = 0$ for all i. Thus, we have

$$\sum_{i=1}^q c_{s,i}\left(r_ix + r_im_i + 1\right) = \sum_{i=1}^q b_{r,i}r_ix + \sum_{i=1}^q b_{r,i}r_im^* + 1 \qquad (2)$$

The monomial r_ix implies $c_{s,i} = b_{r,i}$ for all i, whereas the monomial r_i implies $c_{s,i}m_i = b_{r,i}m^*$. Since we have $c_{s,i} = b_{r,i}$, this means we have $m^* = m_i$ for some i. Hence, the signature (R^*, S^*) is on a message pair $(M_i, \tilde{N}_i)$ that was queried to the sign oracle and thus is not a forgery on a new message. □

---

[1] We remark that we have double verified all of our generic group proofs using the recent generic group tool of Ambrona et al. [9].

We now prove the following theorem regarding the randomizability/strong unforgeability of the scheme.

Theorem 2. *The scheme is strongly existentially-unforgeable against an adversary that queries the signing oracle on each message once at most.*

Proof. For Equality (2) in the proof of Theorem 1 to hold, it is clear that S^* (from which the left-hand side of (2) is constructed) can only be a linear combination of S_i^* part of the signature returned in response to the i-th signing query on the message $(M^*, \tilde{N}^*)$ (if any). Similarly, R^* can only be a linear combination of R_i^*. Since the adversary can make at most one signing query on each message, we have two cases. If the adversary made no signing query on $(M^*, \tilde{N}^*)$, a forgery would contradict Theorem 1. If the adversary made a signing query on $(M^*, \tilde{N}^*)$, then since in this case $q = 1$, we have $r^* = r_i$ since for (2) to hold, we must have $\sum_{i=1}^{q} c_{s,i} = 1$ which implies $b_{r,i} = 1$ and hence the signature (R^*, S^*) is not new. $\qquad\square$

Now consider the following special randomization algorithm for the scheme:

- Randomize† $\left(\mathsf{vk}, (M, \tilde{N}), \{\sigma_i = (R_i, S_i)\}_{i=1}^{2}\right)$: For any two distinct signatures σ_1 and σ_2, i.e. $R_1 \neq R_2$, satisfying $\mathsf{Verify}(\mathsf{vk}, (M, \tilde{N}), \sigma_i) = 1$ for all $i \in [2]$. To obtain a new signature σ' on $(M, \tilde{N})$, choose $a \leftarrow \mathbb{Z}_p$ and let $b = 1 - a$. Now compute $R' := R_1^a \cdot R_2^b$, $S' := S_1^a \cdot S_2^b$. Return $\sigma' := (R', S')$.

Theorem 3. *Signatures output by* Randomize† *are perfectly indistinguishable from those output by* Sign *on the same message.*

Proof. In the Sign algorithm, r is chosen uniformly at random from $\mathbb{Z}_p$, whereas in Randomize†, a (resp. b) is also chosen uniformly at random from $\mathbb{Z}_p$. Moreover, for any possible $r \in \mathbb{Z}_p$ such that $R = G^r$, there is $a \in \mathbb{Z}_p$ such that $r = ar_1 + (1-a)r_2$ for any $r_1, r_2 \in \mathbb{Z}_p$ satisfying $r_1 \neq r_2$. Therefore, the distributions of signatures output by Randomize† and Sign are identical. $\qquad\square$

The above observations makes it possible to achieve combined unforgeability [36] where the same scheme can allow (at the discretion of the signer) either strongly unforgeable signatures or ones that can be re-randomized.

3.2   Construction II

Here we give our second construction which yields publicly re-randomizable signatures. Given the description of Type-III bilinear groups $\mathcal{P}$ output by $\mathcal{BG}(1^\lambda)$, the scheme is as follows:

- KeyGen($\mathcal{P}$): Select $x, y \leftarrow \mathbb{Z}_p^\times$. Set $\mathsf{sk} := (x, y)$ and $\mathsf{vk} := (\tilde{X}, \tilde{Y}) = (\tilde{H}^x, \tilde{H}^y) \in \tilde{\mathbb{H}}^2$.
- Sign($\mathsf{sk}, (M, \tilde{N})$): To sign $(M, \tilde{N}) \in \widehat{\mathbb{GH}}$, select $r \leftarrow \mathbb{Z}_p^\times$, and set $R := G^r$, $S := (G^x \cdot M)^{\frac{r}{y}}$. Return $\sigma := (R, S) \in \mathbb{G}^2$.

- Verify(vk, $(M, \tilde{N}), \sigma = (R, S)$): Return 1 iff $R \in \mathbb{G}^{\times}, S \in \mathbb{G}, (M, \tilde{N}) \in \widehat{\mathbb{GH}}$, and $\hat{e}(S, \tilde{Y}) = \hat{e}(R, \tilde{X} \cdot \tilde{N})$.
- Randomize(vk, $(M, \tilde{N}), \sigma = (R, S)$): Select $r' \leftarrow \mathbb{Z}_p^{\times}$, and set $R' := R^{r'}$, $S' := S^{r'}$. Return $\sigma' := (R', S')$.

Note that R is information-theoretically independent of the message and hence even when proving knowledge of signatures, this component of the signature can be revealed in the clear after re-randomizing it which allows one to verify that $R \neq 1_{\mathbb{G}}$.

Correctness of the scheme follows by inspection and is straightforward to verify. The scheme is perfectly randomizable as the distribution of re-randomized signatures is identical to that of fresh signatures on the same message.

The proof of the following theorem is in the full version [33].

Theorem 4. *The scheme is EUF-CMA secure in the generic group model.*

4   Optimal sEUF-CMA Secure SPS One-Time Schemes

We give here new strongly unforgeable one-time Type-III schemes for unilateral messages matching the optimal one-time scheme in [6] in every measure. By transposing the groups, one can similarly sign messages in $\mathbb{H}^k$. Obtaining a scheme for a vector of Diffie-Hellman messages or a mixture of unilateral and Diffie-Hellman messages from our scheme is straightforward. The scheme for message space $\mathbb{G}^k$ is as follows:

- KeyGen($\mathcal{P}$): Select $x_1, \ldots, x_k, y \leftarrow \mathbb{Z}_p^{\times}$. Set sk $:= (x_1, \ldots, x_k, y)$ and vk $:= (\tilde{X}_1, \ldots, \tilde{X}_k, \tilde{Y}) := (\tilde{H}^{x_1}, \ldots \tilde{H}^{x_k}, \tilde{H}^y) \in \mathbb{H}^{k+1}$.
- Sign(sk, $(M_1, \ldots, M_k) \in \mathbb{G}^k$): Return $\sigma := \left(G^{x_1} \cdot M_1 \cdot \prod_{i=2}^{k} M_i^{x_i}\right)^{\frac{1}{y}} \in \mathbb{G}$.
- Verify(vk, $(M_1, \ldots, M_k), \sigma$): Return 1 iff $\sigma \in \mathbb{G}$, $M_i \in \mathbb{G}$ for $i = 1, \ldots, k$, and $\hat{e}(\sigma, \tilde{Y}) = \hat{e}(G, \tilde{X}_1)\hat{e}(M_1, \tilde{H})\prod_{i=2}^{k} \hat{e}(M_i, \tilde{X}_i)$.

Correctness of the scheme follows by inspection. The Sign algorithm is deterministic and hence for any message there is 1 potential signature. The proof of the following theorem is in the full version [33].

Theorem 5. *The scheme is sEUF-CMA secure against a one-time chosen-message attack.*

5   Optimal Partially Structure-Preserving Signature Scheme for a Vector of Messages

We give here an optimal scheme for the message space $\widehat{\mathbb{GH}} \times \mathbb{Z}_p^k$. We call such a variant *partially structure-preserving* since other than allowing some part of the messages to not be group elements, the scheme conforms to the rest of the requirements of structure-preserving signatures.

Given the description of Type-III bilinear groups $\mathcal{P}$ output by $\mathcal{BG}(1^{\kappa})$, the scheme is as follows:

- KeyGen($\mathcal{P}$): Select $x, y_1, \ldots, y_k, z \leftarrow \mathbb{Z}_p^\times$. Set $\tilde{X} := \tilde{H}^x$, $\tilde{Y}_i := \tilde{H}^{y_i}$ for all $i \in [k]$, $\tilde{Z} := \tilde{H}^z$. Set $\mathsf{sk} := (x, y_1, \ldots, y_k, z)$ and $\mathsf{vk} := (\tilde{X}, \tilde{Y}_1, \ldots, \tilde{Y}_k, \tilde{Z})$.
- Sign$\Big(\mathsf{sk}, \big((M, \tilde{N}), \boldsymbol{u} = (u_1, \ldots, u_k)\big)\Big)$: To sign a Diffie-Hellman pair $(M, \tilde{N}) \in \widehat{\mathbb{GH}}$ and a vector $\boldsymbol{u} = (u_1, \ldots, u_k) \in \mathbb{Z}_p^k$, select $r \leftarrow \mathbb{Z}_p^\times$, and set $R := G^r$, $S := \big(M \cdot G^{x + \sum_{i=1}^k u_i y_i}\big)^{\frac{r}{z}}$. Return $\sigma := (R, S) \in \mathbb{G}^2$.
- Verify$\Big(\mathsf{vk}, \big((M, \tilde{N}), \boldsymbol{u}\big), \sigma = (R, S)\Big)$: Return 1 iff $R \in \mathbb{G}^\times$, $(M, \tilde{N}) \in \widehat{\mathbb{GH}}$, and $\hat{e}(S, \tilde{Z}) = \hat{e}(R, \tilde{N} \cdot \tilde{X} \cdot \prod_{i=1}^k \tilde{Y}_i^{u_i})$.
- Randomize$\Big(\mathsf{vk}, \big((M, \tilde{N}), \boldsymbol{u}\big), \sigma = (R, S)\Big)$: Select $r' \leftarrow \mathbb{Z}_p^\times$, and set $R' := R^{r'}$, $S' := S^{r'}$. Return $\sigma' := (R', S')$.

Correctness of the scheme is straightforward to verify. The signatures are perfectly randomizable. We now prove the following theorem.

Theorem 6. *The scheme is EUF-CMA secure.*

Proof. Let $\mathcal{A}$ be an adversary against the scheme. Using $\mathcal{A}$, we can build an adversary $\mathcal{B}$ against the unforgeability of Scheme II in Sect. 3.2. Adversary $\mathcal{B}$ gets $\mathsf{vk}' = (\tilde{X}', \tilde{Y}')$ from her game where she has access to a sign oracle. She chooses $y_1, \ldots, y_k \leftarrow \mathbb{Z}_p$ and sets $\tilde{Y}_i := \tilde{H}^{y_i}$ for $i = 1, \ldots, k$. She starts $\mathcal{A}$ on the verification key $\mathsf{vk} := (\tilde{X} := \tilde{X}', \tilde{Y}_1, \ldots, \tilde{Y}_k, \tilde{Z} := \tilde{Y}')$. When receiving a query on $\big((M, \tilde{N})_i, \boldsymbol{u}_i\big)$ from $\mathcal{A}$, $\mathcal{B}$ returns $\bot$ if $(M, \tilde{N})_i \notin \widehat{\mathbb{GH}}$. Otherwise, she forwards the message $(M'_i, \tilde{N}'_i) := \left(M_i \cdot G^{\sum_{j=1}^k y_j u_{i,j}}, \tilde{N}_i \cdot \tilde{H}^{\sum_{j=1}^k y_j u_{i,j}} \right) \in \widehat{\mathbb{GH}}$ to her sign oracle and returns the signature she gets to $\mathcal{A}$. Such a signature is a valid signature on the message $\big((M, \tilde{N})_i, \boldsymbol{u}_i\big)$.

Eventually, when $\mathcal{A}$ outputs her forgery σ^* on $\big((M^*, \tilde{N}^*), \boldsymbol{u}^*\big)$, $\mathcal{B}$ returns $\left(\left(M' := M^* \cdot G^{\sum_{j=1}^k y_j u_j^*}, \tilde{N}' := \tilde{N}^* \cdot \tilde{H}^{\sum_{j=1}^k y_j u_j^*} \right), \sigma^* \right)$ in her game. Thus, $\mathcal{B}$ wins her game with the same advantage as that of $\mathcal{A}$ in her game. $\square$

6 Applications

Here we highlight some applications of our new schemes.

Direct Anonymous Attestation (DAA). DAA [15] is a protocol deployed in practice for realizing trusted computing. Bernhard et al. [14] introduced Randomizable Weakly Blind Signature (RwBS) schemes as one of the building blocks for their generic construction of DAA schemes. A RwBS scheme is similar to a standard blind signature scheme [22] but unlike the latter, in the former the signer never gets to see the signed message. DAA is outside of the scope of this paper but for the record we show that combining our publicly re-randomizable scheme from Sect. 3.2 with the SXDH-based Groth-Sahai proofs [37] yields more efficient RwBS schemes (and hence DAA schemes) not relying on random oracles than existing ones [13,32]. The RwBS constructions in [13,32] combine SPS schemes from [30,32], respectively, with SXDH-based Groth-Sahai proofs [37]. The underlying (less efficient) SPS schemes used in [13,32] have the same message space as ours, and similarly to our schemes, enjoy fully randomizable unilateral signatures.

The construction is based on the observation that since signing in those schemes only requires the $\mathbb{G}$ component of the message, whereas verification requires the $\mathbb{H}$ component of the message, it suffices for the user to only submit the $\mathbb{G}$ component of the message along with a zero-knowledge proof of knowledge of the $\mathbb{H}$ component when requesting signatures. The signer then has to accompany the signature she returns with a zero-knowledge proof of correctness of the returned signature. The final RwBS signature is then just a re-randomization of the signature. The RwBS construction as well as the proofs (which can be found in the full version [33]) are very similar to those in [13,32]. The difference lies in the zero-knowledge proofs used in the signing protocol. Our RwBS scheme yields signatures of size $2|\mathbb{G}|$ and require 1 PPE equation (2 pairings in total) to verify and hence is more efficient than those in [13,32].

Attribute-Based Signatures. Attribute-Based Signatures (ABS) [42] allow signers to authenticate messages while enjoying fine-grained control over identifying information. El Kaafarani et al. [24] introduced the notion of Decentralized Traceable Attribute-Based Signatures (DTABS) which adds the traceability feature to standard ABS schemes while allowing attribute authorities to operate in a decentralized manner. Ghadafi [31] revisited the latter notion and provided strengthening of some of the security requirements as well as more efficient constructions. For security definitions and applications refer to [24,31,42].

The most efficient existing DTABS construction not relying on random oracles is the one in [31] which uses the optimal structure-preserving signature scheme from [4] and yields signatures of size $(27|\mathbb{P}| + 19) \cdot |\mathbb{G}| + (22|\mathbb{P}| + 15) \cdot |\mathbb{H}| + (\beta + 3) \cdot |p|$, where $|\mathbb{P}|$ is the number of attributes in the signing policy $\mathbb{P}$, i.e. the number of rows of the span program matrix, whereas β is the number of columns. By instantiating the generic DTABS construction from [31] with the same tools as the instantiations in [31] with the exception of using our partially structure-preserving signature scheme from Sect. 5 to instantiate the tagged signature building block (where the verification key of the user is the Diffie-Hellman component of the message, whereas the attributes are the $\mathbb{Z}_p$ component), we obtain a construction of DTABS not relying on random oracles with signatures of size $(17|\mathbb{P}| + 24) \cdot |\mathbb{G}| + (14|\mathbb{P}| + 18) \cdot |\mathbb{H}| + (\beta + 3) \cdot |p|$ which is shorter than all existing constructions. Security of the instantiation follows from that of the generic construction of [31]. See the full version [33] for details.

7   Lower Bounds and Impossibility Results

Here we prove some lower bounds and impossibility results for USPSDH schemes.

Impossibility of One-Element Signatures. We prove that there is no generic-signer USPSDH scheme with one-element signatures that is EUF-RMA secure against $q > 1$ signing queries.

Theorem 7. *There is no generic-signer USPSDH scheme with one-element signatures that is unforgeable against a random-message attack for $q > 1$ signing queries.*

Proof. Consider the case where the signature $\sigma := S \in \mathbb{G}$, whereas the verification key $\mathsf{vk} = (\tilde{X}_1, \ldots, \tilde{X}_n) \in \mathbb{H}^n$. The proof for the opposite case is similar.

We first prove that it is redundant for a USPSDH scheme (for a single Diffie-Hellman pair) with one-element signatures to have more than 1 verification equation (not counting the cost for verifying the well-formedness of the message).

Lemma 1. *One verification equation is sufficient for a one-element signature scheme.*

Proof. Such a scheme has verification equations of the form of Eq. (3).

$$\prod \hat{e}(S, \tilde{X}_i)^{a_{i,\ell}} \prod \hat{e}(M, \tilde{X}_i)^{b_{i,\ell}} \hat{e}(S, \tilde{N})^{c_\ell} \hat{e}(M, \tilde{N})^{d_\ell} = Z_{\ell_\mathbb{T}} \tag{3}$$

Each of those equations is linear in S. Thus, we can compute a single non-trivial equation linear in S (which uniquely determines S) as a linear combination of all equations and use it for verification. If there is no such combination, the equations must be linearly dependent and hence some of them are redundant. By excluding those, we can reduce them to a single equation linear in S. $\square$

For the scheme to be (perfectly) correct (and publicly verifiable), signatures must verify w.r.t. the (fixed) verification key and (fixed) public parameters (if any). By taking the discrete logarithms of the group elements in the (single) verification equation, we can write the verification equation as

$$s(\sum_{i=1}^{n} a_i x_i + cm) + m(\sum_{i=1}^{n} b_i x_i + dm) = z \tag{4}$$

This implies that there exists at most one potential signature for the message. Since the signing algorithm is generic, a signature σ_i on $(M_i, \tilde{N}_i)$ has the form $\sigma_i = M_i^\alpha \cdot G^\beta$ for some (fixed) $\alpha, \beta \in \mathbb{Z}_p$. Now given signatures σ_1 and σ_2 on distinct random messages $(M_1, \tilde{N}_1), (M_2, \tilde{N}_2)$, respectively, we have $\sigma_1 = M_1^\alpha \cdot G^\beta$ and $\sigma_2 = M_2^\alpha \cdot G^\beta$. By computing $\sigma^* := \sigma_1^\gamma \cdot \sigma_2^{(1-\gamma)}$ we obtain a valid forgery on the message $(M^*, \tilde{N}^*) := \left(M_1^\gamma \cdot M_2^{(1-\gamma)}, \tilde{N}_1^\gamma \cdot \tilde{N}_2^{(1-\gamma)}\right)$ for any $\gamma \in \mathbb{Z}_p$. $\square$

Lower Bounds on the Size of the Verification Key. We prove here that a generic-signer EUF-RMA secure USPSDH scheme with one-element signatures must have at least 2 group elements (excluding the default group generators G and $\tilde{H}$) in the verification key. WLOG, we assume that any public group elements (other than the default group generators) part of the public parameters (if any) are counted as part of the verification key.

Theorem 8. *A generic-signer EUF-RMA secure one-time USPSDH scheme (with one-element signatures) must have at least 2 elements in the verification key.*

Proof. Consider the case where $\sigma = S \in \mathbb{G}$ and $\mathsf{vk} = \tilde{X} \in \mathbb{H}$. The proof for the opposite case is similar. Such a scheme has a verification equation (not counting the check for the well-formedness of the message) of the following form

$$\hat{e}(S, \tilde{X})^a \hat{e}(S, \tilde{H})^b \hat{e}(M, \tilde{X})^c \hat{e}(M, \tilde{H})^d \hat{e}(S, \tilde{N})^u \hat{e}(M, \tilde{N})^v = Z_{\mathbb{T}} \qquad (5)$$

This means that s the discrete logarithm of the signature S has the form

$$s = \frac{z - m(cx + d + vm)}{ax + b + um}$$

A generic signer (who does not know the discrete logarithm m of the message) computes the signature S as $S := M^{\frac{\alpha(x)}{\alpha'(x)}} \cdot G^{\frac{\beta(x)}{\beta'(x)}}$ for some polynomials $\alpha, \alpha', \beta, \beta' \in \mathbb{Z}_p[x]$. Note that none of those polynomials has a term in m. Our proof strategy is to first eliminate some pairings from Eq. (5) which can not be computed by a generic signer which serves to simplify the proof. Note that without knowledge of the discrete logarithm of the message m, it is hard for a generic signer to construct a non-trivial signature S where its discrete logarithm s contains the message m in a term in the denominator. Thus, WLOG we can assume that we have $u = 0$ in Eq. (5). Similarly, it is hard for a generic signer without knowledge of m to construct a signature that contains a term with degree >1 in m (since none of the above polynomials have a term in m). Therefore, we can also WLOG assume that $v = 0$ in Eq. (5).[2]

We now show that any USPSDH scheme with a verification equation of the form of Eq. (6) cannot be secure.

$$\hat{e}(S, \tilde{X})^a \hat{e}(S, \tilde{H})^b \hat{e}(M, \tilde{X})^c \hat{e}(M, \tilde{H})^d = Z_{\mathbb{T}} \qquad (6)$$

Since the verification key (and the public parameters) contain only $\tilde{X}$, G, and $\tilde{H}$, we have $Z_{\mathbb{T}} = \hat{e}(G, \tilde{H})^e \hat{e}(G, \tilde{X})^f$. Note that the exponents $a, b, c, d, e, f \in \mathbb{Z}_p$ are all public. By taking the discrete logarithms of the group elements, we can write the verification equation as

$$s(ax + b) + m(cx + d) = e + fx \qquad (7)$$

---

[2] Refer to the full version [33] for more justification and discussions on why such assumptions do not affect the generality of our proof and how similar cases also apply to other SPS settings.

Note here if $a = b = 0$, the equation is independent of the signature S. Similarly, if $c = d = 0$, the verification equation is independent of the message $(M, \tilde{N})$. Therefore, neither of those cases should occur as otherwise it is obvious that such a scheme is not secure. We now have four cases as follows:

- **Case $bc \neq ad$:** Given a signature $\sigma = S$ on a random message $(M, \tilde{N})$, pick any $\alpha \leftarrow \mathbb{Z}_p \setminus \{1\}$ and let

$$a_m := \frac{ea(\alpha-1) - bf(\alpha-1)}{bc - ad} \qquad \text{and} \qquad a_s := -\frac{ec(\alpha-1) - df(\alpha-1)}{bc - ad}.$$

  By computing $\sigma^* = S^* := G^{a_s} \cdot S^\alpha$, one obtains a valid forgery on $(M^*, \tilde{N}^*)$ $:= \left(G^{a_m} \cdot M^\alpha, \tilde{H}^{a_m} \tilde{N}^\alpha\right)$.

- **Case $bc = ad \neq 0$:** Given a signature $\sigma = S$ on a random message $(M, \tilde{N})$, pick any $\alpha \leftarrow \mathbb{Z}_p^\times$ and compute $\sigma^* = S^* := G^\alpha \cdot S$, which is a valid forgery on $(M^*, \tilde{N}^*) := \left(G^{\frac{-ba}{d}} \cdot M, \tilde{H}^{\frac{-ba}{d}} \cdot \tilde{N}\right)$.

- **Case $bc = ad = 0$, $a \neq 0$ and $c \neq 0$:** Here we have that $b = d = 0$. Given a signature $\sigma = S$ on a random message $(M, \tilde{N})$, $\sigma^* = S^* := G^{\frac{-c\alpha}{a}} \cdot S$ is a valid forgery on $(M^*, \tilde{N}^*) := \left(G^\alpha \cdot M, \tilde{H}^\alpha \cdot \tilde{N}\right)$ for any $\alpha \in \mathbb{Z}_p^\times$.

- **Case $bc = ad = 0$, $b \neq 0$ and $d \neq 0$:** Here we have that $a = c = 0$. Given a signature $\sigma = S$ on a random message $(M, \tilde{N})$, $\sigma^* = S^* := G^{\frac{-d\alpha}{b}} \cdot S$ is a valid forgery on $(M^*, \tilde{N}^*) := \left(G^\alpha \cdot M, \tilde{H}^\alpha \cdot \tilde{N}\right)$ for any $\alpha \in \mathbb{Z}_p^\times$.

This concludes the proof. $\qquad\qquad\qquad\qquad\qquad\qquad\qquad\qquad\qquad\qquad\square$

We now show that the lower bounds for the verification key proved in Theorem 8 holds even if we allow the (generic-signer) signature to have 2 elements.

Theorem 9. *There is no EUF-RMA one-time USPSDH scheme with two-element signatures, 1 PPE verification equation and one-element verification key.*

Proof. Consider the case where the signature $\sigma = (R, S) \in \mathbb{G}^2$ whereas the verification key $\mathsf{vk} := \tilde{X} \in \mathbb{H}$. The proof for the opposite case is similar. Such a scheme has a verification equation of the form of Eq. (8).

$$\hat{e}(R, \tilde{X})^a \hat{e}(R, \tilde{N})^b \hat{e}(R, \tilde{H})^c \hat{e}(S, \tilde{X})^d \hat{e}(S, \tilde{H})^u \hat{e}(M, \tilde{X})^v \hat{e}(M, \tilde{H})^w = Z_\mathbb{T} \qquad (8)$$

As argued in the proof of Theorem 8, since the signing algorithm is generic, WLOG neither R nor S can have a degree >1 of m (the discrete logarithm of the message) or have a term in m in the denominator. It is obvious that a scheme with both signature components independent of the message is insecure. Thus, at least one component of the signature must depend on the message. WLOG, let's assume that S depends on the message while R is independent of the message. If it is the other way around, we just need to replace the term $\hat{e}(R, \tilde{N})^b$ with $\hat{e}(S, \tilde{N})^b$ in Eq. (8) and the proof is similar. If both components of the signature depend on the message, Eq. (8) can be simplified by setting $b = 0$ which is a special case of the cases we prove.

Since we only have $\tilde{X}, G, \tilde{H}$ in the verification key (and the public parameters), we have $Z_{\mathbb{T}} = \hat{e}(G, \tilde{H})^e \hat{e}(G, \tilde{X})^f$. Note $a, b, c, d, e, f, u, v, w \in \mathbb{Z}_p$ are all public. By taking discrete logarithms, we can write the verification equation as

$$r(ax + bm + c) + s(dx + u) + m(vx + w) = e + fx \tag{9}$$

We start by listing 3 trivial forgery cases as follows:

1. **Case $a = b = c = 0$ or $d = u = 0$:** This means the verification equation is independent of one of the signature components and thus we are back into the one-element signature case which is already proven by Theorem 8.
2. **Case $a = d = f = v = 0$:** This means the verification equation is independent of the verification key (and hence σ is independent of sk).
3. **Case $b = v = w = 0$:** This means the verification equation is independent of the message m and hence the signature is valid on any other message.

Excluding the above obvious forgery cases, we can find a forgery by solving the following system of equations in the 9 unknowns $\alpha_m, \beta_m, \alpha_r, \beta_r, \gamma_r, \alpha_s, \beta_s, \gamma_s, \delta_s$

$$u\alpha_s + e\gamma_s - e + b\alpha_r\alpha_m + c\alpha_r + w\alpha_m = 0 \qquad d\alpha_s + f\gamma_s - f + a\alpha_r + v\alpha_m = 0$$

$$u\beta_s - w\gamma_s + b\beta_r\alpha_m + b\alpha_r\beta_m + c\beta_r + w\beta_m = 0 \qquad u\delta_s - c\gamma_s + b\gamma_r\alpha_m + c\gamma_r = 0$$

$$d\delta_s - a\gamma_s + a\gamma_r = 0 \qquad d\beta_s - v\gamma_s + a\beta_r + v\beta_m = 0$$

$$\gamma_s - \gamma_r\beta_m = 0 \qquad \beta_r\beta_m = 0$$

This is a system of 8 equations in 9 unknowns and we get two family of solutions depending on whether $\beta_m = 0$ (where forgeries require no signing queries) or $\beta_m \neq 0$ (where forgeries require a single random-message signing query). Refer to the full version [33] for the full proof. $\qquad \square$

Impossibility of sEUF-CMA Secure Schemes. The following theorem whose proof is in the full version [33] proves that there is no generic-signer USPSDH scheme that is sEUF-CMA against an adversary making $q > 1$ signing queries. We note, however, that there exist sEUF-RMA secure schemes and sEUF-CMA secure schemes, e.g. Scheme I, against an adversary that is not allowed multiple queries on the same message.

Theorem 10. *There is no generic-signer USPSDH scheme that is sEUF-CMA secure against an adversary making $q > 1$ signing queries.*

References

1. Abe, M., Chase, M., David, B., Kohlweiss, M., Nishimaki, R., Ohkubo, M.: Constant-size structure-preserving signatures: generic constructions and simple assumptions. In: Wang, X., Sako, K. (eds.) ASIACRYPT 2012. LNCS, vol. 7658, pp. 4–24. Springer, Heidelberg (2012). doi:10.1007/978-3-642-34961-4_3

2. Abe, M., David, B., Kohlweiss, M., Nishimaki, R., Ohkubo, M.: Tagged one-time signatures: tight security and optimal tag size. In: Kurosawa, K., Hanaoka, G. (eds.) PKC 2013. LNCS, vol. 7778, pp. 312–331. Springer, Heidelberg (2013). doi:10.1007/978-3-642-36362-7_20

3. Abe, M., Fuchsbauer, G., Groth, J., Haralambiev, K., Ohkubo, M.: Structure-preserving signatures and commitments to group elements. In: Rabin, T. (ed.) CRYPTO 2010. LNCS, vol. 6223, pp. 209–236. Springer, Heidelberg (2010). doi:10.1007/978-3-642-14623-7_12

4. Abe, M., Groth, J., Haralambiev, K., Ohkubo, M.: Optimal structure-preserving signatures in asymmetric bilinear groups. In: Rogaway, P. (ed.) CRYPTO 2011. LNCS, vol. 6841, pp. 649–666. Springer, Heidelberg (2011). doi:10.1007/978-3-642-22792-9_37

5. Abe, M., Groth, J., Ohkubo, M.: Separating short structure-preserving signatures from non-interactive assumptions. In: Lee, D.H., Wang, X. (eds.) ASIACRYPT 2011. LNCS, vol. 7073, pp. 628–646. Springer, Heidelberg (2011). doi:10.1007/978-3-642-25385-0_34

6. Abe, M., Groth, J., Ohkubo, M., Tibouchi, M.: Unified, minimal and selectively randomizable structure-preserving signatures. In: Lindell, Y. (ed.) TCC 2014. LNCS, vol. 8349, pp. 688–712. Springer, Heidelberg (2014). doi:10.1007/978-3-642-54242-8_29

7. Abe, M., Groth, J., Ohkubo, M., Tibouchi, M.: Structure-preserving signatures from type ii pairings. In: Garay, J.A., Gennaro, R. (eds.) CRYPTO 2014. LNCS, vol. 8616, pp. 390–407. Springer, Heidelberg (2014). doi:10.1007/978-3-662-44371-2_22

8. Abe, M., Kohlweiss, M., Ohkubo, M., Tibouchi, M.: Fully structure-preserving signatures and shrinking commitments. In: Oswald, E., Fischlin, M. (eds.) EUROCRYPT 2015. LNCS, vol. 9057, pp. 35–65. Springer, Heidelberg (2015). doi:10.1007/978-3-662-46803-6_2

9. Ambrona, M., Barthe, G., Schmidt, B.: Automated unbounded analysis of cryptographic constructions in the generic group model. In: Fischlin, M., Coron, J.-S. (eds.) EUROCRYPT 2016. LNCS, vol. 9666, pp. 822–851. Springer, Heidelberg (2016). doi:10.1007/978-3-662-49896-5_29

10. Attrapadung, N., Libert, B., Peters, T.: Computing on authenticated data: new privacy definitions and constructions. In: Wang, X., Sako, K. (eds.) ASIACRYPT 2012. LNCS, vol. 7658, pp. 367–385. Springer, Heidelberg (2012). doi:10.1007/978-3-642-34961-4_23

11. Baldimtsi, F., Chase, M., Fuchsbauer, G., Kohlweiss, M.: Anonymous transferable e-cash. In: Katz, J. (ed.) PKC 2015. LNCS, vol. 9020, pp. 101–124. Springer, Heidelberg (2015). doi:10.1007/978-3-662-46447-2_5

12. Barthe, G., Fagerholm, E., Fiore, D., Scedrov, A., Schmidt, B., Tibouchi, M.: Strongly-optimal structure preserving signatures from type ii pairings: synthesis and lower bounds. In: Katz, J. (ed.) PKC 2015. LNCS, vol. 9020, pp. 355–376. Springer, Heidelberg (2015). doi:10.1007/978-3-662-46447-2_16

13. Bernhard, D., Fuchsbauer, G., Ghadafi, E.: Efficient signatures of knowledge and DAA in the standard model. In: Jacobson, M., Locasto, M., Mohassel, P., Safavi-Naini, R. (eds.) ACNS 2013. LNCS, vol. 7954, pp. 518–533. Springer, Heidelberg (2013). doi:10.1007/978-3-642-38980-1_33

14. Bernhard, D., Fuchsbauer, G., Ghadafi, E., Smart, N.P., Warinschi, B.: Anonymous attestation with user-controlled linkability. Int. J. Inf. Secur. 12(3), 219–249 (2013)

15. Brickell, E., Camenisch, J., Chen, L.: Direct anonymous attestation. In: CCS 2004, pp. 132–145. ACM (2004)

16. Camenisch, J., Dubovitskaya, M., Haralambiev, K.: Efficient structure-preserving signature scheme from standard assumptions. In: Visconti, I., Prisco, R. (eds.) SCN 2012. LNCS, vol. 7485, pp. 76–94. Springer, Heidelberg (2012). doi:10.1007/978-3-642-32928-9_5

17. Camenisch, J., Dubovitskaya, M., Haralambiev, K., Kohlweiss, M.: Composable and modular anonymous credentials: definitions and practical constructions. In: Iwata, T., Cheon, J.H. (eds.) ASIACRYPT 2015. LNCS, vol. 9453, pp. 262–288. Springer, Heidelberg (2015). doi:10.1007/978-3-662-48800-3_11

18. Camenisch, J., Lysyanskaya, A.: Signature schemes and anonymous credentials from bilinear maps. In: Franklin, M. (ed.) CRYPTO 2004. LNCS, vol. 3152, pp. 56–72. Springer, Heidelberg (2004). doi:10.1007/978-3-540-28628-8_4

19. Chase, M., Kohlweiss, M.: A new hash-and-sign approach and structure-preserving signatures from DLIN. In: Visconti, I., Prisco, R. (eds.) SCN 2012. LNCS, vol. 7485, pp. 131–148. Springer, Heidelberg (2012). doi:10.1007/978-3-642-32928-9_8

20. Chatterjee, S., Hankerson, D., Knapp, E., Menezes, A.: Comparing two pairing-based aggregate signature schemes. Des. Codes Crypt. 55(2010), 141–167 (2010)

21. Chatterjee, S., Menezes, A.: Type 2 structure-preserving signature schemes revisited. In: Iwata, T., Cheon, J.H. (eds.) ASIACRYPT 2015. LNCS, vol. 9452, pp. 286–310. Springer, Heidelberg (2015). doi:10.1007/978-3-662-48797-6_13

22. Chaum, D.: Blind signatures for untraceable payments. In: Chaum, D., Rivest, R.L., Sherman, A.T. (eds.) CRYPTO 1982. LNCS, pp. 199–203. Springer, Boston (1983). doi:10.1007/978-1-4757-0602-4_18

23. ElGamal, T.: A public key cryptosystem and a signature scheme based on discrete logarithms. IEEE Trans. Inf. Theory 31(4), 469–472 (1985)

24. Kaafarani, A., Ghadafi, E., Khader, D.: Decentralized traceable attribute-based signatures. In: Benaloh, J. (ed.) CT-RSA 2014. LNCS, vol. 8366, pp. 327–348. Springer, Cham (2014). doi:10.1007/978-3-319-04852-9_17

25. Fiat, A., Shamir, A.: How to prove yourself: practical solutions to identification and signature problems. In: Odlyzko, A.M. (ed.) CRYPTO 1986. LNCS, vol. 263, pp. 186–194. Springer, Heidelberg (1987). doi:10.1007/3-540-47721-7_12

26. Fuchsbauer, G.: Automorphic Signatures in Bilinear Groups and an Application to Round-Optimal Blind Signatures. Cryptology ePrint Archive, Report 2009/320

27. Fuchsbauer, G.: Commuting signatures and verifiable encryption. In: Paterson, K.G. (ed.) EUROCRYPT 2011. LNCS, vol. 6632, pp. 224–245. Springer, Heidelberg (2011). doi:10.1007/978-3-642-20465-4_14

28. Fuchsbauer, G., Hanser, C., Slamanig, D.: Practical round-optimal blind signatures in the standard model. In: Gennaro, R., Robshaw, M. (eds.) CRYPTO 2015. LNCS, vol. 9216, pp. 233–253. Springer, Heidelberg (2015). doi:10.1007/978-3-662-48000-7_12

29. Galbraith, S., Paterson, K., Smart, N.P.: Pairings for cryptographers. Discrete Appl. Math. 156(2008), 3113–3121 (2008)

30. Ghadafi, E.: Formalizing group blind signatures and practical constructions without random oracles. In: Boyd, C., Simpson, L. (eds.) ACISP 2013. LNCS, vol. 7959, pp. 330–346. Springer, Heidelberg (2013). doi:10.1007/978-3-642-39059-3_23

31. Ghadafi, E.: Stronger security notions for decentralized traceable attribute-based signatures and more efficient constructions. In: Nyberg, K. (ed.) CT-RSA 2015. LNCS, vol. 9048, pp. 391–409. Springer, Cham (2015). doi:10.1007/978-3-319-16715-2_21

32. Ghadafi, E.: Short structure-preserving signatures. In: Sako, K. (ed.) CT-RSA 2016. LNCS, vol. 9610, pp. 305–321. Springer, Cham (2016). doi:10.1007/978-3-319-29485-8_18

33. Ghadafi, E.: More Efficient Structure-Preserving Signatures - Or: Bypassing the Type-III Lower Bounds. Cryptology ePrint Archive, Report 2016/255. http://eprint.iacr.org/2016/255.pdf

34. Green, M., Hohenberger, S.: Universally composable adaptive oblivious transfer. In: Pieprzyk, J. (ed.) ASIACRYPT 2008. LNCS, vol. 5350, pp. 179–197. Springer, Heidelberg (2008). doi:10.1007/978-3-540-89255-7_12

35. Groth, J.: Simulation-sound NIZK proofs for a practical language and constant size group signatures. In: Lai, X., Chen, K. (eds.) ASIACRYPT 2006. LNCS, vol. 4284, pp. 444–459. Springer, Heidelberg (2006). doi:10.1007/11935230_29

36. Groth, J.: Efficient fully structure-preserving signatures for large messages. In: Iwata, T., Cheon, J.H. (eds.) ASIACRYPT 2015. LNCS, vol. 9452, pp. 239–259. Springer, Heidelberg (2015). doi:10.1007/978-3-662-48797-6_11

37. Groth, J., Sahai, A.: Efficient non-interactive proof systems for bilinear groups. SIAM J. Comput. 41(5), 1193–1232 (2012)

38. Hofheinz, D., Jager, T.: Tightly secure signatures and public-key encryption. In: Safavi-Naini, R., Canetti, R. (eds.) CRYPTO 2012. LNCS, vol. 7417, pp. 590–607. Springer, Heidelberg (2012). doi:10.1007/978-3-642-32009-5_35

39. Jutla, C.S., Roy, A.: Improved structure preserving signatures under standard bilinear assumptions. In: Fehr, S. (ed.) PKC 2017. LNCS, vol. 10175, pp. 183–209. Springer, Heidelberg (2017). doi:10.1007/978-3-662-54388-7_7

40. Kiltz, E., Pan, J., Wee, H.: Structure-preserving signatures from standard assumptions, revisited. In: Gennaro, R., Robshaw, M. (eds.) CRYPTO 2015. LNCS, vol. 9216, pp. 275–295. Springer, Heidelberg (2015). doi:10.1007/978-3-662-48000-7_14

41. Libert, B., Peters, T., Yung, M.: Short group signatures via structure-preserving signatures: standard model security from simple assumptions. In: Gennaro, R., Robshaw, M. (eds.) CRYPTO 2015. LNCS, vol. 9216, pp. 296–316. Springer, Heidelberg (2015). doi:10.1007/978-3-662-48000-7_15

42. Maji, H.K., Prabhakaran, M., Rosulek, M.: Attribute-based signatures. In: Kiayias, A. (ed.) CT-RSA 2011. LNCS, vol. 6558, pp. 376–392. Springer, Heidelberg (2011). doi:10.1007/978-3-642-19074-2_24

43. Maurer, U.: Abstract models of computation in cryptography. In: Smart, N.P. (ed.) Cryptography and Coding 2005. LNCS, vol. 3796, pp. 1–12. Springer, Heidelberg (2005). doi:10.1007/11586821_1

44. Pointcheval, D., Sanders, O.: Short randomizable signatures. In: Sako, K. (ed.) CT-RSA 2016. LNCS, vol. 9610, pp. 111–126. Springer, Cham (2016). doi:10.1007/978-3-319-29485-8_7

45. Shoup, V.: Lower bounds for discrete logarithms and related problems. In: Fumy, W. (ed.) EUROCRYPT 1997. LNCS, vol. 1233, pp. 256–266. Springer, Heidelberg (1997). doi:10.1007/3-540-69053-0_18

46. Wang, Y., Zhang, Z., Matsuda, T., Hanaoka, G., Tanaka, K.: How to obtain fully structure-preserving (automorphic) signatures from structure-preserving ones. In: Cheon, J.H., Takagi, T. (eds.) ASIACRYPT 2016. LNCS, vol. 10032, pp. 465–495. Springer, Heidelberg (2016). doi:10.1007/978-3-662-53890-6_16

47. Waters, B.: Efficient identity-based encryption without random oracles. In: Cramer, R. (ed.) EUROCRYPT 2005. LNCS, vol. 3494, pp. 114–127. Springer, Heidelberg (2005). doi:10.1007/11426639_7

Adversarial Examples for Malware Detection

Kathrin Grosse[1]([⊠]), Nicolas Papernot[2], Praveen Manoharan[1],
Michael Backes[1], and Patrick McDaniel[2]

[1] Saarland Informatics Campus, CISPA, Saarland University, Saarbrücken, Germany
kathrin.grosse@cispa.saarland
[2] School of Electrical Engineering and CS, Pennsylvania State University,
State College, USA

Abstract. Machine learning models are known to lack robustness against inputs crafted by an adversary. Such adversarial examples can, for instance, be derived from regular inputs by introducing minor—yet carefully selected—perturbations.

In this work, we expand on existing adversarial example crafting algorithms to construct a highly-effective attack that uses adversarial examples against malware detection models. To this end, we identify and overcome key challenges that prevent existing algorithms from being applied against malware detection: our approach operates in discrete and often binary input domains, whereas previous work operated only in continuous and differentiable domains. In addition, our technique guarantees the malware functionality of the adversarially manipulated program. In our evaluation, we train a neural network for malware detection on the DREBIN data set and achieve classification performance matching state-of-the-art from the literature. Using the augmented adversarial crafting algorithm we then manage to mislead this classifier for 63% of all malware samples. We also present a detailed evaluation of defensive mechanisms previously introduced in the computer vision contexts, including distillation and adversarial training, which show promising results.

1 Introduction

Starting with the use of naive Bayes classifiers for spam detection [1], machine learning has been increasingly applied to solve core security problems. For instance, anomaly detection creates a model of expected behavior in order to detect network intrusions or other instances of malicious activities [35]. Classification with machine learning is also applied to automate the detection of unwanted software like malware [29], or to automate source code analysis [33].

This includes Deep neural networks (DNNs) in security-critical applications, such as malware detection [6,31]. While the benefits applying DNNs are undisputed, previous work has also shown that, as is the case for many machine learning models, they lack robustness to adversarially crafted inputs known as *adversarial examples*. These inputs are derived from legitimate inputs by adding carefully chosen perturbations that force models to output erroneous predictions [9,25,36].

© Springer International Publishing AG 2017
S.N. Foley et al. (Eds.): ESORICS 2017, Part II, LNCS 10493, pp. 62–79, 2017.
DOI: 10.1007/978-3-319-66399-9_4

To evaluate the applicability of adversarial examples to a core security problem, we chose the settings of malware detection. In contrast to the task of image classification, the span of acceptable perturbations is greatly reduced: the model input is now a set of features taking discrete values. Thus, acceptable perturbations must correspond exactly to one of these discrete values. Furthermore, the similarity criteria defined by human perception is replaced by the more challenging requirement that perturbations do not jeopardize the software's malware functionality pursued by the adversary.

In this paper, we show that android malware detection that uses neural networks, with performance comparable to the state-of-the-art, is easy to deceive with adversarial examples. Furthermore, we find that hardening the model to increase its robustness to these attacks is a very difficult task. Our attack approach elaborates on an adversarial example crafting algorithm previously introduced in [25]. Our approach thus generalizes to any malware detection system using a differentiable classification function.

Contributions. We expand the method originally proposed by Papernot et al. [25] to attack Android malware detection. We adapt it to handle binary features while at the same time preserving the Apps malicious functionality.

Applying the attack, *we are able to mislead our best performing malware detector (on the DREBIN dataset [2]) at rates higher than* 63%.

As a second contribution, we investigate potential defense mechanisms for hardening malware detection models trained using DNNs.

We consider defensive distillation [27] and adversarial training [9,36]. The findings of our experimental evaluation of the aforementioned mechanisms is twofold. Applying defensive distillation reduces the rates at which adversarial examples are misclassified, but the improvement observed is often negligible. In comparison, training the model intentionally with adversarially crafted malware applications improves its robustness, as long as the perturbation introduced during adversarial training is carefully chosen.

2 Background

In this section, we explain the general concepts used in this paper. We first give a short introduction to malware detection. Afterwards, we move to the machine learning algorithm we apply, neural networks. Subsequently, we discuss adversarial machine learning with a focus on neural networks. We end the section by briefly reviewing defenses that have been proposed so far.

2.1 Malware Detection

Due to the increasing amount of published programs and applications, malware detection has become application of machine learning. The quality of detection depends then however heavily on the provided features. The literature generally differentiates two types of such features: static and dynamic features. Static features can directly be collected from the application's code and include, for example, n-gram frequencies in the code, opcode usage or control flow graph properties. Dynamic features, the nowadays more popular category, samples features from the application during runtime, observing general behavior, access and communication patterns.

As an example of an approach combining static and dynamic analysis we mention Marvin [20], which extracts features from an application while running it in an analysis sandbox and observing data flow, network behavior and other operations. This approach reaches an accuracy of 98.24% of malicious applications with less than 0.04% false positives.

In malware detection, not only accuracy, but also the false positive and false negative rates matter – classifying malware as benign might lead to a loss of trust by the users, whereas false negatives might lead to great financial loss for companies whose benign applications got classified as malware.

2.2 Neural Networks

We will now have detailed look at neural networks and introduce the required notation and definitions. Neural networks consist of elementary computing units—named *neurons*—organized in interconnected *layers*. Each neuron applies an *activation function* to its input to produce an output. Figure 1 illustrates the general structure of the network used throughout this paper and also introduces the notation used here.

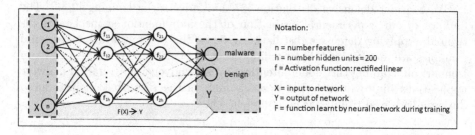

Fig. 1. The structure of deep feed-forward neural network as used in our setting.

Starting with the model input, each network layer produces an output used as input by the next layer. Networks with a single intermediate—*hidden*—layer are qualified as *shallow neural networks* whereas models with multiple hidden layers are *deep neural networks*. Using multiple hidden layers is interpreted as hierarchically extracting representations from the input [8], eventually producing a representation relevant to solve the machine learning task and output a prediction.

A neural network model **F** can be formalized as the composition of multi-dimensional and parametrized functions f_i each corresponding to a layer of the network architecture—and a representation of the input:

$$\mathbf{F} : \boldsymbol{x} \mapsto f_n(...f_2(f_1(\boldsymbol{x}, \theta_1), \theta_2)..., \theta_n) \tag{1}$$

where each vector θ_i parametrizes layer i of the network $\mathbf{F}$ and includes weights for the links connecting layer i to layer $i-1$. The set of model parameters $\theta = \{\theta_i\}$ is learned during training. For instance, in supervised settings, parameter values are fixed by computing prediction errors $f(x) - y$ on a collection of known input-output pairs $(\boldsymbol{x}, \boldsymbol{y})$.

2.3   Adversarial Machine Learning

DNNs, like numerous machine learning models, have been shown to be vulnerable to adversarial manipulations of their inputs [36]. Adversarial goals thereby vary from simple *misclassification* of the input in a class different from the legitimate source class to *source-target misclassification* where samples from any source class are to be misclassified in a chosen *target class*. The space of adversaries was formalized for multi-class deep learning classifiers in a taxonomy [25]. Adversaries can also be taxonomized by the knowledge of the targeted model they must possess to perform their attacks.

Crafting an adversarial example $\boldsymbol{x}^*$—misclassified by model $\mathbf{F}$—from a legitimate sample $\boldsymbol{x}$ can be formalized as the following problem [36]:

$$\boldsymbol{x}^* = \boldsymbol{x} + \delta_{\boldsymbol{x}} = \boldsymbol{x} + \min \|\boldsymbol{z}\| \text{ s.t. } \mathbf{F}(\boldsymbol{x} + \boldsymbol{z}) \neq \mathbf{F}(\boldsymbol{x}) \tag{2}$$

where $\delta_{\boldsymbol{x}}$ is the minimal perturbation $\boldsymbol{z}$ yielding misclassification, according to a norm $\|\cdot\|$ appropriate for the input domain.

Due to the non-linearity and non-convexity of models learned by DNNs, a closed form solution to this problem is hard to find. Thus, algorithms were proposed to select perturbations approximatively minimizing the optimization problem stated in Eq. 2. The *fast gradient sign method* introduced by Goodfellow et al. [9] linearizes the model's cost function around the input to be perturbed and selects a perturbation by differentiating this cost function with respect to the input itself and not the network parameters like is traditionally the case during training. The *forward derivative* based approach introduced by Papernot et al. [25] evaluates the model's output sensitivity to each input component using its Jacobian matrix. From this, we derive a saliency map ranking the individual features by their influence for a particular class.

All previous attack are white-box attacks, since they require access to the differentiable model. Additionally, black-box attacks leveraging both of the previous approaches to target unknown remotely hosted DNNs was proposed in [24]. The attack first approximates the targeted model by querying it for output labels to train a substitute model, which is then used to craft adversarial examples also misclassified by the originally targeted model.

Several approaches have also been presented in the literature to harden classifiers against such crafted inputs. Goodfellow et al. [9] employed an explicit training with adversarial examples. Papernot et al. [27] proposed distillation as another potential defense, of which a simpler alternative—label smoothing—was investigated by Warde-Farley et al. [38]. Since both, adversarial training and distillation, have only been investigated in the image classification setting, we will evaluate their performance for malware detection in Sect. 5.

3   Methodology

This section describes the approach to adversarial crafting for malware detection. We start by describing the data and how we train and configure the DNNs. Thereafter, we describe in detail how we craft adversarial examples, and detail how the perturbation search during adversarial example crafting needs to be adapted to our settings of malware detection.

3.1   Application Model

In the following, we describe the representation of applications we use as input to our malware detector. In this work, we focus on statically determined features of applications. As a feature, we understand some property that the statically evaluated code of the application exhibits. This includes whether the application uses a specific system call or not, as well as a usage of specific hardware components or access to the Internet.

A natural way to represent such features is using *binary indicator vectors*: Given features $1, \ldots, M$, we represent an application using the binary vector $\mathbf{X} \in \{0,1\}^M$, where X_i indicate whether the application exhibits feature i, i.e. $\mathbf{X}_i = 1$, or not, i.e. $\mathbf{X}_i = 0$. Due to the varied nature of applications that are available, M will typically be very large and sparse: each single application only exhibits very few features relatively to the entire feature set. This leads to very sparse feature vectors, and overall, a very sparsely populated space of applications in which we try to successfully separate malicious from benign applications.

3.2   Training the Malware Classifier

In this section, we describe how we train a malware detector using DNNs.

While Dahl et al. [6] use a neural network to classify malware, their approach uses random projections and dynamic data. Since perturbing dynamically gathered features is a lot more challenging than modifying static features, we consider the simpler, static case in this work and leave the dynamic case for future work. Also Saxe et al. [31] proposed a well functioning detection system based on a neural network, which is, to the best of our knowledge, not publicly accessible.

We will thus train out own neural network malware detection system. This also enables us to consider a worst case attacker having full knowledge about model and training data.

Since the binary indicator vector $\mathbf{X}$ we use to represent an application does not possess any particular structural properties or interdependencies, like for example images, we apply a regular, feed-forward neural network as described in Sect. 2 to solve our malware classification task.

We use a rectifier as the activation function for each hidden neuron in our network. As output, we employ a softmax layer for normalization of the output probabilities. the output is thus computed as

Algorithm 1. Crafting adversarial examples for Malware Detection

Input: x, y, F, k, I
1: $\mathbf{x}^* \leftarrow \mathbf{x}$
2: $\Gamma = \{1 \ldots |\mathbf{x}|\}$
3: **while** $\arg\max_j \mathbf{F}_j(\mathbf{x}^*) \neq \mathbf{y}$ and $\|\delta_\mathbf{x}\| < \mathbf{k}$ **do**
4:     Compute forward derivative $\nabla\mathbf{F}(\mathbf{x}^*)$
5:     $i_{max} = \arg\max_{j \in \Gamma \cap \mathbf{I}, X_j = 0} \frac{\partial \mathbf{F}_y(\mathbf{X})}{\partial \mathbf{X}_j}$
6:     **if** $i_{max} \leq 0$ **then**
7:         **return** Failure
8:     **end if**
9:     $\mathbf{x}^*_{i_{max}} = 1$
10:     $\delta_\mathbf{x} \leftarrow \mathbf{x}^* - \mathbf{x}$
11: **end while**
12: **return** $\mathbf{x}^*$

$$\mathbf{F}_i(\mathbf{X}) = \frac{e^{x_i}}{e^{x_0} + e^{x_1}} \; , \; x_i = \sum_{j=1}^{m_n} w_{j,i} \cdot x_j + b_{j,i} \tag{3}$$

To train our network, we use standard gradient descent and standard dropout.

3.3 Crafting Adversarial Malware Examples

We next describe the algorithm that we use to craft adversarial examples against the malware detector we trained in the previous section. The goal of adversarial example crafting in malware detection is to mislead the detection system, causing the output of the classifier for a particular application to change according to the attacker's goal.

More formally, we start with $X \in \{0,1\}^m$, a binary indicator vector that indicates which features are present in an application. Given X, the classifier $\mathbf{F}$ returns a two dimensional vector $\mathbf{F}(\mathbf{X}) = [\mathbf{F}_0(\mathbf{X}), \mathbf{F}_1(\mathbf{X})]$ with $\mathbf{F}_0(\mathbf{X}) + \mathbf{F}_1(\mathbf{X}) = 1$ that encodes the classifiers belief that $\mathbf{X}$ is either benign ($\mathbf{F}_0(\mathbf{X})$) or malicious ($\mathbf{F}_1(\mathbf{X})$). We take as the classification result y the option that has the higher probability, i.e. $y = \arg\max_i \mathbf{F}_i(\mathbf{X})$. The goal of adversarial example crafting now is to find a small perturbation δ such that the classification results y' of $\mathbf{F}(X + \delta)$ is different from the original results, i.e. $y' \neq y$. We denote y' as our *target class* in the adversarial example crafting process.

Our goal is to have a malicious application classified as benign, i.e. given a malicious input $\mathbf{X}$, the classification results $y' = 0$. Note that our approach naturally extends to the symmetric case of misclassifying a benign application.

We adopt the adversarial example crafting algorithm based on the Jacobian matrix

$$\mathbf{J_F} = \frac{\partial \mathbf{F}(\mathbf{X})}{\partial \mathbf{X}} = \left[\frac{\partial \mathbf{F}_i(\mathbf{X})}{\partial \mathbf{X}_j}\right]_{i \in 0,1, j \in [1,m]}$$

of the neural network $\mathbf{F}$ put forward by Papernot et al. [25]. Despite it originally being defined for images, we show that a careful adaptation to a different domain is possible. Note, in particular, that this approach is not restricted to the specific DNN we described in the previous section, but to any differentiable classification function F.

To craft an adversarial example, we take mainly two steps. In the first, we compute the gradient of $\mathbf{F}$ with respect to $\mathbf{X}$ to estimate the direction in which a perturbation in $\mathbf{X}$ would change $\mathbf{F}$'s output. In the second step, we choose a perturbation δ of $\mathbf{X}$ with maximal positive gradient into our target class y'. For malware misclassification, this means that we choose the index $i = \arg \max_{j \in [1,m], \mathbf{X}_j = 0} \mathbf{F}_0(\mathbf{X}_j)$ that maximizes the change into our target class 0 by changing $\mathbf{X}_i$. We repeat this process until either (a) we reached the limit for maximum amount of allowed changes or (b) we successfully cause a misclassification. A pseudo-code implementation of the algorithm is given in Algorithm 1.

Ideally, we keep the change small to make sure that we do not cause a negative change of $\mathbf{F}$ due to intermediate changes of the gradient. For computer vision, this is not an issue since the values of pixels are continuous and can be changed by as arbitrarily small perturbations as permitted by the encoding of the image. In the malware detection case, however, we do not have continuous data, but rather discrete input values: since $\mathbf{X} \in {0,1}^m$ is a binary indicator vector, our only option is to increase one component in $\mathbf{X}$ by exactly 1 to retain a valid input to $\mathbf{F}$. This motivates the changes to the original algorithm in [25].

Note finally that we only consider positive changes for positions j at which $\mathbf{X}_j = 0$, which correspond to adding features the application represented by $\mathbf{X}$ (since $\mathbf{X}$ is a binary indicator vector). We discuss this choice in the next subsection.

3.4   Restrictions on Adversarial Examples

To make sure that modifications caused by the above algorithms do not change the application too much, we bound the maximum distortion δ applied to the original sample. As in the computer vision case, we only allow distortions δ with $\|\delta\| \leq k$. We differ, however, in the norm that we apply: in computer vision, the L_∞ norm is often used to bound the maximum change. In our case, each modification to an entry will always change its value by exactly 1, and we thus use the L_1 norm to bound the overall number of features modified. We further bound the number of features to $k = 20$ (see Appendix B for details).

While the main goal of adversarial example crafting is to achieve misclassification, for malware detection, this cannot happen at the cost of the application's functionality: feature changes determined by Algorithm 1 can cause the application in question to lose its malware functionality in parts or completely. Additionally, interdependencies between features can cause a single line of code that is added to a malware sample to change several features at the same time. We discuss this issue more in detail in Appendix A.

To maintain the functionality of the adversarial example, we restrict the adversarial crafting algorithm as follows: first, we will only change features that result in a single line of code that needs to be added to the real application. Second, we only modify *manifest* features which relate to the `AndroidManifest.xml` file contained in any Android application. Together, both of these restrictions ensure that the original functionality of the application is preserved. Note that this approach only makes the crafting adversarial examples harder: instead of using features that have a high impact on misclassification, we skip those that are not manifest features.

4 Experimental Evaluation

We evaluate the training of the neural network based malware detector and adversarial example-induced misclassification of inputs on it. Through our evaluation, we want to validate the following two hypotheses.

First, that the neural network based malware classifier achieves performance comparable to state-of-the-art malware classifiers (on static features) presented in the literature.

Second, the adversarial example crafting algorithm discussed in Sect. 3.3 allows us to successfully mislead the neural network we trained. As a measure of success, we consider the misclassification rate achieved by this algorithm. The misclassification rate is defined as the percentage of malware samples that are classified as benign after being altered, but are correctly classified before.

We base our evaluations on the DREBIN data set, originally introduced by Arp et al. [2]: DREBIN contains 129.013 android applications, of which 123,453 are benign and 5,560 are malicious. There are 8 feature classes, containing 545,333 static features, each of which is represented by a binary value that indicates whether the feature is present in an application or not. This directly translates to the binary indicator vector $\mathbf{X} \in \{0, 1\}^M$ to represent applications, with $M = 545,333$. A more detailed breakdown of the DREBIN data set can be found in Appendix B.

4.1 DNN Model

We train numerous neural network architecture variants, according to the training procedure described in Sect. 3. Since the DREBIN data set has a fairly unbalanced ratio between malware and benign applications, we experiment with different ratios of malware in each training batch to compare the achieved performance values. The number of training iterations is then set in such a way that all malware samples are at least used once. We evaluate the classification performance of each of these networks using accuracy, false negative and false positive rates as performance measures. We decided to pick an architecture consisting of two hidden layers each consisting of 200 neurons and provide more details about the performance of other architecture is a longer version of this paper. In Table 1 the accuracy as well as positive and negative false negative rates are displayed.

In comparison, Arp et al. [2] achieve a 6.1% false negative rate at a 1% false positive rate. Sayfullina et al. [32] even achieve a 0.1% false negative rate, however at the cost of 17.9% false positives. Saxe and Berlin [31] report 95.2% accuracy given 0.1 false positive rate, where the false negative rate is not reported.

Zhu et al. [39], finally, applied feature selection and decision trees and achieved 1% false positives and 7.5% false negatives. As we can see, our networks are close to this trade-offs and can thus be considered comparable to state-of-the-art.

4.2 Adversarial Malware Crafting

Next, we apply the adversarial example crafting algorithm described in Sect. 3 and observe how often the adversarial inputs are able to successfully mislead our neural network based classifiers. As mentioned previously, we quantify the performance of our algorithm through the achieved misclassification rate, which measures the amount of previously correctly classified malware that is misclassified after the adversarial example crafting. In addition, we also measure the average number of modifications required to achieve misclassification to assess which architecture provided a harder time being mislead. As discussed above, we allow at most 20 modification to any of the malware applications.

The performance results are listed in Table 1. As we can see, we achieve misclassification rates from roughly 63% up to 69%. We can observe that the malware ratio used in the training batches is correlated to the misclassification rate: a higher malware ratio generally results in a lower misclassification rate.

Table 1. Performance of the classifiers. Given are used malware ratio (MWR), accuracy, false negative rate (FNR) and false positive rate (FPR). The misclassification rates (MR) and required average distortion (Dist., in number of added features) with a threshold of 20 modifications are given as well. The last five approaches use the DREBIN data set.

Classifier/MR	Accuracy	FNR	FPR	MR	Dist.
Sayfullina et al. [32]	91%	0.1	17.9	–	–
Arp et al. [2]	93.9%	1	6.1	–	–
Zhu et al. [39]	98.7%	7.5	1	–	–
Ours, 0.3	98.35%	9.73	1.29	63.08	14.52
Ours, 0.4	96.6%	8.13	3.19	64.01	14.84
Ours, 0.5	95.93%	6.37	3.96	69.35	13.47

While the set of frequently modified features across all malware samples differ slightly, we can observe trends for frequently modified features across all networks. For the networks of all malware ratios, the most frequently modified features are permissions, which are modified in roughly 30–45% of the cases. Intents and activities come in at second place, modified in 10–20% of the cases.

More specifically, for the network with ratio 0.3, the feature intent.category.DEFAULT was added to 86.4% of the malware samples. In the networks with the other malware ratios, the most modified feature was permission.MODIFY_AUDIO_SETTINGS (82.7% for malware ratio 0.4 and 87% for malware ratio 0.5).

Other features that are modified frequently are for example `activity`. `SplashScreen`, `android.appwidget.provider` or the GPS feature. And while for all networks the `service_receiver` feature was added to many malware samples, other are specific to the networks: for malware ratio 0.3 it is the `BootReceiver`, for 0.4 the `AlarmReceiver` and for 0.5 the `Monitor`.

Overall, of all features that we decided to modify (i.e. the features in the manifest), only 0.0004%, or 89, are used to mislead the classifier. Of this very small set of features, roughly a quarter occurs in more than $1,000$ adversarially crafted examples. A more detailed breakdown can be found in Table 2.

Table 2. Feature classes from the manifest and how they were used to provoke misclassification. Values in brakets denote number of features used in $>1,000$ Apps.

Feature	Total (0.3)	Total (0.4)	Total (0.5)
Activity	16 (3)	14 (5)	14 (2)
Feature	10 (1)	10 (3)	9 (3)
Intent	18 (7)	19 (5)	15 (5)
Permission	44 (11)	38 (10)	29 (10)
Provider	2 (1)	2 (1)	2 (1)
Service_receiver	8 (1)	6 (1)	8 (1)
Σ	99 (25)	90 (26)	78 (23)

Since our algorithm is able to successfully mislead most networks for a large majority of malware samples, we validate the hypothesis that our adversarial example crafting algorithm for malware can be used to mislead neural network based malware detection systems.

5   Defenses

In this section, we investigate the applicability of two defense mechanisms previously introduced—defensive distillation (Papernot et al. [27]) and adversarial training (Szegedy et al. [36])—in the setting of malware classification. We also investigated feature selection as a defense, but leave the description of the approach a longer version of this paper, since it did not yield conclusive results.

To measure the effectiveness of defensive mechanisms against adversarial examples, we monitor the misclassification rates. The misclassification rate is defined as the percentage of malware samples that are misclassified after the application of the adversarial example crafting algorithm, but were correctly classified before. We simply compare these rates of the original network and the network where the mechanism was applied.

5.1   Distillation

We will investigate now a defense introduced in the context of a computer vision application, distillation, and investigate its applicability in binary, discrete cases such as malware detection. We first introduce the concept of distillation as used by Papernot et al. [27]. Afterwards, we present our evaluation.

While distillation was originally proposed by Hinton et al. [12] as a way to transfer knowledge from large neural networks to a smaller ones, Papernot et al. [27] recently proposed using it as a defensive mechanism against adversarial example crafting. They motivate this through its capability to improve the second network's generalization performance (i.e. classification performance on test samples) and the smoothing effect on the decision boundary.

The idea is, in a nutshell, to use an already existing classifier $\mathbf{F}(\mathbf{X})$ that produces probability distribution over the classes $\mathcal{Y}$. This output is used, as labels, to train a second model F'. Since the new label contain more information about the data $\mathbf{X}$ than the simple class labels, the network will perform similar or better than the original network F. In the original idea, the second trained network is smaller than the first one, whereas in Papernot et al.'s approach, both networks are of the same size.

An important detail in the distillation process is the slight modification of the final softmax layer (cf. Eq. 3) in the original network $\mathbf{F}$: instead of the regular softmax normalization, we use

$$\mathbf{F}_i(X) = \left(\frac{e^{z_i(x)/T}}{\sum_{l=1}^{|\mathcal{Y}|} e^{z_l(x)/T}} \right), \tag{4}$$

where T is a distillation parameter called *temperature*. For $T = 1$, we obtain the regular softmax normalization commonly used in training. If T is large, the output probabilities approach a more uniform distribution, whereas for small T, the output of $\mathbf{F}$ will become more extreme. To achieve a good distillation result, we use the output of the original network $\mathbf{F}$ produced at a high temperature T and use this output to train the new network $\mathbf{F}'$.

The overall procedure for hardening our classifier against adversarial examples can thus be summarized in the following three steps.

1. Given the original classifier $\mathbf{F}$ and the samples $\mathcal{X}$, construct a new training data set $D = \{(\mathbf{X}, \mathbf{F}(X)) \mid \mathbf{X} \in \mathcal{X}\}$ that is labeled with $\mathbf{F}$'s output at high temperature.
2. Construct a new neural network $\mathbf{F}'$ with the same architecture as $\mathbf{F}$.
3. Train $\mathbf{F}'$ on D.

Note that both step two and step three are performed under the same high temperature T to achieve a good distillation performance.

Evaluation. We now apply the above procedure on our originally trained classifiers and examine the impact of distillation as a defensive mechanism against

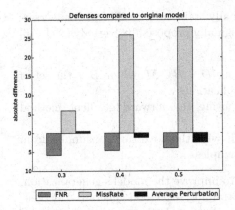

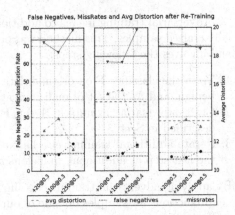

Fig. 2. False negative rates, misclassification rates and average required distortions after applying distillation, original networks are the baseline. For FNR and misclassification rate, higher is better. Average distortion should be negative.

Fig. 3. Misclassification rates, false negative rates and average required distortion achieved on adversarially trained networks. Regular network's performance is given as baseline, indicated by horizontal lines.

adversarial examples in the domain of malware detection. Figure 2 shows the effects of distillation on misclassification compared to the original models. We use a rather low temperature of 10, since we observe a strong decrease of accuracy when distilling on higher temperatures. In general we observe a strong increase of the false negative rate, and a slight increase in the false positive rate. For ratio 0.5, it raises from 4 to 6.4, whereas it is equivalent for 0.3. The accuracy varies in between 93–95%.

We further observe that the misclassification rate drops significantly, in some cases to 38.5% for ratio 0.4. The difference in the average number of perturbed features, however, is rather small. The number of perturbed features is 14 for ratio 0.3 to 16 for the other two.

Using distillation, we can strengthen the neural network against adversarial examples. However, the misclassification rates are still around 40%. Additionally, we pay this robustness with a less good classifier. The effect is further not as strong as on computer vision data. Papernot et al. [27] reported rates around 5% after distillation for images. We further observed that higher temperature (>25), as used in computer vision settings, strongly harms accuracy.

5.2 Adversarial Training

We now apply adversarial training and investigate its influence on the robustness on the resulting classifier. As before, we first introduce the technique of adversarial training and then report the results we observed.

Adversarial training means to additionally train our classifier with adversarially crafted samples. This method was originally proposed by Szegedy et al. [36] and involves the following steps:

1. Train the classifier $\mathbf{F}$ on original data set $D = B \cup M$, where B is the set of benign, and M the set of malicious applications
2. Craft adversarial examples A for $\mathbf{F}$ using the forward gradient method described in Sect. 3.3
3. Iterate additional training epochs on $\mathbf{F}$ with the adversarial examples from the last step as additional, malicious samples.

By applying adversarial training, we aim to improve the model's generalization, i.e. predictions for samples outside of our training set. Good generalization generally makes a classifier less sensitive to small perturbations, and therefore also more resilient to adversarial examples.

Evaluation. We now present the results when applzing adversarial training to our networks. Using $n_1 = 20$, $n_2 = 100$ and $n_3 = 250$ additional adversarial examples, we continued their training. We combined the adversarial examples to create training batches by mixing them with benign samples at each network's malware ratio. We then trained the network for one more epoch on one training batch and re-evaluated their susceptibility against adversarial examples.

Figure 3 illustrates the performance (false negative rate) of the adversarially trained networks and the misclassification rate Algorithm 1 achieved on them (in misclassification rate and average required distortion). We grouped networks by their malware ratio during training.

For the network trained with malware ratio 0.3 and 0.4, we observe a reduction of the misclassification rate, and an increase of the required average distortion for n_1 and n_2 additional training samples. For instance, we achieve a misclassification rate of 67% for the network trained with 100 additional samples at 0.3 malware ratio, from 73% for the original network. A further increase of the adversarial training samples used for adversarial training, however, causes the misclassification rate to increase again to 79% for both malware ratios.

For the networks trained with malware ratio 0.5, the misclassification rate only decreases if we use 250 adversarial training samples. Here, we reach 68% misclassification rate, down from 69% for the original network. For fewer amount of adversarial examples for adversarial training, the misclassification rate remains very similar to the original case. It seems that the network trained with 0.5 malware ratio is fitting very close to the malware samples it was trained on, and therefore requires more adversarial examples to generalize and improve its robustness against adversarial example crafting.

Overall, we can conclude that simple adversarial training does improve the neural network's robustness against adversarial examples. The number of adversarial examples required to improve the robustness depend heavily on the training parameters we chose for training the original networks. However, choosing too many may also further degrade the network's robustness against adversarial examples. This is likely explained by the fact that when too many adversarial examples are used for training, the neural network then overfits to the particular perturbation style used to craft these adversarial examples.

5.3   Summary and Discussion of Evaluation

We evaluated two potential defensive mechanisms, adversarial retraining and distillation.

Adversarial training achieved consistent reduction of misclassification rates across different models. The amount of adversarial training samples has a significant impact on this reduction. Iteratively applying adversarial training to a network may further improve the network's robustness. Unfortunately, this defense is only effective against the perturbation styles that are fed to the model during training.

Distillation does have a positive effect, but does not perform as well as in the computer vision setting. It remains unclear whether this is due to the binary nature or the unbalanced classes of the data. This is left as future work.

Finally, we note that these defenses are non-adaptive: an adversary may exploit knowledge of the defense deployed to evade it.

6   Related Work

The following discussion of related work complements the references included in Sect. 2. The security of machine learning is an active research area [26]. Barreno et al. [3] give a broad overview of attacks against machine learning systems. Previous work showed that adversarial examples can be constructed for different algorithms and also generalize between machine learning techniques in many cases [4, 9, 21, 24, 30, 36].

Many more defenses have been developed than used here. We will thus focus on introducing the main ideas relevant to neural networks and malware. There are many more variants of adversarial training [11, 15, 23], all slightly differing in their objectives from the original version introduced by Goodfellow et al. [9].

Other approaches include blocking the gradient flow [37], changing the activation function [17], or directly classifying adversarial examples as out of distribution [7, 10, 13, 22]. Finally, also the application of statistics has been investigated [19, 28]. An exhaustive study of defenses in a single article is, due to the variety and number of approaches, not feasible. We thus focused on the two most promising approaches.

Related to adversarial examples for malware, Hu and Tan [14] propose another approach to generate examples which is however based on generative adversarial networks.

Further Biggio et al. [4] propose a method that is based on gradient descent. They evaluate their adversarial examples similar to Laskov [18], who show the viability of adversarially crafted inputs against a PDF malware detection system based on random forests. Their adversarial example crafting algorithm, however, focuses on features in the *semantic gap* between the specific classifier they study and PDF renderers, i.e. this gap includes features that are only considered by the classifier, but not by the renderer. While this allows them to generate unobservable adversarial perturbations, their approach does not generalize to arbitrary classifiers.

In contrast, our approach considers all editable features and identifies those that need to be perturbed in order to achieve misclassification. Our technique is applicable to any differentiable machine learning classifier. While this still requires the identification of suitable application perturbations that correspond to feature perturbations, as we discussed in Sect. 3, this is mostly an orthogonal problem that needs to be solved independently.

7   Conclusion and Future Work

In this paper, we investigated the viability of adversarial example crafting against neural networks in a domain different from computer vision and relevant to core security problematics. On the DREBIN data set, we achieved misclassification rates of up to 69% against models that achieve classification performance comparable to state-of-the-art models from the literature. Further, our adversarial examples have no impact on the malware's functionality. Threat vectors like adversarial examples need to be taken into account by defenders.

As a second contribution, we examined two potential defensive mechanisms for hardening our neural networks against adversarial examples. Our evaluations of these mechanisms showed the following: first, distillation does improve misclassification rates, but does not decrease them as strongly as observed in computer vision settings. Secondly, adversarial training achieves consistent reduction of misclassification rates across architectures.

Acknowledgments. Nicolas Papernot is supported by a Google PhD Fellowship in Security. The research leading to these results has received funding from the European Research Council under the European Union's Seventh Framework Programme (FP/2007-2013)/ERC Grant Agreement no. 610150. This work was further partially supported by the German Federal Ministry of Education and Research (BMBF) through funding for the Center for IT-Security, Privacy and Accountability (CISPA) (FKZ: 16KIS0344). This research was also sponsored by the Army Research Laboratory and was accomplished under Cooperative Agreement Number W911NF-13-2-0045 (ARL Cyber Security CRA). The views and conclusions contained in this document are those of the authors and should not be interpreted as representing the official policies, either expressed or implied, of the Army Research Laboratory or the U.S. Government. The U.S. Government is authorized to reproduce and distribute reprints for Government purposes not with standing any copyright notation here on.

A   Generating Suitable Perturbations

Finding suitable perturbations for arbitrary features with interdependencies boils down to an optimization problem where gradient information determined by the adversarial crafting algorithm is used as a fitness function to rate perturbations (by weighing each feature affected by a perturbation with the feature's gradient). This was, in fact, essentially the intuition behind the adversarial saliency maps introduced by [25] to find adversarial image perturbations. Finding a suitable perturbation thus boils down to finding the perturbation with maximal fitness. To this end, it is necessary to identify the set of all possible perturbations that can be performed without altering an applications behavior (as by the restrictions formulated above). This issue is, in general, highly dependent on the specific application domain and orthogonal to the general adversarial crafting problem we examine in this paper. We consider this, however, a very fruitful direction for future work.

B   Data Set

In this Appendix, we provide some more details about the DREBIN data set, originally introduced by Arp et al. [2].

The 8 feature classes in DREBIN cover various aspects of android applications, including: (A) Permissions and hardware component access requested by each application (e.g. for CAMERA or INTERNET access). (B) Restricted and suspicious (i.e. accessing sensitive data, e.g. getDeviceID()) API-calls made by the applications. (C) application components such activities, service, content provider and broadcast receivers used by each applications, and D) intents used by applications to communicate with other applications. Figure 4 lists each feature class and its cardinality.

In Fig. 5 we give average and quantile statistics on the amount of features exhibited by the applications in DREBIN. Given these numbers, we decide to set our distortion bound $k = 20$ – assuming we are modifying an application of average size, it still remains within the two main quartiles when adding at most 20 features.

ID	Name	Manifest	Code	#
S_1	Hardware Components	✓		4513
S_2	Permissions	✓		3812
S_3	Components	✓		218951
S_4	Intents	✓		6379
S_5	Restr. API Calls		✓	733
S_6	Used Permissions		✓	70
S_7	Susp. API Calls		✓	315
S_8	Network Addresses		✓	310447

	benign	malicious
1st Q.	23	35
Mean	48	62
3rd Q.	61	83
max	9661	666

Fig. 4. Feature types, where they are collected and their cardinality.

Fig. 5. Some basic statistics on the number of features per app in the DREBIN data set. Q. denotes Quantiles.

References

1. Androutsopoulos, I., Koutsias, J., Chandrinos, K.V., Paliouras, G., Spyropoulos, C.D.: An evaluation of naive Bayesian anti-spam filtering. arXiv preprint arXiv:cs/0006013 (2000)
2. Arp, D., Spreitzenbarth, M., Hubner, M., Gascon, H., Rieck, K.: DREBIN: effective and explainable detection of android malware in your pocket. In: Proceedings of NDSS (2014)
3. Barreno, M., Nelson, B., Joseph, A.D., Tygar, J.D.: The security of machine learning. Mach. Learn. **81**(2), 121–148 (2010)
4. Biggio, B., Corona, I., Maiorca, D., Nelson, B., Šrndić, N., Laskov, P., Giacinto, G., Roli, F.: Evasion attacks against machine learning at test time. In: Blockeel, H., Kersting, K., Nijssen, S., Železný, F. (eds.) ECML PKDD 2013. LNCS, vol. 8190, pp. 387–402. Springer, Heidelberg (2013). doi:10.1007/978-3-642-40994-3_25
5. Bojarski, M., Del Testa, D., Dworakowski, D., Firner, B., Flepp, B., Goyal, P., Jackel, L.D., Monfort, M., Muller, U., Zhang, J., et al.: End to end learning for self-driving cars. arXiv preprint arXiv:1604.07316 (2016)
6. Dahl, G.E., Stokes, J.W., Deng, L., Yu, D.: Large-scale malware classification using random projections and neural networks. In: Proceedings of the 2013 IEEE ICASSP, pp. 3422–3426 (2013)
7. Gong, Z., Wang, W., Ku, W.-S.: Adversarial and clean data are not twins. arXiv e-prints, April 2017
8. Goodfellow, I., Bengio, Y., Courville, A.: Deep Learning. MIT Press, Cambridge (2016)
9. Goodfellow, I.J., et al.: Explaining and harnessing adversarial examples. In: Proceedings of ICLR 2015 (2015)
10. Grosse, K., Manoharan, P., Papernot, N., Backes, M., McDaniel, P.: On the (statistical) detection of adversarial examples. arXiv e-prints, February 2017
11. Gu, S., Rigazio, L.: Towards deep neural network architectures robust to adversarial examples. CoRR, abs/1412.5068 (2014)
12. Hinton, G., Vinyals, O., Dean, J.: Distilling the knowledge in a neural network. arXiv e-prints (2015)
13. Hosseini, H., Chen, Y., Kannan, S., Zhang, B., Poovendran, R.: Blocking transferability of adversarial examples in black-box learning systems. arXiv e-prints, March 2017
14. Hu, W., Tan, Y.: Generating adversarial malware examples for black-box attacks based on GAN. arXiv e-prints, February 2017
15. Alexander, G., Ororbia, I.I., Giles, C.L., Kifer, D.: Unifying adversarial training algorithms with flexible deep data gradient regularization. CoRR, abs/1601.07213 (2016)
16. Krizhevsky, A., Sutskever, I., Hinton, G.E.: Imagenet classification with deep convolutional neural networks. In: NIPS, pp. 1097–1105 (2012)
17. Krotov, D., Hopfield, J.J.: Dense associative memory is robust to adversarial inputs. arXiv e-prints, January 2017
18. Laskov, P., et al.: Practical evasion of a learning-based classifier: a case study. In: Proceedings of the 36th IEEE S&P, pp. 197–211 (2014)
19. Li, X., Li, F.: Adversarial examples detection in deep networks with convolutional filter statistics. CoRR, abs/1612.07767 (2016)
20. Lindorfer, M., Neugschwandtner, M., Platzer, C.: Marvin: efficient and comprehensive mobile app classification through static and dynamic analysis. In: Proceedings of the 39th Annual International Computers, Software and Applications Conference (COMPSAC) (2015)

21. Liu, Y., Chen, X., Liu, C., Song, D.: Delving into transferable adversarial examples and black-box attacks. CoRR, abs/1611.02770 (2016)
22. Metzen, J.H., Genewein, T., Fischer, V., Bischoff, B.: On detecting adversarial perturbations. CoRR, abs/1702.04267 (2017)
23. Miyato, T., Dai, A.M., Goodfellow, I.J.: Virtual adversarial training for semi-supervised text classification. CoRR, abs/1605.07725 (2016)
24. Papernot, N., McDaniel, P., Goodfellow, I., Jha, S., et al.: Practical black-box attacks against deep learning systems using adversarial examples. arXiv preprint arXiv:1602.02697 (2016)
25. Papernot, N., McDaniel, P., Jha, S., Fredrikson, M., Celik, Z.B., Swami, A.: The limitations of deep learning in adversarial settings. In: Proceedings of IEEE EuroS&P (2016)
26. Papernot, N., McDaniel, P., Sinha, A., Wellman, M.: Towards the science of security and privacy in machine learning. arXiv preprint arXiv:1611.03814 (2016)
27. Papernot, N., McDaniel, P., Wu, X., Jha, S., Swami, A.: Distillation as a defense to adversarial perturbations against deep neural networks. In: Proceedings of IEEE S&P (2015)
28. Shintre, S., Gardner, A.B., Feinman, R., Curtin, R.R.: Detecting adversarial samples from artifacts. CoRR, abs/1703.00410 (2017)
29. Rieck, K., Trinius, P., Willems, C., Holz, T.: Automatic analysis of malware behavior using machine learning. J. Comput. Secur. **19**(4), 639–668 (2011)
30. Rozsa, A., Günther, M., Boult, T.E.: Are accuracy and robustness correlated? arXiv e-prints, October 2016
31. Saxe, J., Berlin, K.: Deep neural network based malware detection using two dimensional binary program features. In: 10th International Conference on Malicious and Unwanted Software, MALWARE, pp. 11–20 (2015)
32. Sayfullina, L., Eirola, E., Komashinsky, D., Palumbo, P., Miché, Y., Lendasse, A., Karhunen, J.: Efficient detection of zero-day android malware using normalized Bernoulli naive Bayes. In: Proceedings of IEEE TrustCom, pp. 198–205 (2015)
33. Shabtai, A., Fledel, Y., Elovici, Y.: Automated static code analysis for classifying android applications using machine learning. In: CIS, pp. 329–333. IEEE (2010)
34. Silver, D., Huang, A., Maddison, C.J., Guez, A., Sifre, L., Van Den Driessche, G., Schrittwieser, J., Antonoglou, I., Panneershelvam, V., Lanctot, M., et al.: Mastering the game of go with deep neural networks and tree search. Nature **529**(7587), 484–489 (2016)
35. Sommer, R., Paxson, V.: Outside the closed world: on using machine learning for network intrusion detection. In: 2010 IEEE S&P, pp. 305–316. IEEE (2010)
36. Szegedy, C., Zaremba, W., Sutskever, I., Bruna, J., Erhan, D., Goodfellow, I., Fergus, R.: Intriguing properties of neural networks. In: Proceedings of ICLR. Computational and Biological Learning Society (2014)
37. Wang, Q., Guo, W., Alexander, G., Ororbia, I. I., Xing, X., Lin, L., Giles, C.L., Liu, X., Liu, P., Xiong, G.: Using non-invertible data transformations to build adversary-resistant deep neural networks. CoRR, abs/1610.01934 (2016)
38. Warde-Farley, D., Goodfellow, I.: Adversarial perturbations of deep neural networks. In: Hazan, T., Papandreou, G., Tarlow, D. (eds.) Advanced Structured Prediction (2016)
39. Zhu, Z., Dumitras, T.: Featuresmith: automatically engineering features for malware detection by mining the security literature. In: Proceedings of ACM SIGSAC, pp. 767–778 (2016)

PerfWeb: How to Violate Web Privacy with Hardware Performance Events

Berk Gulmezoglu[1]([✉]), Andreas Zankl[2], Thomas Eisenbarth[1], and Berk Sunar[1]

[1] Worcester Polytechnic Institute, Worcester, MA, USA
{bgulmezoglu,teisenbarth,sunar}@wpi.edu
[2] Fraunhofer Research Institution AISEC, Munich, Germany
andreas.zankl@aisec.fraunhofer.de

Abstract. The browser history reveals highly sensitive information about users, such as financial status, health conditions, or political views. Private browsing modes and anonymity networks are consequently important tools to preserve the privacy not only of regular users but in particular of whistleblowers and dissidents. Yet, in this work we show how a malicious application can infer opened websites from Google Chrome in Incognito mode and from Tor Browser by exploiting hardware performance events (HPEs). In particular, we analyze the browsers' microarchitectural footprint with the help of advanced Machine Learning techniques: k-th Nearest Neighbors, Decision Trees, Support Vector Machines, and in contrast to previous literature also Convolutional Neural Networks. We profile 40 different websites, 30 of the top Alexa sites and 10 whistleblowing portals, on two machines featuring an Intel and an ARM processor. By monitoring retired instructions, cache accesses, and bus cycles for at most 5 s we manage to classify the selected websites with a success rate of up to 86.3%. The results show that hardware performance events can clearly undermine the privacy of web users. We therefore propose mitigation strategies that impede our attacks and still allow legitimate use of HPEs.

Keywords: Website fingerprinting · Hardware performance events · Machine learning · Incognito mode · Chrome · Tor · Onion routing · Privacy

1 Introduction

Web browsers are indispensable components in our lives. They provide access to news and entertainment, and more importantly serve as a platform through which we perform privacy and security sensitive interactions such as online banking, web enabled healthcare, and social networking. Knowing the websites a user is visiting therefore reveals personal and highly sensitive information. To preserve the privacy of users, browsers consequently implement *private browsing* or *incognito* modes, which leave no traces of visited websites. More comprehensive protection is achieved by *Onion routing*, e.g. *Tor*, which protects users

© Springer International Publishing AG 2017
S.N. Foley et al. (Eds.): ESORICS 2017, Part II, LNCS 10493, pp. 80–97, 2017.
DOI: 10.1007/978-3-319-66399-9_5

against Internet surveillance by obscuring packet routing information. By using a Tor enabled browser users may hide the websites they visit from adversaries monitoring their network communication. This has become indispensable for whistleblowers and dissidents who try to protect their identity against powerful corporations and repressive governments. Besides web browsers, other tools have emerged to mask the identity of the user, e.g. Signal/Redphone, Silent Phone, and Telegram. However, even the installation of such tools can be viewed as subversive action by a repressive regime. In contrast, privacy preserving browsers come pre-installed on many platforms.

While browsers have significantly matured in providing privacy assurances, they are still far from perfect. In 2012, Jana and Shmatikov [15] found that memory footprints of browser processes are unique enough while browsing to detect opened websites. We expand on this observation and show that browsers have a somewhat similar footprint at the hardware level, more specifically in the microarchitecture of processors, and that this footprint can be used to infer web browsing activity with high success. The key to our inference attack is that most applications exhibit different execution behavior depending on the input they are processing. They consequently stress the processor hardware in different ways. Whichever application is able to observe these load patterns can learn a great deal of what is being processed in other programs. Modern processors and operating systems provide such interfaces to their microarchitectural state through hardware performance events (HPEs). While HPEs are legitimately used for debugging purposes and performance analysis, e.g. to keep track of cache misses or branch mispredictions, they can also be leveraged by adversaries. We show that it is feasible for a malicious application to monitor HPEs from user space and to infer opened websites even when users browse in Incognito mode or with the Tor Browser. For the experiments in this work, we use the `perf` subsystem of the Linux kernel, a wide-spread user space interface to hardware performance events. Since HPE based information is incidental and often noisy, advanced methods for data analysis are needed. The recent advances in Machine Learning (ML) provide us with a powerful tool to classify the complex noisy data in an effective manner. We show that while k-th Nearest Neighbors, Support Vector Machines, and Decision Trees are not sufficient to classify the complex and noisy observed data into a high number of different classes, Convolutional Neural Networks, a Deep Learning technique, can efficiently extract meaningful data even in the presence of severe noise. As a result, we demonstrate that it is possible to infer the web activity from HPEs with very high success rates and in a highly automated fashion. This can be a considerable threat in practice, as many of the applications we use every day stem from third-parties and run in the background. We trust these applications, even though we have little control over what is executed on our devices.

Our Contribution. In summary, we use advanced Machine Learning techniques, including Convolutional Neural Networks, to process different types of HPEs that have been acquired through `perf` and combined to get a better classification rate. We cover 40 different websites, including 30 of the top Alexa sites and 10 whistleblowing portals, and detect different web pages of a domain to show that fine-grained browser profiling is possible. We demonstrate that an attacker does not need to precisely synchronize with the browser, as misalignment is compensated by the ML techniques. We also show that it suffices to monitor Google Chrome and Tor Browser for at most 5 s to classify websites with high accuracy. We finally outline possible mitigation strategies that impede website inference while still allowing access to performance profiling.

2 Background and Related Work

This following paragraphs provide background information and related work regarding HPEs and website fingerprinting. Subsequently, we briefly compare our work to previous ones.

Hardware Performance Events. The microarchitectures of modern processors implement a large spectrum of performance enhancing features that speed up memory accesses and code execution. As a compromise, performance enhancements introduce input dependent runtimes and weak separation between executing applications. As a direct consequence, the microarchitectural state of a processor contains crucial information about the processes that are executed on it. Hardware performance events are an interface to this state that is implemented on most modern processors. A dedicated piece of hardware, the performance monitoring unit (PMU), is responsible to keep track of microarchitectural events that occur while executing code on the processor. These events include, e.g., instruction retirements, branch mispredictions, and cache references. They provide a comprehensive picture of a processor's runtime behavior and are therefore interesting for adversaries and developers alike. In literature, clock cycle events have been recognized as a vital timing source for a large class of cache-based attacks [22,35]. Cache miss [30] and branch misprediction events [5] have been exploited in targeted attacks against implementations of AES and RSA. In contrast, HPEs have improved our understanding of attacks [3] and modern processor implementations [23], facilitated the evaluation of software components [34], and helped to analyze malware samples [32]. A large class of previous work is dedicated to the real time detection of attacks and malware infections, a selection of which relies on Machine Learning and related techniques. In particular, naive Bayes [26], probabilistic Markov models [16], k-Nearest Neighbors [10], Decision Trees [10,26], Random Forests [10], Support Vector Machines [4,16,26,28], and (Artificial) Neural Networks [8,10] are studied.

Website Fingerprinting. The protection of the browser history is important to ensure the privacy of web users. Yet, literature offers a large spectrum of history stealing attacks that allow to recover entries of previously visited websites. Most of them are launched by malicious web servers [11,19], but attacks have also been demonstrated on the client side in the form of malicious browser extensions [29]. If no browsing history is stored, e.g. in private browsing modes, it is still possible to detect websites a user is actively visiting. This is investigated in the field of website fingerprinting, to which we contribute with this work. A significant fraction of website fingerprinting literature is dedicated to network traffic analysis [13,27]. Attacks typically require an adversary to sniff network communication between the web server and the client machine. Most of the previous works tolerate encrypted traffic, e.g., generated by SSL/TLS or SSH connections, and some even work with anonymized traffic, e.g., routed over the Tor network. Other website fingerprinting approaches target the browser or the underlying operating system and typically require to execute malicious code, e.g., JavaScript, on the client machine [12,17,31]. Through this attack vector, Jana and Shmatikov [15] measure the memory footprint of browsers that is available through the procfs filesystem in Linux. The authors show that different websites exhibit different footprints and that it is possible to recover opened websites by comparing their footprints to previously recorded ones. Yet other approaches leverage properties of the hardware that runs the web browser. Attacks are typically mounted by malicious code within the browser, by other processes on the same system, or by an external adversary with physical access to the device. Oren et al. [25] demonstrate that websites exhibit different profiles in the processor cache that can be observed from JavaScript. Hornby [14] also fingerprints websites via the cache, but from another process that is running on the same processor as the web browser. Lee et al. [18] demonstrate that websites can be inferred from rendering traces that are retained in GPUs. Booth [6] demonstrates that website fingerprints can also be constructed from the CPU load. Clark et al. [9] measure the power consumption of laptop and desktop systems and attribute different power profiles to different websites. Yang et al. [33] extend this idea to mobile devices that are charged via USB.

Our Work. Similar to Hornby [14] and Lee et al. [18], we assume that a malicious application is running on the same processor as the web browser. In contrast to previous hardware based website fingerprinting, we leverage more than just the processor cache [25] or the processor load [6]. To the best of our knowledge, this work is the first that investigates hardware performance events in the context of website fingerprinting. In compliance with the state of the art in this field, we employ supervised Machine Learning techniques in the form of k-Nearest Neighbors, Decision Trees, and Support Vector Machines. While these are recognized instruments for network based fingerprinting, their application to hardware based website inference attacks is still fragmented [6,9,33]. In this work, we directly compare their effectiveness in multiple practical scenarios. In addition, we demonstrate that Deep Learning (in the form of Convolutional Neural Networks) outperforms traditional Machine Learning techniques that are established in both hardware performance event and website fingerprinting literature. To the best of our knowledge, CNNs have not been investigated in neither of these fields before.

3   Monitoring Hardware Performance Events

The performance monitoring unit (PMU), which is responsible for counting hardware performance events, implements a set of counters that can each be configured to count events of a certain type. The number of available events is often considerably larger than the number of available counters. Consequently, only a limited number of events can be counted in parallel. In order to measure more events, software layers that use the PMU typically implement time multiplexing. All experiments in this work succeed by measuring only as many events as hardware counters are available, i.e., time multiplexing is not needed. Access to PMUs is typically restricted to privileged, i.e., kernel or system level code, but interfaces exist through which user space applications can gather event counts. On Unix and Linux based operating systems, `PAPI` [24] or `perf` [20] interfaces are commonly implemented. In this work, we focus on the `perf` interface that is mainly found on Linux systems. Note that this work demonstrates the general feasibility of website fingerprinting with HPEs. Therefore, similar results are also expected on systems with other HPE interfaces.

Profiling with Perf. The `perf` event monitoring subsystem was added to the Linux kernel in version 2.6.31 and subsequently made available to the user space via the `perf_event_open` system call. Listing 1.1 shows the system call signature.

```
int perf_event_open(struct perf_event_attr *attr,
                     pid_t pid, int cpu,
                     int group_fd,
                     unsigned long flags);
```

Listing 1.1. `perf_event_open` system call signature [21].

The `perf_event_attr` is the main configuration object. It determines the type of event that will be counted and defines a wide range of acquisition properties, which are documented in the Linux man-pages [21]. We focus only on a very limited number of settings and use zero values for all others. This renders our measurements to be reproducible on a larger number of systems. The `type` field in `perf_event_attr` specifies the generic event type. As we focus on hardware based events, we only use `PERF_TYPE_HARDWARE` or `PERF_TYPE_HW_CACHE`. The `config` field determines the specific event type. The event selection used in this work is given in Sect. 4. In addition, we set the `exclude_kernel` option, which avoids counting kernel activity. This improves the applicability of our measurement code, because kernel profiling is prohibited on some systems. Finally, the `size` field is set to the size of the event attribute struct. The `pid` and `cpu` parameters are used to set the scope of the event profiling. In this work, we focus on two profiling scenarios: *process-specific* and *core-wide*. To limit event counting to a single process, `pid` is set to the process identifier and `cpu` is set to -1. Subsequently, events are counted only for the given process, but on any processor core. To enable core-wide counting, `cpu` is set to the core number that should be observed and `pid` is set to -1. Events are then counted only on one processor core, but for all processes running on it. The `group_fd` parameter is used to signal that a selection of events belongs to a group. The `perf` system then counts all members of a group as a unit. Since this is not a strict requirement for our approach, we omit `group_fd` and set it to -1. The `flags` parameter is used to configure advanced settings including the behavior when spawning new processes and monitoring Linux control groups (cgroups). As none of these settings are relevant to our measurement scenarios, we set `flags` to zero.

Once `perf_event_open` succeeds, the returned file descriptor can be used to read and reset event counts, and to enable and disable counting. In our measurements, we read event counts using the standard `read` system call. This yields a sufficiently high sampling frequency and subsequently high success rates during website fingerprinting. On our test systems, the duration of the `read` system call ranges between 1.5 μs and 3.0 μs when reading one counter value.

Access Control. On Linux, access to `perf` can be configured for user space applications. The access level is specified as an integer value that is stored in `/proc/sys/kernel/perf_event_paranoid` in the `procfs` filesystem. A negative value grants user space applications full access to performance profiling. If the `paranoid` level is set to 0, comprehensive profiling of the kernel activity is prohibited. A value of 1 prevents user space applications from core-wide event counting ($pid = -1, cpu \geq 0$). A `paranoid` level of 2 prohibits process-specific event counts while the application gives control to kernel space, e.g., during a system call. Values above 2 disable event counting even in user space and effectively deactivate `perf` for user space applications. Note that the `paranoid` setting is typically overridden by applications started with the CAP_SYS_ADMIN capability, e.g., programs started by the root user.

4   Browser Profiling Scenarios

We investigate the inference of opened websites via HPEs in three distinct scenarios hosted on two Linux test systems. The first system features an ARM Cortex-A53 processor with six programmable hardware counters, the second one comprises an Intel i5-2430M processor with three programmable counters. Given the limited number of counters on both systems, only a selection of HPEs is measured in each experiment. A complete list of events supported by `perf` can be obtained from the Linux man-pages [21]. As we are relying on the standardized `perf_event_open` system call of the Linux kernel, there is no need to change the measurement code when switching between systems. Further details about the profiling scenarios are given in the following paragraphs.

Google Chrome on ARM. In this scenario, we profile the Google Chrome browser (v55.0.2883) with default options on the ARM system. While the browser loads websites, a malicious user space application is measuring six hardware performance events: HW_INSTRUCTIONS, HW_BRANCH_INSTRUCTIONS, HW_-CACHE_REFERENCES, L1_DCACHE_LOADS, L1_ICACHE_LOADS, and HW_BUS_CYCLES. This selection of events covers instruction retirements, cache accesses, and external memory interfaces. It gives a comprehensive view of the microarchitectural load the browser is putting on the processor. The selected events are measured core-wide, hence including noise from other processes and background activity of the operating system. Since we want to assess the feasibility of core-wide profiling, the browser process is bound to the measured processor core. The events are then measured for five seconds.

Google Chrome (Incognito) on Intel. In this scenario, we profile Google Chrome in Incognito mode with default options on the Intel system. Since the number of counters is limited to three on this processor, the malicious user space application is measuring only three events: HW_BRANCH_INSTRUCTIONS, HW_CACHE_REFERENCES, and LLC_LOADS. Moreover, the events are acquired in a process-specific fashion, hence the browser processes float on all processor cores. The events are then measured for one second specifically for the rendering process of the opened website. Compared to the ARM scenario, the reduced event selection still provides a meaningful view of the microarchitectural load. As the browser processes are not bound to one core anymore, we substitute events related to the L1 cache with last-level cache loads. In addition, the bus cycle event is omitted, because it is noisier on the Intel platform. Also, overall retired instructions are omitted, because we found the retired branch instructions to yield more usable information.

Tor Browser on Intel. In this scenario, we profile the Tor Browser (v6.5.1, based on Firefox v45.8.0) on the same Intel platform as before. In contrast to Chrome, the Tor Browser renders all tabs in one process, which is subsequently profiled by the malicious application. While the same three performance events are observed, the measurement duration is prolonged to 5 s. This is because the Tor network introduces significant delays while opening websites.

Synchronization. None of the scenarios require strict synchronization between the browser and the malicious application. Small misalignment is simply passed on to the Machine Learning step. Therefore, we only investigate simple synchronization techniques that can be achieved in practice. For Google Chrome on Intel, the adversary scans the running processes twice per second and checks whether a new rendering process has been spawned. Once a new process is detected, the adversary starts to measure the corresponding process-specific events. The Tor Browser, in contrast, is started freshly for every opened website. Again, the adversary checks all running processes twice per second and once the Tor Browser is detected, the process-specific profiling is started. This includes additional noise as the browser startup phase is also captured. In the ARM scenario, the measurements are precisely aligned with the start of loading a website. This is used to investigate whether more precise alignment yields better results. Such a trigger signal could be derived from a sudden change or characteristic pattern in the event counts, as the load of the system changes when a website is opened.

5   Machine Learning Techniques

Machine Learning provides powerful tools to automate the process of understanding and extracting relevant information from noisy observations. All of the techniques we use in this work are *supervised*, meaning that known samples (training set) are used to derive a model that is subsequently employed to classify unknown samples (test set). The success rate of an ML technique denotes the percentage of unknown samples that are classified correctly. To reliably determine the success rate, classification is performed multiple times with different training and test sets that are derived through statistical sampling. This so-called cross-validation is performed, if the number of overall samples is low. In all our experiments, the acquired hardware performance events are concatenated to create the input data for the Machine Learning techniques. Both training and test sets are normalized to reduce the computation time. All algorithms are implemented in Matlab 2017a and run on a standard dual-core Intel processor. The training phase of the Convolutional Neural Network is reduced with the help of an NVIDIA Tesla K20 GPU accelerator. Further details of the Machine Learning techniques used in our experiments are given in the following paragraphs.

k-th Nearest Neighbor (kNN). The main goal of kNN is to find a training sample that is closest to a test sample according to the Euclidean distance. The smallest distance is taken as the first nearest neighbor and the test sample is marked with the corresponding label. In our experiments, we use the *fitcknn* command to implement kNN and to train our models. By default, the prior probabilities are the respective relative frequencies of the classes in the data, which are initially set to be equal to each other.

Decision Tree (DT). Decision Trees are used to classify samples by creating branches for given data features that yield the best split among all classes. The values for each branch are chosen such that they minimize the entropy. In our experiments, we use the *fitctree* command to train the model. The default value for maximum split is $N - 1$, where N denotes the number of classes. For the training phase, the minimum leaf size is 1 and the minimum parent size is 10.

Support Vector Machine (SVM). In SVM based learning, input data is converted to a multi-dimensional representation by using mapping functions. Hyperplanes are then created to classify the data. The general strategy is to find the optimal decision boundaries between classes by increasing the distance between them. In our experiments, we use `libsvm` [7] to implement multi-class Support Vector Machines. The model is created and trained based on a linear SVM. We set the type of the SVM to C-SVC, where the parameter C is used to regularize the mapping function.

Convolutional Neural Network (CNN). In contrast to the other ML techniques, Convolutional Neural Networks automatically determine important features of the input data. This is achieved by creating nodes between higher and lower dimensional input data mappings. The meaningful features are then extracted by finding the optimal functions for each node. In our experiments, we choose two autoencoders to classify our measurements into N classes. In each autoencoder, different levels of abstraction are learned from the feature vectors and mapped to a lower dimensional space. While the number of layers in the first autoencoder is $100 \cdot N$, the second autoencoder has $10 \cdot N$ layers. The maximum number of iterations is set to 400 and L2 weight regularization is set to 0.001 for both autoencoders. The last layer is the softmax layer. The training data is trained in a supervised fashion using labels. After the neural network is established and first classification results are obtained, the accuracy of the multilayer network model is improved using backpropagation and repeated training using labeled data. While CNNs have many advantages, the most important disadvantage is their memory demands. When we run out of GPU memory, we downsample the input data to reduce the length of the feature vectors.

6   Website Profiling Results

In each of the profiling scenarios described in Sect. 4, we monitor events when loading the homepages of the most visited websites according to Alexa [1]. The tested websites, excluding adult ones, is listed in Appendix A (1–30). This illustrates the general effectiveness of the Machine Learning techniques to classify websites based on HPEs. To demonstrate that also fine-grained profiling is feasible, 10 different sub-pages of the Amazon.com domain are monitored in Google Chrome on Intel. Finally, a selection of whistleblowing websites is measured when visited with the Tor browser. They are also given in Appendix A (31–40).

Google Chrome on ARM. For the experiments on ARM, each website is monitored 20 times to train the models. For each of these visits, 25,000 samples are acquired per hardware performance event. The samples of all events are then concatenated to yield a final measurement size of 150,000 samples. For 30 websites, the total training data size is therefore $90 \cdot 10^6$ samples. Based on this training set, the success rates after cross-validation are 84% for linear SVM, 80% for kNN, and less than 50% for DT and CNN. The low success rates of DT and CNN indicate that not enough samples have been acquired. Figure 1(a) illustrates the success rates for each of the visited websites when classified with SVM. Since the number of samples collected in this scenario is small, 10-fold cross-validation

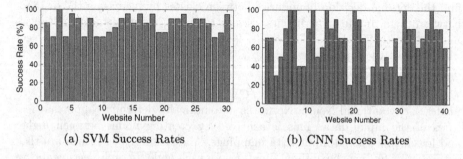

(a) SVM Success Rates   (b) CNN Success Rates

Fig. 1. Success rates per website for (a) Google Chrome on ARM with the dashed line showing an average classification rate of 84%, and (b) Tor Browser on Intel with the dashed line showing an average classification rate of 68%.

is used. The lowest detection rate is 70%, which shows that core-wide profiling is feasible even in the presence of background noise. The average classification rate of 84% is shown as a dashed line in the figure.

Google Chrome (Incognito) on Intel. For the Google Chrome experiments on Intel, the number of measurements per website is increased to 50. As more samples are acquired, fixed training and test sets are derived instead of using cross-validation. Out of the 50 observations, 40 are used for the training phase whereas 10 are collected to test the derived models. Since each website is monitored for only one second, every measurement now consists of 10,000 samples per event. With three observed events, this yields a total training set size of $36 \cdot 10^6$ and a test set size of $9 \cdot 10^6$ samples.

Figure 2(a) shows the success rates over an increasing number of training measurements for all Machine Learning techniques. Clearly, CNN achieves the highest classification rate, if enough training samples are available. In particular, the success rate for 40 training observations per website is 86.3%. If the training data size is small, SVM and kNN achieve similar success rates as CNN. Due to the large size of feature vectors in the training and test data, DT gives lower success rates than other ML techniques. Regarding the computational effort, the training phase of CNN takes 2 h on a GPU and is consequently the longest among the Machine Learning techniques. In contrast, the test phase takes approximately 1 min for every ML technique.

The second experiment for Google Chrome in Incognito mode on Intel assumes that an adversary has detected a website that the user has visited. Consequently, the attacker tries to infer which page of the website the user is interested in. To illustrate the feasibility of this attack, we selected 10 pages of the Amazon.com domain that display different sections of the online store (kitchen, bedroom, etc.). Naturally, this scenario is more challenging, as the difference between web pages of the same domain is smaller than for entirely different websites. Nevertheless, it is still possible to correctly classify the visited web pages with moderate success. This is illustrated in Fig. 2(b). When using CNN and SVM, the success rate is 64%. kNN yields 60% success rate, while DT drops to 52%. For CNN and SVM, we also investigate the success rates when

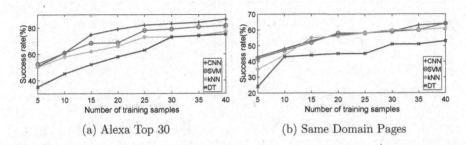

(a) Alexa Top 30

(b) Same Domain Pages

Fig. 2. Success rate vs. number of training measurements for Google Chrome (Incognito), and (a) 30 different websites (b) 10 same domain web pages.

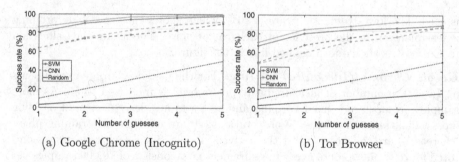

(a) Google Chrome (Incognito)   (b) Tor Browser

Fig. 3. Number of guesses vs. classification rate for (a) Google Chrome (Incognito), and (b) Tor Browser. Solid lines represent results for Alexa Top 30, while the dashed lines illustrate the same domain results.

the number of guesses is increased in Fig. 3(a). If the first 5 result classes are considered, websites can be detected with 99% accuracy for SVM and CNN. Similar results are obtained for the same domain experiments, where both CNN and SVM yield 92% accuracy.

Tor Browser on Intel. For the Tor Browser experiments, the same events as before are observed as well as the same number of measurements are taken for each website. Again, 40 of those measurements are used to construct the training set, while 10 measurements form the test set. As the Tor Browser is monitored for 5 s, 50,000 samples are acquired for each event and website. This yields 150,000 samples for one measurement, $180 \cdot 10^6$ samples for the entire training set, and $45 \cdot 10^6$ samples for the test set.

Figure 4(a) shows the success rates over an increasing number of training measurements for all Machine Learning techniques. CNN yields the highest success rate of 71%. While SVM and kNN have similar success rates around 66%, Decision Tree yields a lower accuracy of 60%. The results show that CNN can handle noisy data and misalignment problems better than other methods, since CNN learns the relations between traces. The experiment results for the 10 web

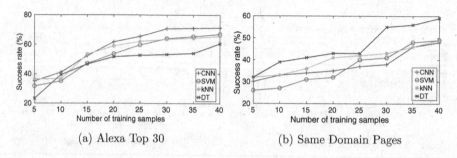

(a) Alexa Top 30   (b) Same Domain Pages

Fig. 4. Success rate vs. number of training measurements for the Tor Browser and (a) 30 different websites, or (b) 10 same domain web pages.

pages on Amazon.com are illustrated in Fig. 4(b). In contrast to the Google
Chrome results, Decision Tree yields the highest success rate of 59%. We believe
the reason is the small number of classes that increases the efficiency of DT.
The remaining algorithms classify the same domain web pages with a similar
success rate of approximately 49%. In addition, Fig. 3(b) shows the success rates
for CNN and SVM over an increasing number of guesses. While the random
selection success rate is around 16% for 5 guesses, CNN achieves a success rate
of 94%. For the same domain web pages, the success rate of CNN is 88% for 5
guesses. SVM achieves slightly worse results.

Finally, we investigate whistleblowing websites, as visiting them anonymously
is an important reason to use the Tor Browser. For this experiment, we select
10 whistleblowing portals from [2] (also given in Appendix A). In the first step,
these websites are classified using all ML techniques. While CNN yields the
best classification rate of 84%, SVM exhibits a success rate of 78%. In contrast,
DT and kNN have lower success rates around 60%. In the second step, the
classification is repeated for all websites considered so far (whistleblowing and
Alexa Top 30). Figure 5(a) illustrates the success rates for all ML techniques.
When classifying 40 websites, CNN yields a success rate of 68%, while SVM
achieves 55%. In contrast, kNN and DT algorithms cannot classify the websites
effectively. When the number of guesses is increased, the success rate improves
again. Figure 5(b) shows the classification rates over an increasing number of
guesses. If only whistleblowing websites and 5 guesses are considered, CNN yields
a success close to 100%. When all websites are considered, the success rate of
CNN is 89.25%. SVM achieves slightly worse results. Individual success rates
for CNN are shown in Fig. 1(b). The lowest success rate is around 20% for
two websites and seven websites are classified correctly with 100% accuracy. An
interesting observation is that among the 40 websites, the whistleblowing portals
are still classified with good success rates. With an average success rate of 68%,
CNN is more capable than other ML techniques to correctly classify websites
opened in Tor browser.

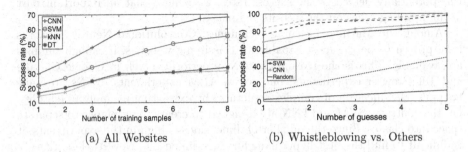

(a) All Websites   (b) Whistleblowing vs. Others

Fig. 5. (a) Success rate vs. number of training measurements for Tor Browser and all
websites. (b) Number of guesses vs. classification rate for whistleblowing (dashed) and
all websites (solid).

7   Discussion

The experiments on ARM were conducted with core-wide measurements, whereas HPEs were acquired in a process-specific fashion on Intel. In general, core-wide acquisition is expected to introduce more noise in the measurements, e.g., from system activity in the background. For process-specific acquisition the activity of the rest of the system does not impair the measurements, as the `perf` subsystem accumulates event counts only when the specified process is running. According to the results presented in the previous section, however, both scenarios allow to classify websites with success rates of over 80% for SVM. This is because the test systems were mostly idling during the experiments. If this is not the case, the effects of increased system load can be countered by increasing the profiling time in order to obtain more information from the renderer process. Furthermore, an adversary can train multiple models for multiple levels of system load to account for an unknown load of the target system. Also, a slight increase of the number of guesses yields a significant increase in classification success. These measures also help against other impairments of the measurement quality, e.g., if multiple websites are opened in parallel in the Tor browser, if direct URLs are used instead of visiting the homepage of a website, if the number of profiled websites grows, or if websites are visited that have not been profiled and cannot be classified as a consequence.

Compared to Google Chrome in Incognito mode, the results of the Tor Browser are worse on average. This can be explained with the browser start-up phase, which is always captured for Tor. Also, random network delays introduce jitter in the observations of the website loading. Large delays require to prolong the event acquisition phase, otherwise the success rates are expected to drop. Another adverse effect is the changing geo-location of the Tor exit nodes. Many websites, particularly news sites like New York Times and Yahoo, customize their appearance based on the location of their visitors and therefore introduce additional noise in the measurements. Similar effects can occur if websites contain personalized advertisements and other frequently changing content. While this potentially decreases the success rates, we believe that an important part of the profiling relies on the website templates.

Among the Machine Learning techniques, Convolutional Neural Networks have proven to be the most capable for classifying websites, if enough samples are available. This is the reason why CNNs performed well in Google Chrome and Tor Browser experiments, but not in ARM experiments. CNNs are built for multi-classification of complex structures by extracting meaningful features. On the contrary, SVM and kNN are designed to create hyperplanes to separate space into classes. Since the number of dimensions is high in the experiments, it is difficult to find the best hyperplane for each dimension. Nevertheless, there is still a need for further studies on CNN, since the results could be improved by modifying the parameters, number of layers and neurons.

In general, the feasibility of website fingerprinting via hardware performance events is not limited to the specific profiling scenarios and test platforms used in our experiments. This is because of the fundamental phenomenon that loading different websites creates different microarchitectural footprints. This a logical consequence of optimized software that is designed to provide best user experience. Therefore, similar results are expected also for other x86 and ARM processors, as well as for other HPE interfaces and web browsers, unless mitigation strategies are implemented.

8 Countermeasures

The website inference technique presented in this work requires that (i) websites loaded by a browser exhibit a unique footprint in the microarchitectural state of a processor, and that (ii) this state can be observed via hardware performance events with sufficient precision. Any efforts impacting these two requirements directly affect the reliability, success, or practicality of our approach. The following two paragraphs discuss such efforts and formulate possible countermeasures.

Displaying Websites. The first requirement of our classification technique implies that the executed operations during downloading and rendering of website elements are closely related to the type and amount of content displayed on a website. From a more abstract perspective this means that the execution flow and memory accesses of the browser vary for different websites. A thorough approach for solving this issue is writing code such that instruction sequences and operand addresses are independent of the input that is processed. While this is reasonable to aspire for security software, it has considerable practical drawbacks in the context of web browsers. First, removing input dependencies almost always impairs performance, because runtime optimizations typically rely on skipping operations and handling special cases differently. As a result, websites take longer to display, which is not in favor of user experience. Second, the larger the code, the more complex it gets to remove input dependencies. For web browsers, at least the code related to networking, storing, and rendering of elements must be changed. Given that security critical software has much smaller code bases and still struggles to remove input dependencies in practice, it is questionable that browser software will successfully implement this in the foreseeable future. If input dependencies cannot be entirely removed, artificial noise can be added to the website loading process. This is, for instance, achieved by introducing random delays between operations, adding functions that process dummy data instead of real inputs, or randomly loading unrelated website elements in the background. While this does not solve the underlying problem, it distorts the microarchitectural footprint each website exhibits while being displayed.

Observing Events. The second requirement is the ability to observe the state of the processor microachitecture with high precision. Since performance monitoring units are dedicated parts of the processor, they cannot simply be removed or permanently deactivated. However, operating systems can block access to them from the software side. On Linux, the kernel can be compiled without the perf subsystem, e.g., by disabling the CONFIG_PERF_EVENTS configuration option. Also, the perf_event_paranoid file can be set to 3 or above to disable event counter access from user space. However, blocking or deactivating `perf` impairs applications that use performance events for legitimate profiling or debugging purposes. If event counting is generally needed, a possible compromise could be more fine-grained profiling restrictions, such that processes can only count events caused by themselves. Profiling any other process is prohibited, even if it belongs to the same user. While this requires changes to the `perf` interface, it provides legitimate applications access to profiling and at the same time impairs the fingerprinting technique presented in this work. This profiling restriction could be added as a dedicated setting in the `perf_event_paranoid` configuration file. An alternative solution is to lower the measurement precision of hardware performance events. This can, for instance, be achieved by artificially adding a certain level of noise to the event counts while retaining a sufficiently high signal-to-noise ratio, or by reducing sampling frequencies with which applications can acquire event counts. Yet again, this would also affect benign applications. A possible solution is to detect malicious programs and then only degrade their observations. However, the presented measurement approach behaves identically to legitimate applications and does not rely on exotic operations or measurement settings.

9   Conclusion

When websites are loaded in the browser, they stress the underlying hardware in a distinct pattern that is closely related to the contents of the website. This pattern is reflected in the microarchitectural state of the processor that executes the browser, which can be observed with high precision by counting hardware performance events. Since these events can be legitimately measured by user space applications, it is feasible to infer opened websites via performance event measurements. We demonstrate this by utilizing Machine Learning techniques and achieve high recognition rates even in the presence of background noise, trace misalignment, and varying network delays. The results show that CNN is able to obtain better classification rates from high number of classes in the presence of noise. By applying CNN, the whistleblowing websites are classified with 79% accuracy among 40 websites while the overall classification rate increases up to 89.25% with 5 guesses in Tor browser. Yet, further work is necessary to investigate practical aspects that go beyond the proof of concept presented in this work. Since many websites change between visits and users, e.g., due to daily news or personalized ads, it is necessary to systematically analyze how geo-location, personalization, and aging affect the classification accuracy. Another direction is investigating the contribution of each website element to the microarchitectural fingerprint and subsequently to the classification success rates. This is especially useful for countermeasures, which could then handle critical elements more carefully.

Acknowledgments. We would like to thank the anonymous reviewers for their valuable comments and suggestions. This work has been supported by the National Science Foundation, under grants CNS-1618837 and CNS-1314770.

A List of Profiled Websites

Table 1 shows the list of profiled websites in this work. Entries 1–30 are taken from the top websites listed by Alexa [1], while URLs 31–40 are a selection of whistleblowing portals from [2].

Table 1. List of profiled websites.

Website numbers and URLs		
(1) Netflix.com	(15) Bing.com	(29) Espn.com
(2) Amazon.com	(16) Imgur.com	(30) Wikia.com
(3) Facebook.com	(17) Ntd.tv	(31) Wikileaks.org
(4) Google.com	(18) Cnn.com	(32) Aljazeera.com/investigations
(5) Yahoo.com	(19) Pinterest.com	(33) Balkanleaks.eu
(6) Youtube.com	(20) Tumblr.com	(34) Unileaks.org
(7) Wikipedia.org	(21) Office.com	(35) Globaleaks.com
(8) Reddit.com	(22) Microsoftonline.com	(36) Liveleak.com
(9) Twitter.com	(23) Chase.com	(37) Globalwitness.org
(10) Ebay.com	(24) Nytimes.com	(38) Wikispooks.com
(11) Linkedin.com	(25) Blogspot.com	(39) Officeleaks.com
(12) Diply.com	(26) Paypal.com	(40) Publeaks.nl
(13) Instagram.com	(27) Imdb.com	
(14) Live.com	(28) Wordpress.com	

References

1. Alexa Internet Inc.: The top 500 sites on the web (2017). http://www.alexa.com/topsites. Accessed 10 May 2017
2. Anonymous Contributors: Leak site directory. http://www.leakdirectory.org/index.php/Leak_Site_Directory
3. Atici, A., Yilmaz, C., Savas, E.: An approach for isolating the sources of information leakage exploited in cache-based side-channel attacks. In: 2013 IEEE 7th International Conference on Software Security and Reliability-Companion (SERE-C), pp. 74–83, June 2013
4. Bahador, M.B., Abadi, M., Tajoddin, A.: HPCMalHunter: behavioral malware detection using hardware performance counters and singular value decomposition. In: 2014 4th International Conference on Computer and Knowledge Engineering (ICCKE), pp. 703–708, October 2014
5. Bhattacharya, S., Mukhopadhyay, D.: Who watches the watchmen?: utilizing performance monitors for compromising keys of RSA on intel platforms. In: Güneysu, T., Handschuh, H. (eds.) CHES 2015. LNCS, vol. 9293, pp. 248–266. Springer, Heidelberg (2015). doi:10.1007/978-3-662-48324-4_13

6. Booth, J.: Not so incognito: exploiting resource-based side channels in JavaScript engines. Master's thesis, School of Engineering and Applied Sciences, Harvard University (2015). http://nrs.harvard.edu/urn-3:HUL.InstRepos:17417578
7. Chang, C.C., Lin, C.J.: LIBSVM: a library for support vector machines. ACM Trans. Intell. Syst. Technol. **2**, 27:1–27:27 (2011). http://www.csie.ntu.edu.tw/~cjlin/libsvm
8. Chiappetta, M., Savas, E., Yilmaz, C.: Real time detection of cache-based side-channel attacks using hardware performance counters. Appl. Soft Comput. **49**, 1162–1174 (2016)
9. Clark, S.S., Mustafa, H., Ransford, B., Sorber, J., Fu, K., Xu, W.: Current events: identifying webpages by tapping the electrical outlet. In: Crampton, J., Jajodia, S., Mayes, K. (eds.) ESORICS 2013. LNCS, vol. 8134, pp. 700–717. Springer, Heidelberg (2013). doi:10.1007/978-3-642-40203-6_39
10. Demme, J., Maycock, M., Schmitz, J., Tang, A., Waksman, A., Sethumadhavan, S., Stolfo, S.: On the feasibility of online malware detection with performance counters. In: Proceedings of the 40th Annual International Symposium on Computer Architecture, ISCA 2013, pp. 559–570. ACM, New York (2013)
11. Felten, E.W., Schneider, M.A.: Timing attacks on web privacy. In: Proceedings of the 7th ACM Conference on Computer and Communications Security, CCS 2000, pp. 25–32. ACM, New York (2000)
12. Gruss, D., Bidner, D., Mangard, S.: Practical memory deduplication attacks in sandboxed javascript. In: Pernul, G., Ryan, P.Y.A., Weippl, E. (eds.) ESORICS 2015. LNCS, vol. 9326, pp. 108–122. Springer, Cham (2015). doi:10.1007/978-3-319-24174-6_6
13. Hayes, J., Danezis, G.: k-fingerprinting: a robust scalable website fingerprinting technique. In: 25th USENIX Security Symposium (USENIX Security 16), pp. 1187–1203. USENIX Association, Austin, (2016). https://www.usenix.org/conference/usenixsecurity16/technical-sessions/presentation/hayes
14. Hornby, T.: Side-channel attacks on everyday applications: distinguishing inputs with FLUSH+RELOAD. Black Hat USA (2016). https://www.blackhat.com/docs/us-16/materials/us-16-Hornby-Side-Channel-Attacks-On-Everyday-Applications-wp.pdf
15. Jana, S., Shmatikov, V.: Memento: Learning secrets from process footprints. In: 2012 IEEE Symposium on Security and Privacy, pp. 143–157, May 2012
16. Kazdagli, M., Reddi, V.J., Tiwari, M.: Quantifying and improving the efficiency of hardware-based mobile malware detectors. In: 2016 49th Annual IEEE/ACM International Symposium on Microarchitecture (MICRO), pp. 1–13, October 2016
17. Kim, H., Lee, S., Kim, J.: Inferring browser activity and status through remote monitoring of storage usage. In: Proceedings of the 32nd Annual Conference on Computer Security Applications, ACSAC 2016, pp. 410–421. ACM, New York (2016)
18. Lee, S., Kim, Y., Kim, J., Kim, J.: Stealing webpages rendered on your browser by exploiting GPU vulnerabilities. In: 2014 IEEE Symposium on Security and Privacy, pp. 19–33, May 2014
19. Liang, B., You, W., Liu, L., Shi, W., Heiderich, M.: Scriptless timing attacks on web browser privacy. In: 2014 44th Annual IEEE/IFIP International Conference on Dependable Systems and Networks, pp. 112–123, June 2014
20. Linux Kernel Developers: perf: Linux profiling with performance counters (2015). https://perf.wiki.kernel.org/index.php/Main_Page
21. Linux Programmer's Manual: perf_event_open - set up performance monitoring (2016). http://man7.org/linux/man-pages/man2/perf_event_open.2.html

22. Lipp, M., Gruss, D., Spreitzer, R., Maurice, C., Mangard, S.: ARMageddon: cache attacks on mobile devices. In: 25th USENIX Security Symposium (USENIX Security 16), pp. 549–564. USENIX Association, Austin (2016). ISBN 978-1-931971-32-4. https://www.usenix.org/conference/usenixsecurity16/technical-sessions/presentation/lipp

23. Maurice, C., Le Scouarnec, N., Neumann, C., Heen, O., Francillon, A.: Reverse engineering intel last-level cache complex addressing using performance counters. In: Bos, H., Monrose, F., Blanc, G. (eds.) RAID 2015. LNCS, vol. 9404, pp. 48–65. Springer, Cham (2015). doi:10.1007/978-3-319-26362-5_3

24. Mucci, P.J., Browne, S., Deane, C., Ho, G.: PAPI: a portable interface to hardware performance counters. In: Proceedings of the Department of Defense HPCMP Users Group Conference, pp. 7–10 (1999)

25. Oren, Y., Kemerlis, V.P., Sethumadhavan, S., Keromytis, A.D.: The spy in the sandbox: practical cache attacks in javascript and their implications. In: Proceedings of the 22nd ACM SIGSAC Conference on Computer and Communications Security, CCS 2015, pp. 1406–1418. ACM, New York (2015)

26. Singh, B., Evtyushkin, D., Elwell, J., Riley, R., Cervesato, I.: On the detection of kernel-level rootkits using hardware performance counters. In: Proceedings of the 2017 ACM on Asia Conference on Computer and Communications Security, pp. 483–493. ACM (2017)

27. Sun, Q., Simon, D.R., Wang, Y.M., Russell, W., Padmanabhan, V.N., Qiu, L.: Statistical identification of encrypted web browsing traffic. In: Proceedings 2002 IEEE Symposium on Security and Privacy, pp. 19–30 (2002)

28. Tang, A., Sethumadhavan, S., Stolfo, S.J.: Unsupervised anomaly-based malware detection using hardware features. In: Stavrou, A., Bos, H., Portokalidis, G. (eds.) RAID 2014. LNCS, vol. 8688, pp. 109–129. Springer, Cham (2014). doi:10.1007/978-3-319-11379-1_6

29. Ter Louw, M., Lim, J.S., Venkatakrishnan, V.N.: Enhancing web browser security against malware extensions. J. Comput. Virol. 4(3), 179–195 (2008)

30. Uhsadel, L., Georges, A., Verbauwhede, I.: Exploiting hardware performance counters. In: 5th Workshop on Fault Diagnosis and Tolerance in Cryptography, FDTC 2008, pp. 59–67, August 2008

31. Vila, P., Köpf, B.: Loophole: timing attacks on shared event loops in chrome. In: 26th USENIX Security Symposium (USENIX Security 17). USENIX Association, Vancouver (2017). https://www.usenix.org/conference/usenixsecurity17/technical-sessions/presentation/vila

32. Willems, C., Hund, R., Fobian, A., Felsch, D., Holz, T., Vasudevan, A.: Down to the bare metal: using processor features for binary analysis. In: Proceedings of the 28th Annual Computer Security Applications Conference, ACSAC 2012, pp. 189–198. ACM, New York (2012)

33. Yang, Q., Gasti, P., Zhou, G., Farajidavar, A., Balagani, K.S.: On inferring browsing activity on smartphones via USB power analysis side-channel. IEEE Trans. Inf. Forensics Secur. 12(5), 1056–1066 (2017)

34. Zankl, A., Miller, K., Heyszl, J., Sigl, G.: Towards efficient evaluation of a time-driven cache attack on modern processors. In: Askoxylakis, I., Ioannidis, S., Katsikas, S., Meadows, C. (eds.) ESORICS 2016. LNCS, vol. 9879, pp. 3–19. Springer, Cham (2016). doi:10.1007/978-3-319-45741-3_1

35. Zhang, N., Sun, K., Shands, D., Lou, W., Hou, Y.T.: TruSpy: cache side-channel information leakage from the secure world on arm devices. Cryptology ePrint Archive, Report 2016/980 (2016). http://eprint.iacr.org/2016/980

Acoustic Data Exfiltration from Speakerless Air-Gapped Computers via Covert Hard-Drive Noise ('DiskFiltration')

Mordechai Guri[(✉)], Yosef Solewicz, Andrey Daidakulov,
and Yuval Elovici

Cyber-Security Research Center, Ben-Gurion University of the Negev,
Beersheba, Israel
{gurim,ysolewicz,daidakul,elovici}@post.bgu.ac.il

Abstract. In the past, it has been shown that malware can exfiltrate data from air-gapped (isolated) networks by transmitting ultrasonic signals via the computer's speakers. However, such a communication relies on the availability of speakers on a computer. In this paper, we present 'DiskFiltration', a method to leak data from speakerless computers via covert acoustic signals emitted from its hard disk drive (HDD) (Video: https://www.youtube.com/watch?v=H7lQXmSLiP8 or http://cyber.bgu.ac.il/advanced-cyber/airgap). Although it is known that HDDs generate acoustical noise, it has never been studied in the context of a malicious covert-channel. Notably, the magnetic HDDs dominate the storage wars, and most PCs, servers, and laptops todays are installed with HDD drive(s). A malware installed on a compromised machine can generate acoustic emissions at specific audio frequencies by controlling the movements of the HDD's *actuator arm*. Binary Information can be modulated over the acoustic signals and then be picked up by a nearby receiver (e.g., microphone, smartphone, laptop, etc.). We examine the HDD anatomy and analyze its acoustical characteristics. We also present signal generation and detection, and data modulation and demodulation algorithms. Based on our proposed method, we developed a transmitter and a receiver for PCs and smartphones, and provide the design and implementation details. We examine the channel capacity and evaluate it on various types of internal and external HDDs in different computer chassis and at various distances. With DiskFiltration we were able to covertly transmit data (e.g., passwords, encryption keys, and keylogging data) between air-gapped computers to a nearby receiver at an effective bit rate of 180 bits/min (10,800 bits/h).

Keywords: Air-gap · Exfiltration · Malware · Acoustic · Covert-channel · Hard-disk drive

1 Introduction

An 'air-gap' is a measure taken in order to keep a computer network (or other type of IT devices) disconnected from public networks such as the Internet. In air-gap isolation, there is no wired or wireless connection between the internal network and the

© Springer International Publishing AG 2017
S.N. Foley et al. (Eds.): ESORICS 2017, Part II, LNCS 10493, pp. 98–115, 2017.
DOI: 10.1007/978-3-319-66399-9_6

outer world. Given the high level of separation, attackers cannot breach the network and steal data using remote attacks launched over the Internet. Military networks, as well as networks within financial organizations, critical infrastructure, and commercial industries [1], are known to be air-gapped due to the sensitive data they store and process. Despite the high level of isolation, an air-gap doesn't provide hermetic protection from breach events. Several incidents in which air-gapped networks have been compromised have been published in the recent years [2]. Infecting such networks can be accomplished through a malicious insider, stolen credentials, physical access, and so on [3].

Once the attacker has a foothold in the target network, he/she may want to exfiltrate valuable data. To that end, the attacker has to overcome the physical isolation by bridging the air-gap. Over the years, different types of covert channels have been proposed by security researchers, enabling exfiltration through an air-gap. Electromagnetic methods that exploit electromagnetic radiation from different components of the computer [4, 5] are likely the oldest type of covert channel researched. Various types of optical [6], thermal [7], and acoustic [8, 9] out-of-band communication channels have also been suggested.

1.1 Speakerless Computers

Most of the acoustic covert channels require a speaker (as a transmitter) and a microphone (as a receiver) to be installed in the air-gapped computers, in order to enable bi-directional covert communication. A malware can encode the data over sonic or ultrasonic frequencies, and subsequently broadcast it through the computer speaker. Another computer with a microphone can receive the transmissions, decode the data, and sent it to the attacker. To avoid such an attack, security policies may prohibit the use of speakers and microphones in a secure network, a measure also referred as an 'audio-gap' [10, 11]. Keeping speakers disconnected from sensitive computers can effectively mitigate the acoustic covert channels based on speakers [12].

In this paper, we introduce 'DiskFiltration', an acoustic channel which works even when speakers (or other audio related hardware) are not present in the infected computer. Our method is based on exploring intrinsic covert noises emitted from the hard disk drive (HDD) which exists on most computers today. We show that malicious code on a compromised computer can perform 'seek' operations, such as the HDDs moving head (the actuator) will induce the generation of such noise patterns at a certain frequency range. Arbitrary binary data can therefore be modulated through these acoustic signals, and the signals can then be received by a nearby device equipped with a microphone (e.g., smartphone), and be decoded and finally sent to the attacker.

1.2 HDD, SSD, and SSHD

Three primary types of mass storage drives exist today:

Hard Disk Drive (HDD). The hard disk drive uses a mechanical arm (actuator) with a read and write head to access information at the correct location on a spinning magnetic platter. The hard disk drive is the most prevalent mass storage medium used in PCs, servers, legacy systems, and laptops ([13], 2017 forecast).

Solid State Drive (SSD). Solid state drives store the data in interconnected flash memory chips (e.g., NAND based flash chips), a type of non-volatile memory. There are no moving or mechanical parts to an SSD, and hence they emit virtually no noise.

Solid State Hard Drive (SSHD). Solid state hybrid drives (SSHDs) combine HDD and SSD technology in the same unit. The flash is used as a cache buffer for frequently used data, while the rest of the data is stored on the magnetic media. SSHD contains the HDD's mechanical parts, and hence emits noise when the data stored on the HDD component is accessed.

Our method is based on the acoustic signals generated by the hard drive's mechanical parts, and therefore is relevant to HDDs and SSHDs, as opposed to SSDs. Generally speaking, SSDs are considered to have advantages over HDDs in term of data access speed, unit size, and reliability. Despite the increased rate of adoption of SSDs, HDD are still the most sold storage devices, mainly due to their low cost. In 2015, 416 million HDD units were sold worldwide, compared to 154 million SSD units. Currently, HDDs still dominate the storage wars, and most PCs, servers, legacy systems, and laptops are installed with HDD drives [13]. This means that our covert channel is available on most of today's desktop and servers.

The rest of this paper is structured as follows. In Sect. 2 we present related work. Section 3 discusses the attack model. Section 4 introduces the anatomy of hard disk drives, and Sect. 5 discusses its acoustic characteristics. Section 6 describes the implementation of the transmitter and receiver. Section 7 present evaluation results. Section 8 proposes countermeasures, and we conclude in Sect. 9.

2   Related Work

Covert channels allowing exfiltration of data from air-gapped computers can be categorized into electromagnetic, optic, thermal, and acoustic. The general technique of spying on information systems through leaking emanations is also referred as a TEMPEST attack [14].

Electromagnetic. Electromagnetic emanations from different computer components have been investigated as a medium for data transmission for more than twenty years. Intentional emissions from a computer screen was first discussed by Kuhn and Anderson [4] and Thiele [15]. More recently, AirHopper malware [16, 17] used the video cable to generate FM radio transmissions, in order to leak data to a nearby mobile phone. In the same manner, GSMem [5] exploit electromagnetic radiation generated from the computer bus to transmit data over the air-gap. Other types of electromagnetic based methods are discussed in [18].

Optic. Optical methods are less discussed in the context of covert channels, since they are visible to the surrounding environment. Data leakage through keyboard LEDs was proposed in [19]. VisiSploit, a covert optical method, was proposed by Guri et al. [20]; in this method, data is leaked from the LCD screen to a remote camera via an invisible image projected on the screen. Other optical methods suggested for exfiltrating data from air-gapped computers are the Hard-Disk-Drive LEDs [6] and routers LEDs [21].

Thermal. Air-gap communication using heat emissions was proposed in [7]. In a method called BitWhisper, the authors demonstrated slow communication between adjacent air-gapped computers via heat exchange. Thermal covert channels on modern multicores (in the same system) have been thoroughly studied by Bartolini et al. [22].

Acoustic. Acoustic methods are based on leaking data over sound waves at sonic and ultrasonic frequencies. Data transmission over audio was first reviewed by Madhavapeddy et al. in 2005 [23] when they discussed audio based communication between two computers. In 2013, Hanspach and Goetz [24] used near-ultrasonic soundwaves to establish a covert channel between air-gapped systems equipped with speakers and microphones. They implemented a botnet which communicated between computers at distance of 19.7 m with a bandwidth of 20 bits/s. The work in [25] extends the ultrasonic covert channel for smartphones, demonstrating how data can be transferred up to 30 m away. Interestingly, in 2013, security researchers claimed to find BIOS level malware in the wild (dubbed BadBios) which communicates between air-gapped laptops using ultrasonic sound [26].

Notably, speakers are sometimes forbidden from certain computers based on regulations and security practices [10]. In 2016, Guri et al. introduced Fansmitter, a malware which facilitates the exfiltration of data from an air-gapped computer via noise intentionally emitted from the PC fans [9]. In this method, the computer does not need to be equipped with audio hardware or an internal or external speaker. Our method uses the acoustic signals emitted from the hard disk drive (HDD). Although it is a known fact that HDDs generate acoustical noise, it has never been studied and analyzed in the context of a covert-channel.

3   Attack Model

DiskFiltration, as an acoustic covert channel, can be used to leak data from air-gapped computers. However, this covert channel can also be used in the case of Internet connected computers (non air-gapped) in which the network traffic is intensively monitored by networked-based intrusion detection (IDS), intrusion prevention (IPS) and data leakage prevention (DLP) systems. In these cases, exfiltration of data though the Internet traffic may be detected, and hence the attacker may want to resort to an out-of-band covert channel.

The adversarial attack model consists of a transmitter and a receiver. The transmitter is usually an ordinary desktop computer or server with at least one HDD installed. The receiver is a nearby device with audio recording capabilities. It can be a smartphone placed on the table, a smartwatch on the user's hand, or a nearby PC with a microphone. Infecting highly secure networks can be accomplished, as demonstrated by incidents such as Stuxnet [27], Agent.Btz [28], and others [29]. Infecting a mobile phone or other recording device, can be accomplished via different attack vectors, using emails, SMS/MMS, malicious apps, and so on [30].

The malware installed on the computer gathers the data to exfiltrate (e.g., passwords or encryption keys), and then transmits it using acoustic signals emitted from the HDD. The acoustic signals are generated by performing intentional seek operations which cause the HDD actuator arm to make mechanical movements. The nearby receiver receives the transmission, decodes the data, and transfers it to the attacker via the Internet Wi-Fi networks, mobile data, or SMS.

4 Anatomy of a Hard Disk Drive

In this section we provide the technical background necessary to understand the way DiskFiltration works. A more comprehensive description of HDD functionality and its internal operation can be found in [31].

The internal view of a hard disk drive is shown in Fig. 1. Hard disk drives store data in disks, or platters, coated with magnetic material (Fig. 1A). The platters rotate at various speeds, depending on the type of HDD. Modern consumer-grade HDDs commonly have rotational speeds of 5400, 7200, or 15,000 revolutions per minute (RPM). The engine that rotates the platters is the spindle motor (Fig. 1B), and it spins at a constant speed that is tied to the RPM of the HDD. Notably, this motor is one of the constant sources of noise from a HDD. The magnetic data is read/written from/to the platters using read-and-write heads (Fig. 1C). These heads are positioned very close to the magnetic surface (at a distance of nanometers from one another) and can detect (read) or change (write) the magnetization of the material passing under it. Modern HDDs have several stacked platters, each of which has its own read-and-write head. All of the read-and-write heads are attached to the actuator arm (Fig. 1D). During read and write operations, the actuator (Fig. 1F) rotates the actuator axis (Fig. 1E) which moves the read-and-write heads on an arc across the platters as they spin. The mechanical movements of the actuator generate noise at different levels and frequencies. Video clips showing HDD internal parts during operation can be found online [32].

The magnetic data is stored on circles on the surface known as tracks (Fig. 2A). Corresponding tracks on all surfaces of a drive (on all platters) make up a cylinder. Two fundamental terms of disk geometry are the geometrical sector and the disk sector. A geometrical sector (Fig. 2B) is a section of a disk between a center, two radii, and a corresponding arc. A disk sector (Fig. 2C) refers to the intersection of a track and geometrical sector. Logically, the disk sector is the minimum storage unit of a hard drive. 'Seek' describes the operation of the actuator arm to move to a specific track of the disk where the data needs to be read or written. The time it takes to move the head to the desired track is called the seek time. As we describe in the following section, the movement of the head assembly on the actuator arm during the seek operation emits acoustic noise.

Fig. 1. A hard disk drive's internal parts.

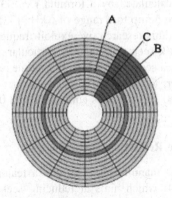

Fig. 2. Basic geometry of an HDD platter

5 HDD Acoustics

An HDD emits noise at different frequencies and intensity levels which are produced by the movements of its internal parts. Notably, although there have been several studies on the acoustic characteristics of a hard drive, the noise emission mechanisms and the precise source of such emissions have not been comprehensively modeled [31, 33].

There are two primary sources of acoustic noise inside a drive: the motor and the actuator. These sources correspond with two type of noises as explained below.

Idle acoustic noise is defined as the noise generated when the HDD spins the disks (platters). Idle noise is generated mainly by the spindle motor and the ball bearings inside the motor. This main frequency of idle noise can be calculated by $IdleMainFreq = RPM/60$ where RPM is the HDD rotation speed. Figure 3 shows the spectrogram of the idle acoustic noise generated by the Western Digital HDD spinning at 7200 RPM. The primary tone is generated at $7200/60 = 120\,\text{Hz}$, and can be seen in the spectrogram as a highlighted continuous frequency peak.

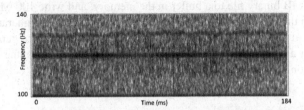

Fig. 3. Spectrogram of the idle acoustic noise generated by a HDD with an RPM of 7200

Seek acoustic noise is generated by the engine of the actuator and its movement during seek, read, and write operations. This noise is produced during file system activities (e.g., file read and write) and is usually louder than the static Idle acoustic noise. Unlike idle acoustic noise, the seek noise depends on many factors (magneto-electric interactions, vibrations, and so on), hence the exact tone frequency cannot be calculated by a formula [31, 33]. The exact seek tone frequency regions (expected to be up to a range of 6 kHz [33]) can be investigated through a waveform analysis. In this research, we exploit frequency regions which are probably rooted on the hard disk seek time, and in particular, on the shortest seek time component, the track-to-track seek time, which is the time required to move from adjacent tracks. As is shown later, the most informative frequency region detected in our experiments is around 2080 Hz, which is equivalent to a 0.48 ms track-to-track seek time.

5.1   Noise Reduction Technologies

Many HDD manufacturers include a feature called automatic acoustic management (AAM) [34] which aims at reducing seek acoustic noise. Such technologies (e.g., Western Digital IntelliSeek [35]) use sophisticated algorithms to regulate the acceleration and positioning of the HDD actuator so that the emitted noise is reduced. Enabling and disabling this feature is possible with the appropriate software or with an API to the HDD controller [36]. During our experiments we *didn't* modify the AAM setting, which is usually set to on by default. The main reason we do so is to keep our covert channel as stealth and quiet as possible in order to evade detection by the user.

5.2   Acoustic Signal Generation

The idle acoustic noise emitted from disk rotation is static and cannot be controlled by software. In order to modulate binary data, we exploit the seek acoustic noise generated by the movements of the actuator. By regulating (starting and stopping) a sequence of seek operations, we control the acoustic signal emitted from the HDD, which in turn can be used to modulate binary '0' and '1'. Next, we examine the seek acoustic noise generated by three types of operations: read, write, and seek.

'Read' and 'Write' Operations. Figure 4 shows the spectrograms of acoustic waveforms generated from the HDD during read (left image) and write (right image) operations as recorded from outside the computer chassis. In this test we read the content of 100 MB binary file to a buffer in the memory, and write 100 MB of random bytes to a file in the disk. During the tests, the cache was disabled to guarantee physical disk access. Read and write operations cause acoustic bursts seen as a general increase in frequency for a short time period. During most of these operations, the head stays at the same position.

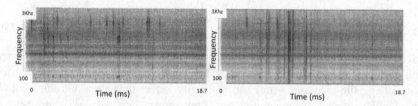

Fig. 4. Spectral views of read (left) and write (right) operations, with minimal head movements.

Acoustic Signal Generation. We also examine the acoustic noise emitted by seek operations when the actuator moves between tracks at different distances. Figure 5 shows the acoustical waveform generated from the HDD during seek operations as recorded from outside the computer chassis. In this test we perform three types of seek operations, (1) seeking and reading repeatedly from the first and last sectors, (2) seeking and reading between two consecutive tracks, and (3) seeking and reading between two consecutive sectors. The seek and read operations cause an acoustic signal to wrap all over the range of 0 to 6000 Hz. There were no significant acoustic differences (frequencies or amplitude) between the three types of seek operations. This indicated that in order to emit a noticeable level of noise it is sufficient to perform seek operations between any two tracks. In our tests we used the seek operation between the first and the last track of the HDD.

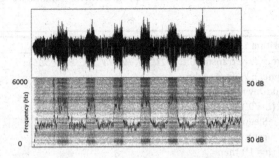

Fig. 5. Spectral view of 'seek' operations between different tracks

6 Implementation

In this section we describe the implementation of the DiskFiltation transmitting software, including signal generation, data modulation, and bit-framing. We also describe the implementation of a receiver as an Android app for the smartphone.

6.1 Transmitter

A program can perform disk operations with two types of addressing: file system addressing and direct disk addressing. In file system addressing, the running process specifies the file name to perform the read or write operations on. In direct addressing, the process specifies the physical location on the HDD layout for the required I/O operation, e.g., specifying a sector number to read from or write to. Modern OSs, such as Windows and Linux, provide APIs for the two type of addressing; in particular, they allowing direct disk addressing [37]. Technically, it means that user-level processes can generate the acoustic signals by performing seek operations by specifying sector numbers or the location within files. Notably, file level operations may not require any special permissions (e.g., root). For example, any process may be able to read and write files from or to temporary or working folders. We choose to use the seek operation, as it generates the highest level of the acoustic signal. The transmitter is a C program which uses the direct addressing system calls using the fopen(), and fseek() systems' calls [38]. For the testing we also implemented a shell script version of the transmitter using the Linux dd command-line utility [39]. This is a low level utility of Linux which can perform a wide range of HDD operations at the file or block level.

6.2   Data Modulation

To transmit binary data we used a simple on-off keying (OOK) modulation. In this digital modulation scheme, data is represented by the presence of a carrier at a specified frequency Fc. More specifically, a binary '0' is represented by the presence of a carrier for a duration of T_1, while its absence for the duration of T_0 represents a binary '0'. Algorithm 1 shows a pseudo code for our C program which handles the transmission of a bit b.

Algorithm 1   *TransmitBit*
1: procedure transmitBit(b, *T0, T1, BEGIN_SEC, END_SEC*)
2:    sync(); //drop cache
3:    hddDev = open(/dev/sda)
4:    if (b='0') then
5:        Sleep (T0);
6:        return;
7:    if (b='1') then
8:        for time T1 do
9:            seek(hddDev, BEGIN_SEC);
10   seek(hddDev, END_SEC);
11:        end for
12: return;

The transmitBit procedure receives the '0' and '1' transmission time (T0, T1) and two sector numbers for the seek operation (BEGIN_SEC, END_SEC). As we previously explained, in signal generation, moving the actuator between the sectors positioned in different tracks produces the highest level of noise. If the bit to transmit is '0', the procedure does nothing by sleeping for duration T0. If the bit to transmit is '1', the procedure invokes seek operations, causing the head to repeatedly move between BEGIN_SEC and END_SEC for duration T1.

Bit Framing. As explained, unlike the idle acoustic noise, seek acoustic noise may vary depending on the type of HDD, and differences in seek acoustic noise can also vary between HDDs of the same model. Although the general range of seek tone frequency is known (e.g., 0–6 kHz [33]), the exact tone frequency cannot be calculated by a formula. This implies that a potential receiver (e.g., an application in a smartphone) needs to scan the frequency range first, in order to find and detect the carrier used for the on-off keying modulation. In addition, T_0 and T_1 may be set differently on each transmitter, and may be unknown to the receiver in advance. To assist the receiver in dynamically synchronizing with the transmitter parameters, we transmit data in small frames. Each frame consists of a preamble sequence of four bits, a cyclic redundancy check (CRC) of 8 bits and a payload of 36 bits (Table 1).

Table 1. A frame consisting of four bits of preamble, followed by a payload of 36 bits

Preamble (4 bits)	CRC-8 (8 bits)	Payload (36 bits)
1010	Checksum	0101110101010101...

The preamble consists of the '1010' sequence and is used by the receiver to periodically determine the carrier frequency. In addition, the preamble header allows the receiver to identify the beginning of a transmission in the area and extract other channel parameters, such as T_0 and T_1. The CRC is computed on the 36 bits payload and added after the preamble. The receiver calculates the CRC for the received payload, and if it differs from the received CRC, an error is detected. For reliable separation of frames we add a time delay of two bits between the transmissions of two consecutive frames.

Stealth. As noted, modern HDDs include a feature called AAM [34] which reduces seek acoustic noise. In order to keep the covert channel as stealth as possible, we did not modify the AAM setting, resulting in quiet HDD operation. Our experiments show that in modern HDDs, the generated acoustic signals blend with the background noise and are not noticeable by the user. Users may notice the HDD activity by seeing the HDD's blinking LED or hearing unusual seek noise. However, such occurrences won't raise suspicions, since they aren't out of ordinary because the HDD is routinely active due to swapping, indexing, backups, and other types of background operations.

6.3   The Receiver

Directly decoding the acoustic information from the transmitted waveform is not efficient, since the relevant information encoded by the induced HDD operations are concentrated in narrowband frequency regions. The signal-to-noise ratio (SNR) of the captured waveform can be significantly improved by exploiting the informative spectral regions, rather than the whole frequency spectrum. In this research, these regions are defined experimentally, because a theoretical modeling of the position of the spectral peaks is quite complex, as discussed earlier.

In order to analyze our distinct encoding, we estimated the SNR in the frequency domain (as opposed to the time domain) as follows. Our "signal" (X) level is estimated by summing the magnitudes of the Fourier transform bins within our defined informative regions (R) during induced seek operations (bit 1). Noise level (N) is estimated in the same way, during an idle noise interval (bit 0). The SNR (in dB) is therefore the logarithm ratio of these two quantities:

$$SNR_R = 20 * log\left(\sum_{k=R}|X_k|/\sum_{k=R}|N_k|\right)$$

The signal adds up coherently in the frequency domain, whereas noise adds up incoherently. Therefore, in order to maximize the SNR, we would like to define R encompassing the most informative frequency bins. Note that the windowing settings and number of spectral bins used should be optimized in order to avoid spectral leaking (single frequencies spread through adjacent bins) and improve the SNR characteristics.

Figure 6 depicts the power spectral density (PSD) for seek and idle wave excerpts from the seek and read operations. The PSD reflects the average power of the signal in a logarithmic scale during a specific time-frequency region. It is expressed in dB relative to the auditory threshold. This wave was captured at a very close distance to the source, at 44.1 kHz, and resampled to 16 kHz. Fast Fourier transform (FFT) was calculated for 160 bins, spanning 50 Hz each. Spectral peaks are clearly spotted in the graphs, and the strongest low frequency peaks correspond to the basic frequency of 120 Hz generated by a 7200 RPM HDD. It can be observed that the 2050–2100 Hz region is the most informative in terms of the SNR. This means that optimal SNR estimation should be focused on this region. For instance, direct SNR calculation on the whole waveform (using all frequency bins) yields an SNR of 1.5 dB, as opposed to 12.0 dB obtained by setting R to 2050–2100 Hz using the bin corresponding to the highest SNR.

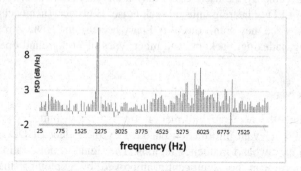

Fig. 6. PSD SNR as function of the frequency

Signal Decoding. From a signal processing perspective, our decoder was implemented as an envelope detector of the waveform energy in the above mentioned frequency regions. In particular, we band-pass filter the received waveform between 2050–2100 Hz and then smooth the narrowband signal, convolving with an analysis window in order to estimate its intensity. The window length should be adjusted according to the bit transmission rate. There are alternative ways of detecting the evolving PSD of a signal on specific frequency region. One could use the Goertzel algorithm [40] which is an efficient FFT implementation for individual frequency bins. Another option would be to use Auto-Regressive (AR) models [41], very useful in describing time-varying random processes. Generally speaking, AR models offer a better frequency resolution but are slower than FFT. These advanced factors should be considered in system design and approached in future research.

Receiver Implementation. The acoustic transmissions can be received by a nearby computer with a microphone, a smartphone placed on the desktop, or other types of recording devices. This subsection briefly describes the receiver implementation. Note that audio sampling and on-off keying (OOK) demodulation are widely used for commutation, and hence are not considered the main contribution of this paper. We refer interested readers to a detailed theoretical explanation and available source-code [42].

We implemented a receiver as an app installed on Samsung Galaxy (S4, S5 and S6) mobile phones with a standard microphone with a sampling rate of 44.1 kHz. The main functionality of the receiver is (1) audio sampling, (2) performing moving windows FFT, (3) preamble detection, and (4) payload demodulation. The receiver continuously samples the audio signals from the recording device - usually the built-in microphone. Technically, this is done by utilizing the `AudioRecord` class in the Android framework [43]. We then transfer the signal to the frequency domain using Fast Furrier transform. In its PAYLOAD state, the code continuously tries to detect a preamble, by scanning for a sequence of "1010" (a sequence of signal, no signal, signal, no signal). Once payload is detected, the channel properties (e.g., transmission time, noise, etc.) are saved, and the state is set to PAYLOAD. In a PAYLOAD state, the code demodulates a sequence of 32 bits using the OOK scheme, then returns to the PRE-AMBLE state. Note that error detection mechanisms, as well as handling of signal loss, are omitted from the description above.

7   Evaluation

In this section we present the evaluation results based on our experiments and analysis.

In our experiments, we used desktop computers installed with the transmitting application as our transmitter. The application can be configured to use 'read', 'write', or 'seek' operations, as well as to operate with specified transmission times and pre-defined sector numbers. During the experiments we checked five different PC desktop workstations with five types of internal HDDs. In addition, we tested external HDDs. The list of the computers and HDDs used during the tests is presented in Table 2.

During our experiments we did not modify the HDD's automatic acoustic management (AAM) setting, which is usually set on by default. The main reason for this is to keep our covert channel as stealth and quiet as possible in order to evade detection by the user. During all of the experiments the HDDs were firmly installed within computer cases in their usual internal drawers (except for the external HDDs). Before the experiments we validated that the computers' cases were firmly enclosed.

We run the transmitter on desktop computers running the Linux Ubuntu OS, 64-Bit version 14.04.3 kernel 3.13.0. We implemented a version of the receiver as an app for the Android OS. All of our tests were conducted using the Samsung Galaxy (S4, S5 and S6) smartphones installed with stock Android. Our testing environment consisted of a computer lab with ordinary background noise, seven workstations, several network switches, and an active air conditioning system.

Table 2. Desktop computers and HDD models tested

#	Type	Model	Chassis
HDD-L	Internal	Seagate Barracuda 7200.12 ST31000524AS 1 TB 7200 RPM 32 MB Cache SATA 6.0 Gb/s 3.5 Inch	Lenovo
HDD-O	Internal	WD Blue 1 TB Desktop Hard Disk Drive - 7200 RPM SATA 6 Gb/s 64 MB Cache 3.5 Inch	Optiplex
HDD-A	Internal	Seagate Barracuda 7200.12 ST3500418AS 500 GB 7200 RPM 16 MB Cache SATA 3.0 Gb/s 3.5 Inch	Antec
HDD-I	Internal	WD Blue 1 TB Desktop Hard Disk Drive - 7200 RPM SATA 6 Gb/s 64 MB Cache 3.5 Inch	Infinity
HDD-G	Internal	Seagate Desktop HDD ST1000DM003 1 TB 64 MB Cache SATA 6.0 Gb/s 3.5 Inch	Gigabyte
HDD-EX	External	WD 500 GB drive 2.5" 5400 RPM	–

Figures 7 and 8 show the acoustical waveform generated from HDD-L, as received by a stationary smartphone placed at a distance of one meter and two meters, respectively, from the transmitter. In the two tests we used the 'seek and write' method for the transmission. Using on-off keying modulation, we transmitted a payload of "101010" when $T_0 = 2$ s and $T_1 = 1$ s. The received waveform was band-pass filtered between 2050–2100 Hz.

Figure 9 shows the acoustical waveforms generated in four tests. HDD-O (Fig. 9a), received by a stationary smartphone placed at a distance of one meter, 'seek and read' method (using dd), and $T_0 = T_1 = 5$ s. HDD-A (Fig. 9b), received by a stationary smartphone placed at a distance of one meter, 'seek & read' method (using dd), and $T_0 = T_1 = 3$ s. HDD-I (Fig. 9c), received by a stationary smartphone placed at a distance of one meter, 'seek & read' method (using dd), and $T_0 = T_1 = 3$ s. HDD-G (Fig. 9d), received by a stationary smartphone placed at a distance of 0.5 m, 'seek & read' method (using dd), and $T_0 = T_1 = 3$ s. The received waveform was band-pass filtered between 2050–2100 Hz. In all tests we used on-off keying modulation to transmit a payload of "101010.". The 128 bits payloads transmitted during the tests were successfully received and demodulated by the smartphone receiver placed up to two meters away with a BER (Bit Error Rate) of 0–10%. We found that with a distance greater than two meters the BER significantly increased, mainly because of the

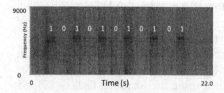

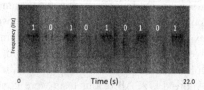

Fig. 7. Spectral view of the signal emitted from HDD-L, as received from a distance of one meter.

Fig. 8. Spectral view of the signal emitted from HDD-L, as received from a distance of two meters

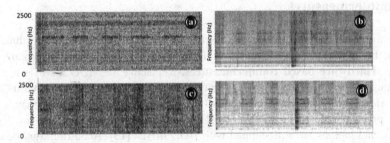

Fig. 9. Spectral view of the signal emitted from four hard drives (HDD-O, HDD-A, HDD-I, and HDD-G)

background noise in the lab. Increasing the distance further with specialized receivers (e.g., microphone array) is left for future work.

7.1 Causal Noise Emission

Since our covert channel is based on HDD activity, casual file operations of other running processes may interfere with the transmissions and interrupt them. Our experiments shows that most applications generate short bursts of noise with only moderate interruptions to the transmission activity. Figure 10 shows the acoustical waveform generated by HDD-I, when the computer was idle, playing video, and performing compilation for a 22 s period. During the idle time, only the system default processes, system services and shell command were active, without additional user application running. During the playing video time, a high definition (HD) video clip was played with the standard VLC media player. During the compilation time, we performed a compilation of medium size C project, using the GCC standard compiler.

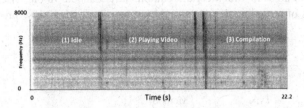

Fig. 10. Spectral view of the signal emitted from HDD-I during different workload

As can be seen, the noise generated by casual operations is fleeting in bursts. There are two main reason for this phenomena. First, applications usually read and write files in a sequential manner, sector by sector. This means that most applications rarely seek between different tracks (e.g., files are stored on the same track), which minimizes the acoustic emission from the HDD. Second, the caching mechanisms (in the OS or in the HDD controller) try to reduce the amount of physical access to the hard drive, which minimizes the number of seek operations, and hence the acoustic emissions.

8 Countermeasures

Countermeasures to mitigate the DiskFiltration attack can be classified into three categories: hardware based, software based, and procedural based, as summarized in Table 3. **Hardware based countermeasures.** Replacing the HDD drives with SSD can eliminate the threat, since SSDs are not mechanical, hence generating virtually no noises. However, replacement of the hard drive in existing infrastructure may not be always practical due to the high cost [13]. In addition, most PCs, servers, legacy systems, and laptops are still shipped with HDD drives [13]. Acquiring a particularly quiet type of HDD [44] or installing the HDD within special enclosures [45] can also limit the range of emitted noise. Another type of hardware product includes signal detection and signal jamming systems. Noise detectors [46] aim at monitoring the background noise at specified frequency ranges. However, such noise detectors are usually limited to use in a quiet environment without noise. Jamming the HDD signal by generating static noise in the background is also possible but not particularly applicable in a work environment due to the disturbance it may cause to users. **Software based countermeasures.** At the software and firmware level, modern HDDs include a feature called automatic acoustic management (AAM) [34] which reduces seek acoustic noise. Ensuring that the AAM settings are at their correct values can limit the range of the emitted signals. As noted, the evaluation in this paper was performed with the default AAM settings, which are configured to their optimal values. Another solution may involve using host intrusion detection systems (HIDS) and host intrusion prevention systems (HIPS) to detect and prevent suspicious 'seek' pattern on HDDs. Such software based countermeasures can be evaded by malware and rootkits at the OS kernel [47]. In addition, distinguishing between legitimate read, write, and seek operations and malicious ones may not be a trivial task. **Procedural based countermeasures.** Procedural countermeasures involve a physical separation of emanating equipment from potential receivers. This approach is referred to as zone separation by United States and NATO standards [11]. In these standards sensitive computers are kept in restricted areas in which certain equipment is banned. In our case, smartphone and other types of recording devices should not be permitted in close proximity of the computer.

Table 3. Different types of countermeasures

Type	Method
Hardware based	• Replacing HDDs with SSDs • Acquiring quiet HDDs • Installing special enclosures • Noise detectors • Signal jammers
Software based	• HIDS/HIPS • Malicious activity detection • Proper configuration of AAM
Procedural	• Zone separation

9   Conclusion

We present a new type of acoustical covert channel code-named DiskFiltration. In this method, an attacker can leak binary data from computers over covert noises emanating from hard disk drives. Unlike most of the existing acoustic covert channels, DiskFiltration can work in computers that are not equipped with speakers or audio hardware. Malicious code installed on the computer can perform intentional seek operations, which cause the HDD head (the *actuator*) to move between different tracks. The mechanical movements generate acoustic signals which can be used for '0' and '1' modulation. The covert signals can be received by a nearby recording device. Despite DiskFiltration's general contribution to the field of covert channels, it is particularly relevant in two adversarial scenarios: (1) in air-gapped networks where there is no network connection between the computer and the Internet, and (2) in computers with heavily monitored (by IDS and IPS systems) Internet connections. In these cases an attacker may resort to out-of-band covert exfiltration channels which are not monitored by existing defense measures. We provided the main technical details regarding the anatomy of modern HDDs and examined the acoustic signals generated by their basic read, write, and seek operations. Based on our observations we designed a rather simple data modulation and demodulation protocol and implemented a prototype of a transmitter (for a computer) and a receiver (for smartphones). We evaluate the covert channel in different types of HDDs and computer chassis, and examine its channel signal quality, channel capacity, and bandwidth. Results shows that DiskFiltration can be used to covertly transfer data to distance of up to two meters (six feet) from the transmitting computer at a bit rate of 180 bits/min.

References

1. McAfee: Defending Critical Infrastructure Without Air Gaps And Stopgap Security, August 2015. https://blogs.mcafee.com/executive-perspectives/defending-critical-infrastructure-without-air-gaps-stopgap-security/. Accessed 01 July 2016
2. SECURELIST: Agent.btz: A Source of Inspiration? (2014). https://securelist.com/blog/virus-watch/58551/agent-btz-a-source-of-inspiration/. Accessed 01 July 2016
3. Goodin, D.: How "omnipotent" hackers tied to NSA hid for 14 years—and were found at last, arstechnica (2015). http://arstechnica.com/security/2015/02/how-omnipotent-hackers-tied-to-the-nsa-hid-for-14-years-and-were-found-at-last/. Accessed 01 July 2016
4. Kuhn, M.G., Anderson, R.J.: Soft tempest: hidden data transmission using electromagnetic emanations. In: Aucsmith, D. (ed.) IH 1998. LNCS, vol. 1525, pp. 124–142. Springer, Heidelberg (1998). doi:10.1007/3-540-49380-8_10
5. Guri, M., Kachlon, A., Hasson, O., Kedma, G., Mirsky, Y., Elovici, Y.: GSMem: data exfiltration from air-gapped computers over GSM frequencies. In: 24th USENIX Security Symposium (USENIX Security 15), Washington, D.C. (2015)
6. Guri, M., Zadov, B., Atias, E., Elovici, Y.: LED-it-GO: leaking (a lot of) data from air-gapped computers via the (small) Hard Drive LED. In: 14th Conference on Detection of Intrusions and Malware & Vulnerability Assessment (DIMVA), Bonn (2017)

7. Mordechai, G., Matan, M., Yiroel, M., Yuval, E.: BitWhisper: covert signaling channel between air-gapped computers using thermal manipulations. In: Computer Security Foundations Symposium (CSF). IEEE (2015)

8. Hanspach, M., Goetz, M.: On covert acoustical mesh networks in air. J. Commun. **8**, 758–767 (2013)

9. Guri, M., Solewicz, Y., Daidakulov, A., Elovici, Y.: Fansmitter: Acoustic Data Exfiltration from (Speakerless) Air-Gapped Computers. arXiv:1606.05915 [cs.CR] (2016)

10. a. Blog: Air Gap Computer Network Security, 30 December 2014. http://abclegaldocs.com/blog-Colorado-Notary/air-gap-computer-network-security/. Accessed 01 July 2016

11. R.I. GUIDANCE: NSTISSAM TEMPEST/2-95, 12 December 1995. https://cryptome.org/tempest-2-95.htm. Accessed 01 July 2016

12. J.-P. Power: Mind the gap: are air-gapped systems safe from breaches? Symantec, 05 Dec 2015. http://www.symantec.com/connect/blogs/mind-gap-are-air-gapped-systems-safe-breaches. Accessed 01 July 2016

13. HDD still dominate the storage wars, June 2013. http://datastorageasean.com/daily-news/hdd-still-dominate-storage-wars. Accessed 01 July 2016

14. S. Institute: An Introduction to TEMPEST. https://www.sans.org/reading-room/whitepapers/privacy/introduction-tempest-981

15. Thiele, E.: Tempest for Eliza (2001). http://www.erikyyy.de/tempest/. Accessed 4 Oct 2013

16. Guri, M., Gabi, K., Assaf, K., Yuval, E.: AirHopper: bridging the air-gap between isolated networks and mobile phones using radio frequencies. In: 2014 9th International Conference on Malicious and Unwanted Software: the Americas (MALWARE), pp. 58–67. IEEE (2014)

17. Guri, M., Monitz, M., Elovici, Y.: Bridging the air gap between isolated networks and mobile phones in a practical cyber-attack. ACM Trans. Intell. Syst. Technol. (TIST) **8**(4) (2017)

18. Guri, M., Monitz, M., Elovici, Y.: USBee: air-gap covert-channel via electromagnetic emission from USB. In: 14th Annual Conference on Privacy, Security and Trust (PST), 2016, Auckland, New Zealand (2016)

19. Loughry, J., Umphress, A.D.: Information leakage from optical emanations. ACM Trans. Inf. Syst. Secur. (TISSEC) **5**(3), 262–289 (2002)

20. Guri, M., Hasson, O., Kedma, G., Elovici, Y.: An optical covert-channel to leak data through an air-gap. In: 14th Annual Conference on Privacy, Security and Trust (PST) (2016)

21. Guri, M., Zadov, B., Daidakulov, A., Elovici, Y.: xLED: Covert Data Exfiltration from Air-Gapped Networks via Router LEDs. arXiv:1706.01140 [cs.CR]

22. Bartolini, D.B., Miedl, P., Thiele, L.: On the capacity of thermal covert channels in multicores. In: Proceedings of the Eleventh European Conference on Computer Systems (EuroSys 2016) (2016)

23. Madhavapeddy, A., Sharp, R., Scott, D., Tse, A.: Audio networking: the forgotten wireless technology. IEEE Pervasive Comput. **4**(3), 55–60 (2005)

24. M. a. G. M. Hanspach: On Covert Acoustical Mesh Networks in Air. arXiv preprint arXiv:1406.1213 (2014)

25. Deshotels, L.: Inaudible sound as a covert channel in mobile devices. In: USENIX Workshop for Offensive Technologies (2014)

26. Goodin, D.: arstechnica (2013). http://arstechnica.com/security/2013/10/meet-badbios-the-mysterious-mac-and-pc-malware-that-jumps-airgaps/

27. Larimer, J.: An inside look at Stuxnet. IBM X-Force (2010)

28. Gostev, A.: Agent.btz: a Source of Inspiration? SecureList, 12 March 2014. http://securelist.com/blog/virus-watch/58551/agent-btz-a-source-of-inspiration/

29. GReAT team: A Fanny Equation: "I am your father, Stuxnet", Kaspersky Labs' Global Research & Analysis Team, 17 February 2015. https://securelist.com/blog/research/68787/a-fanny-equation-i-am-your-father-stuxnet/. Accessed 01 July 2016

30. Symantec: INTERNET SECURITY THREAT REPORT, Apr 2015. https://www4.symantec.com/mktginfo/whitepaper/ISTR/21347932_GA-internet-security-threat-report-volume-20-2015-social_v2.pdf. Accessed 07 Feb 2016

31. Mamun, A.A., Guo, G., Bi, C.: Hard Disk Drive: Mechatronics and Control

32. Inside a Working Hard Drive (Part 1). https://www.youtube.com/watch?v=oIwaNmNMfPU. Accessed 01 July 2016

33. Ying, Y., Feng, G., Fah, Y.F.: Vibro-acoustic Experimental Analysis in Hard Disk Drives. http://www.sea-acustica.es/fileadmin/publicaciones/Sevilla02_sta01001.pdf

34. Wikipedia: Automatic_acoustic_management. https://en.wikipedia.org/wiki/Automatic_acoustic_management. Accessed 01 July 2016

35. Western Digitial, "intelliseek," Western Digitial. http://www.wdc.com/en/flash/index.asp?family=intelliseek

36. https://sourceforge.net/projects/hdparm/

37. http://man7.org/linux/man-pages/man3/fopen.3.html

38. P.P. Manual. http://man7.org/linux/man-pages/man3/fopen.3p.html

39. https://en.wikipedia.org/wiki/Dd_(Unix)

40. Goertzel, G.: An algorithm for the evaluation of finite trigonometric series. Am. Math. Mon. **65**(1), 34–35 (1958). doi:10.2307/2310304

41. Marple, S.L.: Digital Spectral Analysis with Applications. Prentice Hall, Englewood Cliff (1987)

42. Spatula: Modulating and Demodulating Signals in Java. http://spatula.net/mt/blog/2011/02/modulating-and-demodulating-signals-in-java.html. Modulating and Demodulating Signals in Java

43. a. Developer: AudioRecord. https://developer.android.com/reference/android/media/AudioRecord.html

44. Silentpcreview: Recommended Hard Drives. http://www.silentpcreview.com/Recommended_Hard_Drives

45. https://en.wikipedia.org/wiki/Disk_enclosure

46. Pulsar Instruments: Pulsar Instruments for noise meters, sound level meters and noise monitoring equipment. http://pulsarinstruments.com/products/

47. Blunden, B.: The Rootkit Arsenal: Escape and Evasion in the Dark Corners of the System. Jones & Bartlett, Burlington (2012)

DOMPurify: Client-Side Protection Against XSS and Markup Injection

Mario Heiderich$^{(\boxtimes)}$, Christopher Späth, and Jörg Schwenk

Ruhr-University Bochum, Bochum, Germany
mario.heiderich@rub.de

Abstract. To prevent Cross-Site Scripting (XSS) and related attacks, sanitation of untrusted content is usually performed either on the server side, or by client-side filters like XSS Auditor or NoScript. However, modern web applications (including mobile apps) may not be able to rely on these mechanisms any more since untrusted content may pass these filters as ciphertext or may completely be processed within the DOM of the browser/app.

To cope with this problem, XSS sanitation *within* the Document Object Model (DOM) is required. This poses a novel technical challenge: A DOM-based sanitizer must rely on native JavaScript functions. However, in the DOM, any function or property can be overwritten, through a class of attacks called *DOM Clobbering*.

We present a two-part solution: First we show how to embed *any* server or client side filtering technology securely into the DOM. Second, we give an example instantiation of an XSS filter which is highly efficient when implemented in Javascript. Both parts are combined into a working and battle-tested proof-of-concept implementation called DOMPurify.

Keywords: Cross-Site Scripting · JavaScript · DOM Clobbering · Expression injection · Sanitization · Webmail encryption

1 Introduction

Since their introduction to the broader debate in the year 1999[1], XSS and Markup Injection attacks have been recognized as major threats to web applications. New attack classes and sub-classes of XSS are discovered and documented regularly [1–3]. To prevent these attacks and ensure that no malicious scripts are executed, any untrusted input must be sanitized thoroughly (removal of scripts, event handlers, certain styles, expression syntax, and other contextually-risky elements) prior to being rendered in the browser. At the same time, it is crucial that a good sanitizer does not remove too much markup, keeping False Positives at bay.

---

[1] http://blogs.msdn.com/b/dross/archive/2009/12/15/happy-10th-birthday-cross-site-scripting.aspx.

© Springer International Publishing AG 2017
S.N. Foley et al. (Eds.): ESORICS 2017, Part II, LNCS 10493, pp. 116–134, 2017.
DOI: 10.1007/978-3-319-66399-9_7

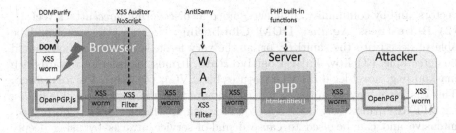

Fig. 1. Standard sanitation points, the position of DOMPurify and a possible attack scenario for an encrypted XSS worm

The sanitization can, for example, take place at the web server, at a dedicated web application firewall (WAF) module, or at a browser-embedded XSS detection module like MSIE's XSS filter, the Webkit/Blink XSS Auditor or NoScript (cf. Fig. 1). Regardless of whether server-side or client-side filters are used, the sanitization takes place *outside* a browser's Document Object Model (DOM), which means before the HTML page is rendered and the JavaScript DOM API is activated for this particular web page. However, sanitization may cease to be possible, given the modern and increasingly complex web application scenarios. For example, if untrusted content is encrypted when passing these filters (see the encrypted webmail example in Sect. 2), or when untrusted content is directly processed in the DOM of a browser/app (see Sect. A for examples).

Thus there is an urgent need for input sanitization *within the DOM*. Such sanitization may range from filtering to completely rewriting the input. However, one new challenge must be faced.

Introducing DOM Clobbering. Any sanitization function must be invoked from JavaScript, e.g. by calling `sanitize()`. An adversary may now overwrite this function by injecting an image with an appropriate `name` attribute, e.g. `<img name="sanitize">`. Calls to the sanitize function will now result in a error. This "overwriting" of important DOM methods is called *DOM Clobbering*, and is an attack technique that uses global variables created by the legacy DOM Version 0 still present in all relevant browsers.

Adversarial Model. We strictly adhere to the well-established *web attacker model* [4], and all our attacks are working in this model. Our adversary is thus able to set up malicious web applications, lure victims to visit and use these applications, may send emails, and may access any open web application on the Internet.

DOM Sanitation Challenges. Each XSS sanitizer that shall operate within the DOM should solve the following (sub-)challenges: **(1) Security Against XSS Attacks.** We used continuous automated testing against all *known* attack vectors, and by community challenges aimed at discovering *novel* attack vectors. **(2) Robustness Against DOM Clobbering.** No web attacker should be able to deactivate the sanitizer, or, at the very least, such deactivation should be detectable. **(3) Low False Positive Rate.** It must be tolerant towards rich markup (e.g. novel legal HTML5 features like SVG). **(4) High Performance.** This challenge may seem trivial but please note that the best server-side filters, e.g. HTMLPurifier, rely on heavy code-rewriting, which is very performance-intensive and can be used to cause denial-of-service attacks by using deeply nested HTML lists or tables. **(5) Easy Deployment.** It must be easy to deploy and use. A safe setting should be default but configuration options should allow for an easy customization. **(6) Broad Deployment.** If the sanitizer is written purely in JavaScript, no changes to the browser engine are required for the sanitizer to work in any browser. The use of browser extensions, Java, Flash or similar technologies should be avoided.

Proposed Solution. The proposed solution mainly consists of two parts: The *DOMPurify HTML sanitizer* (which could be replaced by other filtering solutions) to address challenge 1, and the *DOMPurify DOM Clobbering Detection*, which addresses challenge 2.

To address Challenge 1 (Security against XSS), we answer the following question: which element-attribute combinations can be considered safe and should be white-listed?

For Challenge 2 (Robustness against DOM Clobbering) we have to investigate which attack vectors may influence the functionality of DOMPurify and similar DOM-based sanitizers. We describe how we protect against these attacks. Here we concentrate on DOM Clobbering, because this has only been investigated for complete XSS attack vectors up till now. Again please note that *any* DOM-based sanitizer may be deactivated by a DOM Clobbering vector that does not trigger an XSS attack and thus passes all known filters even if unencrypted.

Challenges 3 and 4 are in scope of an exhaustive investigation using over 1400 emails as discussed in Sect. 4.

Challenge 5 is solved by inclusion as an external script: `<script type="text/javascript" src="purify.js"></script>`. Strings are sanitized by executing the following code: `var clean = DOMPurify.sanitize(dirty);`.

DOMPurify is a DOM-only XSS sanitizer for HTML and SVG. In addition, DOMPurify only makes use of properties and methods available in the XHTML namespace, hence it can also be deployed in scenarios where MIME types such as `text/html` or `application/xml` are being used.

It's written in JavaScript and works in all modern browsers (Safari, Opera (15+), Edge, Internet Explorer (10+, `toStaticHTML()` fallback for older IE), Firefox and Chrome - as well as almost anything else using Blink or WebKit). DOMPurify doesn't break on IE6 or other legacy browsers but rather does nothing there. DOMPurify sanitizes HTML and prevents XSS attacks.

One can feed DOMPurify a string full of dirty HTML and receive a string with clean HTML in return. DOMPurify will remove everything that contains dangerous HTML and thereby prevent XSS attacks and alike. We primarily use the technologies the browser provides and turn them into an XSS filter. The faster a browser DOM engine, the faster DOMPurify.

Advantages of DOM-Based XSS Filters Compared to Existing Solutions. DOM-based XSS filters offer plenty of advantages, especially when compared to their classic pendants on the server-side.

Immunity Against Obfuscation. One major advantage of placing the XSS filter in the DOM is the absence of code obfuscation. Importantly, such obfuscation has already been removed by the browser when loading the markup `dirty.html`. The problem of, for example, Charset XSS does not exist for a DOM-based filter because the browser is already operating in the correct charset setting[2].

Knowledge Advantage. A client-side, DOM-based XSS filter knows exactly the DOM of the browser it runs in. In essence, there is no knowledge gap between a constructed DOM on the server-side (as used by HTMLPurifier or AntiSamy) and the real DOM of the browser. This eliminates situations where a server assumes an element to be harmless but the browser uses it to execute (unwanted) JavaScript – this is for instance possible with mXSS or expression injections. Browser peculiarities that a server-side filter may not be aware of exist in a very limited and marginal capacity.

Performance. A Denial-of-Service attack can be conducted against server-side XSS filters with a use of very longs strings, deeply nested DOM nodes, XML attacks and other similar attack vectors. Once executed, such attacks can affect many users at the same time. If XSS filtering is however performed in the client, the effect of a DoS attack doesn't really extend to the server at all, but exclusively impacts the browsers of the targeted users.

Contributions. This paper presents original work. One of the authors published the first description of DOM Clobbering as a blog post, and is the core maintainer of the software described here. This paper makes the following contributions:

- We propose a framework for the novel problem of markup sanitation within the DOM, which will gain importance with the increasing usage of end-to-end encryption libraries like `OpenPGP.js`.
- As a proof-of-concept, we developed DOMPurify DOM Clobbering Detection, the first constructive solution to this issue which takes into account all of the research challenges. DOMPurify uses novel techniques to detect DOM Clobbering attacks: E.g. it verifies the integrity of a given function during runtime.

---

[2] http://zaynar.co.uk/docs/charset-encoding-xss.html.

- We propose a client-side XSS filter that is as tolerant as possible and doesn't remove benign user-input like forms, ID attributes, SVG and many other elements that are removed by other sanitizers for often no reason.
- We performed an extensive security evaluation of DOMPurify, by using automated tests and challenges to the research community. We also evaluated the performance and usability.

2   Example: An OpenPGP.js Worm

To exemplify the necessity of XSS mitigation within the DOM, let's consider the following case of an encrypted XSS worm as depicted in Fig. 1.

End-to-End Email Encryption. End-to-end encryption (E2E) has always been a desirable goal for IT security, even though we only became aware of its full practical importance in the post-Snowden era. Email is still one of the most important messaging services on the Internet, and the standards (PGP, S/MIME) and implementations (Thunderbird, Enigmail, Outlook, iOS Mail, K9-Mail, etc.) of email encryption are freely available. Nevertheless, the proportion of encrypted email communication is still negligibly low. One of the reasons behind this situation is that the large community of webmail users simply lacked the ability to decrypt or sign mails: browsers supported neither PGP nor S/MIME, and webmail users were thus forced to receive unencrypted mails. Since the publication of the JavaScript library OpenPGP.js, the landscape has changed rapidly: more and more projects are using this library to implement mail encryption for webmail applications. Additionally, Google have started their own end-to-end experiments, introducing yet another open-source E2E library to the market[3].

Possibility of an OpenPGP.js Worm. However, webmail security cannot be reduced to encryption. Since a computer worm can simply copy itself into emails sent to all recipients in the victim's address book, email remains an ideal basis for Internet worm propagation, together with social networking tools. The Samy worm (also known as "JS.Spacehero") is certainly the most famous XSS worm to date. Just eight months later the Yamanner worm used Yahoo! Webmail to spread itself by sending copies of its XSS code to all recipients in the address books of subsequent victims. Webmail XSS worms have already been described back in 2002[4] and a proof-of-concept implementation of a webmail worm which runs in different webmailers has been published in 2007[5]. XSS worms are still a problem[6], but large webmailers today mostly know how to sanitize *unencrypted*

---

[3] https://github.com/google/end-to-end.

[4] http://seclists.org/bugtraq/2002/Oct/119.

[5] http://www.xssed.com/article/9/Paper_A_PoC_of_a_cross_webmail_worm_XWW_called_Nduja_connection/.

[6] http://blog.gdssecurity.com/labs/2013/5/8/writing-an-xss-worm.html.

email traffic (on the server-side) to prevent XSS attacks. However, without utilizing a novel sanitation approach, we may soon face the threat of an "OpenPGP.js Worm" (cf. Fig. 1). This worm would simply contain a script that executes as soon as the decrypted mail is rendered, read all entries in the address book containing a PGP public key, copy its XSS payload to an email, and encrypt its content to avoid sanitation. Precursors of this likely occurrences can already be noted in attacks against ProtonMail and Tutanota, in which un-obfuscated XSS attacks were smuggled into the browser to abuse the mail encryption[7].

Reliability of Browser-Side XSS Filters. Existing browser-side XSS detectors and filters like MSIE's XSS filter, WebKits's XSS Auditor or even NoScript cannot mitigate this problem. Given their position in the markup processing chain, they only see the encrypted content. Content sanitation can solely be done *after* decryption of the message by OpenPGP.js is completed, i.e. only within the DOM of the browser. Please note that the inability of current browser-side XSS filters to mitigate this novel scenario is solely based on the fact that they cannot be called from the DOM: If the DOM API would be extended by a function e.g. called `sanitize()`, which would accept HTML Markup and returned a sanitized version of this markup, then this function could be used as an XSS filter for end-to-end encrypted content, too. *So in principle we can adapt any known filtering solution (e.g. all solutions from* Sect. 5*) to the novel scenario, provided we make them accessible from the DOM by a DOM API call.*

Insecurity of Straightforward Solutions. Regrettably, without additional protection mechanisms, this solution may be easily switched off by an attacker: it is here where techniques like DOM Clobbering come into play! If a client-side XSS filter can be called via a JavaScript function, it must either rely on standard interfaces offered by the DOM, e.g. functions to select certain elements for inspection and traversal, or it must be offered as an extension to the DOM API (e.g. as a function called `sanitize()`). If an attacker manages to deactivate one of these basic functions (or the new function `sanitize()`), and does so by using an attack technique that doesn't count as an XSS attack, then the filtering logic will let it pass. DOM Clobbering is such an attack. The attack works as follows: (1) An attacker sends an initial email which contains no XSS attack vector, but only a DOM Clobbering attack that deactivates a basic DOM API function. If this email is decrypted and rendered, it will simply switch the XSS sanitizer off. (2) Now a full XSS attack vector can be sent with a second mail, which will not be sanitized at all.

DOM Clobbering. These two-stage attacks may seem strange at first, but are actually quite easy to perform: if the first mail contains an element `<img src=""name="getElementsByTagName">`, the rendering of this mail will overwrite one of the most important selector methods available to a

---

JavaScript function, the method `document.getElementsByTagName()`. When this function/method is called afterwards, an exception will be raised stating that `document.getElementsByTagName()` is not a function. This would break most JavaScript based XSS filters, so we have to protect against such attacks. This "overwriting" of important DOM methods is called *DOM Clobbering*, and is an attack techniques that uses global variables created by the legacy DOM Version 0 still present in all browsers.

How DOMPurify Mitigates the OpenPGP.js Worm. In an end-to-end encrypted webmail application, DOMPurify will be applied directly to the result of the OpenPGP.js decryption (cf. Listing 1.1).

```
sanitized_message =
DOMPurify.sanitize(openpgp.decryptMessage(mykey.key,
    openpgp_encrypted_message));
```

Listing 1.1. Filtering of decrypted webmails

DOMPurify has already been implemented in the Mailvelope software that is currently being used to deliver end-to-end encryption features to several large mail providers including government-backed programmes such as de-mail. DOMPurify is in addition being used as the client-side security filter for FastMail and other web-mail providers.

3   DOMPurify

This section is dedicated to a presentation of deployment and basic functionality of our DOM-based XSS filter DOMPurify. This should aid an understanding of the novel security challenges. These newly outlined and challenging issues apply to *all* DOM-based sanitizers. The ways we chose for tackling and ultimately solving these challenges are discussed in the next section.

3.1   Novel Mitigation Paradigms

The following section lists and discusses the abstract mitigation concepts and derives general rules applicable to other client-side validation tools running in similar contexts.

Reviewed List of Element-Attribute Combinations. For an XSS filter and HTML sanitizer a capacity to tell apart "the good" and "the bad" is of paramount importance. This is usually done in two ways. The first option is that a filter employs a black-list of known-bad elements and attributes as well as attribute values. The alternative depends on the creation and subsequent use of a list of benign items that is maintained and enforced as a classic white-list. While this second option may appear tempting, our studies strongly suggest that the majority of XSS filters actually behave in a too strict manner and remove too many benign elements. Therefore, they tend to cripple a user-submitted HTML unnecessarily and negatively impact on the usage experience. Further, only few of the inspected tools allow using SVG and provide a subset of considerably safe HTML and SVG elements and attributes. DOMPurify aims to be as tolerant as possible, which is highlighted in the fact that it supports HTML5+, SVG 1.2 Full and MathML 3.

We thoroughly studied the behavior of different HTML, SVG and MathML elements in all supported browsers. We concluded that the list of permitted elements can be larger than usually perceived and normally implemented by other tools. DOMPurify currently considers 206 different elements safe and permits them for user-submitted HTML, SVG and MathML. We similarly studied the behavior of element-attribute combinations and arrived at the result that deemed allowing 295 different attributes possible, seeing as they were considered safe for usage and incapable of leading to a JavaScript execution. Furthermore, we examined what was necessary for a client-side filter to successfully sanitize Shadow DOM elements. As a result, we implemented code to permit DOMPurify to perform that operation as well. To illustrate this in Sect. 4 we demonstrate that the concept of maximum tolerance is useful for sanitizing the entirety of SVG images used by Wikipedia without overwhelming amounts of false positives.

Exploring the other side of the continuum as well, we managed to identify attributes that are potentially harmful but considered safe by WHATWG and therefore make AngularJS's sanitizer[8] prone to XSS attacks (an attack we reported is currently being fixed):

The WHATWG organization maintains their own list of considerably safe elements and attributes[9]. This list is being used by the sanitizer functionality offered by the AngularJS library. We identified a problem with this list as the WHATWG did not fully test all element-attribute combinations. Thus, once implemented, the presented collection, despite being formerly assumed benign, in fact allows for dangerous XSS attacks. The problematic attributes reside in the SVG namespace and the sample attack vector below shows a full bypass which leads to XSS whenever WHATWG's unadapted list is unreflexively used. A change request was filed to update the WHATWG's list to a safer level. The page is now displaying a deprecation warning.

```
<svg><a xmlns:xlink="http://www.w3.org/1999/xlink" xlink:href
    ="?"><circle r="4000"></circle><animate attributeName="
    xlink:href" begin="0" from="javascript:alert(document.
    domain)" to="&amp;"></animate></a></svg>
```

Listing 1.2. Using xlink:href-animation to cause XSS via SVG

Internal DOM Clobbering Protection. As a library that runs entirely in a browser's DOM, DOMPurify is of course prone to DOM Clobbering attacks. In brief, an attacker could try to craft a HTML string that is to be sanitized by

---

[8] https://docs.angularjs.org/api/ngSanitize/service/%24sanitize.

[9] Sanitization rules, https://wiki.whatwg.org/wiki/Sanitization_rules.

DOMPurify. Upon parsing, the HTML encapsulated by the string could attempt to clobber the DOM and overwrite important functionality needed by DOMPurify to sanitize successfully.

To mitigate DOM Clobbering attacks against DOMPurify and its core functionality, we use the boot-strapping phase between mapping the markup for sanitization into a document implementation, and the initialization of the node iteration. This means a walk over all generated HTML elements after checking if all methods utilized by DOMPurify are really the methods we believe them to be. The same applies to certain DOM properties used by our library - here we use constructor checks as well as instances of operators to verify their identity. In case it turns out that a method is not what we expect it to be, the library simply returns an empty string and no potentially dangerous markup can enter the DOM of the protected website.

External DOM Clobbering Protection. DOMPurify also assures that the markup resulting from a sanitation process cannot clobber the already existing data on the website that the HTML is being used on. Overall, this relies on a generous allowing of ID and NAME attributes, as well as upfront checks against the hosting DOM (to verify if it already uses references of the same name). It is important to note that for those checks an "in" operator is used. We cannot make use of "typeof" since most modern browsers return "undefined" for `typeof document.all`, for instance. Further note that the clobbering protection checks both "window" and "document" in case "ID" attributes are found and only verifies the document if "name" attributes are discovered. This is because Gecko-based browsers (Firefox, etc.) create two rather than just one reference for HTML elements applied with ID attributes – one in the global object and one in "document".

Specifics in DOM Parsing and Traversal. To avoid being vulnerable to certain re-indexing - and mXSS attacks, DOMPurify makes sure that attributes and elements are exclusively parsed and processed in reverse order of appearance in the parent element or container. Note that this feature was also tested extensively in MSIE where the DOM-engine doesn't maintain the original attribute order but also orders attributes of elements in an alphabetic order after applying them to the DOM. This behavior can lead to a race-condition-based bypass of client-side XSS filters and was mitigated in DOMPurify.

3.2   Description

DOMPurify uses a combination of both element and attributes white-lists, which are paired with a very scarce reliance on regular expressions for detecting potentially dangerous values. It comprises two main components: the DOM Clobbering Detection *(DCD)* mainly consists of the function _isClobbered, which checks if references to the actual element being (XSS-)sanitized have been overwritten. Additionally, for each `id` or `name` attribute it is checked if its value could be used to overwrite functions that are essential to DOMPurify. *This DCD can be adapted to protect any XSS mitigation solution proposed in the literature* (Fig. 2).

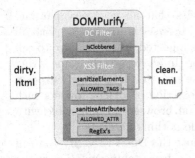

Fig. 2. Block diagram DOMPurify.

The *HTML Sanitizer* is a novel design to implement XSS mitigation in the DOM. Since no obfuscation may be present within the DOM, it uses a combination of whitelists (ALLOWED_TAGS, ALLOWED_ATTR) to skip secure tags/attributes, and carefully crafted regular expressions to delete dangerous attributes.

The function _sanitizeElements() uses the white-list ALLOWED_TAGS to skip secure tags, and the function _isClobbered to check if the markup contains a DOM Clobbering vector. It iterates over all elements in dirty.html. The function _sanitizeAttributes() uses the white-list ALLOWED_ATTR to skip secure attributes and employs some specially crafted regular expressions to ensure the detection of dangerous attributes. Before describing the novel mitigation paradigms - the key foundations of DOMPurify – we have to explain the novel security challenges that a DOM-based XSS sanitizer faces. More importantly, we outline how we coped with these challenges.

One of the additional core features of DOMPurify is the detection and mitigation of DOM Clobbering attacks – both against the library itself and against the surrounding website. This is achieved through the use of strict type checking of all DOM features that the library uses. If one DOM feature appears to have been tampered with, DOMPurify will abort immediately and return an empty string instead of the potentially unsanitized content. Further, DOMPurify allows sanitizing inactive elements inside a Shadow DOM. This works even for recursive Shadow DOM implementations where one Shadow DOM hosts several other, nested Shadow DOM instances.

The clobbering detection happens in two different locations of the library and covers both element clobbering and clobbering of global properties inside window or document. The clobbering tests are being performed for each HTML element or node that is being iterated over. When DOMPurify sanitizes an HTML string containing form nodes, it checks if the DOM it is working in could be clobbered by those form elements. The same takes place for any element applied with an ID or NAME attribute, aiming at avoiding global and document clobbering. If an element in the untrusted HTML string may have clobbering effects on the surrounding document, then it will be removed. In any other case it will be left intact. DOMPurify is therefore the only HTML filter that safely allows the use of ID and NAME attributes in untrusted HTML. This enables DOMPurify to also sanitize full forms and preserves ID attributes that are often important for site navigation via location.hash/anchors. To our knowledge, no other analyzed HTML and XSS filter allows that to occur in a safe manner.

To summarize the description of how DOMPurify works internally to maintain a high level of compatibility to benign markup and at the same time make sure that no form of malicious markup is allowed to pass the filtering mechanisms, a list of interla processing steps has been created:

(1) DOMPurify, upon being started, first verifies that all necessary parameters are set and valid and then checks if the browser is compatible with all required features. If DOMPurify is not fully supported, it will attempt to call a fall-back method such as toStaticHTML or simply return the same string it was receiving for sanitation. This will make sure that DOMPurify exposes maximal compatibility paired with good protection on older browsers such as MSIE8, and have no noticeable impact on browsers incompatible with DOMPurify such as MSIE6 (it will simply do nothing here).

(2) DOMPurify will then perform a check against the DOM to verify that all needed features are indeed trustable and free from tampering (i.e. is the removeChild method really what it claims to be?). DOMPurify will create and store safe references for all verified safe functions and methods to make sure, that an attacker cannot interfere with the library at runtime and exchange important objects and methods in mid flight.

(3) DOMPurify will then determine, how to best create a safe, reliable and isolated document object given the browser it is running on (inert DOM). DOMPurify will preferably chose the DOMParser API and fall back to document.implementation where necessary. The created document object is then being populated with the string or node to be sanitized. Note that depending on not only the browser but also the browser version, different methods need to be chosen to produce a safe document. This is especially for Chrome browsers in versions 12 to 16 and Firefox browsers starting around version 34, as they implement slightly different behaviors, leading to insecure isolated documents if used improperly.

(4) Once the inert DOM has been created and populated, DOMPurify will start iterating over each of the elements in that DOM by using the safely stored and reliable NodeIterator API. Before the first element is being inspected, DOMPurify will call an optionally present hook function. By adding hooks, developers can customize the behavior and extend the feature list. The library offers hooks at all relevant joint-points between unsanitized markup and the sanitization process itself. Any hook method is given the current execution context as parameter to avoid the risk of developers accidentally getting access to a malicious context.

(5) DOMPurify will then inspect the first element, match it to the existing whitelist and either remove it or keep it in the DOM. Two additional hooks can be called during this process for extended customization. If the inspected element is a standard DOM element (such as a DIV or an anchor), DOMPurify will next iterate over all attributes of that element. If the element is however a template element, DOMPurify will invoke a different internal function that allows to recursively sanitize a Shadow DOM before continuing with the next elements. DOMPurify will, if enabled via configuration, in this step also check the element's text nodes for strings that indicate presence of a templating expression and, if instructed to do so, remove it. This was

implemented to protect against XSS via template expressions, popular in AngularJS applications.

(6) Once finished with the basic sanitization of an element itself, DOMPurify will as mentioned iterate over and initially remove all existing attributes in reverse order to respect the internal indexing browsers perform. The attribute name and value will both be matched against the mentioned white-lists, and the library will, if instructed so, also inspect the attribute value for template expressions. In case the attribute is classified to be used in combination with URLs (such as `href` or `action`), DOMPurify will also sanitize this value to prevent XSS and mXSS via URL, especially respecting the risks on XSS via Unicode whitespace and HTML5 character references in Chrome, Opera and Safari. During the process of attribute sanitization, DOMPurify will check for three additional hooks to be present to enable customized behavior. DOMPurify will further check, if the element is applied with attributes that cause DOM Clobbering and check the existing DOM for collisions.

(7) Once DOMPurify checked all attributes, it re-adds the safe ones and returns the sanitized element so it can be added to the safe document and proceeds to the next element selected by the NodeIterator. If no additional element is present, DOMPurify will take the existing DOM tree, serialize it into a string and return it, or, if instructed via configuration, return a DOM fragment or a DOM node. If more elements are present instead, DOMPurify will continue sanitizing the document until the final element has been reached. Note that the attacker cannot inject new elements into the document to sanitize during the process of sanitization, mitigating denial of service risks.

DOMPurify does not store any internal states after a sanitization process, so an attacker cannot bypass the library using multiple sanitization runs in a sequence. This was possible in very early versions of the library thanks to an attack using "Double-Clobbering", namely first changing the library core and then bending the sanitization functionality to produce harmful HTML in a second sanitization run. In the currently deployed version of the library, no bypasses are known.

4   Evaluation

This section discusses the evaluation of DOMPurify's security, performance and false positives.

4.1   Security Evaluation

Methodology. The security of DOMPurify was evaluated in two parts. The first part was a strict empirical analysis where we used automated tests to check the security of DOMPurify against all *known attack vectors*. In the second part we went one step beyond this evaluation, by challenging the security community to test DOMPurify in a white-box test against yet *unknown attack vectors*.

For the first part we used automated testing using a unit test suite, with existing state-of-the-art collections of XSS vectors to automatically check each new version. This is the standard evaluation procedure for any XSS filter, and the collections are constantly being updated to cover each new attack class (e.g. Scriptless Attacks, mXSS, expression injection). We used the following collections: (1) The HTML5 Security Cheatsheet[10], which contains 149 XSS vectors; (2) the OWASP XSS Cheat Sheet, containing 108 XSS vectors.

Second, we received a large number of novel attack vectors by the security community. These consisted of bypasses of early versions of DOMPurify, including numerous DOM Clobbering attack vectors. Altogether we collected 400+ attack vectors. Any bypasses discovered in manual testing were dynamically added to this collection of attacks and will therefore be tracked from this point forward. The vast array of attack vectors used here is publicly available on Github[11].

A public browser-based smoke-test is made available, allowing anyone to test the software quickly and without a need to set up anything. In addition, the security of DOMPurify was tested and further enhanced through a third-party audit in February 2015[12].

Results. We designed DOMPurify to mitigate all known attack vectors from the collections mentioned above. Furthermore we adapted DOMPurify to also mitigate the novel attack vectors. In summary, in the current version of DOMPurify there are neither undetected XSS vectors nor bypasses to DOMPurify.

4.2   Performance and False Positive Evaluation

Methodology. For the evaluation of DOMPurify's performance and false positive rate we subscribed to more than 50 public email marketing lists[13,14] of a range of different topics (politics, sports, psychology, photography, daily digest). We decided to use this data set for several reasons. First, marketing newsletters contain a rich and diverse set of markup in order to attract the customer. Secondly, a wide field of topics and the way its content is presented is more representative for users of different ages, countries, sexes and interests - representing a variety of styles for composing emails. We provide a downloadable copy of the dataset for interested readers [5]. Over two months we accumulated a total of 1421 emails (136 MB of data). All emails were received using a google email account on a locally running Roundcube[15] instance on a Virtual Machine with Ubuntu. Roundcube is a popular web based email client, which we use to take care of the management of emails (load/save).

---

[10] https://html5sec.org/.

[11] https://github.com/cure53/DOMPurify/blob/master/test/expect.json.

[12] https://cure53.de/pentest-report_dompurify.pdf.

[13] https://www.getvero.com/resources/50-email-newsletters/.

[14] https://blog.bufferapp.com/best-newsletters.

[15] https://roundcube.net/.

For the evaluation we proceeded as follows: we created a screenshot of the rendered DOM of both the clean and dirty email with html2canvas[16]. Then we computed the percentual difference between the two versions of the email using resembleJS[17] (e.g. 10%). The performance data constitutes the time taken (ms) by DOMPurify to process a given input file and output the result.

Of the 1421 emails we had to exclude 8 emails from the test set because they were not processed by html2canvas. This left us with a total of 1413 emails as the basis for our evaluation. All tests were executed on a Mac Book Pro Retina[18] on Firefox 52.0.2.

Results - Performance Evaluation. The results of our evaluation are depicted in Fig. 3a. DOMPurify's average processing time of the 1413 emails is 54.7 ms. Our evaluation shows that 62% of input data is processed below the average processing time. 80% of the emails are processed in ≤89 ms (Pareto principle). During our evaluation we observed that factors such as the loading and rendering of images and resources from remote hosts took several seconds up to minutes (for less responsive remote hosts). Summarizing our results, we observed no negative impact on user experience when using DOMPurify as a Sanitizer.

(a) Performance Evaluation: share of emails processed by DOMPurify within a given time frame

(b) False Positive Evaluation: share of emails with a reported difference according to resembleJS

Fig. 3. Performance and false positive evaluation results

Results - False Positives Evaluation. As shown in Fig. 3b, more than 80% of the testset show no visual difference (0.0%) between the original and processed email. For the remaining 20% we investigated the reported impact. We conclude that all reported differences can be attributed to the shifting of text.

To verify these findings we observed the visual display of the emails with the highest reported differences in the browser. For example, consider the rendering of the email with the highest reported difference of 40% in Fig. 4a and b. The astute reader will notice that when manually inspecting these two emails in the

---

[16] https://html2canvas.hertzen.com/.
[17] https://huddle.github.io/Resemble.js/.
[18] OSX 10.12.3 with a 3.1 GHz Intel Core i7 and 16 GB of 1867 MHz DDR RAM.

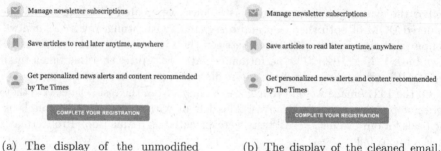

(a) The display of the unmodified email. Screenshot taken manually

(b) The display of the cleaned email. Screenshot taken manually

Fig. 4. Example of a false positive evaluation

browser there is no visual difference between the original and the processed email - except for a shift of a few pixels. However, this shows that DOMPurify has little impact on the processed emails.

We provide a downloadable copy of the highest reported differences including an email with no reported differences for comparison [6].

5   Related Work

XSS Mitigation. Server-side mitigation techniques range from a simple character encoding or replacement, to a full rewrite of the HTML code. The advent of DOM XSS was one of the main reasons behind the introduction of XSS filters embedded into the browser. The IE8 XSS Filter was the first fully integrated solution [7], timely followed by the Webkit XSS Auditor in 2009 [8]. For Firefox, browser-embedded XSS filtering is implemented through the NoScript extension. XSS attacks' mitigation strategies have been covered in numerous publications [1,9–13]. Noncespaces [14] use randomized XML namespace prefixes as an XSS mitigation technique, which would make detection of the injected content reliable. DSI [15] tries to achieve the same goal based on a process of classifying HTML content into trusted and untrusted variety on the server side, subsequently changing browser parsing behavior so that the specified distinction is taken into account. Blueprint [16] generates a model of the user input on the server-side and transfers it, together with the user-contributed content, to the browser, making its behavior modified by an injection of a JavaScript library for processing the model along with the input. Content Security Policy (CSP) comes with a novel feature to block XSS attacks: source whitelisting. Thus even if an attacker may be able to execute a malicious script, he is not able to exfiltrate any security critical information, since he cannot establish a connection to his server. Unfortunately, this feature does not apply to `mailto:` URLs, so this would not block webmail XSS worms. CSP 2.0 and newer (http://www.w3.org/TR/CSP2/) provide a mechanism to distinguish trusted inline script from untrusted script: the `nonce-source` and `hash-source` directives. In both cases, inline scripts are only executed if the value of their nonce-attribute matches the value given in the directive, or if the hash value of the script matches a given value. Note that Weichselbaum et al. discuss the practical value of CSP in great detail, shedding light on shortcomings and implementational problems [17].

Sandboxed iFrames. A straighforward solution to block webmail XSS worms seems to display HTML mails in sandboxed iFrames, a novel HTML5 feature. This works for simply reading emails, but as soon as any action is triggered (e.g. FORWARD or REPLY), the sandboxed iFrame must be opened, and the XSS vectors contained in the mail body will be executed. This is a problem with all of today's webmailers.

Mutation-Based (mXSS) and Scriptless Attacks. Weinberger et al. [18] give an example of the innerHTML being used to execute a DOM-based XSS. Comparable XSS attacks based on changes in the HTML markup have been initially described for client-side XSS filters. Nava and Lindsay [19] and Bates et al. [8] show that the IE8 XSS Filter could have once been used to "weaponize" harmless strings and turn them into valid XSS attack vectors. This relied on applying a mutation through the regular expressions used by the XSS Filter. Zalewski covers concatenation problems based on NUL strings in *inner-HTML* assignments in the *Browser Security Handbook* [20]. Additionally, he later dedicates a section to backtick mutation in his volume "The Tangled Web" [21]. Other mutation-based attacks have been reported by Barth et al. [22]. Hooimeijer et al. describe the dangers associated with the sanitization of content [23] and claim that they were able to produce a string that would result in a valid XSS vector *after* sanitization for every single one of a large number of XSS vectors. The vulnerabilities described by Kolbitsch et al. may form the basis for an extremely targeted attack by web malware [24]. Those authors state that the attack vectors may be prepared for taking into account the mutation behavior of different browser engines. HTML5 introduces a script-like functionality in its different tags, making the so called "Scriptless Attacks" (a term coined in [25]) a real threat. For example, SVG images and their active elements can be used to steal passwords even if JavaScript is deactivated [26].

6   Conclusion and Outlook

Given the current trends in web application and app design, a client-side, DOM-based XSS filtering solution is urgently needed. This concept faces different threats when one compares it with server-side XSS filters. Those are unique to the browser's DOM and need to be discussed in depth. We present DOMPurify, an open-source library designed to reliably filter HTML strings and document objects from XSS attacks. It seeks to allow developers to safely use user-controlled and untrusted HTML in web applications, mobile apps and any other deployment that requires employing a browser(-like) DOM. Its filtering techniques to mitigate DOM Clobbering attacks can form the basis for a framework to include any XSS mitigation technique into the DOM. DOMPurify accompanies and complements CSP 3.0, and closes the gaps that are not covered by the browser itself. Our DOMPurify library implements the current state of the art knowledge in the field of XSS defense. It draws on novel concepts which work surprisingly well in practice. However, as new threats are constantly emerging, the extendibility and configurability of DOMPurify is crucially important. It goes without saying that we encourage future research in this direction. Additional use cases for a security library that resides in the DOM may arise and can now be faced head on in their core rather than in an unrelated and distant layer on the web-server.

Acknowledgements. The research was supported by the German Ministry of research and Education (BMBF) as part of the OpenC3S research project.

A   Deployment

Other Deployment Scenarios

JavaScript MVC (model-view-controller) frameworks are written to move application logic like view-generation, templating and site-interactivity from the server to the client. Example frameworks include AngularJS, EmberJS, KnockoutJS, React and others. They are often maintained by large corporations such as Google, Facebook or Yahoo. Using the frameworks properly requires a change in application design philosophy from the developers' side. While the server generated and delivered the HTML for classic applications, here only a minimal scaffold of HTML is server-generated and delivered. The majority of content is being created in the client and is based on raw JSON from the server containing the data, using static template files, as well as a complex event and widget logic residing almost entirely in the browsers, fuelled by the JavaScript MVC framework. That of course obsoletes server-side HTML and XSS filters as the server doesn't deliver any user-controlled HTML anymore. Now the JavaScript MVC framework must take care of that issue, and this is the point where DOMPurify can be applied as an additional level of mitigation. Note though that DOMPurify is also capable to run on *nodejs* in combination with *jsdom* – therefore it can also protect server-side web-frameworks and template-engines from XSS attacks. The automated tests running for every commit cover this deployment scenario in full.

Actual Deployment

The DOMPurify library is currently downloaded about 52000 times per month on the "npm" JavaScript package manager platform. It is being used by major web mail providers and several commonly known tools used in the context of web-mail end-to-end encryption. DOMPurify is further being utilized by browser extensions who need to sanitize user controlled HTML, giving developers a more fine grained control over what kind of rich text is supposed to be rendered and displayed – beyond what CSP is offering.

References

1. Johns, M.: Code injection vulnerabilities in web applications - exemplified at cross-site scripting. Ph.D. dissertation, University of Passau, Passau, July 2009
2. Heiderich, M., Frosch, T., Jensen, M., Holz, T.: Crouching tiger - hidden payload: security risks of scalable vector graphics. In: Proceedings of the 18th ACM Conference on Computer and Communications Security, pp. 239–250. ACM (2011)
3. Heiderich, M., Schwenk, J., Frosch, T., Magazinius, J., Yang, E.Z.: mXSS attacks: attacking well-secured web-applications by using innerHTML mutations. In: Proceedings of the 2013 ACM SIGSAC Conference on Computer and Communications Security, pp. 777–788. ACM (2013)
4. Akhawe, D., Barth, A., Lam, P.E., Mitchell, J., Song, D.: Towards a formal foundation of web security. In: 23rd IEEE Computer Security Foundations Symposium (CSF) 2010, pp. 290–304. IEEE (2010)
5. Heiderich, M., Späth, C., Schwenk, J.: DOMPurify testset (2017). https://goo.gl/2g2BMz
6. Heiderich, M., Späth, C., Schwenk, J.: Output of ResembleJS (2017). https://goo.gl/9bdmZv
7. Ross, D.: IE8 security part IV: the XSS filter - IEBlog - site home - MSDN blogs (2008).   http://blogs.msdn.com/b/ie/archive/2008/07/02/ie8-security-part-iv-the-xss-filter.aspx
8. Bates, D., Barth, A., Jackson, C.: Regular expressions considered harmful in client-side XSS filters. In: Proceedings of the 19th International Conference on World Wide Web, WWW 2010, pp. 91–100. ACM, New York (2010). http://doi.acm.org/10.1145/1772690.1772701
9. Zuchlinski, G.: The anatomy of cross site scripting. In: Hitchhiker's World, vol. 8, November 2003
10. Bisht, P., Venkatakrishnan, V.N.: XSS-GUARD: precise dynamic prevention of cross-site scripting attacks. In: Conference on Detection of Intrusions and Malware and Vulnerability Assessment (2008)
11. Gebre, M., Lhee, K., Hong, M.: A robust defense against content-sniffing XSS attacks. In: 2010 6th International Conference on Digital Content, Multimedia Technology and its Applications (IDC), pp. 315–320. IEEE (2010)
12. Saxena, P., Molnar, D., Livshits, B.: SCRIPTGARD: automatic context-sensitive sanitization for large-scale legacy web applications. In: Proceedings of the 18th ACM Conference on Computer and Communications Security, pp. 601–614. ACM (2011)
13. Gourdin, B., Soman, C., Bojinov, H., Bursztein, E.: Toward secure embedded web interfaces. In: Proceedings of the USENIX Security Symposium (2011)
14. Gundy, M.V., Chen, H.: Noncespaces: using randomization to defeat cross-site scripting attacks. Comput. Secur. 31(4), 612–628 (2012)
15. Nadji, Y., Saxena, P., Song, D.: Document structure integrity: a robust basis for cross-site scripting defense. In: NDSS. The Internet Society (2009)
16. Louw, M.T., Venkatakrishnan, V.N.: Blueprint: robust prevention of cross-site scripting attacks for existing browsers. In: Proceedings of the 2009 30th IEEE Symposium on Security and Privacy, SP 2009, Washington, DC, USA, pp. 331–346. IEEE Computer Society (2009). http://dx.doi.org/10.1109/SP.2009.33
17. Weichselbaum, L., Spagnuolo, M., Lekies, S., Janc, A.: CSP is dead, long live CSP! On the insecurity of whitelists and the future of content security policy. In: Proceedings of the 23rd ACM Conference on Computer and Communications Security, Vienna, Austria (2016)

18. Weinberger, J., Saxena, P., Akhawe, D., Finifter, M., Shin, R., Song, D.: A systematic analysis of XSS sanitization in web application frameworks. In: Atluri, V., Diaz, C. (eds.) ESORICS 2011. LNCS, vol. 6879, pp. 150–171. Springer, Heidelberg (2011). doi:10.1007/978-3-642-23822-2_9

19. Nava, E.V., Lindsay, D.: Abusing Internet Explorer 8's XSS Filters. http://p42.us/ie8xss/Abusing_IE8s_XSS_Filters.pdf

20. Zalewski, M.: Browser Security Handbook, July 2010. http://code.google.com/p/browsersec/wiki/Main

21. Zalewski, M.: The Tangled Web: A Guide to Securing Modern Web Applications. No Starch Press (2011)

22. Bug 29278: XSSAuditor bypasses from sla.ckers.org. https://bugs.webkit.org/show_bug.cgi?id=29278

23. Hooimeijer, P., Livshits, B., Molnar, D., Saxena, P., Veanes, M.: Fast and precise sanitizer analysis with BEK. In: Proceedings of the 20th USENIX Conference on Security, SEC 2011, Berkeley, CA, USA, p. 1. USENIX Association (2011). http://dl.acm.org/citation.cfm?id=2028067.2028068

24. Kolbitsch, C., Livshits, B., Zorn, B., Seifert, C.: Rozzle: de-cloaking internet malware. In: Proceedings of IEEE Symposium on Security and Privacy (2012)

25. Heiderich, M., Niemietz, M., Schuster, F., Holz, T., Schwenk, J.: Scriptless attacks: stealing the pie without touching the sill. In: Proceedings of the 19th ACM Conference on Computer and Communications Security, pp. 760–771 (2012)

26. Stone, P.: Pixel perfect timing attacks with HTML5. http://contextis.co.uk/files/Browser_Timing_Attacks.pdf

Preventing DNS Amplification Attacks Using the History of DNS Queries with SDN

Soyoung Kim, Sora Lee, Geumhwan Cho, Muhammad Ejaz Ahmed, Jaehoon (Paul) Jeong, and Hyoungshick Kim[✉]

Sungkyunkwan University, Suwon, South Korea
{ksy2608,leesora,geumhwan,ejaz629,pauljeong,hyoung}@skku.edu

Abstract. Domain Name System (DNS) amplification attack is a sophisticated Distributed Denial of Service (DDoS) attack by sending a huge volume of DNS name lookup requests to open DNS servers with the source address spoofed as a victim host. However, from the point of view of an individual network resource such as DNS server and switch, it is not easy to mitigate such attacks because a distributed attack could be performed with multiple DNS servers and/or switches. To overcome this limitation, we propose a novel security framework using Software-Defined Networking (SDN) to store the history of DNS queries as an evidence to distinguish normal DNS responses from attack packets. Our evaluation results demonstrate that the network traffic for DNS amplification attack can completely be blocked under various network conditions without incurring a significant communication overhead.

Keywords: Software-Defined Networking (SDN) · Distributed Denial of Service (DDoS) · Domain Name System (DNS) · DNS amplification attack

1 Introduction

Domain Name System (DNS) amplification attack is a popular form of Distributed Denial of Service (DDoS) attack that relies on the use of publicly accessible open DNS servers to overwhelm a victim system with DNS response traffic [22]. In a typical DNS amplification attack scenario, an attacker uses an extension to the DNS protocol [25] to generate relatively small queries (e.g., about 60 bytes) with a spoofed source address (i.e., the victim's address) to DNS servers. As a result, DNS servers reply with significantly larger responses (e.g., about 4,000 bytes) to exhaust the victim's resources (see Sect. 2.1 for more details). DNS amplification is one of the most notorious and disruptive attack types. In March 2013, a massive 300 Gbps DDoS attack was thrown against the website of Spamhaus which is the anti-spam clearing house organization [9].

However, it is not a trivial task to prevent such attacks since trusted sources (i.e., open DNS servers) are used as the sources of a DDoS attack. Blacklisting the attack machines' IP addresses can also affect legitimate DNS resolutions. To

© Springer International Publishing AG 2017
S.N. Foley et al. (Eds.): ESORICS 2017, Part II, LNCS 10493, pp. 135–152, 2017.
DOI: 10.1007/978-3-319-66399-9_8

make matters worse, DNS requests can easily be spoofed since DNS protocols are based on UDP [3]. Therefore, a proper defense mechanism is needed to mitigate such attacks while minimizing its potential impact on legitimate users.

In recent years, a couple of defense techniques have been developed to mitigate such attacks. Vixie [26] proposed a defense mechanism based on limiting the number of unique responses from a DNS server. However, this defense mechanism could be circumvented by distributing attack packets among a large number of DNS servers.

Another possible strategy is to use the history of DNS queries for checking the "one-to-one mapping" between DNS requests and responses in order to detect orphan DNS responses [8,11,21]. In general, the existing solutions can be categorized into two approaches: (1) using the local memory of switches [8,21] and (2) using the external memory of a remote server [11]. Each approach has its strengths and weaknesses and may not be suitable for certain circumstances. For the first approach (e.g., [8,21]), it is critical to efficiently store the DNS queries because a switch typically has a small memory size. Therefore, the solutions in this category used a space-efficient data structure called Bloom filters to efficiently store this history of DNS queries because a Bloom filter supports probabilistic set membership testing. However, the use of Bloom filters inherently gives erroneous results (i.e., false positives). For the second approach (e.g., [11]), the communication with a remote server is always required to store all DNS query records and check them, which results in a significant communication overhead. In this paper, we proposed a more flexible model by providing a highly robust and scalable data storage for DNS queries using Software-Defined Networking (SDN) [13], which was recently introduced to decouple the data and control planes in network systems. The proposed scheme is designed to store all DNS query records by using an SDN controller even when there is no enough memory to store DNS query records in a switch anymore. Surely, the proposed scheme does not cover all types of DDoS attacks. We focused only on DNS amplification attacks. Our main contributions are as follows:

- We propose a novel mitigation system to fight against DNS amplification attacks by checking the validity of DNS response packets using the history of DNS queries with SDN. The proposed scheme does not need anymore to use a probabilistic method such as Bloom filters and can finally avoid false positives related to DNS amplification attacks (See Sect. 3).
- We show the feasibility of the proposed system by conducting intensive experiments in a controlled environment. Our evaluation results demonstrate that the network traffic for DNS amplification attack can completely be blocked under various network conditions without incurring a significant delay by the communication with the SDN controller (See Sect. 4).

The rest of the paper is organized as follows: Sect. 2 provides the background information about DNS amplification attack and SDN used in the proposed system. Section 3 presents our proposed architecture with the important network components, and our experiment results are presented in Sect. 4. Related work is covered in Sect. 5. Our conclusions and future work are in Sect. 6.

2   Background

In this section, we first explain how a DNS amplification attack can be performed and then provide an overview of SDN usage for the additional storage of the history of a DNS request, when those requests cannot be stored in local switches due to limited memory capacity.

2.1   DNS Amplification Attack

A DNS amplification attack relies on the use of publicly accessible open DNS servers to overwhelm a victim's network bandwidth with DNS response traffic. A DNS server provides the corresponding IP address against the domain name requested by a user. For example, when a user wants to connect to a website, they usually type its domain name (i.e., URL) in the browser. The local DNS server, when receives the domain name request, tries to find the corresponding IP address against the user's request which is then communicated to the user, and that IP address is used to connect to the website. Here, a DNS response packet, delivering the corresponding IP address to the user, is of a much larger size than the user's request. This principle makes a DDoS attack more influential.

Figure 1 shows an overview of the DNS amplification attack. An `Attacker` sends a request using small DNS query with a spoofed IP address (`Victim`'s IP address) to `Open DNS server`. Then `Open DNS server` returns a response to the `Victim` with several times larger packets than the DNS request. Preventing this attack is difficult since DNS requests from the attacker include the spoofed IP address ("`10.0.0.1`"), and DNS responses are sent to the victim with "`10.0.0.1`" as its IP address instead of the original requester. Unlike an ordinary DDoS attack, it is not simple to prevent this form of attacks since trusted sources (i.e., DNS servers) are used for DDoS attack; blocking attack machines' IP addresses might affect and damage normal network operations. To

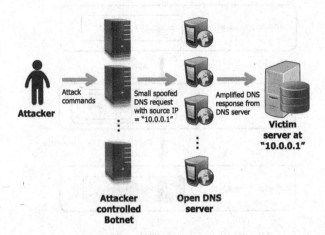

Fig. 1. Overview of DNS amplification attack.

make matters worse, DNS requests can easily be spoofed since DNS protocols are based on UDP. A proper defense mechanism should mitigate attacks, while avoiding a major impact on legitimate users.

In this paper, we consider two types of DNS packets ("A type of packet" and "ANY type of packet"). Normally, when a user requests DNS query, "A type of packet" is used for requesting a query and the response packet is typically less than 512 bytes that contains only an IP address which the user wants to find. Otherwise, if an attacker uses ANY type of packet as a query (about 60 bytes) of the request, it can return a response of about 4,000 bytes, resulting in about 50x amplification [24]. Therefore, the use of ANY type of packet is more effective for the DNS amplification attack.

2.2   Overview of SDN

SDN is a novel networking paradigm that decouples the control plane from the data plane. This separation can be realized by a well-defined programming interface between a switch and an SDN controller [15]. The SDN controller enforces direct control over the data plane elements (e.g., switch) with network applications using an OpenFlow protocol [2], as shown in Fig. 2. The OpenFlow switch performs forwarding functions which allows user space control at flow level processing on the network [1]. The SDN controller can manage and control the OpenFlow switch since the OpenFlow switch forwards packets according to the predefined rules in its flow table received from the SDN controller [16]. For example, a forwarding component in the OpenFlow switch consults the flow table for a proper rule to forward the incoming packet. If the flow rule is found, the component forwards the packet according to the rule. Otherwise, the OpenFlow switch asks the SDN controller, and then a new flow rule is enforced to the OpenFlow switch by the SDN controller. Also, network operators can deploy

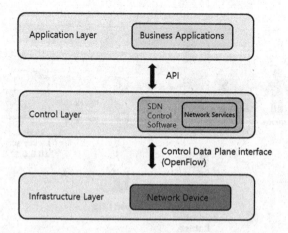

Fig. 2. Overview of SDN architecture.

applications of their choice without manually deploying and excessively configuring the networks. For example, with the use of SDN, network operators can
easily implement a firewall application and deploy it at the application layer.
Besides, the SDN controller enforces the partial functionality of the firewall in
the switch. In this case, the cost of deploying new network resources can be
avoided which results in a cost effective solution.

3   Proposed System

In this section, we explain how the proposed system can be used to block the
packets for a DNS amplification attack.

3.1   Overview

We propose a new DNS amplification attack mitigation scheme using an "one-
to-one strict mapping" method between DNS requests and responses in order to
detect orphan DNS responses. Our proposed scheme can detect such responses
by checking whether there exists a DNS request (generated by a benign host)
that matches to a given DNS response. Consequently, a DNS response, which
matches a DNS query requested by the victim, is only allowed to reach the
victim's machine.

Figure 3 gives an overview of the proposed scheme. To check "one-to-one
strict mapping" between DNS requests and responses, the DNS requests generated by benign hosts are first stored in the local memory of a switch. If the
switch has no available memory space anymore, further DNS requests are stored
in the memory of an external network entity (e.g., the SDN controller or another
remote server).

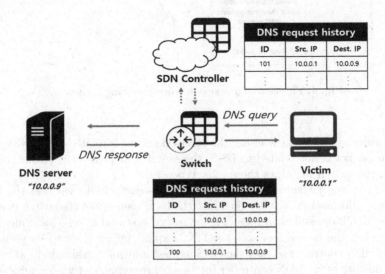

Fig. 3. Logical structure of the proposed scheme.

3.2 Main Components

The proposed system consists of two main components: switch and SDN controller. Here, we describe the primary function of each component to mitigate DNS amplification attacks.

Switch. In the proposed system, we assume that a switch is SDN compatible and has a limited memory capacity. Similar to previous proposals [8,21], the local memory of a switch is used to store the information about DNS request records (e.g., the source and destination IP addresses in a DNS request message). In SDN, unlike traditional network switches, a switch can forward packets based on the rules configured by an SDN controller [14]. We note that each switch constitutes the first line of defense against DNS amplification attacks. When a switch receives a packet, the high-level behaviors of the switch are as follows (see Fig. 4):

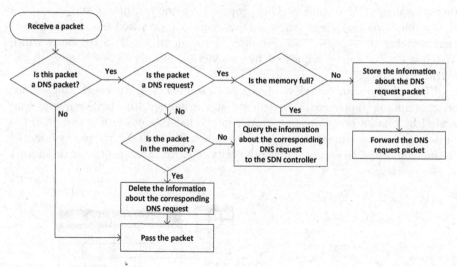

Fig. 4. Flowchart for a switch when receiving a packet.

1. The switch first checks whether the received packet is related to a DNS query. If the packet is not related to DNS, the switch just passes the packet; otherwise, the switch identifies the packet type.
2. If the received packet is "DNS request", the switch checks whether the DNS request information can be stored into the local memory of the switch itself. If the switch has a sufficient memory, the record is stored into its local memory; otherwise, the switch forwards the DNS request information to its predesignated SDN controller so that the DNS request information should be stored in the memory of the SDN controller (or another external host with a sufficiently large memory for storing DNS request records).

3. If the received packet is "DNS response", the switch verifies the validity of the received packet by checking whether there exists the DNS request record exactly matched to the DNS response in its local memory. If the validity of the DNS response is successfully verified, the received packet is passed and then the stored DNS request record is finally deleted because it is already consumed; otherwise, the next step can be redivided into two cases. In First, when its local memory is not full, the packet is simply dropped. Second, when its local memory is full of DNS request records, the switch forwards the DNS response packet to its SDN controller for checking the validity of the DNS response via the SDN controller.

SDN Controller. An SDN controller is a logically centralized network entity that manages flows to enable more flexible, customized, and intelligent networking. Naturally, when there is no enough memory to store DNS query records in a switch anymore, the SDN controller can establish or modify the rules to dynamically forward such information from the switch to an external database server with a large memory capacity needed to store it. Without loss of generality, we assume that an SDN controller itself has a large memory capacity to store the information about DNS request records. That is, the SDN controller can be used as an external storage server to store the history of DNS queries and provide it (if needed). When the SDN controller receives a packet, the high-level behaviors of the SDN controller are as follows (see Fig. 5):

1. The SDN controller first checks whether the received packet is related to a DNS query. If the packet is not related to DNS, the SDN controller processes the packet as normal; otherwise, the SDN controller identifies the packet type.

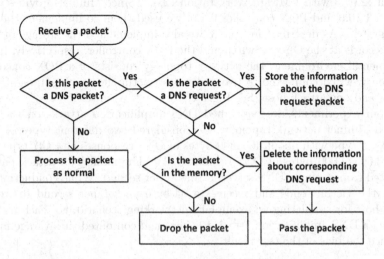

Fig. 5. Flowchart for an SDN controller when receiving a packet.

2. If the received packet is "DNS request", the SDN controller stores the DNS request information into the memory of the SDN controller.

3. If the received packet is "DNS response", the SDN controller verifies the validity of the DNS response message by checking whether there exists the DNS request record exactly matched to the DNS response in its memory. If the validity of the DNS response is successfully verified, the received packet is passed and then the stored DNS request record is finally deleted because it is already consumed; otherwise, the packet is just dropped because it means that the received DNS response is an orphan DNS response which could be used for a DNS amplification attack.

4   Evaluation

This section presents the evaluation results of the proposed scheme against DNS amplification attacks. We conducted experiments with various parameters such as the bandwidth of network link and the number of DNS servers used for DNS amplification attacks.

For evaluation, we measured several metrics such as the ratio of successfully delivered packets and the packet delivery time between normal hosts while performing DNS amplification attacks.

4.1   Experiment Setup and Procedure

To evaluate the performance of the proposed mitigation scheme against DNS amplification attacks, we used Mininet 2.3.0d1 (http://mininet.org/) because we need to conduct large-scale network experiments with varying the important parameters such as the number of DNS servers and bandwidth. Mininet works on Ubuntu 12.04.3 with VMware Workstation 12.5.4. Since Mininet provides Open vSwitch 1.10.0 and POX controller 0.2.0, we used them to implement the proposed system. As described in Sect. 3, we also implemented the storage of DNS query records at the Open vSwitch and the POX controller, respectively. In our experimental environment, the network topology consists of a POX controller, an Open vSwitch connected to two end hosts (victim/benign host), eight DNS servers, and one attack host (See Fig. 6).

In our experiments, we performed DNS amplification attacks on the constructed Mininet network topology. We considered two different types of DNS requests: A type with about 400–500 bytes of DNS responses and ANY type with about 3,000–4,000 bytes of DNS responses [23]. The number of attack packets generated from a single DNS server is 10,000 per second. While conducting the attack, the victim sends and receives a 64-byte packet per second to/from a benign host for simulating an exemplary networking scenario. For each test, we repeated a DNS amplification attack 10 times and computed the average metric to reduce the bias of the test result.

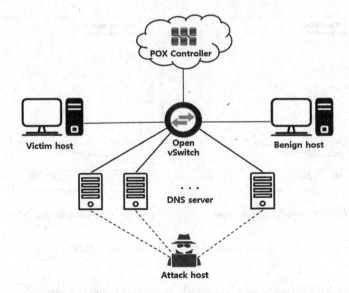

Fig. 6. Mininet network topology for experiments.

4.2 Experiment Results

Effectiveness of the Mitigation Scheme. To evaluate the performance of the proposed scheme, we first analyzed the cumulative amount of the successfully delivered traffic from the benign host to the victim host during 60 s when a DNS amplification attack takes place. We compared this metric with (Protected) and without (Not protected) the proposed mitigation scheme. For the comparison of A type and ANY type, the victim host's bandwidth was set to 5 Mbps since the attack with A type did not work when that bandwidth was more than 5 Mbps. Also, eight DNS servers were used to perform DNS amplification attacks. The experiment results are shown in Fig. 7.

For both A and ANY types, we can see that the cumulative amount of the successfully delivered traffic from the benign host to the victim host increased linearly over time when the proposed scheme was applied (Protected) while that amount tends to increase relatively slow without the proposed scheme (Not protected). In "Not protected", both types received were around 21% of packets; 819 bytes out of 3,840 bytes for A type and 826 bytes out of 3,840 bytes for ANY type, respectively, even when 60 s elapsed. In "Protected", however, the victim host successfully received 100% of the packets from the benign host under the same DNS amplification attack.

Effects of the Victim Host's Bandwidth. We discuss how the performance of the proposed mitigation scheme may change with the victim host's bandwidth. To reduce the impact of DNS amplification attacks, a possible straightforward approach is to increase the victim host's bandwidth. We analyzed how the packet

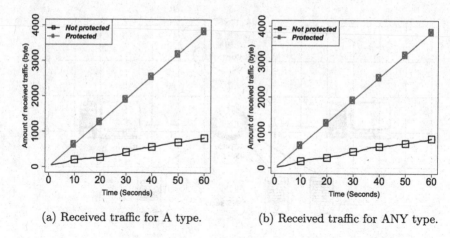

(a) Received traffic for A type.   (b) Received traffic for ANY type.

Fig. 7. Amount of received traffic over time.

delivery time and the ratio of successfully delivered packets were influenced with the victim host's bandwidth.

For an improved analysis of the effects of victim host's bandwidth, we used different experiment parameters for each of A and ANY types since both types of DNS responses have different scales. We used 1 Mbps, 3 Mbps, and 5 Mbps, respectively, as the victim host's bandwidth for A type DNS amplification attacks. We also used 5 Mbps, 10 Mbps, 15 Mbps and 20 Mbps, respectively, as the victim host's bandwidth for ANY type DNS amplification attacks. Also, eight DNS servers were used to perform DNS amplification attacks. The experiment results are shown in Figs. 8 and 9.

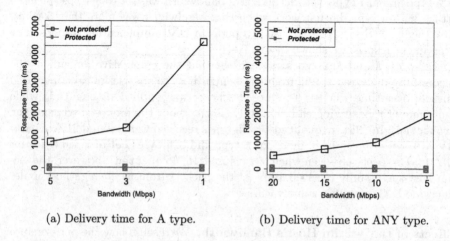

(a) Delivery time for A type.   (b) Delivery time for ANY type.

Fig. 8. Delivery time with bandwidth.

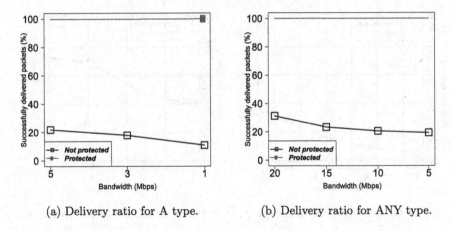

(a) Delivery ratio for A type.   (b) Delivery ratio for ANY type.

Fig. 9. Percentage of successfully delivered packets with bandwidth.

Figure 8 shows how the packet delivery time from the benign host to the victim host changed with the victim host's bandwidth. For both A and ANY types, the packet delivery time in "Protected" is always significantly faster than that in "Not protected". As the victim host's bandwidth decreased, in "Protected", the packet delivery time is still less than 32 ms on average for both types and remains stable regardless of the victim host's bandwidth while, in "Not protected", the packet delivery time greatly increased from 935 to 4,475 ms for A type and from 484 to 1,891 ms for ANY type, respectively.

Figure 9 shows how the ratio for successfully delivered packets sent from the benign host to the victim host changed with the victim host's bandwidth. In "Protected", the victim host successfully received all packets sent from the benign host. However, in "Not protected", for both types of DNS responses, the delivery ratio rather increased with the victim host's bandwidth. When the victim host's bandwidth greatly increased, the packet delivery ratios of A type and ANY type are only 21.83% and 31.33%, respectively.

Effects of the Number of DNS Servers. We now move to the discussion on the performance of the proposed mitigation scheme when the number of DNS servers increased by fixing the victim host's bandwidth as 5 Mbps. It is important to show that the proposed mitigation scheme is highly robust even when many open DNS servers are used for a DNS amplification attack. We analyzed how the packet delivery time and the ratio of successfully delivered packets were influenced with varying the number of DNS servers from 1 to 8.

Figure 10 shows how the packet delivery time from the benign host to the victim host changed with the number of DNS servers. For both A and ANY types, the packet delivery time in "Protected" is always significantly faster than that in "Not protected". As the number of DNS servers increased to 8, in "Protected", the packet delivery time is still less than 29 ms on average for both types and remains stable regardless of the number of DNS servers while,

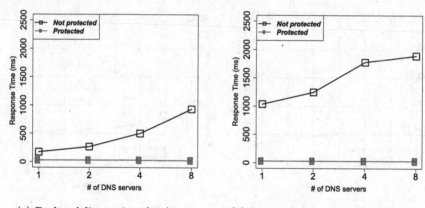

(a) Packet delivery time for A type.   (b) Packet delivery time for ANY type.

Fig. 10. Packet delivery time with the number of DNS servers.

in "Not protected", the packet delivery time continuously increased from 174 to 935 ms for A type and from 1,034 to 1,891 ms for ANY type, respectively.

Figure 11 shows how the ratio for successfully delivered packets sent from the benign host to the victim host changed with the number of DNS servers. In "Protected", the victim host successfully received all packets sent from the benign host. In "Not protected", however, the packet delivery ratio was greatly decreased when the number of DNS servers is 8 for A type; the packet delivery ratio was greatly decreased from 4 to 8 DNS servers for ANY type.

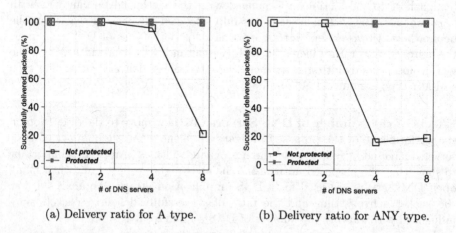

(a) Delivery ratio for A type.   (b) Delivery ratio for ANY type.

Fig. 11. Percentage of successfully delivered packets to the victim from benign host by increasing number of DNS servers, with 5 Mbps of bandwidth.

4.3   Comparison with the Existing Solutions

In this section, we discuss the advantages and disadvantages of the proposed mitigation scheme compared with the existing solutions [8,21] that also used the history of DNS records. Unlike our proposal, those solutions were designed to focus on the construction of efficient storage for DNS query records by using Bloom filters [5]. Bloom filter is a space-efficient probabilistic data structure that uses a one-way hash function. Unfortunately, Bloom filters inherently give false positives when the memory size in a switch is small to cover DNS queries to be stored. The proposed scheme was designed to use external servers' storage when there is no enough memory to store DNS query records in a switch. Therefore, there is no false positive in the proposed scheme since the information about all DNS requests is eventually stored. However, the proposed scheme may incur the communication overhead required to communicate with the external server (i.e., SDN controller). We analyzed how the false positive ratio of the previous solution using a Bloom filter and the communication overhead of the proposed scheme were affected with the available memory size of switch and the communication speed for SDN controller.

Given time T in seconds to keep the information of a DNS request in a Bloom filter, the maximum DNS request packet rate R (packets per second called pps) of a link, and the size M (bits) of the memory required to store DNS request records, false positive P can be calculated by the following formula [8,21]:

$$P = e^{(-1)\cdot(M/2TR)\cdot(\ln 2)^2}$$

Table 1 shows the false positive ratio and the number of error packets in the existing solutions with the available memory size of a switch. We assumed T was 3 s according to previous work [8]. We also assumed that the most widely used network switches (Cisco 350 series, Cisco 500 series, and Cisco 350X series) were deployed, respectively, for the proposed system. Here, the maximum available memory size of each switch can be calculated by excluding the size of the firmware from the overall memory size. The available memory sizes of Cisco 350

Table 1. False positive ratio and number of error packets in the existing solutions using a Bloom filter with the size of available memory in a switch.

Attack rate (pps)	False positive ratio			Number of error packets		
	Cisco 350 series (5.16 MB)	Cisco 500 series (21.94 MB)	Cisco 350X series (230.87 MB)	Cisco 350 series (5.16 MB)	Cisco 500 series (21.94 MB)	Cisco 350X series (230.87 MB)
1,000,000	3%	0%	0%	31,249	0	0
5,000,000	50%	5%	0%	2,499,983	262,205	0
10,000,000	71%	23%	0%	7,071,044	2,289,998	2
15,000,000	79%	37%	0%	11,905,481	5,614,546	485
20,000,000	84%	48%	0%	16,817,900	9,570,784	8,581

series, Cisco 500 series, and Cisco 350X switches are 5.16 MB, 21.94 MB, and 230.87 MB, respectively.

From Table 1, we can see that a large number of false positives occurs when either the memory size is about 5 MB or the attack rate is significantly higher (e.g., 10,000,000 pps). In such environments, existing solutions would not be effective in filtering out attack packets. In contrast to previous approach, as mentioned above, false positives do not appear in the proposed scheme because all DNS request records are stored.

However, the proposed mitigation scheme could incur some communication delay between SDN controller a switch when the memory of a switch is full. We analyzed this overhead with the memory size of a switch. We assumed the communication delay between SDN controller and a switch was 0.0416 ms according to the SDN controller benchmarks in [27]. Table 2 shows the average communication delay per packet between the SDN controller and a switch.

Table 2. Average communication delay for SDN controller and number of requests to be forwarded in the proposed scheme with the size of available memory in a switch.

Attack rate (pps)	Communication delay			Number of requests to SDN controller		
	Cisco 350 series (5.16 MB)	Cisco 500 series (21.94 MB)	Cisco 350X series (230.87 MB)	Cisco 350 series (5.16 MB)	Cisco 500 series (21.94 MB)	Cisco 350X series (230.87 MB)
1,000,000	0.019 ms	0 ms	0 ms	458,984	0	0
5,000,000	0.037 ms	0.022 ms	0 ms	4,458,984	2,698,993	0
10,000,000	0.039 ms	0.032 ms	0 ms	9,458,984	7,698,993	0
15,000,000	0.040 ms	0.035 ms	0 ms	14,458,984	12,698,993	0
20,000,000	0.040 ms	0.037 ms	0 ms	19,458,984	17,698,993	0

From Table 2, we can see that the proposed scheme may incur some communication delay; Cisco 500 series switches take a delay of 0.032 ms on average when the attack rate is 10,000,000 pps. Unsurprisingly, the worst case communication overhead (0.040 ms) can be found when the attack rate is 20,000,000 with Cisco 350 series switches. Those numerical analysis results demonstrate that the communication time overhead incurred by the proposed scheme seems acceptable enough in practice.

5 Related Work

DNS amplification attack is more harmful than other DDoS attacks due to the fact that the attack packets are sent by DNS servers cannot simply be blacklisted because DNS servers are trustworthy network entities. After Vaughn and Evron [23] reported their preliminary results on DNS amplification attacks, a number of countermeasures have been proposed.

The most intuitive approach is to prevent attackers from using spoofed IP addresses. Senie and Ferguson [19] and Katsurai et al. [12] proposed packet filtering methods in which edge routers block packets delivered from invalid sources to a local network. Snoeren et al. [20] proposed a traceback method to find the origins of IP packets. Bremler-Barr and Levy [6] proposed an authentication method to check the authenticity of the source addresses for incoming packets. However, those solutions generally require significant changes to the existing Internet infrastructure which are unlikely to be implemented in the near future. Unlike those solutions, DNS guard [10] did not require such fundamental changes in the Internet infrastructure because it tried to detect spoofed DNS requests using cookies. However, this approach requires the deployment of additional new servers between hosts and root servers, which is also not acceptable for some environments. We can see that the real world Internet is still vulnerable to several types of IP spoofing attacks [4].

A general approach to preventing DDoS attacks is to limit the number of packets delivered from a particular host. For DNS amplification attacks, Vixie [26] particularly proposed a mechanism called response rate limiting to limit the rate of responses from the DNS server and dropping the responses that exceeds the rate limit. However, such solutions are still susceptible to the use of a large number of open DNS servers. Verma et al. [24] proposed a distributed architecture with multiple DNS servers to detect a DNS amplification attack by accumulating the DNS request rates of those DNS servers that are involved in the DNS amplification attack. It needs to deploy the detection system on DNS servers and adjust complicated protocol to share the rate of DNS request between DNS servers.

Another approach is to detect the attacks by analyzing the DNS traffic. Deshpande et al. [7] and Rastegari et al. [18] proposed defense mechanisms using neural networks and a probabilistic model with several traffic statistics, respectively. Lexis and Mekking [17] proposed a visualization method to identify patterns in DNS traffic. Such approaches might be effective in detecting and classifying the attack traffics at the expense of false positives which restrict legitimate users from using DNS servers.

Recently, a promising technique was introduced by using the history of DNS queries to identify orphan DNS responses. Kambourakis et al. [11] proposed a method to check the "one-to-one mapping" relationship between DNS requests and responses. In their proposal, a mapping relationship was stored on an external database server. Consequently, the external database server was always used for storing every DNS request and checking every DNS response, respectively, at which its communication cost may not be acceptable in real world applications. To overcome this limitation, Sun et al. [21] proposed a technique using two Bloom filters in order to store the "one-to-one mapping" relationship between DNS requests and responses in the local memory of a switch. Bloom filters were used to support probabilistic membership queries with a small memory space. Di Paola and Lombardo [8] also proposed a similar technique using Bloom filters with a slight modification of the detection process [5]. Such mitigation techniques and our proposed scheme share a common goal of blocking unmatched DNS responses. Nevertheless, the proposed scheme differentiates itself from other techniques by using a novel network model called SDN that can be used to store the history of DNS request at any network entity in a flexible manner. The proposed scheme aims to avoid the possibility of false-positives that are inherently incurred in previously proposed systems [8, 21] when the number of DNS request increases because a network switch has limited memory space for storing all DNS requests. We propose a hybrid approach that takes the advantages of both approaches in order to support a "one-to-one strict mapping" method and simultaneously minimize the communication overhead with an external network entity such as the database server.

6   Conclusion

DNS amplification attack is a reflection-based DDoS attack. Since trusted severs such as open DNS servers are used as sources of attacks, it is not easy to stop such attacks. Previous defense mechanisms are not effective enough under the resource constrained switches having small memory sizes because they could incur false positives that cannot easily be ignored. In this paper, we propose a novel mitigation scheme against DNS amplification attacks by providing a highly scalable and centralized data storage for DNS request using SDN. Unlike the existing solutions using a probabilistic method, the proposed solution can remove the possibility of false positive packets, thus it can completely prevent DNS amplification attacks without incurring a significant delay by the communication with the SDN controller.

As part of future work, we plan to analyze the overhead for memory lookup procedure for the proposed system in addition to its communication delay. We also intend to conduct real world experiments through the deployment of the proposed system at a university network, and analyze its performance in a real-world setting.

Acknowledgment. This work was supported in part by the MSIP/IITP (No. 2016-0-00078) and the ITRC (IITP-2017-2012-0-00646). Authors would like to thank all the anonymous reviewers for their valuable feedback.

References

1. Open vSwitch. http://openvswitch.org
2. OpenFlow. https://www.opennetworking.org/sdn-resources/openflow
3. Anagnostopoulos, M., Kambourakis, G., Kopanos, P., Louloudakis, G., Gritzalis, S.: DNS amplification attack revisited. Comput. Secur. **39**, 475–485 (2013)
4. Beverly, R., Bauer, S.: The Spoofer project: inferring the extent of source address filtering on the Internet. In: Proceedings of the 1st USENIX Workshop on Steps to Reducing Unwanted Traffic on the Internet (2005)
5. Bloom, B.H.: Space/time trade-offs in hash coding with allowable errors. Commun. ACM **13**, 422–426 (1970)

6. Bremler-Barr, A., Levy, H.: Spoofing prevention method. In: Proceedings of the 24th IEEE International Conference on Computer Communications (2005)
7. Deshpande, T., Katsaros, P., Basagiannis, S., Smolka, S.A.: Formal analysis of the DNS bandwidth amplification attack and its countermeasures using probabilistic model checking. In: Proceedings of the 13rd IEEE Conference on High-Assurance Systems Engineering (2011)
8. Di Paola, S., Lombardo, D.: Protecting against DNS reflection attacks with bloom filters. In: Holz, T., Bos, H. (eds.) DIMVA 2011. LNCS, vol. 6739, pp. 1–16. Springer, Heidelberg (2011). doi:10.1007/978-3-642-22424-9_1
9. Gallagher, S.: How Spamhaus' attackers turned DNS into a weapon of mass destruction (2013). https://arstechnica.com/information-technology/2013/03/how-spamhaus-attackers-turned-dns-into-a-weapon-of-mass-destruction/
10. Guo, F., Chen, J., Chiueh, T.C.: Spoof detection for preventing DoS attacks against DNS servers. In: Proceedings of the 26th IEEE International Conference on Distributed Computing Systems (2006)
11. Kambourakis, G., Moschos, T., Geneiatakis, D., Gritzalis, S.: Detecting DNS amplification attacks. In: Lopez, J., Hämmerli, B.M. (eds.) CRITIS 2007. LNCS, vol. 5141, pp. 185–196. Springer, Heidelberg (2008). doi:10.1007/978-3-540-89173-4_16
12. Katsurai, Y., Nakamura, Y., Takahashi, O.: A proposal of a countermeasure method against DNS amplification attacks using distributed filtering by traffic route changing. In: Proceedings of the 9th International Workshop on Informatics (2015)
13. Kim, H., Feamster, N.: Improving network management with software defined networking. IEEE Commun. Mag. 51, 114–119 (2013)
14. Kloti, R., Kotronis, V., Smith, P.: Openflow: a security analysis. In: Proceedings of the 21st IEEE International Conference on Network Protocols (2013)
15. Kreutz, D., Ramos, F.M., Verissimo, P.E., Rothenberg, C.E., Azodolmolky, S., Uhlig, S.: Software-defined networking: a comprehensive survey. Proc. IEEE 103, 14–76 (2015)
16. Lara, A., Kolasani, A., Ramamurthy, B.: Network innovation using openflow: a survey. IEEE Commun. Surv. Tutor. 16, 493–512 (2014)
17. Lexis, P., Mekking, M.: Identifying patterns in DNS traffic. Technical report, University of Amsterdam (2013)
18. Rastegari, S., Saripan, M.I., Rasid, M.F.A.: Detection of denial of service attacks against domain name system using machine learning classifiers. In: Proceedings of the 18th World Congress on Engineering (2010)
19. Senie, D., Ferguson, P.: Network ingress filtering: defeating denial of service attacks which employ IP source address spoofing. IETF RFC 2827 (1998)
20. Snoeren, A.C., Partridge, C., Sanchez, L.A., Jones, C.E., Tchakountio, F., Kent, S.T., Strayer, W.T.: Hash-based IP traceback. In: Proceedings of the 15th ACM Conference on Applications, Technologies, Architectures, and Protocols for Computer Communications (2001)
21. Sun, C., Liu, B., Shi, L.: Efficient and low-cost hardware defense against DNS amplification attacks. In: Proceedings of the 24th IEEE Global Communications Conference (2008)
22. US-Cert: Alert (TA13-088A) DNS Amplification Attacks. https://www.us-cert.gov/ncas/alerts/TA13-088A (2013)
23. Vaughn, R., Evron, G.: DNS amplification attacks (2006). http://crt.io/DNS-Amplification-Attacks.pdf

24. Verma, S., Hamieh, A., Huh, J.H., Holm, H., Rajagopalan, S.R., Korczynski, M., Fefferman, N.: Stopping amplified DNS DDoS attacks through distributed query rate sharing. In: Proceedings of the 11st International Conference on Availability, Reliability and Security (2016)
25. Vixie, P.: Extension mechanisms for DNS (EDNS0). IETF RFC 2671 (1999)
26. Vixie, P.: DNS Response Rate Limiting (DNS RRL). ISC-TN-2012-1-Draft1 (2012)
27. Zhao, Y., Iannone, L., Riguidel, M.: On the performance of SDN controllers: a reality check. In: Proceedings of the 1st IEEE Conference on Network Function Virtualization and Software Defined Network (2015)

A Traceability Analysis of Monero's Blockchain

Amrit Kumar[✉], Clément Fischer, Shruti Tople, and Prateek Saxena

National University of Singapore, Singapore, Singapore
{amrit,cfischer,shruti90,prateeks}@comp.nus.edu.sg

Abstract. Privacy and anonymity are important desiderata in the use of cryptocurrencies. Monero—a privacy centric cryptocurrency has rapidly gained popularity due to its unlinkability and untraceablity guarantees. It has a market capitalization of USD 290M. In this work, we quantify the efficacy of three attacks on Monero's *untraceability* guarantee, which promises to make it hard to trace the origin of a received fund, by analyzing its blockchain data. To this end, we develop three attack routines and evaluate them on the Monero blockchain. Our results show that in 88% of cases, the origin of the funds can be easily determined with certainty. Moreover, we have compelling evidence that two of the attack routines also extend to Monero RingCTs—the second generation Monero that even hides the transaction amount. We further observe that over 98% of the results can in fact be obtained by a simple temporal analysis. In light of our findings, we discuss mitigations to strengthen Monero against these attacks. We shared our findings with the Monero development team and the general community. This has resulted into several discussions and proposals for fixes.

Keywords: Monero · Cryptocurrency · Blockchain · Traceability · Anonymity

1 Introduction

Since the seminal work by Chaum [3], privacy and anonymity properties have become important desiderata for any e-cash system. Bitcoin, the most popular decentralized cryptocurrency fairs poorly in terms of privacy and anonymity as evidenced by several analyses in the past [6,13,19,21]. In light of the privacy issues in Bitcoin, a new cryptocurrency called *Monero* (XMR) was launched on April 18th 2014. Monero currently has a market capitalization of USD 290M [12] and has the most momentum of all the live privacy-enhancing cryptocurrency projects (*e.g.*, Zcash [1,24], Dash [4], Mimblewimble [9], *etc.*), see [2]. The value of Monero in terms of USD increased by 27 times in the year 2016 from its value in 2015, making it a valuable example of privacy-enhancing cryptocurrencies to study. Its rise to popularity is mainly due to strong privacy properties (compared to Bitcoin) and design simplicity (compared to Zcash).

Background on Monero. As in any other distributed cryptocurrency (such as Bitcoin), Monero coins are spent in the form of a *transaction*, where a sender transfers the coins to a recipient, both often called the *users* of the system.

© Springer International Publishing AG 2017
S.N. Foley et al. (Eds.): ESORICS 2017, Part II, LNCS 10493, pp. 153–173, 2017.
DOI: 10.1007/978-3-319-66399-9_9

Each sender and the recipient has a public and private key pair. The public key uniquely defines the payment *address*. The transaction transfers funds held in the sender's public key to the recipient's public key. A transaction contains a set of *inputs* and *outputs*, wherein inputs consume coins from the sender and outputs transfer them to the recipient, while conserving the total balance. The transaction is digitally signed by the sender to authorize the transfer. It is then broadcast to the network that groups several transactions in the form of a *block* and validates it. Once accepted, the block gets appended to a public ledger called the *blockchain* and in the process a new coin is minted (as a *block reward*). The consensus on which blocks to append is determined by a *proof-of-work* puzzle. Later the recipient can redeem the funds by creating a new transaction that references the previous output as an input. The public blockchain also prevents the *double spend—i.e.*, the ability to spend a coin owned more than once.

An adversary can observe linkages between the addresses involved in transactions on the public blockchain, as evidenced by previous work on Bitcoin, allowing unintended inference of relationships between pseudonymous users [6,13,19,21]. Monero aims to address this privacy issue by requiring the currency to ensure the following two properties (see [22]), paraphrased here:

1. **Unlinkability:** For any two transactions, it should be impossible to deduce that they were sent to the same recipient.
2. **Untraceability:** Given a transaction input, the real output being redeemed in it should be anonymous among a set of other outputs.

In order to guarantee unlinkability, Monero by design introduces the notion of *one-time random addresses* (see Fig. 1). The idea is that each sender of a transaction generates a new one-time random address for the recipient *per output* in a way that only the recipient can spend it using a long-term secret key. If each address is generated using fresh randomness and is used only once, then it should be hard for an adversary to link two addresses. Monero enforces untraceability using a cryptographic primitive called *ring signatures* [7,20]. The primitive allows a sender (the signer)

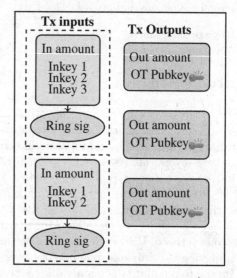

Fig. 1. A schematic representation of a simplified Monero non-RingCT transaction. It has two inputs and three outputs. The first input uses two mix-ins (hence three input keys), while the second one uses one. The sum of all output amounts must be equal to the sum of all input amounts. Ring signatures hide the real input key corresponding to the output being spent.

to anonymously sign the transaction (the message) on behalf of a "ring" or group of other users. As a result, the real output being redeemed remains anonymous amongst the chosen set of outputs (of the same amount) belonging to other users. The extra outputs used to create the ring signature are referred to as the *mix-ins*. As each mix-in is an output of a previous transaction, it is uniquely identified by the corresponding public key. Throughout this paper, we interchangeably use the term output and the public key. The guarantee that Monero aims to achieve through ring signatures is privacy *à la anonymity-set size* [22]. An input using m mix-ins has an anonymity-set size of $m + 1$.

Since January 2017, Monero has further strengthened its privacy guarantees by incorporating *ring confidential transactions* (RingCTs) [16] that also hide the transaction amount preventing several inference attacks. RingCTs are currently optional but are slated to become obligatory starting from September 2017.

Problem Statement. In this work, we focus on Monero's untraceability guarantee. While Monero does provide strong privacy features in theory, it is not known how well it does in real usage scenario, our work attempts to fill this gap. In other words, we aim to study the gap between the *desired anonymity-set size* (from user's perspective) and the *effective anonymity-set size* (from the attacker's perspective) in the presence of a passive adversary. To this end, we develop three attack routines and evaluate them on the Monero blockchain data. Monero designers and developers are aware of the theoretical possibility of the attacks [11,17] and have put in place some measures to mitigate the risks. In light of [11,17], our work has three goals:

1. Quantify through concrete attack strategies both past and existing risks.
2. Demonstrate that the existing measures often fall short in mitigating the risks.
3. Propose better mitigation strategies.

Contributions. We give below our contributions and main findings:

1. One of the most important findings is that over 65% of inputs have an anonymity-set size of one, thereby making them trivially traceable. Attack I leverages this finding to show that such inputs in fact lead to a *cascade effect*, where they affect the untraceability of other inputs with which they have a non-empty anonymity-set intersection. Our evaluation shows that the cascade effect renders another 22% of inputs traceable. The result here is conclusive as Attack I only yields true positives.
2. Attack II exploits the fact that several outputs from a previous transaction are often merged to aggregate funds when creating a new transaction. Such idioms of use leak information on the real outputs being redeemed. On non-RingCTs, Attack II has a true positive rate of 95% when compared to results from Attack I (that provides "ground truth"). We further observe merging of outputs among 1% of RingCTs. We believe that Attack II should extrapolate well even to RingCTs, but the ground truth is not available to scientifically deduce this.

3. Attack III considers an attack based on the temporal analysis of transaction outputs. It considers the most recent output (in terms of block height) in the anonymity-set as the real one being redeemed. Attack III has a true positive rate of 98.5% on non-RingCTs, where the comparison to the Attack I as ground truth is feasible. In light of the results, we propose a better sampling strategy to choose mix-ins. Our method takes into account the actual spending habit of users.

2   Monero Network and Usage Statistics

In this section, we discuss the network and usage statistics of Monero. Our goal is to gain insight into how Monero is used in practice and its ensuing privacy impact. The results obtained here also determine the efficacy of the traceability attacks (presented in Sect. 3). Below, we present the dataset for our statistical analysis. The same dataset will also be used to evaluate the impact of the attack routines.

2.1   Dataset Collection

We acquired the entire Monero history from the first transaction on April 18th 2014 up to and including the last transaction on February 6th 2017. The resulting dataset comprises of a total of 961,463 *non-coinbase transactions*[1] included in 418,910 blocks. The first non-coinbase transaction appears in the block with *height*[2] 110. Our dataset also includes 47,428 RingCTs. The first RingCT appears in the block with height 1,220,517 (on January 10th 2017). We include RingCTs so as to have a more representative dataset. Throughout our analysis, we maintain the raw data in the form of a blockchain and use Monero daemon (monerod) to access it [15].

In the remainder of the section, we present results of our statistical analysis on the dataset. Unless otherwise stated, we do not include *coinbase transactions*. Our analysis focuses on three important aspects: (1) available *liquidity*—the number of outputs that have the same amount. A Monero output can only be mixed with other outputs of the same amount. Hence, a low liquidity implies that it may not always be possible to find sufficient number of mix-ins for a given amount. As a consequence, a desired anonymity-set size may not be achieved. (2) the number of mix-ins used. Clearly, the larger it is the higher is the anonymity; (3) number of input and outputs in a transaction. Roughly speaking larger is the number of inputs and outputs, the higher is the probability that Attack II would work, hence we measure these.

---

[1] Transactions that do not create any new coin. The opposite of coinbase transactions that create new coins.

[2] Height is defined as the number of blocks preceding a particular block on the blockchain.

2.2 Available Liquidity

Since an output can only be mixed with other outputs having the same amount, it is important to have sufficiently large liquidity for each output amount. In order to ensure that sufficient liquidity is maintained, Monero incorporates the notion of denominations. A non-RingCT output amount is $A \times 10^B$, where $1 \leq A \leq 9$ and $B \geq -12$ [11].

There are 1,339,733 different output amounts in the dataset, the largest is 500,000 XMR. We also observe that approximately 85% of all outputs have an amount less than 0.01 XMR ($\approx$0.13 USD [5]). We refer to them as *dust values*. This shows that lower denominations dominate the dataset, and users often transact with small amounts. We further observe that a total of 1,244,165 (93%) output amounts have a frequency of 1. This means that when these outputs have to be redeemed, they cannot be mixed with any other non-RingCT output. The only possible way to create an untraceable transaction redeeming these outputs is to create a RingCT which hides individual mix-in amounts cryptographically (each amount is '0', denoting unknown). These output amounts sum to 1,012,231.3 XMR. Moreover, 84.5% of these outputs correspond to dust values.

Another important observation is regarding the number of output amounts that do not respect the usual denomination format in Monero. We found that 99.98% of these are not denomination compliant. Moreover, 92.8% of these amounts appear only once in the dataset. The total monetary value of the outputs that appear only once and are non-denomination compliant is 12231.27 XMR. The large number of non-denomination compliant output amounts can be attributed to the fact that denomination was not enforced on coinbase transactions in the early years. Moreover, the block reward in Monero is often not denomination compliant by the way it evolves over time.

2.3 Number of Mix-ins

Generally speaking, larger is the number of mix-ins used, the better is the privacy achieved (due to the larger anonymity-set size). However, using a large number of mix-ins leads to a linear increase in the transaction size (in terms of bytes) and a larger transaction size means larger fees. Hence, there is an incentive for users to use low number of mix-ins at the cost of sacrificing privacy. Since March 23rd 2016, Monero enforced a network-wide minimum mix-in of 2.

In fact, a total of 115 different number of mix-ins have been used in our dataset, the minimum and the maximum being 0 and 851 respectively. Table 1 presents the cumulative frequency of the number of mix-ins used in an input. One may observe that lower number of mix-ins, *i.e.*, 0, 1, 2, 3 and 4 correspond to roughly 96% of all mix-ins. Moreover, 65.9% of all inputs have zero mix-ins. Such inputs are traceable by default. In fact, as we show in Sect. 3.1, these inputs may render other inputs traceable as well even if the latter use higher number of mix-ins (through a *cascade effect*).

There are two possible explanations on why smaller mix-ins dominate the dataset. First, it could be possible that at the time a user creates a transaction, he may not find enough suitable outputs to mix with and hence is forced to choose a lower number of mix-ins. This may indeed happen since a majority of the output amounts are non-denomination compliant. Second, even though enough outputs are available at any given time, users deliberately choose a low number of mix-ins, for instance, to lower transaction fees. In order to distinguish the

Table 1. Cumulative frequency of the number of mix-ins (only the first 11 are shown). The last column counts the number of instances where it was possible to choose a higher number of mix-ins.

#Mix-ins	Freq	Cumul. freq. (in %)	Higher #mix-ins possib. (in %)
0	12148623	65.9	10434988 (85.9)
1	707788	69.7	701252 (99.1)
2	2908304	85.5	2902246 (99.8)
3	1313596	92.6	1313530 (99.9)
4	709686	96.5	709681 (99.9)
5	141800	97.3	141797 (99.9)
6	365720	99.2	365718 (99.9)
7	9616	99.3	9614 (99.9)
8	8593	99.3	8593 (100)
9	5369	99.4	5366 (99.9)
10	76524	99.8	76523 (99.9)

cause, we also provide in Table 1, the cumulative frequency of the anonymity-set size varying from 1 to 11 (*i.e.*, number of mix-ins between 0 and 10). The table also presents the percentage of cases when it was possible to choose a higher number of mix-ins. In order to compute these data, we include coinbase transactions. A coinbase transaction output cannot be used as a mix-in for 60 blocks due to system constraints. We observe that in the case of inputs with zero mix-ins, 85.9% of them could have been spent using a higher number of mix-ins. As for the rest, over 99% of the inputs could have been spent using a higher number of mix-ins. These results clearly show that users deliberately create a small anonymity-set (by choosing a small number of mix-ins), which could be to avoid paying a larger transaction fee.

In public communication, it has been mentioned by the Monero developers that Poloniex [18] (an exchange) used to pay to its clients using zero mix-ins (to save on transaction fees) and hence must have contributed to the total number of inputs with zero mix-ins. However, the exact percentage of transactions contributed by Poloniex is hard to obtain without an explicit disclosure from its part.

Lastly, we also observe that there are 9 different mix-in values (7.8%) that are unique in the sense that these many mix-ins are used in only one input (across the entire dataset). The corresponding transactions can be attributed to unique users. In other words, the number of mix-ins used may become an identifying trait of Monero users.

2.4   Number of Inputs and Outputs

The existence of denominations in Monero has a direct impact on the number of inputs and outputs that a transaction can have. To see this, consider a user Alice paying 11 XMR to another user Bob. Since 11 is not denomination compliant, Alice cannot pay 11 XMR in a single output. She has to create two outputs for 10 XMR and 1 XMR. Now, when Bob wishes to redeem the funds, he now needs to create a transaction with two inputs instead of one. Bob's transaction now merges the two previous outputs. Output merging in case of Bitcoin is well known to leak information on the owner of the funds [13]. We show through Attack II (Sect. 3.2) that Monero suffers from a similar privacy leakage. In fact, the efficacy of Attack II depends on the number of inputs and outputs that a transaction can have.

To this end, we present in Fig. 2a, the evolution of the number of inputs and outputs per transaction. We observe that the average number of inputs and outputs per transaction are 19 and 17 respectively. Smaller number of inputs and outputs at the tail can be attributed to RingCTs, which made denominations redundant. With RingCTs, the number of outputs in a transaction can be limited to two: one for the payment to the recipient, the other for the change. We now focus on the impact of RingCTs on the number of inputs and outputs. On an average, a RingCT has 3.7 inputs and only 1.2 output. Figure 2b shows the evolution of these values over time. Clearly, with the advent of RingCTs, the number of outputs per transaction was consistently around 2. The number of inputs however does not show a stable and consistent pattern. The peaks in the curve do however tend to lower. It could be due to the existence of denominations from non-RingCTs. As a result, users were still forced to merge a large number of inputs to reach a desired transaction amount.

To summarize the statistical analysis of this section, we observed that over 65% of inputs use zero mix-ins and that the average number of inputs/outputs per transaction is large for non-RingCTs but considerably small for RingCTs. Attack I and Attack II discussed in the following section leverage these findings.

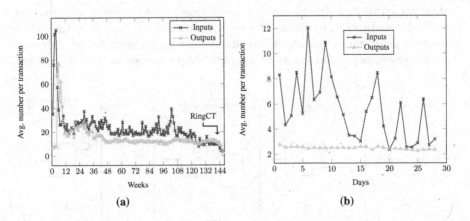

Fig. 2. (a) Average number of inputs and outputs in a transaction. The x-axis represents the number of weeks after the launch of Monero. (b) Average number of inputs and outputs in a RingCT. The x-axis represents the number of days after the launch of RingCTs.

3   Traceability Attacks and Evaluation

In this section, we present three attack strategies on existing Monero transactions. The attacks only assume access to the entire public blockchain. The transactions on the public blockchain are accessible to anyone and hence it justifies our model. We do not assume any active adversary that actively participates in the protocol to undermine the privacy of users. Albeit weak, we show this passive adversary can trace 88% of inputs.

3.1   Attack I: Leveraging Zero Mix-ins

Attack I exploits the presence of inputs spent using zero mix-ins (over 65% in our dataset). Consider the case, where, a user Alice creates a transaction Tx-a with an input that she spends without using any mix-in. Alice's input key can clearly be identified as spent. Now, consider a later transaction Tx-b created by another user Bob who uses Alice's input key as a mix-in for his input. If the number of mix-ins used by Bob is one. Then, any adversary can identify the real input key being spent in Bob's transaction and his input becomes traceable too. More generally, if the number of mix-ins used by Bob is $m > 1$, then the *effective anonymity-set size* now becomes m (instead of the desired size of $m + 1$). A closer look reveals that use of zero mix-in leads to a *cascade effect* where the traceability of an input affects the traceability of another input in a later transaction. Figure 3 schematically presents this cascade effect triggered by Tx-a that uses no mix-in. The cascade effect may not always make an input fully traceable, if for instance, the effective anonymity-set size reduces to a value greater than one.

Our attack routine due to memory restrictions, runs a number of iterations denoted by η. In each iteration, the algorithm makes a pass over the entire blockchain data and finds a set of traceable inputs. In the next iteration, it uses the set of previously found traceable inputs to obtain new set of traceable inputs.

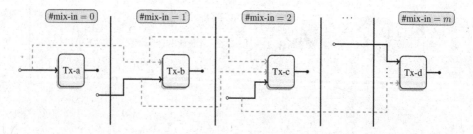

Fig. 3. Attack I: cascade effect due to zero mix-ins. Each transaction has only one input (left of the transaction) and one output (on the right). The number of mix-ins used increases from left to right. Dashed lines represent the input keys identified as a mix-in. Lines in bold are the real input keys being spent.

Results. The impact of Attack I on the traceability of inputs is shown in Figs. 4, 5 and 6. The success of Attack I is due to the fact that 65.9% of inputs do not use any mix-ins and are trivially traceable. This cascades to traceability of another 22% of the inputs, leading to a total of 87.9% of traceable inputs.

In Fig. 4, we present the percentage of traceable inputs for number of mix-ins less than or equal to 10. These together cover 99.8% of all inputs in our dataset. We present histograms for three values of η (1, 3 and 5). With $\eta = 5$, we observe that the set of traceable inputs almost reaches a fixed point. Just after the first iteration ($\eta = 1$), the number of traceable inputs using one mix-in reaches as high as 81%. For $\eta = 5$, this percentage of traceable inputs using one mix-in becomes 87%. The plot also shows the cascade effect as inputs using a high number of mix-ins such as 10 also have a considerable percentage of traceable inputs (27% for $\eta = 5$).

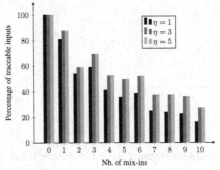

Fig. 4. Results on Attack I: the percentage of traceable inputs as a function of the number of mix-ins.

Figure 5a shows how deep (in terms of number of mix-ins) does the cascade effect propagate. It presents the cumulative percentage of traceable inputs as a function of the number of mix-ins. Clearly, as the number of mix-ins increases, the cascade effect deteriorates and roughly 88% of all inputs become traceable. It is interesting to note that the cascade effect leads to one traceable input that uses 153 mix-ins. This is the largest number of mix-ins that gets affected by the cascade effect.

Figure 5b shows how long (in terms of days) does the cascade effect propagate. It presents the evolution of the percentage of traceable inputs over time grouped by week. Since, the initial transactions did not use any mix-in, a large majority (over 95%) of the inputs were traceable. The maximum percentage of traceable inputs per week is 98.9% (in the 10th week). In fact, the percentage dropped to roughly 62% in the 105th week when the network-wide minimum mix-in of 2 could come into effect. Since then, the percentage of traceable inputs has seen a consistent decline. For the last week, only 8% of all inputs were found to be traceable. Attack I did not find results on RingCTs.

We found several instances where Attack I could not identify a traceable input, but it did nevertheless succeeded in reducing the effective anonymity-set size. Figure 6 presents these findings. For the sake of completeness, it also includes the results presented in Fig. 4. We observe that for $\eta = 5$, roughly 24% of inputs that use 10 mix-ins have an effective anonymity-set size of two. This shows how close Attack I can be in identifying the real input. Moreover, the plot shows that as the number of mix-in increases, the percentage of inputs on

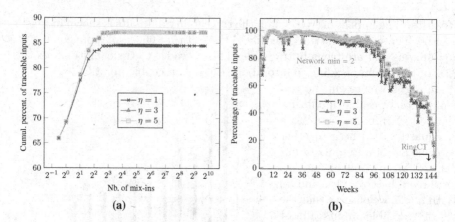

Fig. 5. Results on traceability using Attack I. (a) The cumulative percentage of traceable inputs as a function of the number of mix-ins. (b) The evolution of the percentage of traceable inputs over time. In the x-axis, we have the number of weeks after the launch of Monero.

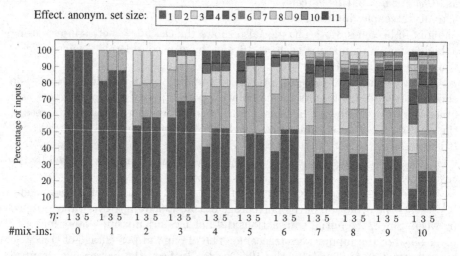

Fig. 6. Results on effective anonymity-set size using Attack I. In x-axis, we have the number of mix-ins from 0 to 10. For each of these mix-ins we plot three stacked bars corresponding to $\eta = 1, 3, 5$. Each stacked bar for a fixed η represents the percentage of inputs that have an effective anonymity-set size between 1 to 11. For instance, for inputs using only 2 mix-ins, and for $\eta = 5$, the percentage of inputs with effective anonymity-set size of 1 is 59%, the percentage of inputs with effective anonymity-set size of 2 is 21% and the percentage of inputs with effective anonymity-set size of 3 is 20%.

which Attack I does not work at all tends to decrease. In fact, for inputs using 10 mix-ins, Attack I does not affect the effective anonymity-set size for only 0.9% of all such inputs.

3.2   Attack II: Leveraging Output Merging

Consider a scenario where a user creates a transaction Tx-a having one input and two outputs O_1, O_2 (Cf. Fig. 7). Without loss of generality, let us assume that only 1 mix-in is used. At a later time, another user creates a transaction Tx-b with two inputs I_1, I_2 and one output. Let us suppose that both the inputs use one mix-in each. The first input I_1 uses one of the outputs O_1 of Tx-a as an input key. Similarly, the second input I_2 uses the other output O_2 of Tx-a as an input key. Attack II then identifies O_1 and O_2 as the real input keys being spent in Tx-b.

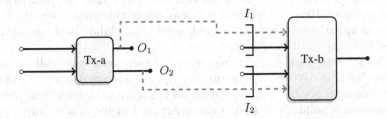

Fig. 7. Attack II. Tx-a is a transaction with one input that uses one mix-in. It has two outputs O_1 and O_2. Tx-b is another transaction that has two inputs I_1 and I_2. Each input again has one mix-in. Both I_1 and I_2 include outputs of Tx-a. According to Attack II, the input keys O_1 and O_2 represented using the dashed line are the real keys being spent in Tx-b.

Attack II functions under the assumption that while creating a transaction, it is unlikely to choose several mix-ins that are outputs of a single previous transaction. Hence, if a transaction includes keys (possibly across several inputs) that are outputs of a single previous transaction, then they are likely to be the real ones being spent. Intuitively, this is true for non-RingCTs, where, due to denominations, several outputs in a transaction may belong to the same recipient. As a result, those outputs will get merged to aggregate funds in a later transaction. Since, mix-ins are randomly chosen, the probability that Attack II gives incorrect result should be small. For RingCTs, denominations are redundant and hence output merging should be less prevalent.

Due to the randomness involved in choosing mix-ins, results obtained from Attack II however cannot always be conclusive and may admit false positives. In this sense, Attack II is weaker than Attack I as the latter does not admit any false positives. As our evaluation later shows, Attack II has a true positive rate of 87.3% on non-RingCTs.

In order to simplify the discussion of Attack II, we refer to transactions of type Tx-a (as in Fig. 7) as a *source* transaction, while, those of type Tx-b as a *destination* transaction. Hence, a destination transaction uses two or more outputs of a source transaction across its inputs. A minimum number of two or more outputs is needed so as to capture the merging of outputs. Attack II may encounter the following scenarios:

- **S1:** It may not find any destination for a given source.
- **S2:** It may find several destinations for a given source.
- **S3:** It may find one (or more) destination for a given source, where the same source output appears in more than one destination input.
- **S4:** It may find one (or more) destination for a given source, where more than one source outputs appear in a single destination input.

S1 means that Attack II failed to yield any result on the given source instance. While, S2 means that the attack has false positives at the transaction level, hence it is hard to ascertain the real destination for a given source. S3 presents the worst case for the attack. It means that the attack has false positives even at the input level. Hence, it is hard to even ascertain the input where the source output was indeed spent. Lastly, S4 yields a set of candidate keys, one of which is probably being spent in the input.

In the following, we conduct experiments to estimate how well Attack II performs. We first measure how frequently the above scenarios occur and then estimate the false positive rate by relying on the results obtained from Attack I as a comparison point. Note that because Attack I yields results only on non-RingCTs, this comparison is limited to non-RingCTs, but the inference extends to RingCTs as well.

Results. Attack II found results on 410,237 different source transactions, which is roughly 43% of all transactions in our dataset. These source transactions also include 636 RingCTs, which is 1% of all RingCTs in the dataset. The low fraction of RingCTs is due to the fact that the average number of inputs and outputs per RingCT is only 3.7 and 1.2 respectively. Recall that Attack II exploits the use of outputs of source transactions in a destination transaction. Hence, a low number of inputs and outputs directly affects the applicability of the attack. Even though, Attack II affects only 1% of RingCTs, it is a serious concern for the Monero developers as exchanges and mining pools are now actively merging RingCT outputs (See Sect. 5 for their feedback).

In Fig. 8a, we present the results obtained on 409,601 non-RingCT sources. Around 60% of all source transactions have only 1 matching destination. The maximum number of destinations found for a source was 146. However, the percentage of source drops exponentially as the number of destinations increases. Similarly, Fig. 8b presents the results obtained on 636 RingCT sources. We observe that a source has at most 3 destinations and a majority of the source transactions (95.1%) have only one destination. The small number of destinations in case of RingCT sources is due to the low number of inputs in RingCTs.

We estimate the accuracy of Attack II by comparing its results with those obtained by Attack I (that yields "ground truth"). Since Attack I does not yield any result on RingCTs, we cannot determine the corresponding accuracy. However, if it performs well on non-RingCTs, then we may extrapolate this result over RingCTs and expect similar accuracy. In order to compare the two attacks, we use the following terms:

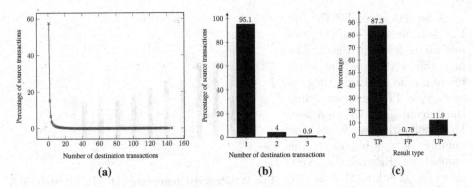

Fig. 8. (a) Result of employing Attack II on non-RingCTs. The x-axis presents all the observed number of destination transactions for a given source transaction. In y-axis, we show the number of source transactions that admit a given number of destination transactions. The number is given as a fraction of 409,601 non-RingCT source transactions. (b) Result of employing Attack II on RingCTs. The x-axis presents all the observed number of destination transactions for a given source transaction. In y-axis, we show the number of source transactions that admit a given number of destination transactions. The number is given as a fraction of 636 RingCT source transactions. (c) Overall observed percentage of TP, FP and UP.

- **True positive (TP):** An input creates a *true positive* if: (a) Attack II identifies a unique key as the one being spent in the input and, (b) the key is the same as the one identified by Attack I. The two attacks are hence in agreement with the conclusion.
- **False positive (FP):** An input creates a *false positive* if all the keys identified as being spent by Attack II were actually found to be spent in a different input by Attack I. In other words, none of the probable keys identified by Attack II was actually the real key being spent in the input. Hence, the two attacks disagree on the real key being spent.
- **Unknown positive (UP):** An input creates an *unknown positive* if at least one of the keys identified by Attack II could not be identified as being spent in any input (of any transaction) by Attack I. The uncertainty comes from Attack I as it does not give ground truth for all inputs.

Now that the terms TP, FP and UP are established, we are ready to present the results on the accuracy of Attack II. The overall accuracy of Attack II computed over all non-RingCT inputs for which it returns a result is given in Fig. 8c. The result shows that Attack II has an overall true positive rate of 87%, while the false positive rate is as low as 0.78%, while the result is inconclusive for around 12% of inputs. The high true positive rate on non-RingCTs clearly demonstrates that it should do equally well even on RingCTs. However, due to the lack of ground truth it is impossible to verify this.

A breakdown of TP, FP and UP as a function of number of mix-ins is given in Fig. 9. The plot shows that as the number of mix-in increases, the percentage of TP decreases, while the percentage of UP increases. Moreover, irrespective of the number of mix-ins used, the number of FP remains very close to 0. All of this is due to the fact that the result of Attack I deteriorates as the number of mix-ins increases and hence it becomes hard to verify the result of Attack II due to a lack of ground truth.

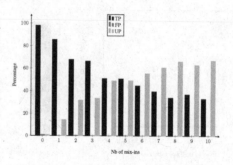

Fig. 9. Observed percentage of TP, FP and UP as a function of number of mix-ins. The result corresponds to non-RingCTs.

Remark 1. Attack II can also be used to break the unlinkability guarantee of Monero. To see this, refer to Fig. 7: If O_1 and O_2 have been determined to be the real input keys being spent in I_1 and I_2, then, they must belong to the same Monero user, hence breaking unlinkability. Since, the focus of this work is on traceability, we do not develop this any further and leave it as a future work.

3.3 Attack III: Temporal Analysis

The third attack leverages the fact that an output does not remain unspent for an infinite time. In general, its probability of being spent should increase with time (eventually becoming 1). Indeed, an output that has been on the blockchain for 100,000 blocks is much more likely to have already been spent than an output that has been on the blockchain for only 100 blocks. In light of this, the Attack III strategy is defined in the following manner: *Given a set of input keys used to create a ring signature, the real key being spent is the one with the highest block height*, where it previously appeared as an output. The strategy applies on both non-RingCTs and RingCTs.

Results. We employed Attack III on our dataset and compared its results with the ones obtained from Attack I ($\eta = 5$). Globally, we observed that Attack III has a true positive rate of 98.1%. This clearly shows that Attack III is very accurate and very often the most recent output is the real one being spent.

In theory, Attack III can be prevented by mixing with only those outputs that are yet to be redeemed. This would however require the ability to distinguish a spent output from an unspent one. Monero's main aim is to make this hard using a ring signature. In order to circumvent this problem, Monero developers have decided since April 5th 2015 to sample mix-ins from a variant of triangular distribution [23].

Table 2. TP: True Positive and FP: False Positive. Breakdown of traceable inputs obtained using Attack I. In the first row, we show the total number of traceable inputs that employ uniform distribution and the variant of triangular distribution (hence *). The second and third row show the true and false positive rate observed on Attack III.

#Inputs	Uniform dist. (until April 4, 2015)	Triangular dist.* (since April 5, 2015)
	9885810	6174801
TP	99.5%	96%
FP	0.5%	4%

The distribution gives higher probability to newer outputs than to ones that are old and hence can potentially mitigate the attack. Prior to April 5th 2015, mix-ins were sampled from a uniform distribution, *i.e.*, each output had the same probability of being a mix-in for any input at any given time. We evaluate how well the current sampling strategy mitigates Attack III. The results are shown in Table 2. While, using the current sampling strategy does help in reducing the number of true positives, the gain over uniform distribution is however marginal, *i.e.*, only 3.5%. Our results clearly show that the existing sampling strategy drastically fails in mitigating Attack III—that is, user spending patterns do not follow the expected (variant of) triangular distribution.

4   Mitigation Strategies and Recommendations

As argued in the Monero Research Lab (MRL) report MRL-004 [11], without a non-interactive zero-knowledge (NIZK) approach, traceability is inevitable. Moreover, it is argued that since NIZK based techniques are computationally intensive, privacy issues should be addressed without employing those techniques. Under these constraints, we propose a mitigation strategy for Attack III that performs better than the variant of the triangular distribution currently employed in Monero. We also propose recommendations to reduce the potential risks associated with Attack I and Attack II.

4.1   Recommendations for Attack I and Attack II

Since Attack I could not find any traceable input on RingCTs, we recommend the Monero development team to make RingCTs obligatory as soon as possible. As long as RingCTs are optional, the possibility of a user creating a non-RingCT cannot be ruled out. Hence, the cascade effect may continue to propagate.

One may argue that enforcing RingCTs must be subject to its acceptance by the community. To this end, we present in Fig. 10, the fraction of RingCTs after its launch. In the fourth day after the launch, the percentage of RingCTs rose as high as 70%. But, in the following two weeks, it remained less than 62%. Looking at the last few days, it appears that RingCTs got well accepted by the Monero users. Indeed, the last day saw a record value of 98%. This is an encouraging result showing the acceptance of RingCTs and hence consolidates our argument that it can be made obligatory.

As for Attack II, it is hard to prevent it completely at the protocol level due to the one-time output addresses. One way to reduce output merging is to warn users when they attempt to do so. Warning can be displayed either when a user creates 2 or more outputs paying the same recipient or when he merges 2 or more outputs from the same transaction. This wallet level solution is certainly not the ideal fix. As a modified version of Attack II can subvert this

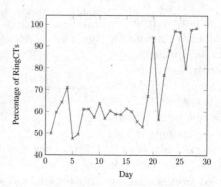

Fig. 10. The percentage of RingCTs among all transactions submitted in a day. The plot only shows data for the days after the launch of RingCT on January 10th 2017.

mitigation measure. To see this, imagine a more general version of Attack II that also considers merging of outputs stemming from different transactions within the same block. We reiterate that information leakage is very hard (if not impossible) to be absolutely prevented without a NIZK based approach.

4.2 Mitigating Threat from Attack III

As we have seen the current sampling strategy for mix-ins fails drastically in preventing temporal analysis. There are two possible strategies towards mitigating the ensuing risks: (a) mimic users' spending behavior or, (b) force mix-ins to be picked according to some "unknown" distribution. Solution (b) can be achieved by employing primitives such as ORAM [8] that will provide cryptographic guarantees on the impossibility to learn information from a passive analysis of the blockchain. However, their applicability to distributed cryptocurrencies seems to require either a trusted party [10] or NIZK proof. We consider them to be important future work. Here, we will focus on (a).

We use the results of Attack I to extract information on when an output (in terms of block height) is created and when it gets spent. We then compute the difference of the two block heights. Since a coinbase output is locked for 60 blocks, its block difference can only be greater than or equal to 60. There is no such restriction on non-coinbase outputs though. Results from Attack I also include a considerable fraction of coinbase outputs (28.9%). This further motivates studying them independently of non-coinbase outputs.

We first observe that users' spending habits can be roughly grouped into four distinct categories characterized by the difference in the block heights (Cf. Table 3). As we see, the percentage of outputs that are spent within the first 1000 blocks is larger among coinbase outputs than among non-coinbase out-

Table 3. Percentage of outputs that remain unspent with a given block interval. The percentage on coinbase is given over coinbase outputs only. Similarly for non-coinbase.

Block difference	Percentage of outputs		
	Coinbase	Non-coinbase	Overall
[0, 10]	0%	0.2%	0.17%
]10, 100]	11.1%	8.4%	9.2%
]100, 1000]	42.6%	22.6%	28.4%
>1000	46.3	68.8%	62.2%

puts. As a general conclusion, coinbase outputs have a larger probability of being spent quickly once unlocked.

The actual frequency distribution on the entire population is shown in Fig. 11a. The curve clearly shows three distinct clusters identified by the block differences: [0, 10],]10, 100] and >100. Figure 11b presents a breakdown according to coinbase and non-coinbase. We observe that both the curves have a long tail starting from a difference of 1000 blocks.

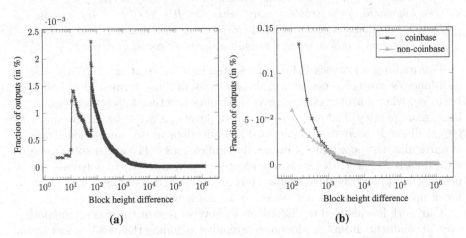

Fig. 11. Spending habit of Monero users. In x-axis, we have the difference between the block height where the output was created and the block height where the output was spent. It measures the duration for which the output remained unspent. In y-axis, we plot the fraction of outputs that share the same difference. Only 1 out of every 100 data points are shown. (a) Combined result on the entire dataset including both coinbase and non-coinbase outputs. (b) Separate results.

In order to mitigate the risks of temporal analysis, we propose replacing the existing sampling method to choose mix-ins. In fact, a better sampling strategy would consist in sampling from the distribution identified by the probability density functions of Fig. 11b. The sampling distribution should moreover depend on whether the output being spent is coinbase or non-coinbase. We estimate the probability density function (PDF) using `descdist()` function of the R statistical tool. For each of the dataset, the underlying heuristic based on the Cullen and Frey graph suggests that the PDF is closest to the gamma distribution ($\Gamma(\alpha, \beta)$) with different parameters α and β. For coinbase outputs, the estimated parameters are $\alpha = 0.24, \beta = 7.97 \times 10^{-6}$, while for non coinbase outputs, the estimated parameters are $\alpha = 0.27, \beta = 5.15 \times 10^{-6}$.

Hence, we hereby recommend Monero developers to employ the corresponding PDFs. However, it should be noted that choosing any static distribution renders the system insensitive to social and economic factors that may influence users' spending behavior.

5   Responsible Disclosure and Feedback

As a part of responsible disclosure, we shared our findings both with the Monero development team and the general community. We received varied feedback through diverse channels including but not limited to e-mail, Twitter and Reddit. Monero development team found our result on Attack II insightful:

> *"We hadn't had it [Attack II] accompanied by a model before, i.e., we've been approaching the problem more generally. It's NOT trivially solvable. Because most users will receive additional outputs and need to combine them; the combination betrays a small amount of correlation data."*

Our findings on Attack II further resulted into the creation of a Github issue on Monero's project repository. The issue was initially termed as a bad user behavior, where, a user merges several outputs together falsely believing it to bring more privacy. The proposed fix was to develop a wallet-based warning system to dissuade users from doing so. The limitations of this mitigation strategy, in particular, the possibility of eventual modifications of the wallet software were also discussed. Later, the issue was identified as non-trivial to solve as output merging is apparently done deliberately by pools and exchanges who want to break up their outputs so payments can be made with locking less change.

Our work has also led to discussions on several Reddit threads accumulating over 50 comments from the Monero community including the development team. Our results on Attack III has also catalyzed the ongoing work on developing better mitigation strategies. Several mitigation measures have been discussed: (1) Sampling mix-ins using our proposed approach of taking into account actual spending behavior, (2) Sampling mix-ins using Zipf distribution, (3) Developing a dynamic sampling procedure, (4) Wallet-specific sampling procedure, *etc*. The ensuing limitations have also been discussed at length. For instance, a dynamic sampling procedure being costly; wallet-specific sampling leading to potential fingerprinting, *etc*.

6   Related Work

Our work is motivated by two prior unpublished works on the privacy analysis of Monero: MRL-001 [17] and MRL-004 [11]. Both of these have been authored by

Monero researchers and developers. The two prior works report on the theoretical possibility of mounting the attacks studied in this paper. However, the impact of the attacks in real usage scenario was unknown. Our work fills this gap by quantifying the existing and the past threat on the blockchain data. It provides a data backed analysis that shows (1) The risks of using no mix-in in practice, (2) How often the risks may arise? (3) How far the cascade effect can propagate? and (4) How the impact has evolved over time? For instance, our work quantifies the severity of cascade effect: it propagates up to 153 mix-ins over a span of three years.

Since the prior works were theoretical and were not backed by real usage behavior, the developers decided on employing a triangular distribution to sample the mix-ins expecting it to mitigate Attack III. Our work shows that a triangular distribution fails drastically in mitigating the attack. This further highlights the difference between the prior work and the new results put forth by our work. Moreover, our work studies the spending habit of users and empirically provides the desired probability distribution function. Our results can be used to improve the current sampling method.

Finally, we are aware of a concurrent work with similar results [14]. The work studies Attack I and Attack III and a countermeasure of Attack III based on real spending behavior. Our work is different from [14] in three contributions: (1) Attack II is not studied in [14] (2) Mitigation for Attack III does not consider coinbase and non-coinbase outputs separately. This may result in a bias as coinbase and non-coinbase outputs have different spending behavior (3) Our network and usage statistics reveal new potential privacy issues in Monero (unknown in [14]) that 7.8% of users are unique in the way they choose their anonymity-set size.

7   Conclusion

This work performs a passive blockchain analysis of Monero and evaluates the efficacy of several attacks on its untraceability guarantees. These attacks are effective as around 88% of inputs are rendered traceable. We also found some traceability results on RingCTs and finally discuss a better strategy (than the one currently employed) to mitigate temporal analysis. Our results hereby reaffirm the weaknesses of anonymity-set size as a privacy metric when implemented in practice. As a future work, we aim to study traceability under active attacks on Monero, where the adversary can take part in the protocol to undermine users' privacy. We are further investigating the use of cryptographic primitives such as zero knowledge proofs and ORAM to strengthen the traceability guarantees beyond the current solutions.

Acknowledgements. Authors would like to thank the anonymous reviewers for their feedback. Amrit Kumar was supported by the research grants R-252-000-560-112 and R-252-000-565-720 from MOE Singapore.

References

1. Ben-Sasson, E., Chiesa, A., Garman, C., Green, M., Miers, I., Tromer, E., Virza, M.: Zerocash: decentralized anonymous payments from bitcoin. In: 2014 IEEE Symposium on Security and Privacy, SP 2014, Berkeley, CA, USA, 18–21 May 2014, pp. 459–474 (2014)
2. Meet the Best Performing Digital Currency of 2016: Monero. http://bit.ly/2pVnaJb. Accessed 22 Apr 2017
3. Chaum, D.: Blind signatures for untraceable payments. In: Advances in Cryptology: Proceedings of CRYPTO 1982, Santa Barbara, California, USA, 23–25 August 1982, pp. 199–203. Plenum Press, New York (1982)
4. Dash (2017). https://www.dash.org/. Accessed 7 Apr 2017
5. https://www.cryptonator.com/rates/XMR-USD. Accessed 23 Feb 2017
6. Fleder, M., Kester, M.S., Pillai, S.: Bitcoin transaction graph analysis (2015). CoRR abs/1502.01657
7. Fujisaki, E., Suzuki, K.: Traceable ring signature. In: Okamoto, T., Wang, X. (eds.) PKC 2007. LNCS, vol. 4450, pp. 181–200. Springer, Heidelberg (2007). doi:10.1007/978-3-540-71677-8_13
8. Goldreich, O., Ostrovsky, R.: Software protection and simulation on oblivious RAMs. J. ACM **43**(3), 431–473 (1996)
9. Jedusor, T.E.: Mimblewimble (2016). Accessed 7 Apr 2017. https://download.wpsoftware.net/bitcoin/wizardry/mimblewimble.txt
10. Jia, Y., Moataz, T., Tople, S., Saxena, P.: OblivP2P: an oblivious peer-to-peer content sharing system. In: 25th USENIX Security Symposium, USENIX Security 2016, Austin, TX, USA, 10–12 August 2016, pp. 945–962 (2016)
11. Mackenzie, A., Noether, S., Monero Core Team: Improving obfuscation in the CryptoNote protocol. Research Bulletin MRL-0004, Monero Research Lab, January 2015
12. https://coinmarketcap.com/currencies/monero/. Accessed 22 Apr 2017
13. Meiklejohn, S., Pomarole, M., Jordan, G., Levchenko, K., McCoy, D., Voelker, G.M., Savage, S.: A fistful of bitcoins: characterizing payments among men with no names. In: Proceedings of the 2013 Internet Measurement Conference, IMC 2013, Barcelona, Spain, 23–25 October 2013, pp. 127–140. ACM (2013)
14. Miller, A., Moeser, M., Lee, K., Narayanan, A.: An Empirical Analysis of Linkability in the Monero Blockchain (2017). https://arxiv.org/abs/1704.04299
15. https://getmonero.org/knowledge-base/developer-guides/wallet-rpc. Accessed 22 Apr 2017
16. Noether, S., Mackenzie, A.: Monero research lab: ring confidential transactions. Ledger **1**, 1–18 (2016)
17. Noether, S., Noether, S., Mackenzie, A.: A note on chain reactions in traceability in CryptoNote 2.0. Research Bulletin MRL-0001, Monero Research Lab, September 2014
18. Poloniex. https://poloniex.com. Accessed 22 Apr 2017
19. Reid, F., Harrigan, M.: An analysis of anonymity in the bitcoin system. In: 2011 IEEE Third International Conference on Privacy, Security, Risk and Trust (PASSAT) and 2011 IEEE Third International Conference on Social Computing (SocialCom), PASSAT/SocialCom 2011, Boston, MA, USA, 9–11 October 2011, pp. 1318–1326. IEEE (2011)
20. Rivest, R.L., Shamir, A., Tauman, Y.: How to leak a secret. In: Boyd, C. (ed.) ASIACRYPT 2001. LNCS, vol. 2248, pp. 552–565. Springer, Heidelberg (2001). doi:10.1007/3-540-45682-1_32

21. Ron, D., Shamir, A.: Quantitative analysis of the full bitcoin transaction graph. In: Sadeghi, A.-R. (ed.) FC 2013. LNCS, vol. 7859, pp. 6–24. Springer, Heidelberg (2013). doi:10.1007/978-3-642-39884-1_2
22. van Saberhagen, N.: CryptoNote v2.0. Technical report, CryptoNote, October 2013
23. https://github.com/monero-project/monero/commit/ f2e8348be0c91c903e68ef582cee687c52411722. Accessed 14 Apr 2017
24. Zerocoin Electric Coin Company: Zcash (2017). https://z.cash/. Accessed 7 Apr 2017

Multi-rate Threshold FlipThem

David Leslie[1], Chris Sherfield[2], and Nigel P. Smart[2(⊠)]

[1] Department Mathematics and Statistics, University of Lancaster, Lancaster, UK
d.leslie@lancaster.ac.uk
[2] Department of Computer Science, University of Bristol, Bristol, UK
c.sherfield@bristol.ac.uk, nigel@cs.bris.ac.uk

Abstract. A standard method to protect data and secrets is to apply threshold cryptography in the form of secret sharing. This is motivated by the acceptance that adversaries will compromise systems at some point; and hence using threshold cryptography provides a defence in depth. The existence of such powerful adversaries has also motivated the introduction of game theoretic techniques into the analysis of systems, e.g. via the FlipIt game of van Dijk et al. This work further analyses the case of FlipIt when used with multiple resources, dubbed FlipThem in prior papers. We examine two key extensions of the FlipThem game to more realistic scenarios; namely separate costs and strategies on each resource, and a learning approach obtained using so-called fictitious play in which players do not know about opponent costs, or assume rationality.

1 Introduction

The traditional methodology of securing systems is to rely solely on cryptographic means to ensure protection of data (via encryption) and authentication (via signatures and secured-passwords). However, both of these techniques rely on some data being kept secure. The advent of attacks such as Advanced Persistent Threats (APTs) means that exfiltration of the underlying cryptographic keys, or other sensitive data, is now a real threat. To model such long term stealthy attacks researchers have turned to game theory [1,22,26,30], adding to a growing body of work looking at game theory in cybersecurity in various scenarios [7,16,35]. Probably the most influential work applying game theory in the security area has been the FlipIt game [10]; with the follow up paper [5] demonstrating applications of FlipIt to various examples including credential management, virtual machine refresh and cloud auditing for service-level-agreement. FlipIt has gained traction and popularity due to the assumption that the adversary can always get into the system; thus aligning with the new rhetoric in the security industry that compromise avoidance is no longer a realistic possibility and it is now about limiting the amount of compromise as quickly and efficiently as possible.

In FlipIt, two players, aptly named the defender and attacker, fight over control of a single resource. Each player has their own button which, when pressed, will give them control over the resource assigning them some form of benefit.

© Springer International Publishing AG 2017
S.N. Foley et al. (Eds.): ESORICS 2017, Part II, LNCS 10493, pp. 174–190, 2017.
DOI: 10.1007/978-3-319-66399-9_10

Pressing the button has a cost associated to it. The FlipIt paper examines this game as a way of modelling attacks in which a stealthy adversary is trying to control a single resource. For example it could be used to model an adversary which compromises passwords (the adversary's button press corresponds to a break of a system password), whilst the defender resets passwords occasionally (via pressing their button in the game). FlipIt has of course been generalised in many different directions [11,17,19,24,27,28].

However, a standard defence against having a single point of failure for secure data (be it real data or cryptographic secrets), is to use some form of distributed cryptography [9], usually using some form of secret sharing [31]. Such techniques can either be used directly as in [4,32], or using secret sharing to actually compute some data as in Multi-Party Computation [2,8]. To capture this and other such situations, Laszka et al. [18] introduce a FlipThem game in which there are multiple resources, each equipped with a button as in FlipIt, and the attacker obtains benefit only by gaining control of every resource in the game. This models the full threshold situation in distributed cryptographic solutions.

The FlipThem game is extended by Leslie et al. [20] to the partial threshold case, where the attacker is not required to gain control of the whole system but only a fraction of the number of resources in order to have some benefit. Assuming both players select the rates of Poisson processes controlling the pressing of buttons, they calculate the proportion of time the attacker will be in control of the system in order to gain some benefit. Nash equilibrium rates of play are calculated which depend on move costs and the threshold of resources required for the attacker to gain any benefit.

A major downside of the analysis in [20] is that the button associated to all resources are given the same cost and move rate for the attacker (and similarly for the defender). So in this current work we introduce the more realistic setting in which a player may have different move rates and costs associated to each resource. For example one resource may be easier to apply patches to than others, or one may be easier to attack due to the operating system it runs. We calculate Nash equilibrium rates of play for this more realistic setting.

We also introduce a framework from the learning in games literature [13] which models the situation where each player responds to the observed actions of the other player, instead of calculating an equilibrium. This adaptive framework is required once we drop the unrealistic assumption that players know their opponent's costs and reward functions, and our version makes considerably weaker assumptions on the information available to the players than the adaptive framework of [10]. In particular we introduce learning into a situation where the FlipThem game is played over a continuing sequence of epochs. We assume players repeatedly calculate the average observed rate of their opponent and respond optimally to that, resulting in a learning rule known as *fictitious play* [6,13]. Performing multiple experiments, we find that when the costs result in a game with an interior equilibrium point (i.e. one in which all players play non-zero rates of all resources) the fictitious play procedure converges to this equilibrium. On the other hand, when there is not an interior equilibrium, we find unstable behaviour in the learning procedure. This result is important in the real world: the fictitious play formulation assumes that players know only their own benefit functions and can observe the play of others, yet the players still manage to converge to the calculated equilibria. Thus in these situations, even if our players are unable to calculate equilibrium strategies, their naïve optimising play will converge to an equilibrium and players' long term rewards are captured by the equilibrium payoffs.

2   Model

Our Multi-rate Threshold FlipThem game has two players, an attacker and defender, fighting for control over the set of n resources, $\mathcal{R} = \{\mathcal{R}_1, \ldots, \mathcal{R}_n\}$. Both players have buttons in front of each resource that when pressed will give them control over that specific resource. For each resource $\mathcal{R}_i$ the defender and attacker will play an exponential rate μ_i and λ_i, respectively, meaning that the times of moves for a player on a given resource will follow a Poisson Process with rate given by μ_i or λ_i. Using Markov Chain theory [14] we can construct explicit values for the proportion of time the each player is in control of resource $\mathcal{R}_i$ depending on their rates of play. This stationary distribution is given by $\pi^i = \left(\pi_0^i, \pi_1^i\right) = \frac{1}{\mu_i + \lambda_i}(\mu_i, \lambda_i)$, and indicates that the defender is in control of the resource $\mathcal{R}_i$ a proportion $\mu_i/(\lambda_i + \mu_i)$ of the time, and the attacker is in control a proportion $\lambda_i/(\lambda_i + \mu_i)$ of the time. We assume that each behaviour on each resource is independent of all the others, and hence the proportion of time that the attacker is control of a particular set of resources C, with the defender in control of the other resources, is simply given by the product of the individual resource proportions: $\prod_{i \in C} \frac{\lambda^i}{\lambda_i + \mu_i} \prod_{i \notin C} \frac{\mu^i}{\lambda^i + \mu_i}$.

At any point in time, the attacker will have compromised k resources, whilst the defender is in control of the remaining $n - k$ resources, for some k. In order for the attacker to have some gain, she must compromise t or more resources: The value t is called the threshold, as used in a number of existing threshold security situations discussed in the introduction. From a game theory point of view, whenever $k \geq t$ the attacker obtains benefit, whilst when $k < t$ the defender obtains benefit.

From this we can construct benefit functions for both players. For the attacker it is the proportion of time she is in control of a number of resources over the threshold, such that $k \geq t$, penalised by a cost for moving. For the defender it is the proportion of time that she is in control of at least $n - t + 1$ resources, again penalised by a cost of moving. Thus, the benefit functions for attacker and defender respectively are given by

$$\beta_D(\boldsymbol{\mu}, \boldsymbol{\lambda}) = 1 - \sum_{\substack{C \subseteq \{1,\dots,n\} \\ |C| \geq t}} \left[\prod_{i \in C} \frac{\lambda_i}{\lambda_i + \mu_i} \right] \cdot \left[\prod_{i \notin C} \frac{\mu_i}{\lambda_i + \mu_i} \right] - \sum_i d_i \cdot \mu_i$$

$$\beta_A(\boldsymbol{\mu}, \boldsymbol{\lambda}) = \sum_{\substack{C \subseteq \{1,\dots,n\} \\ |C| \geq t}} \left[\prod_{i \in C} \frac{\lambda_i}{\lambda_i + \mu_i} \right] \cdot \left[\prod_{i \notin C} \frac{\mu_i}{\lambda_i + \mu_i} \right] - \sum_i a_i \cdot \lambda_i$$

$$(1)$$

where the a_i and d_i are the (relative) move costs on resource i for attacker and defender, which are assumed fixed throughout the game, and $\boldsymbol{\mu}$ and $\boldsymbol{\lambda}$ are the vectors of rates over all resources for the defender and attacker, respectively, constrained to be non-negative. The benefit functions in (1) show that the game is non-zero-sum, meaning we are unable to use standard zero-sum results found in the literature [25].

3   Finding the Equilibria of Multi-rate (n, t)-FlipThem

We begin by finding the equilibria of the multi-rate version of the FlipThem game with n resources. This represents a more realistic scenario than previous studies, by allowing players to favour certain resources based on differential costs of attacking or defending, for example when a company owns multiple servers located in different areas and with different versions of operating systems. We want to find a stationary point or equilibrium of the two benefit functions (1) in terms of purely the costs of moving on each resource. This would mean both players are playing at a rate that maximises their own benefit function with respect to their opponents play and move costs. Thus, they would not wish to deviate from their current playing strategy or rates. This is known as a Nash Equilibrium [23]. Our challenge in this article, compared with previous works such as [20], is that neither benefit function is trivial to optimise simultaneously across the vector of rates.

3.1   Full Threshold: Multi-rate (n, n)-FlipThem

We begin with the full threshold case in which the attacker must control all resources in order to obtain some benefit. The algebra is easier in this case; the partial threshold version is addressed in Sect. 3.2. For this full threshold case, the general benefit functions (1) simplify to

$$\beta_D(\boldsymbol{\mu}, \boldsymbol{\lambda}) = 1 - \prod_{i=1}^{n} \frac{\lambda_i}{\mu_i + \lambda_i} - \sum_{i=1}^{n} d_i \cdot \mu_i$$

$$\beta_A(\boldsymbol{\mu}, \boldsymbol{\lambda}) = \prod_{i=1}^{n} \frac{\lambda_i}{\mu_i + \lambda_i} - \sum_{i=1}^{n} a_i \cdot \lambda_i.$$

$$(2)$$

Note that these benefit functions reduce to those of [20] if we set $\mu_i = \mu, \lambda_i = \lambda$, $a_i = \frac{a}{n}$ and $d_i = \frac{d}{n}$ for all i.

We start by finding the best response function of the defender, which is a function br^D mapping attacker rates $\boldsymbol{\lambda}$ to the set of all defender rates $\boldsymbol{\mu}$ which maximise defender payoff β_D when the attacker plays rates $\boldsymbol{\lambda}$. A necessary, though not sufficient, condition for $\boldsymbol{\mu}$ to maximise β_D is that each μ_i maximises β_D conditional on the other values of $\boldsymbol{\mu}$. Furthermore, maxima with respect to μ_i occur either when the partial derivative $\frac{\partial \beta_D}{\partial \mu_i}$ is 0, or at a boundary of the parameter space. Equating this partial derivative to zero to gives

$$\frac{\partial \beta_D}{\partial \mu_i} = 0 \Rightarrow -\prod_{j=1}^{n} \lambda_j + d_i \cdot (\lambda_i + \mu_i)^2 \cdot \prod_{j=1, j \neq i}^{n} (\mu_j + \lambda_j) = 0.$$

This is a quadratic in μ_i, meaning that fixing the defender's benefit function shown in (2) for all attacker rates $\boldsymbol{\lambda}$ and all defender rates μ_j where $j \neq i$, gives only two turning points. Since β_D decreases to negative infinity as μ_i gets large, the two candidates for a maximising μ_i are at the upper root of this equation, or at $\mu_i = 0$. A non-0 μ_i must therefore satisfy

$$\mu_i = -\lambda_i + \sqrt{\frac{\lambda_i}{d_i} \cdot \prod_{j=1, j \neq i}^{n} \frac{\lambda_j}{(\mu_j + \lambda_j)}}. \tag{3}$$

Of course, a μ_i satisfying this equation could be negative and thus inadmissible as a rate, but all we claim for now is that any non-zero μ_i must be of the this form.

We can use the same method in differentiating the attacker's benefit with respect to her rate λ_i for resource $\mathcal{R}_i$, equating this to zero and manipulating to give

$$\lambda_i = -\mu_i + \sqrt{\frac{\mu_i}{a_i} \cdot \prod_{j=1, j \neq i}^{n} \frac{\lambda_j}{(\mu_j + \lambda_j)}}. \tag{4}$$

Any Nash equilibrium in the interior of the strategy space (i.e. with strictly positive rates on all resources) must be a simultaneous solution of (3) and (4). Note that both equations can be rearranged to express $\lambda_i + \mu_i$ in terms of a square root, and then we can equate the square root terms to find that $\frac{\lambda_i}{\mu_i} = \frac{d_i}{a_i}$. Substituting this relationship back in to (3) and (4) gives

$$\lambda_i^* = \frac{d_i}{(a_i + d_i)^2} \cdot \prod_{\substack{j=1 \\ j \neq i}}^{n} \frac{d_j}{(a_j + d_j)}, \quad \mu_i^* = \frac{a_i}{(a_i + d_i)^2} \cdot \prod_{\substack{j=1 \\ j \neq i}}^{n} \frac{d_j}{(a_j + d_j)}. \tag{5}$$

If a company was reviewing its defensive systems and was able to calculate these equilibria, they can see the rate at which they'd have to move in order to defend their system optimally, under the assumption that the attacker is also playing optimally. (Of course, if the attacker was playing sub-optimally, the defender would be able to gain a larger pay off.) From these equilibria the parties are able to calculate the long run proportion of time each of their resources within the system would be compromised by looking at the stationary distribution shown in Sect. 2. From this information, the company can also calculate the value of the benefit functions for each player when playing these rates. This is useful in the real world as it can be used by companies to make strategic decisions on the design of their systems. We do this by substituting the two equilibria back into the benefit functions (2). We can express these rewards in terms of the ratio between the costs of each resource, $\rho_j = \frac{a_j}{d_j}$, giving the dimensionless expression

$$\beta_D^* = 1 - \prod_{i=1}^{n} \frac{1}{\rho_i + 1} \left[1 + \sum_{j=1}^{n} \frac{\rho_j}{\rho_j + 1} \right],$$

$$\beta_A^* = \prod_{i=1}^{n} \frac{1}{\rho_i + 1} \left[1 - \sum_{j=1}^{n} \frac{\rho_j}{\rho_j + 1} \right]. \tag{6}$$

We have expressed the payoffs to both players at the putative interior equilibrium. If this is an equilibrium, neither player will wish to deviate from these equilibrium rates. However we have thus far ignored the potential maximising μ_i at 0. While no individual μ_i or λ_i will deviate unilaterally to zero (recall that the partial derivatives have only two zeroes, and thus payoff decreases as μ_i decreases to zero), if several rates simultaneously switch the payoff to a player could increase. We therefore consider what happens when rates can switch to zero, starting with the attacker.

By considering the attacker's benefit function (2), we can see that if the attacker plays a zero rate on any resource, then in order to maximise the payoff, she should play zero rates on the rest of the system. In other words, she should drop out of the game and receive zero reward. Thus by comparing the attacker payoff in (6) to zero we can see quickly whether this is indeed a point at which the attacker will be content.

For the defender, things are more complicated. However, we can see from the benefit function (2) that a zero payoff by withdrawing from the game is again an option, and so we compare the equilibrium payoff (6) to zero as a partial check on whether the fixed point (5) is an equilibrium. We do not explicitly discount partial dropout of the defender, but note that by dropping out the defender is effectively reducing the game to a smaller number of servers, and hence should not have invested in the additional servers in the first place. Comparing the benefits in (6) to zero it is easy to see in this full threshold case that the defender's benefit β_D^* is always non-negative when playing (5) meaning dropping out is not an equilibrium point for the defender, whereas β_A^* can drop below 0. We use this to find a condition which must be satisfied for the point (5) to be an equilibrium. In particular, we require β_A^* in (6) to be positive, and therefore

$$1 - \sum_{j=1}^{n} \frac{\rho_j}{\rho_j + 1} > 0. \tag{7}$$

Thus, we have a condition (7) that, if satisfied, the attacker will not drop out of the game. If the condition is not satisfied, the attacker will prefer to drop out of the game entirely than to play at the interior equilibrium. Ensuring condition (7) is met can thus be viewed as an design criterium for system engineers when designing defensive systems.

3.2   Partial Threshold: Multi-rate (n, t)-FlipThem

So far we have extended the full threshold FlipThem game [18] by obtaining the equilibria of the benefit functions constructed from the proportion of time the attacker is in control of the whole system. In order to generalise this further, we return to our partial threshold case in which the attacker gains benefit from controlling only $t < n$ resources. Our general benefit functions for both players are written in (1); the analysis is analogous to methods demonstrated above in Sect. 3.1. In this (n, t)-threshold case, the analogous best response conditions to (3) and (4) are

$$\mu_i = -\lambda_i + \sqrt{\frac{\lambda_i \cdot S_i}{d_i}} \quad \text{and} \quad \lambda_i = -\mu_i + \sqrt{\frac{\mu_i S_i}{a_i}}, \tag{8}$$

where we have introduced S_i to denote

$$\sum_{\substack{C \subseteq \mathcal{A}_i \\ |C| \geq t}} \left[\prod_{j \in C} \frac{\lambda_j}{\lambda_j + \mu_j} \right] \cdot \left[\prod_{j \notin C} \frac{\mu_j}{\lambda_j + \mu_j} \right]$$

and $\mathcal{A}_i = \{1, \ldots, i-1, i+1, \ldots, n\}$. Interestingly, equating the square root terms results in the same relationship $\frac{\mu_i}{a_i} = \frac{\lambda_i}{d_i}$ as in Sect. 3.1. Finally, substituting this relationship back into the best response functions (8) gives us

$$\mu_i^* = \frac{a_i}{(a_i + d_i)^2} \cdot \sum_{\substack{C \subseteq \mathcal{A}_i \\ |C| \geq t}} \left[\prod_{j \in C} \frac{d_j}{a_j + d_j} \right] \cdot \left[\prod_{j \notin C} \frac{a_j}{a_j + d_j} \right],$$

$$\lambda_i^* = \frac{d_i}{(a_i + d_i)^2} \cdot \sum_{\substack{C \subseteq \mathcal{A}_i \\ |C| \geq t}} \left[\prod_{j \in C} \frac{d_j}{a_j + d_j} \right] \cdot \left[\prod_{j \notin C} \frac{a_j}{a_j + d_j} \right]. \tag{9}$$

As in Sect. 3.1, (9) is a Nash equilibrium for the game, unless one or other player can improve their payoff by dropping out of one or more resources. We can substitute these rates back into the players' benefit functions as we did in the full threshold case in Sect. 3.1 to check that the payoffs at this putative equilibrium are non-negative. However, the formulae become very complicated to write down explicitly in general and we leave this to Sect. 4, when we deal with specific examples. Note this also means we do not have a clean condition analogous to (7) to test whether (9) is an equilibrium.

4 Introducing Fictitious Play into Multi-rate (n, t)-FlipThem

While the equilibrium analysis above offers useful insight into the security game Multi-rate Threshold FlipThem, it can be viewed as an unrealistic model of real world play. In particular it is extremely unlikely the players have full knowledge of the payoff and move costs of their opponent, and therefore cannot calculate the equilibrium strategies. We now introduce game-theoretical learning, in which the only knowledge a player has of their opponent is the actions that they take. When the game is repeatedly played through time, players respond to their observations and attempt to improve their payoff. In this article we focus on a method of learning known as *fictitious play* [3,6,13].

We break the game up into periods of fixed length of time. At the end of period τ each player observes the number of times the button of each resource i was pressed by their opponent in that period. Denote by λ_i^τ and μ_i^τ the actual rate played by attacker and defender in period τ, and use $\widetilde{\lambda_i}^\tau$ and $\widetilde{\mu_i}^\tau$ to denote the number of button presses by the attacker and defender respectively, normalised by the length of the time interval. After $\mathcal{T}$ plays of the game, each player averages the observations he has made of the opponent, resulting in estimates for each resource

$$\widehat{\lambda_i^{\mathcal{T}}} = \frac{1}{\mathcal{T}} \sum_{\tau=1}^{\mathcal{T}} \widetilde{\lambda_i^\tau}, \qquad \widehat{\mu_i^{\mathcal{T}}} = \frac{1}{\mathcal{T}} \sum_{\tau=1}^{\mathcal{T}} \widetilde{\mu_i^\tau}.$$

The players select their rates for time period $\mathcal{T}+1$ by playing a best response to their estimates;

$$\mu_i^{\mathcal{T}+1} = \mathrm{br}_i^D(\widehat{\boldsymbol{\lambda}}^{\mathcal{T}}), \qquad \lambda_i^{\mathcal{T}+1} = \mathrm{br}_i^A(\widehat{\boldsymbol{\mu}}^{\mathcal{T}}).$$

where $\widehat{\boldsymbol{\mu}}^{\mathcal{T}}$ and $\widehat{\boldsymbol{\lambda}}^{\mathcal{T}}$ are the defender and attacker's vector of rates played on each resource. If it were the case that opponent rates were constant, the averaging of observations over time would be an optimal estimation of those rates. Since both players are learning, the rates are not constant, and averaging uniformly over time does not result in statistically optimal prediction. However lack of a better informed model of rate evolution means that averaging is retained as the standard mechanism in fictitious play; see [21,34] for attempts to move beyond this assumption.

This fictitious play process is described in Algorithm 1, where we see the simplicity of the learning process and the sparsity of the information required by the players. The only challenging step is in calculating the best response function; as observed in Sect. 3 the best response of each player is not in general a simple analytical function of the rates of the opponent. From the defender's point of view we consider all subsets of the resources; setting the rates of these resources to zero, and solving (8) for the non-zero rates, we find a putative best response; the set of rates with the highest payoff given the fixed belief $\widehat{\boldsymbol{\lambda}}^{\mathcal{T}}$ is

1 Set *maximum* periods to be played;
2 Randomly assign move costs for each player;
3 Randomly choose initial starting rates for both players;
4 One period is played;
5 **while** *Number of periods has not reached the maximum* **do**
6   Each player receives last period's observation of their opponent's play;
7   Each player averages their opponent's history to form a belief;
8   Each player uses their *best response function* to calculate rate for this
      period;
9   Each player plays this rate;
10 **end**

Algorithm 1. Fictitious Play algorithm for multi-rate (n, t)-FlipThem

the best response. The attacker's best response is calculated analogously. An interesting question, which we address, is whether this simple learning process converges to the equilibria calculated previously in Sect. 3.

The process we have defined is a discrete time stochastic process. It is in actual fact a stochastic fictitious play process [12]; since the number of button presses in a period is Poisson with expected value the played rate multiplied by the length of the time interval, the observations can be seen to satisfy

$$\widetilde{\mu}_i^{T+1} = \mathrm{br}_i^D(\widehat{\boldsymbol{\lambda}}^T) + M_{\mu,i}^{T+1}, \qquad \widetilde{\lambda}_i^{T+1} = \mathrm{br}_i^A(\widehat{\boldsymbol{\mu}}^T) + M_{\lambda,i}^{T+1},$$

where $\mathbb{E}(M_{\cdot,\cdot}^{\tau+1}|\mathcal{F}^\tau) = 0$ if $\mathcal{F}^\tau$ denotes the history of the process up to time τ. The methods of [3] then apply directly to show that the convergence (or otherwise) of the discrete stochastic process is governed by the continuous deterministic differential equations

$$\frac{\mathrm{d}\boldsymbol{\lambda}}{\mathrm{d}t} = \mathrm{br}(\boldsymbol{\mu}) - \boldsymbol{\lambda}, \qquad \frac{\mathrm{d}\boldsymbol{\mu}}{\mathrm{d}t} = \mathrm{br}(\boldsymbol{\lambda}) - \boldsymbol{\mu}. \tag{10}$$

In standard fictitious play analyses, one might show that solutions of (10) are globally convergent to the equilibrium set. This is commonly achievable only in some classes of games, and since we do not have a zero-sum game we have not been able to show the required global convergence of (10).

4.1 Original FlipIt

The game of FlipIt can be considered a special case of our game of multi-rate (n, t)-FlipThem, seen by setting $n = t = 1$. This has the advantage that the best responses can be written in closed form, and we can use (10) to set up a two dimensional ordinary differential equation in terms of the players' rates and time. We start by writing the benefit functions for this special case

$$\beta_D(\mu, \lambda) = 1 - \frac{\lambda}{\mu + \lambda} - d\mu, \qquad \beta_A(\mu, \lambda) = \frac{\lambda}{\mu + \lambda} - a\lambda. \tag{11}$$

Differentiating the players' benefit functions (11) in terms of their respective resource rates and then solving for these gives the best response functions

$$\mathrm{br}^{D}(\lambda) = \left(-\lambda + \sqrt{\frac{\lambda}{d}}\right)^{+}, \qquad \mathrm{br}^{A}(\mu) = \left(-\mu + \sqrt{\frac{\mu}{a}}\right)^{+}$$

where $(x)^{+} = \max(x, 0)$. The ordinary differential equation (10) becomes

$$\frac{\mathrm{d}\lambda}{\mathrm{d}t} = \left(-\mu + \sqrt{\frac{\mu}{a}}\right)^{+} - \lambda, \qquad \frac{\mathrm{d}\mu}{\mathrm{d}t} = \left(-\lambda + \sqrt{\frac{\lambda}{d}}\right)^{+} - \mu. \qquad (12)$$

This is a two dimensional ordinary differential equation in terms of the players' rates and time. The plot of the phase portrait of this is shown in Fig. 1. Where we have used $d = 0.1, a = 0.3$ as the move costs. It easy to see that the arrows demonstrating the direction of the rates over time converge upon a single point. This point is the equilibrium we can calculate easily from the more general equilibria derived in Sect. 3.2. We can also use Algorithm 1 to plot trajectories of the system in order to view convergence of the system; the convergence is monotonic and uninteresting so we omit the plots.

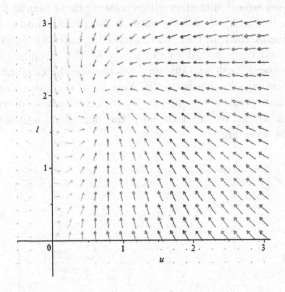

Fig. 1. Phase portrait of (12) with $d = 0.1, a = 0.3$

4.2 (n, t)-FlipThem

A multi-resource example in which we retain one rate per player (as opposed to one rate per resource for each player) is given by the situation in [18, 20];

each player chooses a rate at which to play all resources. Whilst this allows us to retain a two-dimensional system when considering the multiple resource case, unfortunately obtaining explicit best response functions is extremely difficult. Therefore, we revert to Algorithm 1 using time intervals of length 100; we fix this time interval for all further experiments in this article.

As in those previous works, we consider the stationary distribution of the system, with the defender playing with rate μ and attacker rate λ. This results in a stationary distribution for the whole system, given by

$$
\pi = \frac{1}{(\mu + \lambda)^n} \left(\mu^n, n \cdot \lambda \cdot \mu^{n-1}, \ldots, \binom{n}{k} \cdot \mu^{n-k} \cdot \lambda^k, \ldots, n \cdot \mu \cdot \lambda^{n-1}, \lambda^n \right),
$$

where the states correspond to the number of compromised resources, ranging from 0 to n. Benefit functions for both players are given by

$$
\beta_D(\mu, \lambda) = 1 - \sum_{i=t}^{n} \pi_i - d \cdot \mu = 1 - \frac{1}{(\mu + \lambda)^n} \cdot \sum_{i=t}^{n} \binom{n}{i} \cdot \mu^{n-i} \cdot \lambda^i - d \cdot \mu,
$$

$$
\beta_A(\mu, \lambda) = \sum_{i=t}^{n} \pi_i - a \cdot \lambda = \frac{1}{(\mu + \lambda)^n} \cdot \sum_{i=t}^{n} \binom{n}{i} \cdot \mu^{n-i} \cdot \lambda^i - a \cdot \lambda,
$$

and best responses are calculated by differentiating these benefit functions, as in [20] and Sect. 3. In Fig. 2 we plot the rate of the attacker and defender respectively by applying Algorithm 1 to random starting rates for both players, with $(3, 2)$-threshold and costs $a = 0.65$ and $d = 0.5$. The straight horizontal lines represents the players' Nash equilibrium rates that can be calculated as a special case of the general equilibrium from (9). Note that we have chosen these costs in order to produce positive benefits for both players whilst playing the calculated Nash equilibrium. We see that both the defender's and attacker's mean rate converges to these lines.

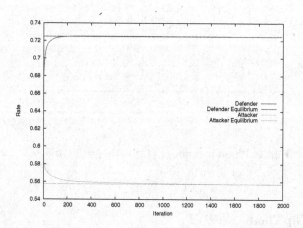

Fig. 2. Mean of the defender's and attacker's rate with $(3, 2)$-threshold and ratio $\rho = \frac{a}{d} = 1.3$.

4.3   Multi-rate (n, t)-FlipThem

Finally, we come to the most general case of the paper, Multi-rate (n, t)-FlipThem. As observed previously, depending on the player's belief of their opponents rates on each resource, they may choose to drop out of playing on a certain resource, or perhaps even all of them. Our best response functions must iterate through all possibilities of setting the resource rates to zero and chooses the configuration with the highest benefit as the best response. This solution is then used as $\mu^{\mathcal{T}+1}$ or $\lambda^{\mathcal{T}+1}$ for the following period $\mathcal{T} + 1$.

We want to find a condition such that we can gain some insight as to whether in this most complicated setting our iterative learning rule will converge to the equilibria we calculated analytically in Sect. 3.2. We experimented with multiple combinations of n and t, randomly simulating costs of both players. From these empirical results, we observe that convergence occurs whenever the internal fixed point (9) results in non-negative benefits to both players.

Specific Case ($n = 3$, $t = 2$): In order to illustrate the outcomes of our fictitious play algorithm we specify our threshold $(n, t) = (3, 2)$, and choose two representative cases of our randomly simulated examples. These particular examples were selected for ease of display, allowing us to illustrate their properties of convergence (or divergence) clearly on just one figure. The first, when the benefits are positive and the internal equilibrium is not ruled out, we term 'success'. The second is an example in which the internal fixed point is not an equilibrium, and we term this case 'failure'.

Success: Our first example is with ratios $(\rho_1, \rho_2, \rho_3) \approx (0.7833, 0.7856, 0.7023)$ and attacker costs $(a_1, a_2, a_3) \approx (0.6237, 0.5959, 0.5149)$. Thus, the benefit values at equilibrium are $\beta_D^* \approx 0.0359$ and $\beta_A^* \approx 0.2429$. Since we have positive payoff for both players we expect convergence of the learning algorithm. This is exactly what we observe in Fig. 3; convergence of rates to the lines representing the equilibria calculated in Sect. 3.2.

Failure: Our second example shows a lack of convergence when conditions are not met. Therefore, we choose ratios to be $(\rho_1, \rho_2, \rho_3) \approx (0.5152, 0.5074, 0.5010)$ and attacker costs $(a_1, a_2, a_3) \approx (0.2597, 0.2570, 0.2555)$. This gives 'equilibrium' benefits for the defender and attacker of $\beta_D^* \approx -0.0354$ and $\beta_A^* \approx 0.4368$. The defender's benefit in this situation is negative, meaning we expect a lack of convergence. Figure 4 shows the development of both players' rates over time. We can see the rates do not approach anywhere near the equilibrium. Intuitively, this makes sense as the defender will not choose to end up playing in a game in which she receives negative payoff when she can drop out of the game completely in order to receive zero payoff.

We can see evidence of this dropping out in Fig. 5, which shows the rates the defender is actually playing on the resource (rather than the mean over time). The defender has certain periods where she drops out of the game entirely. The attacker's mean rates then start to drop until a point when the defender decides to re-enter the game.

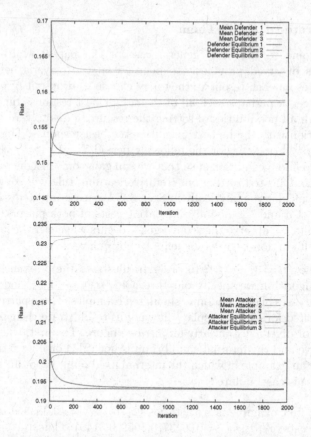

Fig. 3. Mean of the defender's rates (top) and attacker's rates (bottom) on all resources with $(3,2)$-threshold and ratios $(\rho_1, \rho_2, \rho_3) \approx (0.7833, 0.7856, 0.7023)$

To see a reason for this volatility, Fig. 6 shows the defender's payoff surface for nearby attacker strategies on either side of a 'dropout' event from Fig. 5. We fix the defender's rate on resource 1 and plot the benefit surface as the rates on resources 2 and 3 vary. We also plot the plane of zero reward. It's easy to observe that the maximum of this reward surface is above 0 in the left hand plot, but a small perturbation of the attacker rates pushes the maximal defender benefit below zero in the right hand plot, thus forcing the defender to drop out entirely. We conjecture that as the ratios decrease (and therefore become more costly for the defender) the defender drops out of the game more often within this learning environment.

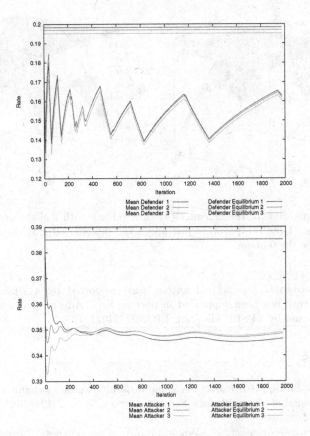

Fig. 4. Mean of the defender's rates (top) and attacker's rates (bottom) on all resources with $(3,2)$-threshold and ratios $(\rho_1, \rho_2, \rho_3) \approx (0.5152, 0.5074, 0.5010)$.

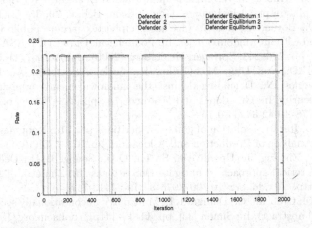

Fig. 5. Defender's actual rates on all resources with $(3,2)$-threshold and ratios $(\rho_1, \rho_2, \rho_3) \approx (0.5152, 0.5074, 0.5010)$.

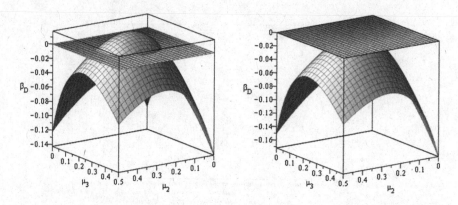

Fig. 6. Two snapshots of the defender's reward surface with a slight perturbation in attackers rates. (Left) the payoff is just above the 0-plane. (Right) the whole payoff surface is below the 0-plane.

Acknowledgements. The second author was supported by a studentship from GCHQ. This work has been supported in part by ERC Advanced Grant ERC-2015-AdG-IMPaCT and by EPSRC via grant EP/N021940/1.

References

1. Bedi, H.S., Shiva, S.G., Roy, S.: A game inspired defense mechanism against distributed denial of service attacks. Secur. Commun. Netw. **7**(12), 2389–2404 (2014). doi:10.1002/sec.949
2. Ben-Or, M., Goldwasser, S., Wigderson, A.: Completeness theorems for non-cryptographic fault-tolerant distributed computation (extended abstract). In: Simon [33], pp. 1–10. http://doi.acm.org/10.1145/62212.62213
3. Benaim, M., Hirsch, M.W.: Mixed equilibria and dynamical systems arising from fictitious play in perturbed games. Games Econ. Behav. **29**, 36–72 (1999)
4. Boneh, D., Boyen, X., Halevi, S.: Chosen ciphertext secure public key threshold encryption without random oracles. In: Pointcheval, D. (ed.) CT-RSA 2006. LNCS, vol. 3860, pp. 226–243. Springer, Heidelberg (2006). doi:10.1007/11605805_15
5. Bowers, K.D., van Dijk, M., Griffin, R., Juels, A., Oprea, A., Rivest, R.L., Triandopoulos, N.: Defending against the unknown enemy: applying FLIPIT to system security. In: Grossklags and Walrand [15], pp. 248–263. http://dx.doi.org/10.1007/978-3-642-34266-0_15
6. Brown, G.: Iterative solution of games by fictitious play. In: Koopmans, T.C. (ed.) Activity Analysis of Production and Allocation, pp. 374–376 (1951)
7. Çeker, H., Zhuang, J., Upadhyaya, S., La, Q.D., Soong, B.-H.: Deception-based game theoretical approach to mitigate DoS attacks. In: Zhu et al. [36], pp. 18–38 (2016). http://dx.doi.org/10.1007/978-3-319-47413-7_2
8. Chaum, D., Crépeau, C., Damgård, I.: Multiparty unconditionally secure protocols (extended abstract). In: Simon [33], pp. 11–19. http://doi.acm.org/10.1145/62212.62214
9. Desmedt, Y.: Threshold cryptography. Eur. Trans. Telecommun. **5**(4), 449–458 (1994). doi:10.1002/ett.4460050407

10. van Dijk, M., Juels, A., Oprea, A., Rivest, R.L.: FLIPIT: the game of "stealthy takeover". J. Cryptol. **26**(4), 655–713 (2013). doi:10.1007/s00145-012-9134-5
11. Farhang, S., Grossklags, J.: FlipLeakage: a game-theoretic approach to protect against stealthy attackers in the presence of information leakage. In: Zhu et al. [36], pp. 195–214. http://dx.doi.org/10.1007/978-3-319-47413-7_12
12. Fudenberg, D., Kreps, D.: Learning mixed equilibria. Games Econ. Behav. **5**, 320–367 (1993)
13. Fudenberg, D., Levine, D.K.: The Theory of Learning in Games, 1st edn. The MIT Press, Cambridge (1998)
14. Grimmett, G., Stirzaker, D.: Probability and Random Processes, 3rd edn. Oxford University Press, Oxford (2001)
15. Grossklags, J., Walrand, J.C. (eds.): GameSec 2012. LNCS, vol. 7638. Springer, Heidelberg (2012). doi:10.1007/978-3-642-34266-0
16. Hota, A.R., Clements, A.A., Sundaram, S., Bagchi, S.: Optimal and game-theoretic deployment of security investments in interdependent assets. In: Zhu et al. [36], pp. 101–113. http://dx.doi.org/10.1007/978-3-319-47413-7_6
17. Hu, P., Li, H., Fu, H., Cansever, D., Mohapatra, P.: Dynamic defense strategy against advanced persistent threat with insiders. In: 2015 IEEE Conference on Computer Communications (INFOCOM), pp. 747–755. IEEE (2015)
18. Laszka, A., Horvath, G., Felegyhazi, M., Buttyán, L.: FlipThem: modeling targeted attacks with FLIPIT for multiple resources. In: Poovendran and Saad [29], pp. 175–194. http://dx.doi.org/10.1007/978-3-319-12601-2_10
19. Laszka, A., Johnson, B., Grossklags, J.: Mitigating covert compromises. In: Chen, Y., Immorlica, N. (eds.) WINE 2013. LNCS, vol. 8289, pp. 319–332. Springer, Heidelberg (2013). doi:10.1007/978-3-642-45046-4_26
20. Leslie, D., Sherfield, C., Smart, N.P.: Threshold FlipThem: when the winner does not need to take all. In: Khouzani, M.H.R., Panaousis, E., Theodorakopoulos, G. (eds.) GameSec 2015. LNCS, vol. 9406, pp. 74–92. Springer, Cham (2015). doi:10.1007/978-3-319-25594-1_5
21. Leslie, D.S., Collins, E.J.: Generalized weakened fictitious play. Games Econ. Behav. **56**, 285–298 (2006)
22. Moayedi, B.Z., Azgomi, M.A.: A game theoretic framework for evaluation of the impacts of hackers diversity on security measures. Reliab. Eng. Syst. Saf. **99**, 45–54 (2012). doi:10.1016/j.ress.2011.11.001
23. Nash, J.: Non-cooperative games. Ann. Math. **54**, 286–295 (1951)
24. Nochenson, A., Grossklags, J.: A behavioral investigation of the FLIPIT game. In: Proceedings of the 12th Workshop on the Economics of Information Security (WEIS) (2013)
25. Osborne, M., Rubinstein, A.: A Course in Game Theory. MIT Press, Cambridge (1994)
26. Panaousis, E., Fielder, A., Malacaria, P., Hankin, C., Smeraldi, F.: Cybersecurity games and investments: a decision support approach. In: Poovendran and Saad [29], pp. 266–286. http://dx.doi.org/10.1007/978-3-319-12601-2_15
27. Pawlick, J., Farhang, S., Zhu, Q.: Flip the cloud: cyber-physical signaling games in the presence of advanced persistent threats. In: Khouzani, M.H.R., Panaousis, E., Theodorakopoulos, G. (eds.) GameSec 2015. LNCS, vol. 9406, pp. 289–308. Springer, Cham (2015). doi:10.1007/978-3-319-25594-1_16
28. Pham, V., Cid, C.: Are we compromised? Modelling security assessment games. In: Grossklags and Walrand [15], pp. 234–247. http://dx.doi.org/10.1007/978-3-642-34266-0_14

29. Poovendran, R., Saad, W. (eds.): GameSec 2014. LNCS, vol. 8840. Springer, Cham (2014). doi:10.1007/978-3-319-12601-2

30. Rass, S., Zhu, Q.: GADAPT: a sequential game-theoretic framework for designing defense-in-depth strategies against advanced persistent threats. In: Zhu et al. [36], pp. 314–326. http://dx.doi.org/10.1007/978-3-319-47413-7_18

31. Shamir, A.: How to share a secret. Commun. ACM **22**(11), 612–613 (1979). doi:10.1145/359168.359176

32. Shoup, V.: Practical threshold signatures. In: Preneel, B. (ed.) EUROCRYPT 2000. LNCS, vol. 1807, pp. 207–220. Springer, Heidelberg (2000). doi:10.1007/3-540-45539-6_15

33. Simon, J. (ed.): Proceedings of the 20th Annual ACM Symposium on Theory of Computing, Chicago, Illinois, USA, 2–4 May 1988. ACM (1988)

34. Smyrnakis, M., Leslie, D.S.: Dynamic opponent modelling in fictitious play. Comput. J. **53**(9), 1344–1359 (2010)

35. Zhou, Z., Bambos, N., Glynn, P.: Dynamics on linear influence network games under stochastic environments. In: Zhu et al. [36], pp. 114–126. http://dx.doi.org/10.1007/978-3-319-47413-7_7

36. Zhu, Q., Alpcan, T., Panaousis, E., Tambe, M., Casey, W. (eds.): GameSec 2016. LNCS, vol. 9996. Springer, Cham (2016). doi:10.1007/978-3-319-47413-7

Practical Keystroke Timing Attacks
in Sandboxed JavaScript

Moritz Lipp[✉], Daniel Gruss, Michael Schwarz, David Bidner,
Clémentine Maurice, and Stefan Mangard

Graz University of Technology, Graz, Austria
moritz.lipp@iaik.tugraz.at

Abstract. Keystrokes trigger interrupts which can be detected through
software side channels to reconstruct keystroke timings. Keystroke timing attacks use these side channels to infer typed words, passphrases, or
create user fingerprints. While keystroke timing attacks are considered
harmful, they typically require native code execution to exploit the side
channels and, thus, may not be practical in many scenarios.

   In this paper, we present the first generic keystroke timing attack
in sandboxed JavaScript, targeting arbitrary other tabs, processes and
programs. This violates same-origin policy, HTTPS security model, and
process isolation. Our attack is based on the interrupt-timing side channel which has previously only been exploited using native code. In contrast to previous attacks, we do not require the victim to run a malicious
binary or interact with the malicious website. Instead, our attack runs in
a background tab, possibly in a minimized browser window, displaying a
malicious online advertisement. We show that we can observe the exact
inter-keystroke timings for a user's PIN or password, infer URLs entered
by the user, and distinguish different users time-sharing a computer. Our
attack works on personal computers, laptops and smartphones, with different operating systems and browsers. As a solution against all known
JavaScript timing attacks, we propose a fine-grained permission model.

Keywords: JavaScript · Side channel · Interrupt · Keystroke ·
Fingerprint

1   Introduction

Keystroke timing attacks are side-channel attacks where an adversary tries to
determine the exact timestamps of user key presses. Keystroke timings con-
vey sensitive information that has been exploited in previous work to recover
words and sentences [39,49]. More recently, microarchitectural attacks have been
demonstrated to obtain keystroke timings [15,25,32,36] in native code. In particular, the interrupt-timing side channel leaks highly accurate keystroke timings
if an adversary has access to a cycle-accurate timing source [36].

   JavaScript is the most widely used scripting language and supported by virtually any browser today. It is commonly used to create interactive website

© Springer International Publishing AG 2017
S.N. Foley et al. (Eds.): ESORICS 2017, Part II, LNCS 10493, pp. 191–209, 2017.
DOI: 10.1007/978-3-319-66399-9_11

elements and enrich the user interface. However, it does not provide access to native instructions, files, or system services. Still, the ability to execute arbitrary code in the JavaScript sandbox inside a website can also be exploited to perform attacks on website visitors, e.g., timing attacks [12].

JavaScript-based timing attacks were first presented by Felten and Schneider [12], showing that access times to website elements are lower if a website has recently been visited. Besides attacks on the browser history [12,21,46], there have also been more fine-grained attacks recovering information on the user or other websites visited by the user [8,16,22,40,41]. Vila and Köpf [43] showed that shared event loops in Google Chrome leak timing information on other browser tabs that share worker processes responsible for rendering or I/O.

Previous work has shown that timing side channels which are introduced on the hardware level or the operating system level, can be exploited from JavaScript. Gruss et al. [14] demonstrated page deduplication attacks, Oren et al. [30] demonstrated cache attacks to infer mouse movements and network activity, and Booth [6] fingerprinted websites based on CPU utilization. Gras et al. [13] showed that accurate timing information in JavaScript can be exploited to defeat address-space layout randomization. Schwarz et al. [37] presented a DRAM timing covert channel in JavaScript.

In this paper, we present the first generic keystroke timing attack in sandboxed JavaScript. Our attack is based on the interrupt-timing side channel which has previously only been exploited using native code. We show that this side channel can be exploited from JavaScript without access to native instructions. Based on instruction throughput variations within equally-sized time windows, we can detect hardware interrupts, such as keyboard inputs. In contrast to previous side-channel attacks in JavaScript, our channel provides a more accurate signal for keystrokes, allowing us to observe exact inter-keystroke timings. We demonstrate how this information can be used to infer URLs entered by the user, and distinguish different users time-sharing a computer.

Our attack is generic and can be applied to any system which uses interrupts for user input. We show that our attack code works both on personal computers and laptops, as well as modern smartphones. An adversary can target other browser tabs and browser processes, as well as arbitrary other programs, circumventing same-origin policy, HTTPS security model, and both operating system and browser-level process isolation. With a low impact on the overall system and browser performance, and a code footprint of less than 256 bytes of code, the attack can easily be hidden in modern JavaScript frameworks and malicious online advertisements. Our attack code utilizes new JavaScript features to run in the background, in a background tab, or on a locked phone. Hence, we can spy on the PIN entry used to unlock the phone.

To verify our results, we implemented our attack also in Java without access to native instructions and only low-accuracy timers. We demonstrate that the same timing measurements as in JavaScript can be observed in our Java implementation with a lower noise level. Furthermore, we demonstrate that in a cross-browser covert channel two websites can communicate through network interrupts. These observations clearly show that the source of the throughput differences is caused by the hardware and not specific software implementations.

Our attack works in two phases, an online phase running in JavaScript, and an offline phase running on the adversary's machine. In the offline phase, we employ machine learning techniques to build accurate classifiers trained on keystroke traces gathered in the online phase. These classifiers enable an adversary to infer which website a victim opens and to fingerprint different users time-sharing the same physical machine (e.g., a family sharing a computer).

Our results show that side-channel attacks are a fundamental problem that is not restricted to local adversaries. We propose a fine-grained permission model as a solution against all known JavaScript timing attacks. The browser restricts access to specific features and prompts the user to grant permissions per domain.

Our key contributions are:

- We show the first generic keystroke timing attack in JavaScript, embedded in a website, targeting arbitrary other tabs, processes and programs.
- We demonstrate our attack on personal computers, laptops and smartphones, with different browsers and operating systems.
- We demonstrate that our attack can obtain the exact inter-keystroke timings for a user's PIN or password, infer URLs entered by the user, and distinguish different users time-sharing a computer based on their input.

Outline. The remaining paper is organized as follows. In Sect. 2, we provide background. We describe our attack in Sect. 3. In Sect. 4, we present the performance of our attack on personal computers and smartphones. We discuss countermeasures in Sect. 5. Finally, we conclude in Sect. 6.

2   Background

2.1   Keystroke Timing Attacks

Keystroke timing attacks acquire accurate timestamps of keystrokes for input sequences. These keystroke timestamps depend on several factors such as bigrams, syllables, words, keyboard layout, and typing experience [33]. An adversary can exploit these timing characteristics to learn information about the user or the user input. Existing attacks use machine learning to infer typed sentences or recover passphrases [38,39,49]. Idrus et al. [19] showed that key press and key release events can be used to fingerprint users.

The Linux operating system exposes information that allows compiling accurate traces of keystroke timings [39,49]. Zhang and Wang [49] demonstrated that instruction and stack pointer, interrupt statistics, and network packet statistics can be used as side channels for keystroke timings. While Song et al. [39] demonstrated that SSH leaks inter-keystroke timings in interactive mode, Hogye et al. [17] showed that network latency in networks with significant traffic conceals these inter-keystroke timings in practice. Ali et al. [3] showed that it is possible to detect keystrokes and classify the typed keys using Wi-Fi Signals. Jana and Shmatikov [20] showed that CPU usage is a much more reliable side channel for keystroke timings than the instruction pointer, or the stack pointer.

Algorithm 1. Online phase of an interrupt-timing attack

input : *threshold*
now ← get_timestamp();
while *true* **do**
 last ← *now*;
 now ← get_timestamp();
 if *now* − *last* > *threshold* **then**
  report(*now, diff*);

Diao et al. [11] demonstrated high-precision keystroke timing attacks based on /proc/interrupts. Mehrnezhad et al. [27] used the JavaScript sensor API to detect touch, hold, scroll, and zoom actions on mobile devices using built-in sensors such as accelerometer and gyroscope.

Cache attacks have also been used to obtain keystroke timings. In a cache attack, the adversary observes effects of the victim's operation on the cache and can then deduce what operations the victim performed. Ristenpart et al. [34] demonstrated a keystroke timing attack using a Prime+Probe cache attack. Gruss et al. [15] demonstrated that Flush+Reload cache attacks can be used for keystroke timing attacks. Similarly, Pessl et al. [32] showed a keystroke timing attack on the Firefox address bar using the DRAM as a side channel.

Recently, it was shown that keystroke interrupt timings can be obtained in a timing attack which continuously measures differences between consecutive rdtsc calls [36]. However, this is not possible if the adversary only controls a website that is visited by the victim. Sandboxed JavaScript running on a website cannot utilize any native instructions such as rdtsc.

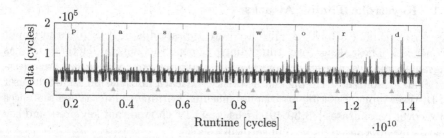

Fig. 1. Native interrupt-timing attack: The difference between consecutive timestamps is measured while a sentence is typed. Every keystroke leads to a significant deviation as the measuring program is interrupted by the keyboard.

2.2 Interrupt-Timing Attacks

Interrupt-timing attacks have recently been demonstrated in native code to recover keystroke timings [36]. The basic idea of interrupt-timing attacks is to continuously acquire a high-resolution timestamp and to monitor differences between subsequent timestamps, *i.e.*, how much time has passed since the last measurement, as outlined in Algorithm 1. Significant differences occur whenever the measuring process is interrupted. The more time the operating system consumes to handle the interrupt, the higher the measured differences are. Especially interrupts triggered by I/O devices—such as keyboards—lead to clearly visible peaks in the measured trace. Figure 1 shows a trace from a native attack implementation while a user typed in a sentence. The exact timestamp where the user pressed a key is clearly visible and can be distinguished from other events. However, the trace does not only contain keyboard interrupts and, thus, allows spying on user input but also on every other event that causes one or more interrupts, e.g., network traffic or redraw events. An adversary can filter relevant peaks by means of post-processing algorithms to monitor entered keystrokes.

2.3   Timing Attacks in Sandboxed JavaScript

JavaScript has evolved to be the most widely supported scripting language, notably because it is supported by virtually every modern browser. With highly-optimized just-in-time compilation, modern JavaScript engines deliver a performance that can compete with native code implementations. The timestamp counter provides a cycle-accurate timestamp to user programs in native code, but it is not accessible from JavaScript. Instead, JavaScript provides the High Resolution Time API [45] (`performance.now`) for sub-millisecond timestamps.

Based on this timing interface, various attacks have been demonstrated. Van Goethem et al. [41] were able to extract private data from users by measuring the differences in the execution time from cross-origin resources. Stone [40] showed that the optimization in SVG filters introduced timing side channels. He showed that this side channel can be used to extract pixel information from iframes. Booth [6] fingerprinted websites based on CPU utilization—interfering with the execution time of a benchmark function—when loading and rendering the page.

Gruss et al. [14] showed that page deduplication timing attacks can be performed in JavaScript to determine which websites the user has currently opened. Oren et al. [30] showed that it is possible to mount cache attacks in JavaScript. They demonstrated how to perform Prime+Probe attacks in the browser to build cache covert channels but also to spy on the user's mouse movements and network activity through the cache. This attack caused all major browsers to decrease the resolution of the `performance.now` method [1,7,10]. The W3C standard now recommends a resolution of 5 µs while the Tor project reduced the resolution in the Tor browser to a more conservative value of 100 ms [28]. Gras et al. [13] showed that accurate timing information in JavaScript can be exploited to defeat address-space layout randomization. Vila and Köpf [43] showed that shared event loops in Google Chrome leak timing information about other browser tabs sharing worker processes for rendering and I/O operations. They exploit this side channel to identify web pages, to build a covert communication channel, and to infer inter-keystroke timings.

Recently, several works investigated timing primitives in JavaScript that allow recovering highly accurate timestamps [13, 24, 37]. We use these timing primitives to build highly accurate keystroke timing attacks in sandboxed JavaScript.

3   Sandboxed Keystroke Timing Attacks Without High-Resolution Timers

Our attack follows the same idea as interrupt-timing attacks in native code [36]. It consists of an online phase where timing traces are acquired on a victim machine and an offline phase for post-processing and evaluation.

Online Phase. In the online phase of our attack, we run an interrupt-timing attack in sandboxed JavaScript. Interrupt-timing attacks have only minimal requirements, most importantly access to the x86 `rdtsc` instruction [36]. Consequently, keystroke interrupt-timing attacks have only been demonstrated in native code. We face several challenges to perform keystroke interrupt-timing attacks from remote websites, as JavaScript can neither execute this instruction nor run endless loops on websites.

There is no high-resolution timestamp available in JavaScript, as the resolution of `performance.now` is limited to 5 µs to mitigate side-channel attacks [45]. Therefore, we implement a counter to simulate a monotonic clock by constantly incrementing a value [13, 24, 37, 47]. The number of increments, *i.e.*, the instruction throughput, is proportional to the time the counter function is scheduled. Thus, any interrupt reduces the instruction throughput and, therefore, leads to a lower number of increments within a fixed time frame. Consequently, we can read the counter value at fixed time intervals and deduce from the number of increments since the last interval whether the counter function was interrupted.

As JavaScript is based on a single-threaded event loop, browsers usually do not allow websites to use endless loops and inform the user when detecting such a construct. The usual solution is to either use `setTimeout` or `setInterval` to constantly trigger execution of the loop body after a specified number of milliseconds have passed. However, these functions enforce a minimum pause of 4 ms before scheduling the same code again, yielding a resolution that is significantly lower than the resolution of `performance.now`.

To work around this limitation, we introduce a new variant of previously published timing primitives [13, 24, 37] called cooperative endless-loop slicing. The idea is to slice the endless loop into smaller finite loops where every loop slice has an execution time of approximately 4 ms. Before running this loop, we schedule the next loop slice using `setTimeout` with a timeout of 4 ms. Thus, in the optimal case, the next slice of the endless loop is executed immediately after the current slice, giving the impression of an actual endless loop. However, as higher priority events, such as user inputs, can still be processed between the loop slices, the browser is responsive and will not stop the endless loop.

Algorithm 2. Interrupt-timing attack implemented in JavaScript

```
Function measure_time(id):
    setTimeout(measure_time, 0, id + 1);
    counter ← 0;
    begin ← window.performance.now();
    while (window.performance.now() - begin) < 5 do
        counter ← counter + 1;
    publish(id, counter);
```

Algorithm 2 illustrates how we use this construct to continuously schedule our counter to obtain continuous timing traces.

The instruction throughput per loop slice, *i.e.*, the counter increments, varies depending on how often and how long the thread was interrupted during this loop slice. Within one loop slice, we achieve on average 72764 increments of the counter, resulting in a resolution of approximately 69 ns ($\sigma = 3$ ns, $n = 4000$) on an Intel i5-6200U. This resolution is three orders of magnitude higher than the result of Vila and Köpf [43] who achieved a resolution of only 25 µs to 100 µs. On ARM, we achieve on average 5038 increments on the Google Nexus 5 and 17 454 increments on the OnePlus 3T, yielding a resolution of 994 ns ($\sigma = 55$ ns, $n = 4000$) and 287 ns ($\sigma = 4$ ns, $n = 4000$) respectively.

A further limitation of JavaScript is that once the user switches the tab or minimizes the browser, the default minimum timeout value of 4 ms is reduced to 1000 ms. Increasing the loop slices to 1000 ms is not practical since it would make the browser unresponsive again. In order to circumvent this issue, we utilize the Web Worker API which explicitly allows JavaScript code to be executed in the background [44]. We discovered that the minimum timeout is not reduced for web workers and we can still measure interrupt timings with a high frequency. This allows us to monitor keystrokes when the victim is visiting a different page or even a different application.

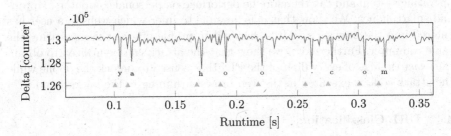

Fig. 2. Interrupt-timing attack in JavaScript: The lower peaks indicate that the measured script has been interrupted, allowing to infer single keystrokes.

Figure 2 shows a measured trace while a user typed the URL https://www.yahoo.com/ into the browser bar. If no interrupt occurs, the counter variable has been incremented for the full time window of 4 ms, defining the baseline. If an interrupt disrupts the measuring JavaScript, the counter variable is not incremented as often in the same time window, yielding to downward-facing peaks. Thus, the typed letters leave clear marks in the measured trace, which allows inferring single keystrokes.

Offline Phase. In the offline phase of the attack, the measurements gathered from the online phase are processed and analyzed. Over time, an adversary can gather thousands of traces in order to learn about the individual typing behavior of the victim or to derive an entered passphrase or PIN code. Depending on the goal of the adversary, different methods to evaluate the gathered data can be applied. In order to detect single keystrokes in a measured trace, we filter the measured trace in order to reduce noise and to deduce threshold values for keystrokes by manually inspecting one recorded trace of the target device. Using this threshold, we can further reduce the number of points in recorded traces to a minimum and, thus, increase the performance of further computations. We build a classifier by calculating the correlation between our training set and the queried trace. In order to classify entered words, we need to take into account that the points in time where a character has been entered can vary in time in our trace. Therefore, we use k-nearest neighbors (k-NN) classification [4] and calculate the correlation of the trace with every other trace in the training set using different alignments. We chose the alignment that yields the highest correlation and decide on the class giving the best match. While more computational expensive methods working with time series [5,35] to build classifiers exist [9,23,48], we show that the features of the recorded measurements are strong enough such that also simpler techniques allow to build an efficient and accurate classifier.

4   Practical Attacks and Evaluation

In this section, we demonstrate the significant attack potential of our JavaScript interrupt-timing attack. Our attack does not depend on any specific browser or operating system and can therefore be performed on personal computers, laptops and smartphones. We show that it is possible to infer which website a user has entered into the browser's address bar and to profile different users sharing the same computer. Furthermore, we show that the attack can be utilized to obtain the exact timings of every digit of the PIN that is used to unlock the phone while the attack code is executed in the web browser running in the background.

4.1   URL Classification

In our first experiment, we demonstrate that using our JavaScript keystroke timing attack on a personal computer in combination with machine learning techniques, we can infer URLs that a user has entered into the address bar of the browser. We train a classifier to successfully label measurement traces of user input sequences for the URLs of the top 10 most visited websites [2]. For this experiment we used an Intel i7-6700K CPU and Firefox 52.0 running on Linux.

Every single trace consists of timestamps with a corresponding counter value (cf. Sect. 3) and the corresponding URL. As there are small timing variations when the user starts typing the URL and whenever the user pressed a key, the length of the trace as well as the position of the features, *i.e.*, the characteristics in the measured values describing a key stroke, within the trace varies. Thus, we need to build our classifier in a way that overcomes those difficulties. In a preparation step, we determine the maximum trace length as well as the timestamp resolution. The resolution can be obtained from the greatest common divisor of all measured timestamps of all samples. Finally, we create a linear interpolation of every sample based on the actual resolution.

The classifier assigns a class label to an unlabeled trace where each class corresponds to one URL that we train our classifier with. In order to classify a new trace, we compute the correlation of the new trace with a fixed number of randomly chosen samples for every class. As the timestamps where the user started entering the URL vary, we need to compute the correlation of two traces for different alignments. Thus, we shift one trace within a fixed time window back and forth in order to find an alignment where the correlation reaches its maximum. The average of the five highest correlations for each class decides which class the trace belongs to, *i.e.*, we choose the highest average correlation.

We evaluate our classifier by using k-fold cross-validation. We first randomly draw 20 samples as *training set* from our collected 100 measurements from every

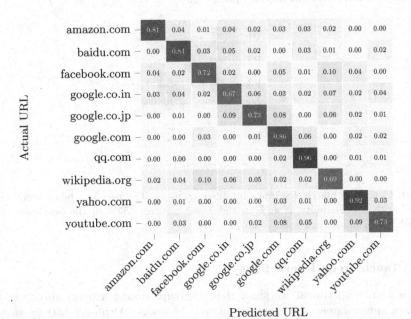

Fig. 3. Confusion matrix for URL input. The user input can be correctly predicted with a probability of 67% in the worst case and 96% in the best case. The probability of random guessing is 10%.

class. We then test the classifier on a randomly drawn set of the remaining 800 samples (80 per class), the *test set*. We cross-validate our classifier by performing this evaluation multiple times with randomly selected training sets.

Figure 3 shows the confusion matrix. Every cell shows the probability that the classifier labels a sample of a class specified by the row into a certain class specified by the column. We can clearly see that for every domain the classifier proposes the correct class with a higher probability than an incorrect one, and a significantly higher probability than random guessing (10%). The identification rate of *qq.com* in comparison with other domains is also very high as the domain contains only a small number of characters to be typed. The overall identification rate of our classifier is 81.75%.

4.2   User Classification

As a second experiment, we evaluate whether it is possible to distinguish different users in order to determine who is actually sitting in front of the personal computer. In order to do so, we have collected only 5 traces of the input of the top 10 most visited websites [2] of 4 different persons to train the classifier. The results with 2 training set and 3 test set traces for each user are illustrated as a confusion matrix in Fig. 4. While it is much harder to determine the user responsible for the given trace, our classifier is with an overall identification rate of 47.5% still better than random guessing.

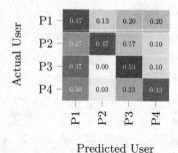

Fig. 4. Confusion matrix for input by different users. The user can be correctly predicted with a probability of 43% in the worst case and 53% in the best case. The probability of random guessing is 25%.

4.3   Touchscreen Interactions

In our third experiment we show that interrupt-timing attacks also work on modern smartphones and on different web browsers. Although battery saving techniques should make attacks harder, the attack can still be applied if the measuring program is executed in a different tab or if the browser app is running in background. Furthermore, we show that the attack can be used to detect when the screen is locked and unlocked.

Mobile phones usually use a soft-keyboard that is displayed on the screen. Every tap on the screen causes a redraw event that is clearly visible in the measured trace, making it easier to detect when a user touches the screen. While the redraw event is sufficient to monitor taps on the keyboard, we want to be able to identify any tap on the device, whether it causes a redraw event or not. Therefore, our test website implemented a custom touch area imitating a PIN pad. This touch area does neither register any events nor does it change its appearance. Thus, a touch onto this PIN pad should not issue any event at all, eliminating all events from the trace that are not caused by the touch interrupt itself. We provide the code for this experiment online.[1]

To cross-check whether we actually observe hardware events and not some browser-internal events, we implemented the same interrupt-detection algorithm in a native Android app. To achieve comparable results for the recorded traces, we reduced the timer resolution to $5\,\mu s$ in the same way as Firefox and Chrome.

For our experiments, we used a Google Nexus 5 with a Qualcomm MSM8974 Snapdragon 800 SoC running Android 6.0.1 with Chrome 44.0.2403.133 and Firefox 54.0a1. Our second testing device is a Xiaomi Redmi Note 3 with a Mediatek MT6795 Helio X10 running Android 5.0.2 with Chrome 57.0.2987.132 and Firefox 52.0.2. In addition, we used all the device listed in Table 1 to record traces using the JavaScript implementation for visual inspection. Table 1 also shows whether we could detect keystrokes and screen locks without machine learning just by visual inspection.

Table 1. Mobile test devices.

Device	SoC	Keystrokes	Screen lock
Google Nexus 5	Qualcomm MSM8974 Snapdragon 800	✓	-
Xiaomi Redmi Note 3	Mediatek MT6795 Helio X10	✓	✓
Homtom HT3	MediaTek MTK6580	✓	✓
Samsung Galaxy S6	Samsung Exynos 7420	-	✓
OnePlus One	Qualcomm MSM8974AC Snapdragon 801	✓	✓
OnePlus 3T	Qualcomm MSM8996 Snapdragon 821	-	-

Keystroke Detection. Figure 5 shows the keystroke timing attack in a native Android app on a Google Nexus 5 where a user tapped the screen twice, before swiping once and tapping it again. The individual interrupts, caused by tapping on the phone, can easily be identified by the two following peaks representing the touch and release event. If the user swipes over the screen, many interrupts are triggered, one for every coordinate change. This results in many visible peaks and, thus, swipes and taps can be distinguished.

Our JavaScript implementation of the keystroke timing attack runs successfully in Chrome and allows distinguishing taps from swipes as illustrated

---

[1] https://github.com/IAIK/interruptjs

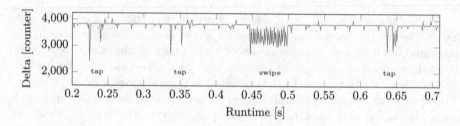

Fig. 5. Keystroke timing attack running in a native app on the Google Nexus 5.

in Fig. 6. While in contrast to the native implementation, the measurements in JavaScript contain much more noise, the exact tap timings can easily be extracted and allow further, more sophisticated attacks.

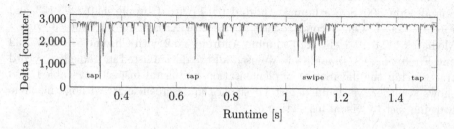

Fig. 6. Keystroke timing attack running in Chrome on the Google Nexus 5.

Figure 7 shows the same trace of two taps, one swipe and one additional tap on the Xiaomi Redmi Note 3. Surprisingly, the peaks caused by the interrupts face upwards instead of downwards as one might expect. We observed that the Xiaomi Redmi Note 3 increases the CPU frequency whenever the screen is touched. Consequently, although the interrupt will consume some CPU time, the counter as described in Sect. 3 can be incremented more often due to the significantly higher CPU frequency. We have verified this behavior by running a benchmark suite on the Xiaomi Redmi Note 3. The benchmark suite has been

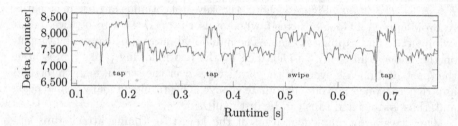

Fig. 7. Keystroke timing attack running in Chrome on the Xiaomi Redmi Note 3. The peaks face upwards instead of downwards as with other devices.

up to 30% faster, when swiping over the screen while the benchmark is executed. While this feature may be useful to handle touch interrupts more efficiently and to appear more responsive, it also opens a new side channel and allows detecting tap and screen events easily. We also verify the same behavior in our native Java implementation with higher peaks which allows detecting tap and swipe events even more reliably. On the OnePlus 3T we were not able to detect keystrokes at all. We suspect that this is due to the big.LITTLE architecture, which moves the CPU-intensive browser task to a high-performance ARM core, while the interrupts are handled by smaller cores. Thus, the browser is not interrupted if a hardware interrupt occurs.

Spying on Other Applications and PIN Unlock. While the attack of Vila and Köpf [43] is limited to spy on tabs or pop-ups opened by the adversary, our attack is not restricted and can be used to monitor any other application running on the system. Indeed, the attack of Vila and Köpf relies on the timing difference caused by the event loop of the render process, thus only tabs or windows sharing the same rendering process can be attacked. In contrast, our interrupt-timing attack is not restricted to the browser and its child processes as it allows monitoring every other event triggering interrupts on the target device. Moreover, our attack also provides a much higher resolution, which allows detecting interrupts triggered by user input more reliably.

Figure 8 shows a trace of a victim opening a website running the measurement code in Chrome on the Xiaomi Redmi Note 3. In addition, the victim opens a tab in incognito mode and taps the screen multiple times. We can even detect these user interactions in different tabs as the attack takes advantage of web workers which are not throttled when running in the background. Thus, the incognito mode offers no protection against our attack.

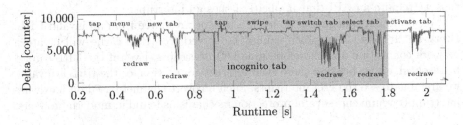

Fig. 8. Keystroke timing attack running while switching to a different tab in the Chrome browser on the Xiaomi Redmi Note 3.

In the next scenario, we show that our attack is not restricted to processes of the browser application but can be used to spy on every other application as well. The victim visits the website running the measuring application in the Firefox app on the Xiaomi Redmi Note 3 and continues using the phone, switching to other tabs or applications, and later locks the screen. After some time the victim turns on the screen again, where the lock screen prompts the victim for the PIN code. Finally, the victim enters the PIN code, unlocking the phone. Figure 9 shows a trace of this scenario. We can clearly observe when the screen is turned off as the CPU frequency is lowered to save battery, as well as when the screen is turned on again. Furthermore, we can extract the exact timestamps where the victim entered the 4-digit PIN and the subsequent redraw event.

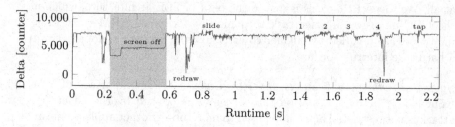

Fig. 9. Keystroke timing attack running in the Firefox browser on the Xiaomi Redmi Note 3. While the user locked the screen, the application still detects keystrokes as long as it is executed on the last used tab. The application extracts the exact inter-keystroke timings for the PIN input used to unlock the device.

4.4 Covert Channel

In our fourth experiment, we implement a covert communication channel based on our attack. This allows us to estimate the maximum number of interrupts we can detect. We establish a unidirectional communication with one sender and one receiver. The receiver simply mounts the interrupt-timing attack to sense any interrupts. The sender has to issue interrupts to send a '1'-bit or idle to send a '0'-bit. There is no JavaScript API which allows to explicitly issue interrupts, thus we require an API that implicitly issues an interrupt.

We use XMLHttpRequests to fetch a network resource from an invalid URL. Every XMLHttpRequest which cannot be served from the cache will create a network connection and therefore issue I/O interrupts. Even if the URL cannot be resolved, either because there is no Internet connection, or the URL is invalid, we are able to see the I/O interrupts. Such a covert channel based on hardware interrupts circumvents several protection mechanisms found in modern browsers.

Cross-Tab Channel. Using the covert channel across tabs breaks two security mechanisms. First, the same origin policy—which prevents any communication between scripts from different domains—does not apply anymore. Thus, scripts can communication across domain borders. Second, due to the security model of browsers, there is no way a HTTPS page is able to load HTTP content. For the covert channel, this security model does not hold anymore.

Cross-Browser Channel. As the interrupt-timing is not limited to a process, the covert channel circumvents policies such as proccess-per-site or process-per-tab which prevent sites or tabs from sharing process resources. The covert channel can even be used as a cross-browser communication channel. We tested a transmission from Firefox to Chrome and achieved the same transmission rate as in the cross-tab scenario. The communication channel can also be established with a browser instance running in incognito mode.

In all scenarios, the receiver uses a constant sampling interval of 40 ms per bit, resulting in a raw transmission rate of 25 bps. Thus, we are also able to spy on 25 interrupts per second in all those scenarios which is sufficient to monitor keystrokes of even the fastest typists [33]. To reliably transmit data over the covert channel, we can apply the techniques proposed by Maurice et al. [26].

5   Countermeasures

5.1   A Fine-Grained Permission Model for JavaScript

In order to impede and mitigate our interrupt-timing attack and other similar side-channel attacks in JavaScript, we propose a more fine-grained permission model for JavaScript running in web browsers. For instance, the existing permission system of Firefox only allows managing the access control to a limited number of APIs. However, as many websites do not require functionality such as web workers. The user should be capable to allow on a per-page level such features. If an online advertisement running potential malicious code requests for permissions to uncommon APIs, the fine-grained permission system prevents its further execution.

5.2   Generic Countermeasures

Myers [29] evaluated how various user-mode keylogging techniques in malware on Windows are implemented and suggested to generate random keyboard activity by injecting phantom keystrokes that will be intercepted by the malware. Furthermore, Ortolani [31] analyzed the statistical properties of noise necessary to impede the detection of real keystrokes in a noisy channel. While both do not protect against the interrupt-timing attack, Schwarz et al. [36] published a proof-of-concept countermeasure that aims to protect against this type of attacks. The countermeasure injects a large number of fake keystrokes that propagate through the kernel driver up to the user space application. We have verified that the countermeasure successfully injects fake keystrokes that cannot be distinguished from real interrupts by our implementation. Figure 10 shows a trace measured on the Google Nexus 5 with the countermeasure enabled. While this countermeasure appears to prevent this attack on personal computers as well, it remains unclear whether it closes the side channel on the Xiaomi Redmi Note 3 where the CPU gets overclocked for every touchscreen input. As the implementation of the countermeasure only supports the touchscreen of the Google Nexus 5 and the OnePlus 3T, we could not evaluate it against our attack on the Xiaomi Redmi Note 3. Therefore, we were unable to verify whether the fake keystrokes injected by the countermeasure also trigger the CPU overclocking and, thus, if the countermeasure protects against this attack on devices with such a behavior.

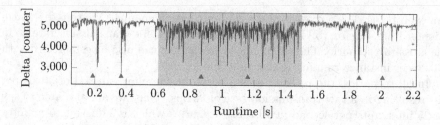

Fig. 10. Measurement of the keystroke timing attack running in the Chrome Browser on the Google Nexus 5. The red rectangles show when the user tapped the screen. In the gray area, we enabled the countermeasure [37], making it infeasible to distinguish real keystrokes from fake keystrokes.

Kohlbrenner and Shacham [24] implemented the fuzzy time concept [18, 42] in order to eliminate high-resolution timers. While this would prevent our attack in its current implementation, we could use the experimental `SharedArrayBuffers` as suggested by Schwarz et al. [37] and Gras et al. [13] in order to obtain a resolution of up to 2 ns and, thus, to re-enable our attack.

6   Conclusion

In this paper, we presented the first JavaScript-based keystroke timing attack which is independent of the browser and the operating system. Our attack is based on capturing interrupt timings and can be mounted on desktop machines, laptops as well as on smartphones. Because of its low code size of less than 256 bytes, it can be easily hidden within modern JavaScript frameworks or within an online advertisement, remaining undetected by the victim. We demonstrated the potential of this attack by inferring accurate timestamps of keystrokes as well as taps and swipes on mobile devices. Based on these keystroke traces, we built classifiers to detect which websites a user has visited and to identify different users time-sharing a computer. Our attack is highly practical, as it works while the browser is running in the background, allowing to spy on other tabs and applications. As the attack is also executed when the phone is locked, we demonstrated that we can monitor the PIN entry that is used to unlock the phone. Finally, as a solution against our attack and other similar side-channel attacks in JavaScript, we proposed a fine-grained permission model for browsers.

Acknowledgments. We would like to thank our anonymous reviewers for their valuable feedback. This project has been supported by the COMET K-Project DeSSnet (grant No. 862235) conducted by the Austrian Research Promotion Agency (FFG) and the European Research Council (ERC) under the European Union's Horizon 2020 research and innovation programme (grant agreement No. 681402).

References

1. Christensen, A.: Reduce resolution of performance.now (2015). https://bugs. webkit.org/show_bug.cgi?id=146531
2. Alexa Internet Inc.: The top. 500 sites on the web, December 2016. http://www. alexa.com/topsites
3. Ali, K., Liu, A.X., Wang, W., Shahzad, M.: Keystroke recognition using wifi signals. In: Proceedings of the 21st Annual International Conference on Mobile Computing and Networking, MobiCom 2015 (2015)
4. Altman, N.S.: An introduction to kernel and nearest-neighbor nonparametric regression. Am. Stat. **46**(3), 175–185 (1992)
5. Berndt, D.J., Clifford, J.: Using dynamic time warping to find patterns in time series. In: Proceedings of the 3rd International Conference on Knowledge Discovery and Data Mining (1994)
6. Booth, J.M.: Not so incognito: exploiting resource-based side channels in JavaScript engines. Bachelor thesis, Harvard School of Engineering and Applied Sciences (2015)
7. Zbarsky, B.: Reduce resolution of performance.now. (2015). https://hg.mozilla. org/integration/mozilla-inbound/rev/48ae8b5e62ab
8. Bortz, A., Boneh, D.: Exposing private information by timing web applications. In: WWW 2007 (2007)
9. Chen, W., Chang, W.: Applying hidden Markov models to keystroke pattern analysis for password verification. In: Proceedings of the 2004 IEEE International Conference on Information Reuse and Integration (2004)
10. Chromium: window.performance.now does not support sub-millisecond precision on Windows (2015). https://bugs.chromium.org/p/chromium/issues/detail? id=158234#c110
11. Diao, W., Liu, X., Li, Z., Zhang, K.: No pardon for the interruption: new inference attacks on android through interrupt timing analysis. In: S&P 2016 (2016)
12. Felten, E.W., Schneider, M.A.: Timing attacks on web privacy. In: CCS 2000 (2000)
13. Gras, B., Razavi, K., Bosman, E., Bos, H., Giuffrida, C.: ASLR on the line: practical cache attacks on the MMU. In: NDSS 2017 (2017)
14. Gruss, D., Bidner, D., Mangard, S.: Practical memory deduplication attacks in sandboxed JavaScript. In: Pernul, G., Ryan, P.Y.A., Weippl, E. (eds.) ESORICS 2015. LNCS, vol. 9326, pp. 108–122. Springer, Cham (2015). doi:10.1007/ 978-3-319-24174-6_6
15. Gruss, D., Spreitzer, R., Mangard, S.: Cache template attacks: automating attacks on inclusive last-level caches. In: USENIX Security Symposium (2015)
16. Heiderich, M., Niemietz, M., Schuster, F., Holz, T., Schwenk, J.: Scriptless attacks: stealing the pie without touching the sill. In: CCS 2012 (2012)
17. Hogye, M.A., Hughes, C.T., Sarfaty, J.M., Wolf, J.D.: Analysis of the feasibility of keystroke timing attacks over SSH connections. School of Engineering and Applied Science University of Virginia, Technical report (2001)
18. Hu, W.-M.: Reducing timing channels with fuzzy time. J. Comput. Secur. **1**(3–4), 233–254 (1992). http://dl.acm.org/citation.cfm?id=2699806.2699810
19. Idrus, S., Cherrier, E., Rosenberger, C., Bours, P.: Soft biometrics for keystroke dynamics: profiling individuals while typing passwords. Comput. Secur. **45**, 147–155 (2014)
20. Jana, S., Shmatikov, V.: Memento: learning secrets from process footprints. In: S&P 2012 (2012)

21. Jang, D., Jhala, R., Lerner, S., Shacham, H.: An empirical study of privacy-violating information flows in JavaScript web applications. In: CCS 2010 (2010)

22. Jia, Y., Dong, X., Liang, Z., Saxena, P.: I know where you've been: geo-inference attacks via the browser cache. IEEE Internet Comput. **19**(1), 44–53 (2015)

23. Kobojek, P., Saeed, K.: Application of recurrent neural networks for user verification based on keystroke dynamics. J. Telecommun. Inf. Technol. **3**, 80 (2016). http://www.itl.waw.pl/publikacje/44-jtit/953-journal-of-telecommunications-and-information-technology-jtit-12012

24. Kohlbrenner, D., Shacham, H.: Trusted browsers for uncertain times. In: USENIX Security Symposium (2016)

25. Lipp, M., Gruss, D., Spreitzer, R., Maurice, C., Mangard, S.: ARMageddon: cache attacks on mobile devices. In: USENIX Security Symposium (2016)

26. Maurice, C., Weber, M., Schwarz, M., Giner, L., Gruss, D., Boano, C.A., Mangard, S., Römer, K.: Hello from the other side: SSH over robust cache covert channels in the cloud. In: NDSS 2017 (2017)

27. Mehrnezhad, M., Toreini, E., Shahandashti, S.F., Hao, F.: Touchsignatures: identification of user touch actions and pins based on mobile sensor data via JavaScript. J. Inf. Secur. Appl. **26**, 23–38 (2016)

28. Perry, M.: Bug 1517: reduce precision of time for JavaScript (2015). https://gitweb.torproject.org/user/mikeperry/tor-browser.git/commit/?h=bug1517

29. Myers, M.: Anti-keylogging with random noise. In: PoC|GTFO, vol. 0x14 (2017)

30. Oren, Y., Kemerlis, V.P., Sethumadhavan, S., Keromytis, A.D.: The spy in the sandbox: practical cache attacks in JavaScript and their implications. In: CCS 2015 (2015)

31. Ortolani, S.: Noisykey: tolerating keyloggers via keystrokes hiding. In: USENIX Workshop on Hot Topics in Security - HotSec (2012)

32. Pessl, P., Gruss, D., Maurice, C., Schwarz, M., Mangard, S.: DRAMA: exploiting dram addressing for cross-CPU attacks. In: USENIX Security Symposium (2016)

33. Pinet, S., Ziegler, J.C., Alario, F.X.: Typing is writing: linguistic properties modulate typing execution. Psychon. Bull. Rev. **23**(6), 1898–1906 (2016)

34. Ristenpart, T., Tromer, E., Shacham, H., Savage, S.: Hey, you, get off of my cloud: exploring information leakage in third-party compute clouds. In: CCS 2009 (2009)

35. Rumelhart, D.E., McClelland, J.L., PDP Research Group, C. (eds.): Parallel Distributed Processing: Explorations in the Microstructure of Cognition, vol. 1: Foundations. MIT Press, Cambridge (1986)

36. Schwarz, M., Lipp, M., Gruss, D., Weiser, S., Maurice, C., Spreitzer, R., Mangard, S.: KeyDrown: eliminating keystroke timing side-channel attacks (2017). arXiv preprint arXiv:1706.06381

37. Schwarz, M., Maurice, C., Gruss, D., Mangard, S.: Fantastic timers and where to find them: high-resolution microarchitectural attacks in JavaScript. In: FC 2017 (2017)

38. Simon, L., Xu, W., Anderson, R.: Don't interrupt me while I type: inferring text entered through gesture typing on android keyboards. In: Proceedings on Privacy Enhancing Technologies (2016)

39. Song, D.X., Wagner, D., Tian, X.: Timing analysis of keystrokes and timing attacks on SSH. In: USENIX Security Symposium (2001)

40. Stone, P.: Pixel perfect timing attacks with HTML5. Context Information Security (White Paper) (2013)

41. Van Goethem, T., Joosen, W., Nikiforakis, N.: The clock is still ticking: timing attacks in the modern web. In: CCS 2015 (2015)

42. Vattikonda, B.C., Das, S., Shacham, H.: Eliminating fine grained timers in Xen. In: CCSW 2011 (2011)

43. Vila, P., Köpf, B.: Loophole: timing attacks on shared event loops in chrome. In: USENIX Security Symposium (2017)

44. W3C: Web Workers - W3C Working Draft, 24 September 2015. https://www.w3. org/TR/workers/

45. W3C: High Resolution Time Level 2 (2016). https://www.w3.org/TR/hr-time/

46. Weinberg, Z., Chen, E.Y., Jayaraman, P.R., Jackson, C.: I still know what you visited last summer: leaking browsing history via user interaction and side channel attacks. In: S&P 2011 (2011)

47. Wray, J.C.: An analysis of covert timing channels. J. Comput. Secur. 1(3–4), 219–232 (1992)

48. Xi, X., Keogh, E., Shelton, C., Wei, L., Ann Ratanamahatana, C.: Fast time series classification using numerosity reduction. In: Proceedings of the 23rd International Conference on Machine Learning (2006)

49. Zhang, K., Wang, X.: Peeping tom in the neighborhood: keystroke eavesdropping on multi-user systems. In: USENIX Security Symposium (2009)

On-Demand Time Blurring to Support Side-Channel Defense

Weijie Liu[1](✉), Debin Gao[2](✉), and Michael K. Reiter[3](✉)

[1] Computer School, Wuhan University, Wuhan, China
liuweijie@whu.edu.cn
[2] Singapore Management University, Singapore, Singapore
dbgao@smu.edu.sg
[3] University of North Carolina, Chapel Hill, NC, USA
reiter@cs.unc.edu

Abstract. Side-channel attacks are a serious threat to multi-tenant public clouds. Past work showed how secret information in one virtual machine (VM) can be leaked to another, co-resident VM using timing side channels. Recent defenses against timing side channels focus on reducing the degree of resource sharing. However, such defenses necessarily limit the flexibility with which resources are shared. In this paper, we propose a technique that dynamically adjusts the granularity of platform time sources, to interfere with timing side-channel attacks. Our proposed technique supposes an interface by which a VM can request the temporary coarsening of platform time sources as seen by all VMs on the platform, which the hypervisor can effect since it virtualizes accesses to those timers. We show that the VM-Function (VMFUNC) mechanism provides a low-overhead such interface, thereby enabling applications to adjust timer granularity with minimal overhead. We present a proof-of-concept implementation using a Xen hypervisor running Linux-based VMs on a cloud server using commodity Intel processors and supporting adjustment of the timestamp-counter (TSC) granularity. We evaluate our implementation and show that our scheme mitigates timing side-channel attacks, while introducing negligible performance penalties.

1 Introduction

Computers that are simultaneously shared by multiple tenants introduce the risk of information leakage between tenants via *access-driven side-channel attacks*. In these attacks, one tenant (the attacker) infers information about another tenant (the victim) by measuring victim's impact on the resources that they share. A predominant form of such side-channel attacks is *timing* attacks, in which the attacker measures victim-induced perturbations in the time between events that the attacker can observe. For example, a widely studied form of access-driven timing attack is one in which the attacker observes which of the attacker's lines the victim evicted from a processor cache when it ran, which the attacker can observe by timing the durations of its own memory fetches when it runs after the victim [11]. Researchers have demonstrated that these attacks can be used to steal a victim VM's cryptographic keys over Xen [17, 40, 42], to collect potentially

© Springer International Publishing AG 2017
S.N. Foley et al. (Eds.): ESORICS 2017, Part II, LNCS 10493, pp. 210–228, 2017.
DOI: 10.1007/978-3-319-66399-9_12

sensitive application data and hijack accounts on a victim web-server in a PaaS cloud [10,43], and others [3,4,9,13].

Many defenses against access-driven timing side channels focus on reducing the degree or granularity of resource sharing (e.g., [2,41,44]). Such defenses, however, necessarily limit the flexibility with which resources are shared, typically with costs to performance, efficiency, and/or utilization. For this reason, in this paper we advance a second class of defense, namely interfering with the adversary's ability to time events. Even though there are theoretically many ways for an adversary to time events [21], timing events with sufficiently fine granularity to extract cryptographic keys, for example, typically leverages the *time stamp counter* (TSC) on x86 platforms (e.g., [23,40]). As such, decreasing the fidelity of the TSC has been advocated in previous research as a method to interfere with the most potent of these attacks (e.g., [25,33]).

The important insight that we contribute in this paper is that the degradation of TSC fidelity need not be constant over time, but can be tuned according to the operations that a tenant application is performing. For example, since AES operations are much faster than RSA operations, the degradation needed to hide timing side channels during AES operations might be much smaller than what would be needed to hide (potentially much larger) timing signals during RSA operations.

In this paper we leverage this insight to advocate for a simple interface by which a tenant application can adjust the fidelity of the TSC observed by tenants on the platform to a specified level, i.e., specified as a number of low-order bits of the TSC to zero before reporting it to a tenant. Our prototype virtualizes the TSC and, at any point in time, zeros a number of bits requested by a tenant on the machine. Moreover, we show that VM-Function (VMFUNC) techniques offer a low-overhead mechanism to VMs to adjust TSC fidelity. Because of the efficiency of these VMFUNC techniques, VMs have the flexibility to adjust TSC fidelity frequently, without incurring significant performance impacts from doing so. We show, for example, that these fidelity adjustments are sufficiently quick to allow fine-grained adjustments to TSC fidelity with virtually no performance impact to, e.g., encryption libraries and web and file servers employing encryption. Moreover, we quantify the degree of TSC degradation that is needed to overcome simple but powerful covert-channel attacks, in which we reveal different settings of the TSC degradation that are "just enough" to disable a last level cache and a memory bus contention attack.

Allowing tenant applications to adjust the fidelity of the TSC could potentially open the platform to detrimental effects caused by tenants overzealously degrading the TSC fidelity for other tenants. We conduct experiments to show that VMs are not particularly sensitive to TSC degradation, but there is obviously a point at which this is no longer true. While our goal here is not to measure the potential for abuse, we note that it is straightforward to impose limits on the amount or duration of degradation that is allowed, e.g., as a cap on the number of bits that will be dropped or a per-tenant budget on the time during which it can request that the TSC fidelity be kept at a reduced level. In the limit, a tenant in a public cloud could be charged extra, in proportion to the time and amount of degradation that it requests, and likewise, tenants could be partially reimbursed for durations in which their executions were subjected to lower TSC fidelity at the request of co-located tenants.

The remainder of the paper is organized as follows. In Sect. 2 we establish our requirements. In Sect. 3 we outline our design and provide in-depth details about our prototype implementations. Section 4 describes the experiments performed using recent, state-of-the-art cross-VM side channels also the performance evaluation of the prototype. Section 5 describes related work and finally Sect. 6 provides brief concluding remarks and discusses limitations of our technique.

2   Threat Model and Requirements

We focus on infrastructure-as-a-service (IaaS) clouds that potentially execute multiple virtual machines from customers on the same, shared computer hardware. Examples of such cloud providers include Amazon EC2 and Rackspace. Due to the nature of shared computer hardware on this architecture, access-driven side-channel attacks become possible among virtual machines (VMs) executing simultaneously, which might originate from different customers.

Threat Model. Our threat model is an attacker VM that tries to infer information about a victim VM running simultaneously on the same computer hardware. Specifically, the attacks that we consider in this paper are those that perform side-channel timing attacks by measuring victim-VM-induced perturbations in the time between certain events on the shared hardware that the attacker VM can observe. We assume that the infrastructure provides reliable access control to prevent the attacker VM from accessing the victim VM directly or via forms of privilege escalation. To this end, we assume that the cloud's virtualization software is trusted.

Under such a threat model, we focus our attention on defense mechanisms that reduce the fidelity of the time stamp counter (TSC) to interfere with the attacker's ability to time events. We consider the following important requirements of a flexible and effective defense.

"Just-Enough" Masking. We want to differentiate various side-channel timing attacks that measure the time between events at different granularities. For example, since AES operations are much faster than RSA operations, their corresponding successful attacks need to obtain timing information at finer granularity. Therefore, a victim might demand that fine-grained timing information be hidden while it performs AES operations and more coarse-grained timing information be hidden during its RSA operations.

On-Demand Protection. While a potential victim has sensitive information in the VM that requires protection and the victim VM knows precisely when sensitive operations involving that data happen, we assume a powerful attacker who also has precise information of such operations (what they are and when they happen) and the corresponding events that the attacker VM can observe in an attempt to infer the sensitive information. That said, we also assume that such operations constitute a small percentage of the entire workload of the victim VM, and so the victim would prefer an "on-demand" protection to minimize the performance overhead. Specifically, we aim for a solution where the victim can dynamically change the protection at low cost, e.g., allowing the victim to enable protection when encrypting blocks of an `https` response (a sensitive operation since the cryptographic key is involved) while turning off the protection when sending out encrypted blocks (a non-sensitive networking operation).

Timing Information Available to VMs. Besides the security features cloud customers desire when running virtual machines on a cloud, they may also demand timing information from the cloud platform for their general computing purposes. For example, a VM running a web server may need timestamp information at microsecond precision for logging purposes. Therefore, a solution to defend against the side-channel timing attacks should not have noticeable impact on such uses of timing information.

3   Design and Implementation

As discussed in Sect. 1, attackers typically need to leverage the time stamp counter (TSC) to obtain fine-grained timing information for the purpose of inferring sensitive information from a victim VM. Therefore, decreasing the fidelity of TSC has been proposed as a potential defense against side-channel timing attacks [25,33]. However, existing such approaches do not satisfy our requirements on just-enough masking and on-demand protection.

Our technique allows a tenant to dynamically adjust the fidelity of the TSC observed by tenants on a virtualized platform to a specified level, i.e., to request a number n of low-order bits of the TSC be zeroed before reporting it to tenants. The request n can be determined by the nature of the sensitive operation that the victim VM is to perform and known exploits available to attacker VMs, so that only *just enough* bits are removed to disable these attacks. After performing its operation, the victim VM can retract its request to coarsen the TSC (i.e., by requesting that $n = 0$ bits be removed).

Figure 1 shows an overview of our design with a hypothetical victim program that performs on-demand requests to reduce the fidelity of TSC. The victim VM in our example performs both AES and RSA operations, while the attacker

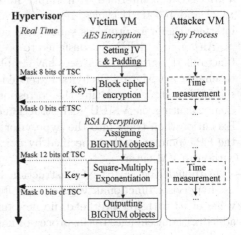

Fig. 1. Overview with hypothetical victim program

VM performs time measurements to exercise a side-channel attack. To defend against such attacks, the victim VM sends on-demand requests to the hypervisor to degrade the fidelity of the TSC during only key-dependent operations that are vulnerable to timing side-channel attacks. Moreover, the degree of degradation is set so that "just enough" low-order bits of TSC are masked for the specific cryptographic operation ($n = 8$ bits for AES and $n = 12$ bits for RSA in Fig. 1).

Although it is relatively simple to enable TSC emulation (by setting the RDTSC_EXITING bit in VMCS) and to zero n bits from TSC readings, two implementation issues require further elaboration. The first is how to set n when multiple threads from multiple VMs request different values of n at overlapping times. In this case, the value of n used should be the maximum among those requested (up to a limit). That is, we take a conservative approach, zeroing the maximum number of bits for which any threads on any guest VMs has a request in effect, which implies that the (lesser) protection requested by other threads/VMs is additionally enforced, *a fortiori*.[1]

The second issue warranting further comment is how to achieve *on-demand* protection without inducing substantial overhead. Specifically, we need to allow a guest VM to dynamically request changing the value of n with little cost. It could make these requests with a VMCALL/hypercall, but doing so causes the guest VM to encounter a VM-exit and so is expected to result in prohibitive overhead when a VM changes n frequently.

Here, we propose leveraging VM-Function (VMFUNC), a feature of the Intel micro-architecture instruction set, to reduce the overhead. VMFUNC allows VMs to use hypervisor functionality without a VM-Exit. We performed a simple experiment to compare the overhead of a VMCALL/hypercall interface and a VMFUNC call interface with empty implementation, and find that they cost 1,622 and 160 CPU cycles, respectively, on our i7-4790 CPU. The VMFUNC interface therefore promises substantial cost savings if it can be used.

Although VMFUNC is designed to be general purpose with up to 64 different functions [1], current processors have implemented only one of them, specifically to enable a VM to switch its Extended Page Table (EPT). A VM specifies the EPT pointer by putting the corresponding index into the ecx register, and then executing the VMFUNC instruction either from user mode or kernel mode. Execution then traps into the hypervisor without any VM-exit, which switches the EPT pointer to that specified by ecx, and subsequently returns to the VM without a VM-enter.

Although the VMFUNC instruction is attractive as a general interface to use hypervisor functionality (in our case to request the hypervisor to change the value of n) with low overhead, no new function besides EPT switching can be added without changes to the processor hardware. To evaluate the corresponding

---

[1] To adjust n to the second highest value when the most demanding thread/VM has finished its sensitive operation, each VM kernel should track all masking requests from its threads and the hypervisor should track all masking requests from VMs. Our evaluation prototype supports this tracking at the VM kernel only, owing to our inability to add or modify VMFUNC instructions, as discussed below.

performance overhead should processor hardware support our functionality using VMFUNC, we commandeered the EPT switching mechanism in our evaluation prototype, reserving a few specific settings of the EPT pointer (`ecx` register value when calling VMFUNC) for the purpose of our on-demand request to change the value of n. That is, when the `ecx` register contains one of these specific values (0 to k in our prototype), we use it to set the value of n for TSC fidelity reduction. This design is not viable in practice, since it disrupts EPT switching and supports TSC degradation requests from only a single VM at a time. However, it suffices to estimate the overheads associated with dynamically adjusting TSC fidelity via the VMFUNC interface, should it be extended to support our mechanism.

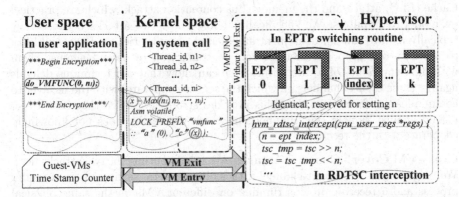

Fig. 2. Design of our evaluation prototype; do_VMFUNC is a system call that tracks requests from VM threads and communicates the VM's current maximum masking request to the hypervisor via VMFUNC invocations

Figure 2 shows the design of our evaluation prototype. We first create a few identical EPT tables denoted EPT 0 to EPT k. A user-space process makes a customized system call to request masking n bits of the TSC. Such a system call is processed by the VM kernel, which keeps track on different requests from different threads and executes a VMFUNC instruction with $ecx \in [0, k]$. In the hypervisor, switching the EPT table thus has no effect on guest execution (due to identical EPT tables). When any `rdtsc` instruction is executed, the hypervisor reconstructs the setting of n by calculating the offset between the current EPT pointer from EPT base address (effectively reconstructing the value of `ecx` in the most recent VMFUNC call) and masks the low-order n bits of TSC value. With this, we create an efficient communication channel from VMs to the hypervisor for on-demand requests to modify n.

4 Evaluation

In this section, we evaluate our proposal. We present two representative covert-channel timing attacks and show how n can be set accordingly to stop them.

Finally, we focus on a number of realistic workloads on virtual machines to illustrate the impact of setting n at various values and modifying n at different granularities.

4.1 Defending Against Timing Attacks

In this subsection, we evaluate our prototype's effectiveness in defending against real timing attacks. Specifically, we want to see how n should be configured dynamically to provide "just-enough" protection to mask out precise time measurement by the attacker VMs to disable the attacks.

We choose two representative covert-channel timing attacks, the Last Level Cache (LLC) attack and the memory bus contention attack, which are practical on modern computers. We specifically choose these two attacks because they typically require time measurement at different granularities, and we would like to see how our proposed method can be configured to defend against them with different values of n. Moreover, if we can show that our technique defends against these *covert* channels, in which the sender cooperates with the receiver to communicate information, then this provides strong assurance that it will also defend against similar *side* channels, in which the sender does not knowingly cooperate with the receiver.

Cross-VM Covert-Channel Attacks. We briefly outline the two attacks here. We target cross-VM covert-channel attacks in a general setting where a sender process and a receiver process running on different VMs on the same physical host are trying to communicate via a covert timing channel.

In the case of the Last Level Cache (LLC) attack [15], the receiver process (1) fills one or more cache sets with its own code or data; (2) waits for the sender process to utilize the same cache set(s); and (3) measures the time to load his code or data again. This follows a typical PRIME+PROBE technique [26] where the sender process sends a bit of information by utilizing (or not utilizing) the same cache sets, which results in different amount of time taken in the receiver's last PROBE operation. We follow the LLC attack by Liu et al. [23] and implement it on two HVM guests running on an Acer Veriton M4630 machine running Xen. We used an eviction set consisting of cache lines from all four cache slices on our i7-4790 CPU to conservatively prime and probe the cache sets.

The memory bus contention attack works in a similar way, while the time measurement is typically more coarse-grained compared to the LLC-based attacks. The sender selectively performs an exotic atomic memory operation that triggers a bus locking behavior [39], which causes longer access time by the receiver and therefore effectively creates the covert channel. We configure the receiver to use the latest Streaming SIMD Extensions (SSE) instructions to access the memory bus bypassing the cache lines to reduce noise from the cache lines (which could mask out the bus locking effect).

In both attacks, we do not implement channel error correction or other accuracy improvements leveraged in previous work, except the necessary encoding mechanism to handle VM scheduling and to provide transmission synchronization. We do this to uncover the impact of reducing fidelity of TSC on the bit-by-bit accuracy of the covert channel.

Impact of Degrading TSC Fidelity on Timing Attacks. Our intention here is to first execute the LLC and memory bus contention attacks with some realistic parameters on an unmodified Xen system and observe the corresponding accuracy of information received at the receiver process. We then turn on our protection and modify the value of n to observe the corresponding impact on the accuracy observed. We also want to enable some coarse comparison between the two different types of covert-channel attacks to demonstrate our scheme's flexibility in handling different types of threats.

To obtain some realistic attack settings, we configure various sending bit rates for both attacks. Since they use different encoding schemes [23,39] (LLC attack uses the RZ encoding while memory bus contention attack uses the Manchester encoding), the sending bit rates are configured indirectly as follows. For the LLC attack, we configure three different pause durations (waiting time between two consecutive bits) of 1 μs, 2 μs and 10 μs, which result in sending bit rates between 27 Kbps and 7 Kbps. For the memory bus contention attack, we set the symbol period T (number of consecutive exotic atomic operations to be repeated in sending out each bit of information) to be 1, 50, and 100, which result in sending bit rates between 8 Kbps and 246 bps.

Under the various sending bit rates, we measure the accuracy at the receiving process. We consider a powerful attacker who has access to our machine to perform experiments to find out the best threshold—a timing threshold used by the receiving process to infer whether the sender had performed the operation (loading data into the cache set for LLC attack or executing the exotic atomic memory operation for the memory bus contention attack) to signal a 1 or 0 on the covert channel. We further assume that the attacker can perform re-calibration of the threshold when we remove different number of bits from the the TSC readings (n). Figure 3 shows the results of our experiments.

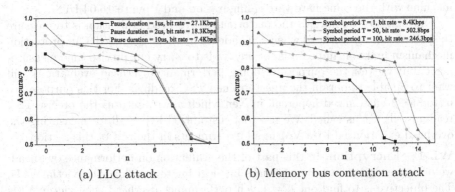

(a) LLC attack   (b) Memory bus contention attack

Fig. 3. Impact on mitigating covert-channel timing attacks

Figure 3 clearly shows that accuracy of the covert-channel attacks decreases when n increases. What is interesting is that the accuracy experiences a much steeper drop when n is greater than a certain number, and the accuracy quickly approaches 50% (the same accuracy as random guessing).

Comparing the two types of attacks, we also notice that our scheme can obtain the same protection (in terms of lowering the accuracy) with smaller n for the LLC attack. This is due to the finer-grained time measurement needed in LLC attacks since the LLC operates much faster than physical memory. This observation reinforces our motivation of this paper—different victim programs and different attacks require different degree of degradation of the TSC fidelity, and the need of dynamically setting the value of n.

4.2   Performance Evaluation

Having shown the effectiveness of our scheme in defending against covert-channel timing attacks, we now focus on the overhead evaluation. More specifically, we want to see the impact in terms of performance overhead when a potential victim VM dynamically sends on-demand requests to the hypervisor to change the value of n. With this, we hope to shed light on the recommended usage of our protection mechanism in striking a balance between timing-attack protection and performance overhead. We consider three different VM workloads in our evaluation that differ in the percentage of instructions that require protection against timing attacks.

Our experiments were carried out on a Dell XPS 8700-R39N8 desktop machine with Xen virtual machine monitor installed. Table 1 shows the hardware and software configurations of our prototype. In some experiments, we have a client-server setting where the server is running as a VM

Table 1. Experiment platform

Server Model:	Dell XPS 8700-R39N8
Processor:	Intel Core i7-4790 3.6 GHz
Memory:	16 GB
VMM:	Xen 4.6.0
Guest OS:	Linux kernel 3.14.60
vCPUs per VM:	1
Memory per VM:	2048 MB

on this machine, and the client is running on a host OS on another physical machine with the same hardware configuration and Ubuntu 16.04 LTS.

One subtlety we have in the performance overhead evaluation is to measure the precise timing overhead when TSC fidelity has been degraded. Our protection mechanism makes it impossible for any VMs to carry out precise time measurement, but we (for the purpose of doing performance overhead evaluation) still want to be able to obtain the finest-grained TSC readings. For this purpose, we introduce a customized hypercall in Xen which always returns the precise TSC readings when it is called. We use this customized hypercall for measuring the overhead experienced by a VM in all experiments in the rest of this section.

WL-1 – Encryption. In this part of the evaluation on performance overhead, we no longer focus on timing attacks but legitimate workloads on victim VMs. The objective is to find out how much performance overhead such victim VMs experience when they request timing-attack protection. The first workloads (WL-1) we consider here include two encryption workloads, one where the victim VM performs AES encryption and the other where the victim VM performs RSA encryption, both using implementations that are vulnerable to cross-VM timing attacks [14,17]. In both cases, the victim VM tries to protect its keys from being compromised via co-residency timing attacks by inserting VMFUNC instructions into its crypto library (`libcrypto.so` in OpenSSL 1.0.2g) to modify n.

When instrumenting OpenSSL source code to insert VMFUNC instructions, we focus on protecting *key-dependent* components. Figure 4 shows an overview of such instrumentation. For AES, we insert VMFUNC instructions before the first round (to turn on TSC masking) and after the last round in each block encryption (to turn off TSC masking), which translates to 32 pairs of VMFUNC instructions executed for each 1 KB text encrypted. For RSA, we insert a pair of VMFUNC instructions in the function `bn_mod_mul_montgomery()`, which performs Montgomery modular multiplications and is usually the target of timing attacks. A noticeable difference between our instrumentation on these two workloads is that our protection (code between a pair of VMFUNC instructions) covers about 90% of AES runtime but only 30–40% of RSA runtime.

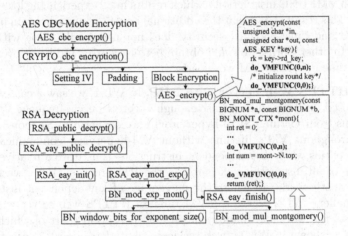

Fig. 4. Instrumenting AES and RSA crypto libraries

Figure 5 shows the normalized runtime overhead with the baseline being an uninstrumented OpenSSL on a VM running on unmodified Xen. Here we try to compare two different strategies of providing timing attack protection: S1 with a constant degradation of TSC fidelity throughout the VM's lifetime (with 8, 16, and 24 bits removed) where no communication is needed between the victim VM and the hypervisor, and S2 with on-demand protection where VMFUNC instructions signal the hypervisor to adjust TSC fidelity. Intuitively, S2 supports on-demand and "just-enough" protection, but experiences additional overhead due to the VMFUNC instructions, especially when they are invoked frequently in the crypto operations.

Surprisingly, our results show that the difference between S1 and S2 is not only small, but sometimes S2 actually outperforms S1, e.g., for RSA when 16 or

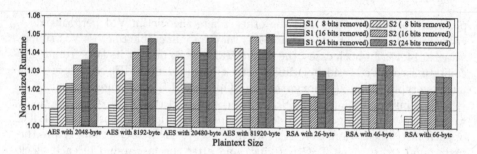

Fig. 5. Runtime overhead in AES/RSA workload

24 bits are masked. This is likely due to the smaller portion of key-dependent instructions in RSA (30% to 40%) compared to that in AES (about 90%). When key-dependent instructions constitute a small percentage, the overhead due to unnecessary protection of key-independent instructions in S1 could outweigh that due to VMFUNC instructions, which results in S2 experiencing lower overall overhead. This result shows that the additional benefit of our scheme in providing on-demand and "just-enough" security does not necessarily come with higher overhead. In other words, we could obtain better security and lower overhead at the same time in certain VM workloads.

WL-2 – HTTPS Web Server with PHP. In WL-1, we saw a case where S2 (our proposed on-demand and "just-enough" protection via frequent VMFUNC instructions from victim VM to hypervisor) may outperform S1 (constant protection throughout VM's lifetime without VM-hypervisor communication) in certain scenarios where key-dependent instructions constitute a relatively small percentage of all instructions executed in the VM program. Here, we focus on another realistic workload where the percentage of key-dependent instructions is even smaller—WL-2 where the VM runs an HTTPS web server with PHP. In this case, the workload mainly consists of encryption (part of which is key-dependent as shown in WL-1), web services (key-independent), and networking (key-independent).

The experiment is on an isolated 1 Gbps LAN. The victim VM runs Apache webserver with HTTPS and PHP, and a client running on another host (not in a VM) executes a webserver load tester Siege (https://www.joedog.org/siege-home/). Siege is configured to send continuous HTTPS requests (with no delay between two consecutive ones) to the webserver for 10 min. One concurrent request is deployed for measuring the response time, while a maximum number of concurrent requests (that result in a maximum throughput) are used as the input for measuring the maximum network I/O performance.

The Apache webserver is configured to use RSA_WITH_AES_256_CBC_SHA for key exchange/agreement and AES256 CBC for data encryption, both of which are key-dependent and require timing protection. We have four different configurations of the Apache webserver. Server A is the unmodified version without any VMFUNC instrumentation, while Server B, C, and D are instrumented to insert VMFUNC instructions to protect key-dependent instructions at decreasing granularity; please see Fig. 6.

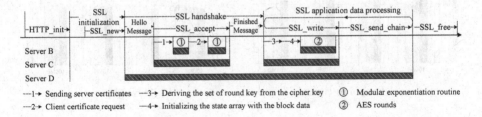

Fig. 6. Instrumenting HTTPS webserver at different granularity

Server B has the finest-grained instrumentation with VMFUNC pairs covering the cryptographic algorithms as described in WL-1. Server C and D have fewer VMFUNC instructions inserted with protection covering some other key-independent instructions of the webserver. Table 2 shows the number of VMFUNC instructions executed in preparing and sending off an HTTPS response. As expected, finer-grained instrumentation results in more VMFUNC instructions called, e.g., in Server B.

Figure 7 shows the normalized response times and normalized throughput for WL-2 for five different configurations: Server A without timing protection (the baseline of normalized response time and throughput), Server B, C, D, and Server A with constant timing protection. We only show results when removing 8 low-order bits of TSC readings here. We performed the same experiment when removing 12 bits, and the results were very similar with slightly bigger variance (due to a more coarse-grained timer).

Table 2. Number of VMFUNC instructions executed in an HTTPS response

	Server			
File size	A	B	C	D
100 KB	0	6576	142	2
1 MB	0	65596	1402	2
10 MB	0	655520	13986	2
100 MB	0	6554006	139824	2

We first make a comparison among the five different configurations of the webserver. Server A without any timing protection (the baseline) obviously gives the best throughput result. What is interesting, though, is that Server C (an instance of S2) very consistently outperforms Server A with constant timing protection (S1), and the advantage is more pronounced for bigger file sizes. The reason is similar to that in WL-1—the savings on unnecessary timing protection on key-independent instructions outweigh the cost of additional VMFUNC instructions called. Server B has the smallest throughput mainly because of its most fine-grained VMFUNC instrumentation.

WL-3 – SCP Server. Both WL-1 and WL-2 show instances where our on-demand and "just-enough" timing protection (S2) outperforms constant timing protection (S1) in specific settings. We now turn to a third workload in which the key-dependent operations account for a very small percentage of the entire

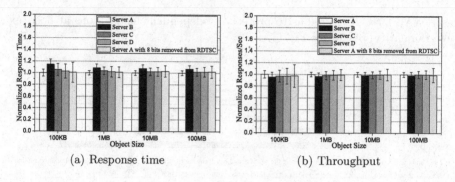

(a) Response time   (b) Throughput

Fig. 7. Evaluation of WL-2

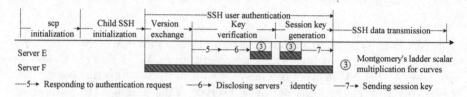

Fig. 8. Instrumenting SCP server at different granularity

workload—WL-3, of a secure file copying (SCP) server. In WL-3, only the very initial part of the transaction involves the authentication key which is to be protected from timing attacks (ECDSA computation in OPENSSL that is vulnerable to a timing attack [8,16]), while the remaining part of the transaction does not need to be protected.

Instrumentation of the SCP server results in Server E and F as shown in Fig. 8, with Server E having finer-grained instrumentation and more VMFUNC instructions (12 VMFUNC instructions executed in Server E compared to 2 in Server F for an SCP transmission).

Transmission rates of the servers are shown in Fig. 9 (showing only results with 8 low-order bits of TSC masked since those with 12 bits masked are very sim-

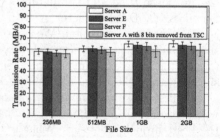

Fig. 9. Network performance in WL-3

ilar). We, again, observe that S2 (Server E and F) outperforms S1 (Server A with timing protection throughout the VM lifetime), except that this time the difference is even more pronounced than that in WL-2, and both instrumentations in S2 outperform that in S1. With these three different workloads and the consistent results obtained, we clearly show that in many realistic workloads, the benefits of the frequent communication from a VM to the hypervisor (which saves on unnecessary timing protection) could outweigh the overhead of the VMFUNC instructions. Therefore, our proposed mechanism of on-demand

and "just-enough" masking of TSC readings not only provides better security, but also in many cases results in lower overhead.

Overhead on VMs that Do Not Need Timing Protection. We now turn to the last part of our performance overhead evaluation, where we measure the impact of one VM demanding n bits of TSC masking on other co-resident "victim" VMs. These other VMs are not under any timing attacks but simply experience some performance overhead due to a co-resident VM that demands higher security.

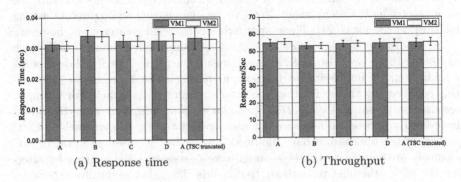

(a) Response time   (b) Throughput

Fig. 10. Results of being co-resident with a security-demanding VM

Figure 10 shows the response time and throughput of individual VMs when VM1 requests $n = 8$ low-order bits of the TSC be masked, while VM2 makes no such requests. Both VMs are running the Apache webservers and connected to a Siege client as in WL-2. These results show that the performance overhead on VM2 is minimal. Server C and its co-resident innocent VM experiences the smallest overhead, which is consistent with the results obtained in WL-2.

Our last experiment includes a VM running a PARSEC benchmark while co-resident with another VM running Server A, B, C, or D with $n = 8$ bits of the TSC masked. Figure 11 shows that, in general, the performance impact is minimal. That said, `canneal` seems to be more affected by the TSC masking. We believe that it is due to `canneal` being most memory intensive, and the large amount of VMFUNC instructions (in the case of Server B) potentially leads to more cache-misses on the other VM.

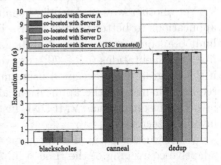

Fig. 11. Overheads of PARSEC benchmarks when co-located with a VM requesting TSC masking

5   Related Work

Many existing works have proposed defenses against co-residence-based timing side-channel attacks. Adding noise to time sources was one of the first timing-attack mitigation schemes [12], and this has been applied specifically to the time stamp counter on Intel platforms [25,33], as discussed previously. Our scheme also belongs to this category; our contribution lies in showing how dynamically coarsening the time stamp counter can provide on-demand protection for very little cost. Other approaches seek to ensure that measurable intervals of executions are independent of secret values, by causing all such measurements to return the same, secret-independent result [2,41] or by aggregating timing events among multiple VM replicas [21]. These approaches come with greater costs, however.

Apart from general-purpose mitigations of timing side-channel attacks such as these, there are also defense mechanisms targeting specific side-channel attacks, i.e., by interfering with resource sharing so as to eliminate information conveyed by the events that the attacker times in its attack. For example, resource partitioning (e.g., [7,27,30]) and access randomization (e.g., [18,35,36]) have been proposed as hardware defenses against timing side channels in CPU caches. Other approaches have modified how caches are used to mitigate side channels in them (e.g., [19,44]). Some have coarsened CPU sharing by altering the CPU scheduler to mitigate timing side channels specifically in per-core caches (e.g., [31,32]). Wang et al. [34] analyzed timing channels through shared memory controllers and proposed techniques to close them. CATalyst uses an Intel-specific cache optimization [22] to fight against LLC-based side channels.

Yet another way of defending against side-channel attacks is to modify the applications to better protect their secrets. These solutions range from tools to limit branching on sensitive data (e.g., [6]) to application-specific side-channel-free implementations (e.g., [20]), or even to execute multiple program paths—as if the program were executed using many secret values [28]. Our proposal also requires changes to the application, although the changes are straightforward, involving inserting some VMFUNC instructions right before and after operations involving secrets.

While we have focused in this paper on demonstrating on-demand defense via adaptive coarsening of the time stamp counter, this technique could be equally well applied to other real-time clocks on the platform. Still, it remains possible for an application to implement its own timer thread that it can use to measure other events in the system [37]. For example, Shwarz et al. [29] and Chen et al. [5] used this technique to build a timer inside an SGX enclave (and thus without access to a real-time clock), for the purposes of mounting and defending against classes of side-channel attacks, respectively. Adapting the techniques we describe here to provide on-demand coarsening of such "clocks" is an intriguing area of future work.

We are not the first to use VMFUNC in the implementation of security techniques. SeCage [24] retrofits VMFUNC and nested paging in Intel processors to transparently provide different memory views for different compartments at a low cost, preventing the disclosure of private keys and memory scanning from rootkits. We, on the other hand, simply leverage VMFUNC as a low-cost interface between the VM and the hypervisor to make frequent communications between them efficient.

6   Conclusion and Limitations

In conclusion, we propose a method to allow VMs to dynamically request that the time stamp counter (TSC) be coarsened temporarily (to a level requested by the VM) on the platform, to mitigate timing side channels that use it. We take advantage of hardware virtualization extensions to provide a lightweight yet effective method to enable system-wide side-channel mitigation. By leveraging the VMFUNC interface in a novel way, our technique allows a VM application to send on-demand requests to the hypervisor to mask just enough low-order bits of the TSC to disable precise time measurements by another co-resident VM. We demonstrated the efficacy of our defense against two covert channels, thereby shedding light on how many TSC bits should be zeroed in these attack scenarios. Our experiments with three different workloads showed that our proposal could have lower performance overhead than existing defenses that provide constant degradation of TSC fidelity throughout the VM's lifetime.

Our design does have a few limitations, however. First, our design depends on hardware support, specifically for invoking a new function via the VMFUNC instruction. Second, any defense that coarsens timing sources (ours or others [25,33,38]) might affect time-critical operations. Third, our approach relies on application developers to locate sensitive portions of the code that are vulnerable to timing side-channel attacks. Fourth, an attacker VM might request large values of n simply to degrade others' use of the TSC. As discussed in Sect. 1, we believe that policies could be put in place to discourage such activities. Lastly, allowing applications to vary n could itself potentially lead to a side-channel leakage by revealing *when* a sensitive operation is occurring. Because attackers can often infer these occurrences based on other circumstances, or even cause them to occur (e.g., by submitting requests to the victim VM), we consider this risk to be minimal.

Acknowledgment. This work was supported in part by NSF grant 1330599.

References

1. Intel 64 and IA-32 Architectures Software Developer's Manual. http://www.intel.com/content/www/us/en/processors/architectures-software-developer-manuals.html
2. Askarov, A., Zhang, D., Myers, A.C.: Predictive black-box mitigation of timing channels. In: 17th ACM Conference on Computer and Communications Security (2010)
3. Barresi, A., Razavi, K., Payer, M., Gross, T.R.: CAIN: silently breaking ASLR in the cloud. In: 9th USENIX Workshop on Offensive Technologies (2015)

4. Benger, N., van de Pol, J., Smart, N.P., Yarom, Y.: "Ooh aah.. just a little bit": a small amount of side channel can go a long way. In: Batina, L., Robshaw, M. (eds.) CHES 2014. LNCS, vol. 8731, pp. 75–92. Springer, Heidelberg (2014). doi:10.1007/978-3-662-44709-3_5

5. Chen, S., Zhang, X., Reiter, M.K., Zhang, Y.: Detecting privileged side-channel attacks in shielded execution with Déjá Vu. In: 12th ACM Asia Conference on Computer and Communications Security (2017)

6. Crane, S., Homescu, A., Brunthaler, S., Larsen, P., Franz, M.: Thwarting cache side-channel attacks through dynamic software diversity. In: ISOC Network and Distributed System Security Symposium (2015)

7. Domnitser, L., Jaleel, A., Loew, J., Abu-Ghazaleh, N., Ponomarev, D.: Non-monopolizable caches: low-complexity mitigation of cache side channel attacks. ACM Trans. Archit. Code Optim. **8**(4), 35 (2012)

8. Genkin, D., Pachmanov, L., Pipman, I., Tromer, E., Yarom, Y.: ECDSA key extraction from mobile devices via nonintrusive physical side channels. In: 23rd ACM Conference on Computer and Communications Security (2016)

9. Gras, B., Razavi, K., Bosman, E., Bos, H., Giuffrida, C.: ASLR on the line: Practical cache attacks on the MMU. In ISOC Network and Distributed System Security Symposium (2017)

10. Gruss, D., Spreitzer, R., Mangard, S.: Cache template attacks: automating attacks on inclusive last-level caches. In: 24th USENIX Security Symposium (2015)

11. Gullasch, D., Bangerter, E., Krenn, S.: Cache games-bringing access-based cache attacks on AES to practice. In: 32nd IEEE Symposium Security and Privacy (2011)

12. Hu, W.-M.: Reducing timing channels with fuzzy time. J. Comput. Secur. **1**(3–4), 233–254 (1992)

13. Hund, R., Willems, C., Holz, T.: Practical timing side channel attacks against kernel space ASLR. In: 34th IEEE Symposium Security and Privacy (2013)

14. Inci, M.S., Gulmezoglu, B., Irazoqui, G., Eisenbarth, T., Sunar, B.: Seriously, get off my cloud! Cross-VM RSA key recovery in a public cloud. IACR Cryptology ePrint Archive, Report 2015/898 (2015)

15. Irazoqui, G., Eisenbarth, T., Sunar, B.: A shared cache attack that works across cores and defies VM sandboxing-and its application to AES. In: 36th IEEE Symposium Security and Privacy (2015)

16. Irazoqui, G., Inci, M.S., Eisenbarth, T., Sunar, B.: Fine grain cross-VM attacks on Xen and VMware. In: 4th IEEE International Conference on Big Data and Cloud Computing (2014)

17. Irazoqui, G., Inci, M.S., Eisenbarth, T., Sunar, B.: Wait a minute! A fast, cross-VM attack on AES. In: Stavrou, A., Bos, H., Portokalidis, G. (eds.) RAID 2014. LNCS, vol. 8688, pp. 299–319. Springer, Cham (2014). doi:10.1007/978-3-319-11379-1_15

18. Keramidas, G., Antonopoulos, A., Serpanos, D.N., Kaxiras, S.: Non deterministic caches: a simple and effective defense against side channel attacks. Des. Autom. Embed. Syst. **12**(3), 221–230 (2008)

19. Kim, T., Peinado, M., Mainar-Ruiz, G.: StealthMem: system-level protection against cache-based side channel attacks in the cloud. In: 21st USENIX Security Symposium (2012)

20. Könighofer, R.: A fast and cache-timing resistant implementation of the AES. In: Malkin, T. (ed.) CT-RSA 2008. LNCS, vol. 4964, pp. 187–202. Springer, Heidelberg (2008). doi:10.1007/978-3-540-79263-5_12

21. Li, P., Gao, D., Reiter, M.K.: StopWatch: a cloud architecture for timing channel mitigation. ACM Trans. Inf. Syst. Secur. **17**(2), 8 (2014)

22. Liu, F., Ge, Q., Yarom, Y., Mckeen, F., Rozas, C., Heiser, G., Lee, R.B.: Catalyst: defeating last-level cache side channel attacks in cloud computing. In: 22nd International Symposium High Performance Computer Architecture (2016)
23. Liu, F., Yarom, Y., Ge, Q., Heiser, G., Lee, R.B.: Last-level cache side-channel attacks are practical. In: 36th IEEE Symposium Security and Privacy (2015)
24. Liu, Y., Zhou, T., Chen, K., Chen, H., Xia, Y.: Thwarting memory disclosure with efficient hypervisor-enforced intra-domain isolation. In: 22nd ACM Conference on Computer and Communications Security (2015)
25. Martin, R., Demme, J., Sethumadhavan, S.: TimeWarp: rethinking timekeeping and performance monitoring mechanisms to mitigate side-channel attacks. In: 39th International Symposium on Computer Architecture (2012)
26. Osvik, D.A., Shamir, A., Tromer, E.: Cache attacks and countermeasures: the case of AES. In: Pointcheval, D. (ed.) CT-RSA 2006. LNCS, vol. 3860, pp. 1–20. Springer, Heidelberg (2006). doi:10.1007/11605805_1
27. Raj, H., Nathuji, R., Singh, A., England, P.: Resource management for isolation enhanced cloud services. In: 1st ACM Cloud Computing Security Workshop (2009)
28. Rane, A., Lin, C., Tiwari, M.: Raccoon: closing digital side-channels through obfuscated execution. In: 24th USENIX Security Symposium (2015)
29. Schwarz, M., Weiser, S., Gruss, D., Maurice, C., Mangard, S.: Malware guard extension: using SGX to conceal cache attacks. arXiv:1702.08719 (2017)
30. Shi, J., Song, X., Chen, H., Zang, B.: Limiting cache-based side-channel in multi-tenant cloud using dynamic page coloring. In: 41st IEEE/IFIP International Conference Dependable Systems and Networks (2011)
31. Stefan, D., Buiras, P., Yang, E.Z., Levy, A., Terei, D., Russo, A., Mazières, D.: Eliminating cache-based timing attacks with instruction-based scheduling. In: Crampton, J., Jajodia, S., Mayes, K. (eds.) ESORICS 2013. LNCS, vol. 8134, pp. 718–735. Springer, Heidelberg (2013). doi:10.1007/978-3-642-40203-6_40
32. Varadarajan, V., Ristenpart, T., Swift, M.: Scheduler-based defenses against cross-VM side-channels. In: 23rd USENIX Security Symposium (2014)
33. Vattikonda, B.C., Das, S., Shacham, H.: Eliminating fine grained timers in Xen. In: 3rd ACM Cloud Computing Security Workshop (2011)
34. Wang, Y., Ferraiuolo, A., Suh, G.E.: Timing channel protection for a shared memory controller. In: 20th International Symposium on High Performance Computer Architecture (2014)
35. Wang, Z., Lee, R.B.: New cache designs for thwarting software cache-based side channel attacks. In: 34th International Symposium on Computer Architecture (2007)
36. Wang, Z., Lee, R.B.: A novel cache architecture with enhanced performance and security. In: 41st IEEE/ACM International Symposium on Microarchitecture (2008)
37. Wray, J.C.: An analysis of covert timing channels. J. Comput. Secur. 1(3–4), 219–232 (1992)
38. Wu, W., Zhai, E., Wolinsky, D.I., Ford, B., Gu, L., Jackowitz, D.: Warding off timing attacks in Deterland. In: Conference on Timely Results in Operating Systems (2015)
39. Wu, Z., Xu, Z., Wang, H.: Whispers in the hyper-space: high-bandwidth and reliable covert channel attacks inside the cloud. IEEE/ACM Trans. Netw. 23(2), 603–614 (2015)
40. Yarom, Y., Falkner, K.: Flush+reload: a high resolution, low noise, L3 cache side-channel attack. In: 23rd USENIX Security Symposium (2014)

41. Zhang, D., Askarov, A., Myers, A.C.: Predictive mitigation of timing channels in interactive systems. In: 18th ACM Conference on Computer and Communications Security (2011)
42. Zhang, Y., Juels, A., Reiter, M.K., Ristenpart, T.: Cross-VM side channels and their use to extract private keys. In: 19th ACM Conference on Computer and Communications Security (2012)
43. Zhang, Y., Juels, A., Reiter, M.K., Ristenpart, T.: Cross-tenant side-channel attacks in PaaS clouds. In: 21st ACM Conference on Computer and Communications Security (2014)
44. Zhou, Z., Reiter, M.K., Zhang, Y.: A software approach to defeating side channels in last-level caches. In: 23rd ACM Conference on Computer and Communications Security (2016)

VuRLE: Automatic Vulnerability Detection and Repair by Learning from Examples

Siqi Ma[1]([⊠]), Ferdian Thung[1], David Lo[1], Cong Sun[2], and Robert H. Deng[1]

[1] Singapore Management University, Singapore, Singapore
{siqi.ma.2013,ferdiant.2013,davidlo,robertdeng}@smu.edu.sg
[2] Xidian University, Xi'an, China
suncong@xidian.edu.cn

Abstract. Vulnerability becomes a major threat to the security of many systems. Attackers can steal private information and perform harmful actions by exploiting unpatched vulnerabilities. Vulnerabilities often remain undetected for a long time as they may not affect typical systems' functionalities. Furthermore, it is often difficult for a developer to fix a vulnerability correctly if he/she is not a security expert. To assist developers to deal with multiple types of vulnerabilities, we propose a new tool, called VuRLE, for automatic detection and repair of vulnerabilities. VuRLE (1) learns transformative edits and their contexts (i.e., code characterizing edit locations) from examples of vulnerable codes and their corresponding repaired codes; (2) clusters similar transformative edits; (3) extracts edit patterns and context patterns to create several repair templates for each cluster. VuRLE uses the context patterns to detect vulnerabilities, and customizes the corresponding edit patterns to repair them. We evaluate VuRLE on 279 vulnerabilities from 48 real-world applications. Under 10-fold cross validation, we compare VuRLE with another automatic repair tool, LASE. Our experiment shows that VuRLE successfully detects 183 out of 279 vulnerabilities, and repairs 101 of them, while LASE can only detect 58 vulnerabilities and repair 21 of them.

Keywords: Automated template generation · Vulnerability detection · Automated program repair

1 Introduction

Vulnerability is a severe threat to computer systems. However, it is difficult for a developer to detect and repair a vulnerability if he/she is not a security expert. Several vulnerability detection tools have been proposed to help developers to detect and repair different kinds of vulnerabilities, such as cryptographic misuse [17], cross-site scripting (XSS) [26], component hijacking vulnerability [28], etc.

Prior studies on automatic vulnerability repair typically focus on one type of vulnerability. These studies require custom manually-generated templates or custom heuristics tailored for a particular vulnerability. CDRep [17] is a tool to

© Springer International Publishing AG 2017
S.N. Foley et al. (Eds.): ESORICS 2017, Part II, LNCS 10493, pp. 229–246, 2017.
DOI: 10.1007/978-3-319-66399-9_13

repair cryptographic vulnerabilities. It detects and repairs the misuses of cryptographic algorithms. By *manually* summarizing repair patterns from correct primitive implementations, repair templates are generated. Similar to CDRep, Wang et al. [26] proposed an approach to repair string vulnerabilities in web applications. They *manually* construct input string patterns and attack patterns. Based on the input-attack patterns, the tool can compute a safe input, and convert a malicious input into a safe input. AppSealer [28] defines *manually* crafted rules for different types of data to repair component hijacking vulnerabilities by using taint analysis. By applying dataflow analysis, it can identify tainted variables, and further repair those variables based on the defined rules.

Manually generating repair templates and defining repair rules are tedious and time consuming activities. As technology and computer systems advance, different vulnerabilities may occur and fixing each of them likely requires different repair patterns. Unfortunately, it is very expensive or even impractical to manually create specific templates or rules for all kinds of vulnerabilities. The above facts highlight the importance of developing techniques that can generate repair templates automatically.

To help developers repair common bugs, Meng et al. [20] proposed LASE that can automatically generate a repair template. LASE automatically learns an edit script from two or more repair examples. However, LASE's inference process has two major limitations. First, it can only generate a general template for a type of bug. However, a bug can be repaired in different ways based on the *context* (i.e., preceding code where a bug appears in). Second, it cannot learn multiple repair templates from a repair example that involves repair multiple bugs.

To address the above limitations, we design and implement a novel tool, called VuRLE (Vulnerability Repair by Learning from Examples), that can help developers automatically detect and repair multiple types of vulnerabilities. VuRLE works as follows:

1. VuRLE analyzes a training set of repair examples and identifies *edit blocks* – each being series of related edits and its context from each example. Each example contains a vulnerable code and its repaired code.
2. VuRLE clusters similar edit blocks in to groups.
3. Next, VuRLE generates several repair templates for each group from pairs of highly similar edits.
4. VuRLE then uses the repair templates to identify vulnerable code.
5. VuRLE eventually selects a suitable repair template and applies the transformative edits in the template to repair a vulnerable code.

VuRLE addresses the first limitation of LASE by generating many repair templates instead of only one. These templates are put into groups and are used collectively to accurately identify vulnerabilities. VuRLE also employs a heuristics that identifies the most appropriate template for a detected vulnerability. It addresses the second limitation by breaking a repair example into several code segments. It then extracts an edit block from each of the code segment. These edit blocks may cover different bugs and can be used to generate different repair templates. This will result in many edit blocks though, and many of which may not be useful in the identification and fixing of vulnerabilities. To deal with this issue, VuRLE employs a heuristics to identify suitable edit blocks that can be generalized into repair templates.

We evaluate VuRLE on 279 vulnerabilities from 48 real-world applications using 10-fold cross validation setting. In this experiment, VuRLE successfully detects 183 (65.59%) out of 279 vulnerabilities, and repairs 101 of them. This is a major improvement when compared to LASE, as it can only detects 58 (20.79%) out of the 279 vulnerabilities, and repairs 21 of them.

The rest of this paper is organized as follows. Section 2 presents an overview of our approach. Section 3 elaborates the learning phase of our approach and Sect. 4 presents the repair phase of our approach. Experimental results are presented in Sect. 5. Related work is presented in Sect. 6. Section 7 concludes the paper.

2   Overview of VuRLE

In this section, we introduce how VuRLE repairs vulnerabilities. Figure 1 shows the workflow of VuRLE. VuRLE contains two phases, **Learning Phase** and **Repair Phase**. We provide an overview of working details of each phase below.

Learning Phase. VuRLE generates templates by analyzing edits from repair examples in three steps (Step 1–3).

1. **Edit Block Extraction.** VuRLE first extracts *edit blocks* by performing Abstract Syntax Tree (AST) *diff* [8] of each vulnerable code and its repaired code in a training set of known repair examples.

    The difference between a pair of vulnerable and repaired code may be in several code segments (i.e., contiguous lines of code). For each pair of vulnerable and repaired code segments, VuRLE outputs an edit block which consists of two parts: (1) a sequence of *edit operations*, and (2) its *context*. The first specifies a sequence of AST node insertion, deletion, update, and move operations to transform the vulnerable code segment to the repaired code segment. The latter specifies a common AST subtree corresponding to code appearing before the two code segments.

2. **Edit Group Generation.** VuRLE compares each edit block with the other edit blocks, and produces groups of similar edit blocks.

    VuRLE creates these *edit groups* in several steps. First, it creates a graph where each edit block is a node, and edges are added between two edit blocks iff they share the longest common substring [11] of edit operations with a substantial size. Next, it extracts connected components [12] from these graphs. Finally, it applies a DBSCAN [5]-inspired clustering algorithm, to divide edit blocks in each connected component into edit groups.

3. **Repair Template Generation.** In each edit group, VuRLE generates a *repair template* for each pair of edit blocks that are adjacent to each other in the connected component (generated as part of Step 2).

Learning Phase

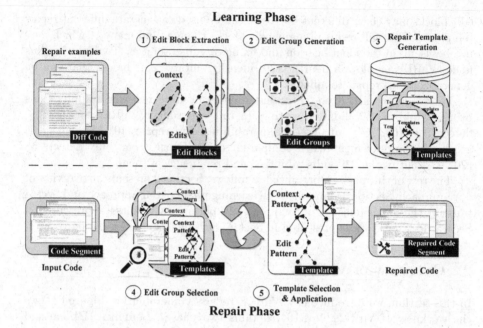

Fig. 1. Workflow of VuRLE: (1) VuRLE generates an edit block by extracting a sequence of edit operations and its context. (2) VuRLE pairs the edit blocks and clusters them into edit groups (3) VuRLE generates repair templates, and each contains an edit pattern and a context pattern. (4) VuRLE selects the best matching edit group to detect for vulnerabilities (5) VuRLE selects and applies the most appropriate repair template within the selected group.

Each repair template has an *edit pattern* and a *context pattern*. An edit pattern specifies a sequence of transformative edits, while a context pattern specifies the location of the code where the transformative edits should be applied. To create the edit pattern, VuRLE identifies the longest common substring of edit operations in the two edit blocks. To create the context pattern, VuRLE compares the code appearing in the context part of the two edit blocks. To generalize the patterns, VuRLE abstracts concrete identifier names and types appearing in the patterns into *placeholders*.

The context pattern is used to identify vulnerable code, while the edit pattern is used to repair identified vulnerabilities in the repair phase.

Repair Phase. VuRLE detects and repairs vulnerabilities by selecting the most appropriate template in two steps (Step 4–5). These two steps are repeated a number of times until no more vulnerable code segments are detected.

4. **Edit Groups Selection.** Given an input code and a set of repair templates, VuRLE compares code segments of the input code with edit groups and identifies an edit group that best matches it.

5. **Template Selection and Application.** The most matched edit group may have multiple templates that match an input code segment. VuRLE enumerates the matched templates one by one, and applies the transformative edits specified in the edit pattern of the template. If the application of the transformative edits results in redundant code, VuRLE proceeds to try the next template. Otherwise, it will flag the code segment as a vulnerability and generates a repaired code segment by applying the transformative edits.

3 Learning Phase: Learning from Repair Examples

In this phase, VuRLE processes a set of vulnerability repair examples to produce groups of similar repair templates. The three steps involved in this phase (Edit Block Extraction, Edit Block Group Extraction, and Repair Template Generation) are presented in more details below.

3.1 Edit Block Extraction

For each repair example, VuRLE uses Falleri et al.'s GumTree [7] to compare the AST of a vulnerable code and its repaired code. Each node in an AST corresponding to a source code file can be represented by a 2-tuple: (*Type, Value*). The first part of the tuple indicates the type of the node, e.g., VariableDeclarationStatement, SimpleType, SimpleName, etc. The second indicates the concrete value stored in the node, e.g., String, readLine, "OziExplorer", etc.

Using GumTree, VuRLE produces for each repair example a set of edit blocks, each corresponds to a specific code segment in the AST diff between a vulnerable code and its repaired code. Each edit block consists of a sequence of edit operations, and its context. The sequence can include one of the following edit operations:

– **Insert(Node** u**, Node** p**, int** k**):** Insert node u as the kth child of parent node p.
– **Delete(Node** u**, Node** p**, int** k**):** Delete node u, which is the kth child of parent node p.
– **Update(Node** u**, Value** v**):** Update the old value of node u to the new value v.
– **Move (Node** u**, Node** p**, int** k**):** Move node u and make it the kth child of parent p. Note that all children of u are moved as well, therefore this moves a whole subtree.

For each sequence of edit operations, VuRLE also identifies its context. To identify this context, VuRLE uses GumTree to extract an AST subtree that appears in both vulnerable and repaired ASTs and is relevant to nodes affected by the edit operations. This subtree is the largest common subtree where each of its leaf nodes is a node with SimpleName type that specifies a variable that is used in the sequence of edit operations. We make use of the `getParents` method of GumTree to find this subtree.

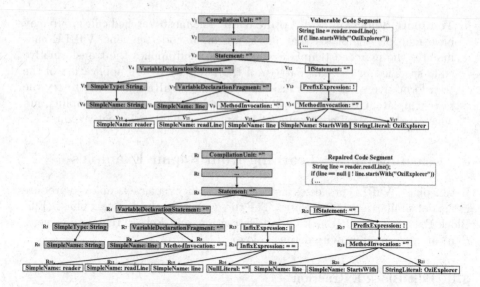

Fig. 2. Vulnerable and repaired code segments and their ASTs

To illustrate the above, consider Fig. 2. It shows the ASTs of a vulnerable code segment and its corresponding repaired code segment. Performing AST diff on these two ASTs produces a sequence of edit operations which results in the deletion of nodes V_{12} to V_{17}, and the insertion of nodes R_{12} to R_{21} into the subtree rooted at V_3. It also produces a context which corresponds to the common AST subtree highlighted in gray.

3.2 Edit Group Generation

VuRLE generates edit groups in two steps: (1) edit graph construction; (2) edit block clustering. We describe these two steps in detail below.

Edit Graph Construction. VuRLE creates a graph, whose nodes are edit blocks extracted in the previous step. The edges in this graph connect similar edit blocks. Two edit blocks are deemed similar iff their edit operations are similar. To check for this similarity, VuRLE extracts the longest common substring (LCS) [11] from their edit operation sequences. The two edit blocks are then considered similar if the length of this LCS is larger than a certain threshold T_{Sim}. Each edge is also weighted by the reciprocal of the corresponding LCS length. This weight represents the distance between the two edit blocks. We denote the distance between two edit blocks e_1 and e_2 as $dist(e_1, e_2)$.

Edit Block Clustering. Given an edit graph, VuRLE first extracts connected components [12] from it. For every connected component, VuRLE clusters edit blocks appearing in it.

To cluster edit blocks in a connected component (CC), VuRLE follows a DBscan-inspired clustering algorithm. It takes in two parameters: ε (maximum cluster radius) and ρ (minimum cluster size). Based on these two parameters, VuRLE returns the following edit groups (EGS):

$$EGS(CC) = \{N_\varepsilon(e_i) \mid e_i \in CC \wedge |N_\varepsilon(e_i)| \geq \rho\} \tag{1}$$

In the above equation, $N_\varepsilon(e_i)$ represents a set of edit blocks in CC whose distance to e_i is at most ε. Formally, it is defined as:

$$N_\varepsilon(e_i) = \{e_j \in CC \mid dist(e_i, e_j) \leq \varepsilon\} \tag{2}$$

The value of ρ is set to be 2 to avoid generating groups consisting of only one edit block. The value of ε is decided by following Kreutzer et al.'s code clustering method [14]. Their heuristic has been shown to work well in their experiments. The detailed steps are as follows:

1. Given an edit graph, VuRLE first computes the distance between each connected edit block. Two edit blocks that are not connected in the edit graph has an infinite distance between them.
2. VuRLE then orders the distances in ascending order. Let $\langle d_1, d_2, \ldots, d_n \rangle$ be the ordered sequence of those distances.
3. VuRLE finally sets the value of ε by finding the largest gap between two consecutive distances $d_{\langle j+1 \rangle}$ and $d_{\langle j \rangle}$ in the ordered sequence. Formally, ε is set as $\varepsilon = d_{\langle j^* \rangle}$, where $j^* = argmax_{1 \leq j \leq n}(\frac{d_{\langle j+1 \rangle}}{d_{\langle j \rangle}})$.

To illustrate the above process, Fig. 3 presents two connected components (CCs), $\{E_1, E_2, E_3, E_5, E_6\}$ and $\{E_0, E_7\}$. VuRLE first orders the distances into $[0.12, 0.14, 0.17, 0.25]$. It then computes the largest gap between two consecutive

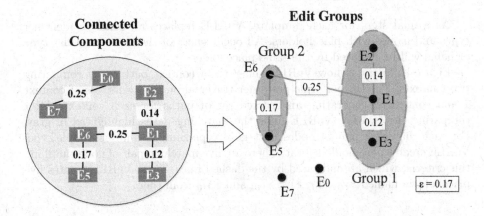

Fig. 3. Edit block clustering: CCs to edit block groups

distances, and identifies a suitable value of ε, which is 0.17. Based on $\varepsilon = 0.17$ and $\rho = 2$, VuRLE creates two groups of edit blocks for the first CC: $\{E_1, E_2, E_3\}$, and $\{E_5, E_6\}$. It generates none for the second CC.

3.3   Templates Generation

For each edit group, VuRLE identifies pairs of edit blocks in it that are adjacent nodes in the edit graph. For each of these *edit pairs*, it creates a repair template. A repair template consists of an edit pattern, which specifies a sequence of transformative edits, and a context pattern, which specifies where the edits should be applied.

To create an edit pattern from a pair of edit blocks, VuRLE compares the edit operation sequences of the two edit blocks. It then extracts the longest common substring (LCS) from the two sequences. This LCS is the edit pattern.

To create a context pattern from a pair of edit blocks, VuRLE processes the context of each edit block. Each context is a subtree. Given a pair of edit block contexts (which is a pair of AST subtrees, ST_1 and ST_2), VuRLE proceeds in the following steps:

1. VuRLE performs pre-order traversal on ST_1 and ST_2.
2. For each subtree, it extracts an ordered set of paths from the root of the subtree to each of its leaf nodes. The two ordered sets PS_1 and PS_2 represent the context of ST_1 and ST_2 respectively. We refer to each of these paths as a *concrete* context sequence.
3. VuRLE then compares the corresponding elements of PS_1 and PS_2. For each pair of paths, if they share a longest common substring (LCS) of size T_{Sim}, we use this LCS to represent both pairs and delete the paths from PS_1 and PS_2. We refer to this LCS as an *abstract* context sequence.
4. VuRLE uses the remaining concrete sequences and identified abstract sequences as the context pattern.

As a final step, for each template, VuRLE replaces all concrete identifier types and names with placeholders. All occurrences of the same identifier type or name will be replaced by the same placeholder.

Figure 4 illustrates how VuRLE generates a context pattern by comparing two contexts. VuRLE performs pre-order traversal on AST subtrees of context 1 and context 2, generating an ordered set of paths for each context. After comparing the two set, VuRLE finds the matching paths highlighted in gray. For each matching pair of nodes that is of type SimpleName or SimpleType, VuRLE creates placeholders for it. There are five matching pair of nodes fulfilling this criteria, which are indicated by the dashed lines. Thus, VuRLE creates five placeholders named V_0, V_1, V_2, T_0, and M_0 from them.

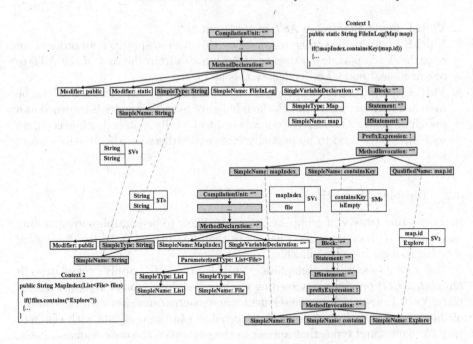

Fig. 4. Context pattern generation

4   Repair Phase: Repairing Vulnerable Applications

In this phase, VuRLE uses repair templates generated in the learning phase to detect whether an input code is vulnerable and simultaneously applies appropriate edits to repair the vulnerability. The two steps involved in this phase (Edit Group Selection and Template Selection) are presented in more details below. They are performed iteratively until VuRLE can no longer detect any vulnerability.

4.1   Edit Group Selection

To detect whether an input code is vulnerable, VuRLE needs to find the edit group with the highest *matching score*. VuRLE compares the input code (IC) with each edit group (EG) and computes the matching score as follows:

$$S_{matching}(IC, EG) = \sum_{T \in templates(EG)} S_{matching}(IC, T) \tag{3}$$

In the above equation, *templates(EG)* is the set of templates corresponding to edit group *EG*, and $S_{matching}(IC, T)$ is the matching score between template *T* and IC. VuRLE computes the matching score between the template *T* and input code *IC* as follows:

1. VuRLE first generates an AST of the input code.
2. VuRLE performs pre-order traversal on this AST to produce an ordered set of paths. Each path is a sequence of AST nodes from the root of the AST to one of its leaf node. Let us denote this as IP.
3. VuRLE compares IP with the context of template T. If sequences in T can be matched with sequences in IP, the number of matching nodes is returned as a matching score. Abstract sequences need to be fully matched, while concrete sequences only need to be partially matched. Otherwise, the matching score is 0.

4.2 Template Selection

In the most matched edit group EG, there are likely to be multiple corresponding templates (i.e., $templates(EG)$ has more than one member). In this final step, we need to pick the most suitable template.

To find a suitable template, VuRLE tries to apply templates in $templates(EG)$ one-by-one according to their matching scores. To apply a template, VuRLE first finds a code segment whose context matches with the context of the template. It then replaces all placeholders in the template with concrete variable names and types that appear in the context of the code segment. Next, VuRLE applies each transformative edits specified in the edit operation sequence of the template to the code segment.

If the application of a template results in redundant code, VuRLE proceeds to try the next template. The template selection step ends when one of the templates can be applied without creating redundant code. The code segment where the template is applied to is marked as being vulnerable and the resultant code after the transformative edits in the template is applied is the corresponding repaired code.

5   Evaluation

This section evaluates the performance of VuRLE by answering two questions below:

RQ1 (Vulnerability Detection). How effective is VuRLE in detecting whether a code is vulnerable?

RQ2 (Vulnerability Repair). How effective is VuRLE in repairing the detected vulnerable codes? Why some vulnerable codes cannot be repaired by VuRLE?

The following sections first describe the settings of our experiments, followed by the results of the experiments which answer the above two questions.

5.1 Experiment Setup

Dataset. We collect 48 applications written in Java from GitHub[1] that have more than 400 stars. These applications consist of Android, web, word-processing and multimedia applications. The size of Android applications range from 3–70 MB while the size of other applications are about 200 MB. Among these applications, we identify vulnerabilities that affects them by manually analyzing commits from each application's repository. In total, we find 279 vulnerabilities. These vulnerabilities belong to several vulnerable types listed in Table 1.

Table 1. Types of vulnerabilities in our dataset

Vulnerability type	Description
Unreleased resource	Failing to release a resource [19] before reusing it. It increases a system's susceptibility to Denial of Service (DoS) attack
Cryptographic vulnerability	Inappropriate usage of encryption algorithm [4,17] or usage of plaintext password storage. It increases a system's susceptibility to Chosen-Plaintext Attack (CPA), brute force attack, etc.
Unchecked return value	Ignoring a method's return value. It may cause an unexpected state and program logic, and possibly a privilege escalation bug
Improper error handling	Showing an inappropriate error handling message. It may cause a privacy leakage, which reveals useful information to potential attackers
SSL vulnerability	Unchecked hostnames or certificates [6,10]. It makes a system susceptible to eavesdroppings and Man-In-The-Middle attacks [2]
SQL injection vulnerability	Unchecked input of SQL. It makes a system susceptible to SQL injection attack, which allows attackers to inject or execute SQL command via the input data [16]

Experiment Design. We use 10-fold cross validation to evaluate the performance of VuRLE. First, we split the data into 10 groups (each containing roughly 28 vulnerabilities). Then, one group is defined as a test group, and the other 9 groups as a training group. The test group is the input of the repair phase, while the training group is the input of the learning phase. We repeat the process 10 times by considering different group as test group. We examine the repaired code manually by comparing it with the real repaired code provided by developers. Furthermore, we compare VuRLE with LASE [20], which is state-of-the-art tool for learning repair templates. When running VuRLE, by default we set T_{Sim} to three.

---

[1] Github: https://github.com/.

To evaluate the vulnerability detection performance of our approach, we use precision and recall as the evaluation metrics, which are defined as follows.

$$Precision = \frac{TP}{TP + FP}$$

$$Recall = \frac{TP}{TP + FN}$$

where TP is the number of correctly detected vulnerabilities, FP is the number of wrongly detected vulnerabilities, and FN is the number of vulnerabilities that are not detected by our approach.

To evaluate the vulnerability detection performance of our approach, we use success rate as the evaluation metric. Success rate is the proportion of the correctly detected vulnerabilities that can be successfully repaired.

5.2   RQ1: Vulnerability Detection

To answer this RQ, we count the number of vulnerabilities that can be detected by VuRLE and compute the precision and recall on the entire dataset.

Table 2. Detection result: VuRLE vs LASE

	# of Detected vulnerabilities	Precision	Recall
VuRLE	183	64.67%	65.59%
LASE	58	52.73%	20.79%

Table 2 shows the number of detected vulnerabilities, precision, and recall of VuRLE and LASE. VuRLE successfully detects 194 vulnerabilities out of the 279 vulnerabilities, achieving a recall of 65.59%. On the other hand, LASE can only detect 58 vulnerabilities out of the 279 vulnerabilities, achieving a recall of only 20.79%. Thus, VuRLE detects 215.52% more vulnerabilities compared to LASE. In terms of precision, VuRLE improves over LASE by 22.64%. It means that VuRLE proportionally generates less false positives than LASE.

5.3   RQ2: Vulnerability Repair

To answer this RQ, we investigate the number of vulnerabilities that can be repaired successfully. We also investigate how VuRLE can repair some bugs than cannot be repaired by LASE. We also discuss some causes on why VuRLE cannot repair some bugs.

Table 3 presents the success rate of VuRLE and LASE. The success rate of VuRLE is much higher than the success rate of LASE. VuRLE successfully

Table 3. Vulnerability repair: VuRLE and LASE

	# of repaired vulnerabilities	Success rate
VuRLE	101	55.19%
LASE	21	36.21%

repairs 101 vulnerabilities (55.19%), and LASE can only repairs 21 vulnerabilities, with a success rate of 36.21%. Thus, VuRLE can repair 380.95% more vulnerabilities compared to LASE. In terms of success rate, it improves over LASE by 52.42%.

Figure 5 provides a repair example generated by LASE and VuRLE on the same input code. The piece of code in the example contains a vulnerability that allows any hostname to be valid. LASE generates an overly general repair template, which only include invocation to `setHostnameVerifier`. It generate such template since each repair example invokes the `setHostNameVerifier` method after they define the `setDefaultHostnameVerifier` method, but the definition of the verifier method itself is different. On the other hand, VuRLE generates two repair templates that can repair this vulnerability. One of the template is for modifying the `verify` method, and another is for invoking the `setDefaultHostnameVerifier` method.

```
  HostnameVerifier allHostsValid = new HostnameVerifier(){
      public Boolean verify(String hostname, SSLSession session){
          return true;
      }
  }
- urlConnection.setDefaultHostnameVerifier(allHostsValid);
+ urlConnection.setHostnameVerifier(allHostsValid);
```

(a) Patch Generated by LASE

```
  HostnameVerifier allHostsValid = new HostnameVerifier(){
      public Boolean verify(String hostname, SSLSession session){
-         return true;
+         HostnameVerifier hv = HttpsURLConnection.getDefaultHostnameVerifier();
+         Return hv.verify(hostname, session);
      }
  }
- urlConnection.setDefaultHostnameVerifier(allHostsValid);
+ urlConnection.setHostnameVerifier(allHostsValid);
```

(b) Patch Generated by VuRLE

Fig. 5. A vulnerability repaired by LASE and VuRLE

Among 183 detected vulnerabilities, VuRLE cannot repair some of them. We discuss the main causes as follows:

Unsuccessful Placeholder Resolution. When replacing placeholders with concrete identifier names and types, VuRLE may use a wrong type or name to fill the placeholders. For example, the required concrete type is "double", but the inferred concrete type is "int". Moreover, VuRLE may not be able to concretize some placeholders since they are not found in the matching contexts.

Lack of Repair Examples. In our dataset, some vulnerabilities, such as *Cryptographic Misuses* and *Unchecked Return Value*, have many examples. Thus, a more comprehensive set of repair templates can be generated for these kinds of vulnerabilities. However, some vulnerabilities, such as *SSL Socket Vulnerability*, only have a few examples. Thus, VuRLE is unable to derive a comprehensive set of repair template to repair these kinds of vulnerabilities.

Partial Repair. For some cases, VuRLE can only generate a partial repair. This may be caused either by the inexistence of similar repairs or because VuRLE only extracts a partial repair pattern.

6   Related Work

This section describes related work on vulnerability detection and automatic vulnerability repair.

Vulnerability Detection. A number of works on detecting software vulnerabilities. Taintscope [26] is a checksum-aware fuzzing tool that is able to detect checksum check points in programs and checksum fields in programs' inputs. Moreover, it is able to automatically create valid input passing the checksum check. TaintScope can detect buffer overflow, integer overflow, double free, null pointer dereference and infinite loop. Sotirov [25] propose a static source analysis technique to detect vulnerabilities, such as buffer overflow, format string bugs and integer overflow. They classify the vulnerabilities and extracted common patterns for each type of vulnerability. Mohammadi et al. [21] focus on the XSS (Cross Site Scripting) vulnerability detection. Instead of analyzing source code, they detect XSS vulnerability that is caused by improper encoding of untrusted input data.

Medeiros et al. [18] propose a combination approach to detect vulnerabilities in web applications. They combine taint analysis and static analysis. Taint analysis is for collecting human coding knowledge about vulnerabilities. Furthermore, they generate several classifiers to label the vulnerable data. These classifiers achieve a low false positive rate. Fu et al. [9] propose a static analysis approach to detect SQL injection vulnerability at compile time. Their approach symbolically executes web applications written in ASP.NET framework and detects an SQL injection vulnerability if it can generates an input string that matches with a certain attack pattern. Kals et al. [13] propose SecuBat, a scanner that can detect vulnerabilites in web applications. SecuBat provides a framework that allows user to add another procedure that can detect a particular vulnerability. Similar like SecuBat, Doupé et al. [3] propose a web vulnerability scanner that is aware of web application state. It infers the web application's state machine by observing effects of user actions on the web application's outputs. This state machine is traversed to discover vulnerabilities. Balduzzi et al. [1] propose an automatic technique to discover HTTP parameter pollution vulnerabilities in web applications. It automatically launches an attack by injecting an encoded parameter into one of the known parameters and discovers a vulnerability if the attack is successful.

Similar like the above works, our work also detects vulnerabilities. However, those works are specialized to detect a certain type of vulnerabilities. On the other hand, our work can detect many types of vulnerabilities, under the condition that examples for repairing the corresponding vulnerabilities can be provided.

Vulnerability Repair. To repair vulnerabilities automatically, it is common to generate a repair pattern for a specific vulnerability. FixMeUp [24] is proposed to repair access-control bugs in web applications. It automatically computes an interprocedural access-control template (ACT), which contains a low-level policy specification and program transformation template. FixMeUp uses ACT to identify a faulty access-control logic and performs the repair. CDRep [17] detects cryptographic misuse in Android applications and repairs vulnerabilities automatically by applying manually-made repair templates. It makes use of seven repair templates, each for a particular type of cryptographic misuse. Yu et al. [27] propose an approach to sanitize user's input in web applications. Given a manually defined input pattern and its corresponding attack pattern, their approach checks whether an input has the same pattern with an input pattern and identifying whether the input is safe from the corresponding attack. If it is not, they convert a malicious input into a benign one. Smirnov and Chiueh [23] proposed DIRA, a tool that can transform program source code to defend against buffer overflow attacks. At running time, the transformed program can detect, identify, and repair itself without terminating its execution. Repair is achieved by restoring programs state to the one before the attack occurs, which was achieved through manually pre-defined procedures. Sidiroglou and Keromytis [22] propose an automated technique to repair buffer overflow vulnerabilities using manually-made code transformation heuristics and testing the repair in a sandboxed environment. Lin et al. [15] propose AutoPAG, a tool that automatically repairs out-of-bound vulnerabilities. It automatically generates a program patch by using pre-defined rules for repairing a particular case of out-of-bound vulnerability.

Different than the above works, our work aims to automatically repair different kinds of vulnerabilities by learning from examples. The closest to our work is LASE [20], which generates a repair template from repair examples. Different than ours, it cannot generate many repair templates from repair examples, which may include fixes for different vulnerabilities. It also cannot generate many sequences of edits when given a repair example, each corresponds to a certain code segment in the example.

7 Conclusion and Future Work

In summary, we propose a tool, called VuRLE, to automatically detect and repair vulnerabilities. It does so by learning repair templates from known repair examples and applying the templates to an input code. Given repair examples, VuRLE extracts edit blocks and groups similar edit blocks into an edit group. Several repair templates are then learned from each edit group. To detect and repair vulnerabilities, VuRLE finds the edit group that matches the most with the input code. In this group, it applies repair templates in order of their matching score until it detects no redundant code (in which case a vulnerability is detected and repaired) or until it has applied all repair templates in the edit group (in which case no vulnerability is detected). VuRLE repeats this detection and repair process until no more vulnerabilities are detected.

We have experimented on 48 applications with 279 real-world vulnerabilities and performed 10-fold cross validation to evaluate VuRLE. On average, VuRLE can automatically detect 183 (65.59%) vulnerabilities and repair 101 (55.19%) of them. On the other hand, the state-of-the-art approach named LASE can only detect 58 (20.79%) vulnerabilities and repair 21 (36.21%) of them. Thus, VuRLE can detect and repair 215.52% and 380.95% more vulnerabilities compared to LASE, respectively.

In the future, we plan to evaluate VuRLE using more vulnerabilities and applications written in various programming languages. We also plan to boost the effectiveness of VuRLE further so that it can detect and repair more vulnerabilities. Additionally, we plan to design a new approach to detect and repair vulnerabilities without examples.

References

1. Balduzzi, M., Gimenez, C.T., Balzarotti, D., Kirda, E.: Automated discovery of parameter pollution vulnerabilities in web applications. In: Network and Distributed System Security Symposium (NDSS) (2011)
2. Conti, M., Dragoni, N., Lesyk, V.: A survey of man in the middle attacks. IEEE Commun. Surv. Tutorials 18(3), 2027–2051 (2016)
3. Doupé, A., Cavedon, L., Kruegel, C., Vigna, G.: Enemy of the state: a state-aware black-box web vulnerability scanner. In: USENIX Security Symposium, vol. 14 (2012)
4. Egele, M., Brumley, D., Fratantonio, Y., Kruegel, C.: An empirical study of cryptographic misuse in android applications. In: Proceedings of the 2013 ACM SIGSAC Conference on Computer and Communications Security, pp. 73–84. ACM (2013)
5. Ester, M., Kriegel, H.P., Sander, J., Xu, X., et al.: A density-based algorithm for discovering clusters in large spatial databases with noise. In: Knowledge Discovery and Data Mining (KDD), vol. 96, no. 34 (1996)
6. Fahl, S., Harbach, M., Muders, T., Baumgärtner, L., Freisleben, B., Smith, M.: Why eve and mallory love android: an analysis of android SSL (in) security. In: Proceedings of the 2012 ACM Conference on Computer and Communications Security, pp. 50–61. ACM (2012)

7. Falleri, J., Morandat, F., Blanc, X., Martinez, M., Monperrus, M.: Fine-grained and accurate source code differencing. In: ACM/IEEE International Conference on Automated Software Engineering, ASE 2014, Vasteras, Sweden, 15–19 September 2014. pp. 313–324 (2014). http://doi.acm.org/10.1145/2642937.2642982

8. Fluri, B., Wuersch, M., PInzger, M., Gall, H.: Change distilling: tree differencing for fine-grained source code change extraction. IEEE Trans. Softw. Eng. **33**(11), 725–743 (2007)

9. Fu, X., Lu, X., Peltsverger, B., Chen, S., Qian, K., Tao, L.: A static analysis framework for detecting SQL injection vulnerabilities. In: 31st Annual International Computer Software and Applications Conference, COMPSAC 2007, vol. 1, pp. 87–96. IEEE (2007)

10. Georgiev, M., Iyengar, S., Jana, S., Anubhai, R., Boneh, D., Shmatikov, V.: The most dangerous code in the world: validating SSL certificates in non-browser software. In: Proceedings of the 2012 ACM Conference on Computer and Communications Security, pp. 38–49. ACM (2012)

11. Gusfield, D.: Algorithms on Strings, Trees and Sequences: Computer Science and Computational Biology. Cambridge University Press, Cambridge (1997)

12. Hopcroft, J., Tarjan, R.: Algorithm 447: efficient algorithms for graph manipulation. Commun. ACM **16**(6), 372–378 (1973)

13. Kals, S., Kirda, E., Kruegel, C., Jovanovic, N.: Secubat: a web vulnerability scanner. In: Proceedings of the 15th International Conference on World Wide Web, pp. 247–256. ACM (2006)

14. Kreutzer, P., Dotzler, G., Ring, M., Eskofier, B.M., Philippsen, M.: Automatic clustering of code changes. In: Proceedings of the 13th International Conference on Mining Software Repositories, pp. 61–72. ACM (2016)

15. Lin, Z., Jiang, X., Xu, D., Mao, B., Xie, L.: AutoPaG: towards automated software patch generation with source code root cause identification and repair. In: Proceedings of the 2nd ACM Symposium on Information, Computer and Communications Security, pp. 329–340. ACM (2007)

16. Livshits, V.B., Lam, M.S.: Finding security vulnerabilities in Java applications with static analysis. In: Usenix Security, vol. 2013 (2005)

17. Ma, S., Lo, D., Li, T., Deng, R.H.: CDRep: automatic repair of cryptographic misuses in android applications. In: Proceedings of the 11th ACM on Asia Conference on Computer and Communications Security, pp. 711–722. ACM (2016)

18. Medeiros, I., Neves, N., Correia, M.: Detecting and removing web application vulnerabilities with static analysis and data mining. IEEE Trans. Reliab. **65**(1), 54–69 (2016)

19. Meghanathan, N.: Source code analysis to remove security vulnerabilities in Java socket programs: a case study. arXiv preprint arXiv:1302.1338 (2013)

20. Meng, N., Kim, M., McKinley, K.S.: LASE: locating and applying systematic edits by learning from examples. In: Proceedings of the 2013 International Conference on Software Engineering, pp. 502–511. IEEE Press (2013)

21. Mohammadi, M., Chu, B., Lipford, H.R., Murphy-Hill, E.: Automatic web security unit testing: XSS vulnerability detection. In: 2016 IEEE/ACM 11th International Workshop in Automation of Software Test (AST), pp. 78–84. IEEE (2016)

22. Sidiroglou, S., Keromytis, A.D.: Countering network worms through automatic patch generation. IEEE Secur. Priv. **3**(6), 41–49 (2005)

23. Smirnov, A., Chiueh, T.C.: DIRA: automatic detection, identification and repair of control-hijacking attacks. In: Network and Distributed System Security Symposium (NDSS) (2005)

24. Son, S., McKinley, K.S., Shmatikov, V.: Fix me up: repairing access-control bugs in web applications. In: Network and Distributed System Security Symposium (NDSS) (2013)
25. Sotirov, A.I.: Automatic vulnerability detection using static source code analysis. In: Ph.D thesis (2005)
26. Wang, T., Wei, T., Gu, G., Zou, W.: TaintScope: a checksum-aware directed fuzzing tool for automatic software vulnerability detection. In: 2010 IEEE Symposium on Security and Privacy (SP), pp. 497–512. IEEE (2010)
27. Yu, F., Shueh, C.Y., Lin, C.H., Chen, Y.F., Wang, B.Y., Bultan, T.: Optimal sanitization synthesis for web application vulnerability repair. In: Proceedings of the 25th International Symposium on Software Testing and Analysis, pp. 189–200. ACM (2016)
28. Zhang, M., Yin, H.: AppSealer: automatic generation of vulnerability-specific patches for preventing component hijacking attacks in android applications. In: Network and Distributed System Security Symposium (NDSS) (2014)

Link-Layer Device Type Classification on Encrypted Wireless Traffic with COTS Radios

Rajib Ranjan Maiti[✉] , Sandra Siby , Ragav Sridharan,
and Nils Ole Tippenhauer

Singapore University of Technology and Design (SUTD),
8 Somapah Road, 487372 Singapore, Singapore
{rajib_maiti,sandra_ds,ragav_sridharan,nils_tippenhauer}@sutd.edu.sg

Abstract. In this work, we design and implement a framework, PrE-
DeC, which enables an attacker to violate user privacy by using the
encrypted link-layer radio traffic to detect device types in a targeted environment. We focus on 802.11 traffic using WPA2 as security protocol.
Data is collected by passive eavesdropping using COTS radios. PrEDeC
(a) extracts features using temporal properties, size of encrypted payload, type and direction of wireless traffic (b) filters features to improve
overall performance (c) builds a classification model to detect different
device types. While designing PrEDeC, we experimentally record the
traffic of 22 IoT devices and manually classify that data into 10 classes
to train three machine learning classifiers: Random Forest, Decision Tree
and SVM. We analyze the performance of the classifiers on different block
sizes (set of frames) and find that a block size of 30k frames with Random
Forest classifier shows above 90% accuracy. Additionally, we observe that
a reduced set of 49 features gives similar accuracy but better efficiency
as compared to taking an entire set of extracted features. We investigate
the significance of these features for classification. We further investigated the number of frames and the amount time required to eavesdrop
them in different traffic scenarios.

Keywords: Encrypted network traffic · Classification · Machine
learning

1 Introduction

According to [7], the number of IoT devices in 2016 has reached 6.4 billion and
is expected to hit the 20 billion mark by 2020. This proliferation of IoT devices
and wireless connectivity brings about questions of security and privacy. The
large volume of data generated by IoT devices can allow those with access to
the data to violate the privacy of the device owners.

Encryption techniques in protocols such as WPA2 are intended to preserve
confidentiality of data transferred over wireless networks. However, traffic analysis can be done even on encrypted link-layer traffic, using header information

© Springer International Publishing AG 2017
S.N. Foley et al. (Eds.): ESORICS 2017, Part II, LNCS 10493, pp. 247–264, 2017.
DOI: 10.1007/978-3-319-66399-9_14

and other parameters such as size and temporal properties. This was demonstrated in works such as [18,19], where features extracted from encrypted link-layer traffic were analyzed to determine a user's online browsing activity and smartphone app usage activity. In this paper, we investigate the possibility of analyzing eavesdropped WiFi link-layer traffic from devices to determine their type. If devices can be classified by type, an attacker can determine which types of devices are present in her surroundings, posing a privacy threat to the users of those devices. For example, an attacker's knowledge about device types on a company's premises would lead to information leakage about the presence and absence of people in particular locations (such as meeting rooms). The attacker might also obtain more details about the company's operations (for example, how many security cameras or laptops are present on the premises) or employees' lifestyles (how many employees are using fitness tracking devices). Furthermore, the attacker can use the knowledge of device types to exploit vulnerabilities associated with a specific type of devices. For example, the article in [13] reported more than 400,000 D-Link cameras, recorders and storage devices that were affected by a single vulnerability. An attacker might detect cameras in her environment and attempt camera-specific attacks on her surrounding devices. The attacker might also be correlate traffic to confidential activities such as the activation of an alarm system.

We propose the Privacy Exposing Device Classifier (PrEDeC), a framework that can be used to detect the presence of different types of devices in a wireless environment. PrEDeC takes eavesdropped encrypted link-layer traffic as input. PrEDeC does not require specialized equipment to obtain the traffic; it uses commercial-off-the-shelf (COTS) radios for eavesdropping. It extracts features from the traffic and uses trained classifiers on them to classify device types. In this paper, we focus on IoT devices such as IP cameras, Amazon smart speakers, smart printers and smartphones that communicate using the 802.11b standard.

We summarize our contributions as follows:

- We propose a framework, PrEDeC, that performs device type classification on eavesdropped encrypted link-layer wireless traffic using machine learning techniques.
- We present an implementation of the proposed framework and discuss which features of the traffic along with classification model are most relevant in device type classification.
- We investigate the accuracy of our implementation by performing experiments with a set of WiFi enabled devices in a controlled environment and compare the performance of three classifiers.

The paper is organized as follows. Section 2 briefly mentions the relevant background for our work. The attacker model and the classification framework is described in Sect. 3. Framework implementation is described in Sect. 4. Section 5 talks about the data sets used in our experiments, and the performance metrics for analysis. Related works are described in Sect. 7. We conclude the paper and discuss possible future work in Sect. 8.

2   Background

In this section, we briefly describe WiFi frame structure and the encryption technique used in WiFi.

2.1   WiFi Frame Structure

We consider wireless traffic that uses the 802.11 standard. A frame in 802.11 has the following fields as shown in Fig. 1:

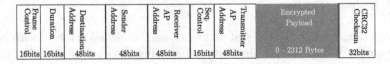

Fig. 1. IEEE 802.11 frame format.

1. Frame Control: This field consists of 11 sub-fields. It provides details about the frame's functions. It specifies the protocol version, type (management, control, data or reserved) and sub-type of the frame. It also has two sub-fields to indicate whether the frame is headed for a distribution system. Other sub-fields provide information such as the fragmentation, power management, order and re-transmission in the frame. Out of these fields, the type and sub-type play an important role in our analysis. Management frames facilitate communication among devices and have 12 sub-types. Control frames help in fair channel access among the contending devices and have 7 sub-types. Data frames carry payload in the frame body and have 9 sub-types.
2. Duration or ID: This field can take different values depending on the type and sender of the frame. It can be a station identifier, a duration or a fixed value. This field is not considered in our analysis.
3. Address: There are up to four address fields. These fields indicates the MAC addresses involved in sending and/or receiving the frame. These fields are used to correlate the device with its activity.
4. Sequence control: This field is used to indicate message order and help in identifying frame duplication. This field is not considered in our analysis.
5. Payload: This indicates the data content of the frame. Since the payload can be encrypted in case of WPA2, we do not use this field in our analysis. We only consider the size of the payload.
6. Frame Check Sequence: This field is used to check the integrity of the frame. This field is not considered in our analysis.

2.2   802.11 and WPA2

WiFi Protected Access 2 (WPA2) was developed to enhance the security mechanisms in WiFi networks. It introduced new protocols (4-way handshake, group key handshake) for key establishment and key change that would enable secure communication among authenticated parties. It also uses a stronger encryption protocol, CCMP, to encrypt the data. A CCMP data unit consists of the frame header, a CCMP header, the data unit, a MIC (Message Integrity Code) and the FCS (Frame Check Sequence). Out of these fields, only the data unit and the MIC (which protects the integrity of the message) are encrypted. The frame header is not encrypted. In this work, we consider only the header information of the frame and the size of the payload for our classification problem.

3   Link-Layer Device Type Classification on Encrypted Wireless Traffic

In this section, we describe the system model, and the attacker model with possible exploits. We then present the Privacy Exposing Device Classifier (PrEDeC), a framework to train classifiers and apply them for device type prediction.

3.1   System and Attacker Model

We consider a scenario where there is a set of devices that can communicate wirelessly. The devices need not be active at all times. In addition, the number of devices in the scenario does not remain constant, i.e., devices can be introduced into or removed from the system.

The attacker model consists of an attacker who can passively eavesdrop the wireless traffic of these devices. The attacker does not have prior knowledge of the devices in the network. Furthermore, she does not perform active probing of the devices and does not attempt to decrypt the wireless traffic. The attacker uses commercial off-the-shelf radios (e.g. wireless adapters in a laptop or raspberry Pi) to perform traffic captures. She has a pre-trained classifier, and eavesdrops for a period of time which allows her to obtain sufficient traffic samples to perform device type classification. The attack scenario is visualized in Fig. 2.

Fig. 2. Attack scenario. Encrypted traffic is observed and devices are classified.

3.2   PrEDeC

Privacy Exposing Device Classifier (PrEDeC) is a framework that enables an attacker to classify device types based on eavesdropped encrypted wireless traffic. An attack using PrEDeC consists of two phases:

Training Phase. This phase is run offline, before the actual attack. During the training phase, the attacker uses wireless traffic from a set of IoT devices to train a machine learning algorithm that can perform device type classification. The attacker performs three actions in this phase—data collection, feature extraction and selection, and model training in this phase. In the data collection step, she uses a COTS radio in monitor mode to passively eavesdrop wireless traffic. She has a number of IoT devices of different types, e.g., smartphone, camera, smart light, etc., from which she gathers traces. The eavesdropped traffic is stored in pcap files for analysis. The second step involves extracting features from the link-layer frames in the files. Features include the type and sub-type, size, direction, inter-arrival time and rate of frames. The feature extraction step produces signatures (a set of features) for every device (represented by its MAC address) present in the trace. The attacker uses certain statistical techniques to obtain a reduced number of features effective for efficient classification. The attacker does not consider MAC address and the manufacturer information that can be obtained from a MAC address as features believing that it may not have any correlation with the type of services provided by a corresponding device. The attacker appropriately labels (which indicates the device types) each of the MAC addresses present in the trace to properly correlate the high level activities performed by the corresponding devices. In the third step, the attacker provides the set of labels and signatures as input to train a model. The attacker can experiment with different models to obtain the best one for classification. The model training step also provides insight into which features were most helpful for classification. This, in turn, can be used as feedback to fine-tune the feature selection process. The attacker can repeat the three steps till she obtains a trained model with an optimized list of features for a large set of device types. She can then use this classification model to attack an unfamiliar environment.

Attack Phase. During the attack phase, the attacker eavesdrops wireless traffic from her target area. She performs feature extraction on the eavesdropped traffic and passes the list of signatures to her trained model. The model outputs the predicted device label for every MAC address present in the trace. The attacker can hence determine what type of devices are present in her environment.

4   Implementation of Framework

In this section, we describe the implementation details of the PrEDeC framework used to perform the attack described in Sect. 3. The framework is shown in Fig. 3. PrEDeC has six modules: data collector (optional), feature extractor, feature pruner, device annotator, model trainer and model tester. Each module is described in detail below.

4.1   Data Collector

The data collector performs passive eavesdropping of WiFi traffic and provides the sniffed WiFi frames as input to the rest of the framework. A number of

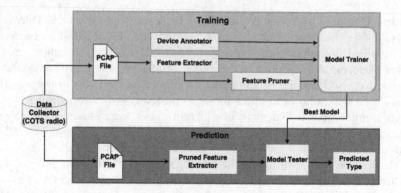

Fig. 3. PrEDec framework.

COTS tools can be used to capture the frames. In our case, we use a TP-Link TL-WN722N wireless adapter (in monitor mode) and Scapy (a python library for packet capture and analysis) to perform the traffic capture [15]. We set the adapter to perform channel hopping, so as to capture traffic on all fourteen WiFi channels. Since the adapter stays on a single channel at a time, frames on channels the adapter is not listening on will not be captured. Hence, the data collector captures a subset of the overall traffic. The sniffed frames are written to pcap files, which are then provided to rest of the framework as input.

4.2   Feature Extractor

The feature extractor extracts features from the frames collected by the data collector. We implement the feature extractor using Scapy. The feature extraction process consists of two steps. In the first step, certain fields are extracted from every frame in the PCAP file. These include the header information, the frame size and the timestamp of frame's capture. We refer to these fields as *basic* features. In the second step, the set of basic features are grouped based on the MAC addresses to compute, what we term as, *processed* features. However, since there may not be any correlation between the service(s) provided or activities performed and the MAC address used by a device, we do not use MAC address or manufacturer information (that can be obtained from a MAC address) as a feature in our work. This step takes one input parameter, called as *block size*. Block size indicates the minimum number of frames that is required to start computing the processed features. If an input pcap file contains more than the block size number of frames, we divide the frames into groups containing the block size number of frames and process each group separately. The processed features can be broadly grouped into five categories: rate, fraction, ratio, load and delta. Parameters used to compute the processed features are shown in Table 1.

Features in the *rate* category describe the rate at which frames are received or sent by a device. They are computed by calculating the number of frames of a particular type or sub-type to the observation window size. Features in

Table 1. Parameters used to calculate processed features.

Notation	Description
$T(f)$	Timestamp of a frame f
$First(mac, tp)$	$T(f)$ of first frame of type/sub-type tp containing MAC address mac
$Last(mac, tp)$	$T(f)$ of last frame of type/sub-type tp containing MAC address mac
$W(mac, tp)$	Observation window size $= Last(mac, tp) - First(mac, tp)$
$C(mac, tp)$	Number/size of frames with MAC address mac and type/sub-type tp
$S(mac, tp)$	Number/size of frames sent by a given mac of type/ sub-type tp
$R(mac, tp)$	Number/size of frames received by a given mac of type/ sub-type tp
$len(mac, tp)$	Size of frame of type/sub-type tp for mac
$gaps(mac, tp)$	Inter-arrival times of frame of type/sub-type tp for mac

the *fraction* category are of two types—aggregated and individual. Aggregated fraction features provide an indication of the contribution of each device to the total traffic. Individual fraction features provide an indication of the frame type composition for each device. The *ratio* category features look at the direction of the traffic and group it into sent and received traffic. Features in the *load* category calculate the mean and standard deviation of the sizes of different frames types. The *delta* category features consider the inter-arrival times of different frame types and calculate the mean and standard deviation of these times. The formulas to calculate the processed features are shown in Table 2. Features in the rate, fraction and ratio categories are computed in terms of both the number of frames and the sum of the sizes of the frames.

Table 2. Processed feature categories.

Feature	Notation	Calculation
Rate	$t(mac, tp)$	$\frac{C(mac, tp)}{W(mac, tp)}$
Fraction	$f_a(mac, tp)$	$\frac{C(mac, tp)}{C(all\_mac, tp)}$
	$f_i(mac, tp)$	$\frac{C(mac, tp)}{C(mac, all\_tp)}$
Ratio	$r_s(mac, tp)$	$\frac{S(mac, tp)}{C(mac, tp)}$
	$r_r(mac, tp)$	$\frac{R(mac, tp)}{C(mac, tp)}$
Load	$s_m(mac, tp)$	$mean(len(mac, tp))$
	$s_d(mac, tp)$	$std(len(mac, tp))$
Delta	$d_m(mac, tp)$	$mean(gaps(mac, tp))$
	$d_d(mac, tp)$	$std(gaps(mac, tp))$

4.3   Device Annotator

The device annotator assigns a label to each MAC address seen in an environment during the training phase. A label is determined by the functionality of a device. If a device has multiple functionality, the label will be assigned based on the discretion of the user of the classifier. In this work, we perform manual labeling of the devices. Table 3 shows the set of devices in our experimental setup—their manufacturers, function(s) performed and the labels assigned by the device annotator, along with a numerical ID. In the rest of the paper, we shall use a device and a MAC address anonymously to indicate a same thing.

Table 3. Devices used in our experiments and their labels.

Label	Manufacturer	Function (s)	Device label
I	Belkin	WiFi access point	Access point
II	Withings/Netatmo	Surveillance camera	Camera
III	Intel	Laptop	Laptop
IV	Belkin	Access point using Ether MAC address	Other AP
V	Alfa	Personal desktop computer with WiFi adapter	PC
VI	HP	Printer, scanner, and fax machine	Printer
VII	Raspberry Pi	WiFi monitoring device	Rasp. Pi
VIII	Philips	Smart light controller	Smart light
IX	LG	Smartphone	Smartphone
X	Amazon Echo	Smart speaker	Speaker

4.4   Feature Pruner

Feature pruner removes those features that may be redundant for efficient classification. Features are extracted, by the extractor module, without looking into any feature-to-feature dependency or correlation. Feature pruner does some simple statistical analysis such as calculating standard deviation and variance inflation factor to identify a set of important features to be used for efficient classification. It follows the steps below to obtain a reduced set of features that can have higher impact on classification:

1. Removes a feature having a constant value (i.e., standard deviation $= 0$) across all the devices, assuming it may not have any impact on the classification. Sometimes, such features can be seen due to the fact that frames with certain sub-types are not seen in the network.
2. Removes a feature from a pair of features having high correlation coefficient. It finds all pairs of independent features with an absolute value of Pearson correlation coefficient greater than 0.5. For each of those pairs, it finds the VIF (Variance Inflation Factor) and discards the one having greater VIF. The procedure is repeated until no pairs have high correlation coefficient. We use 'usdm' package in R for this purpose.

4.5   Model Trainer

The model trainer takes two inputs—the set of signatures from the feature pruner and the set of MAC addresses to device types mapping from device annotator. Note that MAC address is used only for annotating a signature, not for classification. The trainer produces a trained model which will then be used in future predictions. We experiment with three supervised machine learning algorithms for the model trainer—CART (Classification And Regression Tree), RF (Random Forest) and SVM (Support Vector Machine). We implement the model trainer module using the following R packages: 'rpart', 'randomForest' and 'e1071' for CART, RF and SVM respectively. We perform 10-fold cross-validation using the 'caret' package when building the models. The model trainer also provides a ranking of features based on their importance in the classification task. This can help to fine-tune the set of features for future classification tasks.

4.6   Model Tester

The model tester takes a trained model and a set of signatures from the feature extractor and produces a predicted set of labels corresponding to each MAC address present in the signature set. It also provides feedback on the contribution of each feature towards the classification task.

5   Experimental Setup

In this section, we describe the experimental setup and the metrics we use to evaluate PrEDeC.

5.1   Data Collection

In our experimental setup, we use 22 devices which are grouped into eleven types based on functionality (Table 3). We collect three sets of WiFi traffic data under different scenarios and durations. The amount of activity of the devices in the experiments varies based on the scenario. An overview of our test sets is shown in Table 4. Set I is collected in an office environment on a working day, over a period of about 3 h. In this set, the devices have medium usage. Set II is collected over the weekend (36 h of data) when the devices are relatively inactive. Set III is collected under more controlled settings. The devices are placed inside a shielded room [14] and are subjected to heavy usage (high activity scenario) for about 9 h. Note that since Set I and Set II are not conducted inside the shielded room, they have a large number of unknown devices, which we exclude from our analysis. In addition to this, in Set II, there is a OnePlus smartphone which produces several probe requests with random MAC addresses. We do not consider these addresses in our evaluation and plan to explore the impact of MAC randomization on classification in future work. We divide the datasets into training and test sets for our evaluation.

Table 4. Datasets used for performance evaluation.

Set	Purpose	Period (in hours)	Total size (in MB)	#packets (×1000)	#MAC	#Types	#Unknown devices	#known devices
I	Train	2.2	109	450	244	10	224	20
I	Test	0.53	22	100	241	10	219	22
II	Train	28	157	700	252	10	240	22
II	Test	8	40	183	239	10	227	12
III	Train	6.00	891.3	2272	38	10	23	15
III	Test	2.82	372.7	972	37	10	22	15

5.2 Performance Metrics

We use the following metrics to evaluate the performance of PrEDeC:

1. Accuracy – The ratio of the number of correct predictions to the total number of predictions.
2. Precision – The ratio of the number of correct predictions to the total number of predictions for a particular type of device.
3. Recall – The ratio of the number of correct predictions to the number of devices present of a particular type.
4. F-score – The harmonic mean of precision and recall, i.e., f-score $= (2 * \text{precision} * \text{recall})/(\text{precision} + \text{recall})$

While the accuracy measures the overall correctness of the predictions, precision and recall provide an indication of performance on individual device types. F-score is the combined performance of precision and recall of a classification. These metrics can be derived from the confusion matrix.

6 Performance Evaluation

In this section, we evaluate the performance of our classifier, PrEDeC. The feature extractor of the classifier extracts 853 processed features for each distinct MAC address from the corresponding group of frames. Recall that feature extractor, at first, divides the frames in blocks, and then groups the frames in a block based on MAC address. Classification is performed in two phases: first, using all features (about 476 in number) having non-zero standard deviation, and then with features (about 49 in number) having low or no pairwise correlation.

We apply our classification on each data set separately and observe very different performance on every data set. For example, Set I and Set III produce relatively low accuracy (from 70–80% on an average for all the classifiers), whereas Set II produces very high accuracy (about 90% on average). Delving deeper, we observe that Set II has got the data set when the status of individual devices did not change much as it was collected during the weekend. Hence, signatures in both the training and testing data are very similar for every device.

However, Set I and Set III consist of traces where devices were actively used. Hence, the devices changed their statuses, which leads to relatively diverse signatures for them. We combine the data sets into one set to get a good mix of different training and testing signatures. The results reported in the rest of the paper are obtained from this combined set of data. Note that total number of signatures will vary depending on block size, which is an input parameter to our framework. To evaluate performance, we consider the same block size for training and testing in our experiments.

6.1 Classification Using All Features

We first investigate the performance of three classifiers—CART, RF and SVM for different block sizes. This set of experiments is performed using all features having non-zero standard deviation (476 features). Figure 4A shows the variation of overall accuracy with different block sizes (let us denote block size by Ω) for the three classifiers. Accuracy in the CART classifier varies from 45% to 60%, and it achieves maximum accuracy when $\Omega = 5k$, 10k, 20k or 30k. The SVM classifier shows a relatively higher variation in accuracy, between 35–90%, and it achieves more than 80% accuracy only when $\Omega = 30k$. Accuracy turns out to be more than 90% in the RF classifier irrespective of block size. Note that the block size and the number of signatures are inversely proportional. The RF classifier has high overall accuracy with $\Omega = 30k$, 40k or 50k.

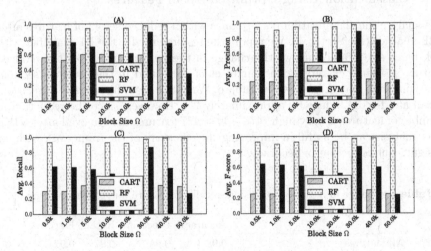

Fig. 4. (A) Overall accuracy (B) Average Precision (C) Average Recall (D) Average F-score for different block sizes in CART, RF, SVM.

Figure 4B shows that the precision (averaged over all device types) varies between 21–27% and 25–90% in CART and SVM respectively. In fact, we observe that the CART classifier fails to detect some types of devices such as the smart speaker during our experiments (results not reported due to space constraints). It shows almost the same precision over $\Omega = 5k$ to 30k. SVM classifier shows a similar trend as in the case of accuracy, with $\Omega = 30k$ producing the highest precision. It is observed that SVM sometimes fails to classify a few types (for example, the Raspberry Pi) when Ω becomes more than 30k. The precision remains above 90% in RF classifier, and $\Omega = 30k$ shows the highest precision though there is no large reduction in precision with higher Ω. This classifier detects all types with more or less same precision with any Ω.

Figure 4C shows that the recall (averaged over all device types) varies between 30–38% and 25–85% approximately in CART and SVM classifier respectively. SVM classifier finds all the devices only in case of $\Omega = 30k$. For other values of Ω, it fails to find 4–5 types of device on average. Again, it is interesting to observe that RF classifier provides consistently good (more than 90%) recall with any block size. Finally, F-score (averaged over all device types) shows that RF classifier outperforms the other two classifiers by a high margin in general, except for that in SVM with $\Omega = 30k$. This set of experiments clearly shows that the RF classifier performs much better than other models irrespective of block size. The block sizes of both 30k and 40k show better results in all three classifiers with any metric in general. However, we chose smaller block size (30k) as it can potentially improve run-time efficiency. Hence, the results in the rest of this paper are reported based on RF classifier with 30k block size.

6.2 Classification Using Optimized Set of Features

We analyze the classification performance with a reduced set 49 of features after VIF analysis (see Sect. 4.4). We report the results only for the RF classifier with 30k block size. Table 5 shows the change in the performance with the reduced feature set when classifying the same set of data used in the previous section. The confusion matrix is shown in Table 6. We notice that the accuracy, precision, recall and f-score reduce by approximately 2%. However, since the reduction in number of features is very high ($476 - 49 = 427$ features are removed after VIF), this analysis can be useful in improving the efficiency of the framework without a significant reduction in accuracy.

Table 5. Change in accuracy, precision, recall and f-score due to feature pruning.

	Accuracy	Precision	Recall	F-score
All features	0.98	0.98	0.97	0.97
% Change with reduced features	−1.64	−1.31	−3.17	−2.29

Furthermore, we look at the distribution of importance of the 49 features in RF classifier to find other avenues for feature reduction. The importance value of each of these features, grouped by category, can be seen in Table 7.

Table 6. Confusion matrix of RF classifier with 30k block size. Columns and rows indicate the number of the actual tags and the predicted tags respectively. Type IDs here are as shown in Table 3.

Type ID	I	II	III	IV	V	VI	VII	VIII	IX	X
I	36	0	0	0	0	0	0	0	0	0
II	0	125	0	0	1	0	0	0	2	1
III	0	0	36	0	0	0	0	0	1	3
IV	0	0	0	32	0	0	0	0	0	0
V	0	4	0	1	111	0	0	1	1	0
VI	0	0	0	0	0	36	0	0	0	0
VII	0	0	0	0	0	0	6	0	0	0
VIII	0	0	0	0	0	0	0	29	0	0
IX	0	2	2	0	0	0	0	0	29	0
X	0	1	0	0	0	0	0	0	0	32

Table 7. Mean and standard deviation of the importance values of the features in reduced set, for each category of features.

Category	Parameter	Mean % importance	Standard deviation
Rate	Frames count	1.21	1.32
	Frame size	0.76	0
Fraction	Frames count	0.02	0.02
	Frame size	2.73	0.90
Ratio	Frame count	0.03	0.02
	Frame size	4.76	4.35
Load	Mean	3.14	3.59
	Standard deviation	1.16	1.61
Delta	Mean	2.12	3.59
	Standard deviation	2.70	0
Number	Frame count	0.21	0.32
	Frame size	2.68	1.74

We observe that only 2 features have a percentage importance greater than 10%. These belong to *ratio* and *delta* category of features. The feature contributing least belongs to *delta* category. We report the distribution of values to the types of devices for two features, the most important and the least important ones (Fig. 5). The most important feature belongs to ratio category, and it is the ratio of the size of the data frames received by a MAC address to the size of all the data frames seen in a block. The least important feature belongs to delta category and it is the mean time gap of the management type frames with sub-type reserved for a MAC address. We see that the printer, camera, smart light and Raspberry Pi show much lower range of values in the ratio feature. The delta feature shows lower spread in Raspberry Pi and smart speaker. We plan to explore the classification efficiency by selecting features based on their importance values in future work.

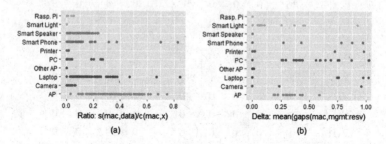

Fig. 5. Distribution of values of the most (A), and least (B) important feature in RF classifier belong to ratio and delta categories respectively (see Sect. 4.2).

6.3 Optimal Traffic Size

In this section, we investigate the number of frames needed to build a set of effective signatures and the time period required to eavesdrop them. We consider only the 30k block size in this analysis.

We see that it takes significantly different time durations on average to sniff 30k frames in the three data sets: about 550 s, 4200 s and 200 s for Set I, Set II and Set III respectively. In addition, standard deviation on time durations is very high in each of the data sets. We then look into average number of frames per group used to build signatures. Recall that frames in a block are grouped based on MAC address. It is observed that there is no direct correlation (Pearson correlation coefficient $= -0.06$) between the number of frames and the observation window size for any particular device in our (both individual and combined) datasets. However, we look for an average frame count and corresponding observation window size to get a rough estimation of the time required to sniff packets in our scenarios. We plan further investigation in this direction as future work.

Table 8 shows the average number of frames and the average observation window size used to build signatures for different types of devices in different data sets. For example, on an average, 1450 frames have been used to build signatures for the cameras and 771 s are needed to sniff those many frames in our combined data set. This analysis can be useful for an attacker to get an estimation of number of WiFi frames and time to eavesdrop them to achieve a certain accuracy.

6.4 Open Environment Experiment

We examine the performance of PrEDeC in an open, i.e., uncontrolled, environment using the RF classifier. We collect 1.1 million frames in 3.64 h in a lounge

Table 8. Number of frames (np) and corresponding window size (ws) per device types when 30k blocks are used.

Device type	Set I		Set II		Set III		Combined set	
	np	ws	np	ws	np	ws	np	ws
AP	5230	525	17088	4310	22245	290	19550	1182
Camera	257	359	2060	4229	1474	271	1450	771
Laptop	35	256	4683	4304	7024	288	5133	1041
Other AP	17	183	214	4126	21	213	67	1143
PC	114	446	1138	4198	142	279	331	1086
Printer	800	512	7271	4301	742	289	2161	1178
Raspberry Pi	16	251	1593	4154	-	-	1120	2983
Smart Light	483	258	150	4093	24	255	102	1181
Smart Phone	844	318	-	-	3094	257	2492	273
Smart Speaker	3543	427	382	4178	1121	269	974	1193
Average	1133.9	353.5	3842.1	4210.3	3987.4	267.8	3338	1203.1

area at our university. The RF classifier is trained using the data sets with 30k block size mentioned in the previous sections. We note that in this scenario we do not have the ground truth. However, by intuition, we would expect to see a larger number of PCs, laptops, and smartphones in a university. We would also expect to see a number of access points and IP cameras.

Table 9. Predicted device types in an open university environment.

Device type	AP	Camera	Laptop	Other AP	PC	Printer	Rasp. Pi	Smart Light	Smart phone	Smart speaker
Count	1	43	34	1	184	3	0	5	256	2

Table 9 shows the results of our prediction using PrEDeC classifier. We get a total of 3446 signatures with 529 unique MAC addresses in this dataset. We observe that PrEDeC detects larger proportion of smartphones and PCs as compared to the other devices. However, PrEDec detects only one access point despite the presence of multiple access points in the test environment. Additionally, the classifier detects 43 cameras, which is higher than the expected number. On closer inspection, we observed that several access points were classified as cameras. This is probably because we have only one access point in our training set. We hope to increase the accuracy of classifying access points by including more number of access points while training our classifier.

7   Related Work

Significant research was conducted in the area of device fingerprinting using link-layer information. Cache [4] used the duration field in 802.11 frames to identify various WiFi drivers. Franklin et al. [6] performed passive fingerprinting of 802.11 drivers by analyzing the inter-arrival times of probe request frames sent by different drivers. They employed a Bayesian classification method to classify 17 drivers. Their approach was fine-tuned in [5] to distinguish different operating systems using the same driver. Since different device types can have the same driver, our work has a more fine-grained classification in comparison to these works. Pang et al. [12] identified four metrics (network destinations, SSID probes, broadcast frame sizes, MAC protocol fields) that would help identify users from a network trace. Out of these, three metrics could be used even with link-layer encryption. In comparison to [12], our work focuses on device classification rather than user identification, and uses a larger set of features.

Hardware specific features such as clock skews [2,8] or radiometric signatures [3,17] were used to identify unauthorized access points and wireless cards. However, these features require precise measurement techniques or modification of the wireless monitor's driver. Hence, we do not consider these techniques in detail in relation to our work.

Another related area of research investigates classification of application behavior rather than device classification. Alshammari and Zincir-Heywood [1] evaluated the performance of five learning algorithms in identifying SSH and Skype traffic using flow based features. Korczyński and Duda [9] identified Skype service flows from TLS encrypted traffic. AppScanner [16], was a framework that used bursts and flows in the network traffic to fingerprint Android apps (using Random Forest). Our work is partly motivated by these works which suggests that encrypted link layer traffic can also become a useful tool to detect the presence of certain type of services provided by the WiFi enabled devices, and such detection would not require any active access to network infrastructure.

Zhang et al. [19] implemented a system to classify the type of online user activity based on link-layer traffic features such as the size distribution, direction, inter-arrival time and type of frames. They used SVM (Support Vector Machine) and RBFN (Radial Basis Function Network) algorithms to perform the classification. Wang et al. [18] employed similar techniques to detect apps used by a user on a smartphone by analyzing the link-layer traffic. They extracted features such as frame size, frame direction and frame inter-arrival time to train a Random Forest classifier and tested their implementation on 13 apps. [18,19] are the most comparable to our work since we utilize a similar, though larger, set of features in our classification framework. In addition, we focus on classifying device types rather than user activity.

Relatively little work has been done so far in IoT device type classification. Miettinen et al. [11] developed the IoT SENTINEL, a system that could identify the type of IP-enabled devices connected to an IoT network and restrict traffic from those identified as vulnerable. Meidan et al. [10] introduced ProfilIoT, a system that analyzed TCP sessions to distinguish IoT and non-IoT devices and identify the device class. Both these works employed machine learning techniques to perform the classification. However, in contrast to our work, they look at wired network traffic and make use of higher layer traffic information for their classification. A comparison of the proposed framework, PrEDeC, and selected related work is shown in Table 10.

Table 10. PrEDeC features vs. related work.

Related work	Layer	Classified entity	Wired/ wireless	Active/ passive	COTS
Proposed work	Link	Device type	Wireless	Passive	Yes
Franklin et al. [6]	Link	Device driver	Wireless	Passive	Yes
Jana and Kasera [8]	Link	Device type	Wireless	Passive	No
Alshammari and Zincir-Heywood [1]	Transport	Service	Wireless	Passive	Yes
Zhang et al. [19]	Link	User	Wireless	Passive	Yes
Miettinen et al. [11]	Multiple*	Device Type	Wired	Passive	No

*uses link, network, transport and application layer features.

8 Conclusion

In this paper, we designed PrEDeC, a framework that allows an attacker to classify device types using encrypted link-layer WiFi traffic obtained by passive eavesdropping with COTS radios. We extracted 853 features from the WiFi frames based on properties such as size, timing and type. We optimized them to a set of 49 features and evaluated three well-known machine learning algorithms: Decision Tree, Random Forest and Support Vector Machine, to classify devices. We evaluated the performance of our classifier using a data set collected in our lab environment of three different traffic scenarios, totaling about 48 h and 5.2 million frames. Our results showed that an accuracy of about 95% can be achieved using the Random Forest classifier. Our investigation revealed that an average of 3300 packets and an observation window size of about 1200s to sniff them are needed to build effective signatures to achieve this accuracy in our scenarios. It is observed that this estimation can vary significantly depending on the status of the devices present in the target network, and further investigation in this direction is planned as a future work. Finally, we have tested our classifier in an open and uncontrolled university area, and we are successful in detecting devices like laptops, smartphones and desktop computers in high numbers. However, our analysis in this case shows that it requires a larger number of devices of certain types like smart lights and cameras to achieve more precise classification.

References

1. Alshammari, R., Zincir-Heywood, A.N.: Machine learning based encrypted traffic classification: identifying SSH and Skype. In: IEEE Symposium on Computational Intelligence for Security and Defense Applications, CISDA 2009, pp. 1–8. IEEE (2009)

2. Arackaparambil, C., Bratus, S., Shubina, A., Kotz, D.: On the reliability of wireless fingerprinting using clock skews. In: Proceedings of ACM Conference on Wireless Security (WiSeC), pp. 169–174. ACM (2010)
3. Brik, V., Banerjee, S., Gruteser, M., Oh, S.: Wireless device identification with radiometric signatures. In: Proceedings of the Conference on Mobile Computing and Networking (MobiCom), pp. 116–127. ACM (2008)
4. Cache, J.: Fingerprinting 802.11 implementations via statistical analysis of the duration field. In: Uninformed.org, vol. 5 (2006)
5. Desmond, L.C.C., Yuan, C.C., Pheng, T.C., Lee, R.S.: Identifying unique devices through wireless fingerprinting. In: Proceedings of ACM Conference on Wireless Security (WiSeC), pp. 46–55 (2008)
6. Franklin, J., McCoy, D., Tabriz, P., Neagoe, V., Van Randwyk, J., Sicker, D.: Passive data link layer 802.11 wireless device driver fingerprinting. In: Proceedings of the USENIX Security Symposium, Berkeley, CA, USA (2006)
7. Gartner (2015). http://www.gartner.com/newsroom/id/3165317
8. Jana, S., Kasera, S.K.: On fast and accurate detection of unauthorized wireless access points using clock skews. IEEE Trans. Mob. Comput. **9**(3), 449–462 (2010)
9. Korczyński, M., Duda, A.: Classifying service flows in the encrypted Skype traffic. In: 2012 IEEE International Conference on Communications (ICC), pp. 1064–1068. IEEE (2012)
10. Meidan, Y., Bohadana, M., Shabtai, A., Guarnizo, J.-D., Ochoa, M., Tippenhauer, N.O., Elovici, Y.: ProfilIoT: a machine learning approach for IoT device identification based on network traffic analysis (poster). In: Proceedings of the Security Track at ACM Symposium on Applied Computing (SAC), April 2017
11. Miettinen, M., Marchal, S., Hafeez, I., Asokan, N., Sadeghi, A.-R., Tarkoma, S.: IoT sentinel: automated device-type identification for security enforcement in IoT. arXiv preprint, December 2016. arXiv:1611.04880v2
12. Pang, J., Greenstein, B., Gummadi, R., Seshan, S., Wetherall, D.: 802.11 user fingerprinting. In: Proceedings of the Conference on Mobile Computing and Networking (MobiCom), pp. 99–110 (2007)
13. SENRIO (2016). http://blog.senr.io/blog/400000-publicly-available-iot-devices-vulnerable-to-single-flaw
14. Siboni, S., Shabtai, A., Elovici, Y., Tippenhauer, N.O., Lee, J.: Advanced security testbed framework for wearable IoT devices. ACM Trans. Internet Technol. (TOIT) **16**(4), 26 (2016)
15. Siby, S., Maiti, R.R., Tippenhauer, N.O.: IoTScanner: detecting privacy threats in IoT neighborhoods. In: Proceedings of the 3rd ACM International Workshop on IoT Privacy, Trust, and Security, pp. 23–30. ACM (2017)
16. Taylor, V.F., Spolaor, R., Conti, M., Martinovic, I.: Appscanner: automatic fingerprinting of smartphone apps from encrypted network traffic. In: Proceedings of the IEEE Symposium on Security and Privacy, pp. 439–454. IEEE (2016)
17. Ureten, O., Serinken, N.: Wireless security through RF fingerprinting. Can. J. Electr. Comput. Eng. **32**(1), 27–33 (2007)
18. Wang, Q., Yahyavi, A., Kemme, B., He, W.: I know what you did on your smartphone: inferring app usage over encrypted data traffic. In: 2015 IEEE Conference on Communications and Network Security (CNS), pp. 433–441. IEEE (2015)
19. Zhang, F., He, W., Liu, X., Bridges, P.G.: Inferring users' online activities through traffic analysis. In: Proceedings of ACM Conference on Wireless Security (WiSeC), pp. 59–70. ACM (2011)

LeaPS: Learning-Based Proactive Security Auditing for Clouds

Suryadipta Majumdar[1]([⊠]), Yosr Jarraya[2], Momen Oqaily[1],
Amir Alimohammadifar[1], Makan Pourzandi[2], Lingyu Wang[1],
and Mourad Debbabi[1]

[1] CIISE, Concordia University, Montreal, QC, Canada
{su_majum,m_oqaily,ami_alim,wang,debbabi}@encs.concordia.ca
[2] Ericsson Security Research, Ericsson Canada, Montreal, QC, Canada
{yosr.jarraya,makan.pourzandi}@ericsson.com

Abstract. Cloud security auditing assures the transparency and accountability of a cloud provider to its tenants. However, the high operational complexity implied by the multi-tenancy and self-service nature, coupled with the sheer size of a cloud, imply that security auditing in the cloud can become quite expensive and non-scalable. Therefore, a proactive auditing approach, which starts the auditing ahead of critical events, has recently been proposed as a promising solution for delivering practical response time. However, a key limitation of such approaches is their reliance on manual efforts to extract the dependency relationships among events, which greatly restricts their practicality and adoptability. In this paper, we propose a fully automated approach, namely *LeaPS*, leveraging learning-based techniques to extract dependency models from runtime events in order to facilitate the proactive security auditing of cloud operations. We integrate LeaPS to OpenStack, a popular cloud platform, and perform extensive experiments in both simulated and real cloud environments that show a practical response time (e.g., 6 ms to audit a cloud of 100,000 VMs) and a significant improvement (e.g., about 50% faster) over existing proactive approaches.

Keywords: Proactive auditing · Security auditing · Cloud security · OpenStack

1 Introduction

Multi-tenancy in cloud has proved to be a double-edged sword leading to both resource optimization capability and inherent security concerns [37]. Moreover, the self-service nature of clouds usually implies significant operational complexity, which may prepare the floor for misconfigurations and vulnerabilities leading to violations of security compliance. Such complexities, coupled with the sheer size of the cloud (e.g., 1,000 tenants and 100,000 users in a decent-sized cloud [35]), can usually render security auditing in cloud expensive and non-scalable. In fact, verifying every user event at runtime can cause considerable

© Springer International Publishing AG 2017
S.N. Foley et al. (Eds.): ESORICS 2017, Part II, LNCS 10493, pp. 265–285, 2017.
DOI: 10.1007/978-3-319-66399-9_15

delays even in a mid-sized cloud (e.g., over four minutes [6]). Since the number of critical events (i.e., events that may potentially breach security properties) to verify usually grows with the number of security properties supported by an auditing system, auditing larger clouds could incur prohibitive costs.

To this end, a promising solution for reducing the response time of security auditing in clouds to a practical level is the proactive approach (e.g., [6,25]). Such an approach prepares for critical events in advance based on the so-called dependency models that indicate which events lead to the critical events [25, 44]. However, a key limitation of existing proactive approaches (including our previous work [25]) is that their dependency models are typically established through manual efforts based on expert knowledge or user experiences, which can be error-prone and tedious especially for large clouds. Moreover, existing dependency models are typically static in nature in the sense that the captured dependencies do not reflect runtime patterns. The manual and static nature of existing proactive auditing approaches prevents them from realizing their full potential, which will be further illustrated through a motivating example in the following.

Motivating Example. The upper part of Fig. 1 depicts several sequences of events in a cloud (from Session N to Session $N + M$). The critical events, which can potentially breach some security properties, are shown shaded (e.g., $E2$, $E5$ and $E7$). The lower part of the figure illustrates two different approaches to auditing such events. We discuss their limitations below to motivate our solution.

- With a traditional runtime verification approach, most of the verification effort (depicted as boxes filled with vertical patterns) is performed after the occurrence of the critical events, while holding the related operations blocked until a decision is made; consequently, such solutions may cause significant delays to operations.
- In contrast, a proactive solution will pre-compute most of the expensive verification tasks well ahead of the critical events in order to minimize the response time. However, this means such a solution would need to first identify patterns of event dependencies, e.g., $E1$ may lead to a critical event ($E2$), such that it may pre-compute as soon as $E1$ happens.
- Manually identifying patterns of event dependencies for a large cloud is likely expensive and non-scalable. Indeed, a typical cloud platform allows more than 400 types of operations [33], which implies 160,000 potential dependency relationship pairs may need to be examined by human experts.
- Furthermore, this only covers the static dependency relationships implied by the cloud design, whereas runtime patterns, e.g., those caused by business routines and user habits, cannot be captured in this way.
- Another critical limitation is that existing dependency models are deterministic in the sense that every event can only lead to a unique subsequent event. Therefore, the case demonstrated in the last two sessions ($N + 2$, $N + M$) where the same event ($E3$) may lead to several others ($E4$ or $E6$) will not be captured by such models.

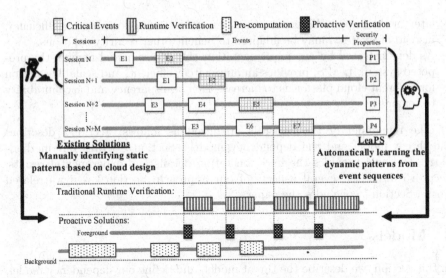

Fig. 1. Identifying the main limitations of both traditional runtime verification and proactive verification solutions and positioning our solution.

To address those limitations, our key idea is to design a probabilistic (instead of deterministic) dependency model, and automatically extract such a model from runtime events through learning techniques. Specifically, we first design a novel probabilistic model for capturing the dependency relationships between event types while taking into consideration the inherent uncertainty in such relationships. Second, we provide detailed methodology and algorithms for our learning-based proactive security auditing system, namely, *LeaPS*. We describe our implementation of the proposed system based on OpenStack [33], and demonstrate how the system may be easily ported to other cloud platforms (e.g., Amazon EC2 [1] and Google GCP [13]). Finally, we evaluate our solution through extensive experiments with both synthetic and real data. The results confirm our solution can achieve practical response time (e.g., 6 ms to audit a cloud of 100,000 VMs) and significant improvement over existing proactive approaches (e.g., about 50% faster).

In summary, our main contributions are threefold.

- To the best of our knowledge, this is the first learning-based, probabilistic approach to proactive security auditing in clouds. First, our probabilistic dependency model allows handling the uncertainty that is inherent to runtime events. Second, our learning-based methodology eliminates the need for impractical manual efforts required by other proactive solutions.
- Unlike most learning-based security solutions, since we are not relying on learning techniques to detect abnormal behaviors, we avoid the well-known limitations of high false positive rates; any inaccuracy in the learning results would only affect the efficiency, as will be demonstrated through experiments

later in the paper. We believe this idea of leveraging learning for efficiency, instead of security, may be adapted to benefit other security solutions.
– As demonstrated by our implementation and experimental results, the proposed system, LeaPS, provides an automated, efficient, and scalable solution for different cloud platforms to increase their transparency and accountability to tenants.

The remainder of the paper is organized as follows. Section 2 describes the threat model and the dependency models. Section 3 details our methodology. Section 4 provides the implementation details and experimental results. Section 5 discusses several aspects of our approach. Section 6 reviews related works. Section 7 concludes the paper.

2   Models

In this section, we describe the threat model, and define our dependency model.

2.1   Threat Model

We assume that the cloud infrastructure management systems (i) may have implementation flaws, misconfigurations and vulnerabilities that can be potentially exploited to violate security properties specified by the cloud tenants, and (ii) may be trusted for the integrity of the API calls, event notifications, logs and database records (existing techniques on trusted computing may be applied to establish a chain of trust from TPM chips embedded inside the cloud hardware, e.g., [3,21]). Though our framework may assist to avoid any violation of specified security properties due to either misconfigurations or exploits of vulnerabilities, our focus is not to detect specific attacks or intrusions. We focus on attacks directed through the cloud management interfaces (e.g., CLI, GUI), and any violation bypassing such interfaces is beyond the scope of this work. We assume a comprehensive list of critical events are provided upon which the accuracy of our auditing solution depends (we provide a guideline on identifying critical events in Appendix A). Our proactive solution mainly targets certain security properties which would require a sequence of operations. To make our discussions more concrete, the following shows an example of in-scope threats based on a real vulnerability.

Running Example. A real world vulnerability in OpenStack[1], CVE-2015-7713 [31], can be exploited to bypass security group rules (which are fine-grained, distributed security mechanisms in several cloud platforms including Amazon EC2, Microsoft Azure and OpenStack to ensure isolation between instances). Figure 2 shows a potential attack scenario exploiting this vulnerability. The prerequisite steps of this scenario are to create VMA1 and VMB1 (*step 1*), create security groups A1 and B1 with two rules (i.e., *allow 1.10.0.7* and *allow*

---

[1] OpenStack [33] is a popular open-source cloud infrastructure management platform.

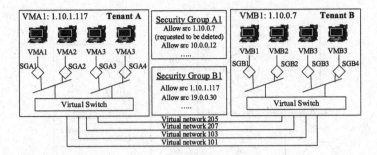

Fig. 2. An exploit of a vulnerability in OpenStack [31], leading to bypassing the security group mechanism.

1.10.1.117) (*step 2*), and start those VMs (*step 3*). Next, when Tenant A tries to delete one of the security rules (e.g., *allow 1.10.0.7*) (*step 4*), the rule is not removed from the security group of the active VMA1 due to the vulnerability. As a result, VMB1 is still able to reach VMA1 even though Tenant A intends to filter out that traffic. According to the vulnerability description, the security group bypass violation occurs only if this specific sequence of events (steps 1–4) happens in the mentioned order (namely, *event sequence*). In the next section, we present our dependency model and how it allows capturing rich and dynamic patterns of event sequences in the cloud.

2.2 The Dependency Model

In this section, we first demonstrate our dependency model through an example and then formally define the model. The model will be the foundation of our proactive auditing solution (detailed in Sect. 3).

Example 1. Figure 3 shows an example of a dependency model, where nodes represent different event types in cloud and edges represent transitions between event types. For example, nodes *create VM* and *create security group* represent the corresponding event types, and the edge from *create VM* to *create security group* indicates the likely order of occurrence of those event types. The label of this edge, 0.625, means 62.5% of the times an instance of the *create VM* event type will be immediately followed by an instance of the *create security group* event type.

Our objective is to automatically construct such a model from logs in clouds. As an example, the following shows an excerpt of the event types *event-type* and historical event sequences *hist* for four days related to the running example of Sect. 2.1.

- *event-type* = {*create VM (CV), create security group (CSG), start VM (SV), delete security group rule (DSG)*}; and

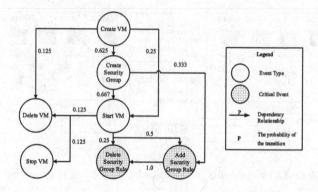

Fig. 3. An example dependency model represented as a Bayesian network.

- $hist = \{day\ 1 : CV, CSG, SV;\ day\ 2 : CSG, SV;\ day\ 3 : CSG, DSG;\ day\ 4 : CV, DSG\}$, where the order of event instances in a sequence indicates the actual order of occurrences.

The dependency model shown in Fig. 3 may be extracted from such data (note above we only show an excerpt of the data needed to construct the complete model, due to space limitations). For instance, in $hist$, CV has three immediate successors (i.e., CSG, SV, DSG), and their probabilities can be calculated as $P(CSG|CV) = 0.5$, $P(SV|CV) = 0.5$ and $P(DSG|CV) = 0.5$.

As demonstrated in the above example, Bayesian network [36] suits our needs for capturing probabilistic patterns of dependencies between events types. A Bayesian network is a probabilistic graphical model that represents a set of random variables as nodes and their conditional dependencies in the form of a directed acyclic graph. We choose Bayesian network to represent our dependency model for the following reasons. Firstly, the event types in cloud and their precedence dependencies can naturally be represented as nodes (random variables) and edges (conditional dependencies) of a Bayesian network. Secondly, the need of our approach for learning the conditional dependencies can be easily implemented as parameter learning in Bayesian network. For instance, in Fig. 3, using the Bayes' theorem we can calculate the probability for an instance of *add security group rule* to occur after observing an instance of *create VM* to be 0.52. More formally, the following defines our dependency model.

Definition 1. Given a list of event types *Event-type* and the log of historical events $hist$, the *dependency model* is defined as a Bayesian network $B = (G, \theta)$, where G is a DAG in which each node corresponds to an event type in *event-type*, and each directed edge between two nodes indicates the first node would immediately precede the other in some event sequences in $hist$ whose probability is part of the list of parameters θ.

We say a *dependency* exists between any two event types if their corresponding nodes are connected by an edge in the dependency model, and we say they are not dependent, otherwise. We assume a subset of the leaf nodes in the dependency model are given as *critical events* that might breach some given *security properties*.

3   LeaPS Auditing System

This section presents our learning-based proactive security auditing system (LeaPS).

3.1   Overview

We briefly describe the auditing process of LeaPS as follows. First, it builds offline a dependency model capturing the probabilistic patterns of event type sequences in the form of a Bayesian network by learning from the runtime event instances captured in cloud event logs. Then, once the model is constructed, it is used by the online modules in order to decide, based on the current observed event instances, the most likely next critical event to occur. This would trigger the proactive modules of our auditing system to pre-compute the required conditions that should be verified, when the critical event actually occurs. We iterate on these tasks to incrementally pre-compute for other likely critical events based on the decreasing order of their conditional probabilities in the model. Once one of these critical events actually occurs, we simply verify the parameters of the events with respect to the pre-computed conditions of that event.

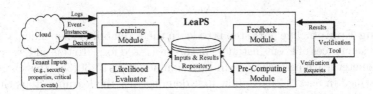

Fig. 4. An overview of LeaPS auditing approach.

Figure 4 shows an overview of LeaPS. LeaPS contains four major modules: learning, pre-computing, likelihood evaluator and feedback. The learning module is mainly responsible for conducting the learning of the probabilistic dependency model. The likelihood evaluator basically triggers the pre-computation based on the model. The pre-computing module prepares the ground for the runtime verification. At runtime, a light-weight verification tool [25], which basically executes queries in the pre-computed results, is leveraged for the verification purpose. Based on the verification result, LeaPS provides a decision on the intercepted critical event instance to the tenant. The feedback module provides feedbacks to different modules (e.g., learning module) to improve the performance of proactive auditing. In LeaPS, the data transfer between modules is performed through a repository. In the following, we detail each module in LeaPS.

3.2 Learning Module

The major steps of this module are: processing logs and learning dependency models.

Log Processor. The event logs in the cloud are used to learn the dependencies between different event types. However, log files generated by the existing cloud platforms are not suitable to be directly fed into the learning engine, as user events are generally mixed up with many other system-initiated events. Furthermore, logs usually contain many implementation specific details (e.g., platform-specific APIs). Therefore, the log processor is responsible for eliminating such system-initiated events and to map the relevant events into implementation-independent event types (more details will be provided in Sect. 5). Also, the log processor groups event sequences based on their dates (i.e., each group of event sequences for each day), and generates inputs (in a specific format) to the learning engine. Table 1 shows examples of OpenStack log entries and the output format of processed logs in LeaPS.

Table 1. Examples of OpenStack logs and output format of processed logs in LeaPS.

OpenStack log entry	Output format of LeaPS
[01/Apr/2017:10:55:41 -0400] "POST /v2/servers HTTP/1.1"	Create VM
[01/Apr/2017:11:00:45 -0400] "POST /v2/os-security-groups HTTP/1.1"	Create security group
[01/Apr/2017:11:01:15 -0400] "GET /v2/os-security-groups HTTP/1.1"	Eliminated

Learning Engine. The next step is to learn the probabilistic dependency model from the sequences of event instances in the processed logs. To this end, we choose the parameter learning technique in Bayesian network [15, 30, 36] (this choice has been justified in Sect. 2.2). We now first demonstrate the learning steps through an example, and then provide further details.

Example 2. Figure 5 shows the dependency model of Fig. 3 with the outcomes of different learning steps as the labels of edges. The first learning step is to define the priori, where the nodes represent the set of event types received as input, and the edges represent possible transitions from an event type, e.g., from *create VM* to *delete VM*, *start VM* and *create security group*. Then, $P(DV|CV)$, $P(CSG|CV)$, $P(SV|CV)$ and other conditional probabilities (between immediate adjacent nodes in the model) are the parameters; all parameters are initialized with equal probabilities. For instance, we use 0.33 to label each of the three outgoing edges from the *create VM* node. The second learning step is to use the historical data to train the model. For instance, the second values in the labels of the edges of Fig. 5 are learned from the processed logs obtained from the log processor. The third values in the labels of Fig. 5 represent an incremental update of the learned model using the feedback from a sequence of runtime events.

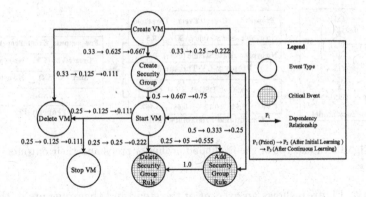

Fig. 5. The outcomes of three learning steps for the dependency model.

This learning mechanism mainly takes two inputs: the structure of the model with its parameters, and the historical data. The structure of the model, meaning the nodes and edges in a Bayesian network, is first derived from the set of event types received as input. To this end, we provide a guideline on identifying such a set of event types in Appendix A. Initially, the system considers every possible edge between nodes (and eventually deletes the edges with probability 0), and conditional probabilities between immediate adjacent nodes (measured as the conditional probability) are chosen as the parameters of the model. We further sparse the structure into smaller groups based on different security properties (the structure in Fig. 5 is one of the examples). The processed logs containing sequences of event instances serve as the input data to the learning engine for learning the parameters. Finally, the parameter learning in Bayesian network is performed as follows: (i) defining a priori (with the structure and initialized parameters of the model), (ii) training the initial model based on the historical data, and (iii) continuously updating the learned model based on incremental feedbacks.

3.3 Likelihood Evaluator

The likelihood evaluator is mainly responsible for triggering the pre-computation. To this end, the evaluator first takes the learned dependency model as input, and derives offline all indirect dependency relationships for each node. Based on these dependency relationships, the evaluator identifies the event types for which an immediate pre-computation is required. Additionally, at runtime the evaluator matches the intercepted event instance with the event type, and decides whether to trigger a pre-computation or verification request.[2] The data manipulated by the likelihood evaluator based on the dependency model will be described using the following example.

---

[2] This is not to respond to the event as in incident response, but to prepare for the auditing, and the incident response following an auditing result is out of the scope of this paper.

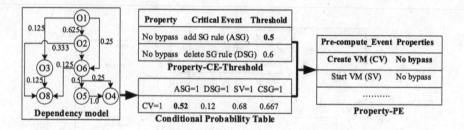

Fig. 6. An excerpt of the likelihood evaluator steps and their outputs.

Example 3. Figure 6 shows an excerpt of the steps and their outputs in the likelihood evaluator module. In this figure, the *Property-CE-Threshold* table maps the *no bypass of security group* property [8] with its critical events (i.e., *add security group rule* and *delete security group rule*) and corresponding thresholds (i.e., 0.5 and 0.6). Then, from the conditional probability in the model, the evaluator infers conditional probabilities of all possible successors (both direct and indirect), and stores in the *Conditional-Probability* table. The conditional probability for *ASG* having *CV* ($P(ASG/CV)$) is 0.52 in the *Conditional-Probability* table in Fig. 6. Next, this value is compared with the thresholds of the *no bypass* property in the *Property-CE-thresholds* table. As the reported probability is higher, the *CV* event type is stored in the *Property-PE* table so that for the next *CV* event instance, the evaluator triggers a pre-computation.

3.4 Pre-computing Module

The purpose of the pre-computing module is to prepare the ground for the runtime verification. In this paper, we mainly discuss watchlist-based pre-computation [25]; where watchlist is a list containing all allowed parameters for different critical events. The specification of contents in a watchlist is defined by the cloud tenant, and is stored in the *Property-WL* table. We assume that at the time LeaPS is launched, we initialize several tables based on the cloud context and tenant inputs. For instance, inputs including the list of security properties, their corresponding critical events, and the specification of contents in watchlists are first stored in the *Property-WL* and *Property-CE-Threshold* tables. The watchlists are also populated from the current cloud context. We maintain a watchlist for each security property. Afterwards, each time the pre-computation is triggered by the likelihood evaluator, this module incrementally updates the watchlist based on the changes applied to the cloud in the mean time. The main functionality of the pre-computing module is described using the following example.

Example 4. Left side of Fig. 7 shows two inputs (*Property-WL* and *Property-PE* tables) to the pre-computing module. We now simulate a sequence of intercepted events (shown in the middle box of the figure) and depict the evolution of a

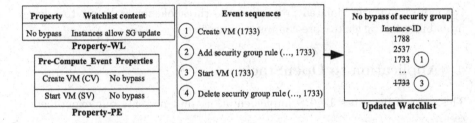

Fig. 7. Showing steps of the updating watchlist for a sample event sequences.

watchlist for the *no bypass* property (right side box of the figure). (1) We intercept the *create VM 1733* event instance, identify the event in the *Property-PE* table, and add VM 1733 to the watchlist without blocking it. (2) After intercepting the *add security group rule (..., 1733)* event instance, we identify that this is a critical event. Therefore, we verify with the watchlist keeping the operation blocked, find that VM 1733 is in the watchlist, and hence we recommend to allow this operation. (3) We intercept *start VM 1733* operation and identify the event in the *Property-PE*. VM 1733 is then removed from the watchlist, as the VM is active. (4) After intercepting the *delete security group rule (..., 1733)* event instance, we identify that this is a critical event. Therefore, we verify with the watchlist keeping the event instance blocked, find that VM 1733 is not in the watchlist, and hence, identify the current situation as a violation of the *no bypass* property.

3.5 Feedback Module

The main purposes of the feedback module are: (i) to provide feedback to the learning engine, and (ii) to provide feedback to the tenant on thresholds for different properties. These purposes are achieved by three steps: storing verification results in the repository, analyzing the results, and providing the necessary feedback to corresponding modules.

Firstly, the feedback module stores the verification results in the repository. Additionally, this module stores the verification result as hit or miss after each critical event, where the hit means the requested parameter is present in the watchlist (meaning no violation), and the miss means the requested parameter is not found in the watchlist (meaning a violation). Additionally, we store the sequence of events for a particular time period (e.g., one day) in a similar format as the processed log described in the learning module. In the next step, we analyze these results along with the models to prepare a feedback for different modules. From the sequence of events, the analyzer identifies whether the pattern is already observed or is a new trend, and accordingly updater prepares a feedback for the learning engine either to fine-tune the parameter or to capture a new trend. From the verification results, the analyzer counts the number of miss for different properties to provide a feedback to the user on their choice of thresholds (stored in the *Property-CE-Threshold* table) for different properties.

For more frequently violated properties, the threshold might be set to a lower probability to trigger the pre-computation earlier.

4   Application to OpenStack

This section describes LeaPS implementation, and presents our experimental results.

4.1   Implementation

In this section, we detail the LeaPS implementation and its integration into OpenStack along with the architecture of LeaPS (Fig. 8) and a detailed algorithm (Algorithm 1).

Background. OpenStack [33] is an open-source cloud management platform in which Neutron is its network component, Nova is its compute component, and Ceilometer is its telemetry for receiving event histories from other components. In this work, we collect Ceilometer logs to later use for learning the dependencies. For learning, we leverage SMILE & GeNIe [2], which is a popular tool for modeling and learning with Bayesian network. SMILE & GeNIe uses the EM algorithm [9,20] for parameter learning.

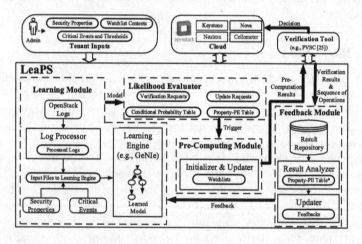

Fig. 8. A high-level architecture of LeaPS auditing system.

Integration to OpenStack. Figure 8 shows a high-level architecture of LeaPS. The learning module is responsible for processing OpenStack logs, preparing inputs for GeNIe, and conducting the learning process using GeNIe. LeaPS first automatically collects logs from different OpenStack components, e.g., Nova,

Neutron, Ceilometer, etc. Then, these logs are converted to the input format (in .dat) of GeNIe. Additionally, the structure of the network and its parameters are provided to GeNIe. We intercept events based on the audit middleware [34] in Keystone, which was previously supported by PyCADF [7], to intercept Neutron and Nova events by enabling the audit middleware and configuring filters. The pre-computing module stores its results into a MySQL database, and the feedback module is implemented in Python. Those modules work together to support the methodology described in Sect. 3, as detailed in Algorithm 1.

Algorithm 1. LeaPS Auditing ($CloudOS$, $Properties$, $critical\text{-}events$, WL)

1: **procedure** LEARN($CloudOS$, $Proeprty\text{-}CE\text{-}Threshold$)
2:     **for** each component $c_i \in CloudOS$ **do**
3:         $processedLogs$ = processLog($c_i.logs$)
4:     **for** each property $p_i \in Properties$ **do**
5:         $structure$ = buildStructure(p_i, $critical\text{-}events$)
6:         $learnedModels$ = learnModel($structure$, $processedLogs$)

7: **procedure** EVALUATE-LIKELIHOOD($CloudOS$, WL, $Property\text{-}PE$, $Event\text{-}Operation$)
8:     **for** each event type $e_i \in CloudOS.event$ **do**
9:         $Conditional\text{-}Probability\text{-}Table$ = inferLikelihood(e_i, $learnedModels$)
10:         **if** checkThreshold($Conditional\text{-}Probability\text{-}Table$, $Property\text{-}CE\text{-}Threshold$) **then**
11:             insertProperty-PE(e_i, $Property\text{-}CE\text{-}Threshold.property$)
12:     $interceptedEvent$ = intercept-and-match($CloudOS$, $Event\text{-}Operation$)
13:     **if** $interceptedEvent \in critical - events$ **then**
14:         $decision$ = verifyWL(WL, $interceptedEvent.params$)
15:         **return** $decision$
16:     **else if** $interceptedEvent \in Property\text{-}PE$ **then**
17:         Pre-compute-update(WL, $property$, $interceptedEvent.params$)

18: **procedure** PRE-COMPUTE-INITIALIZE($CloudOS$, $Property\text{-}WL$)
19:     **for** each property $p_i \in Properties$ **do**
20:         WL_i = initializeWatchlist(p_i, $Property\text{-}WL$, $CloudOS$)
21: **procedure** PRE-COMPUTE-UPDATE(WL, $property$, $parameters$)
22:     updateWatchlist(WL, $property$, $parameters$)

23: **procedure** FEEDBACK($Result$, $learnedModels$)
24:     storeResults($Result$, $learnedModels$)
25:     **if** analyzeSequence($Result.seq$) = "new-trend" **then**
26:         updateModel($Result.seq$, 'new')
27:     **else**
28:         updateModel($Result.seq$, 'old')
29:     **for** each property $p_i \in Properties$ **do**
30:         $change\text{-}in\text{-}threshold[i]$ = analyzeDecision($Result.decision$, p_i)

LeaPS interacts with three external entities (i.e., tenant, cloud platform and the verification tool). Cloud tenants provide security properties, and their thresholds, specification of watchlist contents and critical events to LeaPS. Then, OpenStack is responsible for providing the logs from its different components. We also leverage a verification tool [25], which verifies parameters of an intercepted critical event with the watchlists.

4.2 Experimental Results

In this section, we first describe the experiment settings, and then present LeaPS experimental results with both synthetic and real data.

Experimental Settings. Our test cloud is based on OpenStack version Mitaka. There are one controller node and up to 80 compute nodes, each having Intel i7 dual core CPU and 2 GB memory with the Ubuntu 16.04 server. Based on a recent survey [35] on OpenStack, we simulated an environment with maximum 1,000 tenants and 100,000 VMs. We conduct the experiment for 10 different datasets varying the number of tenants from 100 to 1,000 while keeping the number of VMs fixed to 1,000 per tenant. For learning, we use GeNIe academic version 2.1. We repeat each experiment 100 times.

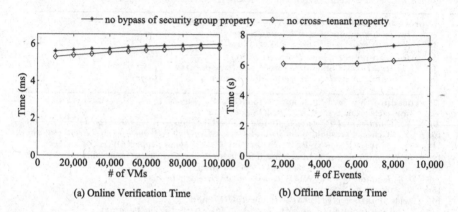

(a) Online Verification Time   (b) Offline Learning Time

Fig. 9. Showing time required for the (a) online runtime verification by varying the number of VMs and (b) offline learning process by varying the number of event instances in the logs for the *no bypass* and *no cross-tenant* properties. The verification time includes the time to perform interception, matching of event type and checking in the watchlist.

Results. The objective of the first set of experiments is to demonstrate the time efficiency of LeaPS. Figure 9(a) shows the time in milliseconds required by LeaPS to verify the *no bypass of security group* [8] and *no cross-tenant port* [18] properties. Our experiment shows the time for both properties remains almost the same for different datasets, because most operations during this step are database queries; SQL queries for our different datasets almost take the same time. Figure 9(b) shows the time (in seconds) required by GeNIe to learn the model while we vary the number of events from 2,000 to 10,000. In Fig. 10(a), we measure the time required for different steps of the offline pre-computing for the *no bypass* property. The total time (including the time of incrementally updating WL and updating PE) required for the largest dataset is about eight seconds which justifies performing the pre-computation proactively. A one-time initialization of pre-computation is performed in 50 s for the largest dataset. Figure 10(b) shows the time in seconds required to update the model and to update the list of pre-compute events. In total, LeaPS requires less than 3.5 s for this step.

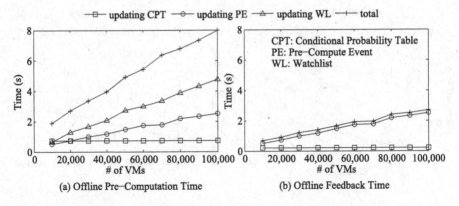

(a) Offline Pre–Computation Time   (b) Offline Feedback Time

Fig. 10. Showing time required in seconds for the (a) pre-computation and (b) feedback modules considering the *no bypass* property by varying the number of instances.

In the second set of experiments, we demonstrate that how much LeaPS may be affected from a wrong prediction resulted from inaccurate learning. For this experiment, we simulate different prediction error rates (PER) of a learning engine ranging from 0 to 0.4 on the likelihood evaluator procedure in Algorithm 1. Figure 11(a) shows in seconds the additional delay in the pre-computation caused by the different PER of a learning engine for three different number of VMs. Note that, the pre-computation in LeaPS is an offline step. The delay caused by 40% PER for up to 100k VMs remains under two seconds, which is still acceptable for most applications.

In the final set of experiments, we compare LeaPS with a baseline approach (similar to [25]), where all possible paths are considered with equal weight, and number of steps in the model is the deciding factor for the pre-computation. Figure 11(b) shows the pre-computation time for both approaches in the average case, and LeaPS performs about 50% faster than the baseline approach (the main reason is that, in contrast to the baseline, LeaPS avoids the pre-computation for half of the critical events on average by leveraging the probabilistic dependency model). For this experiment, we choose the threshold, *N-th* (an input to the baseline), as two, and the number of security properties as four. Increasing both the value of *N-th* and the number of properties increase the pre-computation overhead for the baseline. Note that a longer pre-computation time eventually affects the response time of a proactive auditing.

Experiment with Real Cloud. We further test LeaPS using data collected from a real community cloud hosted at one of the largest telecommunications vendors. The main objective is to evaluate the applicability of our approach in a real cloud environment. To this end, we analyze the management logs (sized more than 1.6 GB text-based logs) and extract 128,264 relevant log entries for the period of more than 500 days. As Ceilometer was not configured in this cloud, we utilize Nova and Neutron logs which increases the log processing efforts significantly. Table 2 summarizes the obtained results. We first measure the time

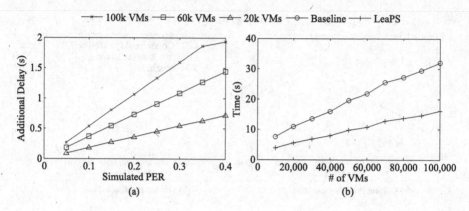

Fig. 11. (a) The additional delay (in seconds) in LeaPS pre-computation time caused by different simulated prediction error rates (PER) of a learning tool, (b) the comparison (in seconds) between LeaPS and a baseline approach.

efficiency of LeaPS. Note that the results obtained are shorter due to the smaller size of the community cloud compared to our much larger simulated environment. Furthermore, we measure the prediction error rate (PER) of the learning tool using another dataset (for 5 days) of this cloud. For the 3.4% of PER, LeaPS affects maximum 9.62 ms additional delay in its pre-computation for the measured properties.

Table 2. Summary of the experimental results with real data. The reported delay is in the pre-computation of LeaPS due to the prediction error (PER) of the learning engine.

Properties	Learning	Pre-compute	Feedback	Verification	PER	Delay*
No bypass	7.2 s	424 ms	327 ms	5.2 ms	0.034	9.62 ms
No cross-tenant	5.97 s	419 ms	315 ms	5 ms	0.034	9.513 ms

5   Discussions

Adapting to Other Cloud Platforms. LeaPS is designed to work with most popular cloud platforms (e.g., OpenStack [33], Amazon EC2 [1], Google GCP [13], Microsoft Azure [28]) with a minimal one-time effort. Once a mapping of the APIs from these platforms to the LeaPS event types are provided, rest of the steps in LeaPS are platform-agnostic. Table 3 enlists some examples of such mappings.

Table 3. Mapping event APIs of different cloud platforms to LeaPS event types.

LeaPS event type	OpenStack [33]	Amazon EC2-VPC [1]	Google GCP [13]	Microsoft Azure [28]
Create VM	POST /servers	aws opsworks − region create-instance	gcloud compute instances create	az vm create 1
Delete VM	DELETE /servers	aws opsworks − region delete-instance − instance-id	gcloud compute instances delete	az vm delete
Update VM	PUT /servers	aws opsworks − region update-instance − instance-id	gcloud compute instances add-tags	az vm update
Create security group	POST /v2.0/security-groups	aws ec2 create-security-group	N/A	az network nsg create
Delete security group	DELETE /v2.0/security-groups/{security_group_id}	aws ec2 delete-security-group − group-name {name}	N/A	az network nsg delete

Possibility of a DoS Attack Against LeaPS. To exploit the fact that a wrong prediction may result a delay in the LeaPS pre-computation, an attacker may conduct a DoS attack to bias the learning model step by generating fake events and hence to exhaust LeaPS pre-computation. However, Fig. 11(a) shows that an attacker requires to inject significantly large amount (e.g., 40% error rate) of biased event instances to even cause a delay of two seconds. Moreover, biasing the model is non-trivial unless the attacker has prior knowledge on patterns of legitimate event sequences. Our future work will further investigate this possibility and its countermeasures.

Granularity of Learning. The above-mentioned learning can be performed for different levels (e.g., cloud level, tenant level and user level). The cloud level learning captures business nature only for companies using a private cloud. The tenant level learning depicts better profile of each business or tenant. This level of learning is mainly suitable for companies following process management strictly where users mainly follow the steps of processes. In contrast, the user level learning is suitable for smaller organizations (where no process management is followed) with fewer users (e.g., admins) who perform cloud events. Conversely, if a company follows process management, user level learning will be an overkill, as different users would exhibit very similar patterns.

6 Related Work

Table 4 summarizes the comparison between existing works and LeaPS. The first and second columns enlist existing works and their verification methods. The next two columns compare the coverage such as supported environment (cloud or non-cloud) and main objectives (auditing or anomaly detection). The next columns compare these works according to different features, i.e., proactiveness, automated and dynamic dependency capturing, cloud-platform-agnostic and probabilistic dependency.

In summary, LeaPS mainly differs from the state-of-the-art works as follows. Firstly, LeaPS is the first proactive auditing approach which captures the dependency automatically from the patterns of event sequences. Secondly, LeaPS is

Table 4. Comparing existing solutions with LeaPS. The symbols (•), (-) and N/A mean supported, not supported and not applicable respectively.

Proposals	Methods	Coverage		Features				
		Environment	Objective	Proactive	Automatic	Dynamic	Agnostic	Probabilistic
Doelitzscher et al. [10]	Custom algorithm	Cloud	Auditing	-	N/A	•	•	N/A
Ullah et al. [40]	Custom algorithm	Cloud	Auditing	-	N/A	-	-	N/A
Majumdar et al. [26]	CSP solver	Cloud	Auditing	-	N/A	-	-	N/A
Madi et al. [24]	CSP solver	Cloud	Auditing	-	N/A	-	-	N/A
Jiang et al. [19]	Regression technique	Non-cloud	Anomaly Det.	•	•	-	N/A	•
Solanas et al. [39]	Classifiers	Cloud	Anomaly Det.	-	•	-	-	•
Ligatti and Reddy [23]	Model checking	Non-cloud	Auditing	•	N/A	•	N/A	-
PVSC [25]	Custom algorithm	Cloud	Auditing	•	-	-	-	-
Weatherman [6]	Graph-theoretic	Cloud	Auditing	•	-	•	-	-
Congress [32]	Datalog	Cloud	Auditing	•	-	-	-	-
LeaPS	Custom + Bayesian	Cloud	Auditing	•	•	•	•	•

the only learning-based work which aims at improving proactive auditing and not (directly) at anomaly detection. Thirdly, the dynamic dependency model allows LeaPS to evolve over time to adapt with new trends. Finally, the LeaPS methodology is cloud-platform agnostic.

Retroactive and Intercept-and-Check Auditing. Retroactive auditing approach (e.g., [10,24,26,40–42] in the cloud is a traditional way to verify the compliance of different components of a cloud. Unlike our proposal, those approaches can detect violations only after they occur, which may expose the system to high risks. Existing intercept-and-check approaches (e.g., [6,32]) perform major verification tasks while holding the event instances blocked, and usually cause significant delay to a user request. Unlike those works, LeaPS provides a proactive auditing approach.

Proactive Auditing. Proactive security analysis in the cloud is comparatively a new domain with fewer works (e.g., [6,25,43]). Weatherman [6] verifies security policies on a future change plan in a virtualized infrastructure using the graph-based model proposed in [4,5]. PVSC [25] proactively verifies security compliance by utilizing the static patterns in dependency models. Both in Weatherman and PVSC, models are captured manually by expert knowledge. In contrast, this work adopts a learning-based approach to automatically derive the dependency model. Congress [32] is an OpenStack project offering similar features as Weatherman. Foley and Neville [12] proposes an algebra for anomaly-free firewall policies for OpenStack. Many state-based formal models (e.g., [11,22,23,38]) are proposed for program monitoring. Our work further expands the proactive monitoring approach into cloud differing in scope and methodology.

Learning-Based Detections. There are many learning-based security solutions (e.g., [14, 16, 17, 19, 27, 29, 39]), which offer anomaly detection. Unlike above-mentioned works, this paper proposes a totally different learning-based techniques to facilitate the proactive auditing.

7   Conclusion

In this paper, we proposed LeaPS, a fully automated system leveraging the learning-based techniques to accelerate the performance of a proactive auditing approach. We integrated LeaPS to OpenStack, and evaluated the performance of LeaPS extensively (using both synthetic and real data) which show LeaPS keeps the response time to a practical level (e.g., about 6 ms to verify 100,000 VMs), and improves the speed up significantly (e.g., about 50%) over existing proactive approaches. As future work, we will investigate the possibility of applying other learning techniques to further improve the efficiency; we will also apply supervised learning to automate the process of identifying critical events and security properties from logs.

Acknowledgements. The authors thank the anonymous reviewers for their valuable comments. We also thank Anandamayee Majumdar for her insightful suggestions. This work is partially supported by the Natural Sciences and Engineering Research Council of Canada and Ericsson Canada under CRD Grant N01566.

A   A Guideline to Choose LeaPS Inputs

We provide a guideline on identifying different inputs of LeaPS. Identifying sets of event types as the input to the learning engine are described as follows: (i) from the property definition, we identify involved cloud components; (ii) we enlist all event types in a cloud platform involving those components; and (iii) we identify the critical events (which is already provided by the tenant) from the list, and further shortlist the event types based on the attack scenario. The specification of watchlist is a LeaPS input from the tenant. The specification of watchlist can be decided as follows: (i) from the property definition, the asset to keep safe is identified; (ii) the objectives of a security property is to be highlighted; and (iii) from the attack scenario, the parameters for the watchlist for each critical event is finalized.

References

1. Amazon: Amazon virtual private cloud. https://aws.amazon.com/vpc
2. BayesFusion: GeNIe and SMILE. https://www.bayesfusion.com

3. Bellare, M., Yee, B.: Forward integrity for secure audit logs. Technical report, Citeseer (1997)
4. Bleikertz, S., Groß, T., Schunter, M., Eriksson, K.: Automated information flow analysis of virtualized infrastructures. In: Atluri, V., Diaz, C. (eds.) ESORICS 2011. LNCS, vol. 6879, pp. 392–415. Springer, Heidelberg (2011). doi:10.1007/978-3-642-23822-2_22
5. Bleikertz, S., Vogel, C., Groß, T., Radar, C.: Near real-time detection of security failures in dynamic virtualized infrastructures. In: ACSAC (2014)
6. Bleikertz, S., Vogel, C., Groß, T., Mödersheim, S.: Proactive security analysis of changes in virtualized infrastructure. In: ACSAC (2015)
7. Cloud Auditing Data Federation: PyCADF: a Python-based CADF library (2015). https://pypi.python.org/pypi/pycadf
8. Cloud Security Alliance: Cloud control matrix CCM v3.0.1 (2014). https://cloudsecurityalliance.org/research/ccm/
9. Dempster, A.P., Laird, N.M., Rubin, D.B.: Maximum likelihood from incomplete data via the EM algorithm. J. Roy. Stat. Soc. **39**, 1–38 (1977)
10. Doelitzscher, F., Fischer, C., Moskal, D., Reich, C., Knahl, M., Clarke, N.: Validating cloud infrastructure changes by cloud audits. In: IEEE Services (2012)
11. Dolzhenko, E., Ligatti, J., Reddy, S.: Modeling runtime enforcement with mandatory results automata. Int. J. Inf. Secur. **14**(1), 47–60 (2014)
12. Foley, S.N., Neville, U.: A firewall algebra for OpenStack. In: IEEE CNS (2015)
13. Google: Google cloud platform. https://cloud.google.com
14. Guha, S.: Attack detection for cyber systems and probabilistic state estimation in partially observable cyber environments. Ph.D. thesis, Arizona State University (2016)
15. Heckerman, D.: A tutorial on learning with Bayesian networks. In: Learning in graphical models (1998)
16. Hemmat, R.A., Hafid, A.: SLA violation prediction in cloud computing: a machine learning perspective. Technical report (2016)
17. Holm, H., Shahzad, K., Buschle, M., Ekstedt, M.: P^2 CySeMoL: predictive, probabilistic cyber security modeling language. IEEE TDSC **12**, 626–639 (2015)
18. ISO Std IEC. ISO 27017: Information technology- security techniques- code of practice for information security controls based on ISO/IEC 27002 for cloud services (DRAFT) (2012). http://www.iso27001security.com/html/27017.html
19. Jiang, Y., Zhang, E.Z., Tian, K., Mao, F., Gethers, M., Shen, X., Gao, Y.: Exploiting statistical correlations for proactive prediction of program behaviors. In: Proceedings of 8th Annual IEEE/ACM International Symposium on Code Generation and Optimization. ACM (2010)
20. Lauritzen, S.L.: The EM algorithm for graphical association models with missing data. Comput Stat. Data Anal. **19**(2), 191–201 (1995)
21. Li, M., Zang, W., Bai, K., Yu, M., Liu, P.: MyCloud: supporting user-configured privacy protection in cloud computing. In: ACSAC (2013)
22. Ligatti, J., Bauer, L., Walker, D.: Run-time enforcement of nonsafety policies. ACM TISSEC **12**, 19 (2009)
23. Ligatti, J., Reddy, S.: A theory of runtime enforcement, with results. In: Gritzalis, D., Preneel, B., Theoharidou, M. (eds.) ESORICS 2010. LNCS, vol. 6345, pp. 87–100. Springer, Heidelberg (2010). doi:10.1007/978-3-642-15497-3_6
24. Madi, T., Majumdar, S., Wang, Y., Jarraya, Y., Pourzandi, M., Wang, L.: Auditing security compliance of the virtualized infrastructure in the cloud: application to OpenStack. In: ACM CODASPY (2016)

25. Majumdar, S., Jarraya, Y., Madi, T., Alimohammadifar, A., Pourzandi, M., Wang, L., Debbabi, M.: Proactive verification of security compliance for clouds through pre-computation: application to OpenStack. In: Askoxylakis, I., Ioannidis, S., Katsikas, S., Meadows, C. (eds.) ESORICS 2016. LNCS, vol. 9878, pp. 47–66. Springer, Cham (2016). doi:10.1007/978-3-319-45744-4_3

26. Majumdar, S., Madi, T., Wang, Y., Jarraya, Y., Pourzandi, M., Wang, L., Debbabi, M.: Security compliance auditing of identity and access management in the cloud: application to OpenStack. In: IEEE CloudCom (2015)

27. Mehnaz, S., Bertino, E.: Ghostbuster: a fine-grained approach for anomaly detection in file system accesses. In: ACM CODASPY (2017)

28. Microsoft: Microsoft Azure virtual network. https://azure.microsoft.com

29. Mitchell, R., Chen, R.: Behavior rule specification-based intrusion detection for safety critical medical cyber physical systems. IEEE TDSC 12, 16–30 (2015)

30. Murphy, K.: A brief introduction to graphical models and Bayesian networks (1998)

31. OpenStack: Nova network security group changes are not applied to running instances (2015). https://security.openstack.org/ossa/OSSA-2015-021.html

32. OpenStack: OpenStack Congress (2015). https://wiki.openstack.org/wiki/Congress

33. OpenStack: OpenStack open source cloud computing software (2015). http://www.openstack.org

34. OpenStack: OpenStack audit middleware (2016). http://docs.openstack.org/developer/keystonemiddleware/audit.html

35. OpenStack: OpenStack user survey (2016). https://www.openstack.org/assets/survey/October2016SurveyReport.pdf

36. Pearl, J.: Causality: models, reasoning and inference (2000)

37. Ren, K., Wang, C., Wang, Q.: Security challenges for the public cloud. IEEE Internet Comput. 1, 69–73 (2012)

38. Schneider, F.B.: Enforceable security policies. ACM TISSEC 3, 30–50 (2000)

39. Solanas, M., Hernandez-Castro, J., Dutta, D.: Detecting fraudulent activity in a cloud using privacy-friendly data aggregates. Technical report, arXiv preprint (2014)

40. Ullah, K., Ahmed, A., Ylitalo, J.: Towards building an automated security compliance tool for the cloud. In: IEEE TrustCom 2013 (2013)

41. Wang, C., Chow, S.S., Wang, Q., Ren, K., Lou, W.: Privacy-preserving public auditing for secure cloud storage. IEEE TC 62, 362–375 (2013)

42. Wang, Y., Wu, Q., Qin, B., Shi, W., Deng, R.H., Hu, J.: Identity-based data outsourcing with comprehensive auditing in clouds. IEEE TIFS 12, 940–953 (2017)

43. Yau, S.S., Buduru, A.B., Nagaraja, V.: Protecting critical cloud infrastructures with predictive capability. In: IEEE CLOUD (2015)

44. Zhu, X., Song, S., Wang, J., Philip, S.Y., Sun, J.: Matching heterogeneous events with patterns. In: IEEE ICDE (2014)

Identifying Multiple Authors in a Binary Program

Xiaozhu Meng[1]([⊠])[iD], Barton P. Miller[1], and Kwang-Sung Jun[2]

[1] Computer Sciences Department, University of Wisconsin - Madison,
Madison, WI, USA
{xmeng,bart}@cs.wisc.edu
[2] Wisconsin Institutes for Discovery, University of Wisconsin - Madison,
Madison, WI, USA
kjun@discovery.wisc.edu

Abstract. Knowing the authors of a binary program has significant application to forensics of malicious software (malware), software supply chain risk management, and software plagiarism detection. Existing techniques assume that a binary is written by a single author, which does not hold true in real world because most modern software, including malware, often contains code from multiple authors. In this paper, we make the first step toward identifying multiple authors in a binary. We present new fine-grained techniques to address the tougher problem of determining the author of each basic block. The decision of attributing authors at the basic block level is based on an empirical study of three large open source software, in which we find that a large fraction of basic blocks can be well attributed to a single author. We present new code features that capture programming style at the basic block level, our approach for identifying external template library code, and a new approach to capture correlations between the authors of basic blocks in a binary. Our experiments show strong evidence that programming styles can be recovered at the basic block level and it is practical to identify multiple authors in a binary.

Keywords: Binary code authorship · Code features · Software forensics

1 Introduction

Binary code authorship identification is the task of determining the authors of a binary program from a set of known authors. This task has significant application to forensic of malicious software (malware) [29], identifying software components from untrusted sources in the software supply chain [11], and detecting software plagiarism [18]. Previous studies [3,8,38] have shown that programming styles survive through the compilation process and can be recovered from binary code. However, these studies operated at the program level and assumed that each binary program is written by a single author, which is not true for real world software and significantly limits their uses in practice. In this paper, we present

© Springer International Publishing AG 2017
S.N. Foley et al. (Eds.): ESORICS 2017, Part II, LNCS 10493, pp. 286–304, 2017.
DOI: 10.1007/978-3-319-66399-9_16

the first study on *fine-grained* binary code authorship identification, with concrete evidence showing that programming styles can be recovered at the *basic block* level and it is practical to perform authorship identification on binaries from multi-author software.

Knowing the authors of a computer program is a key capability for many analysts. Malware analysts want to know who wrote a new malware sample and whether the authors have connections to previous malware samples. This information can be useful to determine the operations and intentions of the new sample. For example, if several cyber attacks use different malware written by closely connected authors, these attacks can be related and can be a part of a bigger offensive plot. In the domain of software supply chain risk management, analysts can identify untrusted code in the supply chain by matching programming styles against known untrusted software such as malware. The idea of matching programming styles can also be used for detecting software plagiarism, where analysts can match programming styles against known code.

Identifying program authors can be performed on either source code or binary code. Source level techniques [6, 7, 9] are not applicable when the source code is not available, which is typically the case when handling malware, proprietary software, and legacy code. Binary level techniques [3, 8, 38] do not have this limitation and can be used under broader scenarios such as when only a code byte stream is discovered in network packets or memory images.

However, existing binary level techniques assume that a binary is written by a single author, which is not true in real world for two reasons. First, modern software, including malware, is often the result of a team effort. Malware development has become similar to normal software development, evolving from an individual hacking to cooperation between multiple programmers [12, 29, 36]. Malware writers share functional components and adapt them [27, 39]. Studies have shown that malware writers share information and code by forming physically co-located teams [28] or virtually through the Internet [1, 5, 21]. These exchanges of information and code gradually develop into underground black markets [2]. Malware writers can then acquire malware functional components such as command and control, key logging, encryption and decryption, beaconing, exfiltration, and domain flux, to facilitate their development of new malware [42]. This trend indicates that current software, including malware, often contains code from multiple authors.

Second, even if the source code is written by a single author, the corresponding binary may contain code that is not written by this author. External library code, such as the Standard Template Library (STL) and Boost C++ Library (Boost), is often inlined in the binary. In addition, compilers may generate binary code that does not correspond to any source code written by this author, such as the default constructor and destructor of a class.

When applied to multi-author binaries, existing single-author techniques have two significant limitations. First, they can identify at most one of the multiple authors or report a merged group identity. Second, these techniques do not distinguish external library code or code solely generated by the compiler from the code written by the authors, which may confuse the styles of these libraries or the compiler with the styles of the authors. Therefore, authorship identification techniques must be fine-grained, identify multiple authors, and recognize library code and compiler introduced code in a binary.

Fine-grained techniques can better help analysts in real world applications. Malware analysts can link the code written by the same author from a set of malware samples and link the authors who cooperated in writing a particular piece of malware. The same-author links can help build profiles of individual malware writers and infer their distinct attacking skills and their roles in cyber attacks. The cooperating-author links can help identify connections among malware writers and infer the structure of physically co-located teams or black markets. Malware analysts can determine who or which organization may be responsible for a new malware sample and relate the new sample to existing samples written by the same authors or even samples written by authors who are linked to the identified authors. In the area of software supply chain risk management and detecting software plagiarism, the untrusted code and plagiarized code may consist of only a small fraction of the whole binary, making fine-grained authorship identification essential in these applications.

Previous single-author techniques provide a foundation for us to develop fine-grained techniques. These techniques have cast binary code authorship identification as a supervised machine learning problem. Given a set of binaries with their author labels as the training set, these techniques extract stylistic code features such as byte n-grams [24,38] and machine instruction sequences [8,24,37,38,40], and use supervised machine learning algorithms such as Support Vector Machine (SVM) [10] or Random Forests [20] to train models to capture the correlations between code features and author labels. The generated machine learning models are then used to predict the author of a new binary.

To develop fine-grained techniques, three additional challenges must be addressed. First, what is the appropriate unit of code for attributing authorship? Fine-grained candidates include the function or the basic block. However, as programmers could change any line of code or even parts of a line, there is no guarantee that a function or a basic block is written by a single author. Therefore, this challenge requires us to balance how likely a unit of code is written by a single author and how much information it carries.

Second, what stylistic code features do we need for a fine-grained unit of code? Code features used in previous program level studies may not be applicable, or may not be effective at a finer code granularity. As we will discuss in Sect. 7, reusing code features in these program level studies does not yield good results in our case. Therefore, it is crucial to design new fine-grained code features.

Third, how do we identify external template library code? Failing to address this challenge may cause authorship identification algorithms to confuse library code with their users' code. However, existing library code identification techniques are designed for only non-template library code. These techniques either create a function fingerprint [16,23] or build a function graph pattern based on the program execution dependencies [33]. When a template function is parameterized with different data types, the final binary code can be significantly different, making function fingerprints or graph patterns ineffective. Therefore, we need new techniques for identifying template library code.

In this paper, we present the first practical fine-grained techniques to identify multiple authors of a binary. We summarize how we address the three fine-grained challenges and how we capture author correlations between code within the same binary to improve accuracy:

- To determine what granularity of authorship attribution is the most appropriate, we conducted an empirical study on three large and long lived open source projects, for which we have authorship ground truth: the Apache HTTP server [4], the Dyninst binary analysis and instrumentation tool suite [32], and GCC [15]. Our results show that 85% of the basic blocks are written by a single author and 88% of the basic blocks have a major author who contributes more than 90% of the basic block. On the other hand, only 50% of the functions are written by a single author and 60% of the functions have a major author who contributes more than 90% of the function. Therefore, the function as a unit of code brings too much imprecision, so we use the basic block as the unit for attribution. See Sect. 3.
- We designed new code features to capture programming styles at the basic block level. These features describe common code properties such as control flow and data flow. We also designed a new type of code features, *context features*, to summarize the context of the function or the loop to which the basic block belongs. See Sect. 4.
- We made an initial step towards more effective library code identification. This step focuses on identifying inlined code from the two most commonly used C++ template libraries: STL and Boost. We add group identities "STL" and "Boost" to represent the code from these libraries and let the machine learning algorithms to distinguish them from their users. See Sect. 5.
- As a programmer typically writes more than one basic block at a time, we hypothesize that adjacent basic blocks are likely written by the same author. To test our hypothesis, we compared *independent classification models*, which make predictions based only on the code features extracted from a basic block, and *joint classification models*, which make predictions based on both code features and the authors of adjacent basic blocks. See Sect. 6.

We evaluated our new techniques on a data set derived from the open source projects used in the empirical study. Our data set consisted of 147 C binaries and 22 C++ binaries, which contained 284 authors and 900,583 basic blocks. The binaries were compiled with GCC 4.8.5 and -O2 optimization. Overall, our new techniques achieved 65% accuracy on classifying 284 authors, as opposed to 0.4% accuracy by random guess. Our techniques can also prioritize investigation: we can rank the correct author among the top five with 77% accuracy and among the top ten with 82% accuracy. These results show that it is practical to attribute program authors at the basic block level. We also conducted experiments to show the effectiveness of our new code features, handling of inlined STL and Boost code, and joint classification models. See Sect. 7.

In summary, our study provides concrete evidence that it is practical to identify multiple program authors at basic block level. Our ultimate goal is to provide automated fine-grained authorship analysis and many research challenges remain. For example, we are currently investigating the impact of compilers or optimization flags on coding styles, and plan to handle the cases when the target author is not in the training data, and apply our techniques to malware samples. In this paper, we make the first step towards practical fine-grained binary code authorship identification and significantly advance the frontier of this field.

2   Background

We discuss two areas of related work as background: designing binary code features that reflect programming style and using machine learning techniques to discover correlations between code features and authors.

2.1   Binary Code Features

Existing binary code features used in authorship identification describe a wide variety of code properties, such as instruction details, control flow, data flow, and external dependencies. These features were extracted at the function and block level and then accumulated to the whole program level. Basic block level features usually included byte n-grams, instruction idioms, and function names of external library call targets [38]. Function level features mainly include graphlets [8,38], which represent subgraphs of a function's CFG, and register flow graphs [3], which captures program data flow. Here, we discuss only basic block level features as the function level features are not applicable at the basic block level.

Byte n-grams represent consecutive n bytes extracted from binary code [24, 38]. Authorship identification techniques typically use small values for n. For example, Rosenblum et al. [38] used $n = 3$ for authorship identification to capture styles reflected on instruction details. While byte n-grams have been shown to be effective, byte n-grams are sensitive to the specific values of immediate operands, and do not capture the structure of programs.

Instruction idioms are consecutive machine instruction sequences [8,24,25, 37,38,40]. Besides the length of instruction idioms, many other variations have been defined, including allowing wild cards [38], ignoring the order of instructions [25], normalizing operands with generic symbols such as representing all immediate operands with a generic symbol [24,38], and classifying opcodes into operation categories such as arithmetic operations, data move operations, and control flow transfer operations [40]. Existing techniques for authorship identification typically used short instruction idioms, ranging from 1 to 3 instructions.

2.2   Workflow of Authorship Identification

Instead of designing complicated features to represent specific aspects of programming styles, existing techniques [3,8,38] define a large number of simple candidate code features and use training data to automatically discover which features are indicative of authorship. This feature design philosophy is a general machine learning practice [17].

Based on this feature design philosophy, a common workflow used in existing studies has four major steps: (1) designing a large number of simple candidate features; (2) extracting the defined features using binary code analysis tools such as Dyninst [32] or IDA Pro [19]; (3) determining a small set of features that are indicative of authorship by using feature selection techniques such as ranking features based on mutual information between features and authors [38]; and (4) applying a supervised machine learning technique, such as Support Vector Machine (SVM) [10] or Random Forests [20], to learn the correlations between code features and authorship. Rosenblum et al. [38] used instruction, control flow, and library call target features, and used SVM for classification. Caliskan-Islam et al. [8] added data flow features, constant data strings, and function names derived from symbol information, and used Random Forests for classification.

Previous projects performed evaluations of their techniques on single author programs, including Google Code Jam, university course projects, and single author programs extracted from Github. Rosenblum et al. reported 51% accuracy for classifying 191 authors on -O0 binaries from Google Code Jam and 38.4% accuracy for classifying 20 authors on -O0 binaries from university course projects. They commented that the university course project data set was significantly more difficult than the Google Code Jam data set, mainly because programs in this data set contained not only code written by individual students, but also skeleton code provided by the course professor. We believe this actually reveals the fundamental limitation of existing program level approaches and motivates our fine-grained techniques.

Caliskan et al. improved Google Code Jam accuracy to 92% for classifying 191 authors on -O0 binaries, and 89% accuracy for classifying 100 authors on -O2 binaries. They also evaluated their technique on single author programs from Github and got 65% accuracy for classifying 50 authors. However, two concerns need further investigations. First, stripping the binaries led to a decrease in accuracy by 24%. In this work, we do not use or depend on symbol information to derive code features. Second, the accuracy of the Github data set is significantly lower than the accuracy of the Google Code Jam data set. They commented two reasons: (1) the binaries from the Github data set were the results of a collaborative effort and each binary had a major author who contributed more than 90% of the code, and (2) the Github data set might contain third party library code that was not written by the major author. Again, we believe our fine-grained techniques can overcome these limitations.

3 Determining Unit of Code

Our fine-grained techniques start with determining whether the function or the basic block is a more appropriate attribution unit. We investigated the authorship characteristics in open source projects to make this granularity decision.

Our study included code from three large and long lived open source projects: the Apache HTTP server [4], the Dyninst binary analysis and instrumentation tool suite [32], and GCC [15]. Intuitively, the more the major author contributes to a function or a basic block, the more appropriate it is to attribute authorship to a single author. We quantify this intuition by first determining how much authorship contribution is from its major author for all basic blocks and functions, and then summarizing these contribution data to compare the basic block with the function.

3.1 Determining Contributions from Major Authors

Our approach to determine the major authors and their contributions can be summarized in three steps:

1. Use *git-author* [30] to get a weight vector of author contribution percentages for all source lines in these projects. Note that well-known tools such as git-blame [35], svn-annotate [43], and CVS-annotate [41] attribute a line of code to the last author who changed it, regardless of the magnitude of the change. We believe *git-author* provides ground truth of higher quality. The source lines of STL and Boost were attributed to author "STL" and "Boost", respectively.
2. Compile these projects with debugging information using GCC 4.8.5 and -O2 optimization, and obtain a mapping between source lines and machine instructions. Note that the compiler may generate binary code that does not correspond to any source line. For example, the compiler may generate a default constructor for a class when the programmer does not provide it. We exclude this code from our study.
3. Derive weight vectors of author contribution percentages for all machine instructions, basic blocks, and functions in the compiled code. We first derived the weight vector for each instruction by averaging the contribution percentages of the corresponding source lines. We then derived the weight vector of a basic block by averaging the vectors of the instructions within the basic block. Similarly, we derived the weight vector of a function by averaging the vectors of the basic blocks within the function.

3.2 Study Results

To compare the function with the basic block, we plot the tail distributions of contribution percentages from the major authors. As shown in Fig. 1, 85% of the basic blocks are written by a single author and 88% of the basic blocks have a major author who contributes more than 90% of the basic block. On the other hand, only 50% of the functions are written by a single author and 60% of the functions have a major author who contributes more than 90% of the function. Therefore, the function as a unit of code brings too much imprecision, so we use the basic block as the unit for attribution.

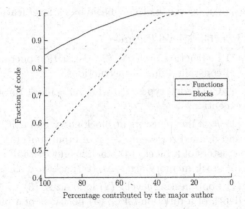

Fig. 1. Tail distributions of major author contribution. The x-axis represents the contribution percentage from the major author. The y-axis represents the fraction of the number of blocks or functions that have a major author who contributed more than a given percentage.

4   New Code Features

We followed an exploratory process for designing new features: designing new features to cover code properties that are not covered, testing new features to see whether they improve accuracy, and keeping those features that turn out to be useful. We have four types of new features: (1) instruction features that describe instruction prefixes, operand sizes, and operand addressing modes, (2) control flow features that describe incoming and outgoing CFG edges and exception-based control flow, (3) data flow features that describe input and output variables of a basic block, stack usages, and data flow dependencies, and (4) *context features* that capture the context of a basic block such as the loops or the functions to which the block belongs. Our new features are summarized in Table 1.

4.1   Instruction Features

There are three new features to describe instruction details.

1. Prefix features: x86 and x86-64 instruction sets contain instruction prefixes that reflect valuable code properties. For example, REP (repeat) prefixes are often used for string operations and REX prefixes are often used to address 64-bit registers. We count how many times each instruction prefix is used.
2. Operand features: Instruction operands represent the data manipulated by programmers, so we designed instruction operand features to capture operand sizes, types, and addressing modes. First, operand sizes capture the granularity of data and may correlate to the data types operated by a programmer. For example, a one-byte operand often represents a char data type in C. We count the number of operands in each operand size. Second, we count the numbers of memory, register, and immediate operands. Third, operand

Table 1. An overview of new basic block level features.

Code property	New block level features
Instruction	(1) Instruction prefixes, (2) instruction operands, (3) constant value in instructions
Control flow	(1) CFG edge types, (2) whether a block throws or catches exceptions
Data flow	(1) # of live registers at block entry and exit, (2) # of used and defined registers, (3) # of input, output, and internal registers of a block, (4) stack height delta of a block, (5) stack memory accesses, (6) backward slices of variables
Context	(1) Loop nesting levels, (2) loop sizes, (3) width and depth of a function CFG, (4) positions of a block in a function CFG

    addressing modes can reflect data access patterns used by programmers. For example, PC-relative addressing often represents accessing a global variable, while scaled indexing often represents accessing an array. We count the number of operands in each addressing mode.

3. Constant value features: We count the number of constant values used in a basic block, such as immediate operands and offsets in relative addressing.

4.2   Control Flow Features

We designed control flow features that describe the incoming and outgoing CFG edges on three dimensions: (1) the control flow transfer type (such as conditional taken, conditional not taken, direct jump, and fall through), (2) whether the edge is interprocedural or intraprocedural, and (3) whether the edge goes to a unknown control flow target such as unresolved indirect jumps or indirect calls.

    In addition, for languages that support exception-based control flow such as C++, we distinguish whether a basic block throws exceptions and whether it catches exceptions.

4.3   Data Flow Features

Our new data flow features can be classified into three categories.

1. Features to describe input variables, output variables, and internal variables of a basic block: We count the number of input, output, and internal registers. To calculate these features, we need to know what registers are live at the block entry and exit, and what registers are used and defined.
2. Features to describe how a basic block uses a stack frame: Features in this category include distinguishing whether a basic block increases, decreases, or does not change the stack frame, and counting the number of stack memory accesses in the basic block. These stack frame features capture uses of local

variables. Note that stack memory accesses are often performed by first creating an alias of the stack pointer, and then performing a relative addressing of the alias to access the stack. So, data flow analysis is necessary to identify aliases of the stack pointer.

3. Features to describe data flow dependencies of variables: Features in this category are based on backward slices of variables within the basic block. A basic block potentially can be decomposed into several disjoint slices [13]. We count the total number of slices, the average and maximum number of nodes in a slice, and the average and maximum length of slices. We also extract slice n-grams of length three to capture common data flow dependency patterns.

4.4   Context Features

Context features capture the loops and the functions to which a basic block belongs. We count loop nesting levels and loop sizes to represent loop contexts. When a basic block is in a nested loop, we extract loop features from the innermost loop that contains this basic block. For function context, we calculated the width and depth of a function's CFG with a breadth first search (BFS), in which we assigned a BFS level to each basic block. We also included the BFS level of a basic block and the number of basic blocks at the same BFS level.

5   External Template Library Code

We must distinguish external library code from the code written by their users. In the study discussed in Sect. 3, about 15% of the total basic blocks are STL and Boost code. If we are not able to identify STL or Boost code, our techniques would wrongly attribute this large amount of code to other authors.

Our experience with STL and Boost is that their source code looks significantly different from other C++ code. So, our initial attempt is to add group identities "STL" to and "Boost" to represent each of these libraries. Our results discussed in Sect. 7 show that both STL and Boost have distinct styles and we are able to identify the inlined code.

6   Classification Models

Our next step is to apply supervised machine learning techniques to learn the correlations between code features and authorship. Commonly used machine learning techniques such as SVM [10] and Random Forest [20] perform prediction solely based on individual features. While this is a reasonable approach when operating at the program level, it may not be the case for the basic block level. Based on the intuition that a programmer typically writes more than one basic block at a time, we hypothesize that adjacent basic blocks are likely written by the same author. To test our hypothesis, we built joint classification models, which perform prediction based on code features and who might be the authors

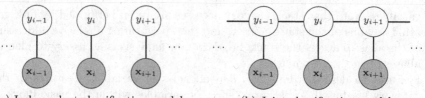

(a) Independent classification models   (b) Joint classification models

Fig. 2. Comparison between independent classification models and joint classification models. Each basic block has an author label y_i and a feature vector x_i. An edge connects two inter-dependent quantities. In both models, the author label and feature vector are dependent. In joint classification models, the author labels of adjacent basic blocks are also inter-dependent.

of adjacent basic blocks, and compare them to independent classification models, which perform prediction solely based on code features. The key difference between the two types of models are illustrated in Fig. 2.

For the independent classification models illustrated inclassification models illustrated in Fig. 2a, we divide a binary into a set of basic blocks $B = \{b_1, b_2, \ldots, b_m\}$. A basic block b_i is abstracted with a tuple $b_i = (y_i, x_i)$, where y_i is the author of this basic block and x_i is a feature vector extracted from the code of this basic block. The training data consists of a set of binaries and we convert them to a collection of training basic blocks B_{train}. Similarly, the testing data consists of a different set of binaries, producing a collection of testing basic blocks B_{test}. The author labels in B_{train} are used for training, while the author labels in B_{test} are not used during prediction and are only used for evaluation. With this modeling, it is straight-forward to use SVM to train independent classification models.

For the joint classification models illustrated in Fig. 2b, we use the same notation $b_i = (y_i, x_i)$ to represent a basic block, where y_i is the author label and x_i is the feature vector. The key difference here is that we convert a binary to a sequence of basic blocks $B = <b_1, b_2, \ldots, b_m>$, where b_i and b_{i+1} are adjacent in the binary. The training data and testing data contain two disjoint collections of basic block sequences. We can then use linear Conditional Random Field (CRF) [26] to train joint classification models.

7   Evaluation

We investigated five aspects of our new techniques: (1) whether we can recover authorship signals at the basic block level, (2) whether our new basic block level features are effective, (3) the impact of the number of selected features, (4) whether the joint classification models based on CRF can achieve better accuracy than the independent classification models based on SVM, and (5) whether we can identify inlined STL and Boost library code. Our evaluations show that:

1. We can effectively capture programming styles at the basic block level. Our new techniques achieved 65% accuracy for classifying 284 authors, compared to 0.4% accuracy by random guess. If a few false positives can be tolerated, we can rank the correct author among the top five with 77% accuracy and among the top ten with 82% accuracy. Our results show that it is practical to perform authorship identification at the basic block level.
2. Our new basic block level features are crucial for practical basic block level authorship identification. F_e represents the existing basic block level features discussed in Sect. 2.1, such as byte n-grams and instruction idioms; F_n represents our new feature set, which is a union of F_e and the new features discussed in Sect. 4. The results of the first row and the sixth row in Table 2 show that adding our new features leads to significant accuracy improvement, adding 26% to 43%, when compared to using only F_e.
3. When operating at the basic block level, we need to select many more features to achieve good accuracy than operating at the program level. As we will discuss in Sect. 7.2, previous program level techniques have selected less than 2,000 features. Our results show that 2,000 features significantly limit the prediction power of our models and we can improve accuracy from 43% to 58% by selecting about 45,000 features at the basic block level, as shown in the sixth and seventh row in Table 2.
4. The CRF models out-perform the SVM models, but CRF requires more training time. As shown in the last two rows in Table 2, the accuracy improved from 58% to 65% when we used CRF for training and prediction. In our experiments, SVM needs about one day for training and CRF needs about 7 times more training time than SVM. Both CRF and SVM can finish predic-

Table 2. Summary of our experiment results. We investigated the impact of three key components of our techniques on the accuracy: our new features, the number of selected features, and the joint classification models. F_e represents the existing basic block level features discussed in Sect. 2.1. We have four types of new features discussed in Sect. 4: instruction, control flow, data flow, and context features, denoted as F_I, F_{CF}, F_{DF}, F_C, respectively. $F_n = F_e \cup F_I \cup F_{CF} \cup F_{DF} \cup F_C$, represents our new feature set.

Classification model	Feature set	Number of selected features	Accuracy
SVM	F_e	2,000	26%
SVM	$F_e \cup F_I$	2,000	31%
SVM	$F_e \cup F_{CF}$	2,000	33%
SVM	$F_e \cup F_{DF}$	2,000	34%
SVM	$F_e \cup F_C$	2,000	38%
SVM	F_n	2,000	43%
SVM	F_n	45,000	58%
CRF	F_n	45,000	65%

tion in a few minutes on binaries of several hundred megabytes. As training new models is an infrequent operation and prediction on new binaries is the major operation in real world applications, it is reasonable to spend more training time on CRF for higher accuracy.

5. We can effectively distinguish STL and Boost code from other code. We calculated the precision, recall, and F1-measure for each author in our data set. Our results show that "STL" has 0.81 F-measure and "Boost" has 0.84 F-measure. For comparison, the average F-measure over all authors is 0.65.

7.1 Methodology

Our evaluations are based on a data set derived from the open source projects used in our empirical study discussed in Sect. 3. Our data set consists of 147 C binaries and 22 C++ binaries, which contains 284 authors and 900,583 basic blocks. C and C++ binaries are compiled on x86-64 Linux with GCC 4.8.5 and -O2 optimization. In practice, newly collected binaries may be compiled with different compilers and optimization levels. We can train separate models for different compilers or optimization levels and then apply compiler provenance techniques [34,37] to determine which model to use. The handling of these cases is the subject of ongoing research.

We used Dynisnt [32] to extract code features, Liblinear [14] for linear SVM, and CRFSuite [31] for linear CRF. We performed the traditional leave-one-out cross validation, where each binary was in turn used as the testing set and all other binaries were used as the training set. Each round of the cross validation had three steps. First, each basic block in the training set was labeled with its major author according to the weight vector of author contribution percentages derived in Sect. 3. Second, we selected the top K features that had the most mutual information with the major authors, where we varied K from 1000 to 50,000 to investigate the how it impacted accuracy. Third, we trained a linear SVM and a linear CRF and predicted the author of each basic block in the testing set. We calculated accuracy as the percentage of correctly attributed basic blocks. We parallelized this cross validation with HTCondor [22], where each round of the cross validation is executed on a separate machine.

An important characteristic of our leave-one-out cross validation is that the author distribution of the training sets is often significantly different from the author distribution of the testing sets. We believe this characteristic represents a real world scenario. For example, an author who wrote a small number of basic blocks in our training data may take a major role and contribute a large number of basic blocks in the new binary. For this reason, we do not stratify our data set, which is to evenly distribute the basic blocks of each author to each testing folds, as stratifying the data set does not represent real world scenarios.

Our data set is also imbalanced in terms of the number of basic blocks written by each author. The most prolific author wrote about 9% of the total basic blocks and the top 58 authors contribute about 90% of the total basic blocks.

We stress that to the best of our knowledge, we are the first project to perform fine-grained binary code authorship identification, so there are no previous basic block or function level techniques with which to compare. We do not compare with any previous program level techniques either, as these techniques can only attribute a multi-author binary to a single author. We experimented with applying program level techniques to our data set to estimate the upper bound accuracy that can be achieved by any program level technique. As a program level technique reports one author per binary, the best scenario is to always attribute all basic blocks in a binary to the major author of the binary. For each binary in our data set, we counted how many basic blocks were written by its major author and got an average accuracy of 31.6%, which is significantly lower than our reported numbers.

7.2 Impact of Features

As we mentioned before, adding our new features can significantly increase the accuracy. We now break down the contribution from each of our new feature type and investigate the impact of number of selected top features.

Our new features can be classified into four types: instruction, control flow, data flow, and context features. We denote these four types of features as F_I, F_{CF}, F_{DF}, and F_C, respectively. To determine the impact of each feature type, we calculated how much accuracy can be gained by adding only this type of new feature to the existing feature set F_e. In this experiment, we used SVM classification and selected top 2,000 features. As shown in the first row of Table 2, the baseline accuracy of using only feature set F_e is 26%. The second to the fifth row of Table 2 show that adding F_I, F_{CF}, F_{DF}, and F_C leads to 31%, 33%, 34%, 38% accuracy, respectively. Therefore, all of our new features provide additional useful information for identifying authors at the basic block level, with the context features providing the most gain.

In terms of the number of selected top features K, previous program level techniques have shown that a small number of features are sufficient to achieve good accuracy. Rosenblum et al [38] selected 1,900 features. Similarly, Caliskan et al. [7] selected 426 features.

We investigate the impact of K and find that the basic block level needs more features. Figure 3 shows how K affects accuracy. We can see that we need over 20,000 features to achieve good accuracy, which is significantly larger than the number used in previous studies. While the number of selected features is large, we have not observed the issue of overfitting: we repeated this experiment with selecting 100,000 features and got the same accuracy as selecting 50,000 features.

7.3 Classification Model Comparison

Our results show that CRF can achieve higher accuracy than SVM, but requires more training time. Specifically, CRF can significantly improve the accuracy for small basic blocks and modestly improve accuracy for large basic blocks. Figure 4a shows how our techniques work with basic blocks of different sizes. We can see that SVM suffers when the sizes of basic blocks are small, which is

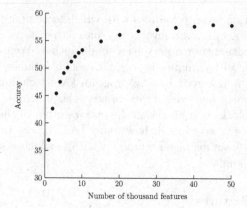

Fig. 3. Experiment results on the impact of the number features. The accuracy results are based on using the new feature set F_n and SVM classification.

not surprising as small basic blocks contain little code, thus few code features and little information. On the other hand, CRF performs better than SVM for all sizes of basic blocks. CRF provides the most benefits when the sizes of basic blocks are small, where we do not have enough information from the code features to make good prediction and have to rely on the adjacency. As the sizes of basic blocks grow, we have more information about these basic blocks and adjacency plays a smaller role in prediction and provides smaller accuracy improvement. We also observe that the accuracy starts to have a large variance when the sizes of basic blocks are larger than 30 bytes. We find that large basic blocks are few in our data set, so their results are unstable.

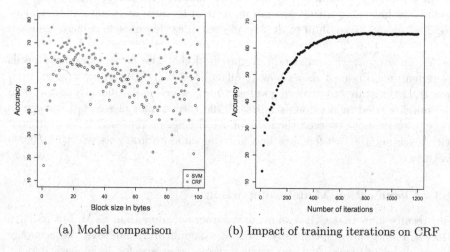

(a) Model comparison   (b) Impact of training iterations on CRF

Fig. 4. Comparison between CRF and SVM. The results of both figures are based on the new feature set F_n and selecting 45 K features.

The accuracy improvement of CRF comes at the cost of more training time. In our experiments, training SVM needs about one day, while training CRF needs about a week. As CRF training consists of iterations of updating feature weights, there is a trade-off between training time and accuracy. Figure 4b shows how the number of iteration of CRF training impacts the accuracy. In our experiments, we can finish about 150 iterations per day. We need about two days for CRF to reach the accuracy achieved by SVM in one day and need about three days for CRF accuracy to converge.

8   Conclusion

We have presented new fine-grained techniques for identifying the author of a basic block, which enables analysts to perform authorship identification on multi-author software. We performed an empirical study of three open source software to determine the most appropriate attribution unit and our study supported using the basic block as the attribution unit. We designed new instruction, control flow, data flow, and context features, handled inlined library code from STL and Boost by representing them with group identities "STL" and "Boost", and captured local authorship consistency between adjacent basic blocks with CRF. We evaluated our new techniques on a data set derived from the open source software used in our empirical study. Our techniques can discriminate 284 authors with 65% accuracy. We showed our new features and new classification models based on CRF can significantly improve accuracy. In summary, we make a concrete step towards practical fine-grained binary code authorship identification.

Acknowledgments. This work is supported in part by Department of Energy grant DE-SC0010474, National Science Foundation Cyber Infrastructure grants ACI-1547272, ACI-1449918, Department of Homeland Security under AFRL Contract FA8750-12-2-0289, and a grant from Intel Corporation. This research was performed using the compute resources and assistance of the UW-Madison Center For High Throughput Computing (CHTC) in the Department of Computer Sciences.

References

1. Abbasi, A., Li, W., Benjamin, V., Hu, S., Chen, H.: Descriptive analytics: examining expert hackers in web forums. In: 2014 IEEE Joint Intelligence and Security Informatics Conference (JISIC), Hague, Netherlands, September 2014
2. Allodi, L., Corradin, M., Massacci, F.: Then and now: on the maturity of the cybercrime markets (the lesson that black-hat marketeers learned). IEEE Trans. Emerg. Top. Comput. 4 (2015)
3. Alrabaee, S., Saleem, N., Preda, S., Wang, L., Debbabi, M.: Oba2: an onion approach to binary code authorship attribution. Digit. Investig. 11(Suppl. 1), S94–S103 (2014)
4. Apache Software Foundation: Apache http server. http://httpd.apache.org

5. Benjamin, V., Chen, H.: Securing cyberspace: identifying key actors in hacker communities. In: 2012 IEEE International Conference on Intelligence and Security Informatics (ISI), Arlington, VA, USA, June 2012
6. Burrows, S.: Source code authorship attribution. Ph.D. thesis, RMIT University, Melbourne, Victoria, Australia (2010)
7. Caliskan-Islam, A., Harang, R., Liu, A., Narayanan, A., Voss, C., Yamaguchi, F., Greenstadt, R.: De-anonymizing programmers via code stylometry. In: 24th USENIX Security Symposium (SEC), Austin, TX, USA, August 2015
8. Caliskan-Islam, A., Yamaguchi, F., Dauber, E., Harang, R., Rieck, K., Greenstadt, R., Narayanan, A.: When coding style survives compilation: de-anonymizing programmers from executable binaries. Technical report. arxiv http://arxiv.org/pdf/1512.08546.pdf
9. Chatzicharalampous, E., Frantzeskou, G., Stamatatos, E.: Author identification in imbalanced sets of source code samples. In: 2012 IEEE 24th International Conference on Tools with Artificial Intelligence (ICTAI), Athens, Greece, November 2012
10. Cortes, C., Vapnik, V.: Support-vector networks. Mach. Learn. **20**(3), 273–297 (1995)
11. Croll, P.R.: Supply chain risk management-understanding vulnerabilities in code you buy, build, or integrate. In: 2011 IEEE International System Conference (SysCon), Montreal, QC, Canada, April 2011
12. de la Cuadra, F.: The geneology of malware. Netw. Secur. **4**, 17–20 (2007)
13. David, Y., Partush, N., Yahav, E.: Statistical similarity of binaries. In: 37th ACM SIGPLAN Conference on Programming Language Design and Implementation (PLDI), Santa Barbara, California, USA, June 2016
14. Fan, R.E., Chang, K.W., Hsieh, C.J., Wang, X.R., Lin, C.J.: Liblinear: a library for large linear classification. J. Mach. Learn. Res. **9**, 1871–1874 (2008)
15. GNU Project: GCC: the GNU compiler collection. http://gcc.gnu.org
16. Guilfanova, I., DataRescue: fast library identificatiion and recognition technology (1997). https://www.hex-rays.com/products/ida/tech/flirt/index.shtml
17. Guyon, I., Elisseeff, A.: An introduction to variable and feature selection. J. Mach. Learn. Res. **3**, 1157–1182 (2003)
18. Hemel, A., Kalleberg, K.T., Vermaas, R., Dolstra, E.: Finding software license violations through binary code clone detection. In: 8th Working Conference on Mining Software Repositories (MSR), Waikiki, Honolulu, HI, USA, May 2011
19. Hex-Rays: IDA. https://www.hex-rays.com/products/ida/
20. Ho, T.K.: Random decision forests. In: 3rd International Conference on Document Analysis and Recognition (ICDAR), Montreal, Canada, August 1995
21. Holt, T.J., Strumsky, D., Smirnova, O., Kilger, M.: Examining the social networks of malware writers and hackers. Int. J. Cyber Criminol. **6**(1), 891–903 (2012)
22. HTCondor: High Throughput Computing (1988). https://research.cs.wisc.edu/htcondor/
23. Jacobson, E.R., Rosenblum, N., Miller, B.P.: Labeling library functions in stripped binaries. In: 10th ACM SIGPLAN-SIGSOFT Workshop on Program Analysis for Software Tools (PASTE), Szeged, Hungary, September 2011
24. Jang, J., Woo, M., Brumley, D.: Towards automatic software lineage inference. In: 22nd USENIX Conference on Security (SEC), Washington, D.C. (2013)
25. Khoo, W.M., Mycroft, A., Anderson, R.: Rendezvous: a search engine for binary code. In: 10th Working Conference on Mining Software Repositories (MSR), San Francisco, CA, USA, May 2013

26. Lafferty, J.D., McCallum, A., Pereira, F.C.N.: Conditional random fields: probabilistic models for segmenting and labeling sequence data. In: 8th International Conference on Machine Learning (ICML), Bellevue, Washington, USA, June 2001

27. Lindorfer, M., Di Federico, A., Maggi, F., Comparetti, P.M., Zanero, S.: Lines of malicious code: insights into the malicious software industry. In: 28th Annual Computer Security Applications Conference (ACSAC), Orlando, Florida, USA, December 2012

28. Mandiant: Mandiant 2013 threat report. Mandiant White paper (2013). https://www2.fireeye.com/WEB-2013-MNDT-RPT-M-Trends-2013_LP.html

29. Marquis-Boire, M., Marschalek, M., Guarnieri, C.: Big game hunting: the peculiarities in nation-state malware research. In: Black Hat, Las Vegas, NV, USA, August 2015

30. Meng, X., Miller, B.P., Williams, W.R., Bernat, A.R.: Mining software repositories for accurate authorship. In: 2013 IEEE International Conference on Software Maintenance (ICSM), Eindhoven, Netherlands, September 2013

31. Okazaki, N.: Crfsuite: a fast implementation of conditional random fields (CRFs) (2007). http://www.chokkan.org/software/crfsuite/

32. Paradyn Project: Dyninst: Putting the Performance in High Performance Computing. http://www.dyninst.org

33. Qiu, J., Su, X., Ma, P.: Library functions identification in binary code by using graph isomorphism testings. In: 2015 IEEE 22nd International Conference on Software Analysis, Evolution, and Reengineering (SANER), Montreal, Quebec, Canada, March 2015

34. Rahimian, A., Shirani, P., Alrbaee, S., Wang, L., Debbabi, M.: Bincomp: a stratified approach to compiler provenance attribution. Digit. Investig. **14**(Suppl. 1), S146–S155 (2015)

35. Rahman, F., Devanbu, P.: Ownership, experience and defects: a fine-grained study of authorship. In: Proceedings of 33rd International Conference on Software Engineering (ICSE), Waikiki, Honolulu, HI, USA, May 2011

36. Roberts, R.: Malware development life cycle. In: Virus Bulletin Conference (VB), October 2008

37. Rosenblum, N., Miller, B.P., Zhu, X.: Recovering the toolchain provenance of binary code. In: 2011 International Symposium on Software Testing and Analysis (ISSTA), Toronto, Ontario, Canada, July 2011

38. Rosenblum, N., Zhu, X., Miller, B.P.: Who wrote this code? Identifying the authors of program binaries. In: 16th European Conference on Research in Computer Security (ESORICS), Leuven, Belgium, September 2011

39. Ruttenberg, B., Miles, C., Kellogg, L., Notani, V., Howard, M., LeDoux, C., Lakhotia, A., Pfeffer, A.: Identifying shared software components to support malware forensics. In: 11th Conference on Detection of Intrusions and Malware, and Vulnerability Assessment (DIMVA), Egham, London, UK, July 2014

40. Sæbjørnsen, A., Willcock, J., Panas, T., Quinlan, D., Su, Z.: Detecting code clones in binary executables. In: 18th International Symposium on Software Testing and Analysis (ISSTA), Chicago, IL, USA, July 2009

41. Śliwerski, J., Zimmermann, T., Zeller, A.: When do changes induce fixes? In: Proceedings of 2005 International Workshop on Mining Software Repositories (MSR), St. Louis, Missouri, USA, May 2005

42. Yavvari, C., Tokhtabayev, A., Rangwala, H., Stavrou, A.: Malware characterization using behavioral components. In: 6th International Conference on Mathematical Methods, Models and Architectures for Computer Network Security (MMM-ACNS), St. Petersburg, Russia, October 2012

Secure IDS Offloading with Nested Virtualization and Deep VM Introspection

Shohei Miyama and Kenichi Kourai[(✉)]

Kyushu Institute of Technology, Iizuka, Fukuoka, Japan
{miyama,kourai}@ksl.ci.kyutech.ac.jp

Abstract. To securely execute intrusion detection systems (IDSes) for virtual machines (VMs), IDS offloading with VM introspection (VMI) is used. In semi-trusted clouds, however, IDS offloading inside an untrusted virtualized system does not guarantee that offloaded IDSes run correctly. Assuming a trusted hypervisor, secure IDS offloading has been proposed, but there are several drawbacks because the hypervisor is tightly coupled with untrusted management components. In this paper, we propose a system called *V-Met*, which offloads IDSes outside the virtualized system using *nested virtualization*. Since V-Met runs an untrusted virtualized system in a VM, the trusted computing base (TCB) is separated more clearly and strictly. V-Met can prevent IDSes from being compromised by untrusted virtualized systems and allows untrusted administrators to manage even the hypervisor. Furthermore, V-Met provides *deep VMI* for offloaded IDSes to obtain the internal state of target VMs inside the VM for running a virtualized system. We have implemented V-Met in Xen and confirmed that the performance of offloaded legacy IDSes was comparable to that in traditional IDS offloading.

Keywords: VM introspection · Nested virtualization · Insider attacks · IDS · Clouds

1 Introduction

In Infrastructure-as-a-Service (IaaS) clouds, users run their services in virtual machines (VMs). They can set up their systems in provided VMs and use them as necessary. As in traditional systems, it is necessary to protect the systems inside VMs from external attackers. For example, intrusion detection systems (IDSes) are useful to monitor the system states, filesystems, and network packets. To prevent IDSes from being compromised by intruders into VMs, *IDS offloading with VM introspection (VMI)* has been proposed [6–8,12]. This technique runs IDSes outside VMs and introspects the internal state of VMs, e.g., the memory, storage, and network. It is difficult that intruders attack IDSes outside VMs.

In semi-trusted clouds, however, it is not guaranteed that offloaded IDSes run correctly. By semi-trusted clouds, we mean that their providers are trusted but some of the system administrators may be untrusted. If untrusted administrators manage virtualized systems for running VMs and offloaded IDSes, offloaded

© Springer International Publishing AG 2017
S.N. Foley et al. (Eds.): ESORICS 2017, Part II, LNCS 10493, pp. 305–323, 2017.
DOI: 10.1007/978-3-319-66399-9_17

IDSes can suffer from insider attacks. Malicious administrators can easily disable offloaded IDSes before attacking VMs. If they do not harden virtualized systems sufficiently, even external attackers can interfere with offloaded IDSes using various system vulnerabilities.

In such semi-trusted clouds, secure IDS offloading has been achieved by assuming a trusted hypervisor inside the virtualized system. Even if insiders on the hypervisor attempt to disable offloaded IDSes, their access to the IDSes is prohibited [3,16]. One drawback of this approach is that the hypervisor can be compromised relatively easily by untrusted administrators because it provides rich interfaces to the other management components on top of the hypervisor. Such interfaces become a broad attack surface. Another drawback is that untrusted administrators cannot manage the hypervisor because the integrity of the hypervisor has to be maintained. Consequently, administrators who may be untrusted cannot manage the entire virtualized system. These problems arise from the fact that a trusted hypervisor and untrusted management components are tightly coupled.

In this paper, we propose *V-Met*, which enables offloading IDSes outside the entire virtualized system. V-Met uses *nested virtualization* [2] to run an untrusted virtualized system in a VM called the cloud VM. Since the interface between the cloud VM and its hypervisor is more restricted, V-Met can separate the trusted computing base (TCB) from untrusted parts more clearly and strictly. Thus, V-Met can prevent offloaded IDSes from being compromised by untrusted virtualized systems confined in the cloud VM. In addition, it allows any administrators to completely manage the entire virtualized system including the hypervisor because the hypervisor has to be no longer trusted.

Deep VMI is a key to offloaded IDSes to monitor the memory, storage, and network of user VMs inside the cloud VM. For *deep memory introspection*, V-Met first finds the memory of a user VM in that of the cloud VM and then obtains data in the user VM. For *deep network introspection*, it captures packets at both boundaries of a user VM and the virtualized system. For *deep storage introspection*, it accesses a virtual disk of a user VM through the analysis of a virtual disk of the cloud VM. Using Transcall [10] with deep VMI, V-Met can offload even legacy IDSes. We have implemented V-Met in Xen and offloaded several legacy IDSes. Then, we confirmed that the performance was comparable to that of traditional IDS offloading.

The organization of this paper is as follows. Section 2 describes issues of IDS offloading in semi-trusted clouds. Section 3 proposes IDS offloading using nested virtualization and deep VMI. Section 4 describes the implementation details of V-Met. Section 5 reports experimental results for examining the effectiveness of V-Met. Section 6 describes related work and Sect. 7 concludes this paper.

2   IDS Offloading in Semi-trusted Clouds

To execute IDSes securely, *IDS offloading* with *VMI* has been proposed [6–8,12]. This technique enables IDSes to run outside their target VMs and monitor the systems inside the VMs from the outside. Even if attackers intrude into a user VM, they cannot disable offloaded IDSes. IDSes are often offloaded to a privileged VM for managing user VMs, e.g., the *management VM* in Xen. Offloaded IDSes can directly obtain detailed information such as the memory, storage, and networks inside user VMs, using VMI. IDSes in the management VM can map memory pages of target VMs and obtain the system state. They can access disk images of user VMs, which are located in the management VM. Also, they can capture packets from virtual network devices created in the management VM.

Although the management VM running offloaded IDSes is managed by system administrators in clouds, not all system administrators are trusted even if cloud providers are trusted. It is reported that 28% of cybercrimes are caused by insiders [27]. One example of insiders is malicious system administrators, who attack systems actively. For example, a site reliability engineer in Google violated user's privacy in 2010 [33]. Another example is curious but honest system administrators, who may eavesdrop on attractive information that they can easily obtain from user VMs. It is revealed that 35% of system administrators access sensitive information without authorization [5].

In such *semi-trusted clouds*, secure IDS offloading using a trusted hypervisor has been proposed. The hypervisor is a part of a virtualized system, which is managed by administrators. For example, BVMD [25] directly runs IDSes inside a trusted hypervisor and protects them from untrusted administrators. SSC [3] enables offloaded IDSes to run only in user's own administrative VMs and prevents system administrators from interfering with those VMs. Remote-Trans [16] offloads IDSes to trusted remote hosts and remotely performs VMI via the trusted hypervisor.

Unfortunately, such a trusted hypervisor is tightly coupled with the untrusted management VM running management components. Therefore, the approach of using a trusted hypervisor has three drawbacks. First, untrusted administrators in the management VM can compromise the hypervisor relatively easily. The hypervisor provides rich interfaces to the management VM to delegate many management tasks. Such interfaces can be abused using vulnerabilities in specification and implementation and become a broad attack surface. Once the hypervisor is penetrated, attackers can disable or compromise IDSes.

Second, it is not allowed that untrusted administrators manage the trusted hypervisor. If untrusted administrators are given such a privilege, they could even replace the hypervisor with a malicious one. This means that administrators who may be untrusted cannot manage the entire virtualized system. In general, the virtualized system is updated using packages like the other software. Since packages have dependency, the entire virtualized system including the hypervisor is usually updated at once. To enable only the hypervisor to be updated separately, it is necessary to largely change the current management method.

Third, the approach of using a trusted hypervisor is only applicable to specific virtualized systems. To trust only the hypervisor, it is necessary that the hypervisor and the other management components are clearly separated. Examples of such virtualized systems are Xen and Hyper-V. In contrast, the hypervisor cannot be separated in KVM because the hypervisor runs inside the host operating system. Although it is possible to trust the entire host operating system, the TCB becomes large because the operating system is much more complex than the hypervisor.

3   V-Met

We propose a system called V-Met for enabling secure IDS offloading outside the virtualized system. We assume that some of the system administrators who manage virtualized systems may be untrusted. The hypervisor and the management VM can be abused by untrusted administrators. On the other hand, we assume that cloud providers are trusted. This assumption is widely accepted [16,17,30,31,35] because a bad reputation is critical for their business. We also assume that the components outside the virtualized system, i.e., V-Met, offloaded IDSes, and hardware, are managed correctly by cloud providers. The integrity of V-Met is guaranteed by remote attestation with TPM at boot time and secure checking with the system management mode (SMM) [1,29,34] or Intel TXT and AMD SVM [21] at runtime.

3.1   Secure IDS Offloading with Nested Virtualization

V-Met runs IDSes outside a virtualized system using a technique called *nested virtualization* [2]. Traditional approaches rely on trusted hardware outside the virtualized system. For example, Copilot [26] detects tampering with the kernel memory on a PCI add-in card. HyperGuard [29] runs IDSes in the SMM of processors. However, it is difficult to run feature-rich legacy IDSes, which monitor high-level system state, filesystems, and network communication. Nested virtualization enables a virtualized system to run in a VM, which is called the *cloud VM*. Figure 1 illustrates the system architecture of V-Met. V-Met offloads IDSes outside the cloud VM and runs them and the cloud VM on top of the *cloud hypervisor*. The IDSes monitor user VMs inside the cloud VM using *deep VMI*, whose details are described in Sect. 3.2.

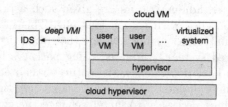

Fig. 1. The system architecture of V-Met.

V-Met can resolve several issues on IDS offloading in semi-trusted clouds. First, V-Met makes insider attack against offloaded IDSes difficult by running a virtualized system inside the cloud VM. This is because the interface between the cloud VM and the cloud hypervisor is narrower than that between the management VM and the hypervisor in the virtualized system. The former hardware-level interface is less vulnerable than the latter rich interface. Therefore, the cloud VM is isolated from the cloud hypervisor more strongly. Second, V-Met allows untrusted administrators to manage the entire virtualized system including the hypervisor. In other words, they can use the traditional management method. This advantage comes from the fact that the responsibility of administrators is more clearly separated at the boundary of virtualization, i.e., between the cloud VM and the cloud hypervisor. Third, V-Met enables clouds to use arbitrary virtualized systems because it does not need to trust specific hypervisors. To achieve this, V-Met provides deep VMI independent of virtualized systems.

In terms of performance, our approach of using nested virtualization is feasible because it is reported that the overhead is 6–8% [2] for common workloads. Special-purpose host hypervisors as used in CloudVisor [35] and TinyChecker [32] can improve the performance of nested virtualization more. Recently, hardware support for nested virtualization has been also added. For example, Intel VMCS Shadowing [11] can eliminate VM exits due to VMREAD and VMWRITE instructions for accessing VMCS. When it is not necessary to run offloaded IDSes, devirtualization [4,13,15,18,24] could largely reduce the overhead of nested virtualization. This is a technique for temporarily disabling virtualization provided by the hypervisor.

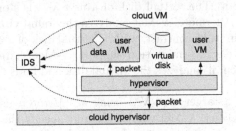

Fig. 2. Deep VMI.

3.2 Deep VMI

Deep VMI enables offloaded IDSes to monitor user VMs inside the cloud VM, as depicted in Fig. 2. For *deep memory introspection*, V-Met finds data of a target user VM from the memory of the cloud VM and provides it to offloaded IDSes. Since the memory of the cloud VM contains the memory of multiple user VMs in general, V-Met has to identify the memory of the target user VM and then the target data inside it. To perform this, V-Met executes address translation *three times*. First, it translates a virtual address of target data into a physical address in a user VM using the page tables stored in the user VM. Second, it translates the address into a physical address in the cloud VM using the extended page tables (EPT) for the user VM, which are stored in the hypervisor inside the cloud VM. Third, it translates the address into a physical address in the entire system using EPT for the cloud VM. In traditional VMI, address translation is only twice.

For *deep network introspection*, V-Met captures packets sent and received by a target user VM at both boundaries of the user VM and the virtualized system. These two methods are called *VM-level* and *system-level* packet capture, respectively. Using VM-level packet capture at the boundary of a user VM, V-Met can monitor sent packets that have not been processed yet by the virtualized system and received ones that have been already processed by that. This means that offloaded IDSes can introspect exact packets sent and received by a user VM. Also, they can introspect packets between user VMs inside the same cloud VM. Using system-level packet capture at the boundary of the virtualized system, on the other hand, V-Met can monitor sent packets that have been already processed by the virtualized system and received ones that have not been processed yet by that. This means that offloaded IDSes can inspect exact communication of a user VM with the outside. Comparing these communication logs of VM-level and system-level packet capture, offloaded IDSes can also detect attacks by insiders in the virtualized system.

For *deep storage introspection*, V-Met supports both local and remote virtual disks. When a virtual disk of a user VM is located in the virtualized system, V-Met first analyzes the virtual disk of the cloud VM and finds a virtual disk of a user VM inside it. The virtual disk of a user VM is stored in the form of a disk image file. Furthermore, V-Met analyzes the found virtual disk and finds data and metadata in it. In contrast, when a virtual disk of a user VM is located in network storage, e.g., for migration support, V-Met shares the virtual disk via the network. Then, it analyzes the virtual disk and finds data and metadata in it.

V-Met identifies a target user VM using a *VM tag* registered by the user VM itself. This is because V-Met cannot securely specify the ID of a user VM, which is managed inside the virtualized system. In V-Met, a user VM registers a unique VM tag to the cloud hypervisor using an *ultracall*. An ultracall is a new mechanism for directly invoking the cloud hypervisor outside the virtualized system. It enables a user VM to securely communicate with the cloud hypervisor without being interfered by the virtualized system. Using the registered VM tag, offloaded IDSes can monitor a target user VM inside the cloud VM uniquely.

3.3 Transcall with Deep VMI

Using deep VMI, legacy IDSes can be run outside the virtualized system in cooperation with Transcall [10]. Transcall provides an execution environment for legacy IDSes to introspect a user VM without any modifications. Transcall consists of the system call emulator, the shadow filesystem, and shadow network devices. The system call emulator traps the system calls issued by IDSes and, if necessary, returns information on the kernel from the memory of a user

VM, using deep memory introspection. The shadow filesystem provides the same filesystem view as that in a user VM, using deep storage introspection. To achieve this, it constructs the shadow proc filesystem, which is a counterpart of the proc filesystem inside a user VM. The proc filesystem provides information on the system such as processes and sockets. The shadow proc filesystem analyzes the memory of a user VM using deep memory introspection and provides files and directories containing system information. In addition, a shadow network device provides a network interface for capturing packets of a user VM, using deep network introspection.

4   Implementation

We have implemented V-Met in Xen 4.4.0. In V-Met, the cloud VM and the cloud management VM run on top of the cloud hypervisor. The *cloud management VM* is a VM that provides virtual devices to the cloud VM and has a privilege for introspecting the cloud VM. The cloud VM runs an existing virtualized system, which consists of the hypervisor, the management VM, and user VMs. To distinguish these components from those of V-Met, we call them the *guest hypervisor* and the *guest management VM*, respectively. V-Met assumes that both the cloud VM and user VMs run in full virtualization using Intel VT-x.

4.1   Deep Memory Introspection

As described in Sect. 3.2, V-Met executes address translation three times to access target data in a user VM inside the cloud VM from the cloud management VM. Figure 3 shows the flow of deep memory introspection. First, V-Met traverses the page tables inside a user VM to translate a virtual address into a physical address in the user VM (guest physical address). It identifies the page tables by the address of the page directory. This address is stored in the CR3 register of a virtual CPU for the user VM. Although that register is maintained by the guest hypervisor, V-Met cannot trust the state of virtual CPUs stored in the untrusted guest hypervisor.

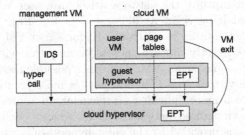

Fig. 3. Deep memory introspection.

Therefore, V-Met obtains the value of the CR3 register without relying on the guest hypervisor. It configures the cloud hypervisor so that a VM exit occurs when a user VM attempts to modify the CR3 register. Since a VM exit does not occur by default at this time, we configured VM-execution control fields in the VMCS of virtual CPUs for a user VM. The VMCS for a user VM is also managed by the untrusted guest hypervisor, but the cloud hypervisor can securely manage it after the VMCS is loaded to a virtual CPU for the cloud VM. When the cloud hypervisor traps access to the control registers including CR3, it first checks whether the access is a write to the CR3 register. If so, it obtains the value that the user VM attempts to write to the register and saves it. Offloaded IDSes in the cloud management VM can obtain the latest value of the CR3 register by issuing a new hypercall to the cloud hypervisor, traverse the page tables, and execute the first address translation.

Second, V-Met traverses EPT inside the guest hypervisor to translate the guest physical address into a physical address in the cloud VM (host physical address). The address of EPT is stored in the VMCS of virtual CPUs for the user VM. When the cloud hypervisor traps access to the CR3 register, it also saves the address of EPT in the VMCS loaded to the virtual CPU. When IDSes in the cloud management VM issue a new hypercall, the cloud hypervisor executes address translation using the saved EPT.

Finally, V-Met translates the host physical into a physical address in the entire system (machine address) using EPT inside the cloud hypervisor. This translation is automatically done by the cloud hypervisor when IDSes issue a hypercall for mapping the memory of the cloud VM.

V-Met assumes that the page tables inside a user VM are protected by the memory isolation technique of CloudVisor [35]. Since CloudVisor restricts access to the memory of a user VM from the virtualized system, insiders cannot tamper with the page tables in the memory of a user VM. Similarly, V-Met protects EPT inside the guest hypervisor by the memory owner tracking technique of CloudVisor. CloudVisor allows only the memory of a user VM to be registered to EPT. Therefore, it is difficult for insiders to modify EPT as they intended.

4.2   Deep Network Introspection

For VM-level packet capture, the network driver in a user VM directly passes packets to the cloud hypervisor, as illustrated in Fig. 4(a). Another possible location of this packet capture is a virtual NIC for a user VM. However, V-Met may not be able to correctly capture packets because that virtual NIC runs in the untrusted guest management VM. The other possible method is to trap all the I/O access of a virtual NIC. This method is more secure, but it is more heavyweight and much more difficult to implement. In addition, it is probably impossible for para-virtualized network devices because such devices strongly depend on mechanisms provided by the guest hypervisor.

The network driver in a user VM uses an ultracall to the cloud hypervisor to prevent the virtualized system in the cloud VM from interfering with packet capture. Since it passes the guest physical address of packet data using the

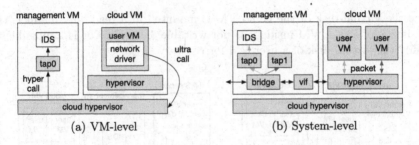

(a) VM-level   (b) System-level

Fig. 4. Deep network introspection.

ultracall, the cloud hypervisor first translates that address into a host physical address using EPT for the user VM. Then, it copies the packet data to the memory of the cloud hypervisor. V-Met periodically issues a new hypercall for obtaining the saved packets and writes them to a TAP device created for each user VM. Offloaded IDSes can capture packets of a user VM from the TAP device.

For system-level packet capture, on the other hand, V-Met can obtain all the packets from the virtual NIC (vif) for the cloud VM, as illustrated in Fig. 4(b). From this virtual NIC, however, the packets sent and received by all the user VMs in the cloud VM are captured. To enable obtaining packets for each user VM separately, V-Met uses the ulog mechanism of ebtables in Linux. ulog is used to pass packets received by the Ethernet bridge to a userland daemon using a netlink socket. After V-Met obtains packets using ulog, it classifies and writes them to a TAP device created for each virtual NIC of user VMs. Offloaded IDSes can capture packets for a user VM from one or some of the TAP devices.

To classify packets without any knowledge of MAC addresses of user VMs, V-Met uses information on sender and receiver devices obtained using ulog. If the sender device of a packet is the virtual NIC of the cloud VM, V-Met automatically creates a TAP device corresponding to the sender's MAC address and writes the packet to the device. In contrast, if the receiver device is the virtual NIC, V-Met writes the packet to a TAP device for the receiver's MAC address. In addition, if such a MAC address is a broadcast address or multicast addresses, V-Met writes a packet to all the TAP devices.

4.3 Deep Storage Introspection

When a virtual disk of a user VM is located in a virtual disk of the cloud VM, as in Fig. 5(a), V-Met first mounts the disk image of the cloud VM in the management VM. Then it mounts the disk image of the user VM in the virtual disk of the cloud VM. This seems to be easy, but the reality is not so simple. These mounts need to be done in a read-only manner because the filesystem in a virtual disk is corrupted if its metadata is simultaneously modified by multiple VMs. However, when the filesystem has to be recovered for various reasons, the virtual disk is temporarily mounted in a writable manner to modify its metadata.

Since the virtual disk of the cloud VM is mounted in a read-only manner, the disk image of a user VM inside it is not writable. Therefore, it is impossible to modify the virtual disk of a user VM for recovery.

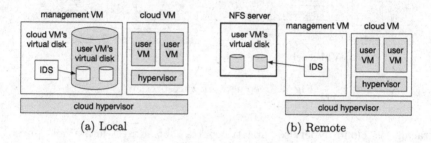

Fig. 5. Deep storage introspection.

To solve this dilemma, V-Met creates a snapshot of the disk image of the cloud VM using dm-thin, which is a mechanism for thin provisioning using the device mapper in Linux. When data is read from the snapshot, dm-thin directly returns the corresponding blocks of the disk image. When data is written to the snapshot, dm-thin allocates new blocks in another disk image and writes the data to them. V-Met mounts the snapshot in a writable manner and then mounts the virtual disk of the user VM inside it. Thus, the virtual disk of the user VM can be recovered by temporarily mounting in a writable manner.

On the other hand, when a disk image of a user VM is located in network storage, as in Fig. 5(b), V-Met first mounts a directory where the disk image is stored in an NFS server and then mounts the disk image in it. The directory is also mounted in the guest management VM to run a user VM. Since NFS is designed for sharing files in mind, the directory in the NFS server can be mounted in a writable manner. Therefore, the disk image can be mounted temporarily in a writable manner if its filesystem has to be recovered.

4.4   Ultracall

An ultracall directly invokes the cloud hypervisor by executing the vmcall instruction. This instruction is originally used for a hypercall to the hypervisor. When a user VM executes the vmcall instruction in the nested virtualization, the cloud hypervisor first traps the instruction and usually redirects it to the guest hypervisor. Then, the guest hypervisor executes the corresponding hypercall for the user VM. In contrast, the cloud hypervisor in V-Met does not redirect the instruction if a user VM sets a special value to the EAX register. Instead, the cloud hypervisor executes an ultracall for the user VM.

4.5   Management of User VMs

In V-Met, the cloud hypervisor manages user VMs inside the cloud VM using VM tags registered by user VMs themselves, the addresses of EPT, and the addresses of the page directories. It binds a VM tag to the address of EPT when the tag is registered. EPT is created at the boot time of a user VM and its address is usually not changed during the execution of the user VM. If EPT is re-created, the cloud hypervisor detects that at a VM exit caused by CR3 access and changes the binding. Also, the cloud hypervisor binds the address of the current page directory to the VM tag. This binding is changed whenever context switches between processes occur in the user VM. These two bindings have to be removed when the user VM is destroyed, but the detection of VM destruction is our future work.

5   Experiments

We conducted experiments to examine the effectiveness of V-Met with deep VMI. We used a PC with an Intel Xeon E3-1270v3 processor, 16 GB of DDR3 SDRAM, 2 TB of SATA III HDD, and Gigabit Ethernet. In this PC, we ran Xen 4.4.0 implemented V-Met. For the cloud VM, we assigned two virtual CPUs, 3 GB of memory, and a virtual disk of 40 GB. We ran vanilla Xen 4.4.0 in this cloud VM. For a user VM inside the cloud VM, we assigned one virtual CPU, 1 GB of memory, and a virtual disk of 8 GB. We ran Linux 3.13 in the cloud and guest management VMs and the user VM. For an NFS server, we used a PC with an Intel Xeon X5675 processor, 32 GB of memory, a RAID 5 disk of 3.75 TB, and Gigabit Ethernet. These PCs were connected using a Gigabit Ethernet switch.

For comparison, we used two systems: the traditional, single-level virtualized system without nested virtualization (Xen-Single) and the virtualized system with nested virtualization (Xen-Nest). For Xen-Single, we ran vanilla Xen with the same resource assignment as that inside the cloud VM. Offloaded IDSes were run in the management VM using traditional VMI. For Xen-Nest, we ran vanilla Xen both on top of hardware and in the cloud VM. Offloaded IDSes were run in the guest management VM inside the cloud VM using traditional VMI.

5.1   Performance of Deep VMI

We measured the performance of VMI in the three systems. First, we examined the performance of memory introspection by reading data in the memory of the user VM. The benchmark tool repeated translating virtual addresses of the user VM, mapping its memory pages, and copying the page contents to measure the throughput. Surprisingly, the throughput in V-Met was 41% higher than that in Xen-Single, as shown in Fig. 6(a).

To clarify why the throughput in V-Met was the highest, we measured the execution time of the hypercalls used for address translation. Figure 6(b) shows the time needed for two new hypercalls. In V-Met, it took 0.64 μs to execute the hypercall for obtaining the address of the page directory of the user VM. In Xen-Single, it took 11 μs because a general-purpose hypercall for obtaining all the state of a virtual CPU was used. The execution time in Xen-Nest was much longer due to the overhead of nested virtualization. Although only V-Met needs

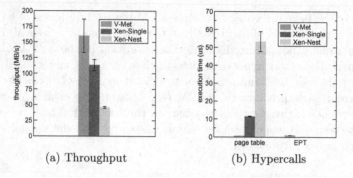

(a) Throughput   (b) Hypercalls

Fig. 6. The performance of memory introspection.

the other hypercall for address translation using EPT, which took $0.92\,\mu s$, the hypercall for the page directory was a dominant factor.

Next, we examined the performance of storage introspection using the IOzone 3.465 benchmark [23]. In this experiment, we created a file of 1 GB in the user VM and measured the throughput of sequentially reading the file using VMI. We flushed the page cache in the cloud management VM, the guest management VM, and the NFS server every run. Figure 7(a) shows the results when we used virtual disks located in the cloud VM and the NFS server. When using a local virtual disk, the throughput in V-Met was 20% higher than that in Xen-Single although V-Met has to access two virtual disks of the cloud VM and the user VM in turn. According to our analysis, this is because read-ahead for the two virtual disks was more effective than that for only one virtual disk used in Xen-Single. The performance in Xen-Nest largely degraded due to increasing the overhead of storage virtualization for the cloud VM. When using a remote virtual disk, V-Met and Xen-Single accessed the virtual disk in exactly the same manner and consequently the throughput was the same. However, the performance was much lower than using a local virtual disk.

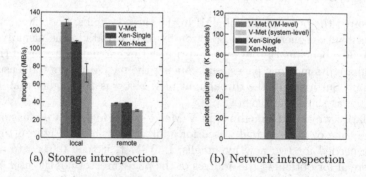

(a) Storage introspection   (b) Network introspection

Fig. 7. The performance of storage and network introspection.

Finally, we examined the performance of network introspection. We transferred 1470-byte UDP datagrams in 500 Mbps to the user VM using iperf 2.0.5 [9] and captured these packets with tcpdump. The maximum rate of packet capture was shown in Fig. 7(b). The rate in Xen-Single was the highest, but the performance degradation in V-Met was only 10% and 8% in VM-level and system-level packet capture, respectively. The overhead of VM-level packet capture comes from writing packets to a TAP device via the cloud hypervisor, while that of system-level packet capture is caused by ebtables. The performance in Xen-Nest was almost the same as that in V-Met.

5.2 Performance of Offloaded IDSes

We examined the performance of legacy IDSes offloaded with Transcall. Since we need to run Transcall before executing IDSes, we first measured the initialization time of Transcall. Transcall constructs the shadow proc filesystem for the user VM and mounts its virtual disk. To construct the filesystem, Transcall gathers information on the operating system using memory introspection. As shown in Fig. 8(a), the construction time in V-Met was only 5 ms shorter than that in Xen-Single although the performance of memory introspection was largely different, as shown in Fig. 6(a). This is because Transcall caches the results of address translation and the portion of memory introspection was relatively small. Figure 8(b) shows the time needed for mounting the virtual disk of the user VM. For a local virtual disk, V-Met took a long time because it had to mount two virtual disks of the cloud VM and the user VM. For a remote virtual disk, the mount time was much shorter.

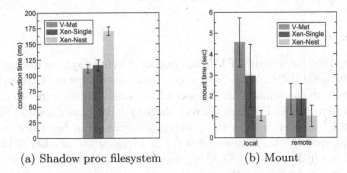

(a) Shadow proc filesystem   (b) Mount

Fig. 8. The initialization time of Transcall.

After Transcall was initialized, we measured the execution time of chkrootkit 0.50 [22], which is an IDS for detecting installed rootkits by inspecting processes, files, and sockets. Figure 9(a) shows the results for local and remote virtual disks. In both storage configurations, the execution time in V-Met was almost the same as that in Xen-Single.

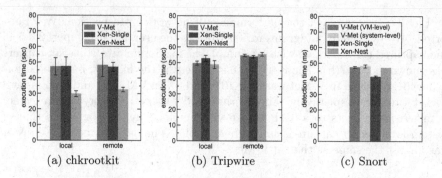

Fig. 9. The performance of offloaded IDSes.

Next, we measured the execution time of Tripwire 2.4 [14], which is an IDS for checking the integrity of filesystems. Figure 9(b) shows the results. For a local virtual disk, the execution time in V-Met was 6% shorter than that in Xen-Single, which came from higher performance of storage introspection. For a remote virtual disk, the execution time in three systems was almost the same.

Finally, we performed a TCP port scan against the user VM using nmap 6.40 [20] and measured the time for detecting this attack. The detection time is from when we started a port scan until Snort 2.9.8.3 [28] detected it. Figure 9(c) shows the results. In V-Met, the detection time increased only by 6 or 7 ms, compared with Xen-Single. When using VM-level packet capture, this delay was caused by passing packets from the user VM to the cloud management VM via the cloud hypervisor. When using system-level packet capture, the overhead of the packet classifier led to the detection delay.

5.3 Overhead

We measured the increase in CPU utilization of the entire system during the execution of offloaded IDSes. While we ran chkrootkit and Tripwire, CPU utilization increased only in the (cloud) management VM, where IDSes were offloaded, for V-Met and Xen-Single. The increase was almost the same, as shown in Fig. 10(a) and Fig. 10(b). In Xen-Nest, CPU utilization increased in both the cloud and guest management VMs. The reason why the increase was smaller is that Xen-Nest could not utilize CPUs effectively due to nested virtualization.

For Snort, we compared CPU utilization when we transferred 1470-byte UDP datagrams in 100 Mbps with and without Snort. For VM-level packet capture in V-Met, the CPU utilization of the cloud management VM increased largely. Although the user VM issued ultracalls many times, its CPU utilization did not increase. For system-level packet capture, in contrast, CPU utilization increased only by 12% point, compared with Xen-Single.

Next, we examined the overhead of causing VM exits for enabling deep memory introspection. While these VM exits are not caused by default, V-Met needs to trap access to the CR3 register. For V-Met and Xen-Nest, we ran UnixBench

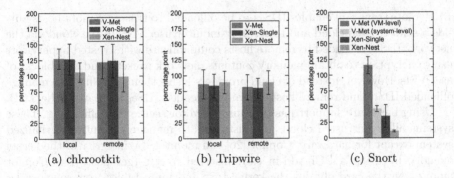

Fig. 10. The increases in CPU utilization during running offloaded IDSes.

5.1.3 [19] in the user VM. Figure 11(a) shows the UnixBench scores and the performance degradation due to VM exits were only 2%.

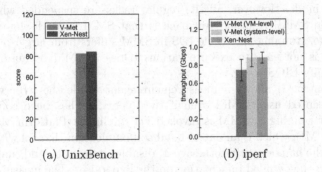

Fig. 11. The overhead of a user VM.

Finally, we examined the impact of deep network introspection on network performance of the user VM. We measured the TCP throughput of the user VM using iperf. As shown in Fig. 11(b), VM-level packet capture degraded the throughput by 16%. In contrast, there was no performance degradation in system-level packet capture.

6   Related Work

Several systems enable secure IDS offloading by using trusted hypervisors. A self-service cloud (SSC) computing platform [3] provides users with privileged VMs called service domains (SDs) to monitor their own VMs. SDs can monitor the memory of target VMs, disk blocks accessed by VMs, and system calls issued by them. Even cloud administrators cannot disable IDSes in SDs. However, a VM called DomB has to be trusted in addition to the hypervisor.

RemoteTrans [16] enables IDSes to be offloaded to trusted remote hosts outside a semi-trusted cloud and to securely monitor user VMs in the cloud via the network. IDSes offloaded to remote hosts communicate with trusted hypervisors using encryption to obtain memory contents, network packets, and disk blocks of user VMs. However, instead of cloud providers, users themselves have to manage offloaded IDSes and remote hosts running offloaded IDSes are part of the TCB.

Using hardware support has been proposed for secure IDS offloading. These systems allow untrusted cloud administrators to manage the entire virtualized system except for hardware. Copilot [26] can monitor the integrity of the kernel memory by using a PCI add-in card inserted in a target host. The Copilot monitor on the card obtains the kernel text and jump tables from memory by DMA and calculates its hash. It sends the results of integrity checking to a remote host via a dedicated network. Due to hardware limitation, it is difficult to run legacy IDSes.

HyperGuard [29] and HyperCheck [34] enable IDSes to securely monitor the integrity of the hypervisor using SMM. In SMM, the CPU can securely execute code in System Management RAM (SMRAM), which cannot be accessed in the normal mode. However, all the regular tasks are suspended while an IDS is running in SMM. Another drawback is that SMM is much slower than the normal mode. Running the whole IDS in SMM suffers from larger overhead. In addition, it is not easy to execute various IDSes in SMM because developers need to modify BIOS.

HyperSentry [1] allows a measurement agent inside the hypervisor to be securely executed using SMM even if the hypervisor has been compromised. The handler running in SMM is invoked via Intelligent Platform Management Interface (IPMI), which is an out-of-band communication channel with a remote host. Then the handler verifies the agent, disables interrupts, and runs the agent for collecting the detailed information on the hypervisor. The measurement output is attested by the remote host. One drawback is that the agent cannot run simultaneously with the other tasks.

Flicker [21] is an infrastructure for executing security-sensitive code using the hardware support such as Intel TXT and AMD SVM. When such code needs to be executed, Flicker suspends the current execution environment, securely executes the code using late launch, and resumes the previous execution environment. Late launch enables code execution without interferences by the attackers. However, it also stops all CPU cores other than the one used by the executed code. While the security-sensitive code is running, the other applications cannot be running.

7   Conclusion

In this paper, we proposed a system called V-Met, which enables IDS offloading outside the virtualized system using nested virtualization. V-Met runs an untrusted virtualized system in a VM and allows offloaded IDSes to securely monitor user VMs inside it using deep VMI. Such clear separation of the TCB can prevent IDSes from being attacked by untrusted virtualized systems. Also, it allows untrusted administrators to manage the entire virtualized system including the hypervisor as traditionally done. We have ported Transcall for offloading the legacy IDSes to V-Met and confirmed that the overhead is comparable to the traditional IDS offloading.

One of our future work is to automatically and securely identify the MAC addresses and the virtual disk used by a user VM. In the current implementation, we assume that these are known in advance. We are also planning to monitor components other than user VMs, e.g., the hypervisor and the management VM in the virtualized system. Another direction is to run other virtualized systems such as KVM. We believe that this is not difficult thanks to the design of V-Met.

Acknowledgment. This work was partially supported by JSPS KAKENHI Grant Number JP16K00101.

References

1. Azab, A., Ning, P., Wang, Z., Jiang, X., Zhang, X., Skalsky, N.: HyperSentry: enabling stealthy in-context measurement of hypervisor integrity. In: Proceedings of ACM Conference Computer and Communications Security, pp. 38–49 (2010)
2. Ben-Yehuda, M., Day, M.D., Dubitzky, Z., Factor, M., Har'El, N., Gordon, A., Liguori, A., Wasserman, O., Yassour, B.A.: The turtles project: design and implementation of nested virtualization. In: Proceedings of USENIX Symposium Operating Systems Design and Implementation, pp. 423–436 (2010)
3. Butt, S., Lagar-Cavilla, H.A., Srivastava, A., Ganapathy, V.: Self-service cloud computing. In: Proceedings of ACM Conference Computer and Communications Security, pp. 253–264 (2012)
4. Chen, H., Chen, R., Zhang, F., Zang, B., Yew, P.C.: Mercury: combining performance with dependability using self-virtualization. In: Proceedings of IEEE International Conference Parallel Processing (2007)
5. CyberArk Software: Global IT Security Service (2009)
6. Dolan-Gavitt, B., Leek, T., Zhivich, M., Giffin, J., Lee, W.: Virtuoso: narrowing the semantic gap in virtual machine introspection. In: Proceedings of IEEE Symposium Security and Privacy, pp. 297–312 (2011)
7. Fu, Y., Lin, Z.: Space traveling across VM: automatically bridging the semantic gap in virtual machine introspection via online kernel data redirection. In: Proceedings of IEEE Symposium Security and Privacy, pp. 586–600 (2012)
8. Garfinkel, T., Rosenblum, M.: A virtual machine introspection based architecture for intrusion detection. In: Proceedings of Network and Distributed Systems Security Symposium, pp. 191–206 (2003)
9. Gates, M., Warshavsky, A.: iperf2. https://sourceforge.net/projects/iperf2/
10. Iida, T., Kourai, K.: Transcall. http://www.ksl.ci.kyutech.ac.jp/oss/transcall/
11. Intel Corp: 4th Generation Intel Core vPro Processors with Intel VMCS Shadowing (2013)
12. Jiang, X., Wang, X., Xu, D.: Stealthy malware detection through VMM-based "out-of-the-box" semantic view reconstruction. In: Proceedings of ACM Conference Computer and Communications Security, pp. 128–138 (2007)

13. Keller, E., Szefer, J., Rexford, J., Lee, R.B.: NoHype: virtualized cloud infrastructure without the virtualization. In: Proceedings of ACM/IEEE International Symposium Computer Architecture, pp. 350–361 (2010)
14. Kim, G., Spafford, E.: The design and implementation of tripwire: a file system integrity checker. In: Proceedings of ACM Conference Computer and Communications Security, pp. 18–29 (1994)
15. Kooburat, T., Swift, M.: The best of both worlds with on-demand virtualization. In: Proceedings of USENIX Workshop on Hot Topics in Operating Systems (2011)
16. Kourai, K., Juda, K.: Secure offloading of legacy IDSes using remote VM introspection in semi-trusted clouds. In: Proc. IEEE Int. Conf. Cloud Computing, pp. 43–50 (2016)
17. Li, C., Raghunathan, A., Jha, N.K.: Secure virtual machine execution under an untrusted management OS. In: Proceedings of IEEE International Conference Cloud Computing, pp. 172–179 (2010)
18. Lowell, D.E., Saito, Y., Samberg, E.J.: Devirtualizable virtual machines enabling general, single-node, online maintenance. In: Proceedings of ACM International Conference Architectural Support for Programming Languages and Operating Systems, pp. 211–223 (2004)
19. Lucas, K.: UnixBench. https://github.com/kdlucas/byte-unixbench
20. Lyon, G.: Nmap - Free Security Scanner for Network Exploration & Security Audits. http://nmap.org/
21. McCune, J., Parno, B., Perrig, A., Reiter, M., Isozaki, H.: Flicker: an execution infrastructure for TCB minimization. In: Proceedings of European Conference Computer Systems, pp. 315–328 (2008)
22. Murilo, N., Steding-Jessen, K.: chkrootkit - Locally Checks for Signs of a Rootkit. http://www.chkrootkit.org/
23. Norcott, W.D.: IOzone Filesystem Benchmark. http://www.iozone.org/
24. Omote, Y., Shinagawa, T., Kato, K.: Improving agility and elasticity in bare-metal clouds. In: Proceedings of ACM International Conference Architectural Support for Programming Languages and Operating Systems, pp. 145–159 (2015)
25. Oyama, Y., Giang, T., Chubachi, Y., Shinagawa, T., Kato, K.: Detecting malware signatures in a thin hypervisor. In: Proceedings of ACM Symposium on Applied Computing, pp. 1807–1814 (2012)
26. Petroni Jr., N., Fraser, T., Molina, J., Arbaugh, W.: Copilot - a coprocessor-based kernel runtime integrity monitor. In: Proceedings of USENIX Security Symposium (2004)
27. PwC: US Cybercrime: Rising Risks, Reduced Readiness (2014)
28. Roesch, M.: Snort - lightweight intrusion detection for networks. In: Proceedings of USENIX System Administration Conference (1999)
29. Rutkowska, J., Wojtczuk, R.: Preventing and detecting Xen hypervisor subversions. Black Hat USA (2008)
30. Santos, N., Gummadi, K.P., Rodrigues, R.: Towards trusted cloud computing. In: Proceedings of Workshop on Hot Topics in Cloud Computing (2009)
31. Tadokoro, H., Kourai, K., Chiba, S.: Preventing information leakage from virtual machines' memory in IaaS clouds. IPSJ Online Trans. **5**, 156–166 (2012)
32. Tan, C., Xia, Y., Chen, H., Zang, B.: TinyChecker: transparent protection of VMs against hypervisor failures with nested virtualization. In: Proceedings of IEEE/IFIP International Workshop on Dependability of Clouds, Data Centers and Virtual Machine Technology (2012)

33. TechSpot News: Google Fired Employees for Breaching User Privacy (2010). http://www.techspot.com/news/40280-google-fired-employees-for-breaching-user-privacy.html
34. Wang, J., Stavrou, A., Ghosh, A.: HyperCheck: a hardware-assisted integrity monitor. In: Proceedings of International Symposium on Recent Advances in Intrusion Detection, pp. 158–177 (2010)
35. Zhang, F., Chen, J., Chen, H., Zang, B.: CloudVisor: retrofitting protection of virtual machines in multi-tenant cloud with nested virtualization. In: Proceedings of ACM Symposium Operating Systems Principles, pp. 203–216 (2011)

Privacy Implications of Room Climate Data

Philipp Morgner[1]([⊠]), Christian Müller[2], Matthias Ring[1], Björn Eskofier[1],
Christian Riess[1], Frederik Armknecht[2], and Zinaida Benenson[1]

[1] Friedrich-Alexander-Universität Erlangen-Nürnberg, Erlangen, Germany
{philipp.morgner,matthias.ring,bjoern.eskofier,christian.riess,
zinaida.benenson}@fau.de
[2] University of Mannheim, Mannheim, Germany
{christian.mueller,armknecht}@uni-mannheim.de

Abstract. Smart heating applications promise to increase energy efficiency and comfort by collecting and processing room climate data. While it has been suspected that the sensed data may leak crucial personal information about the occupants, this belief has up until now not been supported by evidence.

In this work, we investigate privacy risks arising from the collection of room climate measurements. We assume that an attacker has access to the most basic measurements only: temperature and relative humidity. We train machine learning classifiers to predict the presence and actions of room occupants. On data that was collected at three different locations, we show that occupancy can be detected with up to 93.5% accuracy. Moreover, the four actions reading, working on a PC, standing, and walking, can be discriminated with up to 56.8% accuracy, which is also far better than guessing (25%). Constraining the set of actions allows to achieve even higher prediction rates. For example, we discriminate standing and walking occupants with 95.1% accuracy. Our results provide evidence that even the leakage of such 'inconspicuous' data as temperature and relative humidity can seriously violate privacy.

1 Introduction

The vision of the Internet of Things (IoT) is to enhance work processes, energy efficiency, and living comfort by interconnecting actuators, mobile devices and sensors. These networks of embedded technologies enable applications such as smart heating, home automation, and smart metering, among many others. Sensors are of crucial importance in these applications. Data gathered by sensors is used to represent the current state of the environment, for instance in smart heating, sensors measure the room climate. Using these information and a user-defined configuration of the targeted state of room climate, the application regulates heating, ventilation, and air conditioning.

While the collection of room climate data is obviously essential to enable smart heating, it may at the same time impose the risk of privacy violations. Consequently, it is commonly *believed* among security experts that leaking room climate data may result in privacy violations and hence that the data needs to

S.N. Foley et al. (Eds.): ESORICS 2017, Part II, LNCS 10493, pp. 324–343, 2017.
DOI: 10.1007/978-3-319-66399-9_18

be cryptographically protected [4,12,39]. However, these claims have not been supported by scientific *evidence* so far. Thus, one could question whether in practice additional effort for protecting the data would be justified.

The current situation with room climate data is comparable to the area of smart metering [18,24,27,44]. In 1989, Hart [18] was the first to draw attention to the fact that smart metering appliances can be exploited as surveillance devices. Since then, research has shown far-reaching privacy violations through fine-granular power consumption monitoring, ranging from occupancy and everyday activities detection [31] up to recognizing which program a TV was displaying [14].

Various techniques have been proposed over the years to mitigate privacy risks of smart metering [3,25,36,37,44]. This issue has become such a grave concern that the German Federal Office for Information Security published a protection profile for smart meters in 2014 [2]. By considering privacy implications of smart heating, we hope to initiate consumer protection research and policy debate in this area, analogous to the developments in smart metering described above.

Research Questions. In this work, we are the first to investigate room climate data from the perspective of possible privacy violations. More precisely, we address the following research questions:

- *Occupancy detection:* Can an attacker determine the presence of a person in a room using only room climate data, i.e., temperature and relative humidity?
- *Activity recognition:* Can an attacker recognize activities of the occupant in the room using only the temperature and relative humidity data?

Our threat scenario targets buildings with multiple rooms that are similar in size, layout, furnishing, and positions of the sensors. These properties are typical for office buildings, dormitories, cruise ships, and hotels, among others. Assuming that an attacker is able to train a classifier that recognizes pre-defined activities, possible privacy violations are, e.g., tracking presence and working practices of employees in offices, or the disclosure of lifestyle and intimate activities in private spaces. All these situations present intrusions in the privacy of the occupants. In contrast to surveillance cameras and motion sensors, the occupant does not expect to be monitored. Also, legal restrictions regarding privacy might apply to surveillance cameras and motion sensors but not to room climate sensors.

Experiments. To evaluate these threats, we present experiments that consider occupancy detection and activity recognition based on the analysis of room climate data from a privacy perspective. We measured room climate data in three office-like rooms and distinguished between the activities reading, standing, walking, and working on a laptop. Although we assume that in smart heating applications, only one sensor per room is most likely to be installed, each room was equipped with several sensors in order to evaluate different positions of sensors in the room. These sensors measured temperature and relative humidity at a regular time interval of a few seconds. In our procedure, an occupant performed a pre-defined sequence of tasks in the experimental space. In sum, we collected almost 90 h of room climate sensor data from a total of 36 participants. The collected room climate data was analyzed using an off-the-shelf machine learning classification algorithm. To reflect realistic settings, we only evaluated data of a single sensor and did not apply sensor fusion.

Results. Evaluating our collected room climate data, the attacker detects presence of a person with detection rates up to 93.5% depending on location and the sensor position, which is significantly higher than guessing (50%). The attacker can distinguish between four activities (reading, standing, walking, and working on a laptop) with detection rates up to 56.8%, which is also significantly better than guessing (25%). We can also distinguish between three activities (sitting, standing and walking) with detection rates up to 81.0%, as opposed to 33.3% if guessing. Furthermore, we distinguish between standing and walking with detection rates up to 95.1%. Thus, we show that the fears of privacy violation by leaking room climate data are well justified. Furthermore, we analyze the influence of the room size, positions of the sensor, and amount of the measured sensor data on the accuracy. In summary, we provide the first steps in verifying the common belief that room climate data leaks privacy-sensitive information.

Outline. The remainder of this paper is organized as follows. In Sect. 2, we give an overview of related work. Section 3 presents the threat model considered in this work. In Sect. 4, we introduce the experimental design and methods. The results of our experiments are presented and discussed in Sects. 5 and 6, respectively. We draw conclusions in Sect. 7.

2 Related Work

Over the last decade, several experiments have been conducted to detect occupancy in sensor-equipped spaces and to recognize people's activities as summarized in Table 1. Activity recognition has been considered for basic activities, such as leaving or arriving at home, or sleeping [29], as well as for more detailed views, including toileting, showering and eating [41].

Most of the previous research uses types of sensors that are different from temperature and relative humidity. For example, CO_2 represents a useful source for occupancy detection and estimation [43]. Additionally, sensors detecting motion based on passive infrared (PIR) [1,6,15,17,28,46], sound [11,15], barometric pressure [30], and door switches [8,9,45] are utilized for occupancy estimation. For evaluation, different machine learning techniques are used, e.g., HMM [43], ARHMM [17], ANN [11], and decision trees [15,45].

In contrast to previous work, our results rely exclusively on temperature and relative humidity. Previously published experimental results involved other or additional types of sensors, such as CO_2, acoustics, motion, or lighting (the latter

Table 1. Overview of previous experiments on occupancy detection (D), occupancy estimation (E), which aims at determining the number of people in a room, and activity recognition (A) with a focus on selected sensors; AML denotes acoustic, motion, and lighting sensors.

Work	Target	Rel. Humidity	Temperature	CO_2	Ventilation	AML	Switches
van Kasteren et al., 2008 [41]	A	○	○	○	○	○	●
Lam et al., 2009 [28]	E	○	○	●	○	●	○
Dong et al., 2010 [6]	E	●	●	●	○	●	○
Lu et al., 2010 [29]	A	○	○	○	○	●	●
Hailemariam et al., '2011 [15]	D	○	○	○	○	●	○
Han et al., 2012 [17]	E	●	●	●	●	●	○
Zhang et al., 2012 [46]	E	●	●	●	○	●	○
Ekwevugbe et al., 2013 [11]	E	○	○	○	○	●	○
Ebadat et al., 2013 [8]	E	○	●	●	●	○	○
Ai et al., 2014 [1]	E	●	●	●	●	●	●
Wörner et al., 2014 [43]	D	○	○	●	○	○	○
Yang et al., 2014 [45]	D/E	●	●	●	○	●	●
Masood et al., 2015 [30]	E	○	●	●	○	○	○
Ebadat et al., 2015 [9]	E	○	●	●	●	○	●
This work	D/A	●	●	○	○	○	○

three are referred to as AML in Table 1), door switches or states of appliances (also gathered with the help of switches), such as water taps or WC flushes. For this reason, our detection results are also not directly comparable to these works.

3   Threat Model

The overall goal of our work is to understand the potential privacy implications if room climate data is accessed by an attacker. The goal of the attacker is to gain information about the state of occupancy as well as the activity of the occupants without their consent.

Obviously, the more information an attacker can gather, the more likely she can deduce privacy-harming information from the measurements. Therefore, we base our analysis on the attacker model that considers a room climate system where only *one* sensor node is used to derive information. This is a realistic scenario since usually one sensor node per room is sufficient to monitor the room climate. Moreover, we assume that this sensor node takes only the two most basic measurements, temperature and relative humidity. These data are the fundamental properties to describe room climate. Note that our restricted data is in contrast to existing work (cf. Table 1 and Sect. 2) that based their experiments on more types of measurements or used data that is less common to characterize room climate.

We consider a sensor system that measures the climate of a room, denoted as *target location*. At the target location, a temperature and relative humidity sensor is installed that reports the measured values in regular intervals to a central database. We consider an attacker model where the attacker has access to this database and aims to derive information about the occupants at the target location. Furthermore, we assume that the attacker has access to either the target location itself, or a room similar in size, layout, sensor positions, and furniture. Such situations are given, for example, at office buildings, hotels, cruise ships, and student dormitories. This location, denoted as *training location*, is used to train the classifier, which is a machine learning algorithm learning the input data labeled with the groundtruth. As the attacker has full control over the training location, she can freely choose what actions are taking place during the measurements. For example, she could do measurements while no persons are present at the training location, or one person is present and executes a predefined activity.

There are various scenarios, in which an attacker has incentives to collect and analyze room climate data. For example, the management of a company aims at observing the presence and working practices of employees in the offices. In another case, a provider of private spaces (hotels, dormitories, etc.) wants to disclose lifestyle and intimate activities in these spaces. This information may be utilized for targeted advertising or sold to insurance companies. In any case, the evaluation of room climate data provides the attacker with the possibility to undermine the privacy of the occupants.

The procedure of these attacks is as follows: First, the attacker collects training data at a training location, which might be the target location or another room similar in size, layout, sensor positions, and furniture. The attacker also records the groundtruth for all events that shall be distinguished. Examples of events are occupancy and non-occupancy, or different activities such as working, walking, and sleeping. The training data is recorded with a sample rate of a few seconds and split into *windows* (i.e., a temperature curve and a relative humidity curve) of same time lengths, usually one to three minutes. Using the collected training data, the attacker trains a machine learning classifier. After the classifier is trained, it can be used to classify windows of climate data from the target location to determine the events. The classifier works on previously collected data, thus reconstructing past events, and also on live-recorded data, thus determining current events "on-the-fly" at the target location.

4   Experimental Design and Methods

We conducted a study to investigate the feasibility of detecting occupancy and inferring activities in an office environment from temperature and relative humidity: From March to April 2016, we performed experiments at two locations simultaneously, *Location A* and *Location B*, with a distance of approximately 200 km between them. In addition, from January to February 2017, we conducted further experiments at a third location, denoted as *Location C*, which is located in the same building as Location B.

4.1   Experimental Setup and Tasks

The experimental spaces at the three locations are different in size, layout, and positions of the sensors. Thus, each target location is also the training location in our study. At Location A, the room has a floor area of 16.5 m^2 and was equipped with room climate sensors at four positions as shown in Fig. 1(ii). At Location B, the room has a floor area of 30.8 m^2, i.e., roughly twice as much as at Location A, and had room climate sensors installed at three positions as illustrated in Fig. 1(i). Location C has a floor area of 13.9 m^2 and was equipped with room climate sensors at five positions as shown in Fig. 1(iii). In all locations, the room climate sensors measured temperature and relative humidity. The number of deployed sensors varied due to limitations of hardware availability.

Our goal was to determine to which extent the presence and activities of an occupant influences the room climate data. Therefore, we measured temperature and relative humidity during phases of absence as well as phases of occupants' presence. If an occupant was present, this person had to perform one task or a sequence of tasks. We defined the following experimental tasks (see also Fig. 2):

Read: Sit on an office chair next to a desk and read.
Stand: Stand in the middle of the room, try to avoid movements.
Walk: Walk slowly and randomly through the room.
Work: Sit on an office chair next to a desk and use a laptop, which is located on the desk.

To eliminate confounding factors, we defined location default settings applying to all locations. Essentially, all windows were required to remain closed and no person was allowed in the room when not in use for the experiment. The rooms have radiators for heating, which were adjusted to a constant level. At Location A and B, we used shutters fixed in such positions that enough light was provided for reading and working.

4.2   Sensor Data Collection

We used a homogeneous hardware and software setup at all locations for data collection, which is described in the following.

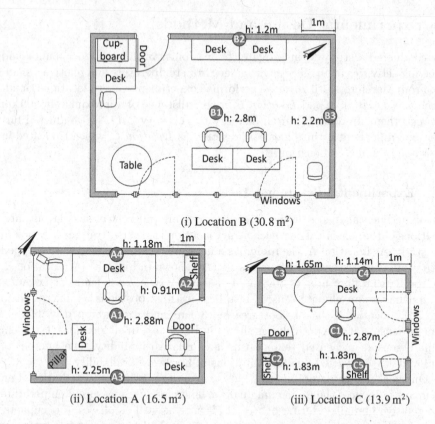

Fig. 1. Floor plans of the experiment spaces including sensor node locations, h indicates the node's height.

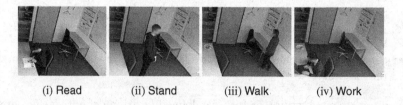

(i) Read   (ii) Stand   (iii) Walk   (iv) Work

Fig. 2. The defined tasks performed by participants at Location A.

Hardware. At each location, we set up a sensor network consisting of several Moteiv Tmote Sky sensor nodes with an integrated IEEE 802.15.4-compliant radio [32] as well as an integrated temperature and relative humidity sensor. The nodes have the Contiki operating system [7] version 2.7 installed. In addition, we deployed a webcam that took pictures in a 3-s interval at Location A. These were used for verification during the data collection phase only, and were not given to the classification algorithms.

Software. For sensor data collection, we customized the *Collect-View* application included in Contiki 2.7, which provides a graphical user interface to manage the sensor network. For our purposes, we implemented an additional control panel offering a customized logging system. The measurement settings of the Collect-View application were set to a report interval of 4 s with a variance of 1 s, i.e., each sensor node reported its current values in a time interval of 4 ± 1 s. The variance is a feature provided by *Collect-View* to decrease the risk of packet collisions during over-the-air transmissions.

Collected Data. We structured data collection in *units* and aimed for a good balance between presence and absence as well as the different tasks among all units, as this is needed for the later analysis using machine learning. Each unit has a fixed time duration, t, where exactly one person was present ($t \in \{10, 30, 60\}$, in minutes) who executed predefined activities. If the presence time was t minutes, then the absence time before and after it, respectively, was determined as $\frac{t}{2}+5$ min, where 5 min served as buffer. This accounts for both, the equal distribution of presence time and absence time, respectively, and the fact that temperature and humidity settle within a 15-min period after the 60-min presence of one person.

Overall, we collected almost 90 h of sensor data, 40 h of which with a person being present. A more extensive overview of the amount of measured sensor data is shown in Table 2. To encourage replication and further investigations, all collected sensor data is available as open data sets on GitHub.[1]

Table 2. Measured sensor data of all locations (in hours)

Variable	Value	Recorded time [h]		
		Location A	Location B	Location C
Occupancy	No	20:38:26	15:21:00	13:21:42
	Yes	14:41:56	11:33:06	13:44:29
Task	Read	4:46:13	2:56:44	3:19:47
	Stand	2:45:27	2:34:20	3:28:27
	Walk	2:43:53	2:37:12	3:20:05
	Work	4:03:33	3:00:20	3:20:52

4.3 Participants and Ethical Principles

For participating in the experiment, 14 subjects volunteered at Location A, 12 subjects at Location B, and 10 subjects at Location C as shown in Table 3. Demographic data of participants was collected in order to facilitate replication and future experiments. All subjects provided written informed consent after the

---

[1] https://github.com/IoTsec/Room-Climate-Datasets.

study protocol was approved by the data protection office.[2] We assigned each participant to a random ID. All collected sensor data as well as the demographic data is only linked to this ID.

Table 3. Demographic data of participants, μ denotes the average, σ denotes the standard deviation.

Characteristic		Location		
		A	B	C
Gender	f:	3	2	5
	m:	11	10	5
Weight [kg]	μ:	74.9	81.7	63.1
	σ:	8.0	12.1	10.0
Height [cm]	μ:	175.9	178.4	170.7
	σ:	9.2	5.3	9.3
Age	μ:	33.7	30.3	25.6
	σ:	8.2	4.8	2.8

4.4   Classifier Design

We used classification to predict occupancy and activities in the rooms. We adopt an approach that has successfully been used in several applications of biosignal processing, namely extraction of a number of statistical descriptors with subsequent feature selection [21, 26].

The features use measurements from short time windows. We experimented with windows of different lengths, namely 60 s, 90 s, 120 s, 150 s, and 180 s. The offset between two consecutive windows was set to 30 s. We excluded all windows where only a part of the measurements belongs to the same activity.

The feature set was composed from a number of statistical descriptors that were computed on temperature and humidity measurements within these windows. These are mean value, variance, skewness, kurtosis, number of nonzero values, entropy, difference between maximum and minimum value of the window (i.e., value range), correlation between temperature and humidity, and mean and slope of the regression line for the measurement window before the current window. Additionally, we subtracted from the measurements their least-square linear regression line, and computed all of the listed statistics on the subtraction residuals. Feature selection was performed using a sequential forward search [42, Chap. 7.1 & 11.8], with an inner leave-one-subject-out cross-validation [19, Chap. 7] to determine the performance of each feature set. For classification, we used the Naïve Bayes classifier. To avoid a bias in the results,

---

[2] Ethical review boards at both locations only consider medical experiments.

we randomly selected identical numbers of windows per class for training, validation and testing. For implementation, we used the ECST software [38], which wraps the WEKA library [16].

As performance measures, we use accuracy (i.e., the number of correctly classified windows divided by the number of all windows), and per-class sensitivity (i.e., the number of correctly classified windows for a specific class divided by the number of all windows of this class). Classification accuracy was deemed statistically significant if it was significantly higher than random guessing which is the best choice if the classifier could not learn any useful information during training. For each experiment, a binomial test with significance level $p < 0.01$ was carried out using the R software [34].

Note that neither the features nor the rather simple Naïve Bayes classifier are particularly tailored to predicting privacy leaks. However, we show that also such an unoptimized system is able to correctly predict occupancy and action types and hence produce privacy leaks. Higher detection rates results can be expected if more advanced classifiers are applied to this task.

5   Results

In this section, we present the experimental results. First, a visual inspection of the collected data is presented, followed by the machine learning-aided occupancy detection and activity recognition.

5.1   Visual Inspection

We started our evaluation by analyzing the *raw* sensor data. Hence, we implemented a visualization script in MATLAB, which plots this data. The visualization of one measurement is exemplary depicted in Fig. 3.

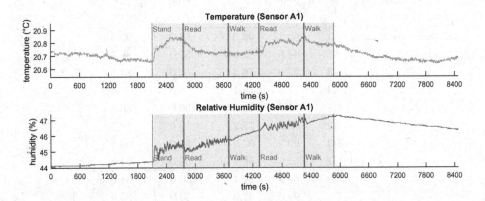

Fig. 3. Visualization of an exemplary room climate measurement. The grey background indicates the presence of the occupant in the experimental space.

The visualization shows an immediate rise of the temperature and humidity as soon as an occupant enters the room. Furthermore, variations in temperature and humidity increase rapidly and can be clearly seen. Thus, one can visually distinguish between phases of occupancy and non-occupancy. One can also notice different patterns during the performance of the tasks. As Fig. 3 shows, an occupant walking in the experimental space causes a constant increase of temperature and humidity with only small variations. In contrast, an occupant standing in the room causes the largest variations of humidity compared to the other defined tasks. The effects of the tasks reading and working on temperature and humidity are very similar: both variables tend to increase showing medium variations.

For further analysis of the data, we used machine learning as outlined in Sect. 4.4.

5.2 Occupancy Detection

Occupancy detection describes the binary detection of occupants in the experimental space based on features from windows with length of 180 s (cf. Sect. 4.4). This is a two-class task, namely to distinguish whether an occupant is present (true) or not (false). We only considered training and testing data within the same room (but separated training and testing both by the days and participants of the acquisition). We randomly selected the same number of positive and negative cases from the data. Thus, simply guessing the state has a success probability of 50%. However, our classification results are considerably higher than that. Table 4 shows that the highest accuracies per location were 93.5%

Table 4. Classification accuracy for occupancy detection. Notations: 'Occup.', sensitivity for class *occupancy*. 'No Occup.', sensitivity for class *no occupancy*. 'Guess', probability of correct guessing. 'Acc.', classification accuracy.

Scenario	Sensor	Sensitivity [%]		Guess [%]	Acc. [%]
		Occup.	No Occup.		
Occupancy	A1	94.1	93.0	50.0	93.5
	A2	94.5	85.0	50.0	89.7
	A3	92.0	76.4	50.0	84.2
	A4	77.8	79.1	50.0	78.4
	B1	91.9	85.1	50.0	88.5
	B2	85.3	77.2	50.0	81.3
	B3	69.7	63.9	50.0	66.8
	C1	92.9	89.2	50.0	91.0
	C2	89.9	87.4	50.0	88.6
	C3	90.0	82.0	50.0	86.0
	C4	89.8	87.6	50.0	88.7
	C5	92.5	88.8	50.0	90.7

(Location A), 88.5% (Location B), and 91.0% (Location C). Considering all sensors of all three locations, detection accuracy ranges between 66.8% (Sensor B3) and 93.5% (Sensor A1) as shown in Fig. 4i. All classification accuracies were statistically significantly different from random guessing. This indicates that an attacker can reveal the presence of occupants in a target location with a high probability.

5.3   Activity Recognition

Activity recognition reports the current activity of an occupant in the experimental space. The four activity tasks are described in Sect. 4.1. The recognition results for these tasks are shown in Fig. 4.

Activity4 classifies between the activities Read, Stand, Walk, Work. As shown in Fig. 4, the accuracy of recognizing activities achieved by the machine learning pipeline ranged from 23.9% (Sensor C1) to 56.8% (Sensor A1). Overall, the

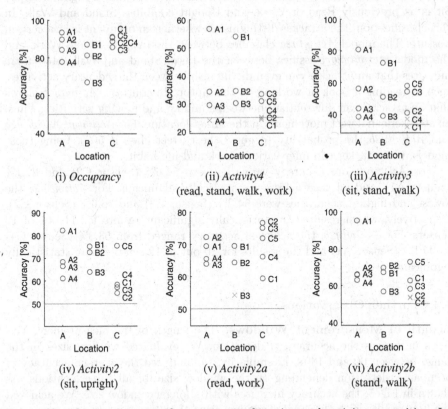

(i) *Occupancy*

(ii) *Activity4*
(read, stand, walk, work)

(iii) *Activity3*
(sit, stand, walk)

(iv) *Activity2*
(sit, upright)

(v) *Activity2a*
(read, work)

(vi) *Activity2b*
(stand, walk)

Fig. 4. Classification accuracy for occupancy detection and activity recognition. In each diagram, the guessing probability is plotted as a line. Each symbol represents the accuracy that we achieved with a single sensor. A blue dot marks a statistically significant result, while a red 'x' represents a statistically insignificant result. (Color figure online)

accuracy of *Activity4* was statistically significantly better than the probability of guessing the correct task (25%) for 8 out of 12 sensors. Thus, the distinction between multiple activities is possible, but depends on the target location and the position of the sensor.

In the next step, we investigated whether an attacker can increase the recognition accuracies by distinguishing between a smaller set of activities. To this end, we combined two tasks to a *meta task*, e.g., the tasks Read and Work became Sit. The model *Activity3* classifies between the tasks Sit, Stand, and Walk. The probability of correct guessing is thus 33.3%. This model is typical to represent activities of an occupant in a private space or an office room. For *Activity3*, the achieved accuracy ranged from 31.8% (Sensor C1) to 81.0% (Sensor A1). Our results were statistically significant for 10 out of the 12 sensors deployed in the three locations. Assuming a known layout of the target location, the attacker might be able to determine the position of the occupant in the space and infer activities such as watching TV, exercising, cooking or eating.

The model *Activity2* classifies between the tasks Sit and Upright, whereby Sit is as previously Read or Work, and Upright combines Stand and Walk. In this classification, the attacker distinguishes whether an occupant is at a certain posture. The model *Activity2a* classifies between the tasks Read and Work, and the model *Activity2b* classifies between the tasks Stand and Walk. *Activity2a* indicates that an attacker can even distinguish between the sedentary activities, such as reading a book or working on the laptop. In contrast, *Activity2b* shows that an attacker can differentiate between standing and moving activities. Thus, an attacker can detect movements at the target location. For *Activity2 Activity2a* and *Activity2b* the probability to guess the correct class is 50%. Using these models, the attacker can infer various work and life habits.

For *Activity2*, our accuracy varies between 54.6% (Sensor C2) and 82.1% (Sensor A1), and all accuracies are statistically significant. For *Activity2a*, the lowest and highest accuracies were 54.2% (Sensor B3) and 76.6% (Sensor C2), respectively, which resulted in statistically significant results for 11 out of 12 sensors. For *Activity2b*, the achieved accuracy ranged from 53.3% (Sensor C4) to 95.1% (Sensor A1) and the results for 10 out of 12 sensors were statistically significant.

5.4   Further Observations

Length of Measurement Windows. The length of the measurement windows influences the accuracy of detection. We evaluated window sizes in the range between 60 and 180 s. Exemplarily, we analyzed the average accuracy of occupancy detection depending on the window size for all three locations. As shown in Fig. 5, the accuracy increases with a longer window size. We achieved the best results with the longest window sizes of 180 s.

This indicates that the highest accuracies are possible if longer time periods are considered. From a practical perspective, it is not advisable to extend the window size to a much larger duration than a few minutes since we assume that the performed activity is consistent for the whole duration of the window.

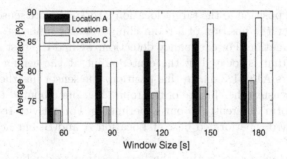

Fig. 5. Average accuracy over all sensors from each location for occupancy detection depending on the window size

Selected Features. To assess the feasibility of an attacker that has only access to either temperature data or relative humidity data, we evaluated whether it might be enough to solely collect one type of room climate data. In the classification process, an attacker derives a set of features from temperature and relative humidity data and selects the best-performing features for each sensor and classification goal automatically (cf. Sect. 4.4). Analysis shows that features computed from temperature and relative humidity are of similar importance. In our evaluation, 57.9% of the selected features are derived from temperature measurements, and 52.3% from relative humidity measurements.[3]

We also compared the features in terms of differences between the three locations as well as differences between occupancy detection and activity recognition. In all these cases, there are no significant differences between the importance of temperature and relative humidity. An attacker restricted to either temperature or relative humidity data will perform worse than with both data.

Size and Layout of Rooms. All our locations are office-like rooms, which have a similar layout (rectangular) but differ in size and furnishing. In our evaluation, the accuracy correlates with the size of the target location. As shown in Fig. 5, we had the highest average accuracy in occupancy detection with Location C, which has also the smallest ground area of $13.9\,\mathrm{m}^2$. Location A has a ground area of $16.5\,\mathrm{m}^2$, and has a slightly lower average accuracy. Location B is almost twice as large ($30.8\,\mathrm{m}^2$) and shows the worst average accuracy compared to the other locations. Thus, our experiment indicates that an increasing room size leads to decreasing accuracy on average. An attacker achieves higher accuracies by monitoring target locations of a small size compared to target locations of larger sizes.

Position of Sensors. According to our threat model in Sect. 3, the attacker controls layout of the target location. Thus, we assume an attacker that can

---

[3] Note that some features are based on both, temperature and relative humidity, which is why the sum of both numbers exceeds 100%.

decide at which position in the target location a room climate sensor is installed. We consider how the position of a room climate sensor influences the accuracy of derived information. For occupancy detection, we had the best accuracy with a sensor node that is located in the center point at the ceiling of the target location (Sensors A1, B1, C1). In this position, the sensor has the largest gathering area to measure the climate of the room. Sensors mounted to the walls or on shelves perform differently in our experiments. For activity recognition, the central sensor nodes performed best at Location A and B, but not at Location C.

From the attacker perspective, the best position to deploy a room climate sensor is at the ceiling in the center of the target location. In large rooms, multiple sensors at the ceiling could be installed, each covering a subsection of the room.

6   Discussion

As our experiments reveal, knowing the temperature and relative humidity of a room allows to detect the presence of people and to recognize certain activities with a significantly higher probability than guessing. By evaluating temperature and relative humidity curves of the length of 180 s, we were able to detect the presence of an occupant in one of our experimental spaces with an accuracy of 93.5% using a single sensor. In terms of activity recognition, we distinguished between four activities with an accuracy up to 56.8%, between three activities up to 81.0%, and between two activities up to 95.1%. Thus, an attacker focusing on the detection of a specific activity is more successful than an attacker that aims to classify a broader variety of activities. In the following, we discuss implications and limitations of our results.

Privacy Implications. We show that an attacker might be able to infer life and work habits of the occupants from the room climate data. Thus, the attacker is able to distinguish between sitting, standing, and moving, which already might reveal the position and activities of the occupant in the room. Moreover, the attacker can distinguish between upright and sedentary activities, between moving and standing, and between working on the laptop or reading a book.

Given the limited amount of recorded sensor data, the achieved accuracies in occupancy detection and activity recognition give a clear indication that occupants are subject to privacy violations according to the threat model described in Sect. 3. However, activity recognition is not straightforward since the achieved accuracies differ between the different sensor positions and locations.

Further experiments are required for a better assessment of the privacy risks induced by the room climate data. Our work provides promising directions for these assessments. For example, we demonstrated the existence of the information leak with the Naïve Bayes classifier. Naïve Bayes is arguably one of the simplest machine learning classifiers. In future work, it would be interesting to explore upper boundaries for the detection of presence/absence and different activities by using more advanced classifiers such as the recently popular deep learning algorithms.

Location-Independent Classification. An important question is whether it is possible to perform location-independent classification, i.e., to train the classifier with sensor data of one location and then use it to classify sensor data at the target location that is not similar to the training location in size, layout, and sensor positions. If this was possible, the service providers of smart heating applications would be able to detect occupancy and to recognize activities without having access to the target locations.

According to their privacy statements, popular smart thermostats from Nest [33], Ecobee [10], and Honeywell [20] send measured climate data to the service providers' databases. To evaluate these privacy threats, we used the room climate data of the best-performing sensor of a location as training data set for other locations. For example, to classify events of an arbitrary sensor of Location A, we trained the classifier with room climate data collected by Sensor B1 or Sensor C1. We gained statistically significant results for a few combinations in occupancy detection but the majority of our occupancy detection results was not significant. For activity recognition, we were not able to gain statistically significant results.

However, the possibility of location-independent attackers cannot be excluded. Absence of significant results in our experiments may be merely due to the limited amount of data. Future studies should be conducted to gather data from various rooms up to a point where the combined results hold for arbitrary locations. Having more data from a multitude of rooms available would help the machine learning classifiers to recognize and ignore data characteristics that are specific to either of the experimental rooms. Consequently, the algorithms could better identify the distinct data characteristics of the different classes in occupancy detection and activity recognition. This would enable location-independent classification of room climate data, in which the training location is not similar to the target location regarding size, layout, furnishing, and positions of the sensors.

In a representative smart home survey of German consumers from 2015, 34% of the participants stated that they are interested in technologies for intelligent heating or are planning to acquire such a system [5]. Another survey with 1,000 US and 600 Canadian consumers found that for 72% of them, the most desired smart home device would be a self-adjusting thermostat, and 37% reported that they were likely to purchase one in the next 12 months [22]. Sharing smart home data with providers and third parties is a popular idea and a controversial issue for consumers. Thus, in a recent representative survey with 461 American adults by Pew Research [35], the participants were presented with a scenario of installing a smart thermostat *"in return for sharing data about some of the basic activities that take place in your house like when people are there and when they move from room to room"*. Of all respondents, 55% said that this scenario was not acceptable for them, 27% said that it was acceptable, with remaining 17% answering "it depends". Furthermore, in a worldwide survey with 9,000 respondents from nine countries (Australia, Brazil, Canada, France, Germany, India, Mexico, the UK, and the US), 54% of respondents said that *"they might be willing to share their personal data collected from their smart home with companies in exchange for money"* [23].[4]

We think that the idea of sharing the smart home data for various benefits will continue to be intensively discussed in the future, and therefore, consumers and policy makers should be made aware of the level of detail inferable from smart home data. Which rewards are actually beneficial for consumers? Moreover, which kind of data sharing is ethically permissible? Only by answering these questions it would be possible to design fair policies and establish beneficial personal data markets [40]. In this work, we take the first step towards informing the policy for the smart heating scenario.

7   Conclusions

We investigated the common belief that the data collected by room climate sensors divulge private information about the occupants. To this end, we conducted experiments that reflect realistic conditions, i.e., considering an attacker who has access to typical room climate data (temperature and relative humidity) only. Our experiments revealed that knowing a sequence of temperature and relative humidity measurements already allows to detect the presence of people and to recognize certain activities with high accuracy. Our results confirm that the assumptions that room climate data needs protection are justified: the leakage of such 'inconspicuous' sensor data as temperature and relative humidity can seriously violate privacy in smart spaces. Future work is required determine the level of privacy invasion in more depth and develop appropriate countermeasures.

Acknowledgement. The work is supported by the German Research Foundation (DFG) under Grant AR 671/3-1: WSNSec – Developing and Applying a Comprehensive Security Framework for Sensor Networks.

References

1. Ai, B., Fan, Z., Gao, R.X.: Occupancy estimation for smart buildings by an autoregressive hidden Markov model. In: American Control Conference, ACC 2014, Portland, OR, USA, 4–6 June 2014, pp. 2234–2239. IEEE (2014)
2. BSI: Protection Profile for the Gateway of a Smart Metering System (Smart Meter Gateway PP). https://www.commoncriteriaportal.org/files/ppfiles/pp0073b_pdf.pdf. Accessed Mar 2014
3. Cavoukian, A., Polonetsky, J., Wolf, C.: SmartPrivacy for the smart grid: embedding privacy into the design of electricity conservation. Identity Inf. Soc. 3(2), 275–294 (2010)
4. Chaos Computer Club: Guidelines for Smart Home Solutions, February 2016. (in German) https://www.ccc.de/en/updates/2016/smarthome

---

[4] Methodological details, such as representativeness, breakdown by country and the exact formulation of the questions, are not known about this survey.

5. Deloitte: Ready for Takeoff? Consumer Survey, July 2015
6. Dong, B., Andrews, B., Lam, K.P., Höynck, M., Zhang, R., Chiou, Y.-S., Benitez, D.: An information technology enabled sustainability test-bed (ITEST) for occupancy detection through an environmental sensing network. Energy Build. **42**(7), 1038–1046 (2010)
7. Dunkels, A., B., Grönvall, B., Voigt, T.: Contiki - a lightweight and flexible operating system for tiny networked sensors. In: 29th Annual IEEE International Conference on Local Computer Networks, pp. 455–462. IEEE (2004)
8. Ebadat, A., Bottegal, G., Varagnolo, D., Wahlberg, B., Johansson, K.H.: Estimation of building occupancy levels through environmental signals deconvolution. In: BuildSys 2013, Proceedings of 5th ACM Workshop On Embedded Systems For Energy-Efficient Buildings, Roma, Italy, 13–14 November 2013, pp. 8:1–8:8 (2013)
9. Ebadat, A., Bottegal, G., Varagnolo, D., Wahlberg, B., Johansson, K.H.: Regularized deconvolution-based approaches for estimating room occupancies. IEEE Trans. Autom. Sci. Eng. **12**(4), 1157–1168 (2015)
10. Ecobee: Privacy policy & terms of use, April 2015
11. Ekwevugbe, T., Brown, N., Pakka, V., Fan, D.: Real-time building occupancy sensing using neural-network based sensor network. In: 7th IEEE International Conference on Digital Ecosystems and Technologies (DEST), pp. 114–119, July 2013
12. European Union Agency For Network And Information Security: Security and Resilience of Smart Home Environments - Good Practices and Recommendations. https://www.enisa.europa.eu. Accessed December 2015
13. Fischer-Hübner, S., Hopper, N. (eds.): Privacy Enhancing Technologies - PETS 2011. LNCS, vol. 6794. Springer, Heidelberg (2011). doi:10.1007/978-3-642-22263-4
14. Greveler, U., Glösekötterz, P., Justusy, B., Loehr, D.: Multimedia content identification through smart meter power usage profiles. In: Proceedings of International Conference on Information and Knowledge Engineering (IKE) (2012)
15. Hailemariam, E., Goldstein, R., Attar, R., Khan, A.: Real-time occupancy detection using decision trees with multiple sensor types. In: 2011 Spring Simulation Multi-conference, SpringSim 2011, Boston, MA, USA, 03–07 April 2011, pp. 141–148 (2011)
16. Hall, M., Frank, E., Holmes, G., Pfahringer, B., Reutemann, P., Witten, I.H.: The WEKA data mining software: an update. SIGKDD Explor. Newsl. **11**(1), 10–18 (2009)
17. Han, Z., Gao, R.X., Fan, Z.: Occupancy and indoor environment quality sensing for smart buildings. In: 2012 IEEE International Instrumentation and Measurement Technology Conference (I2MTC), pp. 882–887, May 2012
18. Hart, G.W.: Residential energy monitoring and computerized surveillance via utility power flows. IEEE Technol. Soc. Mag. **8**(2), 12–16 (1989)
19. Hastie, T., Tibshirani, R., Friedman, J.H.: The Elements of Statistical Learning, 2nd edn. Springer, New York (2009)
20. Honeywell: Honeywell connected home privacy statement, December 2015
21. Huppert, V., Paulus, J., Paulsen, U., Burkart, M., Wullich, B., Eskofier, B.: Quantification of nighttime micturition with an ambulatory sensor-based system. IEEE J. Biomed. Health Inform. **20**(3), 865–872 (2016)
22. icontrol Networks: 2015 State of the Smart Home Report. https://www.icontrol.com/blog/2015-state-of-the-smart-home-report

23. Intel Security: Intel Security's International Internet of Things Smart Home Survey Shows Many Respondents Sharing Personal Data for Money. https://newsroom.intel.com/news-releases/intel-securitys-international-internet-of-things-smart-home-survey

24. Jawurek, M., Johns, M., Kerschbaum, F.: Plug-in privacy for smart metering billing. In: Fischer-Hübner and Hopper [13], pp. 192–210 (2011)

25. Jawurek, M., Kerschbaum, F., Danezis, G.: SoK: privacy technologies for smart grids - a survey of options. Microsoft Research, Cambridge, UK (2012)

26. Jensen, U., Blank, P., Kugler, P., Eskofier, B.: Unobtrusive and energy-efficient swimming exercise tracking using on-node processing. IEEE Sens. J. 16(10), 3972–3980 (2016)

27. Kursawe, K., Danezis, G., Kohlweiss, M.: Privacy-friendly aggregation for the smart-grid. In: Fischer-Hübner and Hopper [13], pp. 175–191 (2011)

28. Lam, K.P., Höynck, M., Dong, B., Andrews, B., Chiou, Y.S., Benitez, D., Choi, J.: Occupancy detection through an extensive environmental sensor network in an open-plan office building. In: Proceedings of Building Simulation 2009, an IBPSA Conference (2009)

29. Lu, J., Sookoor, T., Srinivasan, V., Gao, G., Holben, B., Stankovic, J., Field, E., Whitehouse, K.: The smart thermostat: using occupancy sensors to save energy in homes. In: Proceedings of 8th ACM Conference on Embedded Networked Sensor Systems, pp. 211–224. ACM (2010)

30. Masood, M.K., Soh, Y.C., Chang, V.W., Real-time occupancy estimation using environmental parameters. In: 2015 International Joint Conference on Neural Networks, IJCNN 2015, Killarney, Ireland, 12–17 July 2015, pp. 1–8. IEEE (2015)

31. Molina-Markham, A., Shenoy, P., Fu, K., Cecchet, E., Irwin, D.: Private memoirs of a smart meter. In: Proceedings of 2nd ACM Workshop on Embedded Sensing Systems for Energy-Efficiency in Building, BuildSys 2010, New York, NY, USA, pp. 61–66. ACM (2010)

32. Moteiv Corporation: Tmote Sky Datasheet (2006)

33. Nest: Privacy statement for nest products and services, March 2016

34. R Core Team: A Language and Environment for Statistical Computing. R Foundation for Statistical Computing, Vienna, Austria (2014)

35. Rainie, L., Duggan, M.: Pew Research: Privacy and Information Sharing. http://www.pewinternet.org/2016/01/14/privacy-and-information-sharing. Accessed Jan 2016

36. Reinhardt, A., Englert, F., Christin, D.: Averting the privacy risks of smart metering by local data preprocessing. Pervas. Mob. Comput. 16, 171–183 (2015)

37. Rial, A., Danezis, G.: Privacy-preserving smart metering. In: Proceedings of 10th Annual ACM Workshop on Privacy in the Electronic Society, WPES 2011, pp. 49–60. ACM, New York (2011)

38. Ring, M., Jensen, U., Kugler, P., Eskofier, B.: Software-based performance and complexity analysis for the design of embedded classification systems. In: Proceedings of 21st International Conference on Pattern Recognition, ICPR 2012, Tsukuba, Japan, 11–15 November 2012, pp. 2266–2269. IEEE Computer Society (2012)

39. Selinger, M.: Test: Smart Home Kits Leave the Door Wide Open - for Everyone. https://www.av-test.org/en/news/news-single-view/test-smart-home-kits-leave-the-door-wide-open-for-everyone/. Accessed Apr 2014

40. Spiekermann, S., Acquisti, A., Böhme, R., Hui, K.-L.: The challenges of personal data markets and privacy. Electron. Mark. 25(2), 161–167 (2015)

41. van Kasteren, T., Noulas, A., Englebienne, G., Kröse, B.: Accurate activity recognition in a home setting. In: Proceedings of 10th International Conference on Ubiquitous Computing. ACM (2008)
42. Witten, I.H., Frank, E., Hall, M.A.: Data Mining: Practical Machine Learning Tools and Techniques, 3rd edn. Morgan Kaufmann, Burlington (2011)
43. Wörner, D., von Bomhard, T., Roeschlin, M., Wortmann, F.: Look twice: uncover hidden information in room climate sensor data. In: 4th International Conference on the Internet of Things, IoT 2014, Cambridge, MA, USA, 6–8 October 2014, pp. 25–30. IEEE (2014)
44. Yang, W., Li, N., Qi, Y., Qardaji, W., McLaughlin, S., McDaniel, P.: Minimizing private data disclosures in the smart grid. In: Proceedings of 2012 ACM Conference on Computer and Communications Security, pp. 415–427. ACM (2012)
45. Yang, Z., Li, N., Becerik-Gerber, B., Orosz, M.D.: A systematic approach to occupancy modeling in ambient sensor-rich buildings. Simulation **90**(8), 960–977 (2014)
46. Zhang, R., Lam, K.P., Chiou, Y.-S., Dong, B.: Information-theoretic environment features selection for occupancy detection in open office spaces. Build. Simul. **5**(2), 179–188 (2012)

Network Intrusion Detection Based on Semi-supervised Variational Auto-Encoder

Genki Osada[✉], Kazumasa Omote, and Takashi Nishide

University of Tsukuba, 1-1-1 Tennodai, Tsukuba, Ibaraki 305-8577, Japan
homerunrun@hotmail.com

Abstract. Network intrusion detection systems (NIDSs) based on machine learning have been attracting much attention for its potential ability to detect unknown attacks that are hard for signature-based NIDSs to detect. However, acquisition of a large amount of labeled data that general supervised learning methods need is prohibitively expensive, and this results in making it hard for learning-based NIDS to become widespread in practical use.

In this paper, we tackle this issue by introducing semi-supervised learning, and propose a novel detection method that is realized by means of classification with the latent variable, which represents the causes underlying the traffic we observe. Our proposed model is based on Variational Auto-Encoder, unsupervised deep neural network, and its strength is a scalability to the amount of training data. We demonstrate that our proposed method can make the detection accuracy of attack dramatically improve by simply increasing the amount of unlabeled data, and, in terms of the false negative rate, it outperforms the previous work based on semi-supervised learning method, Laplacian regularized least squares which has cubic complexity in the number of training data records and is too inefficient to leverage a huge amount of unlabeled data.

1 Introduction

Applying machine learning techniques to network intrusion detection systems (NIDSs) has been attracting much attention recently, as it has a potential to detect unknown attacks, which is hard for signature-based ones to capture. Along with the popularization of IoT devices and big data analysis, we can expect that acquisition of data for model training will get easier and that its volume will be much bigger, and hence it is predictable that machine learning will exert stronger presence furthermore in network security research and practice.

However, the need for acquiring labeled data, which is required in general supervised learning, such as classification, exists as a barrier against its widespread adoption. Attacks in the wild are rarely captured, and even then, labeling process to determine whether it is normal or adversarial on every traffic record requires expertise and obviously takes vast times, which ends up with prohibitively high cost. To make matters even more troublesome, the characteristics of traffic data vary from environment to environment. Considering the fact

© Springer International Publishing AG 2017
S.N. Foley et al. (Eds.): ESORICS 2017, Part II, LNCS 10493, pp. 344–361, 2017.
DOI: 10.1007/978-3-319-66399-9_19

that most machine learning methodologies assume that training data and test data should be sampled from independent and identically distributed (i.i.d.) random variables, ideally, it is desirable that data is collected in the actual network environments where the defense system will be deployed, rather than using data that is sampled from other environments. Furthermore, as the trend of network traffic changes day by day even in one environment, it is required to keep the defense systems up-to-date through updating themselves continuously [5]. This necessity means that labeling work is required many times.

We will tackle this issue by introducing semi-supervised learning so that the amount of such labeling operations decreases. Our primal contributions are as follows:

1. We propose a network intrusion detection method based on semi-supervised learning that can reduce the number of labeling operations drastically without sacrificing detection performance. Our proposed method outperforms the previous work of [13] in terms of the false negative rate which is a crucial index for NIDSs: our method gave 4.67%, compared with 10.86% in [13].
2. Our proposed method has the capability to improve its performance dramatically by simply increasing the amount of unlabeled data, which would be easily available. While [13] has proposed NIDSs based on semi-supervised learning, their method, Laplacian regularized least squares, cannot leverage large scale data for training because it has cubic complexity in the number of labeled and unlabeled examples [2]. On the other hand, since our proposed method would be trained by mini-batch gradient descent optimization, it is not restricted in terms of the amount of training data, which is an important aspect to create a synergetic effect with semi-supervised learning. This property also allows us to use the whole training data without the need to extract part of training data. Taking into account the fact that the trend of network traffic changes over a some period as mentioned above, which part of data we extract from the whole data for training can have a great influence on the detection performance. Thus if we are required to extract part of data for training, it means that we need to establish an appropriate extraction method, but such an extraction method would be no longer necessary if there is no limit on the number of processable training data records.
3. In order to realize the above 1 and 2, we propose Forked Variational Auto-Encoder (Forked VAE) as an extension of Variational Auto-Encoder (VAE) [6,11], unsupervised deep neural network. Although there are Deep Generative Model (DGM) [7] and Auxiliary Deep Generative Model [9] as extended the VAE for semi-supervised learning, their objectives are to reconstruct input data, especially images, and they utilized label information for that aim. On the other hand, our objective is to perform classification with the latent variable which is represented with lower dimension and a simpler distribution than the original input data, and for that purpose our Forked VAE utilizes label information.

In this paper, we describe the aforementioned learning model and show experimental results that were done to evaluate its performance as an NIDS using Kyoto2006+ and NSL-KDD datasets.

2   Our Approach

In this section, while we clarify our problem, we describe our detection approach and intention for introducing semi-supervised learning.

2.1   Direction of Attack Detection

Outlier Detection vs. Classification. There are mainly two types of machine learning techniques useful for network intrusion detection systems, namely, outlier detection and classification. As the term of outlier detection is often used interchangeably with anomaly detection, what outlier methods do is to detect a deviation from normal behavior. However, attackers often mimic normal traffic, and in an environment where the users are not imposed a special restriction on their use of network, we can expect that it is very often the case that previously unseen but normal behaviors are observed. We can argue that the aim of outlier detection techniques is just to find unknown behaviors and that distinguishing attacks from benign traffic is out of their scope. In light of this, we choose an approach of classification to judge whether the traffic is normal or not, rather than detecting the outlier.

Unfortunately, classification methods need labeled data to train a model in general. The downside of using labels is the cost of obtaining them as argued before, so outlier detection methods that can be trained in an unsupervised manner without using labels are attractive. However, the upside of using labels is the ability to steer a model in a desired direction, which can only be done by supervised learning methods [15]. The contribution of this paper is mainly to mitigate the above downside of supervised learning classification methods by introducing semi-supervised learning.

Classification with Latent Variable. As mentioned in the above section attackers often mimic benign traffic, so that the observed data can become hard to distinguish from benign traffic. The intent behind the generation of those traffic, however, should clearly be different from that behind benign traffic. Therefore, we work on detecting the presence of malice underneath the generated traffic rather than classifying the raw observed data. To realize this, we bring in the latent variable model, which is a statistical model used in machine learning as a powerful tool. As a latent variable model, let us consider that a single observed traffic data x is generated by a corresponding unobserved continuous random variable z, the latent variable, through some random process. We assume that z is the cause of why traffic x is generated and that each x has corresponding z. If z can be represented in the latent space such that it highlights the presence or absence of malice and with a lower dimension than x in the observation space,

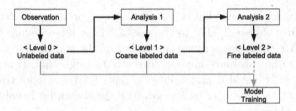

Fig. 1. The whole picture of labeling operation. Black and orange arrows indicate labeling flow and input to model training respectively. (Color figure online)

we can expect that attack detection can be performed in the latent space more efficiently than in the observation space. Together with the discussion so far, what we need to do is to do classification with the latent variable, for which two things are needed:

- To know how to map the observed data x into the corresponding latent variable z. This can be viewed as a matter of posterior distribution inference, and we try to solve this with the technique called approximate inference. As we will describe in detail in Sect. 3.1, we use the VAE as a building block for that.
- To make the representation of latent variables z focus on the presence or absence of malice. For this purpose, we introduce the essence of supervised learning and incorporate it into the VAE, which leads to our new technique, Forked VAE in Sect. 3.2.

2.2 Data Label

Before entering the section for semi-supervised learning, with consideration of actual use, we describe the labels that we assume to put on each traffic record. Figure 1 is the whole picture of labeling operations, from the observed data (i.e., raw data) to the labeled data for model training. First, we define three levels of labels based on the granularity and these levels change through phases of analysis. Level 0 means that no labeling has been done yet, i.e., the observed data has no label. Level 2 indicates either "normal" or the name of attack types, and it would be given through the expert analysis, which corresponds to Analysis 2 of Fig. 1. Here, we assume that a Level 1 label would be attached to the data tentatively before Analysis 2 is finished. An analysis for unknown attacks can often take much time, and until it gets finished, the labeled data for that kind of new attack would be unavailable, which means that the defense system would be left vulnerable during that time. However, even if the expert analysis has not fully figured out the tactics of attackers yet, if the traffic is enough suspicious for us to decide that it is a symptom of attack, immunization of the defense system against those kind of attacks should be started in parallel with Analysis 2. Hence, for the Level 1 label, a bit that indicates whether the traffic is a symptom of attack or not is sufficient, and in order to handle this labeling process automatically in a short time, we assume that a signature based or anomaly detection based NIDS is used in Analysis 1. Due to the use of NIDS, mis-labeling could happen in Analysis 1. We therefore arrange Analysis 2 at the end of the system in Fig. 1 so that every traffic can be re-labeled correctly through that. However, here we focus on using only Level 0 and 1 labeled data for the model training in this paper because these labels are easily obtained timely, and a Level 2 label is out of the scope of this paper.

It is not hard to imagine that once the system gets prepared, it would become possible to collect a massive amount of Level 0 data. Hence, it is desirable that the model has no restriction on the amount of training data so as to fully utilize a vast amount of unlabeled data. In addition, to achieve the property of supervised learning from Level 1 labeled data, we introduce semi-supervised learning.

2.3   Advantage of Semi-supervised Learning

The roles of supervised learning that uses labeled data and unsupervised learning that uses unlabeled one are basically different. The main purpose of supervised learning is clear enough: figuring out how relevant data should be extracted from input data to perform a task at hand (e.g., classification). On the other hand, unsupervised leaning tries to keep as much information about the original data as possible [15]. Semi-supervised learning is known as combination of these two to complement each other.

The detection of unknown attacks is obviously a crucial task for NIDSs, but at the same time it also must be guaranteed that previously unseen normal traffic can pass through the NIDS without being blocked. This can be viewed as a problem of over-fitting, i.e., how well the learned model can handle correctly the data record that was not contained in the training dataset, and we consider this challenge as one of the most important missions for NIDSs. A more in-depth argument about unsupervised learning and over-fitting can be found in other literature, and we just briefly introduce the result of [3], which showed that unsupervised learning outperformed supervised learning in the experiment to verify whether a model can recognize the cluster that did not exist in the training dataset.

The reason why we bring semi-supervised is to take full advantage of the property of unlabeled data, and this leads to the reduction of labeling cost, fast updating of the defense system and the tolerance to over-fitting inherent in unsupervised learning.

3   Proposed Model

On the basis of the discussion so far, our machine learning model needs to have the following functionalities:

- Semi-supervised learning to leverage unlabeled data.
- Scalability to be able to deal with a huge amount of data for training.

- Latent variable modeling by which unobserved latent variables are represented in such a way that the presence or absence of malice underlying the observed traffic data is highlighted.
- Classification with latent variables.

To build our model, we choose the Variational Auto-Encoder (VAE) [6,11] as a building block. In this section, we first describe the VAE and then explain our proposed model named Forked Variational Auto-Encoder (Forked VAE) while comparing it with the Deep Generative Model (DGM) [7], which is previously proposed as a semi-supervised learning version of the VAE.

3.1 Variational Auto-Encoder

Variational Inference. Before going into the description of the VAE, we introduce a general approximating technique called Variational Inference, also known as Variational Bayesian methods. As in Sect. 2.1, we consider a model in which observed data x is considered to be generated from the latent variable z. We assume that the input data and the latent variable consist of some feature variables, and from now on we denote them as $\boldsymbol{x}$ and $\boldsymbol{z}$ respectively. In the context of the NIDS, for example, $\boldsymbol{x}$ corresponds to a single line of network traffic log, and $\boldsymbol{z}$ corresponds to the intention with which $\boldsymbol{x}$ is generated. Our objective is to predict whether $\boldsymbol{x}$ is normal or adversarial. As mentioned in Sect. 2.1, we would like to perform classification with the latent variable, rather than the observed data, and to do so what we have to know is $p(\boldsymbol{z}|\boldsymbol{x})$, which means posterior probability. Suppose $p(\boldsymbol{z}|\boldsymbol{x})$ is parametrized by θ, what we want to do is to optimize the model via tuning θ. Now, rather than trying to obtain $p(\boldsymbol{z}|\boldsymbol{x})$ directly, we introduce an arbitrary simple distribution $q(\boldsymbol{z}|\boldsymbol{x})$, such as Gaussian, and consider approximating $p(\boldsymbol{z}|\boldsymbol{x})$ by using $q(\boldsymbol{z}|\boldsymbol{x})$. Let's suppose that $q(\boldsymbol{z}|\boldsymbol{x})$ is parametrized by ϕ where ϕ is a parameter like the mean and covariance in case $q(\boldsymbol{z}|\boldsymbol{x})$ is Gaussian. Here, logarithm marginal likelihood which we want to maximize can be represented with q as follows:

$$\log p(\boldsymbol{x}) = \int q(\boldsymbol{z}|\boldsymbol{x}) \log p(\boldsymbol{x}) \, d\boldsymbol{z}$$

$$= \int q(\boldsymbol{z}|\boldsymbol{x}) \log \frac{p(\boldsymbol{x},\boldsymbol{z})q(\boldsymbol{z}|\boldsymbol{x})}{p(\boldsymbol{z}|\boldsymbol{x})q(\boldsymbol{z}|\boldsymbol{x})} \, d\boldsymbol{z} \tag{1}$$

$$= L + D_{KL}(q(\boldsymbol{z}|\boldsymbol{x})\|p(\boldsymbol{z}|\boldsymbol{x}))$$

$$\geq L$$

$$L = \int q(\boldsymbol{z}|\boldsymbol{x}) \log \frac{p(\boldsymbol{x},\boldsymbol{z})}{q(\boldsymbol{z}|\boldsymbol{x})} \, d\boldsymbol{z} \tag{2}$$

$$D_{KL}(q(\boldsymbol{z}|\boldsymbol{x})\|p(\boldsymbol{z}|\boldsymbol{x})) = \int q(\boldsymbol{z}|\boldsymbol{x}) \log \frac{q(\boldsymbol{z}|\boldsymbol{x})}{p(\boldsymbol{z}|\boldsymbol{x})} \, d\boldsymbol{z} \tag{3}$$

where the first line of Eq. (1) can be obtained just by insertion of weighted sum by $q(\boldsymbol{z}|\boldsymbol{x})$ that is independent of $p(\boldsymbol{x})$ and whose summation is one. Applying

Bayes rule leads to the second line and it can be transformed into the third line by multiplying both the numerator and the denominator inside the logarithm by $q(z|x)$. There are two goals in this scenario. One is to make marginal likelihood $\log p(x)$ as large as possible, which is equivalent to optimizing the model with regard to θ. The other is to make the shape of approximate distribution $q(z|x)$ closer to true distribution $p(z|x)$ by tuning ϕ, which is equivalent to making Eq. (3) closer to 0. With the fact that the KL divergence, Eq. (3), is nonnegative, $\log p(x)$ is larger than L called variational lower bound, and these two goals can be viewed as a single task, maximization of L. The VAE uses the gradient descent method for this optimization problem in the line of neural networks.

Variational Auto-Encoder. In order to maximize the variational lower bound L of Eq. (2) with regard to both the parameter θ and ϕ, the VAE uses the gradient descent method called Stochastic Gradient Variational Bayes [6] or Stochastic Back-propagation [11]. To derive the object function of VAE, we will do two-step conversion to the variational lower bound L, Monte Calro estimation and a technique called re-parameterization trick. First, we introduce the Monte Carlo sampling, by which the integral at z in Eq. (6) is approximated by taking the average of samples from $q(z|x)$:

$$\int q(z|x)\, f(z)\, dz = \mathbb{E}_{z \sim q(z|x)} [f(z)] \simeq \frac{1}{M} \sum_{m=1}^{M} f(z^{(m)}) \tag{4}$$

where $z \sim q(z|x)$ means that the distribution of the random variable z is consistent with the probabilistic distribution $q(z|x)$, $z^{(m)}$ indicates the m-th sample from $q(z|x)$, M is the number of the Monte Carlo sampling runs and $\mathbb{E}_{z \sim q(z|x)}$ means the expected value over empirical samples from the distribution of $q(z|x)$. Then applying re-parameterization trick, we express the random variable z as a deterministic variable $z = g_\phi(x, \epsilon)$, where ϵ is an auxiliary noise variable and $\epsilon^{(m)} \sim p(\epsilon)$. If we let the variational approximate posterior be a univariate Gaussian, $q(z|x) = \mathcal{N}(z|\mu, \sigma^2)$, the latent variable z can be expressed as $z^{(m)} = \mu + \sigma \epsilon^{(m)}$, where multiplication of σ and $\epsilon^{(m)}$ is done as element-wise. Equation (4) then can be written as:

$$\mathbb{E}_{z \sim q(z|x)} [f(z)] = \mathbb{E}_{\epsilon \sim p(\epsilon)} [f(\mu + \sigma\epsilon)] \simeq \frac{1}{M} \sum_{m=1}^{M} f(\mu + \sigma \epsilon^{(m)}) \tag{5}$$

To make the sampling variance smaller, using the Bayes rule again ($p(x, z) = p(x|z)p(z)$), we convert Eq. (2) as follows:

$$L = \int q(z|x) \log p(x|z)\, dz - D_{KL}(q(z|x)\|p(z)) \tag{6}$$

Note that the KL-divergence between two Gaussians can be integrated analytically. Let $P(z) = \mathcal{N}(\mu_1, \sigma_1)$, $Q(z) = \mathcal{N}(\mu_2, \sigma_2)$ and D be the dimensionality of z, then:

$$D_{KL}(P_1(z)\|P_2(z)) = \frac{1}{2}(\log\frac{|\sigma_2|}{|\sigma_1|} + \text{tr}\{\sigma_2^{-1}\sigma_1\})$$
$$+ \frac{1}{2}(\mu_1 - \mu_2)^{\text{T}}\sigma_2^{-1}(\mu_1 - \mu_2) - \frac{D}{2} \quad (7)$$

In our case, $P_1(z)$ is the posterior approximation $q(z|x) = \mathcal{N}(\mu, \sigma)$ and $P_2(z)$ is $\mathcal{N}(0, I)$ if we set the prior $p(z)$ as a standard normal distribution. Then putting them altogether, the objective function of the VAE for a single data point x ends up as follows:

$$L = \frac{1}{M}\sum_{m=1}^{M} \log p(x|z^{(m)}) - \frac{1}{2}\sum_{d=1}^{D}\left[1 + \log(\sigma_d)^2 - (\mu_d)^2 - (\sigma_d)^2\right] \quad (8)$$

where $z^{(m)} = \mu + \sigma\epsilon^{(m)}$, $\epsilon^{(m)} \sim \mathcal{N}(0, \mathbf{I})$ and μ_d and σ_d denote the d-th element of each vector. If the mean and variance of the approximate posterior, μ and σ^2, are outputs of a fead-forward network $q(z|x)$ parameterized by ϕ which takes x as input, and so is $p(x|z)$ by θ, we can optimize both of them simultaneously as a single neural network whose objective function is L of Eq. (8). It then can be viewed as a kind of Auto-Encoder that consists of the encoder $q(z|x)$ and the decoder $p(x|z)$. In Eq. (8), while the first term corresponds to the reconstruction error similar to typical Auto-Encoders, the second term is the advantage of the VAE. The second term of Eq. (8) works as regularization that makes the shape of the posterior approximation distribution $q(z|x)$ of the latent space close to the one of the prior distribution $p(z)$, which means that in the test time the model would be able to predict a reasonable z to some extent, even for the traffic x that was not contained in the training dataset. Note that, z in the VAE is represented as a continuous variable and the number of its dimensionality can be specified arbitrarily, just in the same way as a usual hidden layer.

3.2 Extension to Semi-supervised Learning

The VAE now enables us to predict a latent representation z for a certain observed traffic x. Additionally, its optimization is done by a mini-batch gradient descent method similarly to usual feedforward neural net models, and the amount of training data that the VAE can handle is unlimited in principle. The other thing we have to do is to add the functionalities of semi-supervised learning and classification using the latent variable to the VAE. Here, we first explain the architecture of the deep generative model (DGM) [7], which is previously proposed as an extension of the VAE to make it possible to generate data conditionally using labels, and then describe our proposed model, Forked VAE.

Deep Generative Model. The deep generative model (DGM) [7], also known as the conditional VAE (CVAE), has been proposed aiming to control the shape of the data that would be generated. Let y be a scalar indicating a label of input data x, and in the context of the NIDS with a Level 1 label in Sect. 2.2, y is a bit indicating whether a certain observed connection x shows a symptom of attack or not. As the graphical model shown in Fig. 2a, the DGM represents the inference model as $q(x, y, z) = q(z|x, y)q(y|x)q(x)$ (the left-hand of Fig. 2a) and the generative model as $p(x, y, z) = p(z|x, y)p(y)p(z)$ (the right-hand of Fig. 2a) respectively[1]. When x with label y is existent, by doing the expression expansion similar to Eq. (1), the variational bound L_ℓ for a single data point (x, y) can be shown as follows:

$$
\begin{aligned}
\log p(x, y) &= \int q(z|x) \log \frac{p(x, y, z)}{p(z|x, y)} \frac{q(z|x, y)}{q(z|x, y)} dz \\
&= \mathbb{E}_{z \sim q(z|x,y)} \left[\log \frac{p(x, y, z)}{q(z|x, y)} \right] - D_{KL}(q(z|x, y)\|p(z|x, y)) \\
&\geq \mathbb{E}_{z \sim q(z|x,y)} \left[\log \frac{p(x, y, z)}{q(z|x, y)} \right] \\
&= L_\ell
\end{aligned}
\tag{9}
$$

For the case where the label is missing, the variational bound L_u for a single data point x with unobserved label y is:

$$
\begin{aligned}
\log p(x) &= \sum_y q(z|x) \int q(z|x) \log \frac{p(x, y, z)q(y, z|x)}{p(y, z|x)q(y, z|x)} dz \\
&= \sum_y q(z|x) \, \mathbb{E}_{z \sim q(z|x)} \left[\log \frac{p(x, y, z)}{q(y, z|x)} \right] - D_{KL}(q(y, z|x)\|p(y, z|x)) \\
&\geq \sum_y q(z|x) \, \mathbb{E}_{z \sim q(z|x)} \left[\log \frac{p(x, y, z)}{q(y, z|x)} \right] \\
&= L_u
\end{aligned}
\tag{10}
$$

Introducing an explicit classification loss $\log q(y|x)$ multiplied by coefficient α so as to improve classification accuracy, the resultant objective function of DGM to be maximized is as follows:

$$
L = \sum_{(x_\ell, y_\ell)} L_\ell + \sum_{x_u} L_u - \alpha \sum_{(x_\ell, y_\ell)} [-\log q(y|x)]
\tag{11}
$$

where (x_ℓ, y_ℓ) indicates a data point x_ℓ with corresponding label y_ℓ and x_u denotes an unlabeled one.

Proposed Model. While the DGM is a semi-supervised learning model, it does not satisfy our requirements. In the left-hand inference model of Fig. 2a, we can see that a label y would be used as additional information to help infer a latent variable z from x, as $q(z|x, y)$, while what we want is exactly the opposite of that, i.e., predicting y given z, as $p(y|z)$[2]. In addition, in a generative model

---

[1] The model shown here is the type named Generative semi-supervised model (M2) in the original paper of [7].

[2] Note that we denote the prediction for y given z as a likelihood $p(y|z)$, not as an approximation posterior $q(y|z)$.

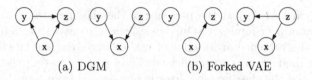

(a) DGM   (b) Forked VAE

Fig. 2. Graphical models of DGM and Forked VAE. Each left one represents inference model $q(\boldsymbol{x}, y, \boldsymbol{z})$ and right one does generative model $p(\boldsymbol{x}, y, \boldsymbol{z})$ respectively.

of Fig. 2a, while the DGM is modeled so that the reconstructed data $\boldsymbol{x}$ would be conditioned by a label y as well as a latent variable $\boldsymbol{z}$, that is, $p(\boldsymbol{x}|y, \boldsymbol{z})$, we consider that such structure is not appropriate for our task. As explained in Sect. 2.2, since the labels we are going to use for NIDSs will be coarse and simply indicate whether an observed data $\boldsymbol{x}$ is benign or not, we consider that it is not natural that such rough labels can decide the actual form of traffic data $\boldsymbol{x}$. The reason why such a difference exists between our expectation and the structure of a DGM is simply that the purpose of a DGM is not a classification task but data generation as well as the VAE, and we can see such a similar structure also in the Auxiliary Deep Generative Model (ADGM) [9], which is an extended model of the DGM.

We therefore propose a model in which labels would not be used for data generation, but only for training of classification. Our model is different from the DGM in the following points:

- Replace $q(\boldsymbol{z}|y)$ with $p(y|\boldsymbol{z})$ so that the classifier for $\boldsymbol{z}$ is trained.
- Use $q(\boldsymbol{z}|\boldsymbol{x})$ instead of $q(\boldsymbol{z}|\boldsymbol{x}, y)q(y|\boldsymbol{x})$ and prohibit y from engaging in producing $\boldsymbol{x}$ via $\boldsymbol{z}$.
- Use $p(\boldsymbol{x}|\boldsymbol{z})$ instead of $p(\boldsymbol{x}|y, \boldsymbol{z})$ and prohibit y from causing $\boldsymbol{x}$.

Figure 2b represents a graphical model of our proposed model in a form in comparison with one of the DGM, where the inference model is $q(\boldsymbol{x}, y, \boldsymbol{z}) = q(\boldsymbol{x}, \boldsymbol{z}) = q(\boldsymbol{z}|\boldsymbol{x})q(\boldsymbol{x})$ and the generative model is $p(\boldsymbol{x}, y, \boldsymbol{z}) = p(\boldsymbol{x}|\boldsymbol{z})p(y|\boldsymbol{z})p(\boldsymbol{z})$. We will also give an intuitive explanation with the whole picture with a single hidden layer h in Fig. 3. We refer to this model as Forked VAE because its graphical model has a form where a generative flow branches from the point of $\boldsymbol{z}$ to two directions, towards $p(y|\boldsymbol{z})$ and towards $p(\boldsymbol{x}|\boldsymbol{z})$. The difference compared

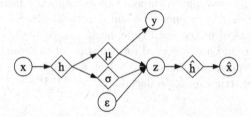

Fig. 3. The graphical model of Forked VAE. Circles are stochastic variables and diamonds are deterministic variables.

with the typical VAE is just the presence of the classifier, the functionality to predict the label y of inputs $\boldsymbol{x}$. Our basic idea is to make the latent variable z subject to the presence or absence of malice by leveraging labeled data $\boldsymbol{x}_\ell$. To do so, the model learns to predict the label y of $\boldsymbol{x}_\ell$, taking the mean of $\boldsymbol{z}$, $\boldsymbol{\mu}$, as inputs, and the classification error is propagated from y to the leftmost $\boldsymbol{x}$ through $\boldsymbol{\mu}$, as a supervised leaning signal. Additionally, for both the labeled data $\boldsymbol{x}_\ell$ and the unlabeled data $\boldsymbol{x}_u$, the model learns to reconstruct each of them, and its unsupervised learning signal is back propagated from the rightmost $\boldsymbol{x}$ to the leftmost $\boldsymbol{x}$. Note that both unsupervised and supervised learning are performed for a labeled data $\boldsymbol{x}_\ell$. The variational lower bound of the marginal likelihood for a single labeled data point is:

$$
\begin{aligned}
\log p(\boldsymbol{x}, y) &= \int q(\boldsymbol{z}|\boldsymbol{x}) \log \frac{p(\boldsymbol{x}, y, \boldsymbol{z}) q(\boldsymbol{z}|\boldsymbol{x})}{p(\boldsymbol{z}|\boldsymbol{x}) q(\boldsymbol{z}|\boldsymbol{x})} \\
&= \mathbb{E}_{z \sim q(z|x)}\left[\log \frac{p(\boldsymbol{x}, y, \boldsymbol{z})}{q(\boldsymbol{z}|\boldsymbol{x})}\right] - D_{KL}(q(\boldsymbol{z}|\boldsymbol{x})\|p(\boldsymbol{z}|\boldsymbol{x})) \\
&\geq \mathbb{E}_{z \sim q(z|x)}\left[\log \frac{p(\boldsymbol{x}, y, \boldsymbol{z})}{q(\boldsymbol{z}|\boldsymbol{x})}\right] \\
&= \mathbb{E}_{z \sim q(z|x)}\left[\log p(\boldsymbol{x}|\boldsymbol{z})\right] + \mathbb{E}_{z \sim q(z|x)}\left[\log p(y|\boldsymbol{z})\right] - D_{KL}(q(\boldsymbol{z}|\boldsymbol{x})\|p(\boldsymbol{z})) \\
&= L_\ell^{(\text{forked})}
\end{aligned}
\tag{12}
$$

where the way of changing mathematical expressions is similar to Eqs. (1) and (9) again, and Bayes rule of $p(\boldsymbol{x}, y) = p(\boldsymbol{x}, y, \boldsymbol{z})/p(\boldsymbol{z}|\boldsymbol{x}, y) = p(\boldsymbol{x}, y, \boldsymbol{z})/p(\boldsymbol{z}|\boldsymbol{x})$ based on the independence of y on $\boldsymbol{z}$ (as the left side of Fig. 2b) is applied in the first line. For a single unlabeled data point, it is simply equal to the variational lower bound of typical VAE, Eq. (2), and we denote that as $L_u^{(\text{forked})}$ here. Adding the classification loss term like the DGM and the ADGM, our objective function to be maximized is as follows:

$$
L^{(\text{forked})} = \sum_{(\boldsymbol{x}_\ell, y_\ell)} L_\ell^{(\text{forked})} + \sum_{\boldsymbol{x}_u} L_u^{(\text{forked})} - \alpha \sum_{(\boldsymbol{x}_\ell, y_\ell)} \mathbb{E}_{z \sim q(z|x_\ell)}\left[-\log p(y|\boldsymbol{z})\right]
\tag{13}
$$

where α is a trade-off hyper-parameter, and since it includes the expected value over samples $\mathbb{E}_{z \sim q(z|x)}$, the number of sampling times M has to be given.

Finally, we present an implementation of multi-layered perceptrons (MLPs) of Fig. 3 as a concrete example. Although this example is relatively simple, there are many possible choices of encoders and decoders. Since $\boldsymbol{x}$ is traffic data in our case and consists of mixed data type, such as a real-valued number for the connection duration and a categorical for the state of the connection, we handle $\boldsymbol{x}$ as real-valued vector, and hence we select a multivariate Gaussian with a diagonal covariance structure for a decoder of our MLP.

$$h = \tanh(\mathbf{W_1}x + \boldsymbol{b_1})$$
$$\boldsymbol{\mu} = \mathbf{W_2}h + \boldsymbol{b_2}$$
$$\log \boldsymbol{\sigma}^2 = \mathbf{W_3}h + \boldsymbol{b_3}$$
$$z^{(m)} = \boldsymbol{\mu} + \boldsymbol{\sigma}\epsilon^{(m)}, \ \epsilon^{(m)} \sim \mathcal{N}(0, \mathbf{I})$$
$$\hat{h} = \mathbf{W_4}z^{(m)} + \boldsymbol{b_{24}} \qquad\qquad (14)$$
$$\hat{\boldsymbol{\mu}} = \tanh(\mathbf{W_5}\hat{h} + \boldsymbol{b_5})$$
$$\log \hat{\boldsymbol{\sigma}}^2 = \tanh(\mathbf{W_6}\hat{h} + \boldsymbol{b_6})$$
$$\hat{x} \sim \mathcal{N}(\hat{\boldsymbol{\mu}}, \hat{\boldsymbol{\sigma}}^2\mathbf{I})$$
$$y = \arg \max_i(\mathrm{softmax}_i(\mathbf{W_{7_i}}z^{(m)} + \boldsymbol{b_7}))$$

where a tanh and multiplication of $\boldsymbol{\sigma}$ and $\epsilon^{(m)}$ are performed as element-wise, and the variances $\boldsymbol{\sigma}^2$ and $\hat{\boldsymbol{\sigma}}^2$ are outputs as a logarithm so that it is guaranteed to be a positive value. The value i in the last line indicates a class label, that is normal or attack traffic, and $\mathbf{W_{7_i}}$ is the i-th row of a weight matrix $\mathbf{W_7}$. The values $\{\mathbf{W_1}, \boldsymbol{b_1}, \mathbf{W_2}, \boldsymbol{b_2}, \mathbf{W_3}, \boldsymbol{b_3}\}$ are the weights and biases of the MLP and corresponding to variational parameters ϕ that composes an encoder $q(z|x)$, and $\{\mathbf{W_4}, \boldsymbol{b_4}, \mathbf{W_5}, \boldsymbol{b_5}, \mathbf{W_6}, \boldsymbol{b_6}, \mathbf{W_7}, \boldsymbol{b_7}\}$ are parameters θ of a decoder $p(x|z)$. Then we obtain the likelihoods used in the objective function Eq. (13) as follows:

$$\log p(x|z) = \log \mathcal{N}(\hat{\boldsymbol{\mu}}, \hat{\boldsymbol{\sigma}}^2\mathbf{I}) \qquad\qquad (15)$$
$$\log p(y|z) = y_\ell \log y + (1 - y_\ell) \log (1 - y) \qquad\qquad (16)$$

As mentioned in the explanation of Eq. (8), $\log p(x|z)$ can be seen as a reconstruction error since it contains the term of squared error. The value $\log p(y|z)$ is simply classification error as cross-entropy loss.

4   Experiments

We evaluate the detection performance of our proposed method using Kyoto2006+ [12] and NSL-KDD [14] datasets, and test it in two settings: one setting is in the semi-supervised learning model where a large amount of unlabeled data and very few labeled data are used, and the other setting is in the unsupervised learning model using only unlabeled data. The detail of the experimental conditions will be described in Sect. 4.2.

Our experimental procedure is simple. We first selected training data and testing data respectively from each dataset, and then put them into the model implemented based on the settings described in Sect. 4.1. Model training and detection test were also performed with the parameters described in Sect. 4.1.

4.1   Preparation

Datasets. Kyoto2006+ dataset covers nearly three years of real network traffic through the end of 2008 over a collection of both honeypots and regular servers that are operationally deployed at Kyoto University, while NSL-KDD is dataset artificially generated over the virtual network nearly two decades ago. Labels provided with Kyoto2006+ just indicates whether each traffic is malicious or non-malicious, whereas labels with NSL-KDD consist of five categories, normal traffic and four types of attack, such as DoS, probing, unauthorized access to local super user (root) privileges and unauthorized access from a remote machine. In this experiment, we deal with the label of NSL-KDD as binary, that is, the presence or absence of malice, similar to Kyoto2006+, with the intent of realization of Level 1 labeling in Sect. 2.2.

For Kyoto2006+, in order to compare the performance with previous works, the condition on how to select the data used for training and for testing was made consistent with [5,13]. Specifically, for Kyoto2006+, we used the traffic data of the day of Jan 1, 2008 for training, which amounts to 111,589 examples and the traffic of 12 days, 10th and 25th of each month from July to December, for testing, which amounts to 1,261,616 examples in total. Note that the data of 10th and 23rd were chosen for testing only in September because the honey pot system was shut down on 25th due to scheduled power outage. For NSL-KDD we used both training data and testing data as they were provided, and the amounts of traffic are 125,973 and 22,543 respectively. More detailed information on datasets can be found in relevant literature.

Parameters. Here, we present the parameters of the model we used in our experiment. Both the inferring and generative models are provided with a hidden layer between an input data layer and a latent variables layer, h in Fig. 3, and the number of units they have is 200 for both. The number of the latent space dimension is 30. As we set the prior distribution $p(z)$ as a standard normal distribution $\mathcal{N}(z|0, \mathbf{I})$, for the sake of the second term of Eq. (6), as the training progresses $q(z|x)$ becomes gradually close to a spherical distribution and each element of z gets independent of each other. However, at the same time we anticipate that at least two clusters corresponding to the attack and the benign would emerge. Therefore, we relieved such regularizing effect stemming from KL divergence a bit by multiplying the second term of Eq. (6) by 0.01. In addition, we let α in Eq. (13) be 100 and let the frequency of Monte Carlo sampling for x, M be 1, and AdaGrad was used as optimization and its learning rate was set to 0.001.

The values for those parameters were chosen heuristically through our experiments. From the difference in the size of the dimension of the input data, the number of units of hidden layers and the size of latent variables are a bit smaller respectively compared with the previous VAE based works, but the remaining parameters ended up with the same as the previous works. For the parameter of Random Forest, we used the default values defined by sickit-learn's API as it is.

Table 1. Summary of experimental conditions.

	Purpose	#Labeled	#Unlabeled	Corresponding Nos. in Tables 2 and 3
1	Unsupervised learning	0	All records	1, 7
2	Semi-supervised learning	100	All records excluding 100	5, 9
3	Semi-supervised learning	100	3,000	3, 8

Environments. The program for our experiments was implemented using Theano 0.7.0 [17], and the specification of the machine used for the experiment is iMac, Intel Core i5 2.7 GHz processor and 12 GB RAM. Although the program runs only on CPU without using GPU, the computational time for the model training was so short that millions of iterations of training for a single mini-batch, that consists of 100 data records, got finished in a couple of hours.

4.2 Experimental Conditions

For comparison, we evaluated our models under three different conditions in terms of the amounts of the training data. Table 1 shows the summary, and the actual number of labeled and unlabeled data records for each condition is shown in Tables 2 and 3, along with their corresponding results.

Condition 1 corresponding to No. 1 in Table 2 and No. 7 in Table 3, is set to aim to evaluate the proposed model as unsupervised learning. The purpose of the experiment of Condition 1 is to qualitatively evaluate the effectiveness of the proposed model in terms of the ability to make the latent representation, i.e., as a feature extractor, for network traffic data. In this evaluation, the latent space is visualized where the raw traffic data is mapped in the unsupervised learning way by using the training dataset without label information. In addition, we also perform a detection experiment that is to classify the latent features extracted by VAE, by using another machine learning classification method. As our proposed model of Condition 1 is equivalent to the normal VAE and does not have a classification function in itself, we chose Random Forest as our classifier, due to its processing speed, the ability to use large amounts of data for training and testing, and ease of implementation[3]. Note that the classification results of Nos. 1 and 7 are done by supervised learning with Random Forest.

Conditions 2 and 3 were set to evaluate our model as semi-supervised learning, which corresponds to Nos. 3, 5, 8 and 9 in Tables 2 and 3. In both conditions the number of labeled data records was only 100 that were selected from the beginning of each training data file, whereas in Condition 2 unlabeled data consists of all but the 100 data records, and in Condition 3 unlabeled data consists of 3,000 records chosen from 101st to 3,100th lines of training file of each datasets. Condition 3 was created to adapt our evaluation to the experimental

---

[3] We use scikit-learn [16].

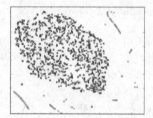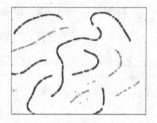

Fig. 4. Visualization of the latent space. Plots on each figure correspond to first 2,000 traffic records of Jul 15, 2008 of Kyoto2006+. According to corresponding labels in the data file, each traffic is plotted as a red point if it is normall or as blue if adversarial. (Left) The model trained in unsupervised learning under Condition 1 (corresponding to No. 1 in Table 2). (Right) The model trained in semi-supervised learning under Condition 2 (corresponding to No. 5 in Table 2). To visualize, the dimensionality is converted from 30 to 2 by using t-SNE. (Color figure online)

condition of [13] where Kyoto2006+ was used in the same way. Indeed, considering that the training data consists of only 3,100 records in total and this number is very small compared with the test data of 1,261,616 records, performance of the trained model is heavily dependent on which records are used for training. Therefore, we tried to match our condition exactly with [13], however unfortunately that could not be realized because in [13] the data had been selected randomly. For NSL-KDD, unlabeled data records for Conditions 2 and 3 were selected in the same way, namely, 3,000 records extracted from 100 line from the beginning of the training data file and all the remaining records except for first 100 lines of that file, which are corresponding to Nos. 8 and 9 in Table 3 respectively.

4.3 Results

Figure 4 shows that how the trained model recognizes the observed traffic data in the latent space z, where each blue plot corresponds to a normal connection and each red does to an attack. Note that all records in the training data have corresponding labels, and hence in the evaluation as the unsupervised model, after we mapped data into the latent space (Fig. 4 left) or performed classification with Random Forest (No. 1 in Table 2 and No. 7 in Table 3), we could distinguish normal from adversarial by using those label information as the ground truth. In the left side of Fig. 4, the plots form concentric circles with different radius between normal traffic and adversarial ones, which can be naturally considered as the manifestation of the effect of the second term of Eq. (6), and although the model has been trained in an unsupervised manner as typical VAE, we can see that it succeeded in isolating adversarial traffic from normal traffic fairly well. The right side of Fig. 4, which is the projection through our Forked VAE, forms no longer a concentric circles nor two clusters. Although the detection accuracy ended up being good as discussed later, there is probably room for the model parameter tuning, especially α in Eq. (13).

Table 2. Classification performance on the Kyoto2006+ dataset.

No	Conditions		Results		
	#Labeled	#Unlabeled	Recall	FP Rate[a]	AUC Score
1 (ours)	0	111,589	0.90893	0.05382	0.90662
2 [13]	0	111,589	N/A	N/A	N/A
3 (ours)	100	3,000	0.62014	0.15330	0.89798
4 [13]	100	3,000	0.89144	0.02667	0.98651
5 (ours)	100	111,489	**0.95326**	0.03439	0.98471
6 [13]	100	111,489	N/A	N/A	N/A

[a] False Positive Rate.

Table 3. Classification performance on the NSL-KDD dataset.

No	Conditions		Results		
	#Labeled	#Unlabeled	Recall	FP Rate[a]	AUC Score
7 (ours)	0	125,973	0.85663	0.12860	0.93713
8 (ours)	100	3,000	0.74267	0.14648	0.86957
9 (ours)	100	125,873	0.85991	0.12106	0.95718

[a] False Positive Rate.

Tables 2 and 3 show the classification results respectively. In both datasets, the relative superiority of Conditions 1, 2 and 3 was as expected. Focusing on Area Under the Curve (AUC), we can see that [13] (No. 4) has still outperformed our result despite the fact that [13] used only 3,000 unlabeled data. However, the results of Conditions 2 and 3 show that the performance of our model was drastically improved with the increase of unlabeled data records. In particular, the recall of our proposed semi-supervised model (No. 5) ends up being remarkably higher than that of [13] (No. 4), and that means our model outperforms [13] in terms of the false negative rate which is a crucial index for NIDSs: our model gave 4.67%, compared with 10.86% in [13][4]. As argued in Sect. 2, our ultimate goal is to construct a defense systems that can fully leverage unlabeled data, which would be available with very low cost, and this results can be regarded as taking the first step towards the realization of that.

5 Related Work

There have been many works related to network intrusion detection system using machine learning techniques. The works [4,8,10] proposed anomaly detection

---

[4] Regarding the N/A in Table 2, the reason why [13] evaluated the performance by using only the small amount of training data records seems that the method they used has the limitation in terms of the amount of the training data records. We confirmed the reason indirectly by the fact that applying the kernel PCA, which is based on kernel computation similarly to Laplacian regularized least squares used in [13], ended up with an out-of-memory error.

methods that measure changes of traffic volume on the basis of entropy. Establishing a way to collect normal data that defines the baseline is a challenge for their methodology, and [10] worked on that issue with the algorithm that makes it possible to sample packets efficiently. While the direction of the detection method of [10] is different from ours, their method can be considered to be related to our objective in terms of data sampling. Once we succeed in reducing the amount of labeling by introducing semi-supervised learning, what would become as the next primary problem is possibly how to select a small amount of data to be labeled efficiently and effectively.

The work [1] proposed an anomaly detection method using the VAE, in which the model was trained only with benign traffic data, and whether observed data is normal or adversarial would be judged based on the likelihood of reconstruction $p(x|z)$. However, acquiring traffic data exclusive of adversarial traffic requires the task that is equivalent to labeling, and hence the need for preparing pure benign traffic data may become problematic when it is put into practical use.

The works [5, 13] dealt with network intrusion detection as a classification task, and especially [13] had much in common with us including the reason why they did not use outlier detection methods. The work [13] is also a pioneering work introducing semi-supervised learning and their method is based on Laplacian regularized least squares. Compared with [13] in terms of the semi-supervised learning based technique, the strength of our proposed Forked VAE is being a more scalable model. As mentioned in Sect. 1, the computation complexity of [13] is a cubic of the number of labeled and unlabeled training data records [2], whereas our model is not much affected by the data volume because, as mentioned in Sect. 3.1, its learning process would be done by gradient descent just as in the other neural network model, which leads to the synergy with semi-supervised learning through making full use of a huge amount of unlabeled data.

6 Summary

In this paper, we have proposed the novel NIDS based on the Forked VAE, a semi-supervised learning model extending the VAE. The strength of our proposed method is the scalability of the model, which makes it possible to train the model with a huge amount of unlabeled data, and in the experiment using Kyoto2006+ dataset, we demonstrated that the false negative rate gets improved from 37.99% to 4.67% by simply increasing the number of unlabeled data records from 3,000 to 111,489 with only 100 labeled data records.

Acknowledgements. This work was supported in part by JSPS KAKENHI Grant Numbers 17K00178 and 16K00183.

References

1. An, J., Cho, S.: Variational Autoencoder based anomaly Detection using Reconstruction Probability (2015). http://dm.snu.ac.kr/static/docs/TR/SNUDM-TR-2015-03.pdf

2. Belkin, M., Niyogi, P., Sindhwani, V.: Manifold regularization: a geometric framework for learning from labeled and unlabeled examples. J. Mach. Learn. Res. **7**(Nov), 2399–2434 (2006)
3. Görnitz, N., Kloft, M., Rieck, K., Brefeld, U.: Toward supervised anomaly detection. J. Artif. Intell. Res. (JAIR) **46**, 235–262 (2013)
4. Gu, Y., McCallum, A., Towsley, D.: Detecting anomalies in network traffic using maximum entropy estimation. In: Proceedings of the 5th ACM SIGCOMM Conference on Internet Measurement, pp. 32–32. USENIX Association, October 2005
5. Kishimoto, K., Yamaki, H., Takakura, H.: Improving performance of anomaly-based ids by combining multiple classifiers. In: 2011 IEEE/IPSJ 11th International Symposium on Applications and the Internet (SAINT), pp. 366–371. IEEE, July 2011
6. Kingma, D.P., Welling, M.: Auto-encoding variational bayes. arXiv preprint arXiv:1312.6114 (2013)
7. Kingma, D.P., Mohamed, S., Rezende, D.J., Welling, M.: Semi-supervised learning with deep generative models. In: Advances in Neural Information Processing Systems, pp. 3581–3589 (2014)
8. Lakhina, A., Crovella, M., Diot, C.: Mining anomalies using traffic feature distributions. In: ACM SIGCOMM Computer Communication Review, vol. 35, no. 4, pp. 217–228. ACM, August 2005
9. Maale, L., Snderby, C.K., Snderby, S.K., Winther, O.: Improving semi-supervised learning with auxiliary deep generative models. In: NIPS Workshop on Advances in Approximate Bayesian Inference (2015)
10. Nawata, S., Uchida, M., Gu, Y., Tsuru, M., Oie, Y.: Unsupervised ensemble anomaly detection through time-periodical packet sampling. In: INFOCOM IEEE Conference on Computer Communications Workshops, pp. 1–6. IEEE, March 2010
11. Rezende, D.J., Mohamed, S., Wierstra, D.: Stochastic backpropagation and approximate inference in deep generative models. arXiv preprint arXiv:1401.4082 (2014)
12. Song, J., Takakura, H., Okabe, Y., Eto, M., Inoue, D., Nakao, K.: Statistical analysis of honeypot data and building of Kyoto 2006+ dataset for NIDS evaluation. In: Proceedings of the First Workshop on Building Analysis Datasets and Gathering Experience Returns for Security, pp. 29–36. ACM, April 2011
13. Symons, C.T., Beaver, J.M.: Nonparametric semi-supervised learning for network intrusion detection: combining performance improvements with realistic in-situ training. In: Proceedings of the 5th ACM Workshop on Security and Artificial Intelligence, pp. 49–58. ACM, October 2012
14. Tavallaee, M., Bagheri, E., Lu, W., Ghorbani, A.A.: A detailed analysis of the KDD CUP 99 data set. In: IEEE Symposium on Computational Intelligence for Security and Defense Applications, CISDA 2009, pp. 1–6. IEEE, July 2009
15. Valpola, H.: From neural PCA to deep unsupervised learning. Adv. Independent Component Anal. Learn. Mach. 143–171 (2015)
16. http://scikit-learn.org/stable/
17. http://deeplearning.net/software/theano/

No Sugar but All the Taste! Memory Encryption Without Architectural Support

Panagiotis Papadopoulos(✉), Giorgos Vasiliadis, Giorgos Christou,
Evangelos Markatos, and Sotiris Ioannidis

FORTH-ICS, Heraklion, Greece
{panpap,gvasil,gchri,markatos,sotiris}@ics.forth.grz

Abstract. The protection of in situ data, typically require solutions that involve different kinds of encryption schemes. Even though the majority of these solutions prioritize the protection of cold data stored on secondary devices, it has been shown that sensitive information like passwords, secrets, and private data can be easily exfiltrated from main memory as well, by adversaries with physical access. As such, the protection of hot data that reside on main memory is equally important.

In this paper, we aim to investigate whether it is possible to achieve memory encryption without any architectural support at a reasonable performance cost. In particular, we propose the first of its kind software-based memory encryption approach, which ensures that sensitive data will remain encrypted in main memory at all times. Our approach is based on commodity off-the-shelf hardware, and is totally transparent to legacy applications. To accommodate different applications needs, we have built two versions of main memory encryption: Full and Selective Memory Encryption. Additionally, we provide a new memory allocation library that allows programmers to manage granular sensitive memory regions according to the specific requirements of each application. We conduct an extensive quantitative evaluation and characterization of the overheads of our software-based memory encryption, using both micro-benchmarks and real-world application workloads. Our results show that the performance overheads due to memory encryption are tolerable in real-world network scenarios, below 17% for HTTP and 27% for HTTPS.

1 Introduction

The theft of sensitive data is an escalating problem. According to a recent study [17], it is estimated that data breaches can cost between $90 and $305 per record exposed, leading to an average cost of around $4.8 million per company per incident. To protect data stored on secondary storage devices, many approaches that provide full disk encryption have been proposed [20,26]. The majority of these approaches encrypt all data stored on the disk using a secret key that is provided, usually, at boot time. As a result, in case of IT hardware equipment theft, physical attack, or industrial espionage, all corporate and sensitive data stored on the hard disk will be protected.

© Springer International Publishing AG 2017
S.N. Foley et al. (Eds.): ESORICS 2017, Part II, LNCS 10493, pp. 362–380, 2017.
DOI: 10.1007/978-3-319-66399-9_20

Besides the protection of (cold) data stored on secondary storage devices, sensitive data can also reside on main memory (*hot data*), where they are typically in clear-text. This permits the launching of memory attacks, and allows the exploitation of main memory and the exfiltration of data used during execution. More importantly, it is not only servers or desktops that are under threat. According to [17], more than 40% of business users leave their laptops in sleep or hibernation mode when traveling, leaving their private or corporate data, keys or passwords residing in memory unprotected. As a consequence, an adversary is able to retrieve all data from the main memory, along with any stored sensitive data, e.g., session keys, passwords, HTTP cookies, SSL key pairs, gaining this way access to online services, bank accounts or local encrypted hard disks. Some of the typical methods adversaries utilize to steal data from main memory are cold boot attacks [11,12,29] and DMA attacks [6,28].

To overcome these problems, many approaches for memory encryption have been proposed [7,21]. These approaches integrate several architectural mechanisms to provide encryption and secure context management of data that reside in off-chip memory regions. Although these systems provide strong security guarantees with acceptable performance, their use in practice is limited, as they require hardware support and cannot be directly applied to commodity systems.

In this paper, we design the first to our knowledge software-based memory encryption approach for commodity, off-the-shelf, systems. With our approach, application data are always encrypted in main memory, using a 128-bit AES key, which is randomly generated every time the application is launched to make it resistant against key guessing attacks [18]. To cope with the computational overhead of memory encryption, we leverage the Advanced Encryption Standard Instruction Set for cryptographic operations, which is currently available in the majority of modern microprocessors. Finally, we experimentally quantify the cost of keeping sensitive data secure in practical, real-world scenarios.

To summarize, the main contributions of this work are the following:

1. We present, to the best of our knowledge, the first of its kind, design and implementation for entirely software-based main memory encryption. Our solution can work transparently without any need to modify the application.
2. We provide a library to allow the users perform partial memory encryption enabling them this way to create, at runtime, fine-grained encrypted segments depending on the application requirements.
3. We conduct an extensive quantitative evaluation of software-based main memory encryption for both static and dynamic instrumentation strategies, using both micro-benchmarks and real-world applications.

2   Our Approach

The goal of our approach is to secure *hot data* of running processes by deploying main memory encryption without any architectural support. To do so, we use code instrumentation to ensure that any process' data will be stored in main memory, encrypted at all time. This way, sensitive data residing in main memory or moving among the different components of an untrusted domain, will always be protected against prying eyes.

2.1   Threat Model

In this section, we describe the classes of physical hardware attacks within our threat model, and additional threats that fall outside the scope of our paper.

In-Scope Threats. We are concerned of adversaries that have physical access to the victim's system where sensitive information is stored, and that the machine can be exposed to physical hardware attacks: or DMA attacks.

Cold Boot Attacks. In a *cold boot attack* [11,12,29], the data remanence effect of RAM is exploited by the adversary to extract the data from the memory. There are two ways of achieving this: (i) an attacker can freeze the RAM modules using a refrigerant [22] which then physically remove from the victim's device and inserts them into a device that is capable to read the contents of the RAM; (ii) an attacker can perform a *warm boot* by running specific attack tools, and retrieve the contents of the residual memory [8]. In this type of side channel attack, the attacker is able to retrieve encryption keys and sensitive data from a running operating system even when the user session is locked. As has been shown in [27], modern SRAM chips can retain about 80% of their data for up to a minute at temperatures above $-20\,°C$.

DMA Attacks. This type of attacks leverage the ability of a DMA interface to allow a peripheral to directly access arbitrary memory regions, and read memory contents without any supervision from the processor or the OS. More specifically, an attacker can program a DMA-capable peripheral to manipulate the DMA controller and read sensitive data stored in memory [24,28]. This type of attack can be carried out over different IO buses, such as the Firewire, PCI, PCI Express or Thunderbolt.

Out-of-Scope Threats. Apart from the above attacks, obviously there are many more threats for the data residing in memory, that fall outside the scope of this paper.

Memory Disclosure Attacks. This type of attacks aim to compromise the software, accessing this way possible secrets and passwords. Such attacks exploit a software vulnerability to install malicious code. Although this type of attacks are quite common and important to consider, this paper focuses on attacks that do not rely on running compromised software.

Side-Channel Attacks. Such type of attacks aim to extract sensitive information by exploiting physical properties (like timing information or power consumption) of the cryptographic implementation. These attacks usually have a limited accuracy and require a relatively high level of sophistication, especially when the attacker cannot run arbitrary code on the device, therefore they fall beyond the threat model of this paper.

Sophisticated Physical Attacks. It is hard to defend against every type of physical attacks. Indeed, there are several Advanced Persistent Threats (APTs), usually deployed for corporate espionage, intelligence stealing from governmental or military infrastructures etc., which under specific circumstances, can achieve severe data breaches. However, such attacks require specialized equipment and can often take several months even when carried out by a skilled attacker.

2.2   Main Assumptions

Our main assumptions, which are in line with the related literature [13], are that the processor provides a secure region, within which sensitive information can reside. As we see in Fig. 1, all components outside of the processor are assumed to be vulnerable, including RAM and its interconnections, like the data and memory bus, I/O devices, etc. Additionally, we assume a trusted kernel in the target system. This is a reasonable assumption, keeping in mind that an adversary capable of controlling the kernel can cause more significant damage than just eavesdropping sensitive data. The core idea of main memory encryption related techniques is to avoid potential data breaches, and make any adversary with the above properties unable of observing, deleting, replacing or modifying any piece of data existing in a victim system.

3   Main Memory Encryption

In this section, we present our technique for main memory encryption, in order to secure the data of running applications. Specifically, we show how we instrument the load and store operations with encryption and decryption instructions.

The instrumentation of load and store instructions can be implemented in two ways, either (i) *statically*: by instrumenting the specific memory access instructions, or (ii) *dynamically*: by running the corresponding binary executable on top of a dynamic instrumentation tool.

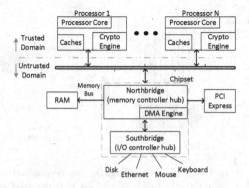

Fig. 1. Data are always encrypted when residing in main memory or moving between the different components of the untrusted domain.

The static instrumentation of the binary executable offers better performance, however requires the static instrumentation of all linked shared libraries as well. On the other hand, dynamic instrumentation is able to handle complex run-time code manipulation cases, such as dynamically generated (JIT), obfuscated or self-modifying code. As such, even though dynamic instrumentation has an extra performance overhead (as we will see in Sect. 4), it is considered more flexible and supports both shared libraries and run-time generated code.

3.1 Full Memory Encryption (FME)

An important design decision, when applying memory encryption, is how to encrypt the memory data. In 64-bit architectures memory operations operate up to 64-bit words. However, the AES algorithm operates in block units, where each block is a minimum of 128 bits. Hence, during each memory operation we need to collect nearby 128-bit aligned data. This is accomplished by making use of two xmm registers, one as a load buffer and one as a store buffer. In case of multiple encryptions, this register helps us temporarily keep data until the next store instruction targeting near data is issued. The sequential store instructions, as can be seen in Fig. 2, will get a couple of words encrypted in the same block and then the block will proceed to be stored in the main memory. In case of decryption, this register allows us to *pre-fetch* data during sequential memory accesses. This way, as seen in Fig. 3, when a process loads a word and then loads its very next one, it will retrieve it directly from the register instead of decrypting again the same block. This solution has the additional benefit of hiding decryption latency when consecutive words are accessed.

We note that it could be possible to use even larger blocks (>128 bits). Such approaches may benefit from less number of performed encryptions and decryptions, which would improve the performance of programs that exhibit cache locality and reduce their overall execution time. However, it would also require quite extensive buffering, which would result to massive utilization of

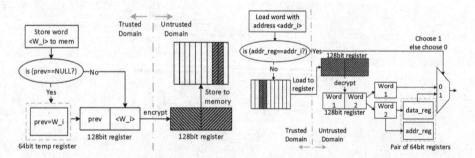

Fig. 2. Subsequent store instructions have words encrypted as a bundle in the same block and are then stored on main memory.

Fig. 3. For sequential memory accesses, the block is decrypted once and the 2nd word is retrieved directly from the register instead of re-decrypting the same block.

registers. The reason behind this is that the data will need to be in the registers for an unknown period of time, until they reach the proper size of the block. More importantly, applications will have performance gains solely in the case of sequential data accesses, while in the case of random memory accesses, a large part of the decrypted data will remain underused and be quickly evicted from the registers. Using the above encryption scheme, all data placed in the memory is encrypted, however they are still not well-protected. Given that each block is encrypted separately, an attacker is able to identify identical ciphertext blocks that yield identical plaintext blocks, after scanning the entire memory. These unprotected data patterns allow trivial attacks available in the adversary's toolchest even in the single-snapshot scenario of the cold boot attack. To remedy this issue, we use a stream cipher encryption mode of operation instead of block cipher. The challenge of such an approach, in our case, is that applications may need to randomly access non-sequential single blocks that need to be decrypted separately. To obtain this random access property during decryption, we employ the CTR mode of operation by using a per-session random nonce and a per-block counter. This way, we turn the block ciphers into a stream cipher, eliminating the potential appearance of patterns.

Handling System Calls. It is quite often for applications to perform specific operations that only the kernel has the privilege to execute. For instance, hardware-related operations (e.g. accessing a hard disk drive), or communication with integral kernel services, such as process scheduling. The request of such privileged applications (i.e. system call) usually is followed by application user data and parameters that need to be passed to the kernel. In our case, all of the data passed from user to kernel space are encrypted. As a consequence, after extracting the calling process `pid`, the kernel obtains the proper process key (see Sect. 3.4 below), and decrypts the parameters before and respectively, encrypts any results after executing the system call. There are system calls that are so frequently used from user-space applications, that can dominate the overall performance. To avoid the expensive performance penalty of system calls and context-switches, the kernel uses a virtual dynamic shared object (vDSO) mechanism. In particular, selected kernel space routines (e.g. `gettimeofday(2)`) are mapped into the address space of user-space applications by the kernel, enhancing thus the performance of these applications. Given that there is no switch to the kernel space, in our case, vDSO is treated like any other shared library object: by having its store and load instructions cryptographically instrumented.

Signals and Non-local Jumps. Another case we need to take into account is signals. When a signal arrives at an application, the used registers and the processor's state must be stored for the execution to smoothly continue afterwards from the current state. That said, in our case, the specific registers may contain sensitive data that we cannot risk to be spilled in memory in plaintext. To overcome this, we modified the kernel by using the proper process key, to encrypt their contents before saving them to `sigcontext` structure. When the specific execution continues, the loaded values are decrypted before restored back to the registers. In a similar way, we deal with the case of non-local jumps (i.e. `setjmp`/`longjmp`). Specifically, in case of `setjmp`, the data from the utilized general purpose registers are being encrypted before stored in a jump buffer in memory. On the other hand, in case of `longjmp` the data are decrypted after restored from the jump buffer to the registers right before the application jumps to the return address set by the `setjmp`.

Handling Context Switches. Typically the CPU loads data at run-time in its registers in order to perform its computations. When context switch evictions take place, all the previously used data from the registers are moved onto the stack, which resides in main memory. Considering that there are cases where this data may be sensitive, sensitive information may find its way unencrypted on main memory, if these evictions are left unhandled. In our case, these evictions may swap out to sensitive states of AES stored in `XMM` registers, even though they were implemented to run solely on CPU. To remedy this, we modified the kernel's typical context switch procedure to encrypt the content of `XMM` registers before they get evicted and decrypt them after the process is switched back. We achieve this by encrypting and decrypting the contents, right before and right after `FXSAVE` (i.e. store to register) and `FXRSTOR` (i.e. restore from register) instructions respectively.

3.2   Selective Memory Encryption (SME)

Having all memory encrypted provides the best protection for all applications. However, our experiments in Sect. 4 show that the overhead, in terms of performance, can increase significantly. To lower the performance overhead of FME, it is feasible to encrypt only the memory regions that contain secret or sensitive data. Indeed, such approach could result in much lower overheads during execution, proportional to the size of the data that need to be protected from memory attacks. Unfortunately, though, the exact location of sensitive data in memory is very difficult to be known in advance. Instead, it will require the developer to define the exact memory regions, the sensitive data will later reside in. One solution would be to use `#pragma` directives to provide additional information about which variables will be encrypted at compile time. However, this would restrict memory encryption to static variables only and do not offer much flexibility to the developer. To address this issue, we implement a secure memory allocator, namely s_malloc to dynamically allocate arbitrary size of memory from the heap. In order to have an integral number of blocks, the memory is allocated in multiples of 128 bits. Any data written in this portion of memory allocated with this allocator will always be encrypted. To achieve this, s_malloc taints the memory regions it allocates to ensure that the corresponding memory addresses have to be encrypted or decrypted when accessed accordingly. For instance, during load operations we can determine if the loaded data originate from s_malloc and need to be first decrypted before being read. s_malloc keeps a structure for each allocation to note the starting memory address that the segment begins along with its allocated size to denote the total length of the tainted area.

De-allocated Memory Pages. Memory pages that have been de-allocated after being allocated by an application handling sensitive data may produce left-overs. These may be readable by attackers, enabling them to retrieve parts or even the entirety of the sensitive information. Even though Linux has a kernel thread responsible for zeroing-out the freed pages, due to internal performance optimizations, there is no guarantee when this will occur. In traditional systems this could pose privacy risks as one may get to read a region of memory that contains sensitive data. In our case, this is not a problem; the reason is that after memory allocation, all sensitive data get always encrypted before being placed in heap. Therefore, sensitive memory disclosure is not possible, as an adversary will read random bits of the ciphertext.

3.3 Protecting Memory from Illegal Access

After ensuring the confidentiality of written-through data, a problem that may arise is in case of DMA attacks, where it is possible not only to read data from memory, but also to write. As a consequence, an attacker could inject the OS with malicious code. To mitigate this issue, we use the commodity Input-Output Memory Management Unit (IOMMU)[1] [16] to prevent malicious memory access through DMA. The IOMMU is an IO mapping mechanism, which translates device-visible virtual addresses to physical addresses using, OS-provided mappings. Besides, it also provides memory protection, where memory is protected either from malicious devices that attempt to perform DMA attacks or from faulty devices that initiate errant memory transfers. This protection is achieved by enabling the OS to restrict *who can access what memory region*. As a result, a device cannot read or write to memory that has not been explicitly allocated or mapped to it. In our case, IOMMU is properly configured in order to forbid any access to in-memory kernel or application data.

3.4 Key Management

In this section we describe how we protect the AES secret keys that are used for encryption and decryption, against all attacks within our threat-model (described in Sect. 2.1). Previous works have shown that it is sufficient to prevent sensitive data and algorithmic state from leaking to RAM by implementing the cryptographic operations using on-chip memory only [9,20].

   In our approach, each process is assigned with a different key, that is stored in the Process Control Block (PCB) data structure. The PCB contains all the information needed to manage a particular process, and is placed at the beginning of the kernel stack of the process. Still, since the kernel memory is vulnerable to cold boot attacks, each *process key* is encrypted before it is stored in the PCB. The process keys are encrypted using a master key which is stored, similar to

---

[1] IOMMU can be considered commodity since both leading x86 vendors (i.e. AMD and Intel) ship their CPUs with this feature supported (see VT-d [1] and AMD-V [2]).

Tresor [20], inside a pair of debug registers[2]. By doing so, we avoid storing any key in main memory. The reason we utilize debug registers is that, by default, they can be accessed only from ring 0 privileged level. As a consequence, they cannot be reached by malicious user-level applications and more importantly, they do not used in procedures like context setjmp/longjmp or signal handling: cases that otherwise one would have to take specific care to prevent them from being spilled into memory. Additionally, we have modified the ptrace system call to respond with EBUSY error to any application that may request the particular registers, preventing them thus from being accessed from user level[3]. We need to note at this point, that there are studies questioning such use of debug registers to store secrets [5]. According to these, an attacker is able to inject and execute code in ring 0 privilege level by deploying a DMA attack, and consequently, disclose the secrets stored in the debug registers. In our case, with the use of IOMMU, we forbid such illegal memory injections and as a result, we eliminate the possibility of such attacks.

Bootstrapping. The master key that encrypts the process keys inside PCB is randomly generated at boot time, ensuring this way, forward secrecy. To achieve that, we modified the kernel to use RDRAND instruction to perform on-chip hardware random number generation and create the next master key. Apparently, the new master key must be present to every core of the processor. The core responsible for the master key generation (core with ID 0), is responsible to distribute it across the rest of the cores. Therefore, the newly generated key will be stored not only in the local debug registers, but also in the Memory Type Range Registers (MTRR), which are visible to all cores. The rest of the cores will spin on a shared variable till core 0 sets the value to true denoting that the new key has been generated and placed in the MTRR. After that, each core can obtain the key, store it in its local debug registers, and finally increment atomically a shared counter. By monitoring this shared counter, core 0 knows how many of the cores have obtain the new key. When they all get informed, it immediately cleans the key from the MTRR registers and the boot process continues normally. Obviously, there are cases where data from the memory need to be swapped-out from memory and stored in the disk. Such data, would not be able to get decrypted after boot if it gets stored encrypted with the current master key. In such cases though, we assume that the users have deployed not only memory encryption but also full disk encryption (FDE). This means that the data will get encrypted with the FDE's key, before swapped out to disk.

---

[2] Chosen from the dr0 - dr3 range group. On 64-bit systems, only 2 are needed to store 2 64-bit words. On 32-bit systems we need 4 for the same amount of data.

[3] Debug registers are used by software debuggers (e.g. GDB) to store breakpoint addresses. However, even without them, debuggers can still operate seamlessly using the rest of the debug register as well as software breakpoints.

4   Performance Evaluation

For the performance measurements we used a server that is equipped with two six-core Intel Xeon E5-2620 operating at 2.00 GHz, with 15 MB L2 cache each. The server contains 8 GB RAM and an Intel 82567 1 GbE network interface.

4.1   Full Memory Encryption

At first, we measure the overhead imposed for encrypting all data stored in main memory. This way, we determine the cost of the most intensive but secure strategy, where every single byte written to memory is encrypted and respectively decrypted before it is read.

Dynamic Instrumentation

One way to keep all data residing in memory encrypted is to instrument dynamically every single memory accessing operation at runtime. By leveraging this technique, we instrumented the memory accessing operations and enhanced them with the appropriate AES-NI instructions. To achieve this, we used the execution environment of the Intel's dynamic binary instrumentation tool PIN [4].

We chose this tool due to its high-versatility and support for multiple architectures (x86, x64, ARM, and more). Additionally, PIN enables the developer to inspect and tamper with an application's original instructions, when at the same time, it operates entirely in user space. It just-in-time compiles (JIT) the application's original instructions along with the instrumentation the developer may have added. This results in producing new code which is placed into a code cache awaiting execution. Dynamic instrumentation with PIN guarantees that any memory access will be intercepted either if it belongs to a dynamic library or self-modifying code etc.

Regarding our memory encryption approach, we insert a callback function to PIN[4], thus intercepting each of the original instructions and we instrument the ones that either load or store data from or to the main memory respectively. We then extract the data from the utilized register and we apply encryption or decryption depending on the instrumented instruction. Both encryption and decryption are performed using the AES-NI instructions. The output of these cryptographic operations replaces the original register's value and the program continue its execution to the next instruction.

To evaluate the performance of our approach along with the overhead imposed by the binary instrumentation, we measure the performance of (i) a vanilla application (listed as Native), (ii) a dynamic instrumentation of the application's store and load instructions using PIN (listed as PIN), and finally (iii) our approach: encryption with AES using dynamic instrumentation (listed as PIN+Encryption). To measure the plain instrumentation overhead produced by PIN (case (ii)), we perform memory instruction instrumentation with empty function calls, instead of any cryptographic operation.

---

[4] The confidentiality of Pintool's code falls beyond the scope of this study, in this paper we only care about the sensitive data of an application.

Benchmarks: In the first experiment, we measure the performance of FME using several representative benchmarks, extracted from the SPEC CPU2006 suite (CINT2006). These benchmarks are comprised of several computational and memory intensive applications aiming to stress both CPU and main memory usage. In Fig. 4, we see the portion of cryptographic operations in each benchmark and in Fig. 5, the slowdown of a simple dynamic instrumentation of the application's load and store instructions (PIN). This number gives us a baseline for the overhead introduced by the PIN tool. In the same figure, we present the results of the instrumentation with the appropriate AES-NI instructions to encrypt or decrypt every chunk of memory that is stored in or loaded from the main memory (PIN+Encryption). As we can see, the run-time overhead of simply instrumenting the application's load and store instructions reaches up to 6 times slowdown for `h264ref` benchmark, while the additional overhead when adding encryption reaches up to 10 times slowdown. The major slowdown in performance arises from the fact that the data are encrypted and decrypted even when residing in the cache. As the caches in `x86` architecture are not addressable, data can reside there in clear-text, without the concern of being leaked. Unfortunately, as it is not possible to check if specific data are cached or not, we cannot benefit from memory locality. In Fig. 6, we measure the instructions per memory access with and without our memory encryption approach. As we see, the average encryption cost is an additional 14–18 instructions. This number is not constant; it depends on the benchmark's synthesis of memory accesses and how sequentially the data are being accessed. Due to our pre-fetching mechanism (described in Figs. 2 and 3): (i) in case of store, encryption takes place only every 2 words (load from register previous word and encrypt the pair - 28 instr.), when (ii) in case of load, the word can be fetched directly from register (8 instr.) or retrieved after decrypting a block (then the unneeded second word has to be stored in the register - 26 instr.).

Real-World Applications: Additionally, we evaluate our approach in a real scenario using two real-world applications. The first, is the SQLite3 relational database management system. We used the C/C++ SQLite interface to implement a simple benchmark that reads a large, 60 MBytes, tab-separated file including 1,000,000 rows of data and updates a table's entries with the respective

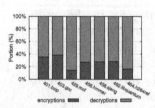 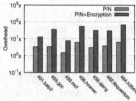 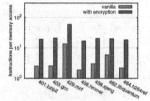

Fig. 4. Portion of cryptographic operations in each SPEC benchmark.

Fig. 5. Runtime overhead of dynamic instrumentation using the SPEC suite.

Fig. 6. Number of instructions per memory access with and without memory encryption (vanilla).

values. Figure 7 shows the achieved throughput, while Fig. 8 shows the slowdown when inserting data into the database as a function of the number of insertions. As expected, the more rows the benchmark updates, the higher the imposed overhead becomes, since the number of memory encryptions increases. In contrast to that, the cost of the instruction instrumentation (PIN) is always proportional to the number of the table insert instructions, resulting to almost linear overhead to the application.

As a second real-world application, we ran the Lighttpd web server both as a vanilla system and with the two versions of dynamic instrumentation In the first experiment, we used a separate machine located on the same local network to repeatedly download a file of 1522 bytes. We synthetically limit the rate of the client's network line to three different network transfer rates: 10, 100 and 1000 Mbit/sec. As can be seen in Fig. 9, when the bandwidth for the client is 10 Mbit/sec, the memory encryption overhead is almost hidden by the the network latency. As a result, the user faces a negligible slowdown of 0.17% for having FME enabled when the cost for the instrumentation is an additional 0.4%. On the other hand, the corresponding overhead for encryption at the higher rate of 1000 Mbit/sec reaches up to 43.7%. Our results indicate that in real-world applications over the Internet the cost for keeping a web server's memory fully encrypted is practically tolerated.

We conduct follow up experiments modifying the usage scenario in the following way. We use the same machine and the same three different network transfer rates to repeatedly download 9 files of different sizes, ranging from 1 KB to 256 MB. We then measure the average requests per second performed for each file. To make this experiment as realistic as possible, we use the most representative workloads found in production web servers. Such workloads include queries for short snippets of HTML (about 1 KB), e.g. user updates in micro-blogging services like Twitter or Tumblr, or portions of articles found in wikis (2.8 KB on average). Other workloads include photo objects of 25 KB size on average, used in photo-sharing sites that serve thumbnails. In general, as reported in [10], the most common file size is between 2–4 KB and regard HTML files, while 95% of all files are less than 64 KB in size. In Fig. 10(a), (b) and (c) we present our results for the same experiment in the network transfer rates used above: 10

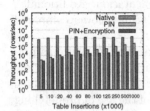

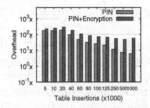

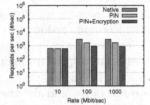

Fig. 7. Achieved throughput when inserting 1M rows into the database.

Fig. 8. Slowdown when inserting 1M rows into the database.

Fig. 9. Req/sec when downloading a file of 1522 bytes using different transfer rates.

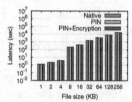 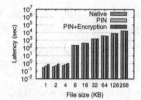 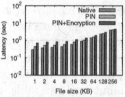

(a) Client is over a 10 Mbps network.   (b) Client is over a 100 Mbps network.   (c) Client is over a 1000 Mbps network.

Fig. 10. Average latency per request when downloading different files from a Lighttpd web server as a function of the requested file's size.

Mbps, 100 Mbps and 1000 Mbps. We immediately notice that in the case of 10 Mbps, the slowdown introduced from the memory encryption is close to zero, regardless the size of the downloaded file. In case of higher rates (i.e. 100 and 1000 Mbps) we observe that bigger files produce higher latency and as a consequence, hide the memory encryption cost. The average performance overhead imposed by encryption as calculated from the results in Fig. 10 is 17%.

Static Instrumentation

The alternative of dynamic instrumentation is to statically parse the executable and instrument the load and store instructions. Although this approach requires the instrumentation of all linked shared libraries as well, however it is able to provide significantly better performance. In the following experiment, we measure this performance, and more specifically, compare the execution time of the two different approaches. We use a very simple application which copies an array of 512 MB size, along with two secure versions of it: The first version, encrypts the array contents before storing them on main memory by dynamically instrumenting the store and load instructions using PIN. The second one statically encrypts the array's cells by utilizing in-line AES-NI assembly instructions. In the first two columns of Table 1 we can see the execution time of each approach as well as the imposed latency overhead compared to the unsecured native application and its binary instrumented version respectively. As we can see, the application with the dynamically instrumented encrypt/decrypt operations on the load and store instructions is 9.56 times slower than the plain instrumentation. Additionally, the static memory encryption makes the application 4.29 times slower compared to the insecure version.

Next, we statically instrument the same benchmarks of SPEC suite as previously and we perform main memory encryption measuring again the run-time overhead. In Fig. 11, we compare the overhead imposed by static and dynamic instrumentation and also the performance improvement of the use of pre-fetching in both cases. As expected static instrumentation performs better (almost 1.7x) than dynamic. In addition, we see that our pre-fetching mechanism, by reducing the number of cryptographic operations in sequential memory accesses, significantly reduces also the performance of our approach (4.9x on average).

Energy Efficiency

To accurately measure the energy efficiency of our approach we used 3 Phidgets high-precision current sensors [23] to constantly monitor the 3 ATX power-supply lines (+12.0a, +12.0b +5.0, +3.3 Volts), similar to [15]. The 12.0 Va line powers the processor, the 5.0 V line powers the memory, and the 3.3 V line powers the rest of the peripherals on the motherboard. For workload, we use the same array copy application from the prior experiment. We measure both versions in our power measurement above and the results are presented in the last two columns of Table 1. We can compare the energy efficiency of the four different approaches: (*i*) unprotected native application, (*ii*) the secure native application that statically encrypts array cells before storing them to memory, (*iii*) the unprotected native application over PIN instrumenting the plain load/store instructions, and (*iv*) the native application over PIN when instrumenting each load and store instruction with the appropriate AES-NI instructions. From the last column, we observe that the additional overhead is 3.6 times higher in case of the static memory encryption compared to native. When we used pin the cost of encryption/decryption is 13.12 times higher compared to the baseline PIN case.

Table 1. Encryption cost in the two implementations, in terms of execution time and power consumption.

	Type	Execution time (sec)	Overhead	Energy efficiency (Joules/mbit)	Overhead
Dynamic	PIN	2.064999	-	0.03983	-
	PIN+Encryption	19.73596	9.56x	0.52276	13.12339x
Static	Native	0.406917	-	0.00849	-
	Native+Encryption	1.745001	4.29x	0.03072	3.61776x

4.2   Selective Memory Encryption

As described in Sect. 3, contrary to Full Memory Encryption one may prefer to follow a more Selective Memory Encryption (SME) strategy to reduce the imposed overhead. To evaluate this strategy, we implemented a s_malloc prototype, to explicitly mark some data as sensitive and only encrypt this data before storing them to memory. Additionally we created a custom benchmark which copies different sized chunks of data from a large array to the heap. Figure 12(a) shows the results for execution time as a function of the portion of data considered as sensitive. As expected, the native application using s_malloc without instrumentation increases with the percentage of sensitive data. On the other hand, the cost of instrumentation is also increasing but not as rapidly since it does not depend on the data being stored in memory. Hence, as can be seen in Fig. 12(b) the instrumentation overhead over native is actually decreasing as the

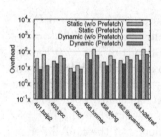

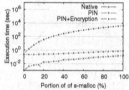

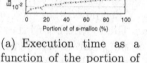

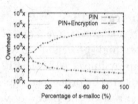

(a) Execution time as a function of the portion of sensitive data.

(b) Overhead over native as a function of the portion of sensitive data.

Fig. 11. Overheads of static and dynamic instrumentation with and without prefetching for the different benchmarks.

Fig. 12. Storing different portion of an array's data to the heap. Data considered as sensitive gets encrypted before sent to main memory.

percentage of data increases. Furthermore, the overhead caused by the memory encryption follows a logarithmic growth with the increasing percentage of data being encrypted. Thus, in case of a chunk of data including 10% of sensitive information, the cost to guarantee its confidentiality is latency 24.90 times higher than the unencrypted case.

In our macro-benchmarks, we used the Lighthttpd web server as a real world application example and the popular Apache HTTP server benchmarking tool of ApacheBench (ab). Web services are a good case of a single physical machine serving multiple users who need to be assured that sessions will be secure during their online transactions. As a result, we can state that the keys used from the web service during the HTTPS protocol are highly sensitive, and in need of protection against unauthorized access.

In our following experiment, we use Lighttpd web server in conjunction with WolfSSL Embedded SSL Library. Inside the latter we integrated s_malloc right at the point that the private key gets stored in memory. This way, while using dynamic instrumentation we are able to selectively encrypt only the particular sensitive information of the key. Figure 13 presents the average latency of the SSL handshake while using SME and considering the server's private key as sensitive. As we can see, this latency has been measured when the client over different network rates (i.e. 10 Mbps, 100 Mbps and 1000 Mbps) downloads different file sizes over the secure channel. It is apparent that since the SSL handshake happens when initializing the connection it is independent from the file size. Still, SSL uses sessions in order to restrict the number of SSL handshakes. As such, for each SSL handshake tens of KBs are typically exchanged over the same session, converging the network latency in both secure and non-secure cases when using a commodity network transfer rate. Consequently, the additional latency caused by SME is concealed by the network latency. The average performance overhead imposed by encryption as calculated from the results in Fig. 13 is below 27%.

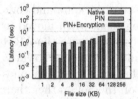
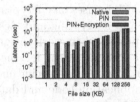
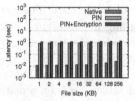

(a) Client is over a 10 Mbps network.
(b) Client is over a 100 Mbps network.
(c) Client is over a 1000 Mbps network.

Fig. 13. Average latency for performing an SSL handshake during a client's connection to a web server where the latter's private key is considered as sensitive.

5   Limitations

A major limitation of memory encryption approaches arises in cases where shared memory is deployed across different processes. To communicate correctly, processes have to maintain the same secret key, or use a different secret key which will use separately for encrypting and decrypting the contents of the shared memory. To deal with such cases, the OS kernel should be responsible for creating different secret keys for each memory segment that is instantiated, and attached it to each participant process. Similar inconveniences also arise for devices that allow data transfers via DMA. The exchanged data have to be unencrypted, since the connected devices are not aware of the encryption scheme. As it is easy to overcome these scenarios in hardware-based implementations (e.g. by performing the corresponding cipher operations at the I/O bus), it is not straightforward to provide a solution in software-only approaches. In some cases, where the device already provides a programmable interface (e.g. Endage DAG network cards, general-purpose graphics cards, etc.), it would be possible to implement the encryption and decryption operations on the device and pre-share the secret key with them.

6   Related Work

There are various approaches proposed, implemented either in software or hardware, aiming to defend against cold-boot attacks in both academia and industry.

Software-Based Mechanisms. Halderman et al. described cold boot attacks [12], and also discussed some forms of mitigation. Mitigations included deleting sensitive data and keys from memory when an encrypted drive is unmounted, obfuscation techniques, and hardware modifications such as intrusion-detection sensors or encased RAM. However, the authors, eventually admit that these solutions do not constitute complete countermeasures, applicable to general-purpose hardware. In [30], the authors assume a powerful attacker with physical access to the machine and able to launch DMA attacks, bus snooping attacks and cold boot attacks in order to disclosure sensitive data residing in the main memory. Their approach focuses on encrypting sensitive data and code residing in the main memory and decrypting and locking them when moved in the cache. Contrary to our approach, their work is tightly woven with the ARM System-on-Chip (SoC) specific features, cache locking and TrustZone. Towards the same direction, Sentry [9], uses ARM-specific mechanisms in smarphones and tablets to keep sensitive application code and data on the SoC rather than on DRAM. They observe that sensitive state data only need to be encrypted when the device is screen-locked. Consequently, Sentry decrypts and encrypts the memory pages of sensitive applications as they are paged in and out, thus avoiding leakage of sensitive information to DRAM when the device is screen-locked. AESSE [19] was designed to provide Full Disk Encryption (FDE) and protect the required keys by storing the encryption key in the Streaming SIMD Extension (SSE) registers of the CPU, while access to these registers is disabled for user-level code. The authors however, admit that many common applications (like multimedia applications e.g. OpenGL) really need SSE registers and therefore there is a significant collision with AESSE. TRESOR [20] is a kernel module and successor of AESSE. Instead of the SSE registers it utilizes the debug registers to store the encryption key. In addition, similar to our approach, it leverages AES-NI instruction set to eliminate cold boot attacks achieving this way far better performance than the AESSE. PrivateCore's commercial product, namely vCage [25], relies on a trusted hypervisor to implement FME for commodity hardware by executing guest VMs entirely in-cache and encrypting their data before they get evicted to main memory. Although it is more cloud-oriented, vCage shares with our approach similar resistance to the same type of physical attacks.

Hardware-Based Mechanisms. Trustwave's BitArmor [17], is a commercial solution that claims to be resistant against cold boot attacks. BitArmor tries to shield the system as soon as abnormal environment conditions are detected. More specifically, it uses temperature sensors and in case a sudden temperature drop is detected it initializes a memory wiping process. As demonstrated in a recent study [11], this approach raises the bar, but it cannot prevent the attack. Finally, Intel provides processors with Software Guard Extensions (SGX) [14]. These extensions aim to enable applications to encrypt specific data by placing them inside secure memory regions, called enclaves. The data that reside in enclaves are protected even in the presence of privileged malware. However, SGX does not allow dynamic creation of enclave pages at runtime, it can currently be used only to encrypt static data, typically secret or private keys [3]. As such, SGX is a complementary technology to our approach, that can be used to provide us with a protected area of storing the secret keys that are used to encrypt the full application's data, that are stored in either statically or dynamically allocated memory areas.

7   Conclusions

In this paper we design the first to our knowledge software-only main memory encryption of a running process and we set out to explore the imposed overhead when following different strategies (full Vs. selective memory encryption-dynamic instrumentation Vs. static patching). Contrary to hardware-based approaches, our work can be directly applied to commodity systems without any architectural support. Our solution leverages AES-NI instructions when our performance analysis uses both benchmarks and real world applications. Results of our work show that the average overhead of the encryption cost in real-world applications was 17% and 27% for HTTP and HTTPS respectively.

Acknowledgements. The research leading to these results has received funding from the European Unions Horizon 2020 Research and Innovation Programme, under Grant Agreement no. 700378 and project H2020 ICT-32-2014 "SHARCS" under Grant Agreement No. 644571.

References

1. Abramson, D., Jackson, J., Muthrasanallur, S., Neiger, G., Regnier, G., Sankaran, R., Schoinas, I., Uhlig, R., Vembu, B., Wiegert, J.: Intel virtualization technology for directed i/o. Intel Technol. J. **10**(3)
2. Advanced Micro Devices Inc. AMD I/O Virtualization Technology (IOMMU). http://support.amd.com/TechDocs/48882_IOMMU.pdf
3. Baumann, A., Peinado, M., Hunt, G.: Shielding applications from an untrusted cloud with haven. TCS **33**(3) (2015)
4. Berkowits, S.: Pin - a dynamic binary instrumentation tool (2012). https://software.intel.com/en-us/articles/pin-a-dynamic-binary-instrumentation-tool
5. Blass, E.-O., Robertson, W.: TRESOR-HUNT: attacking CPU-bound encryption. In: Proceedings of the 28th Annual Computer Security Applications Conference, ACSAC 2012 (2012)
6. Boileau, A.: Hit by a bus: Physical access attacks with firewire. Presentation, Ruxcon
7. Champagne, D., Lee, R.B.: Scalable architectural support for trusted software. In: HPCA - 16 2010 The Sixteenth International Symposium on High-Performance Computer Architecture, HPCA 2010 (2010)
8. Chan, E.M., Carlyle, J.C., David, F.M., Farivar, R., Campbell, R.H.: Bootjacker: compromising computers using forced restarts. In: Proceedings of the 15th ACM Conference on Computer and Communications Security, CCS 2008 (2008)
9. Colp, P., Zhang, J., Gleeson, J., Suneja, S., de Lara, E., Raj, H., Saroiu, S., Wolman, A.: Protecting data on smartphones and tablets from memory attacks. In: Proceedings of the Twentieth International Conference on ASPLOS 2015 (2015)
10. Dilley, J.A.: Web server workload characterization. Hewlett-Packard Laboratories, Technical Publications Department
11. Gruhn, M., Müller, T.: On the practicability of cold boot attacks. In: Proceedings of the 2013 International Conference on ARES 2013 (2013)
12. Halderman, J.A., Schoen, S.D., Heninger, N., Clarkson, W., Paul, W., Calandrino, J.A., Feldman, A.J., Appelbaum, J., Felten, E.W.: Lest we remember: cold-boot attacks on encryption keys. Commun. ACM **52**(5) (2009)

13. Henson, M., Taylor, S.: Memory encryption: a survey of existing techniques. ACM Comput. Surv. **46**(4)

14. Intel Corporation. Software guard extensions programming reference. https:// software.intel.com/sites/default/files/managed/48/88/329298-002.pdf

15. Koromilas, L., Vasiliadis, G., Manousakis, I., Ioannidis, S.: Efficient software packet processing on heterogeneous and asymmetric hardware architectures. In: Proceedings of the Tenth ACM/IEEE Symposium on Architectures for Networking and Communications Systems, ANCS 2014 (2014)

16. Markuze, A., Morrison, A., Tsafrir, D.: True IOMMU protection from DMA attacks: when copy is faster than zero copy. In: Proceedings of the Twenty-First International Conference on Architectural Support for Programming Languages and Operating Systems, ASPLOS 2016 (2016)

17. McGregor, P., Hollebeek, T., Volynkin, A., White, M.: Braving the cold: new methods for preventing cold boot attacks on encryption keys. In: Black Hat Security Conference (2008)

18. Morris, R., Thompson, K.: Password security: a case history. Commun. ACM

19. Müller, T., Dewald, A., Freiling, F.C.: AESSE: a cold-boot resistant implementation of AES. In: Proceedings of the Third European Workshop on System Security, EUROSEC 2010 (2010)

20. Müller, T., Freiling, F.C., Dewald, A.: Tresor runs encryption securely outside ram. In: Proceedings of the 20th USENIX Conference on Security, SEC 2011. USENIX Association (2011)

21. Nagarajan, V., Gupta, R., Krishnaswamy, A.: Compiler-assisted memory encryption for embedded processors. In: Bosschere, K., Kaeli, D., Stenström, P., Whalley, D., Ungerer, T. (eds.) HiPEAC 2007. LNCS, vol. 4367, pp. 7–22. Springer, Heidelberg (2007). doi:10.1007/978-3-540-69338-3_2

22. Ou, G.: Cryogenically frozen ram bypasses all disk encryption methods. http://www.zdnet.com/article/cryogenically-frozen-ram-bypasses-all-disk-encryp tion-methods/

23. Phidgets, Inc. 1122_0 – 30 Amp Current Sensor AC/DC. http://www.phidgets. com/products.php?category=8&product_id=1122_0

24. Piegdon, D.R.: Hacking in physically addressable memory: a proof of concept. http://eh2008.koeln.ccc.de/fahrplan/attachments/1067_SEAT1394-svn-r432 -paper.pdf

25. PrivateCore. Trustworthy computing for OpenStack with vCage. http:// privatecore.com/vcage/

26. Simmons, P.: Security through amnesia: a software-based solution to the cold boot attack on disk encryption. In: Proceedings of the 27th Annual Computer Security Applications Conference, ACSAC 2011 (2011)

27. Skorobogatov, S.: Low temperature data remanence in static ram (2002)

28. Stewin, P., Bystrov, I.: Understanding DMA malware. In: Flegel, U., Markatos, E., Robertson, W. (eds.) DIMVA 2012. LNCS, vol. 7591, pp. 21–41. Springer, Heidelberg (2013). doi:10.1007/978-3-642-37300-8_2

29. Wetzels, J.: Hidden in snow, revealed in thaw: cold boot attacks revisited. CoRR, abs/1408.0725

30. Zhang, N., Sun, K., Lou, W., Hou, Y.T.: Case: cache-assisted secure execution on arm processors. In: 2016 IEEE Symposium on Security and Privacy (SP), S&P 2016 (2016)

Inference-Proof Updating of a Weakened View Under the Modification of Input Parameters

Joachim Biskup[✉] and Marcel Preuß[✉]

Technische Universität Dortmund, Dortmund, Germany
{joachim.biskup,marcel.preuss}@cs.tu-dortmund.de

Abstract. We treat a challenging problem of confidentiality-preserving data publishing: how to repeatedly update a released weakened view under a modification of the input parameter values, while continuously enforcing the confidentiality policy, i.e., without revealing a prohibited piece of information, neither for the updated view nor retrospectively for the previous versions of the view. In our semantically ambitious approach, a weakened view is determined by a two-stage procedure that takes three input parameters: (i) a confidentiality policy consisting of prohibitions in the form of pieces of information that the pertinent receiver of the view should not be able to learn, (ii) the assumed background knowledge of that receiver, and (iii) the actually stored relation instance, or the respective modification requests. Assuming that the receiver is aware of the specification of both the underlying view generation procedure and the proposed updating procedure and additionally of the declared confidentiality policy, the main challenge has been to block all meta-inferences that the receiver could make by relating subsequent views.

Keywords: Background knowledge · Inference-proofness · History-awareness · Meta-inference · Policy of prohibitions · Relational database · Semantic confidentiality · Update · View generation · Weakened information

1 Introduction

Within a framework of cooperating with partners and sharing resources with them, managing the fundamental asset of own information – whether personal or institutional – has evolved as a main challenge of IT-security, leading to diverse computational techniques to enforce all kinds of an owner's interests. This includes confidentiality-preserving data publishing [8] aiming at hiding specific pieces of information while still providing sufficient availability. One class of techniques for confidentiality-preserving data publishing distorts data by weakening the still true information content of released data, e.g., by explicitly erasing sensitive data or by substituting sensitive data items by suitably generalized ones, as for instance applied for k-anonymization with l-diversification [12,15,17].

© Springer International Publishing AG 2017
S.N. Foley et al. (Eds.): ESORICS 2017, Part II, LNCS 10493, pp. 381–401, 2017.
DOI: 10.1007/978-3-319-66399-9_21

Whereas the effectiveness of many such techniques relies on the appropriateness of more or less intuitive concepts, like, e.g., quasi-identifiers, our own approach has more ambitiously been based on a fully formalized notion of semantic confidentiality in terms of inference-proofness. This notion considers an authorized receiver that profits from some background knowledge and unlimited computational resources for rational reasoning. More specifically, in previous work [4] we conceptually designed a two-stage *view generation* procedure that weakens the information content of an actually stored relation instance, and we verified the requested confidentiality property and experimentally evaluated the runtime efficiency. This procedure takes three input parameters, (i) a *confidentiality policy* consisting of prohibitions in the form of pieces of information that the pertinent receiver of the view should not be able to learn, (ii) the assumed *background knowledge* of that receiver in the form of single-premise tuple-generating data dependencies, and (iii) the actually stored *relation instance*.

Example 1 (weakened view). Let R be a relation symbol (table name) with three attributes (columns) with (conceptually) countably infinite domains, having the current relation instance $r = \{(a,b,c),(a,c,c),(b,a,c)\}$ under closed-world assumption. Expressed in terms of first-order logic as a basis for formal semantics of relational databases [1], this means that the three ground atoms $R(a,b,c)$, $R(a,c,c)$ and $R(b,a,c)$ are evaluated to *true*, whereas all other syntactically possible ground atoms are considered to be evaluated to *false*. For the moment still neglecting background knowledge, let us further suppose that the data owner wants to prohibit that the anticipated receiver of the view to be generated could ever learn that $R(a,b,c)$ is *true*, and so for $R(a,b,d)$. Obviously, that view should not reveal that the tuple (a,b,c) is an element of the relation instance r.

The view generation procedure of [4] achieves this goal as follows. In the first stage, only treating the considered prohibitions, the procedure forms a disjunctive template $R(a,b,c) \lor R(a,b,d)$ (notably, the truth evaluation of which is *not* prohibited to be known). In the second stage, the procedure checks each ground atom that is *true* in the instance whether it entails a disjunctive template. If this is the case the procedure replaces the ground atom by all those templates, thus weakening the originally complete information about the ground atom into still *true* disjunctions. Thus, so far, the view consists of the (distorted) *disjunctive part* $R(a,b,c) \lor R(a,b,d)$ and the (untouched) *positive part* formed by $R(a,c,c)$ and $R(b,a,c)$. Moreover, these parts are complemented by an (adapted) *negative part* that replaces the original closed-world assumption by a first-order sentence intuitively expressing that any ground atom that does not entail any element of the disjunctive part and of the positive part should be evaluated to *false*:

$$(\forall X)(\forall Y)(\forall Z)\,[(X \equiv a \land Y \equiv b \land Z \equiv c) \lor (X \equiv a \land Y \equiv b \land Z \equiv d) \lor$$
$$(X \equiv a \land Y \equiv c \land Z \equiv c) \lor (X \equiv b \land Y \equiv a \land Z \equiv c) \lor \neg R(X,Y,Z)\,].$$

The weakened view consisting of the three parts does not entail any of the prohibited sentences. Moreover, capturing the receiver's assumed awareness of the control mechanism, the view is even *inference-proof* in the sense that for each prohibited sentence Ψ there is a fictitious "alternative" relation instance r^{Ψ} that would generate the same view as r and make Ψ *false*. In fact, after seeing the view and in particular learning the truth of the disjunction $R(a, b, c) \lor R(a, b, d)$, the receiver can not distinguish whether only $R(a, b, c)$ is *true* or only $R(a, b, d)$ is *true* or both $R(a, b, c)$ and $R(a, b, d)$ are *true*.

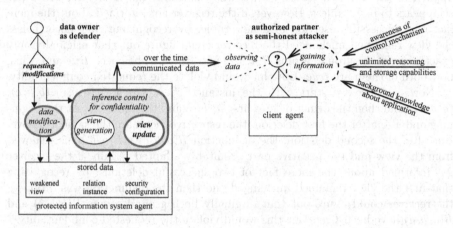

Fig. 1. Visualization of the problem of confidentiality-preserving view updating

Considering the situation roughly visualized in Fig. 1, in the present work we address and solve the problem of efficiently *updating* a released weakened view under a modification of the input parameter values, while *continuously* enforcing the confidentiality policy, i.e., without revealing a prohibited piece of information, neither for the updated view nor retrospectively for the previous versions of the view. Conservatively assuming that the receiver is aware of the specification of both the view generation procedure and the updating procedure and, additionally, of the declared confidentiality policy – and thus of the whole security configuration consisting of the policy and the background knowledge – the main challenge has been to block all *meta-inferences* that the receiver could draw by relating subsequent views. The wanted blocking is achieved by establishing sufficient *indistinguishability* between the actual, possibly harmful situation and a fictitious harmless situation.

In Sect. 2, besides briefly discussing related work, we identify some basic conditions for achieving our goal in a still intuitive style. Then, in Sect. 3 we introduce our formal framework in order to prepare for proving precise assurances about our solution. This solution is presented and analyzed in Sect. 4. Finally, in Sect. 5 we report on the practical efficiency of a prototype implementation.

2   Conditions for Inference-Proof View Updating

Example 2 (instance modification). Continuing Example 1, let the owner now insert the tuple (a, b, d) into the relation instance r. The corresponding ground fact $R(a, b, d)$ entails the disjunctive template $R(a, b, c) \vee R(a, b, d)$, which however is already contained in the view, such that the view generation algorithm applied to the updated relation r' returns the same view as before, which per se appears to be harmless. However, if the receiver got informed about the mere fact of a successful insertion of a new tuple, by recognizing that nevertheless the view remained unchanged the receiver could figure out that originally only exactly one of the ground atoms $R(a, b, c)$ and $R(a, b, d)$ has been *true* and, thus, now both of them are *true*. But this would violate the requested confidentiality.

Now, suppose we start with the instance $r' = \{(a, b, c), (a, c, c), (b, a, c), (a, b, d)\}$ and then the owner deletes first (a, b, c) and then (a, b, d). At the beginning and also after the first deletion, the respective views are the same as above. But after the second deletion, the disjunction $R(a, b, c) \vee R(a, b, d)$ is removed from the view and the negative part is suitably adapted. Again, if the receiver got informed about the mere fact of two successful deletions, by recognizing that first the view remained unchanged and then the disjunction was dropped, the receiver could figure out that originally both ground atoms $R(a, b, c)$ and $R(a, b, d)$ have been *true*. But this would violate the requested confidentiality.

Such a kind of challenge has been identified earlier for diverse and only partially comparable settings, briefly and selectively classified in the following and further surveyed in Table 1; see also Sect. 6 of [8]. The *owner's data* might be either a relation instance focused on individuals [2,7,11,16,18–20] or, more generically, any logic-oriented knowledge or belief base which includes any relation instance under closed world assumption (this work, [3,5,6]). The *protection need* might refer to either the values of a sensitive attribute [2,7,11,16,18–20] or a suitable class of sentences in the underlying logic (this work, [3,5,6]), aiming at either a suitably strengthened version of l-diversity (with match-uncertainty [11]) or a general notion of continuous semantic indistinguishability, respectively. Similarly, the *background knowledge* might dedicatedly consist of either the population concerned [2,7,11,16,18–20] (under uniform publication procedures [11]) or, more generically, of a suitable class of sentences in the underlying logic (this work, [3,5,6]). Regarding *modifications*, there might be either none but only sequential releases of different views [18,20] or independently by other publishers [11], or insertion of tuples only [7,16] or both insertion and deletion of tuples [19] or, additionally, also value modification [2,3,5] or belief modification [6] or transactional modifications of not only the instance but also of the background knowledge and the confidentiality policy (this work). The *modification request* might be issued by either the information owner (this and most other work), or by the attacking receiver [3,5,6], as already earlier studied for mandatory multilevel databases with polyinstantiation. And the main *distortion* kind might be either lying [3] or refusals [5,6] or value generalization [2,7,11,16,18–20] or weakening by disjunctions (this work), the three latter ones possibly complemented by either restricted lying by fake tuples [2,19] or sampling and noise addition [11] or restricted refusals (this work).

Table 1. Properties of selected approaches to confidentiality-preserving updating

Approach/Reference	Original Data	Background Knowledge	Confident. Policy	Kind of Modification	Notion of Confidentiality	Interaction with Receiver	Kind of Distortion	Communicated Data
Yao/Wang Jajodia 2005 [20]	relation instance (about individuals)	represented individuals with their identifiers; functional dependencies	values of a sensitive attribute for individuals	none (fixed set of tuples)	possibilistic k-anonymity for sensitive attribute	sequential release publishing of (select-project views)	none (only checking)	select-project views
Wang/Fung 2006 [18]	relation instance (about individuals)	represented individuals with their identifiers	values of sensitive attributes for individuals	none (fixed set of tuples)	probabilistic l-diversity for sensitive attribute (as (X,Y)-privacy)	sequential release publishing of projections	generalization of attributes leading to a quasi-identifier	anonymized (generalized) projections
Xiao/Tao 2007 [19]	relation instance about individuals	"lifespans" of represented individuals with their quasi-identifiers	values of a sensitive attribute for individuals	tuple insertion and deletion	probabilistic (lifespan-persistent) m-invariance for sensitive attribute	continuous (full) data publishing	generalization of quasi-identifiers and (lied) fake tuples	anonymized (generalized) instances with counts for fake tuples
Byun et al 2009 [7]	relation instance about individuals	"lifespans" of represented individuals with their quasi-identifiers	values of a sensitive attribute for individuals	tuple insertion	probabilistic "cross-version safe" k-anonymity with l-diversity for sensitive attribute	continuous (full) data publishing	generalization of quasi-identifiers with attack-checking of a "history table"	anonymized (generalized) instances
Shmueli/Tassa 2015 [16]	relation instance about individuals	represented individuals with their quasi-identifiers	values of a sensitive attribute for individuals	tuple insertion	probabilistic l-diversity of "possible worlds" for sensitive attribute	sequential release and continuous data publishing (of projections)	generalization of quasi-identifiers using (lied) "fake worlds"	anonymized (generalized) projections
Li/et al 2016 [11]	relation instance about individuals	represented individuals with their quasi-identifiers; uniform publishing	values of a sensitive attribute for individuals	none (fixed set of tuples)	probabilistic uncertainty about matches with independent releases	single (full) publishing, independently of overlapping further releases	generalization of quasi-identifiers and sensitive values; sampling; noise addition	anonymized (generalized, distorted) instance
Anjum et al 2017 [2]	relation instance about individuals	represented individuals with their quasi-identifiers and event-lists	values of a sensitive attribute for individuals	tuple insertion and deletion; modification in quasi-identifiers and sensitive att.	probabilistic τ-safety for sensitive attribute	continuous (full) data publishing	generalization of quasi-identifiers and (lied) fake tuples	anonymized (generalized) instances
Biskup et al 2011 [3]	complete propositional knowledge base	propositional sentences	any propositional sentences	view update transactions; view refreshments	continuous semantic possibilistic indistinguishability	query and update evaluations	lying	controlled (refreshed) query answers and notifications
Biskup/Tadros 2012 [5]	complete propositional knowledge base	propositional sentences	any propositional sentences	view update transactions	continuous or temporary semantic possibilistic indistinguishability	(knowledge) query and update evaluations	refusal	controlled query answers and notifications
Biskup/Tadros 2013 [6]	(incomplete) propositional belief base	initial belief approximation; class of nonmonotonic (belief) reasoning	any propositional sentences	belief revisions	temporary semantic skeptically possibilistic indistinguishability	(belief) query and revision evaluations	refusal	controlled query answers and notifications
published weakened views [this work]	relation instance with closed world assumption	single-premise tuple-generating dependencies	first-order sentences restricted to existential facts	transactions for modification of instance, background and policy	continuous semantic possibilistic indistinguishability	full view publishing	weakening by disjunctions (with some refusals)	positive, disjunctive, negative and refused data; notifications

Example 3 (policy modification). Again extending Example 1, let the owner now specify $R(a,c,c)$ as a new prohibition in the confidentiality policy. The first stage of the view generation procedure would aim at forming a disjunctive template covering the specified new prohibition and also being disjoint from all other templates. To achieve these goals, the procedure has to select an additional (artificial) prohibition, say $R(b,c,c)$, and might then add $R(a,c,c) \lor R(b,c,c)$ as a further disjunctive template. Since the tuple (a,c,c) is an element of the relation instance r, the ground fact $R(a,c,c)$ should no longer appear in the positive part of the modified view generated in the second stage. Instead, the weakening disjunction $R(a,c,c) \lor R(b,c,c)$ should become a further element of the disjunctive part, with the negative part being suitably adapted.

However, if the receiver could be sure that the relation instance r has not been modified, he would still know that $R(a,c,c)$ is *true*. This would violate the new prohibition and, thus, the weakening would be useless. In other words, if previous knowledge about the instance already indicates a violation of the modified policy, then inference-proofness of the updated view can not be achieved. This problem can be resolved by requiring that each modification of the confidentiality policy occurs as part of a *transaction* that might also comprise instance modifications, and thus previous knowledge about the instance could be no longer be valid.

More generally, also dealing with background knowledge as discussed below, we will show that always leaving the receiver uninformed about the kind of the requested modifications – in particular uncertain about additional instance modifications that are not reflected in the new weakened view – is sufficient to enforce the wanted notion of confidentiality. The examples considered so far together with the claimed generalized insights indicate that the underlying view generation procedure enjoys reasonable robustness regarding modifications of the instance and the policy. This behavior mainly results from two fundamental features of the overall approach: the *two-stage design* dealing with the policy and the instance separately, and the *strict isolation* of the three parts of a weakened view regarding entailments. However, achieving this isolation in the presence of *background knowledge*, so far neglected, requires quite subtle considerations presented in [4] and in more detail in [14].

In particular, and only briefly sketched, background knowledge affects the forming of disjunctive templates in the first stage of the view generation procedure in two ways. First, it might become necessary to introduce further prohibitions, which in particular strengthens the needs to clean the (extended) policy from redundancies. Second, the background knowledge has to be partitioned regarding unwanted joint entailment effects such that, roughly described, disjunctive templates have to be formed of suitably "independent" prohibitions that are not affected by sentences of the same partition block. In more general terms, the set of disjunctive templates might be modified. Moreover, in some cases the weakened view has to additionally comprise a *refused* part consisting of so-called *refusals*, i.e., sentences whose truth evaluations are explicitly denied · whatever the stored relation might look like.

Example 4 (background modification). Again continuing Example 1, let now the database application have been changed such that *in future* all relation instances will satisfy the data dependency $R(a, b, d) \Rightarrow R(c, c, c)$. Moreover, let the owner assume that the receiver can henceforth exploit this dependency as his background knowledge. As known to him by the negative part of the view, $(a, b, d) \notin r$ and thus the premise of the dependency is not *true*. So, at first glance the dependency seems to be not helpful for the receiver. A second thought, however, easily indicates that the following inference would be enabled.

Since also $(c, c, c) \notin r$ and thus the conclusion $R(c, c, c)$ of the dependency is not *true* as well, applying the dependency in contraposition, i.e., $\neg R(c, c, c) \Rightarrow \neg R(a, b, d)$, the receiver can learn that $R(a, b, d)$ is *false*. Thus, given the truth of the disjunction $R(a, b, c) \vee R(a, b, d)$, the receiver can conclude that $R(a, b, c)$ is *true*. Hence, without suitable further precautions, the confidentiality policy would be violated. In fact, the underlying view generation procedure would already treat the conclusion $R(c, c, c)$ as a further prohibition.

The insights gained from the given examples and the lessons learnt from elaborating the above sketched solutions lead to the following list of conditions for inference-proof view updating:

– **C1:** (only) **conflict-free requests**:
An initial input control checks whether a modification request of the owner consists of insertions and deletions that are not conflicting. In particular, an item should not be required to be both inserted and deleted within the same modification request, and the items to be modified should be consistent.

– **C2:** (only) **transactions**:
The accepted inputs of the owner are processed as a transaction with semantics that lead to either a commit (all temporary modifications of the relation instance and the security configuration are made persistent) or an abort (the relation instance and the security configuration remain unchanged, i.e., all temporary actions are rollbacked).

– **C3:** (only) **possibly comprehensive transactions**:
Extending condition C2, additionally, (from the point of view of the receiver) the inputs for each transaction might be comprehensive, i.e., they might always comprise *all kinds* of modifications, i.e., simultaneously instance modifications, background modifications and policy modifications.

– **C4:** (only) **state-related invariants**:
Each invariant whose satisfaction is checked for the final decision on either committing or aborting the transaction only refers to the preliminarily generated internal situation, but not to the relationship between the previous one and the still preliminary one.

– **C5: notifications**:
The receiver is always notified about a request of the owner for modifications by either returning the updated weakened view or sending a note about an input rejection or a transaction abort, respectively.

- **C5*:** only **notifications of effective and committed transactions**:
  More restrictively, the receiver is notified about a request of the owner for modifications only if (i) the inputs are not rejected, (ii) the transaction has been committed and (iii) the view update has been effective, i.e., the weakened view has actually been changed. Otherwise, an owner's input attempt is totally invisible to the receiver.
- **C6: observability of the security configuration**:
  The receiver can always learn the somehow "posted" current security configuration which includes the awareness of related requests for modification (but the receiver can never see the current relation instance nor requests for instance modifications).

For most applications, we see no need to inform the receiver about internal modification requests that do not actually change the published view. Accordingly, as expressed by condition C5*, it appears to be reasonable to completely hide the processing of requests that do change the external view. Technically, condition C5* would require to consider possibly differing local times of the owner and of the receiver, respectively. Then, to distinguish points in time local to the owner that are observable by the receiver and those points that are not, we would have to employ a rather complicated formal representation of our approach.

However, under the remaining conditions C1–C6 we can show that our view update procedure is inference-proof even if the receiver can observe the fact (but not the internal effects) of unsuccessful internal processing. Accordingly, to simplify the presentation by avoiding asynchronous local times, we will elaborate our approach based on conditions C1–C6, with a global discrete time for both agents, with points in time $1, 2, \ldots$ used as synchronous timestamps.

3   Basic Concepts and Formal Definitions

We will formally define the *basic concepts* leading to the underlying *view generation* procedure, briefly summarize the assurances proved before in [4,14], and introduce a precise notion of *continuous inference-proofness* to be enforced by the new *view update* procedure. Figure 2 outlines the framework.

3.1   Database Management System

We consider a *relational database* management system, which is operated under the control of the data *owner*. The system is based on a single relational *schema*, which comprises a fixed relation *symbol* (table name) R, a fixed finite set of *attributes* (column names) $\mathcal{A} = \{A_1, \ldots, A_n\}$, each of which has the same *infinite domain Dom* of constants, and some possibly time-varying set SC_t of *semantic constraints*. At each point in time t the system maintains a database *instance* r_t, which is a finite set of tuples over $\mathcal{A}$ with values in Dom, satisfying the current semantic constraints in SC_t. Such an instance is treated as being *complete*: each tuple in r_t represents a fact that is *true* in some fictitious "real world"; whereas,

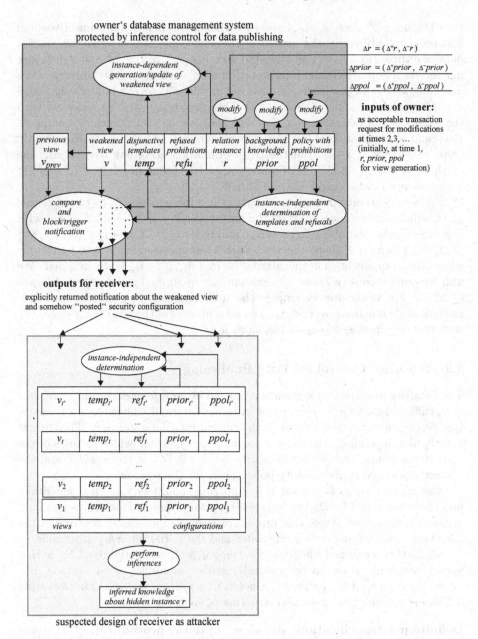

Fig. 2. Outline of the owner's protection (upper part) against the anticipated receiver seen as a rational, omnipotent and too-curious attacker (lower part)

by Closed World Assumption (CWA), each other tuple over $\mathcal{A}$ with values in Dom represents a possible fact which is *false* in that world.

We follow a foundation of the relational model of data in terms of *first-order logic* with equality, as also used, e.g., in [1,10]. Syntactically, the logic is specified by a language $\mathscr{L}$ over $\equiv$, R, $\mathcal{A}$, Dom, variables, propositional connectives and first-order quantifiers in the usual way. Semantically, for this logic we treat a database tuple $(a_1, \ldots, a_n)$ as a ground fact $R(a_1, \ldots, a_n) \in \mathscr{L}$ and a database instance as a finite Herbrand interpretation of $\mathscr{L}$ with the infinite universe Dom assuming *unique names*. Using an instance in this way, we can inductively assign a truth value to each sentence in $\mathscr{L}$. This foundation also provides us with the pertinent notions of *satisfaction* and *entailment*: an instance r, seen as an Herbrand interpretation of the kind described above, *satisfies* a sentence $\Phi \in \mathscr{L}$ (r is a model of Φ, $r \models \Phi$) iff the truth evaluation according to r returns the truth value *true*; a set $S \subseteq \mathscr{L}$ of sentences *entails* a sentence $\Phi \in \mathscr{L}$ ($S \models \Phi$) iff each instance r satisfying S also satisfies Φ.

For confidentiality policies we employ the sublanguage $\mathscr{L}_{exist}$ of *existential facts*, which are sentences in $\mathscr{L}$ of the form $(\exists X_{i_1}) \ldots (\exists X_{i_m}) R(t_1, \ldots, t_n)$ with pairwise different variables $X_{i_1}, \ldots, X_{i_m}$ and terms $t_{i_j} = X_{i_j}$ for $i_j \in \{i_1, \ldots, i_m\} \subseteq \{1, \ldots, n\}$ and $t_i \in Dom$ otherwise. Such a sentence corresponds to a subtuple where the components for the attributes in $\{A_{i_1}, \ldots, A_{i_m}\}$ are dropped. We also see ground facts (without any existentially quantified variables) as elements of $\mathscr{L}_{exist}$. For weakening we employ the sublanguage $\mathscr{L}_{exist}^{\vee}$ of strict and non-redundant *disjunctions* over $\mathscr{L}_{exist}$, i.e., all sentences of the form $\Psi_1 \vee \Psi_2 \vee \ldots \vee \Psi_k$ such that $k \geq 2$, $\Psi_i \in \mathscr{L}_{exist}$ and $\Psi_i \not\models \Psi_j$ for $i \neq j$.

3.2   Inference Control for Data Publishing

The database management system is protected by an *inference control* system for *data publishing*, which for each point in time t internally determines a receiver-specific current weakened view v_t on the current relation instance r_t. The current view v_t also depends on the current *security configuration*, which consists of the currently assumed background knowledge $prior_t \supseteq SC_t$ of the receiver, and the currently declared confidentiality policy $ppol_t$ for the receiver.

The initial view v_1 is generated by applying the underlying *view generation* procedure $vgen$ [4,14], i.e., $v_1 = vgen(r_1, prior_1, ppol_1)$. During its first still instance-independent stage, this procedure $vgen$ also internally determines the initial set $temp_1$ of disjunctive templates and the initial set $refu_1$ of refusals.

All further weakened views v_t, for times $t > 1$, are determined by a *view update* procedure $vupd$, to be presented in the remainder of this article, i.e., $v_t = vupd((\Delta^+ r_t, \Delta^- r_t), (\Delta^+ prior_t, \Delta^- prior_t), (\Delta^+ ppol_t, \Delta^- ppol_t))$. The following definition specifies the envisioned structure of such a procedure.

Definition 1 (specification of view update procedure). *At times* $t = 2, 3, \ldots$ *a view update* procedure *vupd determines a weakened view* $v_t = vupd((\Delta^+ r_t, \Delta^- r_t), (\Delta^+ prior_t, \Delta^- prior_t), (\Delta^+ ppol_t, \Delta^- ppol_t))$, *based on the previous internal owner state, defined by*

$$own_{t-1} = (v_{t-1}, temp_{t-1}, refu_{t-1}, r_{t-1}, prior_{t-1}, ppol_{t-1}), \tag{1}$$

and satisfying the following conditions:

- *The previous internal state own_{t-1} is accessible for the view update procedure vupd, but more aged internal states are not memorized.*
- *The explicit input parameter values $(\Delta^+r_t, \Delta^-r_t)$, $(\Delta^+prior_t, \Delta^-prior_t)$ and $(\Delta^+ppol_t, \Delta^-ppol_t)$ for the requested modifications are internally specified by the owner, for each parameter indicating which elements are to be inserted in and which elements are to be deleted from the previous state.*
- *A requested modification is actually accepted and committed only if (i) the input parameter values are conflict-free and (ii) all pertinent invariants expressed in terms of a state are maintained; otherwise the request would be rejected or aborted, respectively.*
- *The components of the internal state are updated as follows:*
  - $ppol_t := [ppol_{t-1} \cup \Delta^+ppol_t] \setminus \Delta^-ppol_t$;
  - $prior_t := [prior_{t-1} \cup \Delta^+prior_t] \setminus \Delta^-prior_t$;
  - $r_t := [r_{t-1} \cup \Delta^+r_t] \setminus \Delta^-r_t$;
  - $temp_t$ *and* $refu_t$ *are assigned the same results as the underlying view generation procedure vgen would do in its first stage;*
  - v_t *is assigned the return value of the view update procedure vupd.*
- *The receiver always gets notified about the fact of a modification request.*

Cautiously assuming condition C5 and suspecting the memorization of the full history, the observable effects of initial view generation and repeated view updates on the side of the receiver are represented by the sequence of current *attacker states*, each of them defined by $att_t = (v_t, temp_t, refu_t, prior_t, ppol_t)$.

3.3   The Underlying View Generation Procedure

The underlying *view generation* procedure $vgen(r, prior, ppol)$ [4,14] takes three inputs from the owner: a relation instance r, the assumed background knowledge *prior* of the receiver, and the confidentiality policy *ppol* for that receiver. During a first, still instance-independent stage, a subprocedure $vgen\_stage1(prior, ppol)$ internally determines a set *temp* of disjunctive templates and a set *refu* of elements stemming mainly from *ppol* and leading to refusals. In a second, instance-dependent stage, a subprocedure $vgen\_stage2(temp, refu, r)$ generates a weakened view v that consists of four parts: the refused knowledge $v^? := refu$, the positive knowledge v^+, the disjunctive knowledge $v^\vee$, and the negative knowledge v^-. In order to avoid inferences based on the editorial representation of these parts some final *normalization* based on standardized sorting is due. Accordingly, the view generation procedure has the following overall structure:

```
PROCEDURE vgen(r, prior, ppol) {
(temp, refu) := vgen_stage1(prior, ppol);
(v?, v+, v∨, v−) := vgen_stage2(temp, refu, r);
v := norm(v?, v+, v∨, v−);
notify receiver by sending v }
```

Employing first-order logic, all items are formalized by means of suitable subsets of $\mathscr{L}$. Capturing the intuitions and our goals on the one hand and facing the well-known difficulty of the computational unsolvability of the general entailment problem for the full first-order logic language $\mathscr{L}$ on the other hand, see, e.g., [13], we will apply the conventions summarized in the following.

Regarding the input parameters:

- The *relation instance* r is seen as a finite set of ground facts of the form $R(a_1, \ldots, a_n)$, complemented with a pertinent completeness sentence $Comp(r)$; i.e., for $r = \{(a_{1,1}, \ldots, a_{1,n}), \ldots, (a_{m,1}, \ldots, a_{m,n})\}$ we get

$$(\forall X_1) \ldots (\forall X_n)[\bigvee_{(a_{j,1}, \ldots, a_{j,n}) \in r} (\bigwedge_{i \in \{1, \ldots, n\}} X_i \equiv a_{j,i}) \lor \neg R(X_1, \ldots, X_n)].$$

- Establishing knowledge about the relationship of one single fact with another single fact, the *background knowledge prior* is a finite set of single-premise tuple-generating dependencies [1] of the syntactic form[1]

$$(\forall X_1) \ldots (\forall X_k) [R(t_1, \ldots, t_n) \Rightarrow (\exists Y_1) \ldots (\exists Y_l) R(\bar{t}_1, \ldots, \bar{t}_n)], \qquad (2)$$

where $X_1, \ldots, X_k, Y_1, \ldots, Y_l$ are pairwise different variables, each universally quantified variable X_i occurring exactly once in $R(t_1, \ldots, t_n)$ and at most once in $R(\bar{t}_1, \ldots, \bar{t}_n)$, each existentially quantified variable Y_j occurring exactly once in $R(\bar{t}_1, \ldots, \bar{t}_n)$, and – preferably to avoid an overall refusal – in both $R(t_1, \ldots, t_n)$ and $R(\bar{t}_1, \ldots, \bar{t}_n)$ at least one constant of *Dom* occurs.
- The *confidentiality policy ppol* $\subset \mathscr{L}_{exist}$ is a finite set of existential facts.

Regarding the first stage, further outlined below:

- As far as possible, the finite set *temp* of disjunctive *templates* with *temp* $\subset \mathscr{L}^{\lor}_{exist}$ should only be formed by elements of the confidentiality policy, covering all of them. Moreover, all disjunctions seen together should be *mutually independent* in the following sense: for each two different disjunctions $\Psi_1 \lor \Psi_2 \lor \ldots \lor \Psi_k$ and $\bar{\Psi}_1 \lor \bar{\Psi}_2 \lor \ldots \lor \bar{\Psi}_{\bar{k}}$ we have $\Psi_i \not\models \bar{\Psi}_j$ and $\bar{\Psi}_j \not\models \Psi_i$.
- The finite set *refu* of refusals contains selected policy elements and possibly further prohibition sentences and, thus, *refu* $\subset \mathscr{L}_{exist}$.

Regarding the second stage:

- The *refused knowledge* is instance-independent and just comprises the refusals determined in the first stage, i.e., $v^? := refu$.
- The *positive knowledge* gathers all ground facts (tuples) of the relation instance r that entail neither a refusal nor a disjunctive template, i.e., $v^+ := \{\Phi \mid \Phi \in r \text{ and for all } \Psi \in refu : \Phi \not\models \Psi, \text{for all } \tau \in temp : \Phi \not\models \tau\}$.

---

[1] To simplify our treatment, we do not consider definite background knowledge with an empty premise part. Thus, in particular, background knowledge can not per se entail any possible prohibition.

- The *disjunctive knowledge* $v^{\vee}$ is formed as follows. As far as needed for confidentiality, a ground fact (tuple) $R(a_1, \ldots, a_n)$ in the relation instance r is disjunctively *weakened* by replacing it in a *context-free* way by a disjunction $\Psi_1 \vee \Psi_2 \vee \ldots \vee \Psi_k$ taken from the previously, in the first stage determined set of disjunctive templates *temp* such that $R(a_1, \ldots, a_n) \models \Psi_1 \vee \Psi_2 \vee \ldots \vee \Psi_k$. In fact, in order to conveniently capture many simultaneous threats to confidentiality, the replacement is performed with *all* such disjunctions. Formally, $v^{\vee} := \{ \tau \mid \tau \in temp \text{ and there exists } \Phi \in r : \Phi \models \tau \}^2$.
- The *negative knowledge* consists of the suitably adapted pertinent completeness sentence, i.e., $v^{-} := Comp(v^{+}, v^{\vee}, temp, refu)$.

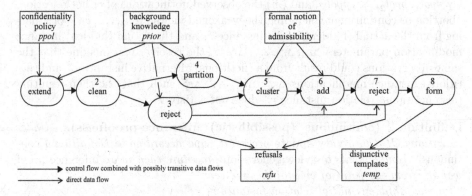

Fig. 3. Direct and transitive data flows and control flow in stage 1

The first stage, which is still independent of r, can be further outlined as follows, and as also visualized in Fig. 3:

1. *extend* the policy by *implicit prohibitions* caused by a single dependency;
2. *clean* the policy from semantically *redundant prohibitions*;
3. *reject* (delete) conflicting prohibitions and establish *refusals* in *refu* instead;
4. *partition* the set of dependencies according to interactions with prohibitions;
5. respecting the partitioning, *cluster* prohibitions into admissible[3] groups;
6. if possible, *add synthetic prohibitions* for completing a partial match;
7. *reject* prohibitions remained isolated and establish additional *refusals* in *refu*;
8. *form templates* of *temp* as disjunctions, one for each group of the clustering.

---

[2] In reference [4], we additionally required a void overlapping with the refused knowledge to ensure unique interactive control decisions; the current weaker requirement is in accordance with the detailed elaboration in reference [14].

[3] As elaborated in [14], the notion of admissibility is intended to formally capture application-oriented needs, in particular aiming at the plausibility of a disjunctive template and an approximate equal likelihood of its disjuncts.

3.4 Continuous Inference-Proofness

Intuitively, as inspired by [9] and closely following [3,5,6], a prohibition sentence $\Psi \in ppol_t$ is intended to express a strong *semantic confidentiality* requirement: from the point of view of the receiver, based on the explicitly returned pieces of data and the somehow "posted" security configurations, at all times $t' \geq t$ it should appear to be *possible* that the prohibition sentence Ψ has *not* been *true* at time t. In other words, even if Ψ has actually been *true* in the (hidden) relation instance r_t, the receiver should not be sure about this situation.

This intuition will be formalized as roughly outlined in the following. Based on (i) his (assumed) time-depending background knowledge $prior_1$, $prior_2, \ldots, prior_{t'}$, (ii) his awareness of the time-depending confidentiality policy $ppol_1, ppol_2, \ldots, ppol_{t'}$, and (iii) the observed notifications of either rejection, abortion or commitment, including the weakened views $v_1, v_2, \ldots, v_{t'}$ – originating from the actual (hidden) initial instance r_1 and the actual (hidden) instance modification parameters $\Delta r_2, \Delta r_3, \ldots, \Delta r_{t'}$ –, the receiver can imagine that the same observations could result from a (fictitious) alternative instance r_1^Ψ and (fictitious) instance modifications $\Delta r_2^\Psi, \Delta r_3^\Psi, \ldots, \Delta r_{t'}^\Psi$ such that the then resulting (also fictitious) relation instance r_t^Ψ does *not* satisfy Ψ.

Definition 2 (continuous (possibilistic) inference-proofness). *Under conditions C1–C6, a* view update *procedure vupd according to Definition 1 continuously* complements *the* view generation *procedure vgen in an inference-proof way iff, from the point of view of the receiver:*
 for each (hidden) initial relation instance r_1,
 for each (known) initial background knowledge $prior_1$,
 for each (known) initial confidentiality policy $ppol_1$ and
  for each (totally hidden) sequence of instance modifications $\Delta r_2, \Delta r_3, \ldots, \Delta r_{t'}$,
   for each (known) sequences of background modifications $\Delta prior_2, \Delta prior_3, \ldots,$
   $\Delta prior_{t'}$ and policy modifications $\Delta ppol_2, \Delta ppol_3, \ldots, \Delta ppol_{t'}$,
    under the procedures vgen and vupd leading to
    ·the (known) attacker states $att_1, att_2, \ldots, att_{t'}$ and
    the (hidden) relation instance r_t at a point in time $t \leq t'$,
     for each prohibition sentence $\Psi \in ppol_t$
there exists an "alternative hidden situation", i.e., there exist a (fictitious) relation instance r_1^Ψ and a (fictitious) sequence of instance modifications $\Delta r_2^\Psi, \Delta r_3^\Psi, \ldots, \Delta r_{t'}^\Psi$ such that

1. *indistinguishability of the alternative hidden situation:*
   under the procedures vgen and vupd, the instance parameters r_1^Ψ and $\Delta r_2^\Psi, \Delta r_3^\Psi, \ldots, \Delta r_{t'}^\Psi$ together with the background parameters $prior_1$ and $\Delta prior_2, \Delta prior_3, \ldots, \Delta prior_{t'}$ and with the policy parameters $ppol_1$ and $\Delta ppol_2, \Delta ppol_3, \ldots, \Delta ppol_{t'}$ generate the same notifications and the same attacker states $att_1^\Psi = att_1, att_2^\Psi = att_2, \ldots, att_{t'}^\Psi = att_{t'}$, in particular the same weakened views, i.e., regarding Ψ, the hidden items are indistinguishable from the fictitious items;

2. credibility of the alternative situation: r_j^Ψ satisfies $prior_j$, for $j = 1, \ldots, t'$;
3. harmlessness of the alternative situation: r_t^Ψ does not satisfy Ψ.

If we restrict Definition 2 to the special case $t' = 1$, i.e., that only initially, at time 1, the view generation procedure *vgen* has been applied but subsequently no modifications have been requested, we just obtain the notion of (static) semantic confidentiality dealt with in our previous work [4,14] and, thus, according to Theorem 1 and Theorem 2 of [4], the following proposition holds.

Proposition 1. *The view generation procedure vgen (restricted to acceptable input parameter values) complies with* static *(possibilistic) inference-proofness, i.e., from the point of view of the receiver: for each (hidden) initial relation instance r_1, for each (known) initial background knowledge $prior_1$, for each (known) initial confidentiality policy $ppol_1$, for each prohibition sentence $\Psi \in ppol_1$ there exists an "alternative hidden situation", i.e., there exists a (fictitious) relation instance r_1^Ψ such that*

1. indistinguishability of the alternative situation: *under the procedure vgen, r_1^Ψ together with $prior_1$ and $ppol_1$ generates the same weakened view v_1;*
2. credibility of the alternative situation: r_1^Ψ satisfies $prior_1$;
3. harmlessness of the alternative situation: r_1^Ψ does not satisfy Ψ.

4 The View Update Procedure

Based on the informally stated conditions C1–C6 identified in Sect. 2 and the formal specifications outlined in Sect. 3, we are now ready to present our main contribution: a concrete view update procedure for weakened views and a verification of its compliance with continuous inference-proofness. As discussed in Sect. 2, to show inference-proofness under as weak conditions as reasonable, we define the procedure in accordance with condition C5 (notifications), such that the receiver gets notified about the fact of any owner request. However, for practical applications, we do not recommend to do so but, following condition C5*, to inform the receiver only about actually changed views. Moreover, condition C6 (observability of security configuration) is not explicitly expressed in the procedure but only employed in its verification assuming an utmost powerful attacking receiver.

PROCEDURE $vupd((\Delta^+r, \Delta^-r), (\Delta^+prior, \Delta^-prior), (\Delta^+ppol, \Delta^-ppol))$ {
IF modification requests are not conflict-free
   THEN notify owner in detail about the detected conflicts;
        notify receiver only about the mere fact of a conflict
  ELSE*****if there are no conflicts
   BEGIN_TRANSACTION
     $own_{prev} := own$;
     $prior := [prior \cup \Delta^+prior] \setminus \Delta^-prior$;
     $r \quad := [r \cup \Delta^+r] \setminus \Delta^-r$;
     IF invariants satisfied (here: *prior* is satisfied by r)

THEN $ppol := [ppol \cup \Delta^+ppol] \setminus \Delta^-ppol$;
　　IF $(prior_{prev}, ppol_{prev}) \neq (prior, ppol)$
　　　THEN $(temp, refu) := vgen\_stage1(prior, ppol)$ FI ;
　　IF $(temp_{prev}, refu_{prev}, r_{prev}) \neq (temp, refu, r)$
　　　THEN $(v^?, v^+, v^\vee, v^-) := vgen\_stage2(temp, refu, r)$;
　　　　　$v := norm(v^?, v^+, v^\vee, v^-)$ FI ;
　　commit (make all modifications persistent);
　　notify owner about commit ;
　　notify receiver about commit by sending v
ELSE　abort (restore previous values of *prior* and r) ;
　　notify owner in detail about violation of invariants ;
　　notify receiver only about the mere fact of a violation
　FI
　END_TRANSACTION
FI }

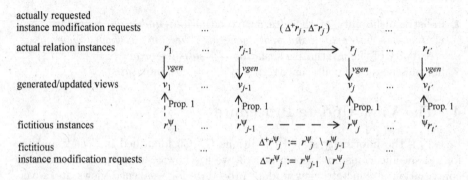

Fig. 4. Construction of "alternative situations" regarding instance modifications

Theorem 1. *Procedure vupd complies with* continuous inference-proofness *in the sense of Definition 2.*

Proof. Let the procedures *vgen* and *vupd* inductively determine a sequence of internal owner states $own_1, own_2, \ldots, own_{t'}$, as defined by (1) within Definition 1. Basically, besides dedicated arguments for conflicting parameter values and transaction abortion, for the standard case of transaction commitment we will apply Proposition 1 for each point in time individually, as indicated in Fig. 4.

More specifically, for $j = 1$, Proposition 1 directly ensures the existence of an "alternative situation" with the same notification.

Inductively, for $j > 1$, according to the declaration of *vupd* we have to distinguish three mutually excluding cases.

Case 1, parameter values conflicting: A conflict can only occur for the following reasons: contradictory insert and delete requests or inconsistent modification requests. Both an actual contradiction and an actual inconsistency could always be imagined to result from alternative fictitious ones, respectively, leading to the same notification and leaving the internal owner state unchanged, and thus the induction hypothesis applies.

Case 2, transaction aborted: The transaction for the modification of the instance and the security configuration is only aborted if the tentatively modified (known) background knowledge $prior_j$ does not satisfy the tentatively modified (hidden) instance r_j. So, there exists a single-premise tuple-generating dependency in $prior_j$ that is violated by r_j and is of the form defined by (2) in Sect. 3.3, e.g.,

$$(\forall X_1)\dots(\forall X_k)\,[\,R(t_1,\dots,t_n) \Rightarrow (\exists Y_1)\dots(\exists Y_l)\,R(\bar{t}_1,\dots,\bar{t}_n)\,]\ .$$

Accordingly, there exists a substitution σ that replaces the universally quantified variables $X_1,\dots,X_k$ with the constants $c_1,\dots,c_k$ such that (i) $\sigma[(t_1,\dots,t_n)] \in r_j$ but (ii) for all constant substitutions τ of the existentially quantified variables $Y_1,\dots,Y_l$ we have $\tau[\sigma[(\bar{t}_1,\dots,\bar{t}_n)]] \notin r_j$.

This actual situation could also result from a fictitious instance modification regarding the fictitious instance r_{j-1}^{Ψ} that requests to insert $\sigma[(t_1,\dots,t_n)]$ and to delete all those (finitely many) $\tau[\sigma[(\bar{t}_1,\dots,\bar{t}_n)]]$ which have been in r_{j-1}^{Ψ}. Accordingly, the abort notification for the actual situation equals the abort notification for the fictitious situation. Moreover, in both situations the internal owner state and thus also the attacker state remains the same as at time $j-1$ such that the induction hypotheses about the situation at time $j-1$ immediately implies the assertion about time j.

Case 3, transaction committed: Consider the committed execution of

$$vupd(\,(\Delta^+r_j, \Delta^-r_j), (\Delta^+prior_j, \Delta^-prior_j), (\Delta^+ppol_j, \Delta^-ppol_j)\,)\ .$$

This execution first determines new components $prior_j$, $ppol_j$ and r_j for the internal state, and then determines the same updated view v_j as the view generation procedure $vgen$ would have done applied to these components. Thus, according to Proposition 1, there exists an "alternative" fictitious instance r_j^{Ψ} leading to the same view v_j under the procedure $vgen$ applied to $prior_j$, $ppol_j$ and r_j^{Ψ}. Now, we observe that this fictitious instance r_j^{Ψ} can also be obtained from the inductively assumed fictitious instance r_{j-1}^{Ψ} by an instance modification request with parameter values

$$\Delta^+r_j^{\Psi} := r_j^{\Psi} \setminus r_{j-1}^{\Psi} \text{ and } \Delta^-r_j^{\Psi} := r_{j-1}^{\Psi} \setminus r_j^{\Psi}\ .$$

Then, the fictitious execution of

$$vupd(\,(\Delta^+r_j^{\Psi}, \Delta^-r_j^{\Psi}), (\Delta^+prior_j, \Delta^-prior_j), (\Delta^+ppol_j, \Delta^-ppol_j)\,)$$

would also generate the same view v_j for the following reasons: by condition C3, these parameter values are possible, and by condition C4, the transaction would commit for these parameter values as well. Accordingly, the notification for the actual situation equals the notification for the fictitious situation. $\square$

5   Experimental Runtime Evaluation

We presented the view *update* procedure *vupd* in a straightforward way in order to facilitate its verification. However, we might attempt to replace the employed *recomputation* of the new internal state by means of the two subprocedures *vgen_stage1* and *vgen_stage2* of the underlying view *generation* procedure *vgen* by a more efficient *incremental* determination of the new internal state.

Regarding the subprocedure *vgen_stage1*, the outline given in Sect. 3.3 and visualized by Fig. 3 already roughly indicates that the final results *temp* and *refu* depend on the inputs *ppol* and *prior* in a transitively dependent way, along the whole chain of the eight steps. For example, the insertion of a new prohibition into *ppol* might raise further extensions in step 1, which in turn might introduce new redundancies that in step 2 can trigger rather involved non-monotonic cleaning effects: a previously kept prohibition is sometimes removed in favor of a new prohibition, but sometimes it remains untouched causing the removal of new prohibitions as being redundant. The alternatives decided in step 2, adjusted by identifying refusals in step 3, further effects all succeeding steps, both by using the result of step 3 as direct input and indirectly via the transitive data flows, in particular incorporated by the partition generated in step 4. A more detailed analysis and corresponding options for optimized, partly incremental computations are beyond the scope of the present work.

Regarding the subprocedure *vgen_stage2*, we can replace its simple call by essentially more refined operations if the results of the first stage, *temp* and *refu*, have remained unchanged. This is an outline of an incremental approach:

- The instance-independent *refused knowledge* remains $v^? := refu$.
- For updating the *positive knowledge*, basically only the elements of the input parameter value $(\Delta^+ r, \Delta^- r)$ have to be processed, rather than the whole modified relation r, i.e., under the precondition $\Delta^+ r \cap \Delta^- r = \emptyset$, $v^+ :=$ $[v_{prev}^+ \cup \{\Phi \,|\, \Phi \in \Delta^+ r$ and for all $\tau \in temp \cup refu : \Phi \not\models \tau\}] \setminus \Delta^- r$.
- For updating the *disjunctive knowledge*, similarly only the elements of the input parameter value $(\Delta^+ r, \Delta^- r)$ have to be processed, i.e., $v^\vee := [v_{prev}^\vee \setminus$ $\{\tau \,|\, \tau \in v_{prev}^\vee$ and for all $\Phi \in r_{prev}$ with $\Phi \models \tau : \Phi \in \Delta^- r\}] \cup \{\tau \,|\, \tau \in temp$ and there exists $\Phi \in \Delta^+ r : \Phi \models \tau\}$.
- The completeness sentence for *negative knowledge* is adapted accordingly.

We also extended the prototype implementation of [4,14] to instantiate the new view update procedure *vupd* in two versions, straightforward and incremental. All crucial subroutines of this implementation, which are employed for view generations and view updates, are developed in Java 8 and parallelized to benefit from modern hardware. The experiments were run under Ubuntu 14.04 on a machine with two "Intel Xeon E5-2690" CPUs, providing a total number of 16 physical and 32 logical cores (due to hyperthreading) running at 2.9 GHz.

Within Experiment 1 an original instance with 1 000 000 database tuples is modified by inserting and deleting the same number of randomly chosen database tuples, varying from 10 000 to 970 000. Comparing the Figs. 5(a) and (b),

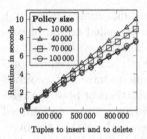
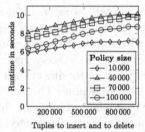
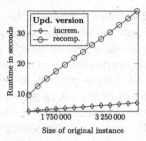

(a) Incremental view updates under varying size of instance modifications

(b) Recomputed view updates under varying size of instance modifications

(c) View updates under increasing size of original instance

Fig. 5. Experimental runtime comparison of the incremental and the straightforward recomputation (of stage 2) version of the view update procedure

it becomes clear that in terms of runtime an incremental view update is nearly always better than a recomputation of a weakened view with *vgen_stage2*. Even if about the full database instance is to be replaced, there is usually little reason *not* to employ the incremental procedure.

Experiment 2 then applies a sequence of instance modifications to an original instance with initially 1 000 000 tuples. Each of these modifications inserts 500 000 random tuples and deletes only 250 000 random tuples, resulting in modified original instances enlarged up to 4 250 000 tuples. A quick look at Fig. 5(c) reveals that the incremental procedure clearly outperforms recomputations.

6   Conclusion

For a specific approach to confidentiality-preserving data publishing, we addressed the challenging problem of how to *update a published view* according to modifications of the underlying original data or of the security configuration *without revealing sensitive information*. Basically, as far as needed for complying with a declarative confidentiality policy, and whenever possible, that approach weakens the knowledge embodied in a tuple of a complete relation instance into a piece of disjunctive knowledge formed from elements of the policy. In a first still instance-independent stage disjunctive templates (and, if required, refusals) are suitably determined, and in a second instance-dependent stage each tuple is inspected individually whether it has to be disjunctively weakened according to one or more of the disjunctive templates (or even be refused). The first stage guarantees that all templates are sufficiently mutually isolated regarding logic entailments – even under background knowledge in the form of data dependencies – such that afterwards in the second stage for any actual relation instance a strong kind of (possibilistic) *semantic confidentiality* will always be achieved (leaving open the problem of probabilistic inference-proofness).

Exploiting the basic features of this approach, namely instance-independent *mutual isolation of templates* (and refusals) in the first stage and *individual* *treatment of tuples* in the second stage, we showed how confidentiality-preserving updating of views is possible while complying with an extended notion of *continuous inference-proofness*. Essentially, this goal can be achieved by conceptually rerunning the two stages of the underlying view generation procedure, provided some precautions are enforced: modification requests have to be formed as *transactions*, in general possibly dealing with modifications of both the relation instance and the security configuration, and *invariants* to be maintained by transaction processing should refer to committed *internal states* of the overall system of the underlying relational database. Due to simplification avoiding asynchronous time, we always made transactions explicit, though essentially the same confidentiality guarantees can be obtained by *completely hiding* rejected, non-committed and non-effective modification requests (see condition C5*).

The updating procedure preserves the *practical efficiency* of the underlying view generation procedure, again due to the basic features summarized above, and as confirmed by runtime experiments with a *prototype implementation*. Moreover, the updating procedure also preserves and extends the *availability* properties of the underlying procedure. As discussed in [4,14], the latter one minimally distorts data only if *locally necessary* under the given setting, and the introductory examples *necessitate some restrictions*, and motivate the concrete ones expressed by conditions C1–C4. However, *global optimization* is likely to be related to NP-hardness and thus would be in conflict with efficiency.

So far, we only deal with a *single* relation governed by single-premise tuple-generating dependencies rather than with a *multi-relational* database with any intrarelational and interrelational constraints. Though any attempt towards the latter goal would be highly worthwhile to enhance practicality, it will always face substantial limitations regarding efficiency or even computability.

References

1. Abiteboul, S., Hull, R., Vianu, V.: Foundations of Databases. Addison-Wesley, Reading (1995)
2. Anjum, A., Raschia, G., Gelgon, M., Khan, A., Malik, S.U.R., Ahmad, N., Ahmed, M., Suhail, S., Alam, M.M.: τ-safety: a privacy model for sequential publication with arbitrary updates. Comput. Secur. **66**, 20–39 (2017)
3. Biskup, J., Gogolin, C., Seiler, J., Weibert, T.: Inference-proof view update transactions with forwarded refreshments. J. Comput. Secur. **19**, 487–529 (2011)
4. Biskup, J., Preuß, M.: Information control by policy-based relational weakening templates. In: Askoxylakis, I., Ioannidis, S., Katsikas, S., Meadows, C. (eds.) ESORICS 2016. LNCS, vol. 9879, pp. 361–381. Springer, Cham (2016). doi:10.1007/978-3-319-45741-3_19
5. Biskup, J., Tadros, C.: Inference-proof view update transactions with minimal refusals. In: Garcia-Alfaro, J., Navarro-Arribas, G., Cuppens-Boulahia, N., de Capitani di Vimercati, S. (eds.) DPM/SETOP -2011. LNCS, vol. 7122, pp. 104–121. Springer, Heidelberg (2012). doi:10.1007/978-3-642-28879-1_8
6. Biskup, J., Tadros, C.: Preserving confidentiality while reacting on iterated queries and belief revisions. Ann. Math. Artif. Intell. **73**(1–2), 75–123 (2015)

7. Byun, J., Li, T., Bertino, E., Li, N., Sohn, Y.: Privacy-preserving incremental data dissemination. J. Comput. Secur. **17**(1), 43–68 (2009)
8. Fung, B.C.M., Wang, K., Chen, R., Yu, P.S.: Privacy-preserving data publishing: a survey of recent developments. ACM Comput. Surv. **42**(4), 14:1–14:53 (2010)
9. Halpern, J.Y., O'Neill, K.R.: Secrecy in multiagent systems. ACM Trans. Inf. Syst. Secur. **12**(1), 5.1–5.47 (2008)
10. Levesque, H.J., Lakemeyer, G.: The Logic of Knowledge Bases. MIT Press, Cambridge (2000)
11. Li, J., Baig, M.M., Sattar, A.H.M.S., Ding, X., Liu, J., Vincent, M.W.: A hybrid approach to prevent composition attacks for independent data releases. Inf. Sci. **367–368**, 324–336 (2016)
12. A. Machanavajjhala, D. Kifer, J. Gehrke, and M. Venkitasubramaniam. ℓ-diversity: privacy beyond k-anonymity. ACM Trans. Knowl. Discov. Data **1**(1) (2007). Article 3
13. Nerode, A., Shore, R.: Logic for Applications, 2nd edn. Springer, Heidelberg (1997)
14. Preuß, M.: Inference-proof materialized views. Ph.D. thesis, Dortmund University of Technology, Germany (2016)
15. Samarati, P.: Protecting respondents' identities in microdata release. IEEE Trans. Knowl. Data Eng. **13**(6), 1010–1027 (2001)
16. Shmueli, E., Tassa, T.: Privacy by diversity in sequential releases of databases. Inf. Sci. **298**, 344–372 (2015)
17. Sweeney, L.: k-anonymity: a model for protecting privacy. Int. J. Uncertainty Fuzziness Knowl.-Based Syst. **10**(5), 557–570 (2002)
18. Wang, K., Fung, B.C.M.: Anonymizing sequential releases. In: Eliassi-Rad, T., Ungar, L.H., Craven, M., Gunopulos, D. (eds.) Knowledge Discovery and Data Mining, KDD 2006, pp. 414–423. ACM (2006)
19. Xiao, X., Tao, Y.: M-invariance: towards privacy preserving re-publication of dynamic datasets. In: Chan, C.Y., Ooi, B.C., Zhou, A. (eds.) Management of Data, SIGMOD 2007, pp. 689–700. ACM (2007)
20. Yao, C., Wang, X.S., Jajodia, S.: Checking for k-anonymity violation by views. In: Böhm, K., Jensen, C.S., Haas, L.M., Kersten, M.L., Larson, P.-Å., Ooi, B.C. (eds.) Very Large Data Bases, VLDB 2005, pp. 910–921. ACM (2005)

Preventing Advanced Persistent Threats in Complex Control Networks

Juan E. Rubio$^{(\boxtimes)}$, Cristina Alcaraz, and Javier Lopez

Department of Computer Science, University of Malaga,
Campus de Teatinos S/n, 29071 Malaga, Spain
{rubio,alcaraz,jlm}@lcc.uma.es

Abstract. An Advanced Persistent Threat (APT) is an emerging attack against Industrial Control and Automation Systems, that is executed over a long period of time and is difficult to detect. In this context, graph theory can be applied to model the interaction among nodes and the complex attacks affecting them, as well as to design recovery techniques that ensure the survivability of the network. Accordingly, we leverage a decision model to study how a set of hierarchically selected nodes can collaborate to detect an APT within the network, concerning the presence of changes in its topology. Moreover, we implement a response service based on redundant links that dynamically uses a secret sharing scheme and applies a flexible routing protocol depending on the severity of the attack. The ultimate goal is twofold: ensuring the reachability between nodes despite the changes and preventing the path followed by messages from being discovered.

Keywords: Advanced · Persistent · Threat · Attack · Detection · Response · Consensus · Opinion · Dynamics · Secret · Sharing · Redundant · Topology

1 Introduction

The interconnection of industrial environments with modern ICT technologies has increased the number of internal and external threats in this context, including those from traditional IT systems (e.g., malware, spyware, and botnets). Among these, the Advanced Persistent Threats (APT) are a new class of sophisticated attacks that are executed by well-resourced adversaries over a long period of time. They usually go undetected because they leverage zero-day vulnerabilities and stealthy and evasive techniques [1]. While APTs originally attacked military organizations, they are now targeting a wide range of industries and governments with multiple purposes: economic (espionage, intellectual property), technical (access to source code), military (revealing information) or political (destabilization of a company). Their goal is to get through the organization's network and take over the industrial control systems.

© Springer International Publishing AG 2017
S.N. Foley et al. (Eds.): ESORICS 2017, Part II, LNCS 10493, pp. 402–418, 2017.
DOI: 10.1007/978-3-319-66399-9_22

Stuxnet was the first attack of this kind, reported in 2010, which sabotaged the Iranian Nuclear Program by causing physical damage to the infrastructure and thereby slowed down the overall process. Ever since, the number of reported vulnerabilities concerning Industrial Control Systems has been dramatically increasing, as the research community has become more involved and new attacks have been revealed. Like Stuxnet, all APTs are tailored to the specific victim's network topology, and they count on a defined succession of steps: firstly, the attacker intrudes on the network by using social engineering (e.g., by means of fraudulent e-mails containing trojans); secondly, they install a backdoor from which the attackers connect to the target network. Then, several exploits and malware are used to compromise as many computers in the victim network as possible, to ultimately modify the productive process or exfiltrate information back to the attacker domain.

On the whole, an APT is a meticulously planned attack adapted to the target infrastructure, one whose complexity makes the use of traditional countermeasures (e.g., antivirus, firewalls) insufficient to tackle them. An additional effort is required to mitigate their effects, by involving the organization in security awareness training and introducing novel services in continuous evolution within the company [2]. For this reason, we propose the design of practical mechanisms to firstly detect and then effectively respond to these attacks, applied to a common network representation. We can summarize our contributions as:

- Modeling the evolution of an APT within the victim network topology.
- Implementation of a multi-agent system for the detection of an APT based on the topological changes suffered in selected parts of the network, observed by hierarchically chosen nodes in accordance with controllability criteria.
- Use of redundancy edges and random routing protocols to overcome the network deformation provoked by the APT and to avoid compromised systems, ensuring the reachability between nodes and the survivability of the network.

The remainder of this paper is organized as follows: Sect. 2 outlines preliminary concepts about dynamic control networks and describes the threat model used for the APT. In Sect. 3 the detection of these attacks is addressed by means of a network decision model. Based on this mechanism, response techniques are implemented in Sect. 4, which are theoretically and experimentally analyzed in Sect. 5.

2 Preliminaries

2.1 Structural Controllability

Considering the cost of the implementation of large control networks from a research point of view, it becomes mandatory to model and simulate the problem through graph theory, taking into account the network topology and the nature of its distribution. Specifically, we focus on topologies of the type power-law $y \propto$

$x^{-\alpha}$ [3], since the vast majority of critical control systems follow these structures, which produce small sub-networks similar to current control substations.

With the purpose of helping the reader understand the underlying theoretical concepts of our model, topics related to structural controllability and power dominance are described here. The concept of structural controllability was introduced by Lin in 1974 [4], which associates the control to a subset of nodes with the maximum capacity of dominance.

Let $G = (V, E)$ be a *directed* graph that represents the network topology, given by its adjacency matrix, that is, a square binary matrix M with dimension $|V|$ where $M(i, j) = 1$ whenever $(v_i, v_j^\cdot) \in E$ and zero otherwise. Through $G(V, E)$, it is possible to characterize dynamic control networks including loops and weighted edges that represent the interconnection of control devices with remote terminal units (e.g., sensors or actuators). These links contain the maximum capacity to conduct the main traffic between two points, which is defined as the *control load capacity* (CLC).

To represent this traffic, we use the edge betweeness centrality (EBC) [5]. It is an indicator that represents the sum of the fraction of the shortest paths that pass through a given edge, so that edges with the highest centrality participate in a large number of shortest paths. The result is a weighted matrix related to $G_w(V, E)$ whose weights are computed as follows:

$$E_{BC} = \sum_{s,t \in V} \frac{\delta(s, t|e)}{\delta(s, t)} \tag{1}$$

where $\delta(s, t)$ denotes the number of shortest (s,t)-paths and $\delta(s, t|e)$ the number of paths passing through the edge e. On the other hand, let the in-neighborhood N_i^{in} of a node i be the set of nodes v_j such that $(v_j, v_i) \in E$, while the out-neighborhood N_i^{out} is the set of nodes v_j such that $(v_i, v_j) \in E$. Consequently, let the in-degree d_i^{in} of a node v_i be the number of its incoming edges, i.e., $d_i^{in} = |N_i^{in}|$, while the out-degree d_i^{out} is the sum of its outgoing edges, i.e., $d_i = |N_i^{out}|$.

Taking these concepts and EBC into account, the Dominating Set (DS) of a graph G can be defined as the minimum subset of nodes $D \subseteq V$ such that for each vertex $v_i \notin D$ is adjacent to at least one member of D, that is $\exists v_k \in D|(v_k, v_i) \in E$. These nodes D with highest control capacity will be those with the highest edge betweeness centrality $E_{BC}(v)$ for all their outgoing edges. The creation of this set is explained in Algorithm 1. Related to this concept, the Power Dominating Set (PDS) consists in an extension of the DS by including new *driver nodes* (denoted by N_D), those with the maximum capacity of dominance. The original formulation of this set was given by Haynes *et al.* in [6], and was later simplified into two fundamental observation rules by Kneis *et al.* in [7]:

OR1 *A vertex in N_D observes itself and all its neighbors, complying with DS.*

OR2 *If an observed vertex v of degree $d^+ \geq 2$ is adjacent to d1 observed vertices, the remaining un-observed vertex becomes observed as well. This also implies that **OR1** $\subseteq$ **OR2** given that the subset of nodes that comply with **OR1** becomes part of the set of nodes that complies with **OR2**.*

For our purpose in this paper, the dominating nodes play the role of agents that detect topological changes in their surroundings that may be derived from an APT attack, and establish backup links that ensure the continuity of the network.

Algorithm 1. DS($G(V, E)$)

---

output ($DS = \{v_i, ..., v_k\}$ where $0 \leq i \leq |V|$)
local: $BC(V)$ representing betweeness centrality of V

Choose $v \in V$ with highest BC
$DS \leftarrow \{v\}$ and $N(DS) \leftarrow \{v_i, ..., v_k\}$ $\forall i \leq j \leq k \setminus (v, v_j) \in E$
while $V - (DS \cup N(DS)) \neq \emptyset$ **do**
    Choose vertex $w \in V - (DS \cup N(DS))$ with highest BC
    $DS \leftarrow DS \cup \{w\}$
    $N(DS) \leftarrow N(DS) \bigcup \{v_i, ..., v_k\}$ where $\forall i \leq j \leq k \setminus (w, v_j) \in E$
end while

2.2 Threat Model: Representation of APT Attacks

Assuming a successful intrusion inside a network represented by a matrix M, we model an APT with a succession of attacks perpetrated on its topology. Specifically, just as an actual APT works, the attacker firstly selects one node and then makes several lateral movements in order to find new nodes to compromise. Since we want to provide realism in this model and consider a scenario of high criticality, we assume the attacker always seeks those nodes with more controllability, that is, those belonging to the DS and hence the ones with the highest betweeness centrality.

In each of the steps in its life cycle, the APT can commit individual attacks on the topology, i.e. changing the edges from the compromised node at a given time instant. This consequently generates a new matrix M'. The types of attacks can be:

* **Removal of an incoming edge:** given the vertex v_i that represents the compromised node such that v_j exists and $M(j, i) = 1$, it implies setting $M(j, i) = 0$.
* **Removal of an outgoing edge:** given the vertex v_i that represents the compromised node such that v_j exists and $M(i, j) = 1$, it implies setting $M'(i, j) = 0$.
* **Addition of an incoming edge:** given the vertex v_i that represents the compromised node such that v_j exists and $M(i, j) = 0$, it implies setting $M'(i, j) = 1$.
* **Addition of an outgoing edge:** given the vertex v_i that represents the compromised node such that v_j exists and $M(i, j) = 0$, it implies setting $M'(i, j) = 1$.

In a simple version of the APT, we suppose that the kind of the attack and the first node compromised within the network are chosen randomly. From that moment on, the attack migrates to the adjacent node with highest betweeness centrality, simulating the fact that the attacker can perform a reconnaissance of the network when looking for potential victims that deal with higher loads of control traffic. The resulting attacker behavior is described in Algorithm 2. An example of an APT with three attacks over a defined network topology is depicted in Fig. 1, where driver nodes are marked in black to show how the APT always migrates to vertices with higher controllability. Firstly, node 4 is selected and an outgoing edge is added towards node 2. Then, the attacker moves to node 6 and removes the edge coming from node 3 and then, since node 6 still has dominance, the attack stays there and removes the edge going to 7.

Algorithm 2. Advanced persistent threat life cycle

output: M' representing the resulting matrix
local: M representing $G(V, E)$, numOfAttacks
attackedNode ← random $v_i \in E$
$M' \leftarrow M$

for i:=1 **to** numOfAttacks **step** 1 **do**
    attack ← randomAttack over attackedNode (edge addition or removal)
    update M' based on attack
    attackedNode ← SELECTNEWATTACKEDNODE(M, attackedNode)
    if attackedNode == null **then**
        attackedNode ← random $v_i \in E$
    end if
end for

function SELECTNEWATTACKEDNODE(M,node)
    childNodes ← vertexes $v_j | M(node, v_j) = 1$
    parentNodes ← vertexes $v_k | M(v_k, node) = 1$
    candidates ← childNodes ∪ parentNodes
    maxCentrality := 0
    attackedNode ← null
    for vertex v in candidates **do**
        centrality ← CALCULATEBETWEENESSCENTRALITY(v)
        if centrality > maxCentrality **then**
            attackedNode ← v
        end if
    end for
    return attackedNode
end function

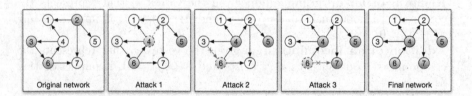

Fig. 1. Example of APT with 3 attacks: 1st: addition of edge from node 4 to node 2. 2nd: removal of edge from node 3 to node 6. 3rd: removal of edge from node 6 to node 7.

3   APT Detection Through Opinion Dynamics

Now we have modeled the effect of an APT over the network topology, in this section we describe a feasible method to allow the network to locate subtle changes in certain parts, making it easier to accurately deploy response techniques to overcome the effect of one of these threats.

We start with the notion introduced before: let us suppose a *power law* distribution network defined by the *directed* graph $G = (V, E)$ and represented by the adjacency matrix M. Let us also suppose the presence of n agents deployed over that network (the DS nodes of the graph G), so each node $v_i \in V$ is connected to one or more agents. We further assume that the agents can also communicate with each other according to a communication network represented by the directed graph $G_c = (V, E_c)$, where for all $(v_i, v_j) \in E_c$, we have that $(v_i, v_j) \in E$. Our goal is to put into practice a distributed cooperative algorithm among these agents to detect precise topology attacks in their neighborhood by exchanging information on changes produced in their observable nodes. In this regard, various decision models can be imported from graph theory, among which we can highlight *consensus* and *opinion dynamics*.

In the consensus approach, a collection of agents cooperate to reach a common objective by sharing information about their state and other environmental conditions [8]. Such negotiation depends on the network topology, so it can be leveraged to collectively build a global indicator of the entire network health at a given moment. Compared to this algorithm, opinion dynamics proposes a model that admits the fragmentation of patterns, so the aforementioned agents may differ in their opinions during the negotiation process [9]. These network partitions will depend on the closeness to the opinion of each node, which is calculated based on the number of topological changes they detect. Therefore, it makes it easier to identify which areas of the network are more affected by the action of the APT and to what extent.

Opinion dynamics originally models the influence among individuals in a group or the entire society, where there is a wide spectrum of opinions. Each agent crafts its own opinion taking into consideration the ones from the rest of agents to a certain extent. Eventually, the opinions are distributed into several clusters. For our purpose, it implies fragmenting the network according to the multiple changes that could occur in separate areas, whose individual consensus value raises an indicator of the severity of the attacks over that particular portion of the topology.

Let us suppose that $x_i(t)$ represents the opinion of a fixed agent i at time t. The vector $x(t) = (x_1(t), ..., x_n(t))$ represents the opinion profile at time t for all the agents. Given an agent i, the weight given to the opinion of any other agent j is denoted by a_{ij}. For simplicity, we consider a_{ii} such that $\sum_{k=1}^{n} a_{ik} = 1$. Therefore, agent i also takes into account its own opinion during the opinion formation process, which can be described as follows:

$$x_i(t+1) = a_{i1}x_1(t) + a_{i2}x_2(t) + ... + a_{in}x_n(t)$$

In a matrix notation it can be written as:

$$x(t+1) = A(t, x(t))x(t)$$

where the matrix $A(t, x(t)) = [a_{ij}]$ is the square matrix that collects the weights, which summarize the relationships between the agents' opinions. These weights can change over time or by opinion, so finally an agent i adjusts its opinion in period $t+1$ by taking a weighted average of the opinion of agent j at time t. When t tends to infinity, the final behavior of the opinion profile may lead to a consensus among all or part of the agents, which can also be visualized graphically.

Returning to our domain, we execute this algorithm assuming that $x_i(0)$ will be calculated for each agent i as follows: let us suppose that $BC(v_i)$ represents the original *betweeness centrality* for each agent i that, as explained, works as an indicator of the controllability of that particular node. If $BC'(v_i)$ is the *betweeness centrality* of the same agent after being victim of a particular attack of those defined in Sect. 2.2 or another node in its neighborhood, we define the initial opinion $x_i(0)$ as

$$x_i(0) = \frac{|BC'(v_i) - BC(v_i)|}{BC(v_i)} \tag{2}$$

Consequently, $x_i(0)$ holds the ratio of change in the controllability of an agent i after an attack, compared to its initial state (due to an increase or decrease of adjacent edges). We assume that when the value was originally zero or the resulting ratio is greater than 1, the result is normalized to the value of 1.

Altogether, if we have the vector $x(0)$ concerning the initial opinion of all agents in the DS, we can run the opinion dynamics algorithm to obtain a value of the change ratio of the network after suffering an individual attack, making it possible to distinguish between different clusters of agents with similar opinion. In this case, the closeness among opinions, which is represented by the matrix A with the weights assigned for each agent, has been modeled according to the difference in the degree of change (the individual opinion each agent holds): for two given agents i and j, if the difference is below a determined epsilon value (e.g., 0.3), they increase the weight given to each other; this models the fact that agents that experiment a similar degree of change in their surrounding topology must agree on the presence of an anomaly in their respective area.

Figure 2 shows the opinion dynamics algorithm for a network of 30 nodes and 17 agents after suffering an APT comprising 10 attacks. The lines represent the evolution in the opinions for each agent, so finally there is multiple consensus between them: in particular, there are only two agents that indicate relatively large changes (more than 0.5 of fluctuation in their betweeness centrality). However, four agents agree on a change of about 0.25 points around their zone of influence, and many of them indicate a fault of approximately 0.1 in the zone governed by these nodes. As can be seen in the figure, a α value has been added to the plot, which holds the ratio of agents that find a consensus on the amount of degree experienced. This value, together with the opinion about the changes in the topology, serves as the criticality indicator that regulates how strong the response technique must be to mitigate the effects of the APT.

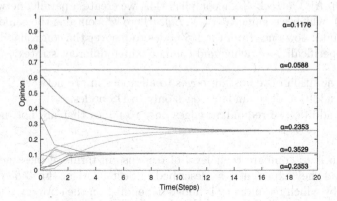

Fig. 2. Calculus of the opinion dynamics for a set of agents

4   APT Response

Once we have obtained a measure of the extent to which the network topology is at risk due to the effect of an APT attack, we are in a position to adopt multiple response techniques. We set the goal of preserving the connectivity for all those nodes in charge of delivering control signals to the rest of nodes of the network. According to the different change ratios raised by the opinion dynamics algorithms, we can apply different techniques in separate nodes of the network.

Specifically, we suppose a scenario where we wish to ensure that one node i belonging to the DS wants to send control messages to another node j in the network. This is done in the presence of an APT that can remove certain edges that originally enabled both nodes to communicate over a defined path, traversing other points of the topology [10]. At the same time, we want to avoid hopping over compromised nodes that may be victims of the APT and hence intercept these sensitive packets, preserving confidentiality by this means. Moreover, it is desirable that the communication pattern (i.e., the paths described by the messages when being transmitted over the network) is as random as possible, so as to guarantee that the attacker cannot easily determine the topology of the network. As a result, we have a security service that ensures the continuity of the network until the APT has been successfully removed from the system. To sum up, we seek these three objectives when designing a response technique:

(a) Ensure the presence of a path between node i and j when possible.
(b) Define a routing protocol that prevents determining the path.
(c) Introduce a mechanism to avoid the interception of messages.

To satisfy objective (a), we propose building an edge-redundant network with hidden edges that are added to the original network topology, so these auxiliary links can be leveraged in the event a path between two given nodes is lost after an APT attack. To accomplish this, we create a parallel network from $G = (V, E)$, which we name $G' = (V, E')$, where E' contains the same edges as E and includes new ones from the DS nodes to recover the controllability of the network. Specifically, we define and compare three different strategies:

- **STG1:** addition of redundant edges to all nodes in the network.
- **STG2:** addition of redundant edges only to DS nodes.
- **STG3:** addition of redundant edges only to nodes that are not included in the DS.

Our aim is to compare their level of response in terms of message loss and the overhead they experience, as described in Sect. 5. Algorithm 3 describes the procedure by which redundancy is added depending on the strategy selected: for each vertex, a set of candidates is created that includes the DS and excludes its parents and the node itself. In the case it is empty, we simply select the DS with maximum out-degree as the new parent of the aforementioned vertex, creating a new edge by this means. It is important to note that during the process, it is ensured that the resulting network $G' = (V, E')$ fulfills OR1 and OR2 conditions, as stated in [11].

On the other hand, to address objectives (b) and (c), we leverage a secret sharing scheme [12]: a secret (i.e., control message) is divided into n shares that are distributed among the sender's neighborhood nodes and follow independent routes, so that the recipient cannot reconstruct the message until it collects, at least, a defined number k of them, where $1 \leq k \leq n$. In the case we have $k = 1$, it can be considered as the basic level of security, as the message in clear is sent over a determined path over the network. If we have $k = n$, then the recipient must collect all the shares to reconstruct the original message. At this point, since our aim is to provide a security mechanism that bases its robustness on the criticality of the attack detected, the election of n will depend on the number of DS agents whose opinion is similar, for which we make use of the α value defined in Sect. 3. Namely, the maximum number of shares to divide the original message into depends on the ratio of agents that have experienced the same severity in the attacks against their surrounding nodes: the greater the number of DS that experience the same criticality, the greater the number of shares. However, the k value can be random (ranging from 1 to n) in order to make the recovery method as stochastic as possible and thereby not leak any information about the topology when analyzing the stream of messages. The resulting methodology, to divide the messages into shares and send them over the network when it has been attacked, and opinion dynamics has been executed, is described in Algorithm 4. It is important to note that the respective shares are arbitrarily sent over the original and redundant links, in order to make the protocol as misleading for the attacker as possible. Figure 3 shows how shares are divided and distributed over the network leveraging a pathfinding algorithm

---

Algorithm 3. hiddenTopology($G(V,E), DS, STG_x$)

---

output ($G' = (V, E')$)
local: $D_r \leftarrow \emptyset$, $E' \leftarrow E$

if $STG_x = 1$ then
    $D_r \leftarrow V$
else if $STG_x = 2$ then
    $D_r \leftarrow DS$
else if $STG_x = 3$ then
    $D_r \leftarrow V - DS$
end if

for vertex v in D_r do
    $F \leftarrow Fathers^a(G(V,E), v)$
    $D_c \leftarrow DS - (F \cup v)$
    $Candidates \leftarrow \emptyset$
    for vertex c in D_c do
        $D \leftarrow Children^b(G(V,E), c) \cap DS$
        $O \leftarrow Children(G(V,E), c) - D$
        comment: checking of **OR1** and **OR2** fulfillment
        if $v \in DS$ and $((|O| \geq 2$ and $|D| \geq 0)$ or $(|O| = 0$ and $|D| \geq 1)$ or $(|D| = 0$ and $|O| = 0))$ then
            $Candidates \leftarrow Candidates \cup c$
        else if $v \notin DS$ and $((|D| \geq 0$ and $|O| \geq 1)$ or $(|D| = 0$ and $|O| = 0)$ then
            $Candidates \leftarrow Candidates \cup c$
        end if
    end for
    if $Candidates = \emptyset$ then
        $Candidates \leftarrow MaxOutDegree^c(G(V,E), DS)$
    end if
    Arbitrarily select vertex $c_1 \in C$
    $E' \leftarrow E' \cup (c_1, v)$
end for

---

[a] Selection of fathers of v, those belonging to its in-neighborhood.
[b] Selection of sons of c, those belonging to its out-neighborhood.
[c] Selection of the DS node with maximum out-degree.

(e.g., *Dijkstra, Breadth-first search (BFS)*) [13,14]. In that example, the secret is divided into three shares with $k = 2$.

5   Theoretical and Practical Analysis

So far in the paper, we have modeled the behavior of an APT against a control network represented with a graph, over which we have applied structural controllability concepts to define a dominance set of nodes. These take the role of agents that make a distributed decision algorithm determine the health of the network based on topological changes detected in their neighbourhood. From this information, they can leverage a parallel hidden topology with redundant links, over which they can continue to deliver their messages with enhanced privacy in the presence of the APT.

In this section, we demonstrate the correctness of this mechanism, as well as offer experimental results to show how effective it is when ensuring the continuity of the network.

Algorithm 4. SecretSharing($G(V, E')$)

---

local: M representing the set of messages to be sent.
for *message m in M* **do**
    agent ← GetRecipient(m)
    alpha ← GetAlpha(agent)
    $n ← alpha * |N_{agent}^{out}|$
    $k ←$ generate random from 1 to n
    $S ← divideSecret(m, n, k)$
    send shares to n neighbours
end for

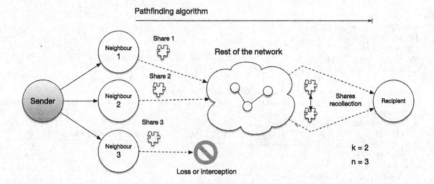

Fig. 3. Secret sharing scheme and shares delivery

5.1 Theoretical Analysis

The correctness proof of the message recovery problem is solved when the following requirements are satisfied: (1) the ratio of lost messages when facing an APT attack decreases when using the redundant topology; (2) the algorithm that crafts the set of redundant edges and sends the messages along the network is able to properly finish in a finite time (termination).

We can show the termination of the algorithm through induction, where we first define the initial and final conditions, and the base cases.

Precondition We assume that the network described by $G(V, E)$ is threatened by one or more attacks, probably causing the removal of available routes from the sender to the destination. In other words, there exists a share s belonging to a message m from sender v_1 whose recipient is v_r for which it is not possible to find a sequence of vertices $v_1, v_2, ..., v_r$ such that $(v_i, v_{i+1}) \in E, \forall i \in 1, .., r$.

Postcondition given the aforementioned message share and redundant network $G'(V, E')$, there exists a sequence of vertices $v_1, v_2, ..., v_r$ such that $(v_i, v_{i+1}) \in E', \forall i \in 1, .., r$. The availability of additional edges in E is subject to the redundancy strategy selected. Either way, the new route is located by a pathfinding algorithm like *BFS* or *Dijkstra*.

Case 1. We have a message m that is divided into n shares, such that $m = \{s_1, s_2, ..., s_n\}$. In the first step, share s_1 is sent to vertex v_2 through $(v_1, v_2) \in E$.

Case 2. In an intermediate step of the path from sender to destination, the share s_1 traverses the node v_l, and the pathfinding algorithm is evaluated to check the availability of a route. According to Algorithm 4, three scenarios can be distinguished in this point:

-Recovery solution: it takes place when the destination is reachable only through the redundant topology G', that is, there exists a route $v_l, v_{l+1}, ..., v_r$ where $(v_l, v_{l+1}) \in E'$ but $(v_l, v_{l+1}) \notin E$.

-Privacy solution: it occurs when multiple routes are available to reach the recipient of the share, using either the original or the redundant topology. Namely, there exists, at least, a route $v_l, v_m, ..., v_r$ where $(v_l, v_m) \in E$ and another one $v_l, v_{l+1}, ..., v_r$ such that $(v_l, v_{l+1}) \in E'$ and $(v_l, v_{l+1}) \notin E$. In this case, the share hops to v_m or v_l arbitrarily, with the aim of making the route as confusing as possible, thereby dodging potentially compromised nodes over which the attacker expects the traffic to flow. At this point, note that the network may experience some delays when delivering such shares (due to extra hops to reach the recipient), which could be the subject of further research. However, since we are considering a critical scenario, we prioritize availability rather than performance.

-Share loss: in the worst-case scenario, the redundant edges are not sufficient to find a path from v_l to v_r and the original path is no longer available due to the APT. In these circumstances, the share is lost and the algorithm terminates. Note, however, that the secret sharing scheme is resistant to share losses with a given threshold, so the rest of shares s_i with $i \neq 1$ can still rebuild the message m. This depends on the n and k parameters: specifically, the message m successfully reaches its recipient with a probability $\frac{k}{n}$. In this regard, we must stress that the choice of n is based on the severity indicator α, as explained in Sect. 4.

Induction finally, after a finite number of steps where the different subcases of Case 2 have been applied (except for a secret loss), the node v_j before the last in the sequence holds the share s_1 and there exists an edge (v_j, v_r). The share is finally delivered and Algorithm 4 terminates, satisfying the postcondition of saving a portion of the messages from getting lost, ensuring the validity of our algorithm.

We can also give a brief analysis of the computational complexity of the response algorithm, which must be performed in two ways: for the secret sharing scheme and for the subsequent delivery of shares over the network by using a pathfinding algorithm. As for the former, processing a given message takes n steps, as many as the number of shares it has been split into (determined by α), having $O(n)$ complexity. With respect to the communication mechanism, the complexity must firstly consider the overhead invested by the pathfinding method, which in the case of BFS is $O(n + e)$, where $n \approx |V|$ and $e \approx |E|$. Secondly, it also implies the complexity associated with the share delivery along the graph. Considering the worst-case scenario of the longest route, such a transmission has a cost of $O(n - 1 + e)$, since the share has to traverse all edges and every node in the network but the sender.

5.2 Experimental Analysis

After successfully designing mechanisms to firstly detect topological changes
by using distributed opinion algorithms and consequently deploying a response
technique to ensure the continuity and preserve privacy in the network, our
aim is to test these services in practice. We have conducted the implementation
in MATLAB of an APT that follows the behavior described in Algorithm 2.
After each attack of the sequence, opinion dynamics is executed on those agents
belonging to the DS, which is calculated based on Algorithm 1. If we run different
test cases, we can check how the opinion of agents evolve to reach a consensus
with each other and form different clusters within the network. Figure 4 shows
how the total number of DSs of three different networks (of 100, 200 and 300
nodes) is divided into substantial sets depending on the degree of change they
experience after suffering a battery of 50 attacks. It is especially significant to
note the presence of a big cluster in each of the three test cases, which indicates
an important effect of the APT (of approximately 0.35, 0.25 and 0.45 ratio of
change).

Opinion dynamics influences the α value that regulates the number of shares
in which the secret messages are divided and distributed from each DS node to
the rest of the network to their destination, as explained in Sect. 4.

To probe the effectiveness of our response technique that leverages a hidden
topology comprising additional edges, we have generated a set of 100 messages

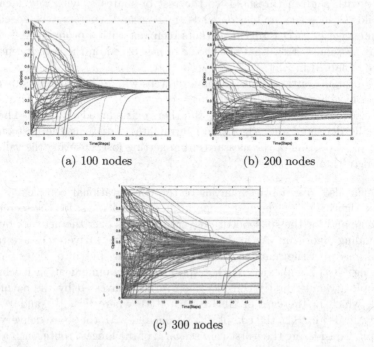

(a) 100 nodes   (b) 200 nodes

(c) 300 nodes

Fig. 4. Opinion dynamics after 50 attacks

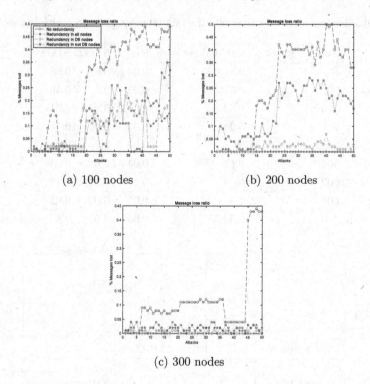

(a) 100 nodes   (b) 200 nodes

(c) 300 nodes

Fig. 5. Message loss ratio with the different strategies, 100 messages and 50 attacks over a network of 100, 200 and 300 nodes

whose sender belongs to the DS and the recipient is any other node within the network. Following the secret sharing scheme of Algorithm 4, each agent divides the message and gives each part to the corresponding neighbors, which are responsible for the delivery by leveraging the BFS algorithm. The path is calculated at each hop when traversing all nodes until the destination, since the topology can change over time, caused by the APT. In the event that the recipient is unreachable from a certain node at a given time, we consider that share to be lost. Consequently, taking into consideration the scheme, we deem a message to be lost if a number of its shares greater than k have been lost, since it is no longer possible for the recipient to construct the message.

Figure 5 shows the ratio of errors (i.e., message loss due to the unavailability of control paths) when using the normal and the hidden topology networks of STG1, STG2, and STG3. In more detail, we have run three test cases with a network of 100, 200 and 300 nodes, against which we perpetrate an APT of 50 attacks. Prior to executing it, we craft a set of 100 random messages for which we ensure the availability of paths from the sender's neighbors to the recipient. From that point on, the attacks take place and we try to send the original messages after each one. As a result, we can check how the loss ratio fluctuates as attacks occur. In this sense, based on the plots, the original network presents

Table 1. Message loss ratio after 50 attacks, 100 messages and multiple topologies

Nodes \Strategy	Original network	STG1	STG2	STG3
10	0.81	0.64	0.64	0.58
50	0.076	0.25	0.3	0.36
100	0.62	0	0.03	0.01
200	0.24	0.04	0.02	0.14
300	0.71	0.02	0	0.21
400	0.07	0.04	0.02	0.03
500	0.39	0.1	0.07	0.19
600	0.4	0.05	0.02	0.03
700	0.32	0.03	0.07	0.1

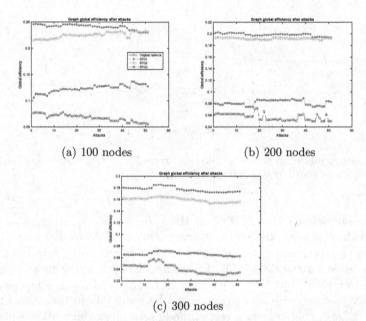

(a) 100 nodes   (b) 200 nodes

(c) 300 nodes

Fig. 6. Global efficiency with different strategies after 50 attacks

a higher quota of lost messages, whereas applying STG1 (i.e., a redundant edge for all nodes) experiments the lowest ratio, as expected in principle. However, we can see how redundancy in DS nodes (STG2) also achieves an acceptable degree of message reachability, comparable with STG1 and even better at certain points when running the same experiment in different topologies, as Table 1 indicates. This can be explained by the fact that attacks always move to nodes that deal with more traffic and hence have higher controllability (i.e. the DS nodes), as described in Sect. 2. Therefore, the addition of extra links to recover the connectivity between DSs results in a robust response that, on the other hand, does not introduce too much overhead because of the lower number of additional edges added.

The supremacy and higher connectivity of STG2 and especially STG1 are visible when analyzing the network global efficiency [15]. This measure indicates the efficiency of the information exchange in the network and how resistant it is to failures. If the distance $d(i, j)$ between any two vertices i and j in the graph is defined as the number of edges in the shortest path between i and j such that $i \neq j$, the efficiency is expressed as $1/d(i, j)$. From this definition, the global efficiency of a graph is the average efficiency over all $i \neq j$. Figure 6 shows the evolution in this indicator when performing an APT attack over the original and redundant topologies, for the three test cases of 100, 200 and 300 nodes.

6 Conclusions

APT attacks must be addressed with innovative techniques that supplement traditional detection and response techniques. As for the former, we have put into practice a dynamic decision mechanism by making use of graph theory and structural controllability concepts and defining a framework of attacks. That allows us to accurately identify topological anomalies in the network with different degrees of criticality. Accordingly, we have proposed the design of a redundant topology that allows the continuity of the network and also preserves privacy by making the routing process as uncertain as possible for an external attacker. Future work will involve the creation of a richer taxonomy of attacks that not only focus on topological changes, but also on the stealthy compromise of selected nodes within the network. The integration of other distributed decision mechanisms will be also studied, together with restoration and recovery services that ensure a better resilience against APT attacks.

Acknowledgements. The first author is supported by the Spanish Ministry of Education through the National F.P.U. Program under Grant Agreement No. FPU15/03213. In addition, this work has been partially supported by the Andalusian Government Research Program through the FISICCO project (P11-TIC-07223) and by the Spanish Ministry of Economy and Competitiveness through the PRECISE project (TIN2014-54427-JIN).

References

1. Chen, P., Desmet, L., Huygens, C.: A study on advanced persistent threats. In: Decker, B., Zúquete, A. (eds.) CMS 2014. LNCS, vol. 8735, pp. 63–72. Springer, Heidelberg (2014). doi:10.1007/978-3-662-44885-4_5
2. Virvilis, N., Gritzalis, D., Apostolopoulos, T.: Trusted computing vs. advanced persistent threats: can a defender win this game? In: Ubiquitous Intelligence and Computing, 2013 IEEE 10th International Conference on and 10th International Conference on Autonomic and Trusted Computing (UIC/ATC), pp. 396–403. IEEE (2013)

3. Pagani, G.A., Aiello, M.: The power grid as a complex network: a survey. Phys. A: Stat. Mech. Appl. **392**(11), 2688–2700 (2013)
4. Lin, C.-T.: Structural controllability. IEEE Trans. Autom. Control **19**(3), 201–208 (1974)
5. Nie, S., Wang, X., Zhang, H., Li, Q., Wang, B.: Robustness of controllability for networks based on edge-attack. PLoS ONE **9**(2), e89066 (2014)
6. Haynes, T.W., Hedetniemi, S.M., Hedetniemi, S.T., Henning, M.A.: Domination in graphs applied to electric power networks. SIAM J. Discrete Math. **15**(4), 519–529 (2002)
7. Kneis, J., Mölle, D., Richter, S., Rossmanith, P.: Parameterized power domination complexity. Inf. Process. Lett. **98**(4), 145–149 (2006)
8. Blondel, V.D., Hendrickx, J.M., Olshevsky, A., Tsitsiklis, J.N.: Convergence in multiagent coordination, consensus, and flocking. In: 44th IEEE Conference on 2005 and 2005 European Control Conference Decision and Control, CDC-ECC 2005, pp. 2996–3000. IEEE (2005)
9. Hegselmann, R., Krause, U., et al.: Opinion dynamics and bounded confidence models, analysis, and simulation. J. Artif. Soc. Soc. Simul. **5**(3) (2002). http://jasss.soc.surrey.ac.uk/5/3/contents.html
10. Alcaraz, C., Lopez, J.: Safeguarding structural controllability in cyber-physical control systems. In: Askoxylakis, I., Ioannidis, S., Katsikas, S., Meadows, C. (eds.) ESORICS 2016. LNCS, vol. 9879, pp. 471–489. Springer, Cham (2016). doi:10.1007/978-3-319-45741-3_24
11. Alcaraz, C., Wolthusen, S.: Recovery of structural controllability for control systems. In: Butts, J., Shenoi, S. (eds.) ICCIP 2014. IAICT, vol. 441, pp. 47–63. Springer, Heidelberg (2014). doi:10.1007/978-3-662-45355-1_4
12. Shamir, A.: How to share a secret. Commun. ACM **22**(11), 612–613 (1979)
13. Dijkstra, E.W.: A note on two problems in connexion with graphs. Numer. Math. **1**(1), 269–271 (1959)
14. Lee, C.Y.: An algorithm for path connections and its applications. IRE Trans. Electron. Comput. **3**, 346–365 (1961)
15. Ek, B., VerSchneider, C., Narayan, D.A.: Global efficiency of graphs. AKCE Int. J. Graphs Comb. **12**(1), 1–13 (2015)

Shortfall-Based Optimal Placement of Security Resources for Mobile IoT Scenarios

Antonino Rullo[1(✉)], Edoardo Serra[2], Elisa Bertino[3], and Jorge Lobo[4]

[1] DIMES Department, Universita della Calabria, 87036 Rende, Italy
n.rullo@dimes.unical.it
[2] Department of Computer Science, Boise State University, Boise, ID 83725, USA
edoardoserra@boisestate.edu
[3] Lawson Computer Science Department, Purdue University,
West Lafayette, IN 47907, USA
bertino@purdue.edu
[4] ICREA and Department of Information and Communication Technologies,
Universitat Pompeu Fabra, 08018 Barcelona, Spain
jorge.lobo@upf.edu

Abstract. We present a method for computing the best provisioning of security resources for Internet of Things (IoT) scenarios characterized by a high degree of mobility. The security infrastructure is specified by a security resource allocation plan computed as the solution of an optimization problem that minimizes the risk of having IoT devices not monitored by any resource. Due the mobile nature of IoT devices, a probabilistic framework for modeling such scenarios is adopted. We adapt the concept of *shortfall* from economics as a risk measure and show how to compute and evaluate the quality of an allocation plan. The proposed approach fits well with applications such as vehicular networks, mobile ad-hoc networks, smart cities, or any IoT environment characterized by mobile devices that needs a monitoring infrastructure.

Keywords: Network security · Internet of Things · Stochastic allocation

1 Introduction

The Internet of Things (IoT) will increase the ubiquity of the Internet by integrating every object for interaction via embedded systems leading to a highly distributed network of devices communicating with human beings as well as other devices [37]. The International Telecommunication Union defines the Internet of Things as "a global infrastructure for the Information Society, enabling advanced services by interconnecting (physical and virtual) things based on, existing and evolving, inter-operable information and communication technologies". [1] These definitions give us a hint to the role IoT will play in the everyday life, and

---

[1] http://www.itu.int/en/ITU-T/Pages/default.aspx.

© Springer International Publishing AG 2017
S.N. Foley et al. (Eds.): ESORICS 2017, Part II, LNCS 10493, pp. 419–436, 2017.
DOI: 10.1007/978-3-319-66399-9_23

the impact it will have in several areas: the inclusion of developing countries in global trade, the use of search engines to the benefit of civil society, combating product counterfeiting, tackling environmental concerns, improving health conditions, securing food supply and monitoring compliance with labor standards [36]. From these observations, it also follows that security will play a very important role in IoT. A security infrastructure will be mandatory for ensuring the integrity of data and reliability of network participants. However, the mobility and heterogeneity of IoT devices make the process of security provisioning more complicated than for traditional computer networks, where both the network topology and the number of network devices are assumed to be static. IoT networks continuously change topology because of mobility and/or (dis)appearance of devices.

In such IoT environments, the geographical distribution and the number of connected devices are not stationary, and vary from spot to spot, according to the different activities taking place in the different areas. A security infrastructure must be able to address such a dynamic nature of IoT networks. To this end, a security resource allocation plan must take into account the numerous shapes the device mobility confers to the system of interest, and ensure a certain security level in the majority of cases.

In this paper we present a method for computing the best allocation plan of security resources for IoT scenarios characterized by a high degree of mobility. By security resources we mean passive monitors of wireless traffic, and by plan, the number and location of such resources. We formalize a model for such scenarios, and provide a heuristic for computing allocation plans that minimize the risk of having IoT devices not monitored by any resource. We employ the key-concept of *shortfall* [3] as a risk measure. Shortfall is mostly used in economics to model the risk associated with an investment by combining in a single (risk) value the return of the investment in the worst scenarios together with the expected return. In fact, an investment might provide a return much more scarce than the expected one due to the significant changes that can affect the market. We adapt the concept of shortfall to model the risk associated with a security solution for which its effectiveness depends on how well the solution is able to address the continuous topology changes that affect the system of interest.

Our contributions can be summarized as follows:

- the formalization of a model for describing a mobile IoT scenario;
- the formalization of the problem of finding an appropriate set of candidate allocation plans of security resources for an IoT environment as an optimization problem;
- the adaptation of the concept of shortfall to our security domain as a risk measure of a security solution.

2   The Framework

The main characteristics of IoT environments are the heterogeneity, due to the simultaneous presence of different types of signals and networks, and the continuous topology changes of the network composed by the devices moving in the area of interest. Simple devices such as RFID tags broadcast messages for others to use, devices paired with other devices use bluetooth or WiFi as communication medium, people equipped with smartphones, laptops, VoIP devices, PDAs, smartwatches, well-being devices etc., move from place to place within a common macro-area. As an example of IoT environment we can think of a university campus where thousand of people with several mobile connected devices continuously change their position. Another well-fitting example is a vehicular network (VANET) that, although more homogeneous in the type of devices, assumes different shapes and different sizes according to the hour and day of the week. In such environments, the traditional security monitoring must be enhanced by security tools *(i)* capable of listening to different types of signals, *(ii)* capable of working in conjunction with other security resources to cover all possible signals, and *(iii)* smartly deployed in the network area in order to monitor as many devices as possible despite continuous changes of the network topology. In this paper we focus on the third aspect, and propose a method for intelligently placing security monitors, such that a certain level of security is ensured even when the system of interest assumes shapes and sizes that are uncommon.

2.1 Threat Model

In such complex IoT ecosystem, different entities have different capabilities and potential to cause security incidents. While our defensive approach is independent from the actual attacks, we assume that the attacker may perform attacks at different layers, and can take any of the steps commonly used to carry out attacks: capturing and reprogramming devices, adding malicious entities to the network to overhear data communications, inject false data and control traffic, intercept and drop data packets, introduce interference, claim multiple identities, exfiltrate data, security credentials or encryption keys, compromise other IoT devices in the network with the help of a compromised device. Also attacks aimed at Internet services are carried through IoT devices. Recent news have in fact reported the use of IoT devices for botnet attacks [10].

2.2 Defender Side

The goal of the defender is to passively monitor all wireless communications the devices moving in the area of interest do. To this end, (s)he needs to choose a set of security resources to monitor traffic and presence of devices, and decide where to deploy them in order to minimize the number of non-monitored devices. There are different kinds of security services the defender may have to use. Intrusion detection systems (IDS) [20,27] as well as attack prevention systems (APS) [29] can be installed in the network area to, respectively, detect ongoing attacks, and prevent future ones; recovery systems [34] can be installed in order to address security problems reported by IDSs and APSs; physical tools, like directional antennas and highly sensitive transceivers can be adopted for enabling security resources collecting data for the services to widen their action range [24]. There are several characteristics of IoT that can be leveraged to design a security resource well fit for IoT. While heterogeneous, most IoT devices communicate and operate on standard mediums and protocols, such as IEEE 802.15.4 [14], WiFi or Bluetooth for mediums, and ZigBee [39] or 6LoWPAN [13] for protocols. Therefore, as long as a device communicates by using any of these mediums and protocols, effective techniques such as promiscuous overhearing and watchdog-based mechanisms [12,21] can be deployed (see e.g. [20]). Notice that a security resource may embed one or more of these services, or may just collect data to be sent to security services located in remote locations. We assume that different kinds of security resources act independently and hence, are independently deployed.

The geographical distribution and the number of connected devices in the area of interest are key parameters for the task of computing the best placement of security resources. Such distributions can be learned during a training period long enough to be a representative sample of the monitored eco-system. Following the two examples of IoT environments described above, in a campus area, most students follow patterns that repeat every day, and can be learned in a few months of an academic year: during the morning and the afternoon they are located at the classrooms; at lunch/dinner time they move to the dining areas; during the night they stay in the dorms or other in-campus accommodations. Such patterns can be learned by analyzing the network traces produced by the interaction between users' devices, or between access points and the devices. In a VANET, where cars move according to the hour and day of the week, such patterns can be learned from data collected by road side units (RSUs). Commuting patterns are also predictable by stochastic processes that capture local mobility decisions. Such processes help analytically derive commuting and mobility fluxes that require as input only information on the population distribution. The resulting model predicts mobility patterns in good agreement with mobility and transport patterns observed in a wide range of phenomena, from long-term migration patterns to communication volume between different regions [33].

In the next sections we show that for a security manager, the problem of computing the best allocation plan of security monitors for a changing IoT environment can be interpreted as the problem an investor faces when choosing an investment that maximizes the return, considering the continuous changes that affect the market.

3   Shortfall

In this section we briefly introduce the concept of shortfall, clarify the motivations that have lead us to adopt it in our formalization, and show how we manipulate it in order to obtain a more appropriate solution to our situation.

3.1   Definition

Shortfall is a risk measure used in economics which has conceptual, computational and practical advantages over other commonly used risk measures [3]. The shortfall, or more precisely, the *shortfall at level* α, measures how large losses, below the expected return, can be expected if the return of the investment drops below its α-quantile. Given all the possible market trends, we can compute the set of all possible returns of our investment. The shortfall at level α is the difference between the expected return and the average of the returns of the worst $\alpha\%$ of cases. Given an investment x and a value $\alpha \in (0,1)$, the shortfall $s_\alpha(x)$ is defined as follows:

$$s_\alpha(x) = E[R] - E[R|R \leq q_\alpha(R)] \tag{1}$$

where $E[R]$ is the expected return of the investment, and $q_\alpha(X)$ is the α-quantile of a random variable X:

$$q_\alpha(X) = inf\{x|P(X \leq x) \geq \alpha\} \tag{2}$$

According to Levy and Kroll [18], for an investment x chosen to minimize $s_\alpha(x)$ for a fixed α and a given target mean μ_t, there is no other investment with the same mean which would be preferred to x, because less profitable in the worst $\alpha\%$ of cases. Thus, one is naturally led to minimize the quantity $s_\alpha(x)$ for some $\alpha \in (0,1)$ as follows:

$$\begin{aligned} \min \quad & s_\alpha(x) \\ \text{subject to} \quad & E[R] = \mu_t \end{aligned} \tag{3}$$

3.2 From the Minimum Shortfall to the Best Choice

The solution we obtain by solving Problem 3 depends on the target mean μ_t we choose. In fact, given a target mean, we obtain the best investment (i.e., the one with minimum shortfall) among those with the same expected value, but we do not know whether there exists a better investment for different values of μ_t. In other words, there might exist a *dominating* investment, i.e., of a higher mean and a smaller shortfall, or alternatively, a *non-dominated* investment, i.e., of a higher (resp. lower) mean and a greater (resp. smaller) shortfall, which may be preferred by the investor. A possible solution is that of solving Problem 3 with different μ_t, and finally select the investment that best meets our needs. However, this solution is not efficient because it might compute some dominated investment, i.e., which would not be preferred to any other because of a lower expected value and a greater shortfall than those of the other ones. Consequently the time needed to compute such dominated solutions would be wasted. As alternative, we propose to adapt Problem 3 in such a way that it computes only non dominated solutions. This is possible by turning Problem 3 into a bi-objective optimization problem. First of all, we start considering the following equivalent problem:

$$\begin{aligned} \max \quad & E_\alpha[R] \\ \text{subject to} \quad & E[R] = \mu_t \end{aligned} \tag{4}$$

where $E_\alpha[R] = E[R|R \leq q_\alpha(R)]$ is the mean of the worst $\alpha\%$ of cases, namely, the subtrahend in Eq. 1. Problem 4 is equivalent to Problem 3 because for a target mean μ_t, minimizing $E[R] - E_\alpha[R]$ is equivalent to maximizing $E_\alpha[R]$. Since we want to compute a set of non dominated investments based on their $E[R]$ and $E_\alpha[R]$ values, we place the expected value as an objective of the optimization problem, and we impose two inequality constraints on the values of $E[R]$ and $E_\alpha[R]$, in order to restrict the computation only to the cases we are interested in. The resulting problem is as follows:

$$\begin{aligned} \max \quad & E[R], E_\alpha[R] \\ \text{subject to} \quad & E[R] \geq \mu_t \\ & E_\alpha[R] \geq \mu_\alpha \end{aligned} \qquad (5)$$

Problem 5 is a less restricted version of Problem 3, where we split the two terms of the shortfall, $E[R]$ and $E_\alpha[R]$, and optimize them separately. The output is a Pareto frontier PF [19] whose points are non dominated investments x with values of $E[R]$ and $E_\alpha[R]$ below the desired thresholds. Formally, PF is defined as follows:

$$PF = \{(E[R], E_\alpha[R]) | \nexists (E'[R], E'_\alpha[R]) \in PF \text{ such that}$$
$$(E[R] \geq E'[R] \land E_\alpha[R] \geq E'_\alpha[R]) \land (E[R] > E'[R] \lor E_\alpha[R] > E'_\alpha[R])\}$$

An investor can thus conduct a cost-benefit analysis on the solutions of the Pareto frontier, and finally choose the one that best fits his/her requirements. In the next sections we show that the shortfall is well suited for describing the risk associated with an allocation plan, such that a certain level of security is ensured for every variation in the topology of the monitored environment.

4 Problem Definition

4.1 Preliminaries

We define an IoT environment as a set of n geographic areas $R_k, k = 1, \ldots, n$, that we call *regions*. We divide each region in *locations*, i.e., space units where IoT devices or security resources could reside.

Definition 1 (region). *A region R is a tuple $\langle L_R, P_R \rangle$, where:*

- *L_R is the set of locations of R;*
- *P_R is the probability distribution over a discrete random variable X that takes integer values in the interval $[0, \infty)$. $P_R(X = x)$ is the probability that there are x devices in R.*

Definition 2 (security resource). *A security resource sr is a tuple $\langle c, r, P_{sr} \rangle$, where:*

- *c is the cost;*
- *r (from radius) is the maximum action range;*

– P_{sr} is the probability distribution over a discrete random variable Y that takes values in the interval $[0, r]$. $P_{sr}(Y = y)$ is the probability that sr is able to monitor a device located at a distance y.

Furthermore, we define $\mathcal{R} = \bigcup_{k=1}^{n} R_k$ as the set of all regions, and $\mathcal{L} = \{loc : loc \in \mathcal{R}\}$, as the set of all locations in $\mathcal{R}$. In the rest of the paper we will use the notation $sr.c$ to denote the cost c of a security resource sr.

Security resources have an associated probability distribution, that describes how likely a device at a certain distance is seen by a resource. This choice is driven by the fact that the typical assumptions about all radios having circular range and perfect coverage in that range is far from real [17]. More realistic models take into account antenna height and orientation, terrain and obstacles, surface reflection and absorption, and so forth. It is often difficult in reality to estimate whether or not one has a functioning radio link between nodes, because signals fluctuate greatly due to mobility and fading as well as interference. Several signal attenuation models have thus been proposed [9, 25], and there are a few that can be used in concrete implementations of our model. For example, the Okumura model, the Hata model for urban areas, the Hata model for open areas, are models for outdoor attenuation; instead, the ITU model and the Log-distance path loss model are models for indoor attenuation. One of these models, or a combination of them, can be adopted for modeling the attenuation of a device according to its radio characteristics.

4.2   From Economics to the IoT Domain

The problem we face is that of computing the optimal security resource allocation plan for IoT scenarios characterized by a high degree of mobility. This problem can be reduced to Problem 5 if we consider an allocation plan along with its cost as an investment, and all the possible configurations a set of IoT devices may assume in the area of interest as all the possible market trends. A security manager (the investor) knows that the number of devices moving within a region R_k follows a certain probability distribution P_{R_k}, and that the resource allocation plan to choose must be able to provide a good security level not only in the average cases of P_{R_k}, but also in the rare ones. In fact, rare device configurations may result in high losses if not addressed by an adequate security infrastructure. We use $E[R]$ and $E_\alpha[R]$ as evaluation metrics of an allocation plan for an IoT environment, where the multitude of device configurations is wide because mobility. The optimal plan is the one that minimizes the expected number of IoT devices not reached by any security resource. We call this quantity the *risk* associated with the allocation plan (AP), denoted by $risk_{AP}$. We adopt the risk as a negative return of an allocation plan, such that the smaller the risk is, the more effective the plan. Being the risk a negative return, we need to adapt the definition of α-quantile given in Eq. 2 as follows:

$$q_\alpha(risk) = inf\{x | P(risk \geq x) \geq \alpha\} \tag{6}$$

Given a set of regions $\mathcal{R}$ (i.e., an IoT environment), and a fixed security budget b, we define an allocation plan for $\mathcal{R}$ as the set

$$AP = \{(sr_i, loc_j) | \sum_i sr_i.c \leq b, loc_j \in \mathcal{L}\} \qquad (7)$$

Given the set of all possible device configurations, we can compute the set of all possible returns of an AP in terms of risk, and thus compute $E[risk_{AP}]$ and $E_\alpha[risk_{AP}]$. The adaptation of Problem 5 to our application domain is as follows:

$$\max_{AP \in \mathcal{AP}} - E[risk_{AP}], -E_\alpha[risk_{AP}]$$

subject to

$$E[risk_{AP}] \leq \mu_t \qquad (8)$$
$$E_\alpha[risk_{AP}] \leq \mu_\alpha$$

$$\sum_{sr \in AP} sr.c \leq b$$

where $\mathcal{AP}$ is the set of all possible allocation plans. The minus sign before the two objectives means that we are actually minimizing the two measures, being the risk a negative return. For the same reason, μ_t and μ_α are upper bounds for $E[risk_{AP}]$ and $E_\alpha[risk_{AP}]$, respectively, and not lower bounds as in Problem 5. Note that without the constraint on the maximum budget, Problem 8 becomes meaningless because it would compute a unique allocation plan possibly with an unreasonable number of resources, providing risk 0 for any device configuration, which is surely the most effective solution, but also unlikely the most efficient because it would be very expensive in terms of cost.

Once a security manager has obtained the set of solutions to Problem 8, (s)he can choose the allocation plan that best fits his/her security requirements. However, there may be cases for which there is no solution, i.e., solving Problem 8 outputs an empty set. This can happen for two reason:

1. no allocation plan exists able to satisfy the constraints, because the security budget is too small to provide a value of $E[risk_{AP}]$ and $E_\alpha[risk_{AP}]$ below the desired thresholds;
2. the α-quantile is too small to admit $E_\alpha[risk_{AP}] \leq \mu_\alpha$.

In case (1), the security manager can try to increase the security budget until at least one solution is returned, or alternatively can turn Problem 8 in a three-objective optimization problem by placing the cost as a further objective as follows:

$$\max_{AP \in \mathcal{AP}} - E[risk_{AP}], -E_\alpha[risk_{AP}], -cost_{AP}$$

subject to

$$E[risk_{AP}] \leq \mu_t \qquad (9)$$
$$E_\alpha[risk_{AP}] \leq \mu_\alpha$$
$$minCost \leq cost_{AP} \leq maxCost$$

where $cost_{AP} = \sum_{sr \in AP} sr.c$. This way, the security manager can have a comprehensive view of cost-benefit, by determining the minimum cost required to ensure a certain security level. However, this problem takes more time to solve than Problem 8, proportionally to the quantity $maxCost - minCost$.

In case (2), the security manager may decide to increase μ_α, or to tolerate a higher risk by having a larger quantile. In fact, α can be intended as a "measure of the risk tolerance": by increasing α, the value of $q_\alpha(risk)$ decreases, and Problem 8 computes $E_\alpha[risk]$ over a larger set of cases, which means that cases with high risk are more tolerated. On the contrary, when α decreases, $q_\alpha(risk)$ tends to the maximum value of risk, thus restricting the cases over which $E_\alpha[risk]$ is computed, meaning that we tolerate fewer cases with high risk.

5 Evaluation Algorithm

To solve Problem 8 an algorithm should enumerate all possible allocation plans $\mathcal{AP}$, and evaluate each $AP \in \mathcal{AP}$ over all possible configurations the IoT devices can take within the geographic area of interest $\mathcal{R}$. It easy to see that such an algorithm would take an unreasonable amount of time to solve the problem. In fact, for each region $R_k \in \mathcal{R}$, the number of possible configurations is the cardinality of the power set of L_{R_k}, and the size of $\mathcal{AP}$ is upper-bounded by the number of all subsets of $\mathcal{L}$ of cardinality at most s, where s is the maximum number of security resources allowed by the security budget. This lead us to look for approximations in place of an exact solution. A standard tool for approximation is the use of genetic algorithms. There exist several genetic algorithms for computing a Pareto frontier, one of the most commonly used is NSGA-II [8], an evolutionary genetic algorithm able to find an approximation of the Pareto frontier for multi-objective optimization problems. The main difference between NSGA-II and other evolutionary genetic algorithms is the selection phase: NSGA-II has no unique fitness function but one for each objective. During the selection phase, the selected points are only the non dominated ones. When some constraints exist the selection phase will remove all points that do not satisfy the constraints.

In Problem 8 there are two objectives $-E[risk_{AP}]$ and $-E_\alpha[risk_{AP}]$. To compute their fitness at each iteration, the NSGA-II algorithm needs to evaluate the current AP over the set of all possible device configurations. An AP is implemented as an individual of the population of the genetic algorithm, where each gene is the id of the location where a security resource has been placed. As stated before, for each region R_k the set of different configurations C_k is too big to be employed in the evaluation process without incurring in scalability problems. In its place we generate a subset of C_k with a Monte Carlo method [28], whose elements are generated according to the probability distribution P_{R_k} associated with the region R_k. More precisely, for a given region R_k, a device configuration is a set of locations chosen randomly, with cardinality equal to an integer randomly generated from P_{R_k}. Algorithms 1 and 2 illustrate the fitness function NSGA-II used for evaluating an allocation plan. Algorithm 1 takes as input an

---

Algorithm 1

1: **procedure** COMPUTEFITNESS(AP, n)
2:     $\vec{risk}_{AP} = $ MONTECARLO(AP, n);
3:     $q_\alpha = \alpha$-quantile of $\vec{risk}_{AP}$;
4:     $E[risk_{AP}] = 0$;
5:     $E_\alpha[risk_{AP}] = 0$;
6:     $count = 0$;
7:     **for** $r \in \vec{risk}_{AP}$ **do**
8:         $E[risk_{AP}] + = r$;
9:         **if** $r \geq q_\alpha$ **then**
10:             $E_\alpha[risk_{AP}] + = r$;
11:             $count + +$;
12:         **end if**
13:     **end for**
14:     $E[risk_{AP}] = E[risk_{AP}]/\vec{risk}_{AP}.length$;
15:     $E_\alpha[risk_{AP}] = E_\alpha[risk_{AP}]/count$;
16:     **return** $E[risk_{AP}], E_\alpha[risk_{AP}]$;
17: **end procedure**

Algorithm 2

1: **procedure** MONTECARLO(AP, n)
2:     $\vec{risk}_{AP} = [\ ]$;
3:     **while** $n > 0$ **do**
4:         $devicesLocations = \emptyset$;
5:         **for** $R_k \in \mathcal{R}$ **do**
6:             $numberOfDevices = P_k.nextInt()$;
7:             **while** $numberOfDevices > 0$ **do**
8:                 $loc = $ a location $\in R_k$ chosen randomly;
9:                 $devicesLocations.add(loc)$;
10:                 $numberOfDevices - -$;
11:             **end while**
12:         **end for**
13:         $risk = $ COMPUTERISK($AP, devicesLocations$);
14:         add $risk$ to $\vec{risk}_{AP}$;
15:         $n - -$;
16:     **end while**
17:     **return** $\vec{risk}_{AP}$;
18: **end procedure**

---

allocation plan AP and an integer n. In Line 2, the MONTECARLO procedure returns a vector of length n with the risks associated with AP evaluated over n different device configurations. In Line 3, q_α is the value of the α-quantile of the vector $\vec{risk}_{AP}$. In Algorithm 2, the MONTECARLO procedure produces n different device configurations over which it evaluates AP. The number of devices for each region R_k is chosen randomly according to the probability distribution P_{R_k} (Line 6). In Line 13, the procedure COMPUTERISK computes the number of devices not monitored by any security resource $sr \in AP$ for each configuration, according to P_{sr} (the probability that sr is able to monitor a device located at a certain distance). The exact positions where to place the sensors are identified by each single gene of the individual corresponding to the chosen Pareto point.

6   Results Analysis

In this section we show the steps a security manager has to follow for computing the allocation plan that best fits his/her security requirements, according to his/her security budget. To this end, we report results related to the simulation of an area of $2000\,\mathrm{m}^2$ and consisting of three regions divided in locations of $1\,\mathrm{m}^2$. The details are shown in the following figure:

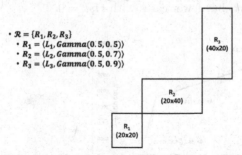

$Gamma(\alpha, \beta)$ is the Gamma probability distribution, adopted for simulating the devices distribution over each region.

Suppose the security manager has at his/her disposal a security budget of 30 monetary units, and only one type of security resource, based on the watchdog mechanism, with action range of 8 space units, and unitary cost. The security level (s)he wants to achieve is at most 30 unmonitored devices in no more than 10% of cases. This is formally translated as:

- $\forall$ security resource $sr, sr = \langle 1, 8, LDPL \rangle$;
- $\alpha = 0.1$;
- $b = 30$;
- $\mu_t = \infty$, $\mu_\alpha = 30$.

where $LDPL$ is the Log-distance path loss model [9], adopted as the signal attenuation model for the security resources. In order to compute the set of plans that satisfy his/her security constraints, the security manager solves Problem 8 with an NSGA-II algorithm, and set the Monte Carlo simulation with $n = 100K$ (see the MonteCarlo procedure shown in Algorithm 2) such that each plan is evaluated over a set of 100 K different device configurations. Figure 1 shows the Pareto frontier (left), and the risk distribution of its plans (right). Looking at the Pareto frontier the security manager would choose the AP having the best combination of $E[risk]$ and $E_\alpha[risk]$. $AP\_30.1$ would be a better plan than $AP\_30.2$ and $AP\_30.3$ because $E[risk]$ is almost the same in the three cases and $E_\alpha[risk]$ is 25% lower. Looking at the risk distributions of Fig. 1 (right), (s)he can also base his/her decision on additional information and conduct a more in-depth analysis. Over 100 K different device configurations, each plan provides a minimum risk of 0 and a maximum risk of 45. $AP\_30.2$ is the plan that provides more cases with risk 0, thus a lower probability of an attack to happen in the network area. $AP\_30.1$, although it provides the lowest number of cases with risk in the range bounded by the α-quantile, it also provides the lowest number of cases with risk 0, thus the highest probability to have an attack.[2] The trade-off between $E[risk]$, $E_\alpha[risk]$, and the probability of having an attack, is at

---

[2] The probability to have an attack is computed as the ratio between the number of cases with $risk > 0$ and the total number of cases.

the basis of the reasoning a security manager may want to follow to choose a plan. In this situation, a security manager interested in minimizing the cases with $risk > 0$ would choose $AP\_30.2$, since $AP\_30.3$ provides similar values of $E[risk]$ and $E_\alpha[risk]$ but fewer cases with $risk = 0$.

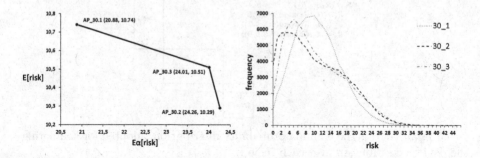

Fig. 1. Pareto frontier (left), and the risk distribution of its allocation plans (right).

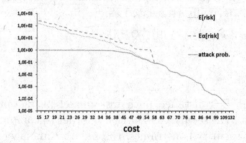

Fig. 2. The relation between cost, $E[risk]$, $E_\alpha[risk]$, and the probability to have an attack, of plans computed with $\alpha = 0.1$, $\mu_t = \infty$, $\mu_\alpha = 30$, $minCost = 15$ and $maxCost = 132$.

Now suppose that the security manager wants to know how much to rise the budget to achieve higher security performances. In this case (s)he can solve Problem 9 and plot the values of $E[risk]$ and $E_\alpha[risk]$ along with the attack probability as shown in Fig. 2. It can be noticed that, although $E[risk]$ and $E_\alpha[risk]$ decrease of two orders of magnitude from $cost = 15$ to $cost = 40$, the probability of having an attack remains around 1, which means that there are very few cases (possibly none) with $risk = 0$. This way, the security manager would know (s)he needs a security budget greater than 40 for ensuring a higher level of security.

7   Case Study

In this section we show how we applied our method to a real case scenario, and demonstrate its validity by comparing it with other heuristics.

7.1   The Dartmouth College Data

In [16] Kotz et al. analyze an extensive network trace from a mature 802.11 WLAN, including more than 550 Access Points (AcP) and 7000 users over seventeen weeks in the Dartmouth College area. This work reports several statistics about the movement of people equipped with various IoT devices within the campus area. All these data plus some additional data collected covering more than 160 weeks over the same population have been made publicly available.[3] We used this dataset for testing our method on a simulation of a real IoT environment, intended as a set of regions (the area covered by each AcP), and with real device distributions. Those were computed as follows. Each location data entry is associated with the MAC address of a mobile device that generated the data point. By grouping the devices that were connected at the same hour of the day in the same AcP, we counted how many devices were observed in each hour over the entire period in each AcP. We also added up the number of different devices observed during a day (a period of 24 h) in each AcP. In this way we could compute the device distribution for each region/AcP of the campus area. Other experimental settings are as follows: we divided each region/AcP in locations of $1\,m^2$, for a total of $183279\,m^2$; we adopted watchdog-like devices as security resources with an action range of 15 m and unitary cost; we adopted *LDPL* [9] as the signal attenuation model for the security resources; we set $\alpha = 0.1$; we used the data of the first 3 months as training set for computing the Pareto frontier. Finally, we tested the plan of the Pareto frontier with the lowest $E[risk]$ on the data relative to the remaining 21 months.

7.2   Evaluation Methodology

In order to evaluate our method, we compare the allocation plans obtained by running Problem 8 on the IoT environment described above, with those obtained by using other heuristics that follow different approaches for solving the placement problem. We implemented four heuristics: *(1) square lattice, (2) triangular lattice, (3) max coverage,* and *(4) greedy*.

Methods *(1)* and *(2)* are placements typically used by system engineers to model the structure of a set of base stations (BSs) in cellular networks [4]. We have chosen those models because the BSs placement problem is similar to the problem of placing security monitors in an IoT environment, since both mobile phones and IoT devices are mobile, while BSs and security monitors are not. Method *(3)* is implemented as a single-objective optimization problem solved by an NSGA-II algorithm with the objective of maximizing the number of locations that fall under the action range of security resources, given a fixed budget. Method *(4)* is an algorithm that computes the placement in a greedy manner, i.e., given a fixed budget b, at each iteration it chooses the security resource which maximizes the number of covered locations without exceeding b. We ran experiments with different security budgets on the network area built, and with

---

[3] http://crawdad.org/dartmouth/campus/20090909.

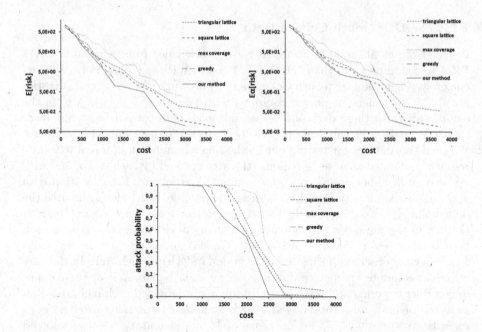

Fig. 3. Values of $E[risk]$ (top-left), $E_\alpha[risk]$ (top-right), and attack probability (bottom), computed for different values of cost, with five different heuristics.

the device distributions computed from the Dartmouth College dataset.[4] The results are reported in Fig. 3. It can be noticed that our method computes allocation plans with $E[risk]$, $E_\alpha[risk]$ and an attack probability lower than those provided by the other methods. Furthermore, we recall that evolutionary algorithms compute solutions that are an approximation of the optimal one. The results of Fig. 3 were obtained by running the NSGA-II algorithm with 50 generations, thus one can obtain better plans by just rising the number of generations, or also by adjusting other parameters like the mutation method, mutation probability, and algorithm seed.

8   Related Work

We are not the first to use shortfall to characterize risk in a security context. Molloy et al. [23] adapt shortfall to take security decisions (such as access-control decisions or spam filtering decisions) under uncertainty when the benefit of doing so outweighs the need to absolutely guarantee that these decisions are correct. Molloy et al. have also put forward a more general vision on economic models

---

[4] Method (4) was run with budgets not greater than 1298, i.e., the cheapest budget for covering all locations; running such a greedy algorithm with a budget greater than 1298 is meaningless because the objective of covering as much locations as possible would be already reached.

for security [22]. We also would like to mention the risk-aware security solutions by Chen et Crampton incorporating the notion of risk into the RBAC model [5]. The problem of computing the best placement of network devices for mobile scenarios has been mostly addressed in the area of cellular networks. In such networks, the optimal placement of base stations (BSs) is crucial for the correct functioning of the communication system. The similarity with our scenarios is in the presence of mobile devices that have to be covered by the action range of static entities. However, the roaming problem, that has to be taken into account in the computation of the optimal BS placement, makes those solutions not suitable for the IoT scenario. We refer the reader to [11] for a more comprehensive discussion on this topic. The problem of finding efficient security solutions in the domain of computer networks with the help of the Pareto analysis has been extensively investigated In [31] the Pareto analysis has been used to compute the best combination between cost of patching vulnerabilities and cost of deactivating products within an enterprise system. Chang and Zhuang propose an approach based on a node clustering algorithm, with effective tax-based sub-carrier allocation, tailored for wireless mesh networks with QoS support [6]. Here, the Pareto analysis is used for the optimal resource management. Signal attenuation models have also been widely investigated. Shen et al. propose an indoor wireless propagation model in WiFi radio-over-fiber network architecture for received signal strength (RSS) based localization in the IoT [32]. The proposed model adds attenuation terms of obstacles in each sub-space by dividing the room into several sub-spaces according to the obstacles' distribution. Alwajeeh et al. [2] propose an intelligent method to associate known models with spatial zones according to the electromagnetic interactions. Past work on IoT security focuses on protection mechanisms against specific attacks [1,35,38], investigates ISO/OSI layer-related security problems [15], or proposes architectures for intrusion detection, attack prevention, or recovery systems [27,29]. Raza et al. [26] propose an IPsec extension of 6LoWPAN, and show that IPsec is a feasible option for securing the IoT in terms of packet size, energy consumption, memory usage, and processing time. Chigan et al. [7] propose a resource-aware self-adaptive network security provisioning scheme for the resource constraint Mobile Ad-hoc Networks (MANET), in order to avoid security provisioning Denial of Service (SPDoS) attack. While we model efficiency and effectiveness of a security solution as cost and risk, Chigan et al. model them as two indexes, performance index (PI) and security index (SI), respectively. SI quantitatively reflects the security contribution of a secure protocol to a MANET system, while PI quantitatively reflects network performance perspectives of a secure protocol. The problem of finding the optimal security resource allocation plan for IoT networks has already been investigated by Rullo et al. [30]. However, such approach only works for static networks for the topology changes due to the occasional (dis)appearance of devices.

9   Conclusion

In this paper we built upon the concept of security resources specialized for the IoT. These security resources monitor traffic generated by devices possibly using different protocols and wireless networks. Our proposed framework takes into consideration the possibility that the security resources are not able to monitor all the devices at all times. Our framework provides different security resource deployment plans based on cost and risk. We measure the risk associated with an allocation plan as the expected number of devices left uncovered. Considering the cost of the plan as an investment, and the expected risk as the expected return of the investment, we were able to borrow the concept of shortfall from economics, that looks at the worst possible outcomes of an investment to make better decisions from investments with similar expected returns. Hence, our framework produces resource allocation plans that are the outcomes of bi-objective optimization of expected risks and expected worst risk scenarios. We have developed a reference implementation of the framework and ran simulations that incorporate mobility patterns from real data. The reference implementation uses standard genetic algorithms to find approximate solutions to the optimization problem. In our experimental setting we employed just one type of security resource for simplicity, but with some modeling effort, NSGA-II algorithm can be tuned to work with individuals of different types, such that a wider range of security scenarios can be addressed.

Acknowledgment. Jorge Lobo was partially supported by the Secretaria de Universitats i Recerca de la Generalitat de Catalunya, the Maria de Maeztu Units of Excellence Programme and the Spanish Ministry for Economy and Competitiveness (MINECO) under Grant Ref.: TIN2016-81032-P.

References

1. Altman, E., Avrachenkov, K., Gamaev, A.: Jamming in wireless networks: the case of several jammers. In: Proceedings of the First ICST International Conference on Game Theory for Networks (2009)
2. Alwajeeh, T., Combeau, P., Bounceur, A., Vauzelle, R.: Efficient method for associating radio propagation models with spatial partitioning for smart city applications. In: Proceedings of the International Conference on Internet of Things and Cloud Computing, p. 8. ACM (2016)
3. Bertsimas, D., Lauprete, G.J., Samarov, A.: Shortfall as a risk measure: properties, optimization and applications. J. Econ. Dyn. Control **28**(7), 1353–1381 (2004)
4. Charoen, P., Ohtsuki, T.: Codebook based interference mitigation with base station cooperation in multi-cell cellular network. In: 2011 IEEE Vehicular Technology Conference (VTC Fall), pp. 1–5. IEEE (2011)
5. Chen, L., Crampton, J.: Risk-aware role-based access control. In: Meadows, C., Fernandez-Gago, C. (eds.) STM 2011. LNCS, vol. 7170, pp. 140–156. Springer, Heidelberg (2012). doi:10.1007/978-3-642-29963-6_11
6. Cheng, H.T., Zhuang, W.: Pareto optimal resource management for wireless mesh networks with QoS assurance: joint node clustering and subcarrier allocation. IEEE Trans. Wireless Commun. (2009)
7. Chigan, C., Li, L., Ye, Y.: Resource-aware self-adaptive security provisioning in mobile ad hoc networks. In: 2005 IEEE Wireless Communications and Networking Conference, vol. 4, pp. 2118–2124. IEEE (2005)

8. Deb, K., Pratap, A., Agarwal, S., Meyarivan, T.: A fast elitist multi-objective genetic algorithm: NSGA-II. IEEE Trans. Evol. Comput. **6**, 182–197 (2000)
9. Goldhirsh, J., Vogel, W.J.: Handbook of propagation effects for vehicular and personal mobile satellite systems. NASA Ref. Publ. **1274**, 40–67 (1998)
10. Gonsalves, A.: New toolkit seeks routers, internet of things for DDoS botnet (2014). http://www.csoonline.com/article/2687653/data-protection/new-toolkit-seeks-/routers-internet-of-things-for-ddos-botnet.html. Accessed May 2016
11. Guo, A., Haenggi, M.: Spatial stochastic models and metrics for the structure of base stations in cellular networks. IEEE Trans. Wireless Commun. **12**(11), 5800–5812 (2013)
12. Huang, Y.A., Lee, W.: A cooperative intrusion detection system for ad hoc networks. In: Proceedings of the 1st ACM Workshop on Security of Ad Hoc and Sensor Networks, SASN 2003, pp. 135–147. ACM, New York (2003). http://doi.acm.org/10.1145/986858.986877
13. Hui, J., Culler, D., Chakrabarti, S.: 6LoWPAN: incorporating IEEE 802.15.4 into the IP architecture. IPSO Alliance White Paper 3 (2009)
14. IEEE: IEEE 802.15 WPAN Task Group 4 (TG4). http://www.ieee802.org/15/pub/TG4.html
15. Jinwala, D., Patel, D., Dasgupta, K.: FlexiSec: a configurable link layer security architecture for wireless sensor networks. arXiv preprint (2012). arXiv:1203.4697
16. Kotz, D., Henderson, T., Abyzov, I., Yeo, J.: CRAWDAD dataset dartmouth/campus (v. 2009–09–09), September 2009
17. Kotz, D., Newport, C., Gray, R.S., Liu, J., Yuan, Y., Elliott, C.: Experimental evaluation of wireless simulation assumptions. In: Proceedings of the 7th ACM International Symposium on Modeling, Analysis and Simulation of Wireless and Mobile Systems, pp. 78–82. ACM (2004)
18. Levy, H., Kroll, Y.: Ordering uncertain options with borrowing and lending. J. Finance **33**(2), 553–574 (1978)
19. Messac, A., Ismail-Yahaya, A., Mattson, C.A.: The normalized normal constraint method for generating the pareto frontier. Struct. Multidiscip. Optim. **25**(2), 86–98 (2003)
20. Midi, D., Rullo, A., Mudgerikar, A., Bertino, E.: Kalis: a system for knowledge-driven adaptable intrusion detection for the internet of things. In: IEEE 37th International Conference on Distributed Computing Systems (ICDCS) (2017)
21. Mishra, A., Nadkarni, K., Patcha, A.: Intrusion detection in wireless ad hoc networks. IEEE Wireless Commun. **11**(1), 48–60 (2004)
22. Molloy, I., Cheng, P.C., Rohatgi, P.: Trading in risk: using markets to improve access control. In: Proceedings of the 2008 Workshop on New Security Paradigms, pp. 107–125. ACM (2009)
23. Molloy, I., Dickens, L., Morisset, C., Cheng, P.C., Lobo, J., Russo, A.: Risk-based security decisions under uncertainty. In: Proceedings of the Second ACM Conference on Data and Application Security and Privacy, pp. 157–168. ACM (2012)
24. Nasipuri, A., Li, K.: A directionality based location discovery scheme for wireless sensor networks. In: Proceedings of 1st ACM International Workshop on Wireless Sensor Networks and Applications. ACM (2002)
25. Rappaport, T.S., et al.: Wireless Communications: Principles and Practice, vol. 2. Prentice Hall PTR, Upper Saddle River (1996)
26. Raza, S., Duquennoy, S., Höglund, J., Roedig, U., Voigt, T.: Secure communication for the internet of things–a comparison of link-layer security and IPsec for 6LoWPAN. Secur. Commun. Netw. (2012)

27. Raza, S., Wallgren, L., Voigt, T.: SVELTE: real-time intrusion detection in the internet of things. Ad Hoc Netw. (2013)
28. Robert, C., Casella, G.: Monte Carlo Statistical Methods. Springer Science & Business Media, Berlin (2013)
29. Roman, R., Alcaraz, C., Lopez, J., Sklavos, N.: Key management systems for sensor networks in the context of the internet of things. Comput. Electr. Eng. **37**(2), 147–159 (2011)
30. Rullo, A., Midi, D., Serra, E., Bertino, E.: A game of things: strategic allocation of security resources for IoT. In: ACM/IEEE 2nd International Conference on Internet of Things Design and Implementation (IoTDI 2017), p. 6 (2017)
31. Serra, E., Jajodia, S., Pugliese, A., Rullo, A., Subrahmanian, V.: Pareto-optimal adversarial defense of enterprise systems. ACM Trans. Inf. Syst. Secur. (TISSEC) (2015)
32. Shen, X., Xu, K., Sun, X., Wu, J., Lin, J.: Optimized indoor wireless propagation model in WIFI-RoF network architecture for RSS-based localization in the internet of things. In: 2011 International Topical Meeting on & Microwave Photonics Conference Microwave Photonics, 2011 Asia-Pacific, MWP/APMP, pp. 274–277. IEEE (2011)
33. Simini, F., González, M.C., Maritan, A., Barabási, A.L.: A universal model for mobility and migration patterns. Nature **484**(7392), 96–100 (2012)
34. Sultana, S., Midi, D., Bertino, E.: Kinesis: a security incident response and prevention system for wireless sensor networks. In: Proceedings of ACM SensSys (2014)
35. Tumrongwittayapak, C., Varakulsiripunth, R.: Detecting sinkhole attack and selective forwarding attack in wireless sensor networks. In: ICICS 2009 (2009)
36. Weber, R.H., Weber, R.: Internet of Things, vol. 12. Springer, Heidelberg (2010)
37. Xia, F., Yang, L.T., Wang, L., Vinel, A.: Internet of things. Int. J. Commun. Syst. **25**(9), 1101 (2012)
38. Zhu, Q., Li, H., Han, Z., Basar, T.: A stochastic game model for jamming in multi-channel cognitive radio systems. In: IEEE ICC (2010)
39. ZigBee Alliance and others: Zigbee specification (2006)

Boot Attestation: Secure Remote Reporting with Off-The-Shelf IoT Sensors

Steffen Schulz[1]([✉]), André Schaller[2], Florian Kohnhäuser[2],
and Stefan Katzenbeisser[2]

[1] Intel Labs, 64293 Darmstadt, Germany
steffen.schulz@intel.com
[2] Security Engineering Group, TU Darmstadt, CYSEC,
Mornewegstrasse 32, 64293 Darmstadt, Germany
{schaller,kohnhaeuser,katzenbeisser}@seceng.informatik.tu-darmstadt.de

Abstract. A major challenge in computer security is about establishing the trustworthiness of remote platforms. Remote attestation is the most common approach to this challenge. It allows a remote platform to measure and report its system state in a secure way to a third party. Unfortunately, existing attestation solutions either provide low security, as they rely on unrealistic assumptions, or are not applicable to commodity low-cost and resource-constrained devices, as they require custom secure hardware extensions that are difficult to adopt across IoT vendors. In this work, we propose a novel remote attestation scheme, named Boot Attestation, that is particularly optimized for low-cost and resource-constrained embedded devices. In Boot Attestation, software integrity measurements are immediately committed to during boot, thus relaxing the traditional requirement for secure storage and reporting. Our scheme is very light on cryptographic requirements and storage, allowing efficient implementations, even on the most low-end IoT platforms available today. We also describe extensions for more flexible management of ownership and third party (public-key) attestation that may be desired in fully Internet-enabled devices. Our scheme is supported by many existing off-the-shelf devices. To this end, we review the hardware protection capabilities for a number of popular device types and present implementation results for two such commercially available platforms.

1 Introduction

In the Internet-of-Things (IoT) low-cost and resource-constrained devices are becoming the fundamental building blocks for many facets of life. Innovation in this space is not only fueled by making devices ever more powerful, but also by a steady stream of even smaller, cheaper, and less energy-consuming "things' that enable new features and greater automation in home automation, transportation, smart factories and cities.

Unfortunately, the novelty of this space combined with dominating market forces to minimize cost and time-to-market also has a devastating impact on security. While it may be tolerable that deployed firmware is not free of bugs [12]

© Springer International Publishing AG 2017
S.N. Foley et al. (Eds.): ESORICS 2017, Part II, LNCS 10493, pp. 437–455, 2017.
DOI: 10.1007/978-3-319-66399-9_24

and vendors have varying opinions about privacy and access control in this new space [21,35], an arguably critical requirement for survivable IoT infrastructures is the capability to apply security patches and recover from compromises [15,37].

The ability to recognize and establish trust in low-cost devices is becoming relevant even in scenarios where devices are not connected to the Internet or not intended to receive firmware updates at all. For instance, SD-cards and USB sticks that are exchanged with third parties can be infected or replaced by malicious hardware in order to attack the host [29]. Bluetooth devices may offer an even larger attack surface, since typically employed security mechanisms were shown to be insufficient [34,42]. Remote attestation is a key security capability in this context, as it allows a third party to identify a remote device and verify its software integrity.

Existing attestation schemes can be classified as timing-based or hardware-based. Timing-based schemes require no secure hardware and thus are applicable to a broad range of devices [20,23,41]. However, they rely on assumptions like exact time measurements, time-optimal checksum functions, and a passive adversary, which have been proven to be hard to achieve in practice [4,10,22]. In contrast, hardware-based attestation schemes provide much stronger security guarantees by relying on secure hardware components. Recent works specifically target the needs of embedded devices to perform remote attestation with a minimum set of secure hardware requirements [13,14,17,30]. Unfortunately, these hardware security features are currently not available in commodity embedded devices. Another direction of research specifically focuses on a major use case of attestation, the verification of firmware integrity after updates. These works often target device classes that cannot be secured using hardware-based attestation approaches, such as legacy and low-end devices [16,18,32,39]. Yet they only address a subset of attestation usages, suffer from the similar limitations as software-based attestation approaches, or employ costly algorithms that involve a high memory and computational overhead.

Contributions. We present a novel approach to remote attestation which is based on load-time authentication. Our scheme is very efficient and well-suited for resource- constrained, embedded devices (cf. Sect. 2). In more detail:

Boot Attestation Concept: Instead of recording measurements in a secure environment, as in traditional TPM-like attestation, our integrity measurements are immediately authenticated as the platform boots. We will argue in Sect. 3, that for the very simple hardware and firmware configurations found in low-end IoT devices, this construction can meet the key goals of remote attestation which many prior works tried to tackle.

Provisioning and 3rd Party Verification: In Sect. 4 we describe two extensions that further increase the practicality and completeness of Boot Attestation. First, a key provisioning extension to take ownership of potentially untrustworthy devices. Second, an extension to enable attestation towards untrustworthy third-party verifiers. The latter is a capability that is missing in prior work, but essential when applying a symmetric attestation scheme in the IoT use case.

Minimal HW/SW Requirements: Our proposed attestation scheme offers a new middle-ground between previously proposed timing-based and hardware-based attestation approaches. Boot Attestation does not depend on timing or other execution-side effects which turned out to be difficult to achieve in practice. As we will discuss in Sect. 5, Boot Attestation side-steps hardware requirements that were deemed essential for remote attestation until now [13]. In contrast to prior work, our approach merely requires memory access control enforcement, secure on-DIE SRAM and debug protection.

Analysis and Implementation: In Sect. 6, we examine hardware protection capabilities for a range of existing Commercial Off-the-Shelf Microcontroller Units (COTS MCUs) and describe how they can be programmed to support Boot Attestation *today*. We then describe two concrete implementations, highlighting the practicality and efficiency of our design.

2   System Model and Goals

In this section, we specify our system model, discuss the adversaries' capabilities and describe the general procedure of remote attestation.

2.1   System Model

We consider a setting with two parties, a verifier $\mathcal{V}$ and a prover $\mathcal{P}$. $\mathcal{V}$ is interested in validating whether $\mathcal{P}$ is in a *known-good* software state, and for this purpose engages in a remote attestation protocol with $\mathcal{P}$.

$\mathcal{P}$ is modeled as a commodity, low-cost IoT device as it may be found in personal gadgets, or smart home and smart factory appliances. In order to minimize manufacturing cost and power consumption, such devices tend to be single-purpose MCUs with often just the minimum memory and compute capabilities required to meet their intended application. Modern MCUs combine CPU, memory, basic peripherals, and selected communication interfaces on a single System on Chip (SoC), as illustrated in Fig. 1. Common on-DIE memory comprises SRAM, flash memory, and EEPROM. Additional peripheral devices and bulk memory are often connected externally.

On the software side, MCUs are often programmed bare-metal, with the SDK building necessary drivers and libraries into a single application binary (firmware image). Some platforms also implement additional stages, e.g. a smart watch loading "companion apps" at runtime. The firmware image is typically initialized by an immutable component, such as a boot ROM or bootloader, which reduces the risk of permanently disabling a device ("bricking"). When programmed via low-level interfaces such as JTAG, many devices also allow to customize this early stage(s) of boot. We will revisit this property when implementing our Root of Trust (RoT) in Sect. 6.

Note that in the IoT context, the attestation verifier $\mathcal{V}$ is typically the owner of $\mathcal{P}$ (e.g., fitness trackers or USB thumb drives) or an operator who is responsible for managing $\mathcal{P}$ on behalf of the owner (e.g., smart factory or smart city).

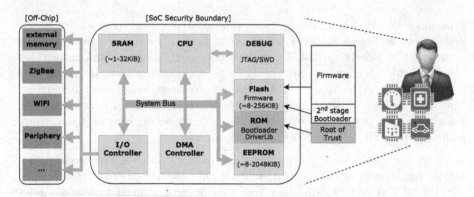

Fig. 1. Typical hardware configuration of a IoT MCU. We consider on-chip components as secure against "simple" hardware attacks (SoC Security Boundary).

2.2 Adversary Model

The adversary $\mathcal{A}$ controls the communication between $\mathcal{V}$ and $\mathcal{P}$ and can compromise the firmware of $\mathcal{P}$ at will. In more detail, $\mathcal{A}$ is granted full control over the communication channel (Dolev-Yao model) and thus can eavesdrop, inject, modify, or delete any messages between $\mathcal{V}$ and $\mathcal{P}$. $\mathcal{A}$ can also compromise the higher-level firmware on $\mathcal{P}$, i.e., the MCU application, whereupon $\mathcal{A}$ has full control over the execution and can read from and write to any memory.

However, we assume that $\mathcal{A}$ is unable to bypass hardware protection mechanisms, such as reading data from memory regions that are explicitly protected by hardware. We also exclude a comprehensive discussion of physical attacks as these require an in-depth analysis of the particular hardware design and are outside the scope of this work. Instead, we consider only a simple hardware adversary who may attempt to access documented interfaces such as JTAG, and replace or manipulate external SoC components like external memory or radios (cf. Fig. 1). We also assume that the verifier does not collaborate with $\mathcal{A}$, in particular, $\mathcal{V}$ will not disclose the attestation key to $\mathcal{A}$. However, this assumption is reduced when introducing third party verifiers in Sect. 4.

2.3 Remote Attestation Game

Remote Attestation is a security scheme where a verifier $\mathcal{V}$ wants to gain assurance that the firmware state of the prover $\mathcal{P}$ has not been subject to compromise by $\mathcal{A}$. Following the common load-time attestation model [31], we define the firmware state of $\mathcal{P}$ as an ordered set of k binary measurements $M = (m_1, m_2, \ldots, m_k)$ that are taken as $\mathcal{P}$ loads its firmware for execution. Since the chain of measurements is started by the platform's Root of Trust (RoT), it is assumed that any modification to the firmware state is reliably reflected in at least one measurement m_x.

To gain assurance on the actual state M' of $\mathcal{P}$, $\mathcal{V}$ and $\mathcal{P}$ engage in a challenge-response protocol. This culminates in the construction of an attestation report

$r \leftarrow attest_{\mathsf{AK}}(c, M')$ at $\mathcal{P}$, where c is a random challenge and AK is an attestation key agreed between $\mathcal{P}$ and $\mathcal{V}$. $\mathcal{V}$ accepts $\mathcal{P}$ as trustworthy, i.e., not compromised, if the response r is valid under chosen values (c, AK) and an expected known-good state M (i.e., $M' = M$).

3 Boot Attestation

In this section, we introduce our Boot Attestation concept and protocol, extract hardware requirements and analyze its security with regard to Sect. 2.3.

3.1 Implicit Chain of Trust

Traditional attestation schemes collect measurements in a secure environment, such as a TPM or TEE, which can be queried at a later time to produce an attestation report. They support complex software stacks comprising a large set of measurements and allow a multitude of verifiers to request subsets of these measurements, depending on privacy and validation requirements.

In contrast, our approach is to authenticate measurements m_x of the next firmware stage x immediately into an authenticated state M_x, before handing control to the next firmware stage. This way, m_x is protected from manipulations by any subsequently loaded application firmware. The new state M_x is generated pseudo-randomly and the previous state M_{x-1} is discarded. This prevents an adversary from reconstructing prior or alternative measurement states. The final state M_k, seen by the application, comprises an authenticated representation of the complete measurement chain for reporting to $\mathcal{V}$:

$$M_x \leftarrow PRF_{\mathsf{AK}}(M_{x-1}, m_x)$$

As typically no secure hardware is available to protect AK in this usage, we generate pseudo-random sub-keys AK_x and again discard prior keys AK_{x-1} before initiating stage x:

$$\mathsf{AK}_x \leftarrow KDF_{\mathsf{AK}_{x-1}}(m_x), \text{ with } \mathsf{AK}_0 \leftarrow \mathsf{AK}$$

Note that we can instantiate PRF and KDF using a single HMAC. The measurement state M_x has become implicit in AK_x and does not have to be recorded separately.

The approach is limited in the sense that the boot flow at $\mathcal{P}$ dictates the accumulation of measurements in one or more implicit trust chains M. However, for the small, single-purpose IoT platforms we target here, there is typically no need to attest subsets of the firmware state as it is possible with TPM PCRs. The next section expands this idea into a full remote attestation protocol.

3.2   Remote Attestation Protocol

Figure 2 provides an overview of a possible remote attestation protocol utilizing the implicit chain of trust and a symmetric shared attestation key AK. On the right-hand side, the prover $\mathcal{P}$ builds its chain of trust from the Root of Trust to a possible stage 1 (bootloader) and stage 2 (application). Once booted, the prover may be challenged by $\mathcal{V}$ to report its firmware state by demonstrating possession of the implicitly authenticated measurement state AK_2.

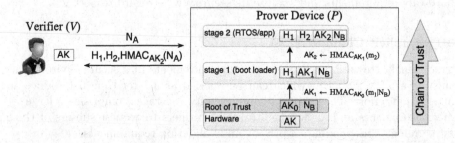

Fig. 2. Schematic overview of one possible instantiation of our Boot Attestation scheme as part of a remote attestation protocol.

The detailed protocol works as follows. The prover hardware starts execution at the platform Root of Trust (RoT). This "stage 0" has exclusive access to the root attestation key $AK_0 \leftarrow AK$ and an optional boot nonce N_B. It derives AK_1 as $HMAC_{AK_0}(N_B, m_1)$, with $m_1 := (start_1, size_1, H_1)$ defined as the binary measurement of the firmware stage 1. Before launching stage 1, the RoT must purge intermediate secrets from memory and lock AK against further access by application firmware. Execution then continues at stage 1 using the intermediate attestation key AK_1 and measurement log $(H_1, N_B)^1$.

The scheme continues through other boot stages $x \in \{1, \ldots, k\}$ until the main application/runtime has launched in stage k. In each stage, a measurement m_{x+1} of the next firmware stage is taken and extended into the measurement state as $AK_{x+1} \leftarrow HMAC_{AK_x}(m_{x+1})$. The prior attestation key AK_x and intermediate values of the $HMAC()$ operation are purged from memory so that they cannot be accessed by stage $x + 1$. Finally, the measurement log is extended to aid the later reconstruction and verification of the firmware state at $\mathcal{V}$.

Once $\mathcal{P}$ has launched the final stage k, it may accept challenges $c \leftarrow N_A$ by a remote verifier to attest its firmware state. For $\mathcal{P}$, this simply involves computing a proof of knowledge $r \leftarrow HMAC_{AK_k}(N_A)$ and sending it to $\mathcal{V}$ together with the measurement log. Using this response, the verifier $\mathcal{V}$ can reconstruct the state $M' = (m'_1, \ldots, m'_k)$ claimed by $\mathcal{P}$ and the associated AK_k. $\mathcal{V}$ can then validate and accept $\mathcal{P}$ if $M' = M$ and $r = HMAC_{AK_k}(N_A)$.

---

[1] We consider $(start_x, size_x)$ as well-known parameters here, since the individual m_x would typically encompass the complete firmware image at a particular stage.

Note that for the devices we target, k tends to be very low. Typical MCUs load only one or two stages of firmware, which helps keeping the validation effort at $\mathcal{V}$ manageable even for large amounts of valid platforms (AK, M).

We emphasize that the protocol described here only considers the core attestation scheme. A complete solution should also consider authorizing $\mathcal{V}$ towards $\mathcal{P}$, protecting the confidentiality of the attestation report and linking the attestation to a session or otherwise exchanged data. As part of an authorized attestation challenge c', $\mathcal{V}$ may also include a command to update N_B and reboot $\mathcal{P}$ to refresh all AK_x. However, while the implications of managing N_B are discussed in Sect. 3.3, the detailed choices and goals are application-dependent and outside the scope of this work.

3.3   Security Analysis

In the following, we analyze the security of Boot Attestation based on the adversary model and attestation game defined in Sects. 2.2 and 2.3. We will show that Boot Attestation is able to provide the same security as all load-time attestation approaches, such as TPM-based attestation schemes [28]. For this purpose, we consider the relevant attack surface in terms of *network, physical/side-channel* as well as *load-time* and *runtime* compromise attacks.

Network Attacks. The adversary $\mathcal{A}$ can eavesdrop, synthesize, manipulate, and drop any network data. However, the employed challenge-response protocol using the shared secret AK trivially mitigates these attacks. More specifically, any manipulation of assets exposed on the network, including H_1, H_2, N_A or the attestation response r, is detected by $\mathcal{V}$ when reconstructing AK_k and validating $r = HMAC_{\mathsf{AK}_k}(N_A)$. The attestation nonce N_A mitigates network replay attacks. $\mathcal{A}$ can cause a DoS by dropping messages, but $\mathcal{V}$ will still not accept $\mathcal{P}$.

Since AK is a device-specific secret, the intermediate keys AK_x and final response r are uniquely bound to each individual device. This allows Boot Attestation to function seamlessly with emerging swarm- attestation schemes, where the same nonce N_A is used to attest many devices at once [1,6,9].

Physical and Side-Channel Attacks. $\mathcal{A}$ may attempt simple hardware attacks, using SoC-external interfaces to gather information on intermediate attestation keys AK_x or manipulate SoC- external memory and I/O. Boot Attestation assumes basic hardware mechanisms to protect debug ports and protect intermediate values in memory (cf. Sect. 5). Otherwise, the resilience against hardware attacks heavily depends on the SoC implementation and is outside our scope.

$\mathcal{A}$ could also attempt software side-channel attacks, such as cache, data remanence, or timing attacks. However, as each stage i clears any data besides $\mathsf{N}, H_{i+1}, \mathsf{AK}_{i+1}$, there is no confidential data that a malware could extract from cache, RAM, or flash. Furthermore, the risk of timing side-channels is drastically reduced as root keys are only used initially by the RoT. Implementing a constant-time HMAC operation in the typically used non- paged, tightly coupled SRAM is straightforward.

Load-Time Compromise. $\mathcal{A}$ may compromise the firmware stage a of $\mathcal{P}$ before it is loaded and hence, measured. In this case, $\mathcal{A}$ can access all intermediate measurements $(m_1, \ldots, m_k)$, the nonces (N_B, N_A), and any subsequent attestation keys $(\mathsf{AK}_a, \ldots, \mathsf{AK}_k)$. Note that compromising the RoT (i.e., the initial stage) is outside the capabilities of $\mathcal{A}$. This is a reasonable assumption due to RoT's hardware protection (cf. Sect. 5) and miniscule code complexity (cf. Table 2).

Compromising the intermediate measurement state and keys allows $\mathcal{A}$ building alternative measurement states M'_{a+n} and associated attestation keys AK'_{a+n} for positive integers n. However, $\mathcal{A}$ cannot recover the attestation keys of prior stages $a - n$, as they have been wiped from memory prior to invoking stage a. In particular, $\mathcal{A}$ cannot access the root attestation key AK, which can only be accessed by the RoT. As a result, $\mathcal{A}$ can only construct attestation responses that *extend* on the measurement state M'_a and the associated attestation key AK_a. Moreover, load-time attestation assumes that the measurement chain is appropriately setup to record the compromise, so that (M'_a, AK'_a) already reflect the compromise and cannot be expanded to spoof a valid firmware state M_k.

In practice, successfully recording M'_a will typically require a persistent manipulation or explicit code loading action by the adversary. However, this is a well-known limitation of load-time attestation and also affects the TPM and other load-time attestation schemes.

Following a firmware patch to return stage a into a well-known, trustworthy component, a new measurement and associated key chain is produced starting at stage a. $\mathcal{A}$ is unable to forsee this renewed key chain, as this would require access to at least AK_{a-1}.

Runtime Compromise. $\mathcal{A}$ may also compromise the firmware stage a at runtime, after is measured, e.g., by exploiting a vulnerability that leads to arbitrary code execution. In this case, $\mathcal{A}$ would have access to the correct (unmodified) attestation key AK_a, could bypass the chain of trust, and thus win the attestation game. Note that this is a generic attack affecting all load-time attestation schemes, including the TPM [28]. Even platforms supporting a Dynamic Root of Trust for Measurement (DRTM) cannot detect runtime attacks after the measurement was performed. However, Boot Attestation performs slightly worse in this case since $\mathcal{A}$ may additionally record AK_a and replay it later on to simulate alternative measurement states and win the attestation game, even after reboot. Nevertheless, Boot Attestation allows recovering the platform and returning into a trustworthy state, in the same way as with other load-time attestation schemes, by patching the vulnerable firmware stage a and performing a reboot. This leads to a refresh of attestation keys $\mathsf{AK}_a, \ldots, \mathsf{AK}_k$ in a way that is unpredictable to $\mathcal{A}$, thus enabling $\mathcal{V}$ to attest the proper recovery of $\mathcal{P}$ and possibly reprovision application secrets.

To further mitigate the risk of a compromised AK_a, $\mathcal{V}$ may also manage an additional boot nonce N_B as introduced in Sect. 3.2. Depending on the particular usage and implementation of $\mathcal{P}$, N_B could be incremented to cause a refresh of the measurement chain without provisioning new firmware. For instance, MCUs in an automotive on-board network may regularly receive new boot nonces for use on next boot/validation cycle.

4   Extensions for Real-World Use

In the following, we discuss extensions to our attestation scheme that are commonly not considered in prior work, but which are fundamental for real-world application in IoT. The first extension provides support for provisioning an attestation key and requires a slight extension of our HW requirements. The second extension is a software-only solution to support verification of attestation reports by untrusted third parties.

4.1   Attestation Key Provisioning

In many cases, it is desirable to provision a new root attestation key AK to a possibly compromised platform. Examples include a user taking ownership of a new or second-hand device, or issuing a fresh AK after compromise of the verifier. To realize this, we follow the TCG concept of provisioning a device-unique *endorsement key* EK as part of manufacturing of $\mathcal{P}$. EK is a symmetric key shared between $\mathcal{P}$ and the manufacturer $\mathcal{M}$. This allows $\mathcal{M}$ to authorize AK key provisioning requests from $\mathcal{V}$ to $\mathcal{P}$, while at the same time ensuring the authenticity of the provisioning target $\mathcal{P}$ to $\mathcal{V}$.

Provisioning AK based on EK can be realized with a number of key exchange or key transport protocols implemented in RoT. We omit a detailed instantiation here due to the lack of space. However, we like to call out the slightly extended key protection requirement for supporting such a scheme. In particular, AK provisioning requires the AK storage to be writable by RoT but read/write-locked for subsequent FW stages (cf. Sect. 5).

4.2   Third-Party Verification

In many IoT usages, MCUs operate not just with a single trusted device owner or manager, but can establish a variety of interactions with user platforms, infrastructure components and cloud backends.

However, as the final attestation key AK_k is a critical asset during attestation, sharing it with all possible verifiers would significantly reduce the confidence into the scheme. To tackle this issue, which is shared by all existing symmetric attestation schemes [13,30], we extend Boot Attestation to allow for potentially untrusted third-party verifiers.

For this purpose, we turn the original verifier $\mathcal{V}$ into a Certification Authority $(\mathcal{CA})$. $\mathcal{CA}$ and $\mathcal{P}$ do not use AK_k directly, but instead generate a key pair based on the pseudo-random input AK_k. In order to attest $\mathcal{P}$ by third-party verifies $\mathcal{V}'$, only the public key computed from AK_k must be distributed.

In practice, one would store AK in a secure environment at the owner or manufactuer and only distribute and use valid public keys based on expected firmware measurements. The detailed protocol works as follows:

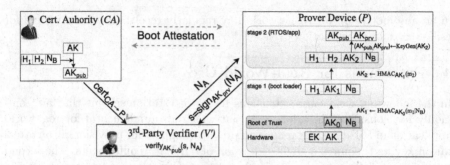

Fig. 3. Third-party verification using a trusted $\mathcal{CA}$. The optional boot attestation phase is depicted with dashed arrows.

Initially, $\mathcal{P}$ and $\mathcal{CA}$ share a common secret AK and that $\mathcal{P}$ was initialized according to Sect. 3.1, i.e. has derived the correct key AK_k.

This time, $\mathcal{P}$ uses AK_k as pseudo-random input to generate a key pair $(AK_{prv}, AK_{pub}) \leftarrow KeyGen(AK_k)$. This can be done deterministically for example using ECC key generation. Subsequently, $\mathcal{CA}$ receives $(H_1, \ldots, H_k, N, r = HMAC_{AK_k}(c))$ from $\mathcal{P}$. Using the intermediate hashes $(H_1, \ldots, H_k)$ and AK, $\mathcal{CA}$ can reproduce AK_k and $\mathcal{P}$'s public key AK_{pub} and publish a certificate $cert_{\mathcal{CA} \rightarrow \mathcal{P}} \leftarrow Sign_{\mathcal{CA}_{prv}}(AK_{pub})$.

The third party $\mathcal{V}'$ initiates attestation by querying $\mathcal{CA}$ for $\mathcal{P}$'s signed public key $cert_{\mathcal{CA} \rightarrow \mathcal{P}}$. Subsequently $\mathcal{V}'$ challenges the (valid) prover $\mathcal{P}$ for a fresh signature, using a nonce N_A. In turn, $\mathcal{P}$ creates a signature s of N_A $s \leftarrow Sign_{AK_{prv}}(N_A)$ and sends s to $\mathcal{V}'$. The third party is now able to infer statements about $\mathcal{P}$'s identity and firmware state. At the same time AK_k is kept secret from $\mathcal{V}'$. An overview of the scheme is shown in Fig. 3.

5 Hardware Requirements

In this section, we describe the hardware requirements of our Boot Attestation scheme in detail. We formulate these as results here and not as system assumptions in Sect. 2.1, since the exploration of alternative remote attestation schemes with minimal hardware requirements has been a major research challenge in recent years [13,14,17,30]. In particular, remote attestation schemes proposed so far still require a secure co-processor or custom hardware security extensions in order to support the secure recording and signing of measurements. Alternative approaches using a software-only root of trust still require strong assumptions on the operating environment and implementation correctness, which has precluded them as a generic attestation solution for IoT [10,22].

Leveraging the implicit chain of trust, our Boot Attestation scheme avoids the requirement for a hardware-isolated attestation runtime. Specifically, we only require the following hardware security features:

[I] RoT Integrity: The RoT is critical to initializing the chain of trust and protecting fundamental platform assets such as AK. Our scheme requires RoT integrity in the sense that it must be impossible for the adversary $\mathcal{A}$ to manipulate the RoT firmware, and that the RoT must be reliably and consistently executed at platform reset. In practice, this requires hardware access control on the RoT code and data region, but also hardware logic to consistently reset the SoC's caches, DMA engines and other interrupt-capable devices in order to reliably execute RoT on power-cycle, soft-reset, deep sleep, and similar events. While RoT integrity is well-understood in terms of supporting secure boot or firmware management, we know of no COTS MCU which natively supports a RoT for attestation. To realize Boot Attestation on COTS MCUs we therefore require an extension of the RoT integrity requirement: The device owner must be able to customize or extend the initial boot phase to implement an attestation RoT, and then lock or otherwise protect it from any further manipulation. As we will show, many COTS MCUs actually offer this level of customization prior to enabling production use.

[II] AK Protection: Boot attestation requires that the root attestation key AK is read-/write-locked ahead of execution of the firmware application. This typically requires the RoT to initialize some form of memory access control and then lock it down, such that it cannot be disabled by subsequent firmware stages. While such lock-able key storage is not a standard feature, we found that most COTS MCUs offer some kind of memory locking or hiding that can be used to meet this requirement (cf. Sect. 3.3).

[II*] AK Provisioning: Provisioning of a new attestation key AK_{new} involves replacement of its previous instance, conducted by the RoT (cf. Sect. 4.1). Hence, in order to support provisioning, AK must further be writable by the RoT exclusively. However, this procedure is preceded by the secure negotiation of AK_{new}. During this process the endorsement key EK is used to provide authorization and confidentiality of the new attestation key AK_{new}. Thus, during key provisioning the RoT must read EK and then lock it against read attempts by latter firmware stages, basically resembling requirement **[II]**.

[III] State Protection: When calculating measurements m_x and attestation keys AK_x, the respective firmware stage must be able to operate in a secure memory that cannot be accessed by later firmware stages or other unauthorized platform components. This includes protecting intermediate values of the HMAC calculation as well as the stack. In practice, this requirement breaks down to operating in memory that is shielded against simple hardware attacks (cf. Sect. 2.2), such as the SoC on-DIE SRAM, and clearing sensitive intermediate values from memory before handing control to the respective next stage.

[IV] Debug Protection: Once programmed and provisioned, the device should reject unauthorized access via external interfaces such as UART consoles, JTAG or SWD debug interfaces [11]. Strictly speaking this requirement is sufficiently addressed if the above integrity and confidentiality requirements are met. However, we list it here as separate requirement since debug access and re-programming protections are typically implemented and enabled separately from the above general implementation requirements.

Overall, we can see that Boot Attestation side-steps requirements for protecting the initial call into the secure environment and inhibiting interrupts during execution - including resets - which are not achievable with established hardware protection mechanisms and therefore also not feasible on commodity COTS MCUs [13,14].

6   Proof of Concept Implementation

We reviewed specifications for a range of popular COTS MCUs with regard to meeting the hardware requirements of Boot Attestation (cf. Sect. 5), including support for AK Provisioning (req. [II] *).

All of the platforms we investigated support executing firmware completely within the confines of the SoC, ensuring confidentiality and integrity against external HW manipulation (req. [III]). Most of the chips also offer one or more lock bits to disable debug access for production use ([IV]). Differences could be observed mainly in the memory access control facilities, with a large variety in the number, granularity and permissions available per physical memory block. In contrast, all of the investigated devices support customization and subsequent locking of the boot "ROM", allowing developers to customize and then integrity-protect the platform Root of Trust in one way or another (req. [I]).

An overview of the results is provided in Table 1. Apart from [I] RoT Integrity and [IV] Debug Protection, we also list the respective options for protecting AK and EK in the AK Provisioning scenario (req. [II] *)[2]. As can be seen, Boot Attestation is potentially supported by a wide range of devices. Naturally, a full implementation and validation is required to ensure the respective platform controls are accurately documented and sufficient in practice.

We selected two rather different device types, the Stellaris LM4F120 and the Quark D2000, to evaluate different implementation options and provide an overview of the associated costs. In both cases, the implementation of our scheme comprised extending the RoT for measuring the FW application image and deriving an attestation key, as well as initializing the hardware key protection for AK and EK. Note also that there is no intermediate bootloader stage on these devices as the application image is directly executed by RoT. An overview of the implementation footprint is provided in Table 2.

6.1   Prototype I: TI Stellaris LaunchPad

The TI Stellaris Launchpad [44] implements an ARM Cortex-M4F operating at 80 MHz[3], 32 kB SRAM, 32 kB flash memory and 2 kB EEPROM. The platform is typically used in industrial automation, point of sale terminals and network

---

[2] If no AK provisioning is desired, EK protection is sufficient to store AK_0 (req. [II]).

[3] In our experiments we set the operating frequency to 50 MHz to allow for better comparison with the Intel MCU.

Table 1. List of COTS MCUs and how they meet our hardware requirements.

Device type	CPU	SRAM (kB)/ Flash (kB)/ EEPROM (kB)	RoT Integrity	AK protection	EK protection	Debug protection
ATmega328P	AVR	2/32/1024	Flash	Flash	Flash/PUF	✓
PIC16F1825	PIC16	1/8/256	Flash	Flash/ EEPROM	Flash/ EEPROM	✓
LPC1200	Cortex-M0	4–8/32–128/–	Flash	✗	✗	✓
STM32F100Rx	Cortex-M3	8/64–128/–	Flash	✗	PUF	✗
Stellaris LM4F120	Cortex-M4F	32/256/2048	Flash	Flash	Flash/ EEPROM	✓
Quark MCU D2000	Quark D2000	8/44/–	Flash	Flash (main)	Flash (OTP)	✓
Arduino/ Genuino101	Quark SE C1000	80/392/–	Flash	Flash	Flash	✓

appliances. We use FreeRTOS [33] as a firmware stack, as it is freely available, pre-configured for the Stellaris and as it exhibits a small memory footprint.

Integrity Protected RoT. The Stellaris supports RoT code integrity by enabling execute-only protection to those flash blocks that store the boot loader. In particular, by setting register values of FMPPEn and FMPREn to '0', read and write access to the bootloader section is disabled while keeping it executable.

Protection of AK and EK. Although the Stellaris provides memory protection for flash [5], we decide not to use it for secure key storage. Despite the fact that individual blocks of flash memory can be read-protected, it is yet possible to execute said blocks. This could allow an attacker $\mathcal{A}$ to extract bits of AK or EK. $\mathcal{A}$ can try to execute respective memory regions and infer information by interpreting resulting execution errors. Instead, we securely store AK and EK on the internal EEPROM module. The Stellaris platform provides register EEHIDE that allows for hiding individual 32 B EEPROM blocks until subsequent reset.

PUF-Based Storage of EK. It is also possible to securely store EK using a fraction of the on-chip SRAM as a PUF. Previous work supports the use of SRAM as PUFs for key storage [27,38]. Indeed, the SRAM-based PUF instance of the Stellaris has already been characterized in [19]. Using PUFs as a key storage significantly increases the level of protection, as PUF-based keys are existent only for a limited period [3]. Especially for long-term keys, such as EK, this is a desirable property, which is otherwise hard to achieve on low-cost devices. To evaluate this option, we implemented a Fuzzy Extractor construction based on [7]. On start-up of the device, a fraction of the SRAM start-up values are used as a (noisy) PUF measurement X. Using X and public Helper Data W that was created during a prior enrollment phase, the Fuzzy Extractor can reconstruct EK. For details on the the interaction with SRAM-based PUFs, we refer to [36]. Assuming a conservative noise level of 15 % in the PUF measurements X, which is a common value used in literature [7], and applying a $(15, 1, 15)$ repetition code as part of the Fuzzy Extractor, we achieve an error probability of 10^{-9}.

Debug Protection. The bootloader is further protected from attempts to replace it by malicious code by disabling access to JTAG pins. For this purpose bits DBG0, DBG1 and NW, part of register BOOTCFG are set to '0'. This leaves a subset of standard IEEE instructions intact (such as boundary scan operations), but blocks any access to the processor and peripherals.

6.2   Prototype II: Intel Quark D2000

The Intel Quark Microcontroller D2000 employs an x86 Quark CPU operating at 32 MHz, 8 kB SRAM, 32 kB main flash memory, as well as two regions (4 kB and 4 kB) of One-Time-Programmable (OTP) flash memory. The Intel D2000 is tailored towards IoT scenarios, where low energy consumption is required. We use the Intel Quark Microcontroller Software Interface (QMSI) [25] and Zephyr RTOS [26] as the standard firmware stack.

Integrity Protected RoT and Debug Protection. The D2000 boots directly from an 8 kB OTP flash partition. A hardware-enforced OTP lock permanently disables write accesses to the OTP partition of the flash memory. It further deactivates mass erase capability of the OPT partition and at the same time disables JTAG debug access. Locking the OTP partition is done by setting bit '0' at offset 0 x 0 of the flash memory region to '0'.

Protection of AK and EK. We store AK in main flash to support updates via key provisioning. One of the D2000 flash protection regions (FPR) is setup and locked by the RoT to prevent read access by later firmware stages. In order to store the long-term key EK, we use the OTP flash region of the D2000. The 8 kB OTP supports read-locking of the upper and lower 4 kB regions of OTP flash. As this read protection also inhibits execute access, we store EK at the upper end of OTP memory and set the read-lock just at the very end of RoT execution. The read-lock for the lower and upper OTP region is activated by programming bits ROM_RD_DIS_L and ROM_RD_DIS_U of the CTRL register.

6.3   Performance Evaluation

In the following, we present evaluation results for both device types, with focus on memory footprint and runtime. Numbers are given for the RoT and key protection logic. Values for the RoT are further separated with respect to RoT base logic (memory management, setup of data structures) and the HMAC implementation. Runtime results of the HMAC functionality are given for a memory range of 256 bit, i.e., a single HMAC data block, and a 32 kB region that reflects larger firmware measurements. For both, memory footprint and runtime, we further provide numbers with respect to two different compile time optimizations. The detailed results are given in Table 2.

Memory. For memory consumption we consider static code segments (.text) and read-only data (.rodata) segments of the firmware image. Table 2 lists results for compile optimizations towards size (-Os) and runtime (-O1). Using

Table 2. Implementation overhead with respect to runtime in milliseconds (left) and memory overhead in Bytes (right) for the TI Stellaris (ARM) and the Intel D2000 (x86), with optimizations for size (-Os) and runtime (-O1).

	Size (Bytes)				Runtime (ms)			
	ARM		x86		ARM		x86	
Component	-Os	-O1	-Os	-O1	-Os	-O1	-Os	-O1
Base ROM	702	712	1955	2115	0.79	0.63	6.11	5.93
Root of Trust (RoT)								
Base Logic	336	340	168	193	<0.01	<0.01	<0.01	<0.01
HMAC-SHA2 (256 bit)	1828	1836	1819	2061	3.04	3.04	1.54	1.44
HMAC-SHA2 (32 kB)	1828	1836	1819	2061	312.26	312.26	148.23	145.37
AK Protection								
Flash	—	—	295	337	—	—	0.02	0.02
EEPROM	516	580	—	—	0.01	<0.01	—	—
EK Protection								
Flash	—	—	378	448	—	—	<0.01	0.002
EEPROM	516	580	—	—	0.01	<0.01	—	—
SRAM PUF	1662	1980	—	—	46.44	46.42	—	—

the most memory-efficient setting, the scheme requires a total of $\approx 3.1\,$kB on the Stellaris. This may seem large compared to the 700 B footprint of the base ROM image (i.e., excluding the application), but is only 1.22 % of the total available flash. On Intel D2000, our RoT extension consumes 2.6 kB on top of the QMSI stock ROM of 2 kB. This fits well within the total 8 KB available for boot loader code. The application flash is left for use by applications, except for the small part reserved for AK storage.

Runtime. Additional runtime introduced by our scheme mainly results from HMAC operations in order to compute attestation measurements, with the key protection logic introducing only little overhead. The right hand side of Table 2 lists runtime overhead of our implementation. As to be expected, the main overhead is caused by the HMAC function which depends on the concrete size of the next stage to be measured. We give 256 B and 32 kB as reference points to estimate the cost hashing the KDF output and a larger firmware, respectively. The D2000 is more than two times faster in computing authenticated measurements over various memory regions, which is much likely due to faster flash access. In particular, the D2000 requires only 145 ms for hashing 32 kB, whereas the Stellaris takes 312 ms. In contrast, the key protection logic adds negligible runtime for both device types. It takes less than 0.02 ms on the Stellaris and 0.04 ms on the Intel D2000, in the worst-case. Lastly, the SRAM PUF is by far the slowest key storage solution for EK on the Stellaris, taking almost half a second. This is due to costly error correction of the PUF measurements. As a reference, the unmodified base ROM, without our extension, takes on average 0.7 ms on the Stellaris and 6 ms on the Intel D2000.

7   Related Work

Previous work on attestation addresses *hardware-based* or *timing-based* attestation, *scalable attestation* for groups of devices, and *secure code updates*. verifier, to check the integrity of the software on a remote device, named prover. Prior work is related to *timing-based* or *hardware- based* attestation, *scalable attestation* for groups of devices, or *secure code updates*.

Hardware-based attestation schemes rely on secure hardware, such as Intel SGX or a Trusted Platform Module (TPM) [2,28], that is installed on the prover. Since such secure hardware is typically too expensive and complex to be integrated in low-cost embedded devices, recent works focused on the advancement of new minimalist security architectures [13,14,17,30] which enable hardware-based remote attestation capabilities for small embedded devices. However, these lightweight architectures have not yet reached the market, and hence are not available in commodity low-end embedded devices. Furthermore, even when they are available, there is still the need to secure old systems.

By contrast, timing-based attestation schemes do not require secure hardware and thus are applicable to legacy systems [20,24,40,41]. However, they rely on assumptions that have proven to be hard to achieve in prac tice [4,10,22]. Such assumptions include an optimal implementation and execution of the protocol, exact time measurements, and an adversary who is passive during attestation.

Recent works address a scalable attestation of groups of devices (i.e., device swarms) that are interconnected in large mesh networks [1,6,9]. The basic idea is that neighboring devices mutually attest each other in order to distribute the attestation burden across the entire network. Since these works rely on hardware-based attestation schemes, such as [8,13,17], they could leverage our Boot Attestation scheme to be applicable to a broader range of embedded devices.

The field of secure code updates specifically addresses the challenge of verifying the integrity firmware after ist has been updated. Initial approaches employ software-based attestation techniques [39], and hence inherit their characteristics, mentioned above. Later on, the notion of Proofs of Secure Erasure (PoSE) was introduced to secure code updates [16,32]. PoSE-based approaches build on a challenge-response protocol that requires the prover to fill its entire memory with data, in turn overwriting any malicious code. Although such solutions can be applied to many devices, as they require a small amount of read-only memory, they assume an network adversary to only communicate with the verifier but not the prover device, which is a strong limitation. Recent work focuses on scalable updates in large mesh networks [18]. In contrast to our work, it imposes the use of asymmetric cryptography, involving heavy computational overhead and a large memory footprint. There are also platform-specific security extensions such as cryptoBSL [45] and STM32 PCROP [43]. While they are focused on secure boot and IP protection, it would be interesting to evaluate their use in context of remote attestation and recovery.

8   Conclusions and Future Work

In this work, we explored a novel lightweight remote attestation scheme for low-cost COTS MCUs. We showed that it is possible to narrow down hardware requirements of the targeted MCUs and even to enable the extension of already deployed devices. We demonstrated practicability and efficiency of implementing our scheme on two representative MCUs and proposed extensions for usage in real-world scenarios. For future work, we will investigate support of additional device types, to widen to scope of applicability. A second effort will be taken to refine existing and develop further protocol extensions, such as symmetric sealing of assets (i.e., sensor values, etc.), establishment of trusted channels or means to log provenance of such assets, especially if they are computed on flash-based media that employ or scheme.

Acknowledgments. This work has been partly funded by the DFG as part of project P3 within the CRC 1119 CROSSING and the LOEWE initiative (Hessen, Germany) within the NICER project. The authors would also like to thank the anonymous reviewers for their valuable comments.

References

1. Ambrosin, M., Conti, M., Ibrahim, A., Neven, G., Sadeghi, A.-R., Schunter, M.: SANA: secure and scalable aggregate network attestation. In: CCS. ACM (2016)
2. Anati, I., Gueron, S., Johnson, S., Scarlata, V.: Innovative technology for CPU based attestation and sealing. In: HASP (2013)
3. Armknecht, F., Maes, R., Sadeghi, A.-R., Sunar, B., Tuyls, P.: Memory leakage-resilient encryption based on physically unclonable functions. In: Towards Hardware-Intrinsic Security (2010)
4. Armknecht, F., Sadeghi, A.-R., Schulz, S., Wachsmann, C.: A security framework for the analysis and design of software attestation. In: CCS. ACM (2013)
5. Ahuja, A.: SPMA044A - Using Execute, Write, and Erase-Only Flash Protection on Stellaris Microcontrollers Using Code Composer Studio
6. Asokan, N., Brasser, F., Ibrahim, A., Sadeghi, A.-R., Schunter, M., Tsudik, G., Wachsmann, C.: SEDA: scalable embedded device attestation. In: CCS (2015)
7. Bösch, C., Guajardo, J., Sadeghi, A.-R., Shokrollahi, J., Tuyls, P.: Efficient helper data key extractor on FPGAs. In: Oswald, E., Rohatgi, P. (eds.) CHES 2008. LNCS, vol. 5154, pp. 181–197. Springer, Heidelberg (2008). doi:10.1007/978-3-540-85053-3_12
8. Brasser, F., El Mahjoub, B., Sadeghi, A.-R., Wachsmann, C., Koeberl, P.: TyTAN: tiny trust anchor for tiny devices. In: DAC (2015)
9. Carpent, X., ElDefrawy, K., Rattanavipanon, N., Tsudik, G.: Lightweight swarm attestation: a tale of two LISA-s. In: AsiaCCS. ACM (2017)
10. Castelluccia, C., Francillon, A., Perito, D., Soriente, C.: On the difficulty of software-based attestation of embedded devices. In: CCS. ACM (2009)
11. Chen, W., Bhadra, J., Wang, L.-C.: SoC security and debug. In: Bhunia, S., Ray, S., Sur-Kolay, S. (eds.) Fundamentals of IP and SoC Security, pp. 29–48. Springer, Cham (2017). doi:10.1007/978-3-319-50057-7_3

12. Costin, A., Zaddach, J., Francillon, A., Balzarotti, D.: A large-scale analysis of the security of embedded firmwares. In: USENIX Security (2014)
13. Eldefrawy, K., Tsudik, G., Francillon, A., Perito, D.: SMART: secure and minimal architecture for (establishing dynamic) root of trust. In: NDSS (2012)
14. Francillon, A., Nguyen, Q., Rasmussen, K.B., Tsudik, G.: A minimalist approach to remote attestation. In: DATE (2014)
15. Hern, A.: Chinese webcam maker recalls devices after cyberattack link, October 2016. https://www.theguardian.com/technology/2016/oct/24/chinese-webcam-ma ker-recalls-devices-cyberattack-ddos-internet-of-things-xiongmai. Accessed 19 Apr 2017 ·
16. Karame, G.O., Li, W.: Secure erasure and code update in legacy sensors. In: Conti, M., Schunter, M., Askoxylakis, I. (eds.) Trust 2015. LNCS, vol. 9229, pp. 283–299. Springer, Cham (2015). doi:10.1007/978-3-319-22846-4_17
17. Koeberl, P., Schulz, S., Sadeghi, A.-R., Varadharajan, V.: TrustLite: a security architecture for tiny embedded devices. In: EuroSys (2014)
18. Kohnhäuser, F., Katzenbeisser, S.: Secure code updates for mesh networked commodity low-end embedded devices. In: Askoxylakis, I., Ioannidis, S., Katsikas, S., Meadows, C. (eds.) ESORICS 2016. LNCS, vol. 9879, pp. 320–338. Springer, Cham (2016). doi:10.1007/978-3-319-45741-3_17
19. Kohnhäuser, F., Schaller, A., Katzenbeisser, S.: PUF-based software protection for low-end embedded devices. In: Conti, M., Schunter, M., Askoxylakis, I. (eds.) Trust 2015. LNCS, vol. 9229, pp. 3–21. Springer, Cham (2015). doi:10.1007/978-3-319-22846-4_1
20. Kovah, X., Kallenberg, C., Weathers, C., Herzog, A., Albin, M., Butterworth, J.: New results for timing-based attestation. In: Security & Privacy (2012)
21. Krebs, B.: Who Makes the IoT Things Under Attack? October 2016. https://krebsonsecurity.com/2016/10/who-makes-the-iot-things-under-attack/. Accessed 19 Apr 2017
22. Li, Y., Cheng, Y., Gligor, V., Perrig, A.: Establishing software-only root of trust on embedded systems: facts and fiction. In: Christianson, B., Švenda, P., Matyáš, V., Malcolm, J., Stajano, F., Anderson, J. (eds.) Security Protocols 2015. LNCS, vol. 9379, pp. 50–68. Springer, Cham (2015). doi:10.1007/978-3-319-26096-9_7
23. Li, Y., McCune, J.M., Perrig, A.: SBAP: software-based attestation for peripherals. In: Acquisti, A., Smith, S.W., Sadeghi, A.-R. (eds.) Trust 2010. LNCS, vol. 6101, pp. 16–29. Springer, Heidelberg (2010). doi:10.1007/978-3-642-13869-0_2
24. Li, Y., McCune, J.M., Perrig, A.: VIPER: verifying the integrity of PERipherals' firmware. In: CCS. ACM (2011)
25. Linux Foundation: Intel Quark Microcontroller Software Interface. Accessed 19 Apr 2017
26. Linux Foundation: Zephyr Project. https://www.zephyrproject.org/. Accessed 19 Apr 2017
27. Maes, R., Tuyls, P., Verbauwhede, I.: Low-overhead implementation of a soft decision helper data algorithm for SRAM PUFs. In: Clavier, C., Gaj, K. (eds.) CHES 2009. LNCS, vol. 5747, pp. 332–347. Springer, Heidelberg (2009). doi:10.1007/978-3-642-04138-9_24
28. Trusted Computing Group: TPM Main Specification. http://www.trustedcompu tinggroup.org/resources/tpm_main_specification. Accessed 19 Apr 2017
29. Nohl, K., Krißler, S., Lell, J.: BadUSB - On accessories that turn evil (2014). https://opensource.srlabs.de/projects/badusb. Accessed 19 Apr 2017

30. Noorman, J., Agten, P., Daniels, W., Strackx, R., Van Herrewege, A., Huygens, C., Preneel, B., Verbauwhede, I., Piessens, F.: Sancus: low-cost trustworthy extensible networked devices with a zero-software trusted computing base. In: USENIX Security (2013)
31. Parno, B., McCune, J.M., Perrig, A.: Bootstrapping Trust in Modern Computers. Springer, New York (2011)
32. Perito, D., Tsudik, G.: Secure code update for embedded devices via proofs of secure erasure. In: Gritzalis, D., Preneel, B., Theoharidou, M. (eds.) ESORICS 2010. LNCS, vol. 6345, pp. 643–662. Springer, Heidelberg (2010). doi:10.1007/978-3-642-15497-3_39
33. Real Time Engineers Ltd.: FreeRTOS Website. Accessed 9 Dec 2015
34. Ryan, M.: Bluetooth: with low energy comes low security. In: WOOT (2013)
35. Saponas, T.S., Lester, J., Hartung, C., Agarwal, S., Kohno, T.: Devices that tell on you: privacy trends in consumer ubiquitous computing. In: USENIX Security (2007)
36. Schaller, A., Arul, T., van der Leest, V., Katzenbeisser, S.: Lightweight anti-counterfeiting solution for low-end commodity hardware using inherent PUFs. In: Holz, T., Ioannidis, S. (eds.) Trust 2014. LNCS, vol. 8564, pp. 83–100. Springer, Cham (2014). doi:10.1007/978-3-319-08593-7_6
37. Schneier, B.: The internet of things is wildly insecure and often unpatchable. Wired, January 2014
38. Schrijen, G.-J., van der Leest, V.: Comparative analysis of SRAM memories used as PUF primitives. In: DATE (2012)
39. Seshadri, A., Luk, M., Perrig, A., van Doorn, L., Khosla, P.: SCUBA: secure code update by attestation in sensor networks. In: WiSe (2006)
40. Seshadri, A., Luk, M., Shi, E., Perrig, A., van Doorn, L., Khosla, P.: Pioneer: verifying code integrity and enforcing untampered code execution on legacy systems. In: SOSP (2005)
41. Seshadri, A., Perrig, A., van Doorn, L., Khosla, P.: SWATT: software-based attestation for embedded devices. In: Security & Privacy. IEEE (2004)
42. Shaked, Y., Wool, A.: Cracking the Bluetooth PIN. In: MobiSys (2005)
43. STMicroelectronics: Proprietary code read-out protection on microcontrollers of the STM32L4 series. Accessed 23 June 2017
44. Texas Instruments: Stellaris LM4F120 LaunchPad Evaluation Kit. http://www.ti.com/tool/ek-lm4f120xl. Accessed 19 Apr 2017
45. Texas Instruments: Crypto-Bootloader (CryptoBSL) for MSP430FR59xx and MSP430FR69xx MCUs. Accessed 23 June 2017

RingCT 2.0: A Compact Accumulator-Based (Linkable Ring Signature) Protocol for Blockchain Cryptocurrency Monero

Shi-Feng Sun[1,2], Man Ho Au[1(✉)], Joseph K. Liu[3], and Tsz Hon Yuen[4]

[1] Hong Kong Polytechnic University, Hung Hom, Hong Kong
{csssun,csallen}@comp.polyu.edu.hk
[2] Shanghai Jiao Tong University, Shanghai, China
[3] Monash University, Melbourne, Australia
joseph.liu@monash.edu
[4] Huawei, Singapore, Singapore
YUEN.TSZ.HON@huawei.com

Abstract. In this work, we initially study the necessary properties and security requirements of Ring Confidential Transaction (RingCT) protocol deployed in the popular anonymous cryptocurrency Monero. Firstly, we formalize the syntax of RingCT protocol and present several formal security definitions according to its application in Monero. Based on our observations on the underlying (linkable) ring signature and commitment schemes, we then put forward a new efficient RingCT protocol (RingCT 2.0), which is built upon the well-known Pedersen commitment, accumulator with one-way domain and signature of knowledge (which altogether perform the functions of a linkable ring signature). Besides, we show that it satisfies the security requirements if the underlying building blocks are secure in the random oracle model. In comparison with the original RingCT protocol, our RingCT 2.0 protocol presents a significant space saving, namely, the transaction size is independent of the number of groups of input accounts included in the generalized ring while the original RingCT suffers a linear growth with the number of groups, which would allow each block to process more transactions.

1 Introduction

1.1 Monero: A Blockchain-Based Cryptocurrency

A cryptocurrency is a digital asset designed to work as a medium of exchange using cryptography to secure the transactions and to control the creation of additional units of the currency. Bitcoin became the first decentralized cryptocurrency in 2009. Since then, numerous cryptocurrencies have been created. Bitcoin and its derivatives use decentralized control as opposed to centralized electronic money or centralized banking systems. The decentralized control is related to the use of blockchain transaction database in the role of a distributed ledger.

© Springer International Publishing AG 2017
S.N. Foley et al. (Eds.): ESORICS 2017, Part II, LNCS 10493, pp. 456–474, 2017.
DOI: 10.1007/978-3-319-66399-9_25

Major advantages of cryptocurrency include decentralized control and anonymous payment, when compared to the traditional credit card or debit card system. However, the anonymity provided by bitcoin has been questioned in the sense it offers pseudonymity instead of offering a true anonymity. For instance, there is a research that identifyies ownership relationships between Bitcoin addresses and IP addresses [20]. Bitcoin proxy or even other users may still compute the actual identity of a bitcoin's owner. Although there are various improvements to enhance the anonymity of bitcoin (e.g. [31]), they are far from practical and satisfactory.

One of the first attempt to provide anonymity in cryptocurrency is Dash (released in 2014), which anonymizes the transaction process by mixing coins. Nevertheless, it does not formally provide cryptographic anonymity. Another attempt to provide anonymity in cryptocurrency is ZCash [8] (released in 2016), which uses zero-knowledge succinct non-interactive argument of knowledge (zk-SNARKs) [9]. They provide anonymity with a formal security proof. They used zk-SNARKs to prove the knowledge of pre-image of hash functions in which the proof generation process is rather expensive. Therefore, the efficiency is much worse than the normal bitcoin transaction (for the sender side, it takes a few minutes to perform a spent computation).

Monero is an open-source cryptocurrency created in April 2014 that focuses on privacy, decentralisation and scalability. The current market value of Monero is already over US$750M[1], which is one of the largest cryptocurrencies. Unlike many cryptocurrencies that are derivatives of Bitcoin, Monero is based on the CryptoNote protocol and possesses significant algorithmic differences relating to blockchain obfuscation. Monero daemon is mainly based on the original CryptoNote protocol, which deploys "one-time ring signatures" as the cored crypto-primitive to provide anonymity. Monero further improves the protocol by using a variant of linkable ring signature [22], which is called **Ring Confidential Transactions (RingCT)** [24].

On 10 January 2017, RingCT has been put into Monero transactions, starting at block #1220516. RingCT transactions are enabled by default at this stage, but it is still possible to send a transaction without RingCT until the next hard fork in September 2017. In the first month after implementation, it has been reported that approximately 50–60% of transactions used the optional RingCT feature.[2]

Upon the enhancement of privacy, a major trade-off is the increase of size for the transaction, due to the size of the linkable ring signature in the RingCT protocol. Although RingCT has already shortened the size of the ring signature by 50% when compared to the original CryptoNote protocol, it is still linear with the number of public keys included in the ring.

---

[1] At the time of June 2017. Market info is referenced from https://coinmarketcap.com/.

[2] https://web.archive.org/web/20170127204814/http://moneroblocks.info/stats/ringct-transactions.

1.2 Ring Signature and Linkable Ring Signature

A ring signature scheme (e.g., [1,26,33]) allows a member of a group to sign messages on behalf of the group without revealing his identities, i.e. signer anonymity. In addition, it is not possible to decide whether two signatures have been issued by the same group member. Different from a group signature scheme (e.g., [6,10,12]), the group formation is spontaneous and there is no group manager to revoke the identity of the signer. That is, under the assumption that each user is already associated with a public key of some standard signature scheme, a user can form a group by simply collecting the public keys of all the group members including his/her own. These diversion group members can be totally unaware of being conscripted into the group.

Ring signature provides perfect (or unconditional) anonymity. However, it may be too strong in some scenario. For example, in the case of anonymous e-voting, it is necessary to detect if someone has submitted his vote more than once so that the second casting should not be counted. Similar concerns should be applied into anonymous e-cash system. A double-spent payment should be discarded. In both scenarios, a linkable-anonymity is necessary, instead of the strongest form, unconditional anonymity. Linkable ring signature [22] provides a perfect characteristic of linkable anonymity: verifier knows nothing about the signer, except that s/he is one of the users in the group (represented by the list of public keys/identities). Yet given any two linkable signatures, the verifier knows that whether they are generated by the same signer (even though the verifier still does not know who the actual signer is).

1.3 Our Contributions

The contributions of this paper are twofold. First, we give a rigorous security definition and requirement of RingCT protocol. We note that in the original paper of RingCT [24], there is no rigorous security definition but just a direct instantiation of the protocol. A rigorous security definition would definitely help future researchers to develop better improvement of RingCT. Second, we target to reduce the size of the RingCT protocol. Our new RingCT protocol (we call it RingCT 2.0) is based on the well-known Pedersen commitment, accumulator with one-way domain and signature of knowledge related to the accumulator. The accumulator and the signature of knowledge together perform the functions of a linkable ring signature. In particular, the size of signature in our protocol is independent to the number of groups of input accounts in a transaction. We argue that it can significantly shorten the size of each block, when compared to the original protocol (which is linear with the number of groups of accounts included in the generalized ring for the anonymizing purpose) especially when the number of groups grows larger. More importantly, our construction fits perfectly into the framework of the RingCT definition, which makes it suitable to be deployed in Monero.

2   Related Works

Linkable ring signature was first proposed by Liu et al. [22] in 2004 (they named it as *Linkable Spontaneous Anonymous Group* Signature which is actually linkable ring signature). There are many variants in different types of cryptosystems with different features. We summarize their features in Table 1.

Table 1. Comparison of linkable ring signatures

Scheme	Signature size	Cryptosystem
Liu *et al.* [22]	$\mathcal{O}(n)$	public key
Tsang and Wei [29]	$\mathcal{O}(1)$	public key
Liu and Wong [23]	$\mathcal{O}(n)$	public key
Au *et al.* [2]	$\mathcal{O}(1)$	public key
Au *et al.* [3]	$\mathcal{O}(n)$	certificate-based
Zheng *et al.* [34]	$\mathcal{O}(n)$	public key
Tsang *et al.* [30]	$\mathcal{O}(n)$	public key
Tsang *et al.* [28]	$\mathcal{O}(n)$	identity-based
Chow *et al.* [13]	$\mathcal{O}(1)$	identity-based
Fujisaki and Suzuki [18]	$\mathcal{O}(n)$	public key
Fujisaki [17]	$\mathcal{O}(\sqrt{n})$	public key
Au *et al.* [4]	$\mathcal{O}(1)$	identity-based
Yuen *et al.* [32]	$\mathcal{O}(\sqrt{n})$	public key
Liu *et al.* [21]	$\mathcal{O}(n)$	public key

As we can see from the table, there are only a few constant size linkable ring signature existed in the literature. In our discussion, we focus on public key only because both identity-based and certificate-based cryptosystems are not suitable for blockchain paradigm as they require a Private Key Generator (PKG) to issue user keys, which contradicts to the decentralized concept of blockchain. Among them, [29] requires the Certificate Authority (CA) to generate the user key. [2] is an improvement over [29] but it still requires an interaction between the user and the CA during the user key generation process. Neither of them is suitable for blockchain.

We note that not all linkable ring signature schemes are suitable for Monero. There are some requirements that should be satisfied in order to be compatible with RingCT. We will discuss more on this in Sect. 4.

3   Preliminaries

In this section, we first give some notations used in the rest of this paper. We use $[n]$ to denote the set of integers $\{1, 2, \ldots, n\}$ for some positive integer $n \in \mathbb{N}$. For a randomized algorithm $A(\cdot)$, we write $y = A(x; r)$ to denote the unique output of A on input x and randomness r, and denote by $y \leftarrow A(x)$ the process of picking randomness r at random and setting $y = A(x; r)$. Also, we write $x \leftarrow S$ for sampling an element uniformly at random from a set S, and use $negl(\lambda)$ to denote some negligible function in a security parameter λ.

3.1 Mathematical Assumptions

Bilinear Pairings. Let $\mathbb{G}_1$ and $\mathbb{G}_2$ be two cyclic groups of prime order p, and g be a generator of $\mathbb{G}_1$. A function $e : \mathbb{G}_1 \times \mathbb{G}_1 \rightarrow \mathbb{G}_2$ is a bilinear map if the following properties hold:

- Bilinearity: $e(A^x, B^y) = e(A, B)^{xy}$ for all $A, B \in \mathbb{G}_1$ and $x, y \in \mathbb{Z}_p$;
- Non-degeneracy: $e(g, g) \neq 1$, where 1 is the identity of $\mathbb{G}_2$;
- Efficient computability: there exists an algorithm that can efficiently compute $e(A, B)$ for all $A, B \in \mathbb{G}_1$.

Decisional Diffie-Hellman (DDH) Assumption. Let $\mathbb{G}$ be a group where $|\mathbb{G}| = q$ and $g \in \mathbb{G}$ such that $\langle g \rangle = \mathbb{G}$. There exists no probabilistic polynomial time (PPT) algorithm that can distinguish the distributions (g, g^a, g^b, g^{ab}) and (g, g^a, g^b, g^c) with non-negligible probability over $1/2$ in time polynomial in q, where a, b, c are chosen uniformly at random from $\mathbb{Z}_q$.

k-Strong Diffie-Hellman (k-SDH) Assumption. There exists no PPT algorithm which, on input a $k + 1$-tuple $(g_0, g_0^\alpha, g_0^{\alpha^2}, \ldots, g_0^{\alpha^k}) \in \mathbb{G}^{k+1}$, returns a pair $(w, y) \in \mathbb{G} \times \mathbb{Z}_p^*$, where $\mathbb{G} = \langle g_0 \rangle$ and p is the order of $\mathbb{G}$, such that $w^{\alpha+y} = g_0$, with non-negligible probability and in time polynomial in λ.

3.2 Building Blocks

In this section, we briefly recall the basic primitives used to construct our RingCT protocol, which include accumulator with one-way domain, signature of knowledge and homomorphic commitment scheme.

ACCUMULATORS WITH ONE-WAY DOMAIN. As defined in [5,14], an accumulator *accumulates* multiple values into one single value such that, for each value accumulated, there is a witness proving that it has indeed been accumulated. Formally, let $\mathcal{F} = \{F_\lambda\}$ be a sequence of families of functions and $\mathcal{X} = \{X_\lambda\}$ a sequence of families of finite sets, such that $F_\lambda = \{f : U_f \times X_f \rightarrow U_f\}$ and $X_\lambda \subseteq X_f$ for all $\lambda \in \mathbb{N}$, we call the pair $(\mathcal{F}, \mathcal{X})$ *an accumulator family with one-way domain* if the following conditions hold:

- quasi-commutativity: for all $\lambda \in \mathbb{N}, f \in F_\lambda, u \in U_f$ and $x_1, x_2 \in X_\lambda$, it holds that $f(f(u, x_1), x_2) = f(f(u, x_2), x_1)$. $\{X_\lambda\}$ is always referred to as the domain of this accumulator. For any $X = \{x_1, x_2, \cdots, x_n\} \subset X_\lambda$, we further refer to $f(\cdots f(u, x_1) \cdots x_n)$ as the accumulated value of X over u, which will be denoted by $f(u, X)$ thanks to this quasi-commutative property.

- collision-resistance: for all $\lambda \in \mathbb{N}$ and efficient adversaries $\mathcal{A}$, it holds that

$$\Pr \left[\begin{array}{l} X \subset X_\lambda \wedge (x \in X_f \backslash X) \\ (w \in U_f) \wedge (f(w,x) = f(u,X)) \end{array} : \begin{array}{l} f \leftarrow F_\lambda; u \leftarrow U_f; \\ (x, w, X) \leftarrow \mathcal{A}(f, U_f, u) \end{array} \right] \leq negl(\lambda).$$

- one-way domain: let $\{Y_\lambda\}, \{R_\lambda\}$ be two sequences of families of sets associated with $\{X_\lambda\}$, such that each R_λ is an *efficiently verifiable, samplable* relation over $Y_\lambda \times X_\lambda$ and it is infeasible to efficiently compute a witness $y' \in Y_\lambda$ for an x sampled from X_λ. That is,

$$\Pr\left[(y', x) \in R_\lambda : (y, x) \leftarrow \mathsf{Samp}(1^\lambda); y' \leftarrow \mathcal{A}(1^\lambda, x)\right] \leq negl(\lambda),$$

where Samp denotes the efficient sampling algorithm over R_λ.
- efficient generation: there exists an efficient algorithm denoted by ACC.Gen that on input a security parameter λ outputs a description desc of a random element of F_λ, possibly including some auxiliary information.
- efficient evaluation: for $\lambda \in \mathbb{N}, f \in F_\lambda, u \in U_f$ and $X \subset X_\lambda$, $w \in U_f$ is called a witness for the fact that $x \in X$ has been accumulated within $v \doteq f(u, X) \in U_f$ iff $f(w, x) = v$. There exists two algorithms denoted by ACC.Eval and ACC.Wit that on input (desc, X) and (desc, x, X) can efficiently evaluate the accumulated value $f(u, X)$ and the witness for x in $f(u, X)$, respectively.

For sake of simplicity, we will denote by ACC $=$ (ACC.Gen, ACC.Eval, ACC.Wit) such an *accumulator with one-way domain* in the following.

SIGNATURE OF KNOWLEDGE. Every three-move Proof of Knowledge protocols (PoKs) that is Honest-Verifier Zero-Knowledge (HVZK) can be transformed into a signature scheme by setting the challenge to the hash value of the commitment concatenated with the message to be signed [16]. Signature schemes generated as such are provably secure [25] against existential forgery under adaptively chosen message attack in the random oracle model [7]. They are sometimes referred to as *Signatures of Knowledge*, SoK for short [10]. As an example, we denote by SoK$\{(x) : y = g^x\}(m)$, where m is the message, the signature scheme derived from the zero-knowledge proof of the discrete logarithm of y using the above technique. Before presenting the formal definition of SoK, we first let R be a fixed NP-hard relation with the corresponding language L $= \{y : \exists \ x \ s.t \ (x, y) \in$ R$\}$. Recall that a relation is called hard if it is infeasible for any efficient algorithm, given some instance y, to compute a valid witness such that $(x, y) \in$ R. In general, signature of knowledge protocol for R over message space $\mathcal{M}$ comprises of a triple of poly-time algorithms (Gen, Sign, Verf) with the following syntax:

- Gen(1^λ): on input a security parameter λ, the algorithm outputs public parameters par, which will be implicitly taken as part input of the following algorithms. Also, we assume that λ is efficiently recoverable from par.
- Sign(m, x, y): on input a message $m \in \mathcal{M}$ and a valid pair $(x, y) \in$ R, the algorithm outputs an SoK π.
- Verf(m, π, y): on input a message m, an SoK π and a statement y, the algorithm outputs 0/1 indicating the in/validity of the SoK.

Definition 1 (SimExt Security of SoK [11]). *An SoK protocol* $SoK = (Gen,$ *Sign, Verf) for hard relation R is called SimExt-secure if it satisfies the correct, simulatable and extractable properties as defined below.*

Correctness. *For any message $m \in \mathcal{M}$ and valid pair $(x, y) \in R$, it holds that*

$$\Pr\left[Verf(m, \pi, y) = 1 : par \leftarrow Gen(1^\lambda); \pi \leftarrow Sign(m, x, y)\right] \geq 1 - negl(\lambda),$$

where if the probability is exactly 1 we call SoK perfectly correct.

Simulatability. *There exists a poly-time simulator $Sim = (SimGen, SimSign)$ such that for any PPT adversary $\mathcal{A}$, it holds that*

$$\left|\Pr\left[b = 1 : (par, td) \leftarrow SimGen(1^\lambda); b \leftarrow \mathcal{A}^{Sim(td, \cdot, \cdot, \cdot)}(par)\right] -\right.$$
$$\left.\Pr\left[b = 1 : par \leftarrow Gen(1^\lambda); b \leftarrow \mathcal{A}^{Sign(\cdot, \cdot, \cdot)}(par)\right]\right| \leq negl(\lambda),$$

where Sim receives an input (m, x, y), checks the validity of y and returns $\pi \leftarrow SimSign(m, x, y)$ if $(x, y) \in R$. In addition, td is the additional trapdoor information used by Sim to simulate signatures without knowing a witness.

Extraction. *In addition to Sim, there exists an efficient extractor Ext such that for any PPT adversary $\mathcal{A}$, it holds that*

$$\Pr\left[\begin{array}{l} (x, y) \in R \vee (m, y) \in Q \\ \vee\ Verf(m, y, \pi) = 0 \end{array} : \begin{array}{l} (par, td) \leftarrow SimGen(1^\lambda); \\ (m, y, \pi) \leftarrow \mathcal{A}^{Sim(td, \cdot, \cdot, \cdot)}(par) \\ x \leftarrow Ext(par, td, m, y, \pi). \end{array}\right] \geq 1 - negl(\lambda).$$

where Q denotes the set of all queries (m, y) that $\mathcal{A}$ has made to Sim.

HOMOMORPHIC COMMITMENT SCHEMES. Informally, a (non-interactive) commitment scheme includes two phases: in commit phase, a sender chooses a value and constructs a commitment to it; later in the reveal phase the sender may open the commitment and reveal the value. After that, the receiver can verify that it is exactly the value that was committed at first. More formally, a commitment scheme consists of a pair of poly-time algorithms (CKGen, Com): on input a security parameter λ, CKGen(1^λ) outputs a public commitment key ctk, which specifies a message space $\mathcal{M}_{ctk}$ and a commitment space $\mathcal{C}_{ctk}$; on input a message $m \in \mathcal{M}_{ctk}$, Com(ctk, m) generates a commitment $c \leftarrow$ Com(ctk, m) to m, where ctk is often omitted when it is clear from the context. Normally, a commitment scheme should satisfy the hiding and binding properties, as defined below.

Definition 2 (Security of HCom [19]). *A non-interactive scheme HCom = (CKGen, Com) is called a secure homomorphic commitment scheme if it satisfies the following properties.*

Hiding *This property means that the commitment does not reveal the committed value. More precisely, HCom is called hiding if for all PPT adversaries $\mathcal{A}$, it holds that*

$$\left| \Pr\left[\mathcal{A}(c) = b : \begin{array}{l} ctk \leftarrow CKGen(1^\lambda); (m_0, m_1) \leftarrow \mathcal{A}(ctk); \\ b \leftarrow \{0,1\}; c \leftarrow Com(ctk, m_b) \end{array} \right] - \frac{1}{2} \right| \leq negl(\lambda),$$

where $m_0, m_1 \in \mathcal{M}_{ctk}$ and HCom is called perfectly hiding if the probability of $\mathcal{A}$ guessing b is exactly $1/2$.

Binding. *This property means that a commitment cannot be opened to two different values. More precisely, HCom is called binding if for all PPT adversaries $\mathcal{A}$, it holds that*

$$\Pr\left[\begin{array}{l} m_0 \neq m_1 \wedge \\ Com(m_0; r_0) = Com(m_1; r_1) \end{array} : \begin{array}{l} ctk \leftarrow CKGen(1^\lambda); \\ (m_0, r_0, m_1, r_1) \leftarrow \mathcal{A}(ctk) \end{array} \right] \leq negl(\lambda),$$

where $m_0, m_1 \in \mathcal{M}_{ctk}$ and r_0, r_1 are random coins of Com. HCom is called perfectly binding if the probability is exactly 0. Moreover, we call HCom strongly binding if the probability holds even for the condition $(m_0, r_0) \neq (m_1, r_1)$ rather than $m_0 \neq m_1$.

Homomorphic. *For this property, we assume that for each well-formed ctk, the commitment space $\mathcal{C}_{ck}$ is a multiplicative group of order q and both the messages and random coins are from $\mathbb{Z}_q$. This property says that for all $\lambda \in \mathbb{N}$, $ctk \leftarrow CKGen(1^\lambda)$, $m_0, m_1 \in \mathbb{Z}_q$ and $r_0, r_1 \in \mathbb{Z}_q$, it holds that*

$$Com(m_0; r_0) \cdot Com(m_1; r_1) = Com(m_0 + m_1; r_0 + r_1).$$

4   RingCT Protocol for Monero

In this section, we formalize ring confidential transaction (RingCT) protocol for Monero. Recall that Monero is based on CryptoNote, where each user may have a number of distinct accounts. Each account consists of a one-time address and a coin, and it is always associated with an account key used to authorize its spending. In each transaction, a user can spend many of her/his accounts with the corresponding keys. The goal of ring confidential transaction (RingCT) protocol is to protect the anonymity of spenders as well as the privacy of transactions.

Informally, a RingCT protocol mainly comprises of two phases: the generation and the verification of ring confidential transactions, which are operated by the spender and recipients respectively. When a user would like to spend m of her/his accounts, w.l.o.g., denoted by $A_s = \{(pk_s^{(k)}, cn_s^{(k)})\}_{k \in [m]}$ where $pk_s^{(k)}$ is the user's k-th account address and $cn_s^{(k)}$ is the coin w.r.t. this account, s/he first chooses t output accounts $\{(pk_{out,j}, cn_{out,j})\}_{j \in [t]}$ for all output addresses $R = \{pk_{out,j}\}_{j \in [t]}$ accordingly, such that the sum of balances of her/his input accounts equals to that of output accounts, and then additionally selects $n - 1$

groups of input accounts with each containing m different accounts to anonymously spend A_s for some payments (i.e., creating a ring confidential transaction). Whenever receiving this transaction from the P2P blockchain network, the miners check the validity of the transaction with public information along with it and add it to a (new) block if valid.

By a thorough analysis of the protocol in [24], we find that the RingCT protocol essentially involves ring signatures and commitments (that are used to hide account balance). To be compatible within the protocol, these two cryptographic primitives should satisfy the following properties simultaneously:

- Public keys generated by the key generation algorithm of ring signature should be homomorphic.
- Commitments should be homomorphic with respect to (w.r.t.) the same operation as public keys.
- Commitments to zero are well-formed public keys, each corresponding secret key of which can be derived from the randomness of commitments.

To further capture the essential properties and securities required by the ring confidential transaction protocol for Monero, we initiate the formalization of RingCT protocol and its security models, the details of which are shown in the following subsections.

4.1 Technical Description

In general, a RingCT protocol consists of a tuple of poly-time algorithms (Setup, KeyGen, Mint, Spend, Verify), the syntax of which are described as follows:

- $pp \leftarrow$ Setup(1^λ): the *Setup* algorithm takes a security parameter $\lambda \in \mathbb{N}$, and outputs the public system parameters pp. All algorithms below have implicitly pp as part of their inputs.
- $(sk, pk) \leftarrow$ KeyGen(pp): the *key generation* algorithm takes as input pp and outputs a public and secret key pair (pk, sk). In the context of Monero, pk is always set as a one-time address, which together with a coin constitutes an account.
- $(cn, ck) \leftarrow$ Mint(pk, a): the *Mint* algorithm takes as input an amount a and a valid address pk s.t. $(pk, sk) \leftarrow$ KeyGen(pp), and outputs a coin cn for pk as well as the associated coin key ck^3. The coin cn together with address pk forms an account $act \doteq (pk, cn)$, the corresponding secret key of which is $ask \doteq (sk, ck)$ that is required for authorizing its spending.
- $(tx, \pi, S) \leftarrow$ Spend($\mathsf{m}, K_s, A_s, A, R$): on input a group A_s of accounts together with the corresponding account secret keys K_s, an arbitrary set A of groups of input accounts containing A_s, a set R of out addresses and some transaction string $\mathsf{m} \in \{0, 1\}^*$, the algorithm outputs a transaction tx (containing m, A and A_R which denotes the set of output accounts w.r.t. R), a proof π and a set S of serial numbers.

---

[3] We note that ck will be privately sent to the user possessing account address pk, e.g., by private public key encryption.

- $1/0 \leftarrow \mathsf{Verify}(tx, \pi, S)$: on input the transaction tx containing $\mathbf{m}, A$ and A_R, proof π and serial numbers S, the algorithm verifies whether a set of accounts with serial numbers S is spent properly for the transaction tx towards addresses R, and outputs 1 or 0, meaning a valid or invalid spending respectively.

4.2   Security Definitions

A RingCT protocol should at least satisfy the properties formalized below.

Definition 3 (Perfect Correctness). *This property requires that a user can spend any group of her accounts w.r.t. an arbitrary set of groups of input accounts, each group containing the same number of accounts as the group she intends to spend. Specifically, a RingCT protocol $\Pi = (\mathsf{Setup}, \mathsf{KeyGen}, \mathsf{Mint}, \mathsf{Spend}, \mathsf{Verify})$ is called perfectly correct if for all PPT adversaries $\mathcal{A}$, it holds that*

$$\Pr\left[\mathsf{Verify}(tx, \pi, S) = 1: \begin{array}{l} pp \leftarrow \mathsf{Setup}(1^\lambda); \ (\mathbf{m}, A, R) \leftarrow \mathcal{A}(pp, A_s, K_s) \\ where \ (A_s, K_s) = \left\{ \left((pk, cn), (sk, ck)\right) \right\} \ s.t. \\ (pk, sk) \leftarrow \mathsf{KeyGen}(pp), (cn, ck) \leftarrow \mathsf{Mint}(pk, a); \\ (tx, \pi, S) \leftarrow \mathsf{Spend}(\mathbf{m}, K_s, A_s, A, R). \end{array}\right] = 1.$$

Definition 4 (Balance). *This property requires that any malicious user cannot (1) spend any account without her control and (2) spend her own/controllable accounts with a larger output amount. Specifically, a RingCT protocol $\Pi = (\mathsf{Setup}, \mathsf{KeyGen}, \mathsf{Mint}, \mathsf{Spend}, \mathsf{Verify})$ is called balanced w.r.t. insider corruption if for all PPT adversaries $\mathcal{A}$, it holds that*

$$\Pr\left[\mathcal{A} \ Wins: \begin{array}{l} pp \leftarrow \mathsf{Setup}(1^\lambda); \ (\{act_i'\}_{i=1}^\mu, \{\mathcal{S}_i\}_{i=1}^\nu) \\ \leftarrow \mathcal{A}^{AddGen, ActGen, Spend, Corrupt}(pp) \end{array}\right] \leq negl(\lambda),$$

where all oracles AddGen, ActGen, Spend *and* Corrupt *are defined as below:*

- AddGen*(i): on input a query number i, picks randomness τ_i, runs algorithm $(sk_i, pk_i) \leftarrow \mathsf{KeyGen}(pp; \tau_i)$ and returns address pk_i.*
- ActGen*(i, a_i): on input address index i and an amount a_i, runs algorithm $(cn_i, ck_i) \leftarrow \mathsf{Mint}(pk_i, a_i)$, then adds i and account $act_i = (pk_i, cn_i)$ to initially empty lists $\mathcal{I}$ and $\mathcal{G}$ respectively, and outputs (act_i, ck_i) for address pk_i, where pk_i is assumed to have been generated by* AddGen*. The associated secret key with account act_i is $ask_i \doteq (sk_i, ck_i)$. The oracle also uses ask_i to determine the serial number s_i of act_i and adds it to initially empty list S.*
- Spend*($\mathbf{m}, A_s, A, R$): takes in transaction string $\mathbf{m}$, input accounts A containing A_s and output addresses R, runs $(tx, \pi, S) \leftarrow \mathsf{Spend}(\mathbf{m}, K_s, A_s, A, R)$ and returns (tx, π, S) after adding it to list $\mathcal{T}$, where $A_s \subset \mathcal{G}$ and we assume that at least one account/address in A_s has not been corrupted so far.*
- Corrupt*(i): on input query number $i \in \mathcal{I}$, uses account key ask_i to determine the serial number s_i of account act_i with address pk_i, then adds s_i and (s_i, a_i) to lists $\mathcal{C}$ and $\mathcal{B}$ respectively, where a_i is the balance of the account with address pk_i, and finally returns τ_i.*

At last, $\mathcal{A}$ outputs all her spends with some new accounts $(act'_1, act'_2, \cdots, act'_\mu, S_1, S_2, \cdots, S_\nu)$ such that $S_i = (tx_i, \pi_i, S_i)$, where all spends are payed to, w.l.o.g., the challenger with account address pk_c[4], i.e., $tx_i = (\mathfrak{m}_i, A_i, A_{\{pk_c\}})$, and $A_i \subset \mathcal{G} \cup \{act'_i\}_{i=1}^\mu$ for all $i \in [\nu]$. We call $\mathcal{A}$ wins in the experiment if her outputs satisfy the following conditions:

1. $\mathsf{Verify}(tx_i, \pi_i, S_i) = 1$ for all $i \in [\nu]$.
2. $S_i \notin \mathcal{T} \wedge S_i \subset \mathcal{S}$ for all $i \in [\nu]$, and $S_j \cap S_k = \emptyset$ for any different $j, k \in [\nu]$.
3. Let $S_i = \{s_{i,j}\}$ and $E = \bigcup_{i=1}^\nu \{a_{i,j} : (s_{i,j}, a_{i,j}) \in \mathcal{B} \wedge s_{i,j} \in S_i \cap \mathcal{C}\}$, it holds that $\sum_{a_{i,j} \in E} a_{i,j} < \sum_{i=1}^\nu a_{out,i}$, where $a_{out,i}$ denotes the balance of output account in S_i.

Definition 5 (Anonymity). *This property requires that two proofs of spending with the same transaction string* $\mathfrak{m}$, *input accounts* A, *output addresses* R *and distinct spent accounts* $A_{s_0}, A_{s_1} \in A$ *are (computationally) indistinguishable, meaning that the spender's accounts are successfully hidden among all the honestly generated accounts. Specifically, a RingCT protocol* $\Pi = (\mathsf{Setup}, \mathsf{KeyGen}, \mathsf{Mint}, \mathsf{Spend}, \mathsf{Verify})$ *is called anonymous if for all PPT adversaries* $\mathcal{A} = (\mathcal{A}_1, \mathcal{A}_2)$, *it holds that*

$$\left| \Pr \left[b' = b : \begin{array}{l} pp \leftarrow \mathsf{Setup}(1^\lambda); \; (\mathfrak{m}, A_{s_0}, A_{s_1}, A, R) \leftarrow \\ \mathcal{A}_1^{AddGen, ActGen, Spend, Corrupt}(pp); \; b \leftarrow \{0, 1\}, \\ (tx^*, \pi^*, S^*) \leftarrow \mathsf{Spend}(\mathfrak{m}, K_{s_b}, A_{s_b}, A, R); \\ b' \leftarrow \mathcal{A}_2^{Spend, Corrupt}(pp, (tx^*, \pi^*, S^*)) \end{array} \right] - \frac{1}{2} \right| \leq negl(\lambda),$$

where all oracles are defined as before, $A_{s_i} \in A$ *and* $A_{s_i} \subset \mathcal{G}$ *for* $i \in \{0, 1\}$. *In addition, the following restrictions should be satisfied:*

- *For all* $i \in \{0, 1\}$, *any account in* A_{s_i} *has not been corrupted.*
- *Any query in the form of* $(\cdot, A_s, \cdot, \cdot)$ *s.t.* $A_s \cap A_{s_i} \neq \emptyset$ *has not been issued to* Spend *oracle.*

Definition 6 (Non-Slanderability). *This property requires that a malicious user cannot slander any honest user after observing an honestly generated spending. That is, it is infeasible for any malicious user to produce a valid spending that share at least one serial number with a previously generated honest spending. Specifically, a RingCT protocol* $\Pi = (\mathsf{Setup}, \mathsf{KeyGen}, \mathsf{Mint}, \mathsf{Spend}, \mathsf{Verify})$ *is called non-slanderable if for all PPT adversaries* $\mathcal{A}$, *it holds that*

$$\Pr \left[\mathcal{A} \; Wins : \begin{array}{l} pp \leftarrow \mathsf{Setup}(1^\lambda); \; ((\hat{tx}, \hat{\pi}, \hat{S}), (tx^*, \pi^*, S^*)) \\ \leftarrow \mathcal{A}^{AddGen, ActGen, Spend, Corrupt}(pp) \end{array} \right] \leq negl(\lambda),$$

where all oracles are defined as before, and $(\hat{tx}, \hat{\pi}, \hat{S})$ *is one output of the oracle* Spend *for some* $(\mathfrak{m}, A_s, A, R)$. *We call* $\mathcal{A}$ *succeeds if the output satisfies the following conditions: (1)* $\mathsf{Verify}(tx^*, \pi^*, S^*) = 1$; *(2)* $(tx^*, \pi^*, S^*) \notin \mathcal{T}$; *(3)* $\hat{S} \cap \mathcal{C} = \emptyset$ *but* $\hat{S} \cap S^* \neq \emptyset$.

---

[4] Note that in this case, assuming pk_c has been generated by AddGen, the challenger knows all balances of the spent accounts and output accounts involved in the adversarial spends $\{S\}_{i=1}^\nu$.

We note that our non-slanderability definition already covers *linkability* property of a linkable ring signature. Thus we do not need to explicitly define linkability.

5 Our RingCT 2.0 Protocol

In this section, we present a new RingCT protocol under our formalized syntax. Specifically, our protocol is constructed based on a generic accumulator with one-way domain ACC, a signature of knowledge SoK and the well-known Pedersen commitment. Proceeding to present the details, we first give an intuition of our protocol. Without loss of generality, we denote all, say, n groups of input accounts by $A = \{(pk_{in,i}^{(k)}, cn_{in,i}^{(k)})\}_{i \in [n], k \in [m]}$ (including the group of m accounts the user intends to spend) and set the spender's group as the s-th group, i.e., $A_s = \{(pk_{in,s}^{(k)}, cn_{in,s}^{(k)})\}_{k \in [m]}$. Conceptually, our idea is to arrange the account groups key into a matrix in which each group corresponds to a column. To shorten the size of transaction, the public keys in the same row is accumulated into one value. Then, the spender proves that he is using one account of each row in the spending. To ensure that the spender is using the account of the same column, the accumulated elements in protocol are formed as $pk_{in,i}^{(k)} \cdot u^s$ instead of $pk_{in,i}^{(k)}$, as shown in the matrix below.

To further guarantee the total balance in each transaction is conserved, the spender computes extra public keys $\widetilde{pk}_i$ based on the input accounts and the output accounts. Looking ahead, knowledge of the secret key that corresponds to $\widetilde{pk}_i$ implies that the balance in accounts A_i is equal to the balance of the output accounts.

$$
\begin{pmatrix}
pk_{in,1}^{(1)} \cdot u^1 & \cdots & pk_{in,s}^{(1)} \cdot u^s & \cdots & pk_{in,n}^{(1)} \cdot u^n \\
\vdots & \ddots & \vdots & \ddots & \vdots \\
pk_{in,1}^{(k)} \cdot u^1 & \cdots & pk_{in,s}^{(k)} \cdot u^s & \cdots & pk_{in,n}^{(k)} \cdot u^n \\
\vdots & & \vdots & \ddots & \vdots \\
pk_{in,1}^{(m)} \cdot u^1 & \cdots & pk_{in,s}^{(m)} \cdot u^s & \cdots & pk_{in,n}^{(m)} \cdot u^n \\
\boxed{\widetilde{pk}_1 \cdot u^1} & \cdots & \boxed{\widetilde{pk}_s \cdot u^s} & \cdots & \boxed{\widetilde{pk}_n \cdot u^n}
\end{pmatrix}
\begin{matrix}
\Rightarrow \\ \vdots \\ \Rightarrow \\ \vdots \\ \Rightarrow \\ \Rightarrow
\end{matrix}
\begin{pmatrix}
v_1 \\ \vdots \\ v_k \\ \vdots \\ v_m \\ v_{m+1}
\end{pmatrix}
$$

5.1 Protocol Description

Let $\mathsf{ACC} = (\mathsf{ACC.Gen}, \mathsf{ACC.Eval}, \mathsf{ACC.Wit})$ be an accumulator with one-way domain and $\mathsf{SoK} = (\mathsf{Gen}, \mathsf{Sign}, \mathsf{Verf})$ be a signature of knowledge as defined in Sect. 3.2. Based on these primitives and the Pedersen commitment, our RingCT protocol $\mathsf{RCT} = (\mathsf{Setup}, \mathsf{KeyGen}, \mathsf{Mint}, \mathsf{Spend}, \mathsf{Verify})$ is designed as follows:

$\mathsf{Setup}(1^\lambda)$: on input a security parameter λ, the algorithm prepares a collision-resistant accumulator f with one-way domain $\mathbb{G}_q$, together with its description desc, by calling ACC.Gen(1^λ), and generates par by running Gen(1^λ). Then it randomly picks generators h_0, $h_1, u \in \mathbb{G}_q$, chooses a random hash function H, and outputs the system parameters $pp = (1^\lambda, \text{desc}, \text{par}, h_0, h_1, u, H)$.

KeyGen(pp): on input pp, the algorithm generates a key pair $(sk, pk) := (x, y = h_0^x) \in \mathbb{Z}_q \times \mathbb{G}_q$ by executing the sampling algorithm of the one-way relation associated with the domain of f. In the context of Monero, the public key pk is always set as a one-time address, which combining with a coin constitutes a user's account.

Mint(pk, a): on input address pk and an amount $a \in \mathbb{Z}_q$, the algorithm mints a coin for pk: chooses $r \in \mathbb{Z}_q$ uniformly at random, computes commitment $c = h_0^r h_1^a$, where r is called a secret hiding factor and a is the balance of account pk, and then returns $(cn, ck) = (c, (r, a))$. The coin cn together with pk forms the account $act \doteq (pk, cn)$, to which the corresponding secret key is $ask \doteq (sk, ck)$.

Spend($\mathsf{m}, K_s, A_s, A, R$): on input a set of secret keys K_s associated with the group of input accounts A_s, some transaction string $\mathsf{m} \in \{0,1\}^*$, an arbitrary set A of groups of input accounts containing A_s, and a set R of output addresses, the algorithm produces an SoK π and the corresponding serial numbers S w.r.t. A_s as follows. Without loss of generality, we denote all, say, n groups (including the group the user intends to spend) of input accounts by $A = \{(pk_{in,i}^{(k)}, cn_{in,i}^{(k)})\}_{i \in [n], k \in [m]}$ and set the spender's group as the s-th group, i.e., $A_s = \{(pk_{in,s}^{(k)}, cn_{in,s}^{(k)})\}_{k \in [m]}$, the corresponding secret keys of which are $K_s = \{ask_s^{(k)} = (sk_{in,s}^{(k)}, (r_{in,s}^{(k)}, a_{in,s}^{(k)}))\}_{k \in [m]}$, and denote the intended output addresses by $R = \{pk_{out,j}\}_{j \in [t]}$.

1. Set $a_{out,j} \in \mathbb{Z}_q$ for all output address $pk_{out,j} \in R$, such that the input and output balances satisfy $\sum_{k=1}^{m} a_{in,s}^{(k)} = \sum_{j=1}^{t} a_{out,j}$, then pick uniformly at random $r_{out,j} \in \mathbb{Z}_q$ and mint coin $cn_{out,j} = c_{out,j} = h_0^{r_{out,j}} h_1^{a_{out,j}}$. After that, add output account $act_{out,j} = (pk_{out,j}, cn_{out,j})$ to A_R, and privately send the coin key $ck_{out,j} = (r_{our,j}, a_{out,j})$ to the user holding address $pk_{out,j}$.

2. Compute $\widetilde{sk}_s = \sum_{k=1}^{m} sk_{in,s}^{(k)} + \sum_{k=1}^{m} r_{in,s}^{(k)} - \sum_{j=1}^{t} r_{out,j}$ and $\widetilde{pk}_i = \prod_{k=1}^{m} pk_{in,i}^{(k)} \cdot$ $\prod_{k=1}^{m} cn_{in,i}^{(k)} / \prod_{j=1}^{t} cn_{out,j}$ for each $i \in [n]$. Clearly, it holds that $\widetilde{pk}_s = h_0^{\widetilde{sk}_s}$, which follows from the fact that $\sum_{k=1}^{m} a_{in,s}^{(k)} = \sum_{j=1}^{t} a_{out,j}$. For convenience, we denote $\widetilde{pk}_i$ and $\widetilde{sk}_s$ by $y_i^{(m+1)}$ and $x_s^{(m+1)}$ respectively hereafter, i.e., $\widetilde{pk}_i \doteq y_i^{(m+1)}$ and $\widetilde{sk}_s \doteq x_s^{(m+1)}$.

3. Generate a proof π that the group of coins A_s was spent properly for a transaction tx, which consists of m, input accounts A and output accounts $A_R = \{act_{out,j}\}$, as follows. For clarity, we denote $sk_{in,s}^{(k)} = x_s^{(k)}$ for all $k \in [m]$ and $pk_{in,i}^{(k)} = y_i^{(k)}$ for all $i \in [n]$ and $k \in [m]$. Recall that $\widetilde{pk}_i \doteq y_i^{(m+1)}$ for all $i \in [n]$ and $\widetilde{sk}_s \doteq x_s^{(m+1)}$.

(a) For each $k \in [m+1]$, compute the accumulated value $v_k = \mathsf{ACC.Eval}(\mathsf{desc}, \{y_i^{(k)} \cdot u^i\})$ and the witness $w_s^{(k)} = \mathsf{ACC.Wit}(\mathsf{desc}, \{y_i^{(k)} \cdot u^i | i \neq s\})$ for the fact that $y_s^{(k)} \cdot u^s$ has been accumulated within v_k (i.e., computing the witness $w_s^{(k)}$ s.t. $f(w_s^{(k)}, y_s^{(k)} \cdot u^s) = v_k$). Then compute $s_k = H(y_s^{(k)})^{x_s^{(k)}}$ for all $k \in [m]$. For simplicity, we denote $z_s^{(k)} = y_s^{(k)} \cdot u^s$ hereafter.

(b) Use Sign to produce a signature of knowledge π on tx as:

$$\mathsf{SoK}\left\{ (\{w_k, z_k, x_k\}_{k=1}^{m+1}, \gamma) : \begin{array}{l} f(w_{m+1}, z_{m+1}) = v_{m+1} \wedge z_{m+1} = h_0^{x_{m+1}} u^\gamma \wedge \\ f(w_1, z_1) = v_1 \wedge z_1 = h_0^{x_1} u^\gamma \wedge s_1 = H(y_s^{(1)})^{x_1} \wedge \\ \vdots \\ f(w_m, z_m) = v_m \wedge z_m = h_0^{x_m} u^\gamma \wedge s_m = H(y_s^{(m)})^{x_m} \end{array} \right\} \quad (tx)$$

(c) Eventually, return (tx, π, S), where $S = \{s_1, s_2, \ldots, s_m\}$. We note that the serial number s_k is uniquely determined by the address key $sk_{in,s}^{(k)}$ for every $k \in [m]$, and thus they can be used to prevent double-spending.

$\mathsf{Verify}(tx, \pi, S)$: receiving a transaction tx containing m, A and A_R, the associated SoK π for tx and the serial numbers $S = \{s_i\}$, the recipient verifies that a set of accounts with serial numbers $\{s_i\}$ from input accounts A was spent for a transaction tx (towards output addresses R) with string m, as follows:

1. Use $A = \{(pk_{in,i}^{(k)}, cn_{in,i}^{(k)})\}_{i \in [n], k \in [m]}$ and $A_R = \{(pk_{out,j}, cn_{out,j})\}_{j \in [t]}$ (contained in tx) to compute $\widetilde{pk}_i = \prod_{k=1}^{m} pk_{in,i}^{(k)} \cdot \prod_{k=1}^{m} cn_{in,i}^{(k)} / \prod_{j=1}^{t} cn_{out,j}$ for all $i \in [n]$, and then compute the accumulated values $v_k = \mathsf{ACC.Eval}(\mathsf{desc}, \{pk_{in,i}^{(k)} \cdot u^i\})$ for all $k \in [m]$ and $v_{m+1} = \mathsf{ACC.Eval}(\mathsf{desc}, \{\widetilde{pk}_i \cdot u^i\})$.

2. Take as input accumulated values $(v_1, \cdots, v_{m+1})$, serial numbers $S = (s_1, \cdots, s_m)$, transaction tx and π to verify whether it is a *valid* spending by checking $\mathsf{Verf}(tx, (v_1, \cdots, v_{m+1}, s_1, \cdots, s_m), \pi) \stackrel{?}{=} 1$. If true, accept this transaction, otherwise reject it.

The correctness of this protocol follows directly from that of the underlying signature of knowledge protocol SoK. We do not give more details here.

5.2 Security Analysis

In this part, the securities of our RingCT protocol are collectively analyzed under the formalized security models, which are indicated as the following theorems.

Theorem 1. *Assuming the discrete logarithm (DL) problem in $\mathbb{G}_q$ is hard, ACC is an accumulator with one-way domain and SoK is a SimExt-secure signature of knowledge, then the proposed RingCT protocol RCT is balanced w.r.t. insider corruption.*

Theorem 2. *Let HComp be the Pedersen commitment, ACC be an accumulator with one-way domain and SoK a SimExt-secure signature of knowledge, then the proposed RingCT protocol RCT is anonymous under the DDH assumption.*

Theorem 3. *Assuming the DL problem in $\mathbb{G}_q$ is hard, ACC is an accumulator with one-way domain and SoK is a SimExt-secure signature of knowledge, then the proposed RingCT protocol RCT is non-slanderable w.r.t. insider corruption.*

Proofs for Theorems 1, 2 and 3 can be found in the full version of this paper [27].

5.3   Instantiations

Our RingCT protocol is constructed based on a well-known homomorphic commitment, i.e., the Pedersen commitment, a generic accumulator with one-way domain ACC and a signature of knowledge SoK for a specific language related to ACC. Next we give an instantiation of ACC and SoK, and briefly recall the Pedersen commitment for completeness.

Accumulator with One-Way Domain. A specific (universal) accumulator for DDH groups presented in [5] is well suited to our protocol, the algorithms of which are described as follows:

- ACC.Gen(1^λ): generate cyclic groups $\mathbb{G}_1 = \langle g_0 \rangle$ and $\mathbb{G}_2$ of prime order p, equipped with a bilinear pairing $e : \mathbb{G}_1 \times \mathbb{G}_1 \to \mathbb{G}_2$, and an accumulating function $g \circ f : \mathbb{Z}_p^* \times \mathbb{Z}_p^* \to \mathbb{G}_1$, where f is defined as $f : \mathbb{Z}_p^* \times \mathbb{Z}_p^* \to \mathbb{Z}_p^*$ such that $f : (u, x) \mapsto u(x + \alpha)$ for some auxiliary information α randomly chosen from $\mathbb{Z}_p^*$ (for simplicity, u is always set as the identity element of $\mathbb{Z}_p^*$) and g is defined as $g : \mathbb{Z}_p^* \to \mathbb{G}_1$ such that $g : x \mapsto g_0^x$. The domain of accumulatable elements is $\mathbb{G}_q = \langle h \rangle$, which is a cyclic group of prime order q such that $\mathbb{G}_q \subset \mathbb{Z}_p^*$. At last, output the description $\mathsf{desc} = (\mathbb{G}_1, \mathbb{G}_2, \mathbb{G}_q, e, g_0, g_0^\alpha, g_0^{\alpha^2}, \cdots, g_0^{\alpha^n}, g \circ f)$, where n is the maximum number of elements to be accumulated.
- ACC.Eval(desc, X): compute the accumulated value $g \circ f(1, X)$ for X by evaluating $\prod_{i=0}^{n}(g_0^{\alpha^i})^{u_i}$ with public information $\{g_0^{\alpha^i}\}_{i \in [n]}$, where u_i is the coefficient of the polynomial $\prod_{x \in X}(x + \alpha) = \prod_{i=0}^{n}(u_i \alpha^i)$.
- ACC.Wit(desc, x_s, X): the relation Ω w.r.t. this accumulator is defined as $\Omega(w, x, v) = 1$ iff $e(w, g_0^x g_0^\alpha) = e(v, g_0)$, a witness w_s for the element $x_s \in X := \{x_1, x_2, \cdots, x_n\}$ s.t. $s \in [n]$ is computed as $w_s = g \circ f(1, X \backslash \{x_s\}) = \prod_{i=0}^{n-1}(g_0^{\alpha^i})^{u_i}$ with public information $\{g_0^{\alpha^i}\}_{i \in [n-1]}$, where u_i is the coefficient of the polynomial $\prod_{i=1, i \neq s}^{n}(x_i + \alpha) = \prod_{i=0}^{n-1}(u_i \alpha^i)$.

Regarding this accumulator, the domain of accumulatable elements is $\mathbb{G}_q = \langle h \rangle$, the one-way relation for which is defined as $\mathsf{R}_q \doteq \{(y, x) \in \mathbb{Z}_q \times \mathbb{G}_q : x = h^y\}$. Moreover, the relation R_q is *efficiently verifiable, efficiently samplable* and *one-way*, as defined before.

Theorem 4 [5]. *Under the n-SDH assumption in group $\mathbb{G}_1$, the above accumulator ACC is a secure universal accumulator. Moreover, under the DL assumption in group $\mathbb{G}_q$, it is an accumulator with one-way domain.*

As to the associated SoK with this concrete ACC, it can be easily obtained by applying the Fiat-Shamir paradigm [15] to the associated interactive zero-knowledge protocol given in [5].

Pedersen Commitment. As shown in [19], the Pedersen commitment is naturally a homomorphic commitment scheme. Its key generation algorithm CKGen and commit algorithm Com are described respectively as:

- CKGen(1^λ): on input a security parameter 1^λ, outputs the commitment key $ctk = (\mathbb{G}_q, q, g, h)$, where $\mathbb{G}_q$ is a cyclic group of prime order q and g, h are random generators of $\mathbb{G}_q$.
- Com(ctk, m): to commit to a message $m \in \mathbb{Z}_q$, the algorithm randomly picks $r \in \mathbb{Z}_q$ and computes $c = g^m h^r$.

As well known, this commitment scheme is perfectly hiding and computationally strongly binding under the discrete logarithm assumption in $\mathbb{G}_q$.

6 Efficiency Analysis

In this section, we give a brief comparison of the efficiency of our RingCT protocol with that of [24]. In particular, the anonymity of our protocol relies heavily on the underlying accumulator with one-way domain, which compacts a group of input accounts to a shorter value, while the RingCT protocol given in [24] is directly constructed on the basis of a linkable ring signature. As shown in [24], the size of signature in their protocol increases linearly with the number n of group accounts. More concretely, it is almost $\mathcal{O}(n(m+1))$ where m is the number of accounts contained in each group. In contrast, the communication complexity of our protocol is $\mathcal{O}(m)$, which is independent of the number of groups. Clearly, the proposed protocol presents a significant space/bandwidth saving.

7 Conclusion

In this work, we first formalize the syntax of RingCT protocol and present some rigorous security definitions by capturing the necessary security requirements for its application in Monero, which is the core part for Monero. Next, we propose a new RingCT protocol (RingCT 2.0) based on a specific homomorphic commitment, accumulator with one-way domain and the related signature of knowledge. The size of the RingCT 2.0 protocol is independent to the number of groups of input accounts included in the generalized ring while the original RingCT protocol suffers from the linear growing size with the number of groups. We believe the significant space complexity improvement in RingCT 2.0 will improve the overall efficiency of Monero.

Acknowledgement. This work is supported by National Natural Science Foundation of China (61602396, 61472083).

References

1. Abe, M., Ohkubo, M., Suzuki, K.: 1-out-of-n signatures from a variety of keys. In: Zheng, Y. (ed.) ASIACRYPT 2002. LNCS, vol. 2501, pp. 415–432. Springer, Heidelberg (2002). doi:10.1007/3-540-36178-2_26
2. Au, M.H., Chow, S.S.M., Susilo, W., Tsang, P.P.: Short linkable ring signatures revisited. In: Atzeni, A.S., Lioy, A. (eds.) EuroPKI 2006. LNCS, vol. 4043, pp. 101–115. Springer, Heidelberg (2006). doi:10.1007/11774716_9
3. Au, M.H., Liu, J.K., Susilo, W., Yuen, T.H.: Certificate based (linkable) ring signature. In: Dawson, E., Wong, D.S. (eds.) ISPEC 2007. LNCS, vol. 4464, pp. 79–92. Springer, Heidelberg (2007). doi:10.1007/978-3-540-72163-5_8
4. Au, M.H., Liu, J.K., Susilo, W., Yuen, T.H.: Secure id-based linkable and revocable-iff-linked ring signature with constant-size construction. Theor. Comput. Sci. **469**, 1–14 (2013)
5. Au, M.H., Tsang, P.P., Susilo, W., Mu, Y.: Dynamic universal accumulators for DDH groups and their application to attribute-based anonymous credential systems. In: Fischlin, M. (ed.) CT-RSA 2009. LNCS, vol. 5473, pp. 295–308. Springer, Heidelberg (2009). doi:10.1007/978-3-642-00862-7_20
6. Bellare, M., Micciancio, D., Warinschi, B.: Foundations of group signatures: formal definitions, simplified requirements, and a construction based on general assumptions. In: Biham, E. (ed.) EUROCRYPT 2003. LNCS, vol. 2656, pp. 614–629. Springer, Heidelberg (2003). doi:10.1007/3-540-39200-9_38
7. Bellare, M., Rogaway, P.: Random oracles are practical: a paradigm for designing efficient protocols. In: 1st ACM Conference on Computer and Communications Security, pp. 62–73. ACM Press (1993)
8. Ben-Sasson, E., Chiesa, A., Garman, C., Green, M., Miers, I., Tromer, E., Virza, M.: Zerocash: decentralized anonymous payments from bitcoin. In: 2014 IEEE Symposium on Security and Privacy, SP 2014, Berkeley, CA, USA, 18–21 May 2014, pp. 459–474 (2014)
9. Ben-Sasson, E., Chiesa, A., Tromer, E., Virza, M.: Succinct non-interactive zero knowledge for a von Neumann architecture. In: Proceedings of the 23rd USENIX Security Symposium, San Diego, CA, USA, 20–22 August 2014, pp. 781–796 (2014)
10. Camenisch, J., Stadler, M.: Efficient group signature schemes for large groups. In: Kaliski, B.S. (ed.) CRYPTO 1997. LNCS, vol. 1294, pp. 410–424. Springer, Heidelberg (1997). doi:10.1007/BFb0052252
11. Chase, M., Lysyanskaya, A.: On signatures of knowledge. In: Proceedings 26th Annual International Cryptology Conference on Advances in Cryptology - CRYPTO 2006, Santa Barbara, California, USA, 20–24 August 2006, pp. 78–96 (2006)
12. Chaum, D., Heyst, E.: Group signatures. In: Davies, D.W. (ed.) EUROCRYPT 1991. LNCS, vol. 547, pp. 257–265. Springer, Heidelberg (1991). doi:10.1007/3-540-46416-6_22
13. Chow, S.S.M., Susilo, W., Yuen, T.H.: Escrowed linkability of ring signatures and its applications. In: Nguyen, P.Q. (ed.) VIETCRYPT 2006. LNCS, vol. 4341, pp. 175–192. Springer, Heidelberg (2006). doi:10.1007/11958239_12
14. Dodis, Y., Kiayias, A., Nicolosi, A., Shoup, V.: Anonymous identification in *ad hoc* groups. In: Cachin, C., Camenisch, J.L. (eds.) EUROCRYPT 2004. LNCS, vol. 3027, pp. 609–626. Springer, Heidelberg (2004). doi:10.1007/978-3-540-24676-3_36
15. Fiat, A., Shamir, A.: How to prove yourself: practical solutions to identification and signature problems. In: Odlyzko, A.M. (ed.) CRYPTO 1986. LNCS, vol. 263, pp. 186–194. Springer, Heidelberg (1987). doi:10.1007/3-540-47721-7_12

16. Fiege, U., Fiat, A., Shamir, A.: Zero knowledge proofs of identity. In: STOC 1987: 19th Annual ACM conference on Theory of Computing, pp. 210–217. ACM Press, New York (1987)

17. Fujisaki, E.: Sub-linear size traceable ring signatures without random oracles. In: Kiayias, A. (ed.) CT-RSA 2011. LNCS, vol. 6558, pp. 393–415. Springer, Heidelberg (2011). doi:10.1007/978-3-642-19074-2_25

18. Fujisaki, E., Suzuki, K.: Traceable ring signature. In: Okamoto, T., Wang, X. (eds.) PKC 2007. LNCS, vol. 4450, pp. 181–200. Springer, Heidelberg (2007). doi:10.1007/978-3-540-71677-8_13

19. Groth, J., Kohlweiss, M.: One-out-of-many proofs: or how to leak a secret and spend a coin. In: Oswald, E., Fischlin, M. (eds.) EUROCRYPT 2015. LNCS, vol. 9057, pp. 253–280. Springer, Heidelberg (2015). doi:10.1007/978-3-662-46803-6_9

20. Koshy, P., Koshy, D., McDaniel, P.: An analysis of anonymity in bitcoin using P2P network traffic. In: Christin, N., Safavi-Naini, R. (eds.) FC 2014. LNCS, vol. 8437, pp. 469–485. Springer, Heidelberg (2014). doi:10.1007/978-3-662-45472-5_30

21. Liu, J.K., Au, M.H., Susilo, W., Zhou, J.: Linkable ring signature with unconditional anonymity. IEEE Trans. Knowl. Data Eng. **26**(1), 157–165 (2014)

22. Liu, J.K., Wei, V.K., Wong, D.S.: Linkable spontaneous anonymous group signature for ad hoc groups. In: Wang, H., Pieprzyk, J., Varadharajan, V. (eds.) ACISP 2004. LNCS, vol. 3108, pp. 325–335. Springer, Heidelberg (2004). doi:10.1007/978-3-540-27800-9_28

23. Liu, J.K., Wong, D.S.: Linkable ring signatures: security models and new schemes. In: Gervasi, O., Gavrilova, M.L., Kumar, V., Laganà, A., Lee, H.P., Mun, Y., Taniar, D., Tan, C.J.K. (eds.) ICCSA 2005. LNCS, vol. 3481, pp. 614–623. Springer, Heidelberg (2005). doi:10.1007/11424826_65

24. Noether, S.: Ring signature confidential transactions for Monero. Cryptology ePrint Archive, Report 2015/1098 (2015). http://eprint.iacr.org/

25. Pointcheval, D., Stern, J.: Security proofs for signature schemes. In: Maurer, U. (ed.) EUROCRYPT 1996. LNCS, vol. 1070, pp. 387–398. Springer, Heidelberg (1996). doi:10.1007/3-540-68339-9_33

26. Rivest, R.L., Shamir, A., Tauman, Y.: How to leak a secret. In: Boyd, C. (ed.) ASIACRYPT 2001. LNCS, vol. 2248, pp. 552–565. Springer, Heidelberg (2001). doi:10.1007/3-540-45682-1_32

27. Sun, S.-F., Au, M.H., Liu, J.K., Yuen, T.H.: RingCT 2.0: a compact accumulator-based (linkable ring signature) protocol for blockchain cryptocurrency Monero (Full Version). Cryptology ePrint Archive, Report 2017 (2017). http://eprint.iacr.org/

28. Tsang, P.P., Au, M.H., Liu, J.K., Susilo, W., Wong, D.S.: A suite of non-pairing ID-based threshold ring signature schemes with different levels of anonymity (extended abstract). In: Heng, S.-H., Kurosawa, K. (eds.) ProvSec 2010. LNCS, vol. 6402, pp. 166–183. Springer, Heidelberg (2010). doi:10.1007/978-3-642-16280-0_11

29. Tsang, P.P., Wei, V.K.: Short linkable ring signatures for e-voting, e-cash and attestation. In: Deng, R.H., Bao, F., Pang, H.H., Zhou, J. (eds.) ISPEC 2005. LNCS, vol. 3439, pp. 48–60. Springer, Heidelberg (2005). doi:10.1007/978-3-540-31979-5_5

30. Tsang, P.P., Wei, V.K., Chan, T.K., Au, M.H., Liu, J.K., Wong, D.S.: Separable linkable threshold ring signatures. In: Canteaut, A., Viswanathan, K. (eds.) INDOCRYPT 2004. LNCS, vol. 3348, pp. 384–398. Springer, Heidelberg (2004). doi:10.1007/978-3-540-30556-9_30

31. Wijaya, D.A., Liu, J.K., Steinfeld, R., Sun, S.-F., Huang, X.: Anonymizing bitcoin transaction. In: Bao, F., Chen, L., Deng, R.H., Wang, G. (eds.) ISPEC 2016. LNCS, vol. 10060, pp. 271–283. Springer, Cham (2016). doi:10.1007/978-3-319-49151-6_19

32. Yuen, T.H., Liu, J.K., Au, M.H., Susilo, W., Zhou, J.: Efficient linkable and/or threshold ring signature without random oracles. Comput. J. **56**(4), 407–421 (2013)
33. Zhang, F., Kim, K.: ID-based blind signature and ring signature from pairings. In: Zheng, Y. (ed.) ASIACRYPT 2002. LNCS, vol. 2501, pp. 533–547. Springer, Heidelberg (2002). doi:10.1007/3-540-36178-2_33
34. Zheng, D., Li, X., Chen, K., Li, J.: Linkable ring signatures from linear feedback shift register. In: Denko, M.K., et al. (eds.) EUC 2007. LNCS, vol. 4809, pp. 716–727. Springer, Heidelberg (2007). doi:10.1007/978-3-540-77090-9_66

SePCAR: A Secure and Privacy-Enhancing Protocol for Car Access Provision

Iraklis Symeonidis[1(✉)], Abdelrahaman Aly[1], Mustafa Asan Mustafa[1],
Bart Mennink[2], Siemen Dhooghe[1], and Bart Preneel[1]

[1] imec-COSIC, KU Leuven, Leuven, Belgium
{iraklis.symeonidis,abdelrahaman.aly,mustafa.mustafa,
siemen.dhooghe,bart.preneel}@esat.kuleuven.be
[2] Radboud University, Nijmegen, The Netherlands
b.mennink@cs.ru.nl

Abstract. We present an efficient secure and privacy-enhancing protocol for car access provision, named SePCAR. The protocol is fully decentralised and allows users to share their cars conveniently without sacrificing their security and privacy. It provides generation, update, revocation, and distribution mechanisms for access tokens to shared cars, as well as procedures to solve disputes and to deal with law enforcement requests, for instance in the case of car incidents. We prove that SePCAR meets its appropriate security and privacy requirements and that it is efficient: our practical efficiency analysis through a proof-of-concept implementation shows that SePCAR takes only 1.55 s for a car access provision.

1 Introduction

As opposed to the traditional car ownership, the idea of car sharing, which allows users to share their cars in a convenient way, is gaining popularity. Statistics have shown that the worldwide number of users for car sharing services has grown from 2012 to 2014 by 170% (4.94 million) [15] with a tendency to increase by 2021 [7]. With the use of portable devices and in-vehicle telematics, physical car keys are slowly becoming obsolete. Keyless car Sharing Systems (KSSs) allow car owners to rather use their portable devices such as smartphones to distribute temporary digital car keys (access tokens) to other users. Several companies (including Volvo [48], BMW [8], Toyota [47], and Apple [46]) have started investing in such systems. Moreover, unlike traditional car rental companies, KSSs can provide a relatively inexpensive alternative to users who need a car occasionally and on-demand [49]. Their use can also contribute to a decrease in the number of cars, effectively reducing CO_2 emissions [39] and the need for parking space [32].

In spite of these advantages, information collection in car sharing systems does not only jeopardise a system's security, but also the users' privacy. Uber used a tool called "Hell" to spy on their rival company drivers [41], whereas their mobile app *always* tracks their users' location [13]. Moreover, it is possible to reach high identification rates of drivers, from 87% to 99% accuracy, based on data collected by the sensors of a car from 15 min of open-road driving [16].

© Springer International Publishing AG 2017
S.N. Foley et al. (Eds.): ESORICS 2017, Part II, LNCS 10493, pp. 475–493, 2017.
DOI: 10.1007/978-3-319-66399-9_26

In short, an adversary may try to eavesdrop and collect information exchanged within the KSS, tamper with the car sharing details, extract the key of a car stored in untrusted devices, generate a rogue access token to maliciously access a car or to deny having accessed a car. Regarding users' privacy, an adversary may try to correlate and link two car sharing requests of the same user or the car, to identify car usage patterns and deduce the users' sharing preferences. These preferences can be established by collecting information about sharing patterns such as rental time, duration, pickup location, when, where and with whom someone is sharing a car. An adversary may even attempt to infer sensitive information about users such as racial and religious beliefs [37] or their health status, by identifying users who use cars for disabled passengers. Sensitive personal data are related to *fundamental rights and freedoms*, and merit protection regarding the collection and processing as articulated in the new EU General Data Protection Regulation (GDPR) [9]. In addition, a KSS may introduce various other concerns with respect to connectivity issues [15], car key revocations when a user's device is stolen [21], and the fact that malicious users may attempt to manipulate or even destroy potential forensic evidence on the car or their devices.

Related Work. Troncoso et al. [44] proposed a pay-as-you-drive scheme to enhance the location privacy of drivers by sending aggregated data to insurance companies. Balasch et al. [2] proposed an electronic toll pricing protocol where a car's on-board unit calculates locally the driver's annual toll fee while disclosing a minimum amount of location information. For colluding (dishonest) users [2], Kerschbaum et al. [27] presented a privacy-preserving spot checking protocol that allows observations in public spaces. Mustafa et al. [31] proposed an anonymous electric vehicle charging protocol with billing support. EVITA [17] and PRESERVE [34] are designated projects on the design and specification of the secure architecture of on-board units. Driven by the PRESERVE instantiation, Raya et al. [36] described the need for a Vehicular Public-Key Infrastructure (VPKI), and Khodaei et al. [28] proposed a generic pseudonymization approach to preserve the unlinkability of messages exchanged between vehicles and VPKI servers. None of these solutions provides a full-fledged keyless car sharing system.

Our work is closely related to the protocol proposed by Dmitrienko and Plappert [15]. They designed a centralised and secure free-floating car sharing system that uses two-factor authentication including mobile devices and RFID tags, e.g., smart-cards. However, in contrast to our solution, their protocol assumes a fully trusted car sharing provider who has access to the master key of smart-cards and also collects and stores all the information exchanged between the car provider and their users for every car access provision.

Our Contributions. We design a concrete and fully decentralised secure and privacy-enhancing protocol for car access provision, named SePCAR. The protocol provides generation and distribution of access tokens for car access provision, as well as update and revocation operations used for facilitating mutually agreed modifications of the booking details and protecting against misbehaving consumers, respectively. It internally uses secure multiparty computation to facilitate forensic evidence provision in the case of car incidents or at the request of law enforcement. SePCAR is described in detail in Sect. 4.

We prove that the protocol fulfils the desired security and privacy requirements bound to the standards of connected cars. First, departing from Symeonidis et al. [40], we give a detailed list of security and privacy requirements in Sect. 2. Then, in Sect. 5, we prove that SePCAR meets its security and privacy requirements as long as its underlying cryptographic primitives (listed in Sect. 3) are secure. Our theoretical complexity and practical efficiency analysis in Sect. 6 demonstrates SePCAR's competitiveness. In particular, we implemented a prototype as a proof-of-concept in C++ and we achieved a car access provision in ≈ 1.55 s.

2   System Model and Requirements

We describe the system model and functionalities of a KSS. Moreover, we specify the threat model, the security, privacy and functional requirements which it needs to satisfy, and our assumptions about the system.

System Model. We follow the KSS system model of Symeonidis et al. [40] (see also Fig. 1). *Users* are individuals who are willing to share their cars, *owners* (u_o), and use cars which are available for sharing, *consumers* (u_c); both use of *Portable Devices* (PDs) such as smartphones. An *On-Board Unit* (OBU) is an embedded or a standalone hardware/software component [25] that is part of the secure access management system of a *car*. It has a wireless interface such as Bluetooth, NFC or LTE. The *Car manufacturer* (CM) is responsible for generating and embedding a digital key into each car. These keys are used for car sharing and are stored in the manufacturers' *Database* (DB). The *Keyless Sharing Management System* (KSMS) is a complex of multiparty computation (MPC) *servers* that assists owners with car access token generation, distribution, update and revocation. Each *server* individually retrieves its share of the car key,

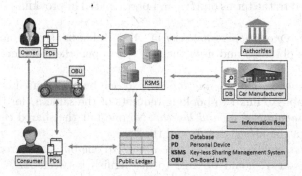

Fig. 1. System model of a physical Keyless car Sharing System (KSS) [40].

K^{car}, and the servers jointly encrypt the booking details, M^B, to generate an access token, AT^{car}. The access token is published on a *Public Ledger* (PL), which serves as a public bulletin board that guarantees the integrity of the data [30]. The booking details are typically agreed upon by owner and consumer prior to the beginning of the protocol.

Threat Model. Within the KSS, the KSMS, the CM and the PL are considered honest-but-curious entities. They will perform the protocol honestly, but they are curious to extract private information about users. Owners are passive adversaries while consumers and outsiders may be malicious. The car's OBU is trusted and equipped with a Hardware Security Module (HSM) [34,45] that supports secure key storage and cryptographic operations such as symmetric and public-key encryption, following the EVITA [17] and PRESERVE [34] specifications. Users' PDs are untrusted as they can get stolen, lost or broken.

Protocol Design Requirements. The keyless car sharing system should satisfy the following security, privacy and functional requirements [40], which we denote by *SR*, *PR* and *FR*, respectively. Here, we recall that M^B refers to the booking details, AT^{car} the access token to the car and K^{car} the car key.

- *SR1 - Confidentiality of M^B.* No one but the shared car, u_o and u_c should have access to M^B.
- *SR2 - Authenticity of M^B.* The shared car should verify the origin and integrity of M^B from u_o.
- *SR3 - Confidentiality of AT^{car}.* No one but the shared car and u_c should have access to AT^{car}.
- *SR4 - Confidentiality of K^{car}.* No one but the shared car and the CM should have access to K^{car}.
- *SR5 - Backward and forward secrecy of AT^{car}.* Compromise of a key used to encrypt any AT^{car} should not compromise other tokens (future and past) published on the PL of any honest u_c.
- *SR6 - Non-repudiation of origin of AT^{car}.* The u_o should not be able to deny it has agreed to the terms of M^B, and participated in providing the respective AT^{car}.
- *SR7 - Non-repudiation of delivery of AT^{car}.* The u_c should not be able to deny it has obtained and used the AT^{car} to open the car (once it has done so).
- *PR1 - Unlinkability of u_c and the car.* No one but the shared car, u_o and u_c should be able to link two booking requests of the same u_c for the car.
- *PR2 - Anonymity of u_c and the car.* No one but the shared car, u_o and u_c should learn the identity of u_c and the car.
- *PR3 - Undetectability of AT^{car} operation.* No one but the shared car, u_o and u_c (if necessary) should be able to distinguish between AT^{car} generation, update and revocation.

- *PR4 - Forensic evidence provision.* The KSMS should be able to provide authorities with the transaction details of an access provision to a car at the request of law enforcement without violating the other users' privacy.
- *FR1 - Offline authentication.* Access provision should be provided for locations where cars have limited (or no) network connection.

Assumptions. For SePCAR, we assume that before every evaluation, the booking details are agreed upon by owner and consumer, but that both keep these booking details confidential against external parties. SePCAR relies on a PKI infrastructure [34], and we assume that each entity has her private/public-key pair with their corresponding digital certificates. The communication channels are secure and authenticated among entities using SSL-TLS and NFC. OBU is equipped with a HSM [34, 45], and it is designed to resist deliberate or accidental physical destruction (i.e., black box). The MPC servers are held by non-colluding organisations, i.e., organisations with conflicting interests such as authorities, car owner unions and car manufacturers.

3 Cryptographic Building Blocks

This section specifies, the cryptographic functionalities that are used across this paper, as well as the MPC functionalities and cryptographic building blocks.

Cryptographic Functionalities. SePCAR uses the following cryptographic building blocks. The suggested instantiations are the ones used in our proof-of-concept implementation.

- $\sigma \leftarrow \mathsf{sign}(Sk, m)$ and true/false $\leftarrow \mathsf{verify}(Pk, m, \sigma)$ are public-key operations for signing and verification respectively. These can be implemented using RSA as defined in the PKCS #1 v2.0 specifications [23].
- $z \leftarrow \mathsf{prf}(K, counter)$ is a pseudo-random function (PRF) that uses as input a key and a counter. This function can be implemented using CTR mode with AES (as the message input is small).
- $c \leftarrow \mathsf{enc}(Pk, m)$ and $m \leftarrow \mathsf{dec}(Sk, c)$ are public-key encryption and decryption functions. These can be implemented using RSA as defined in the RSA-KEM specifications [24].
- $c \leftarrow \mathsf{E}(K, m)$ and $m \leftarrow \mathsf{D}(K, c)$ are symmetric key encryption and decryption functions. These can be implemented using CTR mode with AES.
- $v \leftarrow \mathsf{mac}(K, m)$ is a symmetric key MAC function. This function can be implemented using CBC-MAC with AES.[1]
- $z \leftarrow \mathsf{hash}(m)$ is a cryptographic hash function. This function can be implemented using SHA-2 or SHA-3.

---

[1] CBC-MAC is proven to be secure as long as it is *only* evaluated on equal-size messages (or on prefix-free messages) [5], which is the case for SePCAR. For variable length messages, one should resort to *encrypted* CBC-MAC or replace the key for the last block [22].

We will furthermore use the notation $z \leftarrow \mathsf{query}(x, y)$ to denote the retrieval of the xth value from the yth database DB (to be defined in Sect. 4), and $z \leftarrow \mathsf{query\_an}(y)$ to denote the retrieval of the yth value from the PL through an anonymous communication channel such as Tor [43], aiming to anonymously retrieve a published record submitted using the $\mathsf{publish}(y)$ function.

Multiparty Computation. Ben-Or et al. [6] (commonly referred to as BGW) proved that it is possible to calculate any function with perfect security in the presence of active and passive adversaries under the information-theoretic model, as long as there is an honest majority: 1/2 for passive and 2/3 for active adversaries. The former can be achieved by assuming the use of private channels among the servers and the latter using Verifiable Secret Sharing.

Our protocol is *MPC-agnostic*, meaning that it does not depend on the solution that implements the MPC functionality; example protocols that could be executed within our protocol are SPDZ [12] or MASCOT [26]. However, the three-party protocol for Boolean circuits that was introduced by Araki et al. [1,18] is fairly suited for our current needs, given its performance and threshold properties. Hence, we use this protocol in our simulation. It can perform non-linear operations with relatively high throughput and somewhat low latency (when tested on 10 Gbps connections). The scheme provides threshold security against semi-honest and malicious parties.

On an Incremental Setup for KSMS. Our protocol can support an incremental setup and deployment where an $(l > 2)$-case of KSMS servers is trivial, e.g., using BGW [6]. The 2-party case setting could also be achieved with MPC protocols such as SPDZ [12], however, the forensic properties of our setup would no longer be attainable.

Multiparty Computation Functionalities. SePCAR uses the following cryptographic functionalities for MPC:

- $[x] \leftarrow \mathsf{share}(x)$ is used to secretly share an input. This function can be instantiated using Araki et al.'s sharing functionality.
- $x \leftarrow \mathsf{open}([x])$ reconstructs the private input based on the secret shares.
- $[z] \leftarrow \mathsf{XOR}([x], [y])$ outputs a secret shared bit, representing the XOR of secret shared inputs $[x]$ and $[y]$. Note that for both arithmetic or Boolean circuits, such functionality could be implemented without requiring any communication cost.
- $[z] \leftarrow \mathsf{AND}([x], [y])$ outputs a secret shared bit, representing the AND of two secret shared inputs $[x]$ and $[y]$. This function can be instantiated using Araki et al.'s AND operation.
- $[z] \leftarrow \mathsf{eqz}([x], [y])$ outputs a secret shared bit, corresponding to an equality test of two secret shared inputs $[x]$ and $[y]$. This is equivalent to computing $[z] \leftarrow [x] \overset{?}{=} [y]$ where $z \in \{0, 1\}$.

- $[C] \leftarrow \mathsf{E}([K], [M])$ secretly computes a symmetric encryption from a secret shared key $[K]$ and a secret shared message $[M]$. We include a succinct review on how to implement AES below.
- $[V] \leftarrow \mathsf{mac}([K], [M])$ secretly computes a MAC from a secret shared key $[K]$ and a secret shared message $[M]$.

On the Secure Equality Test. Various protocols have been proposed to implement the equality tests (previously referred to an eqz functionality). Common approaches provide either constant rounds or a logarithmic number of them in the bit size of its inputs, which could be proven more efficient for sufficiently small sizes. Furthermore, they also offer different security levels, i.e., perfect or statistical security [10, 29]. In this paper we assume the use of any logarithmic depth construction, which matches the current state of the art.

On AES over MPC. AES has been the typical functionality used for benchmarking MPC protocols during the last few years. This fact and its usability for MPC based applications have motivated faster and leaner MPC implementations of the cipher. As it was previously stated, they consider the case where the MPC parties hold a secret shared key K and a secret shared message M. The product of the operation is a secret shared AES encrypted ciphertext. Note that in this paper we assume the use of the methods proposed by Damgård and Keller [11] with some minor code optimisations.

4   SePCAR

This section provides a detailed description of SePCAR. For simplicity and without loss of generality, we consider a single owner, consumer and a shared car. The description straightforwardly scales to a larger set of owners, consumers, and cars.

SePCAR consists of four steps: *session keys generation and data distribution, access token generation, access token distribution and verification* and *car access*. We will discuss these steps in detail in the remainder of the section. We first discuss a few *prerequisite* steps which have to be performed. After the discussion of the fourth (and last) step, we complete the section with an overview of the possible operations after SePCAR: *access token update and revocation*.

Prerequisite. Before SePCAR can commence, two prerequisite steps need to take place: *car key distribution* and setting the details for the *car booking*.

Car key distribution takes place immediately after the xth owner, $ID_x^{u_o}$, has registered her yth car, $ID_y^{car_{u_o}}$, with the KSMS. The KSMS forwards $ID_y^{car_{u_o}}$ to the CM to request the symmetric key, $K_y^{car_{u_o}}$, of the car. The CM retrieves $K_y^{car_{u_o}}$ from its DB, DB^{CM} and generates ℓ secret shares of $K_y^{car_{u_o}}$ and $ID_y^{car_{u_o}}$, denoted by $[K_y^{car_{u_o}}]$ and $[ID_y^{car_{u_o}}]$, respectively. Then, it forwards each share to the corresponding KSMS server, i.e., S_i. Upon receipt of the shares, each S_i stores ID^{u_o} together with the shares, $[ID_y^{car_{u_o}}]$ and $[K_y^{car_{u_o}}]$, in its local DB, DB^{S_i}.

The representations of the DB of CM and S_i are shown in Fig. 2. For simplicity, in some parts of SePCAR we will use ID^{u_o}, ID^{car} and K^{car} instead of $ID_x^{u_o}$, $ID_y^{car_{u_o}}$ and $K_y^{car_{u_o}}$.

$$DB^{CM} = \begin{pmatrix} ID_1^{u_o} & ID_1^{car_{u_o}} & K_1^{car_{u_o}} \\ \vdots & \vdots & \vdots \\ ID_x^{u_o} & ID_y^{car_{u_o}} & K_y^{car_{u_o}} \\ \vdots & \vdots & \vdots \\ ID_m^{u_o} & ID_n^{car_{u_o}} & K_n^{car_{u_o}} \end{pmatrix} \qquad DB^{S_i} = \begin{pmatrix} ID_1^{u_o} & [ID_1^{car_{u_o}}] & [K_1^{car_{u_o}}] \\ \vdots & \vdots & \vdots \\ ID_x^{u_o} & [ID_y^{car_{u_o}}] & [K_y^{car_{u_o}}] \\ \vdots & \vdots & \vdots \\ ID_m^{u_o} & [ID_n^{car_{u_o}}] & [K_n^{car_{u_o}}] \end{pmatrix}$$

Fig. 2. The DB of CM (left) and the DB of the ith server S_i (right).

Car booking allows u_o and u_c to agree on the booking details, i.e., $M^B = \{\mathsf{hash}(Cert^{u_c}), ID^{car}, L^{car}, CD^{u_c}, AC^{u_c}, ID^B\}$, where $\mathsf{hash}(Cert^{u_c})$ is the hash of the digital certificate of u_c, L^{car} is the pick-up location of the car, CD^{u_c} is the set of conditions under which u_c is allowed to use the car (e.g., restrictions on locations, time period), AC^{u_c} are the access control rights under which u_c is allowed to access the car and ID^B is the booking identifier. Recall that it is assumed that an owner and a consumer agree on the booking details beforehand.

Step 1: Session Keys Generation and Data Distribution. u_c generates two symmetric session keys, $K_1^{u_c}$ and $K_2^{u_c}$. Key $K_1^{u_c}$ will be used by each S_i to encrypt the access token, such that only u_c has access to it. $K_2^{u_c}$ will be used to generate an authentication tag which will allow u_c to verify that the access token contains M^B which was agreed upon during the *car booking*. In addition, u_o sends the necessary data to each S_i, such that the access token can be generated. In detail, as shown in Fig. 3, u_o sends a session-keys-generation request, $SES\_K\_GEN\_REQ$, along with ID^B to u_c. Upon receipt of the request, u_c generates $K_1^{u_c}$ and $K_2^{u_c}$ using the prf() function instantiated by u_c's master key, i.e., K^{u_c} and *counter* and *counter* + 1. Then, u_c transforms these into ℓ

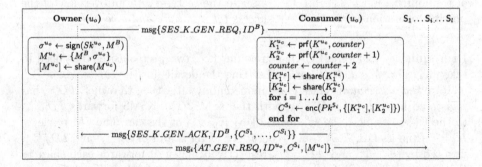

Fig. 3. Step 1: session keys generation and data distribution.

secret shares, $[K_1^{u_c}]$ and $[K_2^{u_c}]$, one for each S_i in such a way that none of the servers will have access to the keys but that they can jointly evaluate functions using these keys securely. Then, it encrypts $[K_1^{u_c}]$ and $[K_2^{u_c}]$ with the public-key of each S_i, $C^{S_i} = \mathsf{enc}(Pk^{S_i}, \{[K_1^{u_c}], [K_2^{u_c}]\})$, such that only the corresponding S_i can access the corresponding shares. Finally, u_c forwards to u_o an acknowledgment message, $SES\_K\_GEN\_ACK$, along with ID^B and $\{C^{S_1}, \ldots, C^{S_l}\}$.

While waiting for the response of u_c, the owner u_o signs M^B with her private key, i.e., $\sigma^{u_o} = \mathsf{sign}(Sk^{u_o}, M^B)$. In a later stage, the car will use σ^{u_o} to verify that M^B has been approved by u_o. Then u_o transforms $M^{u_c} = \{M^B, \sigma^{u_o}\}$ into ℓ secret shares, i.e., $[M^{u_c}]$. Upon receipt of the response of u_c, u_o forwards to each S_i an access-token-generation request, AT_GEN_REQ, along with ID^{u_o}, the corresponding C^{S_i} and $[M^{u_c}]$.

Step 2: Access Token Generation. The servers generate an access token and publish it on the PL. In detail, as shown in Fig. 4, upon receipt of AT_GEN_REQ from u_o, each S_i uses the ID^{u_o} to extract $[K^{car}]$ from DB^{S_i} as follows. Initially, each S_i uses ID^{u_o} to retrieve the list of identities of all cars and car key shares related to the set of records that correspond to u_o. The result is stored in a vector $\vec{D}^{u_o}$ of size $n \times 3$, i.e.,

$$\vec{D}^{u_o} = \begin{pmatrix} ID^{u_o} & [ID_1^{car_{u_o}}] & [K_1^{car}] \\ \vdots & \vdots & \vdots \\ ID^{u_o} & [ID_y^{car_{u_o}}] & [K_y^{car}] \\ \vdots & \vdots & \vdots \\ ID^{u_o} & [ID_n^{car_{u_o}}] & [K_n^{car}] \end{pmatrix},$$

where n is the number of cars which u_o has registered with the KSS.

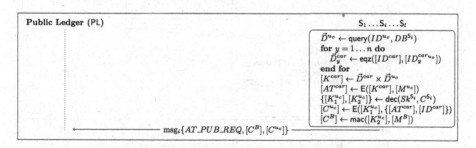

Fig. 4. Step 2: access token generation.

To retrieve the record for the car to be shared, each S_i extracts $[ID^{car}]$ from $[M^{u_c}]$ and performs a comparison with each of the n records of $\vec{D}^{u_o}$ using the $\mathsf{eqz}()$ function. The comparison outcomes 0 for mismatch and 1 for identifying the car at position y. The result of each iteration is stored in a vector $\vec{D}^{car}$ of length n, i.e.,

$$\vec{D}^{car} = \left(\overset{1}{[0]} \cdots [0] \overset{y}{[1]} [0] \cdots \overset{n}{[0]} \right).$$

Each S_i then multiplies $\vec{D}^{car}$ and $\vec{D}^{u_o}$ to generate a third vector of length 3, i.e.,

$$\vec{D}^{car} \times \vec{D}^{u_o} = \left(ID^{u_o} \, [ID_y^{car_{u_o}}] \, [K_y^{car_{u_o}}] \right),$$

from which the share of the car's secret key, $[K^{car}]$, can be retrieved. Then, the KSMS servers S_i collaboratively encrypt $[M^{u_c}]$ using the retrieved $[K^{car}]$ to generate an access token for the car in shared form, $[AT^{car}]$.

As AT^{car} and ID^{car} need to be available only to u_c, a second layer of encryption is performed using $K_1^{u_c}$. To retrieve the shares of the session keys, $\{[K_1^{u_c}], [K_2^{u_c}]\}$, each S_i decrypts C^{S_i} using its private key. Then, the servers encrypt $[AT^{car}]$ and $[ID^{car}]$ with $[K_1^{u_c}]$ to generate $[C^{u_c}]$. In addition, they generate an authentication tag, $[C^B]$, using the mac() function with $[K_2^{u_c}]$ and $[M^B]$ as inputs. Finally, each S_i sends to PL an access-token-publication request, AT_PUB_REQ, along with $[C^B]$ and $[C^{u_c}]$.

Step 3: Access Token Distribution and Verification. The PL publishes the shares of the encrypted access token which are then retrieved by u_c. Once retrieved, u_c can obtain the access token and use it to access the car. In detail, as shown in Fig. 5, upon receipt of AT_PUB_REQ, PL publishes $[C^B]$, $[C^{u_c}]$ and TS^{Pub}, which is the time-stamp of the publication of the encrypted token. Then PL sends an acknowledgement of the publication, AT_PUB_ACK, along with TS_i^{Pub} to at least one S_i which forwards it to u_o who, in turn, forwards it to u_c.

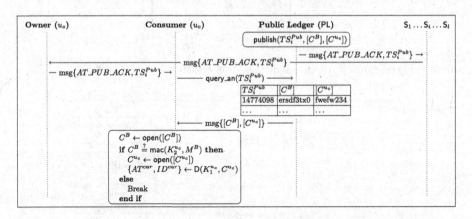

Fig. 5. Step 3: access token distribution and verification.

Upon receipt of AT_PUB_ACK, u_c uses TS_i^{Pub} and the query_an() function to anonymously retrieve $[C^{u_c}]$ and $[C^B]$ from PL, such that PL cannot identify u_c. Then, u_c uses the open() function to reconstruct C^B and C^{u_c} using the retrieved shares. Next, u_c verifies the authentication tag C^B locally using the mac() function with $K_2^{u_c}$ and M^B as inputs. In the case of successful verification, u_c is assured that the token contains the same details as the ones agreed during *car booking*. Then, u_c decrypts C^{u_c} using $K_1^{u_c}$ to obtain the access token and the car identity, $\{AT^{car}, ID^{car}\}$.

Step 4: Car Access. The consumer uses the access token to obtain access to the car. In detail, u_c sends $\{AT^{car}, ID^{car}, Cert^{u_c}\}$ to the car using a secure and close range communication channel such as NFC or Bluetooth (see Fig. 6). Upon receipt, the car's OBU obtains $M^{u_c} = \{M^B, \sigma^{u_o}\}$ by decrypting AT^{car} with K^{car}. It then performs three verifications. It checks if the access attempt satisfies the conditions specified in M^B. Then, it verifies σ^{u_o} to be assured that the booking details, M^B, have not been modified and have been indeed approved by the car owner. Finally, it verifies the identity of u_c. For the last verification, as the OBU receives $Cert^{u_c}$ (along with the hash($Cert^{u_c}$) in M^B), it can use any challenge-response protocol based on public/private key [14] and RFIDs [15]. If any of these verifications fails, the OBU terminates the car access process and denies access to the car. Otherwise, it grants u_c access to the car, signs $\{M^B, TS^{car}_{Access}\}$, where TS^{car}_{Access} is the time-stamp of granting the access and asynchronously sends msg$\{\sigma^{car}_{Access}, TS^{car}_{Access}\}$ to u_o.

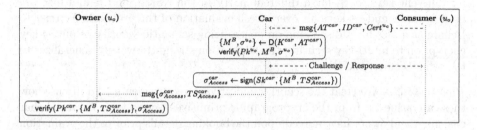

Fig. 6. Step 4: car access. Dashed lines represent close range communication.

Access Token Update and Revocation. Upon an agreement between u_o and u_c to update or revoke an access token, SePCAR can be performed as described in steps 1–3. The values of an update request can be changed according to new booking details, $\hat{M}^B$, whereas for revocation, each of the parameters in $\hat{M}^B$ can receive a predefined value indicating the revocation action. However, there are occasions when u_o may need to enforce an update or revocation of an access token. To prevent u_c from blocking such operations, SePCAR should be executed only by u_o, without the involvement of u_c. More specifically, u_o generates session keys, requests an access token, queries the PL, and sends the token to the car using long range asynchronous communication channel such as LTE.

5 Security and Privacy Analysis

We prove that SePCAR satisfies the security and privacy requirements of Sect. 2, provided that its underlying cryptographic primitives are sufficiently secure. The theorem statement and the proof given below are informal; a formal description of the security models and the proof is given in the full version of the paper.

Theorem 1. *If communication takes place over private channels, the MPC is statistically secure,*

- *the signature scheme* sign *is multi-key existentially unforgeable* [20],
- *the pseudo-random function* prf *is multi-key secure* [19],
- *the public-key encryption scheme* enc *is multi-key semantically secure* [3],
- *the symmetric key encryption scheme* E *is multi-key chosen-plaintext secure* [4],
- *the MAC function* mac *is multi-key existentially unforgeable* [20], *and*
- *the hash function* hash *is collision resistant* [38],

then SePCAR fulfils the security and privacy requirements of Sect. 2.

Note that, indeed, for each of the keyed cryptographic primitives we require security in the *multi-key* setting, as these are evaluated under different keys. For example, sign is used by all owners, each with a different key; enc is used for different keys, each for a different party in the KSMS, and E and mac are used for independent keys for every fresh evaluation of the protocol. We refer to Bellare et al. [3] for a discussion on generalizing semantic security of public-key encryption to multi-key security; the adaptation straightforwardly generalizes to the other security models.

Proof (sketch). We treat the security and privacy requirements, and discuss how these are achieved from the cryptographic primitives, separately. We recall that consumer and owner have agreed upon the booking details prior to the evaluation of SePCAR, hence they know each other.

SR1 - Confidentiality of M^B. In one evaluation of the protocol, u_c, u_o, and the shared car learn the booking details by default or design. The KSMS servers only learn shares of the booking data, and under the assumption that the MPC is statistically secure, nothing about the booking data is revealed during the MPC. The outcomes of the MPC are C^B and C^{u_c} satisfying

$$C^B = \mathsf{mac}(K_2^{u_c}, M^B), \tag{1}$$

$$C^{u_c} = \mathsf{E}(K_1^{u_c}, \{\mathsf{E}(K_y^{car_{u_o}}, \{M^B, \sigma^{u_o}\}), ID^{car}\}), \tag{2}$$

both of which reveal nothing about M^B to a malicious outsider due to the assumed security of mac, E, and the independent uniform drawing of the keys $K_1^{u_c}$ and $K_2^{u_c}$. The nested encryption E does not influence the analysis due to the mutual independence of the keys $K_1^{u_c}$ and $K_y^{car_{u_o}}$.

SR2 - Authenticity of M^B. An owner who initiates the access token generation and distribution, first signs the booking details using its private key before sending those to the KSMS in shares. Therefore, once the car receives the token and obtains the booking details, it can verify the owner's signature on the booking details. In other words, the car can verify the source of the booking details, the owner and their integrity. Suppose, to the contrary, that a malicious consumer can get access to a car of an owner u_o. This particularly means that it created a tuple (M^B, σ^{u_o}) such that $\mathsf{verify}(Pk^{u_o}, M^B, \sigma^{u_o})$ holds. If σ^{u_o} is new, this means that u_c forges a signature for the secret signing key Sk^{u_o}. This is impossible by assumption that the signature scheme is existentially unforgeable. On the other hand, if (M^B, σ^{u_o}) is old but the evaluation is fresh, this means a collision $\mathsf{hash}(Cert^{u_c}) = \mathsf{hash}(Cert^{u_c\prime})$, which is computationally infeasible as hash is collision resistant.

SR3 - Confidentiality of AT^{car}. The access token is generated by the KSMS servers obliviously (as the MPC is statistically secure), and only revealed to the public in encrypted form, through C^{u_c} of (2). Due to the uniform drawing of the key $K_1^{u_c}$ (and the security of the public-key encryption scheme used to transmit this key), only the legitimate user can decrypt and learn the access token. It shares it with the car over a secure and private channel.

SR4 - Confidentiality of K^{car}. Only the car manufacturer and the car itself hold copies of the car key. The KSMS servers learn these in shared form, hence learn nothing about it by virtue of the statistical security of the MPC. Retrieving a car key from encryptions made under this key constitutes a key recovery attack, which in turn allows to break the chosen-plaintext security of the symmetric key encryption scheme.

SR5 - Backward and forward secrecy of AT^{car}. The access token is published on the public ledger as C^{u_c} of (2), encrypted under symmetric key $K_1^{u_c}$. Every honest consumer generates a fresh key $K_1^{u_c}$ for every new evaluation, using a pseudo-random function prf that is secure, i.e., that is indistinguishable from a random function. This implies that all session keys are drawn independently and uniformly at random. In addition, the symmetric encryption scheme E is multi-key secure. Concluding, all encryptions C^{u_c} are independent and reveal nothing of each other. (Note that nothing can be said about access tokens for malicious users who may deviate from the protocol and reuse one-time keys.)

SR6 - Non-repudiation of origin of AT^{car}. The car, who is a trusted identity, verifies the origin through verification of the signature, $\mathsf{verify}(Pk^{u_o}, M^B, \sigma^{u_o})$. The consumer u_c verifies the origin through the verification of the MAC algorithm, $C^B \overset{?}{=} \mathsf{mac}(K_2^{u_c}, M^B)$. Note that the consumer does not effectively verify AT^{car}, but rather C^B, which suffices under the assumption that the MPC servers evaluate their protocol correctly. In either case, security fails only if the asymmetric signature scheme or the MAC function are forgeable.

SR7 - Non-repudiation of delivery of AT^{car}. The owner can verify correct delivery through the verification of the message sent by the car to the owner, $\mathsf{verify}(Pk^{car}, \{M^B, TS^{car}_{Access}\}, \sigma^{car}_{Access})$ at the end of the protocol. Security breaks only if the signature scheme is forgeable.

PR1 - Unlinkability of u_c and the car. The only consumer-identifiable data is in the consumer's certificate included in the booking details. Note that these are agreed upon between the consumer and the owner, so the owner learns the identity of the consumer by default. Beyond that, the consumer only communicates with the car, which is supposed to learn the consumer's identity so that it can perform proper access control. The consumer consults the public ledger over an anonymous channel. The booking details are transferred to and from the

KSMS, but these are encrypted and do not leak by virtue of their confidentiality (security requirement SR1).

PR2 - Anonymity of u_c and the car. The reasoning is identical to that of PR1.

PR3 - Undetectability of AT^{car} operation. Access token generation, update, or revocation is performed using the same steps and the same type of messages sent to the KSMS and PL. Hence, outsiders and system entities cannot distinguish which operation has been requested.

PR4 - Forensic evidence provision. In the case of disputes, the information related to a specific transaction (and only this information) may need to be reconstructed. This reconstruction can be done only if the KSMS servers collude and reveal their shares. In our setting, these servers have competing interests, thus they would not collude unless law authorities enforce them to do so. Due to the properties of threshold secret sharing, the private inputs can be reconstructed by a majority coalition. This is, if the KSMS consists of three parties, it suffices two of such parties to reconstruct the secrets (for semi-honest and malicious cases).

FR1 - Offline authentication. Note that steps 1–3 of the protocol require a network connection, but step 4, car access, is performed using close range communication and with no need of a network connection. The decryption and verification of the access token can be performed by the car offline (it has its key K^{car} and the owner's public-key Pk^{u_o} stored). Sending the confirmation signature σ_{Access}^{car} can also be done offline.   □

6   Performance Evaluation

Below we analyse the theoretical complexity and efficiency of SePCAR.

Theoretical Complexity. The complexity of MPC protocols is typically measured by the number of communication rounds produced by non-linear operations, as linear operations can usually be performed without any information exchange and are virtually free of charge. In one evaluation of SePCAR, the non-linear operations performed by the KSMS servers are (i) the retrieval of the car key through multiple calls of the eqz functionality using the ID^{car} and their counterparts in $\vec{D}^{car}$ as parameters, and (ii) have two evaluations of the encryption scheme E and one evaluation of mac.

For (i) the evaluations of the eqz functionality, we consider a multiplicative depth of $\lceil \log(|ID^{car}|) \rceil + 1$, where $|ID^{car}|$ is the amount of bits in ID^{car}. Note that we can parallelize the eqz call for all $\vec{D}^{car}$ entries. Therefore, the bulk of the overhead of extracting the car key comes from implementing the equality test in logarithmic depth [29]. Besides executing the eqz tests, we also have to perform an extra communication round since we need to multiply the result of each equality test with its corresponding car key. The total number of communication rounds for (i) is thus $\lceil \log(|ID^{car}|) \rceil + 1$.

For (ii) the two evaluations of the encryption scheme E and the single evaluation of mac we use, as mentioned in Sect. 3, CTR mode with AES and CBC-MAC with AES, respectively. Note that in a single AES evaluation the number of non-linear operations equals the number of S-Boxes evaluated in these functions, but many can be parallelized. Denote by ν the number of communication rounds needed to encrypt a single 128-bit block using AES. The two evaluations of CTR mode can be performed in parallel, and cost $2 \cdot \nu$ rounds. The evaluation of CBC-MAC is inherently sequential and costs $\left\lceil \frac{|M^B|}{128} \right\rceil \cdot \nu$ communication rounds. The total number of communication rounds can thus be expressed as:

$$\left(\lceil \log(|ID^{car}|) \rceil + 1 \right) + 2 \cdot \nu + \left\lceil \frac{|M^B|}{128} \right\rceil \cdot \nu. \tag{3}$$

Efficiency. Our protocol is agnostic towards the underlying multiparty protocol. In our experiments we have incorporated the 3-party semi-honest protocol by Araki et al. [1], given its relative efficiency of AES calls compared to alternatives such as, [12, 26]. The upshot of our experiments is that SePCAR needs only 1.55 s for a car access provision. We elaborate on our simulation below, following the steps of Sect. 4. An allocation of the time on the different steps is provided in Table 1.

Table 1. Performance of SePCAR, where time is averaged over 1000 runs.

Phase	Description	Time (in sec)
Step 1	Sharing the booking details and keys	0.220 ± 0.027
Step 2	Extracting car key and making access token	1.274 ± 0.032
Step 3	Verifying the access token	0.055 (+1 Tor [42])
Total		1.551 ± 0.043 (+1 Tor)

Step 1. Recall that step 1 handles the preparation and sharing of the booking details and generation of keys. For enc we use RSA with 2048-bit keys (≈ 2 ms) and for sign we use RSA with SHA-2 with a 512-bit output (≈ 50 ms). The prf is implemented using AES in CTR mode ($\approx 2 \mu s$). For all these functions we use OpenSSL [33]. The share function is implemented by the sharing primitive introduced by Araki et al. [1].

Step 2. In this step, the KSMS servers retrieve the car key and perform the corresponding encryption and other subroutines linked to generating the MAC. We consider the following message configuration size: hash($Cert^{u_c}$) of 512-bits, ID^{car} of 32-bits, L^{car} of 64-bits, CD^{u_c} of 96-bits, AC^{u_c} of 8-bits, ID^B of 32-bits and σ^{u_c} of 512-bits. The booking details M^B are of size 768-bits (including padding) and the final access token AT^{u_c} is of size 1408-bits (including padding). For the dec function we use RSA with 2048-bit keys (≈ 2 ms). The symmetric encryption E is implemented in CTR mode and the mac in CBC mode. As mentioned before, the functions E, mac, and eqz use the primitives proposed by Araki et al. [1], and we use the multiparty AES method of Damgård and Keller [11]. Using this method, a single S-Box evaluation takes 5 communication rounds. A single evaluation of AES consists of 20 sequential evaluations of an S-Box, where we included the key expansion and took into account that parallelizable S-Boxes do not add up to the number of communication rounds, hence encryption requires $\nu = 100$ communication rounds. From (3) we obtain that in our simulation the total number of communication rounds is

$$\left(5+1\right) + 2 \cdot 100 + 6 \cdot 100 = 806.$$

Key expansion for different keys needs to be performed only once, and for multiple evaluations of SePCAR for the same car the round complexity reduces.

Step 3. In this step the consumer retrieves, reconstructs, and verifies the assigned access token. The PL is implemented using SQLite. The implementation of open again follows the primitive of Araki et al. [1], and mac is implemented using AES in CBC mode ($\approx$13 ms).

Step 4. The final step consists of a challenge-response protocol between u_c and the car, but it does not directly affect the performance of SePCAR and we omit it from our implementation.

Environment Settings. We implemented our simulation for SePCAR in C++ and evaluated it using a machine equipped with an Intel $i7$, 2.6 Ghz CPU and 8 GB of RAM.[2] The communication within the KSMS was simulated using socket calls and latency parameters. We used the setting from Araki et al. [1] to simulate the LAN latency ($\approx$0.13 ms) and from Ramamurthy et al. [35] for Wi-Fi ($\approx$0.50 ms). We did not assume any specific network configuration for our experimentation.

7   Conclusion

SePCAR is proven to be secure and privacy-enhancing, efficiently performing in $\approx$1.55 s for a car access provision. We presented a formal analysis of the security and privacy requirements of our protocol and we designed a prototype as proof-of-concept. SePCAR provides a complementary solution to physical keys, aiming for those that hold portable devices and want a dynamic and efficient way to access to a car. As future work, we plan to extend SePCAR to support additional operations such as booking and payment. It would also be interesting to investigate potential modifications of the protocol, in order to provide security and privacy guarantees while KSMS, CM, and PL are active adversaries.

Acknowledgments. This work was supported in part by the Research Council KU Leuven: C16/15/058 and GOA TENSE (GOA/11/007). Bart Mennink is supported by a postdoctoral fellowship from the Netherlands Organisation for Scientific Research (NWO) under Veni grant 016.Veni.173.017.

---

[2] The implementation can be obtained from https://bitbucket.org/Siemen11/sepcar.

References

1. Araki, T., Furukawa, J., Lindell, Y., Nof, A., Ohara, K.: High-throughput semi-honest secure three-party computation with an honest majority. In: Proceedings of the 2016 ACM SIGSAC CCS, pp. 805–817 (2016)
2. Balasch, J., Rial, A., Troncoso, C., Preneel, B., Verbauwhede, I., Geuens, C.: PrETP: privacy-preserving electronic toll pricing. In: USENIX, pp. 63–78 (2010)
3. Bellare, M., Boldyreva, A., Micali, S.: Public-key encryption in a multi-user setting: security proofs and improvements. In: Preneel, B. (ed.) EUROCRYPT 2000. LNCS, vol. 1807, pp. 259–274. Springer, Heidelberg (2000). doi:10.1007/3-540-45539-6_18
4. Bellare, M., Desai, A., Jokipii, E., Rogaway, P.: A concrete security treatment of symmetric encryption. In: FOCS, pp. 394–403 (1997)
5. Bellare, M., Kilian, J., Rogaway, P.: The security of the cipher block chaining message authentication code. J. Comput. Syst. Sci. **61**(3), 362–399 (2000). http://dx.doi.org/10.1006/jcss.1999.1694
6. Ben-Or, M., Goldwasser, S., Wigderson, A.: Completeness theorems for non-cryptographic fault-tolerant distributed computation. In: STOC, pp. 1–10. ACM (1988)
7. Bert, J., Collie, B., Gerrits, M., Xu, G.: What's ahead for car sharing?: the new mobility and its impact on vehicle sales. https://goo.gl/ZmPZ5t. Accessed June 2017
8. BMW: DriveNow Car Sharing. https://drive-now.com/. Accessed Nov 2016
9. Council of the EU Final Compromised Resolution: General Data Protection Regulation. http://www.europarl.europa.eu. Accessed Feb 2015
10. Damgård, I., Fitzi, M., Kiltz, E., Nielsen, J.B., Toft, T.: Unconditionally secure constant-rounds multi-party computation for equality, comparison, bits and exponentiation. In: Halevi, S., Rabin, T. (eds.) TCC 2006. LNCS, vol. 3876, pp. 285–304. Springer, Heidelberg (2006). doi:10.1007/11681878_15
11. Damgård, I., Keller, M.: Secure multiparty AES. In: Sion, R. (ed.) FC 2010. LNCS, vol. 6052, pp. 367–374. Springer, Heidelberg (2010). doi:10.1007/978-3-642-14577-3_31
12. Damgård, I., Pastro, V., Smart, N., Zakarias, S.: Multiparty computation from somewhat homomorphic encryption. In: Safavi-Naini, R., Canetti, R. (eds.) CRYPTO 2012. LNCS, vol. 7417, pp. 643–662. Springer, Heidelberg (2012). doi:10.1007/978-3-642-32009-5_38
13. Fireball, D.: Regarding Uber's New 'Always' Location Tracking. https://goo.gl/L1Elve. Accessed Apr 2017
14. Diffie, W., van Oorschot, P.C., Wiener, M.J.: Authentication and authenticated key exchanges. Des. Codes Crypt. **2**(2), 107–125 (1992). http://dx.doi.org/10.1007/BF00124891
15. Dmitrienko, A., Plappert, C.: Secure free-floating car sharing for offline cars. In: ACM CODASPY, pp. 349–360 (2017)
16. Enev, M., Takakuwa, A., Koscher, K., Kohno, T.: Automobile driver fingerprinting. PoPETs **2016**(1), 34–50 (2016)
17. EVITA: E-safety Vehicle Intrusion Protected Applications (EVITA). http://www.evita-project.org/. Accessed Nov 2016
18. Furukawa, J., Lindell, Y., Nof, A., Weinstein, O.: High-throughput secure three-party computation for malicious adversaries and an honest majority. In: Coron, J.-S., Nielsen, J.B. (eds.) EUROCRYPT 2017. LNCS, vol. 10211, pp. 225–255. Springer, Cham (2017). doi:10.1007/978-3-319-56614-6_8

19. Goldreich, O., Goldwasser, S., Micali, S.: How to construct random functions. J. ACM **33**(4), 792–807 (1986)
20. Goldwasser, S., Micali, S., Rivest, R.L.: A digital signature scheme secure against adaptive chosen-message attacks. SIAM J. Comput. **17**(2), 281–308 (1988)
21. GOV.UK: reducing mobile phone theft and improving security. https://goo.gl/o2v99g. Accessed Apr 2017
22. International Organization for Standardization: ISO/IEC 9797-1:2011. https://www.iso.org/standard/50375.html. Accessed June 2017
23. Internet Engineering Task Force: PKCS #1: RSA Cryptography Specifications Version 2.0. https://tools.ietf.org/html/rfc2437. Accessed June 2017
24. Internet Engineering Task Force: Use of the RSA-KEM Key Transport Algorithm in the Cryptographic Message Syntax (CMS). https://tools.ietf.org/html/rfc5990. Accessed June 2017
25. INVERS: Make Mobility Shareable. https://invers.com/. Accessed Apr 2017
26. Keller, M., Orsini, E., Scholl, P.: MASCOT: faster malicious arithmetic secure computation with oblivious transfer. In: ACM SIGSAC, pp. 830–842 (2016)
27. Kerschbaum, F., Lim, H.W.: Privacy-preserving observation in public spaces. In: Pernul, G., Ryan, P.Y.A., Weippl, E. (eds.) ESORICS 2015. LNCS, vol. 9327, pp. 81–100. Springer, Cham (2015). doi:10.1007/978-3-319-24177-7_5
28. Khodaei, M., Jin, H., Papadimitratos, P.: Towards deploying a scalable & robust vehicular identity and credential management infrastructure. CoRR (2016)
29. Lipmaa, H., Toft, T.: Secure equality and greater-than tests with sublinear online complexity. In: Fomin, F.V., Freivalds, R., Kwiatkowska, M., Peleg, D. (eds.) ICALP 2013. LNCS, vol. 7966, pp. 645–656. Springer, Heidelberg (2013). doi:10.1007/978-3-642-39212-2_56
30. Micali, S.: Algorand: the efficient and democratic ledger (2016). arXiv:1607.01341
31. Mustafa, M.A., Zhang, N., Kalogridis, G., Fan, Z.: Roaming electric vehicle charging and billing: An anonymous multi-user protocol. In: IEEE SmartGridComm, pp. 939–945 (2014)
32. Naphade, M.R., Banavar, G., Harrison, C., Paraszczak, J., Morris, R.: Smarter cities and their innovation challenges. IEEE Comput. **44**(6), 32–39 (2011)
33. OpenSSL: Cryptography and SSL/TLS Toolkit. https://www.openssl.org/. Accessed Apr 2017
34. PRESERVE: Preparing Secure Vehicle-to-X Communication Systems (PRESERVE). https://www.preserve-project.eu/. Accessed Nov 2016
35. Ramamurthy, H., Prabhu, B., Gadh, R., Madni, A.M.: Wireless industrial monitoring and control using a smart sensor platform. IEEE Sens. J. **7**(5), 611–618 (2007)
36. Raya, M., Papadimitratos, P., Hubaux, J.: Securing vehicular communications. IEEE Wirel. Commun. **13**(5), 8–15 (2006)
37. reddit: identifying Muslim cabbies from trip data and prayer times. https://goo.gl/vLrW1s. Accessed Apr 2017
38. Rogaway, P., Shrimpton, T.: Cryptographic hash-function basics: definitions, implications, and separations for preimage resistance, second-preimage resistance, and collision resistance. In: Roy, B., Meier, W. (eds.) FSE 2004. LNCS, vol. 3017, pp. 371–388. Springer, Heidelberg (2004). doi:10.1007/978-3-540-25937-4_24
39. Shaheen, S.A., Cohen, A.P.: Car sharing and personal vehicle services: worldwide market developments and emerging trends. Int. J. Sustain. Transp. **7**(1), 5–34 (2013)
40. Symeonidis, I., Mustafa, M.A., Preneel, B.: Keyless car sharing system: a security and privacy analysis. In: IEEE ISC2, pp. 1–7 (2016)

41. Guardian, T.: Hell of a ride: even a PR powerhouse couldn't get Uber on track. https://goo.gl/UcIihE. Accessed Apr 2017

42. Tor: METRICS. https://metrics.torproject.org/torperf.html. Accessed Apr 2017

43. Tor Project: protect your privacy. Defend yourself against network surveillance and traffic analysis. https://www.torproject.org/. Accessed Apr 2017

44. Troncoso, C., Danezis, G., Kosta, E., Balasch, J., Preneel, B.: PriPAYD: privacy-friendly pay-as-you-drive insurance. IEEE TDSC 8(5), 742–755 (2011)

45. Trusted Computing Group: TPM 2.0 Library Profile for Automotive-Thin. https://goo.gl/fy3DxD. Accessed June 2016

46. United States Patent, Trademark Office. Applicant: Apple Inc.: accessing a vehicle using portable devices. https://goo.gl/a9pyX7. Accessed June 2017

47. USA TODAY: Toyota will test keyless car sharing. https://goo.gl/C9iq34. Accessed Nov 2016

48. Volvo: Worth a Detour. https://www.sunfleet.com/. Accessed Nov 2016

49. Wielinski, G., Trépanier, M., Morency, C.: Electric and hybrid car use in a free-floating carsharing system. Int. J. Sustain. Transp. 11(3), 161–169 (2017)

Privacy-Preserving Decision Trees Evaluation via Linear Functions

Raymond K.H. Tai$^{(\boxtimes)}$, Jack P.K. Ma, Yongjun Zhao, and Sherman S.M. Chow

Information Engineering Department,
Chinese University of Hong Kong, Shatin, Hong Kong
{tkh016,mpk016,zy113,sherman}@ie.cuhk.edu.hk

Abstract. The combination of cloud-based computing paradigm and machine learning algorithms has enabled many complex analytic services, such as face recognition in a crowd or valuation of immovable properties. Companies can charge clients who do not have the expertise or resource to build such complex models for the prediction or classification service. In this work, we focus on machine learning classification with decision tree (or random forests) as the analytic model, which is popular for its effectiveness and simplicity. We propose privacy-preserving decision tree evaluation protocols which hide the sensitive inputs (model and query) from the counterparty. Comparing with the state-of-the-art, we made a significant improvement in efficiency by cleverly exploiting the structure of decision trees, which avoids an exponential number of encryptions in the depth of the decision tree. Our experiment results show that our protocols are especially efficient for deep but sparse decision trees, which are typical for classification models trained from real datasets, ranging from cancer diagnosis to spam classification.

1 Introduction

Machine learning analyzes the pattern of past data for predicting the outcome when given new data as a query. It is widely applicable, say, to credit risk assessment, object recognition, recommendation systems, *etc*. Taking diagnosis of ischemic heart disease as an example, applying machine learning to the past client records help the symptoms evaluation and electrocardiography [21].

Typical machine learning algorithms reveal the query of client and the corresponding classification result to the server. The clients (or users) using these services may not want to reveal their sensitive information. For example, consider revealing every single email to the spam classification server, or food allergy to a diagnosis server. Leakage of sensitive information can be a life-or-death issue.

Another approach is to simply ask the server to give the model to the clients, who then perform the classification themselves. Yet, the computation for a complex classification model is time-consuming for a typical client. Moreover, the

Sherman Chow is supported by the Early Career Scheme and the Early Career Award (CUHK 439713), and General Research Funds (CUHK 14201914) of the Research Grants Council, University Grant Committee of Hong Kong.

S.N. Foley et al. (Eds.): ESORICS 2017, Part II, LNCS 10493, pp. 494–512, 2017.
DOI: 10.1007/978-3-319-66399-9_27

classifier itself, as the result of dedicated research effort which spent a considerable amount of resources, is a valuable asset of the company. This means revealing such "business secret" in clear is not an option. Also, the model is built from, and hence can reveal, sensitive training data such as financial statements or medical records. Recent work by Fredrikson *et al.* [10,11] showed a model inversion attack which can recover information about the training data when given access to the model but can be avoided by taking privacy-aware model training [10]. A comprehensive survey [28] summarized attacks and defenses throughout the process of machine learning, with a focus on confidentiality of training data and differential privacy. Leaking the model not only hurts the reputation of the company due to the compromise of the collected sensitive data, but may even violate laws and regulations such as Health Insurance Portability and Accountability Act (HIPAA). This further motivates the need for the client to send the (encrypted) query for the server to apply the model on it locally.

Ideally, users do not want the server to infer anything about their data, including the classification result, while the server aims to prevent leaking any information about the model. Simply put, the users should only know the classification result[1] and the server should learn nothing.

This paper focuses on preserving privacy in classification using a decision tree, a classifier known for its effectiveness and simplicity. Comparing to deep learning approaches which are more powerful, decision tree approach is more efficient when the data has a hierarchical structure and requires less parameter tuning as well as training cost. Furthermore, in general, the more complicated the underlying (non-privacy-preserving) machine learning it is, the less efficient will be the corresponding privacy-preserving version. Figure 1 gives an overview of the supervised machine learning model. The model w is a decision tree computed from training data. In classification phase, a server holding w receives a *feature vector* from the user as a query, and returns the result by applying w on it.

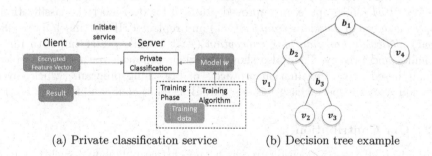

(a) Private classification service   (b) Decision tree example

Fig. 1. Machine learning service under the decision tree model

Decision tree, illustrated in Fig. 1b, is a binary tree structure storing a collection of decision nodes and leaf nodes. Starting at the root, the classifier compares one attribute in the feature vector with a node-specific threshold at a time

---

[1] Of course, all such systems require a rate-limiting mechanism on the user queries.

and outputs a bit b_i denoting which node to traverse. This process is iterated until arriving at some leaf node, which represents the classification result v_i. The result can be a fixed class or a probability distribution. Recent privacy-preserving machine learning classification protocols [4, 35] are built upon decision tree.

In general, it is a secure multi-party computation problem, where one may employ garbled circuit (GC) [16, 19, 20, 23, 25] and fully homomorphic encryption (FHE) [14] to implement different kinds of classifiers. However, this approach typically incurs a high cost even for cloud servers. A comprehensive discussion on generic methods can be found in [35]. Tailor-made schemes for specific classifier can be far more efficient [4, 12, 17, 27, 35].

1.1 Related Work

Earlier works in the privacy-preserving machine learning mostly focus on protecting data in the training phase [9, 15, 18, 24, 31, 34]. Some of them use cryptographic techniques including somewhat homomorphic encryption [14], and some leverage differential privacy. Recently, big data analytics and cloud services are gaining popularity. There are many privacy-preserving protocols for cloud-based computation (*e.g.*, feature extraction from encrypted images [29, 33]). Following the trend, privacy-preserving machine learning classification is getting more and more attention [2–4, 35]. Mohassel and Niksefat [26] proposed protocols that evaluate decision program obliviously, but with the assumption that clients already knew the comparison results, *i.e.*, the comparison nodes are public.

Bost *et al.* [4] build privacy-preserving protocols for hyperplane decision, naïve Bayes, and decision tree classifiers. They first identify what are the core operations of these classifiers, including addition, multiplication, dot products, argmax, and comparison over encrypted data. Many of these can be achieved by semi-homomorphic encryption. However, their construction treats a decision tree as a high-degree polynomial, evaluation thus requires using FHE.

Wu *et al.* [35] propose an improved protocol for decision tree classification. They make use of *oblivious transfer* (OT) and replace FHE by (much more efficient) *additively homomorphic encryption* (AHE), while preserving both functionality and privacy. They also show that their protocols outperform garbled circuit based private evaluation protocols of branching program (which cover decision tree as a special case) proposed by Brickell *et al.* [5] and Barni *et al.* [1].

1.2 Our Contribution

Bost *et al.* [4] treat a decision tree as a high-degree polynomial such that the server can evaluate the result by homomorphic operation on the client's FHE encrypted input. To avoid using heavy FHE, Wu *et al.* [35] require the server to send the decision tree to the client. For security, the server needs to transform it into a randomized and complete tree before sending it to the client. However, this results in the server complexity growing exponentially in the depth of the tree.

Instead of representing a decision tree as a high-degree polynomial, we represent it in the form of linear functions. We exploit the structure of the decision tree and leverage the concept of path cost. Specifically, we compute the path cost of each leaf node by a linear function and use it to determinate whether a leaf node contains the classification result. This is to avoid multiplications between encrypted messages. In this way, we require neither heavy FHE nor sending randomized complete tree to the client, and achieve by far the most efficient privacy-preserving decision-tree evaluation protocols while keeping the communication cost minimal. The overall performance beats the state-of-the-art asymptotically and empirically. Our basic construction is secure under the semi-honest model which only requires AHE. Moreover, it only requires 4 *communication rounds*, where one sending/receiving action is considered as one round. Let n and t be the *dimension* and the *bit-size* for *each feature* of a feature vector respectively, and m be the *number of decision nodes*. The complexity of our protocol is $O((n + m)t)$ for clients and $O(mt)$ for the server.

We extend our basic construction to achieve one-sided security against malicious client. The only existing one-sided secure protocol is from Wu *et al.* [35], which requires the server to send a randomized complete tree to the client for achieving one-sided security, *even for sparse trees*. Its complexity thus grows exponentially in the *depth of the tree* denoted by d. For the first time, with our new way of decision tree evaluation, we obtain a one-sided secure protocol which does not require this exponential blow-up in both time and space complexities. Notably, it achieves the same asymptotic complexity as the semi-honest one.

Depending only on m, our protocols work well for deep but sparse trees. Table 1 shows a comparison. In practice, the differences between m and 2^d can be huge. Table 2 demonstrates this according to the parameters of UCI dataset [22] considered by Wu *et al.* [35]. The ratios of $2^d/m$ for the listed datasets are $1.6, 3.2, 21.3, 89.0$, and 2259.9. It is practically relevant to consider sparse trees.

Table 1. Summary (t/n: size/number of feature, d/m: depth/number of nodes)

Protocol	Complexity		Number	Encryption	Leakage	
	Client	Server	of rounds	scheme	Client	Server
Bost *et al.* [4] (semi-honest)	$O((n + m)t)$	$O(mt)$	≥ 6	Leveled-FHE	None	m
Wu *et al.* [35] (semi-honest)	$O((n + m)t + d)$	$O(mt + 2^d)$	6	AHE	None	m, d
This work (**semi-honest**)	$O((n + m)t)$	$O(mt)$	4	AHE	None	m
Wu *et al.* [35] (One-sided)	$O((n + d)t)$	$O(2^d t)$	2	AHE	None	d
This work (**one-sided**)	$O((n + m)t)$	$O(mt)$	4	AHE	None	m

2   Preliminaries

2.1   Decision Tree Classifiers and Important Notations

Let the user input be in the form of an n-dimensional feature vector $x = (x_1, \ldots, x_n) \in \mathbb{Z}^n$, and the number of decision nodes of the tree be m. Without loss of generality, we assume the decision tree is a *full binary tree*, namely, every node has either 0 or 2 children. For a full binary tree with m non-leaf nodes, the number of leaf nodes is $m + 1$. Let $\mathcal{T} : \mathbb{Z}^n \longmapsto \{v_1, \ldots, v_{m+1}\}$ be the decision tree evaluation function with m decision nodes. Its output $v = \mathcal{T}(x)$ is the classification result which represents the class that x belongs. Each non-leaf node denotes a test on the input attributes. Evaluation starts from the root, descends to the left or right branch based on the test on the current node, and continues until arriving at some leaf node storing $\mathcal{T}(x)$.

2.2   Building Blocks

Homomorphic Encryption. Our protocols use an *additively homomorphic encryption* (AHE) called lifted ElGamal encryption [13] which is like ElGamal but encodes the messages as exponents. Our particular choice of this encryption scheme is for a fairer and easier comparison with prior work [35].

We denote by $[m]$ an encryption of the plaintext m. Lifted ElGamal consists of the following PPT algorithms: Let g be a generator of $\mathbb{G}$. KGen takes in security parameter λ and outputs public key pk and secret key sk. Enc outputs ciphertext $[m]$ when given plaintext (as an exponent) m while DEC outputs g^m when given $[m]$. Of course, one can also encrypt $V = g^v$ without knowing v as regular ElGamal. Add takes in ciphertexts $[m_1]$, $[m_2]$ and outputs a ciphertext $[m_1 + m_2]$. ScalarMul takes in $[m]$ and a scalar n, and outputs $[n \cdot m]$. Again, ScalarMul also works for a regular ElGamal ciphertext of $V = g^v$ without knowing v.

We stress that we do not require recovering the plaintext from the exponents as we only use it to encrypt either a bit or we use the group element as is. Thus our usage does not require solving any discrete logarithm problem. In particular, our constructions simply encrypts key k or classification v using regular ElGamal. Ciphertext $[k']$ of lifted ElGamal is equivalent to a regular ElGamal encryption of the key $k = g^{k'}$. Likewise, classification result can be directly represented by $g^{v'}$ while neither the server nor the client needs to know v'. To avoid clumsy notation, our protocol description simply treats the implicit exponent as the classification result to be encrypted. For actual operation, the server can simply encrypt the group element and multiply its ElGamal ciphertext with another.

Comparison Protocols. Here we review the functionality of the *private comparison protocol* PvtCmp [32] and the private comparison protocol *with conditional key transfer* PvtCmpOT [35] used by our schemes. The main idea of the protocol is that, $x = \sum_{i=1}^{t} 2^{t-i} \cdot x_i > y = \sum_{i=1}^{t} 2^{t-i} \cdot y_i$ if and only if there exist i such that $x_i - y_i - 1 + 3 \cdot \sum_{j<i} x_j \oplus y_j = 0$ where t is a number larger than the length of both x and y. It is easy to see that the equation can be computed over

x encrypted with additively homomorphic encryption and plaintext y. Therefore it can be used to achieve private comparison. More formally, let $[\mathbf{x}]$ be an (additively homomorphic) encryption of x in binary form, $\mathbf{y}$ denote y in binary form, b_1 is a bit chosen randomly as part of the input (which also serves as a secret share), and (k_0, k_1) are the two secret keys (for the protocol with key transfer). The functionalities of these protocols are:

$$\mathsf{PvtCmp}([\mathbf{x}], (\mathbf{y}, b_1)) \longmapsto (b_2, \perp),$$
$$\mathsf{PvtCmpOT}([\mathbf{x}], (\mathbf{y}, b_1, (k_0, k_1))) \longmapsto ((b_2, k_{b_2}), \perp)$$

The bit b_2 is set such that $b_1 \oplus b_2 = (x < y)$, e.g., when $x < y$ and $b_1 = 1$, we have $(x < y) = 1$, so $b_2 = 0$.

Looking ahead, our schemes make black-box use of these protocols. We iterate them over i to perform comparison at each node D_i to decide the traversal. We use $\mathsf{PvtCmp_s}$ and $\mathsf{PvtCmp_c}$ to denote the two stages of the protocol, which is respectively initiated by the server and executed by the client upon receiving the output of the server. Similar notation will be adopted for $\mathsf{PvtCmpOT}$. Figure 2 gives the constructions of the above protocols. For their correctness and security proofs, we refer to [35, Sects. 3.2, 4.2].

Proof of Knowledge. Zero-knowledge proofs can protect the privacy of some inputs while we need to assert a certain property about them. We use the notion of Camenisch and Stadler [6] to represent a zero-knowledge proof of knowledge (PoK). For example, $\mathsf{PoK}\{(\alpha) : c = g^\alpha\}$ denotes a PoK to prove that $c = g^\alpha$ holds for a secret α. Everything else in the equation (c and g here) are public.

Our schemes require proving certain equality for lifted ElGamal and the following disjunctive (DisJ) proof [7]. $\mathsf{PfDisj_{pk}}$ takes in a ciphertext $[m_b]$ and the corresponding randomness used to encrypt, the bit b, $M_0 = g^{m_0}$ and $M_1 = g^{m_1}$, and outputs $\pi = (c_0, f_0, c_1, f_1)$ as a proof that $[m_b]$ encrypted m_0 or m_1. $\mathsf{VerDisj_{pk}}$ takes $[m]$, π, M_0 and M_1, and outputs a bit indicating if π is valid. To turn it into a non-interactive proof, we use a hash function $H : \{0,1\}^* \to \mathbb{Z}_p$.

With input $[\mathbf{x}] = ([x_1], \cdots, [x_t])$, $\mathsf{PfDisj_{pk}}$ is run t times, each with input $[x_q]$ and output π_q, $q \in \{1, \cdots, t\}$. With input $[\boldsymbol{\pi}]$, $\mathsf{VerDisj_{pk}}$ is run t times, each with input $([x_q], \pi_q)$. Figure 3 shows the instantiation of $\mathsf{PfDisj_{pk}}$ and $\mathsf{VerDisj_{pk}}$.

3   Proposed Main Construction

Our main construction is secure under semi-honest adversary. If both parties follow the protocol, it guarantees the client only learns the number of decision nodes and the correct classification result while the server learns nothing.

In the rest of paper, we denote n as dimension of the feature space, t as bits needed to represent one feature, m as number of decision nodes in a decision tree, d as depth of a decision tree. D_i indicates i^{th} decision node, $E_{i,0}$ ($E_{i,1}$) indicates left (right) edge of D_i, $ec_{i,j}$ indicates edge cost of $E_{i,j}$, L_k indicates k^{th} leaf node, P_k indicates path of L_k from the root, and pc_k indicates the

$\mathsf{PvtCmp_s}([\mathbf{x}], (\mathbf{y}, b_1)), \mathbf{y} = (y_0, \ldots, y_{t-1}) \in \{0,1\}^t$ $\quad$ $\mathsf{PvtCmp_c}(C)$

$[\mathbf{x}] = ([x_1], \cdots [x_t])$

$\quad\quad$ For $i \in \{1, \ldots, t\}$

$$y = \sum_{i=1}^{t} 2^{t-i} \cdot y_i$$

$\quad\quad\quad$ If $\mathsf{Dec_{sk}}([c_i]) = 0$

$\quad\quad\quad\quad$ return $b_2 = 1$

$s \leftarrow 1 - 2 \cdot b_1$

$\quad\quad$ return $b_2 = 0$

For $i \in \{1, \ldots, t\}$

$\quad r_i \leftarrow \mathbb{Z}_p^*$

$\quad [c_i] \leftarrow [r_i \cdot (x_i - y_i + s + 3 \cdot \sum_{j<i} x_j \oplus y_j)]$

return $C = ([c_1], \cdots, [c_t])$

(a) Details of $\mathsf{PvtCmp_s}$ and $\mathsf{PvtCmp_c}$

$\mathsf{PvtCmpOT_s}([\mathbf{x}], (\mathbf{y}, b_1, (k_0, k_1)))$ $\quad\quad$ $\mathsf{PvtCmpOT_c}(C)$

$[\mathbf{x}] = ([x_1], \cdots [x_t])$

$\quad\quad$ For $i \in \{1, \ldots, t\}$

$$y = \sum_{i=1}^{t} 2^{t-i} \cdot y_i, \quad s \leftarrow 1 - 2 \cdot b_1$$

$\quad\quad\quad k \leftarrow \mathsf{Dec_{sk}}([c_i])$

$\quad\quad\quad K \leftarrow g^k$

For $i \in \{1, \ldots, t\}$

$\quad\quad\quad$ If $K = K_0$

$\quad r_i \leftarrow \mathbb{Z}_p^*, K_0 \leftarrow g^{k_0}, K_1 \leftarrow g^{k_1}$

$\quad\quad\quad\quad$ return $(b_2 = 0, k_0 = k)$

$\quad$ If $(-y_i - s = 0)$ or $(-y_i - s = -1)$

$\quad\quad\quad$ If $K = K_1$

$\quad\quad [c_i] \leftarrow [k_0 + r_i \cdot (x_i - y_i - s + 2 \cdot \sum_{j<i} x_j \oplus y_j)]$

$\quad\quad\quad\quad$ return $(b_2' = 1, k_1 = k)$

$\quad$ Else

$\quad\quad [c_i] \leftarrow [k_1 + r_i \cdot (x_i - y_i + s + 2 \cdot \sum_{j<i} x_j \oplus y_j)]$

return $C = ([c_1], \cdots, [c_t]), K_0, K_1$

(b) Details of $\mathsf{PvtCmpOT_s}$ and $\mathsf{PvtCmpOT_c}$

Fig. 2. Comparison protocols

corresponding path cost, while v_k indicates classification result belongs to L_k. $[m]$ denotes encryption of message m, $k_{i,j}$ denotes key belongs to $\mathsf{E}_{i,j}$ and $\mathbf{x}$ denotes binary representation of $x = x_1, \cdots, x_t$. $b \leftarrow_\$ \{0,1\}$ means randomly picking a bit and assign it to b, $c \leftarrow f(b)$ means assigning the output of $f(b)$ to c and $(x < y)$ is a bit equals 1 if the predicate $x < y$ is true, 0 otherwise.

3.1 Intuition

When using a binary decision tree to do classification, each decision node D_i outputs a boolean value $b_i = (x_i < y_i)$ by comparing a given attribute x_i in

$\mathsf{PfDisj}_{\mathsf{pk}}((\mathsf{ct}_0, \mathsf{ct}_1), b, M_0, M_1)$	$\mathsf{VerDisj}_{\mathsf{pk}}((\mathsf{ct}_0, \mathsf{ct}_1), (c_0, f_0, c_1, f_1), M_0, M_1)$
$\mathsf{pk} = (g, g^s), (\mathsf{ct}_0, \mathsf{ct}_1) = (g^r, g^{sr+m}; r)$	$\mathsf{pk} = (g, g^s), (\mathsf{ct}_0, \mathsf{ct}_1) = (g^r, g^{sr+m})$
$a_{1-b}, c_b, f_b \leftarrow_\$ \mathbb{Z}_p$	$c \leftarrow c_0 + c_1$
$A_{1-b} \leftarrow g^{a_{1-b}}, B_{1-b} \leftarrow (g^s)^{a_{1-b}},$	$A_0 \leftarrow \dfrac{g^{f_0}}{\mathsf{ct}_0^{c_0}},\ B_0 \leftarrow \dfrac{(g^s)^{f_0}}{(\mathsf{ct}_1/M_0)^{c_0}},$
$A_b \leftarrow \dfrac{g^{f_b}}{\mathsf{ct}_0^{c_b}}, B_b \leftarrow \dfrac{(g^s)^{f_b}}{(\mathsf{ct}_1/M_b)^{c_b}}$	$A_1 \leftarrow \dfrac{g^{f_1}}{\mathsf{ct}_0^{c_1}},\ B_1 \leftarrow \dfrac{(g^s)^{f_1}}{(\mathsf{ct}_1/M_1)^{c_1}}$
$c \leftarrow H(A_{1-b}, B_{1-b}, A_b, B_b)$	$c' \leftarrow H(A_0, B_0, A_1, B_1)$
$c_{1-b} \leftarrow c - c_b,\ f_{1-b} \leftarrow a_{1-b} + c_{1-b}r$	
return $\pi = (c_0, f_0, c_1, f_1)$	**return** $(c \stackrel{?}{=} c')$

Fig. 3. Proof of knowledge for lifted ElGamal encryption

the query and the threshold y_i stored in D_i. The boolean value $b_i = 0$ (or 1) indicates the classification result v is in the left (or right) subtree of D_i. After eliminating all impossible leaf nodes, we will get the unique classification result.

Each leaf node L_k has a unique path P_k from the root of the decision tree. This path consists of a unique collection of edges. Observing that each of the leaf node L_k in the right (left) subtree of D_i has path P_k containing the right (left) outgoing edge $E_{i,1}$ ($E_{i,0}$) of D_i.

Combining the above two observations, we can get the unique classification result by using each b_i to eliminate leaf nodes that have path containing $E_{i,1-b_i}$.

In our constructions, we introduce *edge cost* $\mathsf{ec}_{i,j}$ for each edge $E_{i,j}$ and define *path cost* pc_k as the summation of all $\mathsf{ec}_{i,j}$'s along the path P_k. By setting edge cost ec_{i,b_i} of edge E_{i,b_i} to be zero and edge cost $\mathsf{ec}_{i,1-b_i}$ of edge $E_{i,1-b_i}$ to be non-zero, path P_k that contains edge $E_{i,1-b_i}$ will have path cost pc_k being non-zero. Finally, we have v_k being the classification result if and only if $\mathsf{pc}_k = 0$.

Referring to the example in Fig. 1b, setting the edge costs $\mathsf{ec}_{i,0} = b_i$ and $\mathsf{ec}_{i,1} = 1 - b_i$ for every node D_i, the path cost pc_k for each leaf node L_k are: $\mathsf{pc}_1 = b_1 + b_2;\ \mathsf{pc}_2 = b_1 + (1-b_2) + b_3;\ \mathsf{pc}_3 = b_1 + (1-b_2) + (1-b_3);\ \mathsf{pc}_4 = 1 - b_1$.

By using ABY framework [8], one can switch the underlying primitives to achieve better performance on different operations. However, in our construction, the server needs to hide from the client which attribute is being compared in each node as well as how the path costs are added up. To the best of our knowledge, AHE is the best primitive to achieve our purpose.

3.2 Details of Algorithms

Let $(\mathsf{pk}, \mathsf{sk})$ be a key pair for lifted ElGamal over $\mathbb{G}$ of prime order p. The client holds secret key sk. A feature vector is defined as $(x_1, \ldots, x_n) \in \mathbb{Z}^n$. Let t be the bit-length of x_i, and $\mathbf{x}_i$ denotes the binary representation of x_i.

In Steps 1–3 in Fig. 4, the server and the client interact to derive the comparison results b_i of *every* decision node. The client outputs a bit $b_{i,2}$ such that $b_{i,1} \oplus b_{i,2} = b_i = (x_i < y_i)$ where $b_{i,1}$ is chosen by the server.

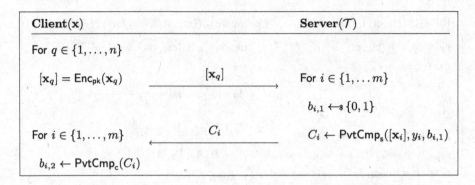

Fig. 4. Private decision tree evaluation in the honest-but-curious model (Steps 1–3)

1. **Client:** Encrypts each component of the feature vector $x_1, \ldots, x_n$ in bits then sends the ciphertexts $[\mathbf{x}_1], \ldots, [\mathbf{x}_n]$ to the server.
2. **Server:** For each decision node D_i, $i \in \{1, \cdots, m\}$: chooses a random bit $b_{i,1} \leftarrow_\$ \{0, 1\}$, applies PvtCmp (in Sect. 2.2) on attribute $[\mathbf{x}_i]$, threshold y_i, and bit $b_{i,1}$. After the loop, sends the results of all comparisons to the client.
3. **Client:** For $i \in \{1, \cdots, m\}$: obtains bit $b_{i,2}$, a share of the comparison result.

In Steps 4–6 in Fig. 5, the server returns an encryption of the classification result according to the comparison done in Steps 1–3. Firstly, the client encrypts its share bit $b_{i,2}$ and sends $[b_{i,2}]$ to the server. The server then computes $[b_i] = [b_{i,1} \oplus b_{i,2}]$. We set $\mathsf{ec}_{i,0} = b_i$ to be the edge cost of $E_{i,0}$ and $\mathsf{ec}_{i,1} = 1 - b_i$ to be the edge cost of $E_{i,1}$. Then we compute the path cost $\mathsf{pc}_k = \sum_{E_{i,j} \in P_k} \mathsf{ec}_{i,j}$ for each leaf node L_k. Finally, the server sends the randomized path cost $[\tilde{\mathsf{pc}}_k] = [r_k \cdot \mathsf{pc}_k]$ with randomized classification result $[\tilde{v}_k] = [r'_k \cdot \mathsf{pc}_k + v_k]$ to the client such that the client can only check whether the path cost $[\mathsf{pc}_k]$ equals zero and can only get the corresponding classification result v_k when pc_k equals zero.

4. **Client:** Sends encryptions of comparison results $[b_{1,2}], \ldots, [b_{m,2}]$ to the server.
5. **Server:**
   For $i \in \{1, \cdots, m\}$: computes $[b_i] \leftarrow [b_{i,1} \oplus b_{i,2}]$.
   For $k \in \{1, \cdots, m+1\}$: computes path cost pc_k of leaf node L_k by taking $([b_1], \ldots, [b_m])$ and the decision tree as input. Chooses $r_k, r'_k \leftarrow_\$ \mathbb{Z}_p^*$. Then computes randomized path cost $\tilde{\mathsf{pc}}_k \leftarrow [r_k \cdot \mathsf{pc}_k]$ and randomized classification result $[\tilde{v}_k] \leftarrow [r'_k \cdot \mathsf{pc}_k + v_k]$ for leaf node L_k.
   After the loop, chooses a random permutation P over $\{1, \ldots, m+1\}$ and sends $([\tilde{\mathsf{pc}}_{P(1)}], [\tilde{v}_{P(1)}]), \ldots, ([\tilde{\mathsf{pc}}_{P(m+1)}], [\tilde{v}_{P(m+1)}])$ to the client.
6. **Client:** For $k' \in \{1, \cdots m+1\}$: checks if $[\tilde{\mathsf{pc}}_{k'}] = [0]$. If so, outputs $v \leftarrow \mathsf{DEC}_{\mathsf{sk}}([\tilde{v}_{k'}])$.

The following lemma shows that our protocol is correct.

Lemma 1. *If both client and server follow our protocol, the client learns the classification results $T(x)$ at the end.*

Client(x)	Server($\mathcal{T}$)
For $i \in \{1, \dots, m\}$	
$[b_{i,2}] \leftarrow \mathsf{Enc}_{\mathsf{pk}}(b_{i,2})$ $\xrightarrow{\quad [b_{i,2}] \quad}$	For $i \in \{1, \dots, m\}$
	$[b_i] \leftarrow [b_{i,1} \oplus b_{i,2}]$
	$[\mathsf{ec}_{i,0}] \leftarrow [b_i], \; [\mathsf{ec}_{i,1}] \leftarrow [1 - b_i]$
	For $k \in \{1, \dots, m+1\}$
	$[\mathsf{pc}_k] \leftarrow [\sum_{\mathsf{E}_{i,j} \in \mathsf{P}_k} \mathsf{ec}_{i,j}], \; r_k, r'_k \leftarrow_\$ \mathbb{Z}_p^*$
	$[\tilde{\mathsf{pc}}_k] \leftarrow [r_k \cdot \mathsf{pc}_k]$
	$[\tilde{v}_k] \leftarrow [r'_k \cdot \mathsf{pc}_k + v_k]$
For $k' \in \{1, \dots, m+1\}$ $\xleftarrow{\quad ([\tilde{\mathsf{pc}}_{P(k)}], [\tilde{v}_{P(k)}]) \quad}$	Chooses a random permutation P
If $\mathsf{Dec}_{\mathsf{sk}}([\tilde{\mathsf{pc}}_{k'}]) = 0$	
$v \leftarrow \mathsf{Dec}_{\mathsf{sk}}([\tilde{v}_{k'}])$	
return v	

Fig. 5. Private decision tree evaluation in the honest-but-curious model (Steps 4–6)

Proof. By the tree construction, $\mathsf{E}_{i,0} \in \mathsf{P}_k$ indicates $x_i < y_i$ is a constraint of getting v_k, while $\mathsf{E}_{i,1} \in \mathsf{P}_k$ indicates $x_i \geq y_i$ is a constraint of getting v_k. The server obtains $[b_i]$ from the comparison protocol where $b_i = (x_i < y_i)$. The edge costs $\mathsf{ec}_{i,0}, \mathsf{ec}_{i,1}$ are defined as b_i and $1 - b_i$ respectively, so that $\mathsf{ec}_{i,0} = (x_i < y_i)$, and $\mathsf{ec}_{i,1} = (x_i \geq y_i)$. The path cost pc_k of classification v_k is defined to be $\sum_{\mathsf{E}_{i,j} \in \mathsf{P}_k} \mathsf{ec}_{i,j}$. Thus, we have v_k is the classification result if and only if $\forall \mathsf{E}_{i,j} \in \mathsf{P}_k, \mathsf{ec}_{i,j} = 0$, that is $\mathsf{pc}_k = 0$. Moreover, we have $\tilde{\mathsf{pc}}_k = r_k \cdot \mathsf{pc}_k = 0 \iff \mathsf{pc}_k = 0$ and $\tilde{v}_k = r'_k \cdot \mathsf{pc}_k + v_k = v_k \iff \mathsf{pc}_k = 0$. Therefore the protocol is correct.

3.3 Random Forest Extension

To extend our constructions to random forest, the simplest way is asking the server to send the comparison results of all trees in the forest in Step 2 and likewise all outputs in Step 5 to the client. In this way, the client only knows the total number of decision nodes of all trees, but does not know the number of decision nodes of an individual tree. In addition, we can use the trick of additive secret sharing [35] to further hide each output value v from a tree.

To handle numeric attributes, one can multiply the numeric attributes with a large number to make it an integer. For categorical attributes C_i, we require the client to send encryption of its category $[C]$ to the server. In malicious setting, the client is also required to prove that $[C] = [C_i]$ for some i. Then the server chooses $r_i \leftarrow_\$ \mathbb{Z}_p^*$ and sets the edge cost ec_i as $r_i \cdot (C_i - C)$.

4 One-Sided Secure Extension

A client that does not follow the protocol specification can learn some information about the threshold or structure of the model in the semi-honest construction. For example, the client can send feature vector not in binary form or send false responses in the comparison protocol.

In the one-sided secure extension, similar to the existing protocol [35], we use *proof of knowledge* and *conditional oblivious transfer* to protect against malicious clients. In particular, the client needs to prove that the encrypted feature vector consists of encryption of either 0 or 1. To ensure the client sends true responses in the comparison protocol, the server uses conditional OT to transfer the keys, such that the client gets either key k_0 or k_1 at each comparison depending on the comparison result. The client needs to prove the response is encryption of either k_0 or k_1. We only require the input attribute values to be in encrypted binary form while the range of attribute values are not restricted (except the bound 2^t) as inputting abnormal attribute values only leads to a corrupted classification result. For this extension, a malicious server can only give corrupted result but learns nothing, while a malicious client can only learn the classification result and the number of decision nodes m.

Figures 6 and 7 show the details of our extension. In Steps 1–3, PoKs are sent along with encrypted inputs to ensure that they are encryption of bits. The

Client(x)		Server($\mathcal{T}$)
For $q \in \{1, \dots, n\}$		
$[\mathbf{x}_q] \leftarrow \mathsf{Enc}_{\mathsf{pk}}(\mathbf{x}_q)$		
$\pi_q \leftarrow \mathsf{PfDisj}_{\mathsf{pk}}([\mathbf{x}_q], \mathbf{x}_q, g^0, g^1)$ $\xrightarrow{([\mathbf{x}_q], \pi_q)}$		For $q \in \{1, \dots, n\}$
		If $\neg\mathsf{VerDisj}_{\mathsf{pk}}([\mathbf{x}_q], \pi_q, g^0, g^1)$
		abort
		For $i \in \{1, \dots, m\}$
		$b_{i,1} \leftarrow_\$ \{0,1\}$, $k_{i,0}, k_{i,1} \leftarrow_\$ \mathbb{Z}_p$
		$K_{i,0} \leftarrow g^{k_{i,b_{i,1}}}$
		$K_{i,1} \leftarrow g^{k_{i,1-b_{i,1}}}$
		$input \leftarrow [\mathbf{x}_i], y_i, b_{i,1}, k_{i,0}, k_{i,1}$
For $i \in \{1, \dots, m\}$	$\xleftarrow{C_i}$	$C_i \leftarrow \mathsf{PvtCmpOT}_{\mathsf{s}}(input)$
$(b_{i,2}, k_{i,b_{i,2}}) \leftarrow$		
$\mathsf{PvtCmpOT}_{\mathsf{c}}(C_i, K_{i,0}, K_{i,1})$		

Fig. 6. One-sided secure decision tree evaluation (Steps 1–3)

$\textbf{Client}(\mathbf{x})$ (let $b' = b_{i,2}$)		$\textbf{Server}(\mathcal{T})$ (let $b = b_{i,1}, b' = b_{i,2}$)
For $i \in \{1,\ldots,m\}$		
$[k_{i,b'}] \leftarrow \mathsf{Enc}_{\mathsf{pk}}(k_{i,b'})$		
$\pi_i \leftarrow$		
$\mathsf{PfDisj}_{\mathsf{pk}}([k_{i,b'}], b', \mathbf{K}_i)$	$\xrightarrow{\ ([k_{i,b'}], \pi_i)\ }$	For $i \in \{1,\ldots,m\}$
		If $\neg\mathsf{VerDisj}_{\mathsf{pk}}([k_{i,b'}], \pi_i, \mathbf{K}_i)$
		$\quad$abort
		$[\mathsf{ec}_{i,0}] \leftarrow [k_{i,b} - k_{i,b'}]$
		$[\mathsf{ec}_{i,1}] \leftarrow [k_{i,1-b} - k_{i,b'}]$
		For $k \in \{1,\ldots,m+1\}$
		$\quad [\mathsf{pc}_k] \leftarrow [\sum_{E_{i,j} \in P_k} \mathsf{ec}_{i,j}]$
		$\quad r_k, r'_k \leftarrow_\$ \mathbb{Z}_p^*$
		$\quad [\tilde{\mathsf{pc}}_k] \leftarrow [r_k \cdot \mathsf{pc}_k]$
		$\quad [\tilde{v}_k] \leftarrow [r'_k \cdot \mathsf{pc}_k + v_k]$
For $k' \in \{1,\ldots,m+1\}$	$\xleftarrow{\ ([\tilde{\mathsf{pc}}_{P(k)}], [\tilde{v}_{P(k)}])\ }$	Chooses a random permutation P
If $\mathsf{Dec}_{\mathsf{sk}}([\tilde{\mathsf{pc}}_{k'}]) = 0$		
$\quad$return $v \leftarrow \mathsf{Dec}_{\mathsf{sk}}([\tilde{v}_{k'}])$		

Fig. 7. One-sided secure decision tree evaluation (Steps 4–6)

server and the client involve in comparison protocol with OT. The client outputs $b_{i,2}$ such that $b_{i,1} \oplus b_{i,2} = (x_i < y_i)$ and key $k_{i,b_{i,2}}$ where $b_{i,1}$ is chosen by server.

1. **Client:** Encrypts the feature vector in bits and computes proofs showing the ciphertexts are encryption of 0 or 1. Then sends encrypted feature vector in bits with proofs $([\mathbf{x}_1], \boldsymbol{\pi}_1), \cdots, ([\mathbf{x}_n], \boldsymbol{\pi}_n)$ to the server.
2. **Server:** Verifies all proofs. Aborts if any proofs fail.
   For $i \in \{1, \cdots, m\}$: chooses $b_{i,1} \leftarrow_\$ \{0,1\}$ and keys $k_{i,0}, k_{i,1} \leftarrow_\$ \mathbb{Z}_p$.
   Computes $K_{i,0} \leftarrow g^{k_{i,b_{i,1}}}$, $K_{i,1} \leftarrow g^{k_{i,1-b_{i,1}}}$. Then applies $\mathsf{PvtCmpOT}$ (in Sect. 2.2) on attribute $[x_i]$, threshold y_i, bit $b_{i,1}$, and keys $k_{i,0}, k_{i,1}$.
   After the loop, sends $(K_{1,0}, K_{1,1}), \ldots, (K_{m,0}, K_{m,1})$ and all messages for m comparisons with OT to the client.
3. **Client:** For $i \in \{1, \cdots, m\}$: computes the comparison result $(b_{i,2}, k_{i,b_{i,2}})$.

In Steps 4–6 in Fig. 7, PoKs are sent along with encrypted keys $[k_{i,b_{i,2}}]$ to ensure that the client sends the correct comparison results. Instead of using $b_{i,2}$, the server uses $k_{b_{i,2}}$ to define the edge cost and compute path cost pc_k. The edge cost $\mathsf{ec}_{i,j}$ is defined as $\mathsf{ec}_{i,j} \leftarrow k_{i,j} - k_{i,b_i}$. As mentioned in Sect. 2.2, the client does not need to solve discrete logarithm to get the keys or the result.

4. **Client:** For $i \in \{1, \cdots, m\}$: encrypts comparison result $k_{i,b_{i,2}}$ and produces proof π_i showing $[k_{i,b_{i,2}}]$ encrypted either one element in K_i where $\mathbf{K}_i = \{g^{k_{i,0}}, g^{k_{i,1}}\}$. Then sends $(([k_{1,b_{1,2}}], \pi_1), \ldots, ([k_{m,b_{m,2}}], \pi_m))$ to server.
5. **Server:** Let $\mathbf{K}_i = \{g^{k_{i,0}}, g^{k_{i,1}}\}$. Verifies all the proofs, aborts if any one fails. For $k \in \{1, \cdots, m+1\}$: computes path cost pc_k of leaf node L_k by taking $([k_{1,b_{1,2}}], \ldots, [k_{m,b_{m,2}}]), (k_{1,b_{1,1}}, \ldots, k_{m,b_{m,1}}), (k_{1,b_{1,2}}, \ldots, k_{m,b_{m,2}})$ and tree $\mathcal{T}$ as input.
   Chooses $r_k, r'_k \leftarrow_\$ \mathbb{Z}_p^*$. Then computes $\tilde{\mathsf{pc}}_k \leftarrow [r_k \cdot \mathsf{pc}_k]$ and $[\tilde{v}_k] \leftarrow [r'_k \cdot \mathsf{pc}_k + v_k]$. After the loop, chooses a random permutation P over $\{1, \ldots, m+1\}$ and sends $([\tilde{\mathsf{pc}}_{P(1)}], [\tilde{v}_{P(1)}]), \ldots, ([\tilde{\mathsf{pc}}_{P(m+1)}], [\tilde{v}_{P(m+1)}])$ to the client.
6. **Client:** For $k' \in \{1, \cdots, m+1\}$: checks if $[\tilde{\mathsf{pc}}_{k'}] = [0]$. If so, outputs $v \leftarrow \mathsf{DEC}_{\mathsf{sk}}([\tilde{v}_{k'}])$.

5   Performance Analysis

5.1   Complexity

In the semi-honest construction, the client needs to encrypt its feature vector in binary form, which results in nt ciphertext to be sent to the server. When computing the comparison results, the server computes mt ciphertexts and sends to the client. The client decrypts at most mt ciphertexts and encrypts m responses to the server. Finally, the server computes $2(m+1)$ ciphertexts and sends to the client. The client outputs the result by decrypting at most $(m+2)$ ciphertexts.

The one-sided secure construction requires the client to do additional PoKs. The client sends nt ciphertexts and nt PoKs in the first round. The server verifies all nt PoKs. When computing the comparison results, the server computes mt ciphertexts and sends to the client. The server also computes $2m$ exponentiation (for the g^k term) and sends the results to the client. The client decrypts at most mt ciphertexts and mt exponentiations to get the comparison results. The client then encrypts m responses to the server with m PoKs. The server verifies all m PoKs. Finally, the server computes $2(m+1)$ ciphertexts and sends to the client. The client outputs the result by decrypting at most $(m+2)$ ciphertexts.

5.2   Experiment Setup

We also evaluate our protocols empirically. We implement the lifted ElGamal over elliptic curve secp256k1 with key size 256 bits using mcl library[2] which contains an implementation of lifted ElGamal cryptosystem [30].

For the comparison protocol, we instantiate it with an AHE-based one. While one can easily change the AHE-based comparison protocol to one based on garbled circuits (GC) [19,20,23]; however, if we adapt GC in a trivial way, the client will know what attribute is utilized in each comparison. More concretely, in a decision tree, one attribute may be reused in comparison nodes or not being used (if it is a dummy one), revealing which attribute is used to compare will

---

[2] https://github.com/herumi/mcl/.

leak information of the decision tree to the client. One can, again, prevent such leakage by utilizing AHE, but this defeats the purpose of replacing it with GC. In addition, the experiment done by Wu et al. [35] is based on AHE, so we only consider comparison protocol in AHE for a fairer comparison.

We run our tests on a commodity desktop computer equipped with Intel Core i7-6700 CPU (3.40 GHz) running Ubuntu 16.04 on VMware Workstation allocated with one core and 4 GB of RAM. The times reported are an average over 10 trials. For an easier comparison, we use the Nursery dataset from UCI machine learning repository [22] as in the previous benchmarks [4,35]. We set $t = 64$ as the bit-size for representing a single feature following [35].

5.3   Comparison

Table 2 shows the comparison between our protocols and the existing works. The timing figures for [4,35], marked with "()", are from the experiments performed by Bost et al. [4] and Wu et al. [35]. Those marked with "($\sim$)", e.g., ($\sim$290) are read off from the chart which cannot be precise due to the scale. The comparison below used those numbers as is. While we used a similar platform and same security parameter for the experiment, those numbers are for references only.

Table 2. Computation time comparison (n: vector dim., d: depth, m: no. of nodes)

Dataset	n	d	m	Protocol		Computation (s)		Bandwidth (MB)
						Client	Server	
Nursery	8	4	4	Semi-honest	Bost et al. [4]	(1.58)	(0.80)	(2.58)
					Wu et al. [35]	(0.11)	(0.13)	(0.10)
					This work	**0.11**	**0.06**	**0.10**
				One-sided	Wu et al. [35]	(0.22)	(0.94)	(0.70)
					This work	**0.40**	**0.51**	**0.25**
(Sparse) tree	16	20	500	Semi-honest	Wu et al. [35]	($\sim$2)	($\sim$102)	($\sim$145)
					This work	**2.54**	**7.88**	**4.15**
	16	12	300	One-sided	Wu et al. [35]	($\sim$0.5)	($\sim$290)	($\sim$130)
					This work	**2.35**	**10.01**	**5.06**

For tree with $m \approx 2^d$, e.g., nursery data with $d = m = 4$, ours perform similarly to Wu et al. [35]. For a sparse tree with $m \ll 2^d$, which are abundant as we argued in the introduction, our protocols perform much better. Note that one-sided secure protocol of Wu et al. [35] has to transform a non-complete tree to a complete tree, resulting in $O(2^d t)$ complexity for the server (see Table 1). While the server is more powerful than the clients in general, yet it is serving multiple clients. Since all these protocols are interactive, a client still needs to wait for the server to complete its computation before getting the final results, the running time of the server unavoidably affects the user experiences.

For concrete benchmark, we consider a sparse tree with $m = 25d$ (following [35]). For $d = 20$, our semi-honest protocol takes 7.88 s for the server which is 13 times better. The total bandwidth required by our protocol is only 4.15 MB, which is only 2.86% of [35]. For a sparse tree of depth 12 with 300 nodes, the one-sided secure protocol of Wu *et al.* [35] operates on a complete tree of $2^d = 4096$ nodes. Our protocol takes 10.01 s for the server which is 29 times better. For both cases, the client takes less than 3 s. The total bandwidth required by our protocol is 5.06 MB, which is only 3.9% of [35].

In general, our protocol greatly reduces the computation time for the server when $m \ll 2^d$ while maintaining similar performance for clients. More importantly, we avoid the exponential (in the tree depth) bandwidth required by the one-sided protocol of Wu *et al.* [35]. It is desirable to save both the local storage and the downloading bandwidth requirement for the client. In favor of existing works, the above figures exclude our saving in network communication time.

5.4 Benchmark on Real Datasets

Table 3 shows that our protocols give good performance in various real datasets. Even for housing data which introduces a large number of decision nodes, or spambase date which has high dimension feature vectors and introduces a deep tree, our semi-honest protocol requires less than 2.5 s to complete the classification, and the bandwidth required is less than 1 MB. Our semi-honest protocol outperforms the semi-honest protocol of Wu *et al.* [35] in all datasets. Although the performance of one-sided secure protocol of Wu *et al.* [35] is not provided, by referring to Table 2, we can see that it requires more than 5 min and 130 MB for housing and spambase data due to the great depth, which is not practical. For our one-sided secure protocol, the computation time required is less than 8 s while the bandwidth required is less than 2.5 MB.

Table 3. Performance of semi-honest and one-sided secure protocol on UCL datasets

Dataset	n	d	m	Computation (s)				Bandwidth (MB)			
				Semi-honest			One-sided	Semi-honest			One-sided
				This work	[35]	Difference	This work	This work	[35]	Difference	This work
Heart-disease	13	3	5	0.25	(0.37)	−33%	1.42	0.14	(0.11)	+25%	0.39
Credit-screening	15	4	5	0.27	(0.55)	−50%	1.59	0.16	(0.09)	+70%	0.43
Breast-cancer	9	8	12	0.34	(0.55)	−47%	1.30	0.17	(0.20)	−16%	0.41
Housing	13	13	92	1.98	(4.08)	−51%	4.56	0.85	(1.87)	−54%	1.80
spambase	57	17	58	1.80	(16.60)	−89%	7.47	0.92	(17.41)	−95%	2.28

In both protocols, the bandwidth and computation required by the server grows linearly with the number of decision nodes m. When $m \gg n$ (*e.g.*, for spam), the computation required by clients also grows linearly with m.

Figure 8 shows the bandwidth required and the performance of our protocol.

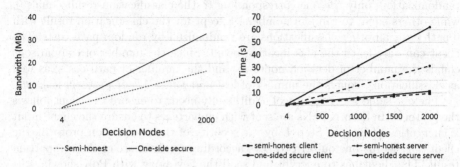

(a) Total bandwidth vs. number of nodes (b) Computation time vs. number of nodes

Fig. 8. Performance of semi-honest and one sided secure protocol

6 Conclusion

We proposed new privacy-preserving protocols for decision tree classifier. The complexity of the state-of-the-art [35] is exponential in the depth of the decision tree. The major improvement is that the complexity of our protocols grows only linearly with the number of decision nodes. Many models in the form of a decision tree are deep but sparse [22,35]. This makes our protocols more desirable.

Our experiment results show a significant improvement for our semi-honest protocol and one-sided secure protocol. The total bandwidth and the server computation are greatly reduced which makes the one-sided protocol practical. We hope our techniques of exploiting the structure of decision tree will spark future improvement on the efficiency while maintaining security.

A   Outline of Security Analysis

Security of Client. In the semi-honest protocol, all the client sends to the server are encrypted feature vector in Step 1 and encrypted share of comparison results in Step 4. The server can thus learn nothing from the client. In the one-sided secure protocol, the server additionally receives PoKs along with ciphertexts in Step 1 and Step 4. By the zero-knowledge property of the PoK, the PoKs leak no information about the client input.

Security of Server. In the semi-honest protocol, all the server sends to the client are secret shares of comparison results in Step 2, and randomized path costs and randomized classifications in Step 5. Without the knowledge of another share (hidden by the server), the share of comparison results appears to be random.

In Step 5, by the correctness of our protocol, only the path cost corresponding to the classification result equals 0 and others equal to non-zero numbers. After randomization, only the one corresponding to the classification result equals 0, while others equal to random numbers. Except for the classification result with 0 path cost, all other classifications are randomized by random path costs. The client can only learn the classification result. Since the number of comparisons equals the number of decision nodes m, and the number of path costs, as well as classifications, equals the number of leaf nodes $m + 1$, our protocol leaks m.

The one-sided secure protocol additionally needs to ensure the client follows the protocol. In Step 1, PoKs are sent with ciphertexts to ensure the client input is encryption of bits. In Step 4, by the security of the comparison protocol, the client only learns one out of two keys according to the share of the comparison result. The client has to encrypt and send the key along with PoK showing the encrypted key is one of the two keys corresponding to the comparison. This ensures the comparison response sent by the client is correct as the client only learns one key and it has to send back either key as the response. As long as the correctness of the client input is ensured, the messages sent in Step 2 and Step 5 leak no information about the server input as the semi-honest setting.

References

1. Barni, M., Failla, P., Kolesnikov, V., Lazzeretti, R., Sadeghi, A.-R., Schneider, T.: Secure evaluation of private linear branching programs with medical applications. In: Backes, M., Ning, P. (eds.) ESORICS 2009. LNCS, vol. 5789, pp. 424–439. Springer, Heidelberg (2009). doi:10.1007/978-3-642-04444-1_26

2. Barni, M., Failla, P., Lazzeretti, R., Sadeghi, A., Schneider, T.: Privacy-preserving ECG classification with branching programs and neural networks. Trans. Inf. Forensics Secur. **6**(2), 452–468 (2011)

3. Bos, J.W., Lauter, K.E., Naehrig, M.: Private predictive analysis on encrypted medical data. J. Biomed. Inform. **50**, 234–243 (2014)

4. Bost, R., Popa, R.A., Tu, S., Goldwasser, S.: Machine learning classification over encrypted data. In: NDSS (2015)

5. Brickell, J., Porter, D.E., Shmatikov, V., Witchel, E.: Privacy-preserving remote diagnostics. In: ACM CCS (2007)

6. Camenisch J., Stadler, M.: Efficient group signature schemes for large groups (extended abstract). In: CRYPTO (1997)

7. Chaum, D., Pedersen, T.P.: Wallet databases with observers. In: Brickell, E.F. (ed.) CRYPTO 1992. LNCS, vol. 740, pp. 89–105. Springer, Heidelberg (1993). doi:10.1007/3-540-48071-4_7

8. Demmler, D., Schneider, T., Zohner, M.: ABY - a framework for efficient mixed-protocol secure two-party computation. In: NDSS (2015)

9. Du, W., Han, Y.S. Chen, S.: Privacy-preserving multivariate statistical analysis: linear regression and classification. In: SDM (2004)

10. Fredrikson, M., Jha, S., Ristenpart, T.: Model inversion attacks that exploit confidence information and basic countermeasures. In: ACM CCS (2015)

11. Fredrikson, M., Lantz, E., Jha, S., Lin, D., Page, D., Ristenpart, T.: Privacy in pharmacogenetics: an end-to-end case study of personalized Warfarin dosing. In: USENIX Security (2014)

12. Frikken, K.B.: Practical private DNA string searching and matching through efficient oblivious automata evaluation. In: DBSec (2009)
13. ElGamal, T.: A public key cryptosystem and a signature scheme based on discrete logarithms. In: Blakley, G.R., Chaum, D. (eds.) CRYPTO 1984. LNCS, vol. 196, pp. 10–18. Springer, Heidelberg (1985). doi:10.1007/3-540-39568-7_2
14. Gentry, C.: A fully homomorphic encryption scheme. Ph.D. thesis, Stanford University, Stanford, CA, USA, AAI3382729 (2009)
15. Graepel, T., Lauter, K., Naehrig, M.: ML confidential: machine learning on encrypted data. In: Kwon, T., Lee, M.-K., Kwon, D. (eds.) ICISC 2012. LNCS, vol. 7839, pp. 1–21. Springer, Heidelberg (2013). doi:10.1007/978-3-642-37682-5_1
16. Hazay, C., Lindell, Y.: Efficient Secure Two-Party Protocols - Techniques and Constructions. Information Security and Cryptography. Springer, Heidelberg (2010)
17. Ishai, Y., Paskin, A.: Evaluating branching programs on encrypted data. In: TCC (2007)
18. Jagannathan, G., Pillaipakkamnatt, K., Wright, R.N.: A practical differentially private random decision tree classifier. Trans. Data Priv. **5**(1), 273–295 (2012)
19. Kolesnikov, V., Mohassel, P., Rosulek, M.: FleXOR: flexible garbling for XOR Gates that beats free-XOR. In: Garay, J.A., Gennaro, R. (eds.) CRYPTO 2014 Part II. LNCS, vol. 8617, pp. 440–457. Springer, Heidelberg (2014). doi:10.1007/978-3-662-44381-1_25
20. Kolesnikov, V., Schneider, T.: Improved garbled circuit: free XOR gates and applications. In: Aceto, L., Damgård, I., Goldberg, L.A., Halldórsson, M.M., Ingólfsdóttir, A., Walukiewicz, I. (eds.) ICALP 2008 Part II. LNCS, vol. 5126, pp. 486–498. Springer, Heidelberg (2008). doi:10.1007/978-3-540-70583-3_40
21. Kononenko, I.: Machine learning for medical diagnosis: history, state of the art and perspective. Artif. Intell. Med. **23**(1), 89–109 (2001)
22. Lichman, M.: UCI machine learning repository. School of Information and Computer Sciences, University of California, Irvine (2013). http://archive.ics.uci.edu/ml
23. Lindell, Y.: Fast cut-and-choose based protocols for malicious and covert adversaries. In: Canetti, R., Garay, J.A. (eds.) CRYPTO 2013 Part II. LNCS, vol. 8043, pp. 1–17. Springer, Heidelberg (2013). doi:10.1007/978-3-642-40084-1_1
24. Lindell, Y., Pinkas, B.: Privacy Preserving Data Mining. Springer, Heidelberg (2000)
25. Lindell, Y., Pinkas, B.: An efficient protocol for secure two-party computation in the presence of malicious adversaries. J. Cryptol. **28**(2), 312–350 (2015)
26. Mohassel, P., Niksefat, S.: Oblivious decision programs from oblivious transfer: efficient reductions. In: Keromytis, A.D. (ed.) FC 2012. LNCS, vol. 7397, pp. 269–284. Springer, Heidelberg (2012). doi:10.1007/978-3-642-32946-3_20
27. Mohassel, P., Niksefat, S., Sadeghian, S., Sadeghiyan, B.: An efficient protocol for oblivious DFA evaluation and applications. In: Dunkelman, O. (ed.) CT-RSA 2012. LNCS, vol. 7178, pp. 398–415. Springer, Heidelberg (2012). doi:10.1007/978-3-642-27954-6_25
28. Papernot, N., McDaniel, P.D., Sinha, A., Wellman, M.P.: Towards the science of security and privacy in machine learning. CoRR, abs/1611.03814 (2016)
29. Qin, Z., Yan, K. Ren, K., Chen, C.W., Wang, C.: Towards efficient privacy-preserving image feature extraction in cloud computing. In: ACM Multimedia (2014)
30. Sakai, Y., Emura, K., Hanaoka, G., Kawai, Y., Omote, K.: Methods for restricting message space in public-key encryption. IEICE Trans. **96**(6), 156–1168 (2013)
31. Vaidya, J., Kantarcioglu, M., Clifton, C.: Privacy-preserving naïve Bayes classification. VLDB J. **17**(4), 879–898 (2008)

32. Veugen, T.: Improving the DGK comparison protocol. In: WIFS (2012)
33. Wang, Q., He, M., Du, M., Chow, S.S.M., Lai, R.W.F., Zou, Q.: Searchable encryption over feature-rich data. IEEE Trans. Dependable Sec. Comput. (2017)
34. Wright, R.N., Yang, Z.: Privacy-preserving Bayesian network structure computation on distributed heterogeneous data. In: SIGKDD (2004)
35. Wu, D.J., Feng, T., Naehrig, M., Lauter, K.: Privately evaluating decision trees and random forests. PoPETs **4**, 335–355 (2016)

Stringer: Measuring the Importance of Static Data Comparisons to Detect Backdoors and Undocumented Functionality

Sam L. Thomas[✉], Tom Chothia, and Flavio D. Garcia

School of Computer Science, University of Birmingham, Birmingham B15 2TT, UK
{s.l.thomas,t.p.chothia,f.garcia}@cs.bham.ac.uk

Abstract. Finding undocumented functionality in commercial off-the-shelf (COTS) device firmware is an important and challenging task. This paper proposes a new static analysis method that measures the influence individual pieces of static data (such as strings) have upon the control flow of binaries in firmware. Our method automatically identifies static data comparison functions within binaries, then labels each function's basic blocks with the set of sequences of static data that must be matched against to reach them. Then using these sets, it assigns a score to each function, which measures the extent to which the function's branching is influenced by static data. Special keywords triggering backdoor functionality will have a large impact on the program flow. This allows us to identify three authentication backdoors – two of which previously undocumented. Moreover, we show our method is effective in aiding the recovery of both previously known and proprietary text-based protocols. We have developed a tool, `Stringer` which implements our technique; we demonstrate the effectiveness of our approach as well as its applicability to lightweight analysis by running it on a data set of 2,451,532 binaries from 30 different COTS device vendors.

1 Introduction

The current state of commercial off-the-shelf (COTS) embedded device security needs much improvement: from manufacturers deploying outdated, vulnerable software components within device firmware, to so-called *debug* interfaces being *accidentally* enabled within production versions of firmware[1]. Several backdoors, undocumented commands and daemons have been reported[2,3,4,5]. The impact of these malicious or simply bad practices is exacerbated by the sheer number of devices available, with each device potentially having multiple firmware versions.

---

[1] e.g., https://github.com/elvanderb/TCP-32764.

[2] https://ics-cert.us-cert.gov/advisories/ICSA-13-136-01.

[3] https://w00tsec.blogspot.nl/2015/11/arris-cable-modem-has-backdoor-in.html.

[4] http://www.devttys0.com/2013/10/reverse-engineering-a-d-link-backdoor/.

[5] https://www.sec-consult.com/fxdata/seccons/prod/temedia/advisories_txt/2016012
1-0_AMX_Deliberately_hidden_backdoor_account_v10.txt.

© Springer International Publishing AG 2017
S.N. Foley et al. (Eds.): ESORICS 2017, Part II, LNCS 10493, pp. 513–531, 2017.
DOI: 10.1007/978-3-319-66399-9_28

Organizations handling sensitive data or critical infrastructure need a mean to determine the trustworthiness of a device before bringing it into their systems or networks. This work is currently either simply not done or is carried out manually by an expert analyst who dissembles the devices firmware with IDA Pro or similar tools. This is a very costly process that does not scale. Moreover, because the evaluation is so expensive and it needs to be done for each firmware version, it has the negative effect of motivating corporations to not update the device's firmware, leaving them exposed to known security vulnerabilities.

This work aims to reduce the effort of manual analysis by automating the identification of *interesting* code structures and functions within binaries from Linux-based embedded device firmware. This analysis is performed in a lightweight, scalable manner and is thus applicable to processing large collections of binaries from both device firmware and commodity hardware.

We say that a section of code is *interesting* when it exhibits unexpected behaviour. This behaviour is generally triggered when certain conditions are met – such as on the input of a *special* keyword. The code executed as a result of successful comparison with a *special* keyword is often not accessible by any other means, and is thus, uniquely *guarded* by that keyword.

This work automates much of the process of identifying functions that may contain functionality that is guarded by such keywords. Our method first automatically identifies the static data comparison functions within a binary. Following this, for each function we contruct the sets of sequences of static data that must be successfully compared against to reach each basic block within said function. We then use these sets to compute a score, which provides a measure of how much of a function's conditional processing is dependent on comparisons with static data.

We show that using our methods, we are able to find three backdoors, which manifest as hard-coded credential checks. In addition, we are able to demonstrate the recovery of both a known text-based protocol and a previously unknown proprietary protocol. In the case of text-based protocols, our method allows a human analyst with knowledge of known protocols to first isolate the function responsible for parsing the protocol and then identify superfluous (which are often indicative of additional, undocumented functionality) protocol messages with relative ease compared to manual analysis with tools such as IDA Pro, `strings` or `grep`.

1.1 Our Contribution

This paper proposes a method for lightweight large-scale static analysis of commodity embedded device firmware. We implement our techniques in a tool `Stringer`, which we use to demonstrate the effectiveness of our methods through identification of three backdoors, which we later present as case-studies in Sect. 5.2. Concretely, the overall contributions of this paper are:

- A set of heuristics for automatically identifying static data comparison functions.

- A metric for measuring the degree a binary's functions branching is influenced by comparisons with static data.
- The result of applying `Stringer` to a set of 7,590 firmware images, which exposes a number of backdoors. Additionally, we demonstrate how our methods can automatically identify static data processing routines. Specifically:
  - We demonstrate the recovery of the full FTP command set handled by a variant of `vsftpd` from Linksys firmware and the recovery of the SOAP-based RPC command set from a Netgear firmware's web-server.
  - We identify two previously undiscovered authentication backdoors relying on hard-coded credentials: one in a Q-See DVR and the other in a TRENDnet router.
  - We identify a third (previously reported) backdoor in firmware from Ray Sharp.

1.2 Related Work

Cojocar et al. [6] explore the notion of a function-level metric to discover general parsing routines; they employ a fully automated approach in a similar manner to that proposed by this work; it is however, unclear of the applicability of their metric for use on a large-scale. Further, their metric relies on purely discrete counts of particular code features as opposed to more complex properties as utilised in our metric. McCabe [13] defines so-called cyclomatic complexity as a metric for computing the complexity of control flow graph (CFG); it quantifies the number of linearly independent paths through the CFG – and is hence a reasonable estimate of the branching complexity within a given CFG.

While the field of program analysis is mature, adapting traditional techniques to embedded devices is relatively new and challenging. Zaddach et al. [19], propose a framework, Avatar, for performing semi-automated dynamic analysis upon embedded device firmware. This is done through insertion of a minimal debugger stub into the firmware itself – and hence, requires physical access to the device. A hybrid approach is taken to the dynamic analysis – relying on S^2E [5] and KLEE [3], where execution is performed both on commodity hardware through emulation and symbolic execution and in a *standard* manner upon the device itself. Similarly, FIE [11] by Davidson, et al., is a symbolic execution engine based upon KLEE, which is geared towards finding vulnerabilities in embedded microcontrollers. FIRMADYNE [4] is a framework by Chen et al. that like Avatar, allows for dynamic analysis via emulation of embedded device firmware; In contrast to Avatar, it does this in a completely automated manner without the need for physical access to the hardware under analysis, at the cost of only being able to analyse Linux-based firmware. Subramanyan et al. [17] also use symbolic execution, in this case to verify the information flow properties of firmware. Firmalice [16], provides a means of identifying authentication bypass vulnerabilities, or backdoors, within device firmware, again by use of a symbolic execution engine; their techniques are however not practical for lightweight, large-scale use due to the inherent performance limitations imposed by symbolic execution (taking between 12 to 705 min to complete on the examples presented – which were binaries of moderate complexity). Pewny et al. [14] propose a means of identification of bugs and vulnerabilities across different architectures and apply their technique to identify a previously known software backdoor amongst a number of firmware images from various differing vendors. Schuster and Holz [15] attempt to identify potentially malicious, or anomalous code-paths in binaries on a number of architectures, including those from embedded device firmware. Their technique relies on dynamically interacting with the binary in order to explore the effect of sending specific protocol messages; thus, relies on prior knowledge of the protocol used within the binary. Thomas et al. [18] use a hybrid approach of machine and a domain specific language to identify anomalous behaviour (including backdoors) in binaries from embedded device firmware. Both [8,9] rovide a large-scale analysis of consumer embedded device firmware, which in the former case identified a number of known vulnerabilities within firmware; whilst the latter applies particular focus to web-frontend based vulnerabilities, the former is a more general, high-level analysis.

All of [2,7,10,12] propose methods for automatic protocol reverse-engineering. Although it is not the primary goal of our method, Stringer is able to extract text-based protocol messages in a lightweight, semi-automated manner.

2   Methodology

For a given binary, our method works as follows:

1. First we identify all possible static data comparison functions.
2. Then we label the basic blocks of all functions with the sets of static data sequences that must be matched against to reach them.
3. Then using the computed sets, we calculate a score for each element of static data.
4. Finally, using the scores for each item of static data we compute a score for each function.

While one approach to identifying static data comparison functions might rely on the symbol names of imported functions and look for references such as strcmp or strncmp, many binaries in firmware have their symbols stripped. Furthermore, in the case of statically linked binaries, there is no list of imported functions to extract such information. We therefore have developed a means to automatically identify static data comparison functions which overcomes both of these problems. We do this by looking for function calls where at least one of the arguments passed is static data and the result of the function call influences control flow. Following this we rank the functions based on how they are used overall within the binary – such as the properties of the arguments they are passed and the number of arguments they are passed; Sect. 3 provides the complete details.

Once the static data comparison functions have been identified, we label the basic blocks of each function within the binary with a set of static data sequences. These sets dictate the sequences of static data that must be matched to reach that block. Then we calculate a score for each static data item based on how it influences the branching within the function. Finally we calculate a score for each function based on the scores assigned to the static data.

The score assigned to a function is dependent on the scores assigned to its static data. This score is used to impose an ordering of functions where those that score highly are those which contain complex decision logic that is dependent on comparisons with static data. In general, functions that implement protocol handling or contain parsing functionality are scored the highest. Further analysis of the static data and corresponding scores of those functions enables us to identify additional, undocumented functionality and (possible) backdoor functionality.

For the proof of concept tool we have developed, Stringer, we leverage components of BAP [1] and IDA Pro[6] in order to perform analysis upon concrete binaries. We rely on a number of useful components provided by BAP; in particular, the IL (intermediate language) it uses: BIL, its code-lifting components and the extensive set of algorithms implemented for handling graphs.

2.1 Notation

In this section we outline the notation used for the remainder of the paper. We denote an arbitrary binary as B where B is the set of its functions, denoted as $f \in B$. f_{blocks} defines the set of basic blocks for a function f. For a given block b, b_{addr} denotes the entry address of the block and b_{insns} denotes the sequence of lifted (BIL) instructions of b. $succs(b)$ and $preds(b)$ compute the set of successor and predecessor blocks of a block b.

We use the abstract notion of "sections" to denote regions of program memory that have particular properties. We assume three basic sections exist: $section_{data}$ which corresponds to the section holding data that can both be read and written and $section_{rodata}$ which corresponds to the section with constant, read-only data; we use $section_*$ to denote the union of the other two sections.

We use the notation m_k where m is a map to evaluate to the value corresponding to the key k within m. $m_k \leftarrow v$ associates the value v with the key k within m.

3   Heuristics for Identifying Static Data Comparisons

In general, COTS Linux-based firmware images contain binaries that use a mixture of static and dynamic linking to call external library routines (such as the C standard library). Additionally, both Linux-based binaries and standalone firmware images (which in themselves can be seen as a homogeneous binary) are often devoid of symbol names. Therefore, it is both unreliable and restrictive

---

[6] https://www.hex-rays.com/products/ida/.

to rely on symbol names to indicate functions used for static data comparison. To remedy this, we propose a collection of heuristics which together are able to reliably identify static data comparison functions, based on their usage within a binary. We list below the properties we expect calls to potential static data comparisons to have.

Argument References. At least one function argument is either a pointer or a direct reference to either read-only program memory, or the initialised data section. From our analysis, those arguments are generally unique in functions that perform a substantial amount of static data processing.

Function Arity. A comparison is made between at least two items, therefore the arity, or number of rguments to a data comparison function should be at least two.

Branching Properties. From observation, the result of a call to a data comparison function generally influences a branching condition. Thus, one of the variables influencing the branch should be tainted by the return value of said comparison function. Further, a literal value of 0 should be compared against in the branching condition – which, in a boolean (i.e. matched/not matched) context represents *true* or *false*.

Local Call Frequency. We observe that data processing routines such as protocol parsers generally utilise the same comparison function many times with different static data arguments as opposed to different comparison functions for each element of static data to be compared against. Therefore, we should score functions used in this way relatively highly.

Data Properties. From our analysis of binaries, where comparison functions are used in protocol or message–based parsing routines we see that the static data is contained within either $section_{rodata}$ or $section_{data}$ and it is generally an ASCII-based, NUL terminated string. The string itself also satisfies certain properties:

- It does not contain any characters (or combination of characters) that are indicative of a format string. Concretely, we scan the string for the '%' character followed by common format directives such as 'd', 's', etc.
- It does not contain certain whitespace characters other than new line, line feed and space, such as: tab ('\t'), vertical tab ('\v'), etc. or those characters that are used as control characters.

3.1   An Algorithm for Finding Static Data Comparisons

We now outline our algorithm for identifying static data comparison functions. For each function in the binary, we identify all blocks that contain function calls. Of those function calls, we filter out those that don't influence branching conditions where that condition is a comparison against 0. Of the remaining function calls, we analyse the arguments passed. For those arguments we define two cases: the ideal case and a "catch-all" se.

The ideal case occurs when the function invocation involves at least two arguments where one of those is a reference to static data that conforms to the properties outlined in Sect. 3. In addition to those constraints upon the data references, at least two of the arguments should not be register-based constants such as integers or floating point numbers (that are not also address references to $section_*$). We impose this restriction as we expect a comparison to make two references to data – one static, the other dynamic. The general "catch-all" case occurs when at least two of the arguments identified do not reference constant data.

The result of applying our algorithm is a set of comparison functions along with a score representing the likelihood that that function is a comparison function.

```
 1: function COMPUTEHEURISTICSCORES(ς, δ, μ₊, α₋, α∗, B)
 2:     ν ← {}
 3:     for each f ∈ B do
 4:         ν' ← {}
 5:         for each b ∈ {b | b ∈ f_blocks ∧ branchesOnCall(b) ∧ branchesOnZCmp(b)} do
 6:             args_data ← ∅, args_rodata ← ∅, args_other ← ∅
 7:             for each arg ∈ dependentArgs(b, 3) do
 8:                 if arg ∈ section_rodata then
 9:                     arg_rodata ← arg_rodata ∪ {arg}
10:                 else if arg ∈ section_data then
11:                     arg_data ← arg_data ∪ {arg}
12:                 else if arg ∉ section∗ then
13:                     arg_other ← arg_other ∪ {arg}
14:                 end if
15:             end for
16:             addr ← f_addr
17:             if |arg_rodata| + |arg_data| + |arg_other| ≥ 2 ∧ containsIdealSD(args) then
18:                 ν'_addr ← ν'_addr + ς
19:             else if |arg_data| + |arg∗| ≥ 2 then
20:                 ν'_addr ← ν'_addr + δ · ς
21:             end if
22:         end for
23:         ν ← mergeScores(ν, applyRewards(applyPenalties(ν', α₋, α∗), μ₊))
24:     end for
25:     return ν
26: end function
```

Fig. 1. Algorithm to compute heuristic scores

We use the notation ν_{addr} to represent the heuristic score for the function with entry point at address $addr$. ς represents the value to increase ν_{addr} by when a block satisfying the ideal case is encountered. When the ideal case is not encountered, we use a multiplier δ to scale ς such that $0 < \delta \leq 1$ prior to incrementing.

After processing the function f, local scores for each possible data comparison function are merged into a global map of scores. Prior to this merge, we apply two modifiers as *rewards* and *penalties*: we scale up the score of the suspected static data comparison function with the highest number of call-site occurrences within f by a constant μ_+, where $\mu_+ \geq 1$ (local call frequency), we scale down the score of every function h that references the same static data multiple times by α_-, where $0 < \alpha_- \leq 1$ (argument references). We apply further scaling of α_- by α_* which is raised to the number of non-unique data references n, used as arguments to h. That is, if h has the address h_{addr}, $h_{addr} \leftarrow h_{addr} \cdot \alpha_- \cdot \alpha_*^n$.

The algorithm in Fig. 1 outlines the computation performed to calculate the heuristic scores for all possible comparison functions within B. For brevity, the algorithm makes reference to a number of functions: $containsIdealSD$ which evaluates to $true$ if at least one of the expressions in the set passed as an argument satisfy the aforementioned data constraints; $branchesOnCall$ evaluates to $true$ if any variable in the conditional expression of the block is tainted by the last function invocation within the block; $branchesOnZCmp$ evaluates to $true$ if the conditional expression of the block depends on a comparison with 0 (or a semantically equivalent boolean comparison); deg_{in}/deg_{out} evaluate to the number of incoming/outgoing edges from the block; $dependentCall$ evaluates to the function that would cause $branchesOnCall$ to evaluate to $true$; $dependentArgs$ evaluates to a map of at most n expressions that correspond the arguments passed to the function call that $dependentCall$ evaluates to. $applyPenalties$ and $applyRewards$ perform the previously outlined score modifications. While $mergeScores$ merges the locally computed scores (on a function-level basis) into the global map of scores. For each function, we use a $local$ map, ν' to store the computed values for that function prior to merging into μ. In our implementation, the variables are assigned values based on small-scale experiments; in all cases (50 binaries) the C standard string comparison functions are identified.

4   A Metric for Scoring the Importance of Code

This section defines our metric that is used to determine the degree to which a given piece of static data influences the execution of a function. Our metric provides:

- A means to discover those branches within each function that are dependent upon static data and assign them and the associated static data a score of relative importance in relation to other such branches within that function based upon how much unique functionality they guard.
- A function-level score that signifies which functions contain a relatively high density of decision logic that depends on comparison with static data (i.e. a large amount of their decision logic is influenced by comparison with static data).

4.1   Requirements of the Metric

Our metric's goal is to score functions that contain decision logic that depends upon static data comparisons where that static data tends to uniquely isolate functionality within a function highly.

We assign a score to a given element of static data depending on how it isolates functionality within a function's CFG – if the only way to reach part of the CFG is via successful comparison with an item of static data, that static data shall score highly. The scores for each piece of static data are computed based on the successor blocks following the use of that static data as an argument to a comparison function.

Within CFGs there are a number of possibilities how to propagate values; we base those on observations of basic block properties:

Number of Incident Blocks. A block that has many incident edges can be considered a *join-point*, that is its functionality is of less importance to the functionality of a single isolated code path as it is reachable by many paths throughout the function. Thus, the influence that such a block should have upon its predecessor blocks should be distributed relative to the number of incident edges (i.e. $deg_{in}(b)$).

Branches as "guards" of Functionality. We associate the code of successor blocks with the branch that is *guarded* by the branch condition evaluating to *true*. For any given static data comparison, the degree it divides the overall CFG along the branch which is followed when the comparison is *true* is a general indicator of the importance of that string comparison. The static data which guards large amounts of functionality should have a higher score than that that does not. Applying this directly to a scoring metric however would cause those comparisons that happen first within the CFG to be assigned significantly higher scores than those that happen later. A notion of dependence and a means to be able to diminish the value of that dependence in a manner proportional to the distance along the path of static data comparisons required to reach a given point within the CFG should overcome this.

4.2   Definition of the Metric

The calculation of our metric is performed as a two stage process: we first construct sets of static data sequences at each block within the CFG; then using these computed sets we perform a single pass over all blocks within the CFG and assign a score to each branching block that contains a comparison with static data.

The computed static data sequence set for a block represents all possible positive static data comparisons taken to reach that block. For instance in Fig. 2, if we consider both nodes 1 and 2 static data comparisons where the branches from $1 \rightarrow 2$ and $2 \rightarrow 3$ are taken if the comparisons at 1 and 2 evaluate to *true*. Then the sets we compute are as in Fig. 3. We use the notation s_i to represent the static data compared against at node i.

We compute the sets by using the algorithm in Fig. 4; it is applied to each block until the computed static data sequences reach a fixpoint. The notation $+\!\!+$ is used to denote the concatenation operator on sequences, $branchData(b)$ computes the static data compared to at block b, $branchesOnStaticData(b)$ evaluates to *true* if the block b's branching is dependent upon a comparison

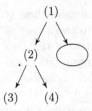

Label	Computed string sequence set
1	$\{[]\}$
2	$\{[s_1]\}$
3	$\{[s_2, s_1]\}$
4	$\{[s_1]\}$

Fig. 2. Example CFG with static data comparisons

Fig. 3. Computed string sequence sets for Fig. 2

with static data. Loops are ignored when determining if a fixpoint is reached; this ensures termination and avoids the construction of sequences with repeated sub-sequences.

In COMPUTESDS(B), if after iterating over all of $preds(b)$, b_s is equivalent to $\emptyset$, then we set b_s to $\{[]\}$. This represents there is no known path to reach b that is dependent upon successful comparison with static data.

We compute the scores for each block using the algorithm in Fig. 5. In our implementation, the function to compute basic block

```
1: function COMPUTESDS(b)
2:     for each p ∈ preds(b) do
3:         if branchesOnStaticData(p) then
4:             s_p ← branchData(p)
5:             b_s ← b_s ∪ {S_i ⧺ s_p|S_i ∈ p_s}
6:         else
7:             b_s ← b_s ∪ p_s
8:         end if
9:     end for
10:    if b_s = ∅ then
11:        b_s ← {[]}
12:    end if
13: end function
```

Fig. 4. Algorithm to compute static data sequences

complexity ($\omega(b)$) evaluates to $|b_{insns}|$ – the number of lifted (BIL) instructions within the block. The algorithm takes each previously computed static data sequence and computes a score for each block that is associated with a static data comparison. For each block, we take the set of static data sequences S and update the score of each element of static data found within those sequences. The final result is a map of static data and corresponding scores.

For each block, the computation is approached in two sub-phases: the first constructs a mapping of static data to the number of times said element of static data s occurs within the sequences within the set of static data sequences. This count is used to determine a scaling factor which is a fraction of the total number of sequences and the count of those that s is present in. This value is representative of how much the reachability of a given block depends upon successful comparison with a given element of static data: if the static data *has* to be matched to reach the block then the fraction shall be equivalent to 1. Following this, for each element of static data within the previously discussed map, we compute the sum of the base score assigned to the block (computed by $\omega(b)$) scaled by the mentioned scaling factors and the current score assigned.

```
 1: function COMPUTESCORES(ω, f)
 2:     M ← {}
 3:     for each b ∈ f_blocks do
 4:         S ← b_S, baseScore ← ω(b), numChains ← |S|, countMap ← {}
 5:         for each S_i ∈ S do
 6:             for each s ∈ S_i do
 7:                 countMap_s ← countMap_s + 1
 8:             end for
 9:         end for
10:         for each s ∈ countMap do
11:             occScale ← countMap_s / numChains
12:             M_s ← M_s + baseScore × ln(1 + occScale × 1/deg_in(b))
13:         end for
14:     end for
15:     return M
16: end function
```

Fig. 5. Algorithm to compute scores

An additional scaling factor is also computed which is equivalent to the inverse of the number of incident edges to the block: i.e. $\frac{1}{deg_{in}(b)}$.

The previous two phases compute a block-level score. We define the *importance* of a function as the sum of scores assigned to each element of static data. This allows us to identify functions where decision logic is largely influenced by comparisons with static data.

5   Results

We have implemented the aforementioned heuristics and metric within our tool, Stringer which automates the entire analysis process: firmware acquisition, unpacking and report generation. In this section we discuss the outcomes of running our tool upon a firmware collection totalling 7,590 successfully unpacked firmware images, equating to 2,451,532 individual binaries.

5.1   Experiment Methodology

While Stringer automates the majority of the analysis process, a degree of manual intervention is required to discern the most *interesting* binaries from the processed data-set.

First we use a web and FTP crawler to download 15,438 firmware images from 30 different vendors. For each firmware image downloaded, we attempt to extract its filesystem using existing tools: binwalk, sasquash and jefferson. Our resulting data-set consists of 7,590 successfully unpacked firmware images. With the resulting filesystems, we search for binaries and each of the 2,451,532 binaries are passed to Stringer, which generates a report for each.

Then we perform semi-automated analysis of the generated reports. We attempt to discover routines handling common protocols; for this we devise some simple models of what static data we expect to be grouped together within a single function. For instance, for a web-server we expect the terms GET and POST and possibly, PUT, HEAD and DELETE. Additional static data found within these routines is further analysed manually. In addition to this, we use grep to search the reports for *interesting*, "low-hanging fruit" by searching for terms such as admin, Administrator and root. Our report format details the highest scoring functions along with the associated static data, which is tagged with the score it contributes to the overall score for the function.

Once an interesting binary is identified, we perform manual analysis using IDA Pro. The standard manual analysis process is aided by the fact the functions and strings of interest are available from the generated reports and so anomalous functionality such as backdoors or undocumented commands can quickly be checked for, and confirmed.

Due to the modest amount of backdoors publically available that are both present in embedded device firmware and also backdoors that are of the class that can be detected by Stringer, calculating the FP rate of our technique is infeasible.

5.2   Case-Studies

Due to the large amount of binaries processed as part of the analysis, we present a selection of case-studies. Each case-study follows a similar form: we first present the scores and ranking of possible comparison functions as computed by application of our heuristics. Then we present *interesting* functions identified by application of our metric.

5.2.1   Identification of the FTP Command Set

The vsftpd FTP server, shared amongst numerous Linksys device firmware images provides a clear example of the effectiveness of our approach. The binary analysed, contains a total of 600 functions, uses static linking and is stripped of symbol information. Our heuristic identifies 44 potential comparison functions; those ranked highest are: sub_10814 (394.84), sub_1622C (35.00), sub_10754 (27.20), and sub_139FC (12.20). As vsftpd is open-source software, we are able to discover that sub_10814 corresponds to the function str_equal_text – a string equality check for the vsftpd's custom string implementation.

The metric finds the highest ranking function to be the main protocol parsing routine: sub_C4F0 which is assigned a score of 942.08 (and corresponds to process_post_login). The FTP command set handled by vsftpd is extensive; we therefore omit the specific output of the tool and associated CFG due to its size.

The metric scores for sub_C4F0 group the protocol messages; the uniformity that is apparent reflects the implementation of the state-machine used to handle connections. That is, following matching the input with a protocol message; a secondary function is called which handles further processing of the input or the functionality of a specific command. The group of highest scoring protocol messages (HELP, ...) have scores of 16.00, while the lowest (such as PROT) score

8.03. The largest group of commands with uniform scores of 10.00 contains the core command set (STOR, RETR, PASV, PORT, LIST, QUIT, . . .).

5.2.2   Hard-Coded Credential Backdoor #1

In a number of firmware images for QSee DVR products, Stringer identifies numerous hard-coded credentials – to the best of our knowledge, this backdoor is previously undiscovered – which provide differing levels of access to the device. The binary used for this case study, td3520 contains a total of 15, 669 functions and is statically linked. The heuristics identify a possible 911 comparison functions, those that are ranked highest are: strcmp (1464.70), strncmp (779.33), CRYPTO_malloc (685.10) (from the statically linked OpenSSL library), _ZNKSs7compareEPKc (C++'s string equality operator) (376.20), strstr (306.00) and strcasecmp (196.00). All but one of those functions is a static data comparison function; a single false positive, CRYPTO_malloc is identified due to its usage patterns being almost identical to that of an expected comparison function.

We identify the third highest ranked function by our metric as _ZN9CLoginDl-g5LogInEPKcS1_b (scoring 421.38) which contains a hard-coded credential checking routine. Figure 6 shows the scores and sets of static data sequences of the static data extracted from that function, while Fig. 7 shows the simplified CFG with static data labelled using those in Fig. 6.

Label	Score	Static Data	Function	Depends
1	171.39	admin	strcmp	{[]}
2	58.92	ppttzz51shezhi	strcmp	{[admin]}
3	45.13	6036logo	strcmp	{[admin]}
4	42.14	6036adws	strcmp	{[admin]}
5	37.54	6036huanyuan	strcmp	{[admin]}
6	35.21	6036market	strcmp	{[admin]}
7	31.05	jiamijiami6036	strcmp	{[admin]}

Fig. 6. Scores for _ZN9CLoginDlg5LogInEPKcS1_b

We observe that successor nodes that are dependent on the highest ranked static data (admin) follow from the left branch of the comparison node. All other static data comparisons are dependent upon a successful comparison with admin. The static data ranked as second most important isolates most unique functionality relative to the other identified static data (in this case that past the node labelled with a +: this is the functionality associated with a successful login with administrative credentials.

This binary was first located by searching through the reports generated by Stringer for common privileged usernames: namely, admin; verification of the backdoor was performed manually using IDA Pro.

5.2.3 Hard-Coded Credential Backdoor #2

`Stringer` also finds a hard-coded credential check within firmware from Ray Sharp – a popular CCTV DVR vendor. The binary containing the backdoor, `raysharp_dvr` contains a total of 7,605 functions, is dynamically linked and stripped of local symbol names. The heuristics reveal the highest ranked comparison functions to be those from the C standard library: `strcmp` (ranked highest) (5170.30), `strncmp` (1109.73), `strstr` (353.93) and `memcmp` (222.00). Additionally, `sub_1C7EC` (1351.96) is ranked second – which from manual analysis with IDA Pro is identified as a wrapper around `strcmp`.

The functions our metric scores highest consist of complex parsing routines – indicated by their relatively high scores compared to other *interesting* functions identified. `sub_60118` contains the functionality responsible for the backdoor. Figure 9 details the CFG of the function along with the scores assigned to the username and password combination and Fig. 8 shows the scores as assigned by the metric as well as computed static data sequence sets. Figure 10 shows an IDA Pro CFG snippet of the backdoor.

This binary was identified by searching the logs for common usernames that are associated with privileged user accounts: in this case, `root`.

A posteriori research online shows that (in contrast to the other case studies) this discovery was not original. The backdoor has been previously documented[7] and is present in a multitude of devices from many vendors: Swann, Lorex, URMET, KGuard, Defender, DEAPA/DSP Cop, SVAT, Zmodo, BCS, Bolide, EyeForce, Atlantis, Protectron, Greatek, Soyo, Hi-View, Cosmos, and J2000.

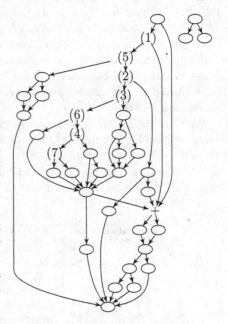

Fig. 7.   CFG   for `_ZN9CLoginDlg5LogInEPKcS1_b`

5.2.4 Additional Functionality Within Standard Protocols

In the bundled web-server found within the firmware of a number of TRENDnet devices, `Stringer` identifies a hard-coded credential

Label	Score	Static Data	Function	Depends
1	30.23	664225	strcmp	{[]}
2	2.77	root	strcmp	{[664225]}

Fig. 8. Scores for `sub_60118`

---
[7] https://community.rapid7.com/community/metasploit/blog/2013/01/28/ray-sharp-cctv-dvr-password-retrieval-remote-root.

pair within the routine handling basic HTTP authentication. The comparisons are performed via standard string comparison (strcmp) – which is ranked by the heuristic as the most likely static data comparison function. It identifies 40 such functions out of a total of 391 functions within the entire binary. strcmp is ranked highest by a large margin with a score of 1635.01, followed by strstr (481.20), nvram_get (413.10), strncmp (265.45) and sub_A2D0 (131.00). sub_A2D0 provides a wrapper around hsearch_r – a lookup function for hash tables, evaluating to 0 on failure. Both nvram_get and sub_A2D0 may be regarded as false-positives: the former provides a lookup of the embedded devices NVRAM (Non-Volatile RAM – an area on the device usually used for storing configuration that can persist across device restarts).

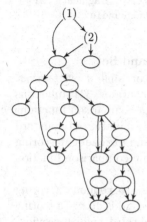
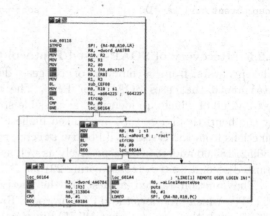

Fig. 9. Ray Sharp hard-coded credential check

Fig. 10. IDA Pro CFG snippet of the Ray Sharp backdoor

The additional functionality is embedded within the eighth highest scoring function – sub_B958, with a score of 827.99. Whilst validating the credentials for HTTP basic authentication, an additional code path checks for the hard-coded username/password pair: emptyuserrrrrrrrrrrr and emptypassworddddddddd both via strcmp, which score 106.00 and 103.47, respectively and rank as the second and fourth most important strings. The most important string is the string comparison to detect if basic authentication is being used and scores 151.84. We omit a diagrammatic representation of the CFG due to space considerations.

This binary was located by matching the logs against the common authentication header strings used in HTTP authentication. To the best of our knowledge, the hard-coded credentials have not been previously documented. Again, manual analysis was performed using IDA Pro.

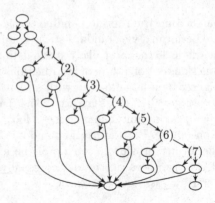

Label	Score	Static Data
1	7.64	EnableTrafficMeter
2	7.64	SetTrafficMeterOptions
3	7.64	SetGuestAccessEnabled
4	7.64	SetGuestAccessEnabled2
5	7.64	SetGuestAccessNetwork
6	7.64	SetWLANNoSecurity
7	7.64	SetWLANWPAPSKByPassphrase

Fig. 11. Selection of static data from soap_parent_ctrl_handle

Fig. 12. CFG fragment for soap_parent_ctrl_handle

5.2.5 Recovery of SOAP-based Protocol Command Set

The firmware from a number of Netgear devices contains a web-server, mini_httpd that uses SOAP[8] for RPC. The binary contains 331 functions in total, 60 of which are identified as possible static data comparison functions by the heuristic. Those that are ranked highest are a combination of standard functions from the C standard library: strcmp, strstr and strcasecmp scoring 380.52, 185.00 and 184.00, respectively as well as a custom comparison function (ranked second): safestrcmp scoring 221.00.

The function ranked highest by the metric is handle_request (scoring 952.91) – which processes the HTTP protocol. Ranked second is do_file scoring 486.47, while the *main* (scoring 449.55) function is ranked third – which provides argument parsing for the binary. soap_parent_ctrl_handle is assigned a score of 328.75 and is ranked fourth; it handles the processing of the SOAP command set. This function exemplifies the effectiveness of Stringer in extracting protocol command sets that are previously unknown to the analyst. The scores assigned to individual command strings within the function are uniform. Figure 12 is a fragment of the CFG for soap_parent_ctrl_handle and Fig. 11 contains the scores of the static data present in that fragment.

The command set was discovered by searching logs for web-server related protocol strings, in this case: GET. This string existed (amongst other HTTP commands) in the higher scoring function handle_request; soap_parent_ctrl_handle was located by looking at other high ranking functions within the binary.

5.3 Performance

On average a firmware image contains a total of 379 binaries; with each binary taking 1.31 s to process. Larger binaries, with a greater number of functions or larger CFGs take considerably longer; though, the performance is still acceptable

---

[8] https://www.w3.org/TR/soap12/.

for large scale analysis. As a concrete example, the binary td3520 (Sect. 5.2.2) which contains 15,669 functions, took 46.043 s. A significant portion of the total runtime for Stringer is due to the invocation of IDA Pro to export data required for CFG recovery. The total time taken to invoke IDA takes on average 11.26% of the total execution time. Processing this data takes on average 0.63% of the total time. The remainder of the time is due to computation of the heuristic and metric scores.

5.4   Comparison with Naïve Techniques

The techniques we have shown improve upon existing techniques for identification of interesting static data. Past work has used a combination of linux functions strings, to extract stings from binaries, and grep, to find interesting terms, or more advanced processing methods such as using IDA Pro with IDAPython to export static data coupled with function names with further processing performed using grep. Neither of these existing tool combinations provide any indication of the importance of a given piece of static data in relation to any other. Furthermore, neither provide a means of ranking the importance of functions in relation to how much of their conditional processing is influenced by static data. The lack of both of these properties limit the effectiveness of these methods, meaning that a large amount of manual analysis, and some luck are required when analysing large pieces of firmware. Moreover, these techniques only scale to locate functionality based upon *known* protocols or easily recognisable strings.

6   Conclusion

We have presented a novel approach to identify static data comparison functions within binaries, which when combined with our function-level scoring metric, as demonstrated, is effective in discovering undocumented functionality and recovery of text-based protocol messages and commands. In the case of the former, we have identified a three instances of authentication backdoors in commodity firmware images from a number of vendors. Our approach is shown to be suitable for large-scale analysis – with methods presented for reducing the effort required by a human analyst processing the resulting data. With our technique we are able to isolate functions of interest ranking them within the first tens of functions as opposed to an analyst having to trawl through potentially thousands of functions. A concrete example of this is from our case-study in Sect. 5.2.2, whereby the most interesting function for an analyst is ranked as third most important out of 15, 669 functions.

Our approach improves on existing large-scale analysis methods upon embedded device firmware by performing more complex static analysis – that considers the control-flow properties of code – as opposed to propagating known bitstring patterns over the data-set. Moreover, we introduce a new means of identifying potential functionality for binary analysis – which is applicable beyond binaries within embedded device firmware.

References

1. Brumley, D., Jager, I., Avgerinos, T., Schwartz, E.J.: BAP: a binary analysis platform. In: Gopalakrishnan, G., Qadeer, S. (eds.) CAV 2011. LNCS, vol. 6806, pp. 463–469. Springer, Heidelberg (2011). doi:10.1007/978-3-642-22110-1_37
2. Caballero, J., Yin, H., Liang, Z., Song, D.: Polyglot: automatic extraction of protocol message format using dynamic binary analysis. In: Proceedings of the 14th ACM Conference on Computer and Communications Security, CCS 2007. ACM (2007)
3. Cadar, C., Dunbar, D., Engler, D.: KLEE: unassisted and automatic generation of high-coverage tests for complex systems programs. In: Proceedings of the 8th USENIX Conference on Operating Systems Design and Implementation, OSDI 2008. USENIX Association (2008)
4. Chen, D.D., Egele, M., Woo, M., Brumley, D.: Towards automated dynamic analysis for Linux-based embedded firmware. In: Network and Distributed System Security (NDSS) Symposium, NDSS 2016 (2016)
5. Chipounov, V., Kuznetsov, V., Candea, G.: S2E: a platform for in-vivo multipath analysis of software systems. In: Proceedings of the Sixteenth International Conference on Architectural Support for Programming Languages and Operating Systems, ASPLOS XVI. ACM (2011)
6. Cojocar, L., Zaddach, J., Verdult, R., Bos, H., Francillon, A., Balzarotti, D.: PIE: parser identification in embedded systems. In: Proceedings of the 31st Annual Computer Security Applications Conference. ACM (2015)
7. Comparetti, P.M., Wondracek, G., Kruegel, C., Kirda, E.: Prospex: protocol specification extraction. In: 2009 IEEE Symposium on Security and Privacy (2009)
8. Costin, A., Zaddach, J., Francillon, A., Balzarotti, D.: A large-scale analysis of the security of embedded firmwares. In: 23rd USENIX Security Symposium, USENIX Security 2014 (2014)
9. Costin, A., Zarras, A., Francillon, A.: Automated dynamic firmware analysis at scale: a case study on embedded web interfaces. In: 11th ACM Asia Conference on Computer and Communications Security (AsiaCCS), ASIACCS 2016 (2016)
10. Cui, W., Peinado, M., Chen, K., Wang, H.J., Irun-Briz, L.: Tupni: automatic reverse engineering of input formats. In: Proceedings of the 15th ACM Conference on Computer and Communications Security, CCS 2008. ACM (2008)
11. Davidson, D., Moench, B., Ristenpart, T., Jha, S.: Fie on firmware: finding vulnerabilities in embedded systems using symbolic execution. In: 22nd USENIX Security Symposium (USENIX Security 2013) (2013).
12. Lin, Z., Jiang, X., Xu, D., Zhang, X.: Automatic protocol format reverse engineering through context-aware monitored execution. In: NDSS 2008 (2008)
13. McCabe, T.J.: A complexity measure. IEEE Trans. Softw. Eng. **2**, 308–320 (1976)
14. Pewny, J., Garmany, B., Gawlik, R., Rossow, C., Holz, T.: Cross-architecture bug search in binary executables. In: 2015 IEEE Symposium on Security and Privacy (2015)
15. Schuster, F., Holz, T.: Towards reducing the attack surface of software backdoors. In: Proceedings of the 2013 ACM SIGSAC Conference on Computer & Communications Security, CCS 2013. ACM (2013)
16. Shoshitaishvili, Y., Wang, R., Hauser, C., Kruegel, C., Vigna, G.: Firmalice - automatic detection of authentication bypass vulnerabilities in binary firmware. In: Network and Distributed System Security (NDSS) Symposium, NDSS 2015 (2015)

17. Subramanyan, P., Malik, S., Khattri, H., Maiti, A., Fung, J.: Verifying information flow properties of firmware using symbolic execution. In: 2016 Design, Automation & Test in Europe Conference & Exhibition (DATE). IEEE (2016)
18. Thomas, S.L., Garcia, F.D., Chothia, T.: HumIDIFy: a tool for hidden functionality detection in firmware. In: Polychronakis, M., Meier, M. (eds.) Detection of Intrusions and Malware, and Vulnerability Assessment, pp. 279–300. Springer, Cham (2017). doi:10.1007/978-3-319-60876-1_13
19. Zaddach, J., Bruno, L., Francillon, A., Balzarotti, D.: Avatar: a framework to support dynamic security analysis of embedded systems' firmwares. In: Network and Distributed System Security (NDSS) Symposium, NDSS 2014 (2014)

Generic Constructions for Fully Secure Revocable Attribute-Based Encryption

Kotoko Yamada[1,2]([✉]), Nuttapong Attrapadung[2], Keita Emura[3], Goichiro Hanaoka[2], and Keisuke Tanaka[1]

[1] Tokyo Institute of Technology, Tokyo, Japan
yamada3@is.titech.ac.jp
[2] National Institute of Advanced Industrial Science and Technology (AIST), Tokyo, Japan
[3] National Institute of Information and Communications Technology (NICT), Tokyo, Japan

Abstract. Attribute-based encryption (ABE) is a cryptographic primitive that realizes fine-grained access control. Due to its attractive functionality, several systems based on ABE have been widely constructed so far. In such cryptographic systems, revocation functionality is indispensable in practice to handle withdrawal of users, secret key exposure, and others. While many ABE schemes with various functionalities have been proposed, only a few of these are revocable ABE (RABE). In this paper, we propose two generic constructions of RABE from ABE. Our first construction employs the pair encoding framework (Attrapadung, EUROCRYPT 2014), and combines identity-based revocation and ABE via the generic conjunctive conversion of Attrapadung and Yamada (CT-RSA 2015). Our second construction directly converts ABE to RABE when ABE supports Boolean formulae. Since our constructions preserve functionalities of the underlying ABE, we can instantiate various fully secure RABE schemes for the first time, e.g., supporting regular languages, with unbounded attribute size and policy structure, and with constant-size ciphertext and secret key.

1 Introduction

Cryptographic primitives are widely employed for constructing a secure system, and attribute-based encryption (ABE), introduced by Sahai and Waters [27], is one of the most popular cryptographic primitives for constructing secure systems due to its high affinity to flexible access control. An encryptor specifies ciphertext attributes, and a user can decrypt a ciphertext only when his/her attributes match the decryption policy.

When users enroll the system they generate or are issued cryptographic keys such as a decryption key or a signing key. Thus, towards constructing a secure system and its long-term usage, a functionality of key revocation is quite important and indispensable to deal with withdrawal of users from the system,

© Springer International Publishing AG 2017
S.N. Foley et al. (Eds.): ESORICS 2017, Part II, LNCS 10493, pp. 532–551, 2017.
DOI: 10.1007/978-3-319-66399-9_29

key exposure, and others. Especially, in ABE-based systems, it is non-trivial to revoke specific users since the users may share common attributes.

To handle revocation in the ABE context, *revocable ABE* (RABE) has been proposed [5,6] where a user secret key is associated with not only attributes but also an identity. An encryptor specifies a set of identities of revoked users in addition to ciphertext attributes, and a user can decrypt a ciphertext only when his/her attributes match the decryption policy *and* he/she is not specified in the revoked user list. As an encryptor directly specifies the revoked set, this type of RABE is called *direct revocation*. Another flavor called *indirect revocation* has also been proposed [5,10,28], where the revocation mechanism is indirectly enabled via key update (required to be done by all non-revoked users). In this paper, we focus on the *direct* flavor, where the key update is not required.

Currently, "non-revocable" ordinary ABEs with various functionalities have been widely constructed, e.g., key-policy (KP), ciphertext-policy (CP), supporting regular languages [2,31], with unbounded attribute size and policy structure [2,22,26], and with constant-size ciphertext or secret key [1,2,4,8]. Moreover, a generic framework for constructing fully secure ABEs called the pair encoding framework [2] has been proposed. Since the framework yields fully secure ABEs with various functionalities, methodologies to realize a fully secure ABE scheme have been (not completely but significantly) clarified.

However, in contrast to ordinary ABEs, currently just a few RABE schemes have been proposed [5,6,13,14,20,30], and all of them except [14,20] provide only selective security, which is a weaker security model than the full security. Moreover, all of them are *specific* constructions, i.e., they are based on algebraic structures according to each functionality to be focused in each paper. One obvious disadvantage of specific approaches is that the designing process would be inefficient: RABE has to be designed anew each time one by one to match desired functionalities. To construct RABE schemes with various functionalities, it is thus desirable to propose a *generic* construction of RABE from ABE in such a way that it preserves the functionalities of the underlying ABE.

1.1   Our Contributions

Generic Constructions. We propose two generic constructions of RABE from ABE. Both have different kinds of generality and complement each other. The first construction, C_1, is generic in the sense that it can deal with ABE for *any predicate*, while the construction must reside in the pair encoding framework [2, 3]. On the other hand, the second construction, C_2, is generic in the sense that it is applicable to *any construction* of ABE not necessarily in the pair encoding framework, albeit confined to only predicates that imply Boolean formulae.

Implied Instantiations. Since our constructions preserve functionalities of the underlying ABE, we can instantiate several fully secure RABE schemes *for the first time* including:

- KP, CP-RABE supporting regular languages
- KP, CP-RABE with unbounded attribute size and policy structure

- KP, CP-RABE with constant-size ciphertext
- KP, CP-RABE with constant-size secret key

Moreover, our constructions cover fully secure KP, CP-RABE from simple assumptions as in [14]. We give more detailed comparisons in Sect. 5.

1.2 Our Approaches

Basic Idea of Construction C_1. As mentioned above, in RABE, an encryptor specifies not only attributes but also a set of revoked user's identities. Our observation is that the latter functionality resembles that of identity-based revocation (IBR) [7,21]. Hence, *conjunctively* combining ABE and IBR to construct RABE would be a natural idea. However, straightforward combinations, such as double encryption, would amount to collusion attacks. To this end, we utilize the generic conjunctive conversion of [9], which allows to conjunctively combine any two ABE schemes, albeit in the pair encoding framework, securely. Therefore, the input to the conversion C_1 is any ABE in such a framework.

On the other hand, to the best of our knowledge, no IBR described within the pair encoding framework has been proposed so far. Thus, we newly propose such IBRs. To achieve flexibility, we provide at least three IBR schemes: one is specific, and the other two are generic. Their properties diverse: basically, the first achieves constant-size ciphertext but allows only bounded number of revoked users, the latter ones allow unbounded number of revoked users in some instantiations. These properties will be inherited to the resulting RABE.

The first IBR we provide is that of Attrapadung et al. [8]. We show that their scheme can be described in the pair encoding framework with required security.

The second and third IBR are based on the combinatorial methods proposed in [23] called Complete-Subtree (CS) and Subset-Difference (SD), respectively. Both schemes have different advantages in key and ciphertext sizes (see Sects. 3.2 and 4.2). These schemes are originally symmetric-key schemes [23], and are converted to public-key variants (and can be considered as IBR) by Dodis and Fazio [15], who employ identity-based encryption (IBE) [11,29] and hierarchical IBE (HIBE) [17,19] for the CS and SD schemes respectively. Their IBRs are known to be fully secure when the underlying IBE or HIBE is fully secure. However, when casting their schemes as pair encodings (as required by the conjunctive conversion), we found that the security of pair encoding representing IBE to that of the CS-based IBR *does not preserve*, and similarly for that of HIBE to the SD-based IBR. Concretely, we can show attacks against the CS-based IBR scheme and the SD-based IBR scheme if they are constructed from IBE and HIBE respectively. We will show these attacks in the full version of this paper due to the page limitation.

To overcome this problem, for the CS-based scheme, instead of using IBE as in [15], we employ ABE that covers Boolean formulae. As for the SD-based scheme, instead of using HIBE as in [15], we employ ABE for "prefix predicate". The latter is a new primitive and we show that it is implied by key-policy doubly spatial encryption (KP-DSE) [2].

Basic Idea of Construction C_2. Though the pair encoding framework covers various ABEs, some are still left out, such as DLIN-based ABEs by Okamoto and Takashima [24, 25]. Our second generic construction allows to convert any ABEs which support Boolean formulae into RABE for also Boolean formulae. The original ABE is not required to fit the pair encoding framework.

Our observation is that RABE is the conjunctive (AND) between ABE and IBR; therefore, we thus connect the original policy in ABE to the policy which represents revocation (for IBR) by AND. To be able to do so, both ABE/IBR must hence support Boolean formulae. The latter policy can be obtained exactly by our representation of the CS method using ABE as in the scheme C_1.

2 Preliminary

In this section we define some notations and cryptographic primitives.

Notations. If $\mathcal{A}$ is a probabilistic polynomial time (PPT) algorithm, $y \leftarrow \mathcal{A}(x)$ denotes assigning y to the output of $\mathcal{A}$ on an input x. If $\mathcal{S}$ is a finite set, $x \xleftarrow{\$} \mathcal{S}$ denotes that x is chosen uniformly at random from $\mathcal{S}$, and $2^{\mathcal{S}}$ denotes power set of $\mathcal{S}$. $O^{a \times b}$ denotes a $a \times b$ zero matrix, and E^a denotes a $a \times a$ identity matrix.

Tree Structures. We assume a full binary tree $\mathcal{T}$ of depth ℓ. Let $\mathbb{L}_{\mathcal{T}}$ be a set of all nodes in $\mathcal{T}$. Each node is described by a string in $\{0,1\}^{\leq \ell}$. The root node is the starting node denoted by the empty string ε, and the children of root node are 0 and 1. For a node v, the left and the right children are denoted by $v\|0$ and $v\|1$ respectively. For each node $v \in \mathbb{L}_{\mathcal{T}}$, the sibling node $\mathsf{Sibling}(v)$ is the node which shares the parent node with v. For a node v in the tree $\mathcal{T}$, let $\mathsf{Path}(v)$ be the set of nodes on the path from the root node to v, $\mathsf{Parent}(v)$ be the parent node of v, and $\mathsf{Leaves}(v)$ be the node set of leaves in the subtree whose root node is v. For nodes $v, w \in \mathbb{L}_{\mathcal{T}}$, $\mathsf{path}(v, w)$ denotes the path from v to w.

2.1 Revocable Attribute Based Encryption

In this section, we define the syntax of revocable attribute-based encryption (RABE). Since RABE can be defined as ABE for specific predicate, first we define the syntax of ABE, and the syntax of RABE will be obtained. The same can be said for the security definition, but due to limited space, we refer the (standard) definition of full security of ABE to [2].

Predicate Family [2]. We consider a predicate family $\mathsf{R} = \{\mathsf{R}_{\kappa}\}_{\kappa \in \mathbb{N}^c}$, for some constant $c \in \mathbb{N}$. A relation $\mathsf{R}_{\kappa} : \mathbb{X}_{\kappa} \times \mathbb{Y}_{\kappa} \to \{0,1\}$ is a predicate function which maps a pair of key attribute in a space $\mathbb{X}_{\kappa}$ and ciphertext attribute in a space $\mathbb{Y}_{\kappa}$ to $\{0,1\}$. The index $\kappa = (n_1, n_2, \ldots)$ specifies description of a predicate from the family. Some parameters in κ specify the bounds on attribute universe, policy structure or attribute size. When those are unbounded, we denote that by "-". We will often omit κ for simplicity.

Attribute Based Encryption (ABE). An ABE scheme for predicate family R consists of four algorithms (Setup, KeyGen, Encrypt, Decrypt).

Setup: The setup algorithm takes as input a security parameter 1^λ and a family index κ of predicate family R, and outputs a master public key PK and a master secret key MSK.

KeyGen: The key generation algorithm takes as input a key attribute $X \in \mathbb{X}_\kappa$ and the master secret key MSK, and outputs a secret key SK.

Encrypt: The encryption algorithm takes as input a ciphertext attribute $Y \in \mathbb{Y}_\kappa$, a message $M \in \mathcal{M}$ and a public key PK where $\mathcal{M}$ is a message space, and outputs a ciphertext CT.

Decrypt: The decryption algorithm takes as input a ciphertext CT and a secret key SK, and outputs a message M or $\bot$.

Correctness. For all indexes κ, all $M \in \mathcal{M}$, $X \in \mathbb{X}_\kappa$ and $Y \in \mathbb{Y}_\kappa$ such that $R_\kappa(X, Y) = 1$, if (PK, MSK) $\leftarrow$ Setup($1^\lambda, \kappa$), SK $\leftarrow$ KeyGen(X, MSK, PK) and CT $\leftarrow$ Encrypt(Y, M, PK), then Decrypt(CT, SK) $= M$ holds.

Revocable Attribute-Based Encryption (RABE). Next, we define RABE. As mentioned before, RABE can be defines as ABE for specific predicate. Briefly, in RABE each user has a unique identity ID $\in \mathcal{ID}$ in addition to a key attribute X, and an encryptor specifies a list of revoked users RL in addition to a ciphertext attribute Y. A user can decrypt the ciphertext if both ID $\notin$ RL and $R(X, Y) = 1$ hold. Due to this functionality, RABE for predicate family R can be seen as ABE for the following predicate P_R defined as follows.

- **Parameter:** It is specified by (κ, m, R), where κ is a parameter of the predicate family R, m denotes the size of identity space $\mathcal{ID} = \{0, 1\}^{\log m}$, and R denotes the maximum size of a revocation list RL.
- **Key Attribute:** It is specified by a pair $(X, \text{ID}) \in \mathbb{X} \times \mathcal{ID}$. $X \in \mathbb{X}$ is a key attribute for predicate R, and ID $\in \mathcal{ID}$ is user identity information.
- **Ciphertext Attribute:** It is specified by a pair $(Y, \text{RL}) \in \mathbb{Y} \times 2^{\mathcal{ID}}$, such that $|\text{RL}| \leq R$. $Y \in \mathbb{Y}$ is a ciphertext attribute for predicate R, and RL $\in 2^{\mathcal{ID}}$ is a revoked user set.
- **Predicate:** $P_R((X, \text{ID}), (Y, \text{RL})) = \begin{cases} 1 & \text{if } R(X, Y) = 1 \land \text{ID} \notin \text{RL} \\ 0 & \text{otherwise} \end{cases}$

2.2   Identity Based Revocation and Other Predicates

In our constructions, we employ identity-based revocation (IBR), ABE for Boolean formula and ABE for prefix predicate as its building blocks. As in RABE, these primitives can also be defined as ABE for specific predicate.

Identity Based Revocation (IBR). In IBR, a secret key of each receiver is associated with his identity ID, and the encryptor specifies a list RL of revoked users. A receiver can decrypt the ciphertext and get message iff ID $\notin$ RL. An IBR scheme is an ABE scheme for following predicate I and attributes.

- **Parameter:** It is specified by (m, R), where m denotes the size of identity space $\mathcal{ID}$, and R denotes the maximum size of a revocation list RL.

- **Key Attribute**: It is specified by user identity information $\mathsf{ID} \in \mathcal{ID}$.
- **Ciphertext Attribute**: It is specified by a set $\mathsf{RL} \in 2^{\mathcal{ID}}$ of revoked users, such that $|\mathsf{RL}| \leq R$.
- **Predicate**: $\mathsf{I}(\mathsf{ID}, \mathsf{RL}) = \begin{cases} 1 & \text{if } \mathsf{ID} \notin \mathsf{RL} \\ 0 & \text{otherwise} \end{cases}$

Boolean Formulae Predicate. A KP-ABE scheme for Boolean formulae over a set $\mathcal{U}$ is an ABE scheme for following predicate $\mathsf{R}^{\mathsf{Bool}}$ and attributes.

- **Parameter**: It is specified by (U, K, S, T), where U denotes the size of attribute space $|\mathcal{U}|$, K denotes the maximum length of Boolean formulae, S denotes the maximum size of attribute set and T denotes the maximum number of appearances of the same attribute in a Boolean formula.
- **Key Attribute**: It is specified by a Boolean formula f over $\mathcal{U}$. That is a string in which some elements in $\mathcal{U}$ are connected by "∨" or "∧".
- **Ciphertext Attribute**: It is specified by a set $Y \subset \mathcal{U}$.
- **Predicate**: $\mathsf{R}^{\mathsf{Bool}}(f, Y) = \begin{cases} 1 & \text{if } f|_{\{x=\mathtt{true}|x \in Y\}} = \mathtt{true} \\ 0 & \text{otherwise} \end{cases}$

Note that the predicate of CP-ABE for Boolean formulae can be defined by switching the roles of key attribute and ciphertext attribute.

Prefix Predicate. We introduce new predicate: prefix predicate. We construct IBR from ABE for prefix predicate, and ABE for prefix predicate is implied by key-policy doubly spatial encryption (KP-DSE) [2]. Therefore IBR can be constructed from KP-DSE. We discuss about that in Appendix A. The prefix predicate is defined as follows:

- **Parameter**: It is specified by (N, ℓ, S_1, S_2), where N defines a universe $\mathbb{Z}_N$ of elements in vectors, ℓ denotes the maximum size of vectors, and S_1 and S_2 denote the maximum size of a key attribute set and a ciphertext attribute set respectively.
- **Key Attribute**: It is specified by a set $X \subset \mathbb{Z}_N^{\leq \ell}$.
- **Ciphertext Attribute**: It is specified by a set $Y \subset \mathbb{Z}_N^{\leq \ell}$.
- **Predicate**:
  $\mathsf{R}^{\mathsf{prefix}}(X, Y) = \begin{cases} 1 & \text{if there exist } \boldsymbol{x} \in X \text{ and } \boldsymbol{y} \in Y \text{ s.t. } \boldsymbol{x} \text{ is a prefix of } \boldsymbol{y} \\ 0 & \text{otherwise} \end{cases}$

For example, considering $X = \{(2, 56), (3, 24, 2), (11, 97, 47)\}$ and $Y = \{(2, 56, 7), (8, 5)\}$, we have $\mathsf{R}^{\mathsf{prefix}}(X, Y) = 1$ because $(2, 56) \in X$ is a prefix of $(2, 56, 7) \in Y$.

2.3 Pair Encoding Framework

In this section we recall the pair encoding framework introduced by Attrapadung [2]. We employ this framework in our construction C_1. He introduced pair encoding, and showed that an ABE scheme for predicate family R can be constructed from a pair encoding scheme for predicate family R, and that if the pair encoding scheme satisfies its security notion, the constructed ABE scheme is fully secure. Because the security of pair encoding schemes can be proven more easily than full security of ABE schemes, through this framework, we can construct fully secure ABE schemes more easily than constructing them directly. Though the framework [2] employs composite order bilinear groups, later Attrapadung [3] proposed another pair encoding framework on prime order bilinear groups. Though our generic construction can employ both composite and prime order groups, in this paper we focus on prime order groups due to its efficiency.

Syntax of Pair Encoding Scheme [3]. A pair encoding scheme for predicate family R consists of four deterministic algorithms given by $\mathcal{PE} = (\mathsf{Param}, \mathsf{Enc1}, \mathsf{Enc2}, \mathsf{Pair})$ as follows, where a prime number p denotes the size of the group.

- $\mathsf{Param}(\kappa) \to n$. It takes as input an index κ and outputs an integer n, which specifies the number of common variables in Enc1 and Enc2. For the default notation, let $\boldsymbol{h} = (h_1, \ldots, h_n)$ denote the list of common variables.
- $\mathsf{Enc1}(X) \to (\boldsymbol{k}; m_2)$. It takes as inputs $X \in \mathbb{X}_\kappa$, and outputs a sequence of polynomials $\boldsymbol{k} = \{k_i\}_{i \in [1, m_1]}$ with coefficients in $\mathbb{Z}_p$, and $m_2 \in \mathbb{N}$. We require that each polynomial k_i is a linear combination of monomials $\alpha, r_j, h_k r_j$, where $\alpha, r_1, \ldots, r_{m_2}, h_1, \ldots, h_n$ are variables. Denote $\boldsymbol{r} = (r_1, \ldots, r_{m_2})$.
- $\mathsf{Enc2}(Y) \to (\boldsymbol{c}; w_2)$. It takes as inputs $Y \in \mathbb{Y}_\kappa$, and outputs a sequence of polynomials $\boldsymbol{c} = \{c_i\}_{i \in [1, w_1]}$ with coefficients in $\mathbb{Z}_p$, and $w_2 \in \mathbb{N}$. We require that each polynomial c_i is a linear combination of monomials $s_j, h_k s_j$, where $s_0, s_1, \ldots, s_{w_2}, h_1, \ldots, h_n$ are variables. Denote $\boldsymbol{s} = (s_0, s_1, \ldots, s_{w_2})$.

Correctness. The correctness requirement is defined as follows. Let $(\boldsymbol{k}; m_2) \leftarrow \mathsf{Enc1}(X)$, $(\boldsymbol{c}; w_2) \leftarrow \mathsf{Enc2}(Y)$, and $\boldsymbol{E} \leftarrow \mathsf{Pair}(X, Y)$. We have that if $\mathsf{R}(X, Y) = 1$, then $\boldsymbol{k}\boldsymbol{E}\boldsymbol{c}^\top = \alpha s_0$, where the equality holds symbolically.

Attrapadung [2,3] proposed security notions and another property called regularity of pair encoding. We omit the definition of them due to limitations of space. Refer those papers for detail. Moreover, he constructed ABE $\mathcal{ABE}(\mathcal{PE})$ on prime order groups from pair encoding schemes. We employ this construction in our construction C_1, but it is not described in this paper. Refer [3] for detail. He showed the following lemma.

Lemma 1 (Theorem 4 in [3]). *If $\mathcal{PE}$ is master-key hiding and if the matrix Diffie-Hellman assumption [16] holds in $\mathcal{G}$, then $\mathcal{ABE}(\mathcal{PE})$ is fully secure.*

2.4 Embedding Lemma

In this section, we recall embedding lemma [4,12]. We will show the implication between ABEs or pair encodings through this lemma.

The lemma considers two arbitrary predicate families: $\mathsf{R}_\kappa : \mathbb{X}_\kappa \times \mathbb{Y}_\kappa \to \{0, 1\}$ and $\mathsf{R}'_{\kappa'} : \mathbb{X}'_{\kappa'} \times \mathbb{Y}'_{\kappa'} \to \{0, 1\}$, which are parametrized by $\kappa \in \mathcal{K}$ and $\kappa' \in \mathcal{K}'$ respectively. We say that the embedding relation holds iff there exist three efficient mappings $g_\mathsf{p} : \mathcal{K}' \to \mathcal{K}$, $g_\mathsf{k} : \mathbb{X}'_{\kappa'} \to \mathbb{X}_{g_\mathsf{p}(\kappa')}$ and $f_\mathsf{e} : \mathbb{Y}'_{\kappa'} \to \mathbb{Y}_{g_\mathsf{p}(\kappa')}$, which map parameters, ciphertext attributes and key attributes, respectively, such that for all $X' \in \mathbb{X}'_{\kappa'}, Y' \in \mathbb{Y}'_{\kappa'}$, $\mathsf{R}'_{\kappa'}(X', Y') = 1 \Leftrightarrow \mathsf{R}_{g_\mathsf{p}(\kappa')}(g_\mathsf{k}(X'), f_\mathsf{e}(Y')) = 1$ holds.

Lemma 2 (Embedding lemma [4,12]**).** *Suppose the embedding relation between R_κ and $R'_{\kappa'}$ holds and fully secure ABE scheme for predicate R_κ exists. Then we can construct fully secure ABE scheme for predicate $R'_{\kappa'}$ efficiently.*

For pair encoding schemes, a similar lemma holds but we omit the proof of the lemma due to limitations of space. It can be proven straightforwardly, and we will show it in the full version of this paper.

3   Generic Constructions for RABE

In this section, we give two generic constructions of RABE from ABE. The first generic construction C_1 employs ABE and IBR as building blocks, and both are required to be described with the pair encoding framework. As mentioned before, several ABE schemes with various functionalities can be constructed in the pair encoding framework. We can employ all of them as building blocks of the construction C_1. On the other hand, to the best of our knowledge, no IBR described with the pair encoding framework has been proposed so far. Thus, we newly propose such IBRs in Sect. 4.

Unlike the first construction, in the second generic construction C_2, the underlying ABE is not required to be described in the pair encoding framework. Instead, predicates of the underlying ABE is required to cover Boolean formulae. The construction C_2 allows us to instantiate RABE schemes which are not covered by the construction C_1.

3.1 C_1: RABE Construction from Pair Encoding

In our first generic construction C_1, we construct RABE from ABE and IBR. Precisely, we construct a pair encoding scheme $\mathcal{PE}$ for P_R from a pair encoding scheme $\mathcal{PE}_{abe}$ for R and a pair encoding scheme $\mathcal{PE}_{ibr}$ for I. Note that the pair encoding schemes $\mathcal{PE}_{abe}$ and $\mathcal{PE}_{ibr}$ are extracted from the underlying ABE scheme $\mathcal{ABE}$ and IBR scheme $\mathcal{IBR}$ respectively. Then, we compile $\mathcal{PE}$ into an ABE scheme $C_1(\mathcal{ABE}, \mathcal{IBR})$ for P_R. As mentioned in Sect. 2.1, ABE for P_R is RABE for R.

Remark that if ABE for R and IBR are naively combined, then it does not provide collusion resistance. That is, if two users conspire, whose attributes satisfy R and I respectively, they can decrypt the ciphertext together, even though each of them is not allowed to decrypt it. Thus, we employ the technique proposed by Attrapadung and Yamada [9] which can securely combine pair encoding schemes for providing collusion resistance. Then, a user can decrypt a ciphertext only if its attributes satisfy both R and I. See Theorem 9 in [9] for details.

Our construction C_1 is given as follows.

The Construction C_1. Let $\mathcal{PE}_{abe} = (\mathsf{Param}_{abe}, \mathsf{Enc1}_{abe}, \mathsf{Enc2}_{abe}, \mathsf{Pair}_{abe})$ be a pair encoding scheme for predicate family R, and $\mathcal{PE}_{ibr} = (\mathsf{Param}_{ibr}, \mathsf{Enc1}_{ibr}, \mathsf{Enc2}_{ibr}, \mathsf{Pair}_{ibr})$ be a pair encoding scheme for predicate family I. The pair encoding scheme $\mathcal{PE} = (\mathsf{Param}, \mathsf{Enc1}, \mathsf{Enc2}, \mathsf{Pair})$ for predicate family P_R is as follows:

$\mathsf{Param}(\kappa)$: Run $n_{\mathsf{abe}} \leftarrow \mathsf{Param}_{\mathsf{abe}}(\kappa)$, $n_{\mathsf{ibr}} \leftarrow \mathsf{Param}_{\mathsf{ibr}}(\kappa)$. Output $n := n_{\mathsf{abe}} + n_{\mathsf{ibr}}$.

$\mathsf{Enc1}((X, \mathsf{ID}), N)$: Run $(\boldsymbol{k}_{\mathsf{abe}}; m_2^{\mathsf{abe}}) \leftarrow \mathsf{Enc1}_{\mathsf{abe}}(X, N)$ and $(\boldsymbol{k}_{\mathsf{ibr}}; m_2^{\mathsf{ibr}}) \leftarrow$
$\mathsf{Enc1}_{\mathsf{ibr}}(\mathsf{ID}, N)$. Output $(\boldsymbol{k}; m_2^{\mathsf{abe}} + m_2^{\mathsf{ibr}} + 1)$, where $\boldsymbol{k}$ is defined as follows:
$$\boldsymbol{k}(\alpha, (\boldsymbol{r}_{\mathsf{abe}}, \boldsymbol{r}_{\mathsf{ibr}}, r'), (\boldsymbol{h}_{\mathsf{abe}}, \boldsymbol{h}_{\mathsf{ibr}})) = (\boldsymbol{k}_{\mathsf{abe}}(r', \boldsymbol{r}_{\mathsf{abe}}, \boldsymbol{h}_{\mathsf{abe}}), \boldsymbol{k}_{\mathsf{ibr}}(\alpha - r', \boldsymbol{r}_{\mathsf{ibr}}, \boldsymbol{h}_{\mathsf{ibr}})).$$

$\mathsf{Enc2}((Y, \mathsf{RL}), N)$: Run $(\boldsymbol{c}_{\mathsf{abe}}; w_2^{\mathsf{abe}}) \leftarrow \mathsf{Enc2}_{\mathsf{abe}}(Y, N)$ and $(\boldsymbol{c}_{\mathsf{ibr}}; w_2^{\mathsf{ibr}}) \leftarrow$
$\mathsf{Enc2}_{\mathsf{ibr}}(\mathsf{RL}, N)$. Output $(\boldsymbol{c}; w_2^{\mathsf{abe}} + w_2^{\mathsf{ibr}})$, where $\boldsymbol{c}$ is defined as follows:
$$\boldsymbol{c}((s_0, \boldsymbol{s}_{\mathsf{abe}}, \boldsymbol{s}_{\mathsf{ibr}}), (\boldsymbol{h}_{\mathsf{abe}}, \boldsymbol{h}_{\mathsf{ibr}})) = (\boldsymbol{c}_{\mathsf{abe}}((s_0, \boldsymbol{s}_{\mathsf{abe}}), \boldsymbol{h}_{\mathsf{abe}}), \boldsymbol{c}_{\mathsf{ibr}}((s_0, \boldsymbol{s}_{\mathsf{ibr}}), \boldsymbol{h}_{\mathsf{ibr}})).$$

$\mathsf{Pair}((X, \mathsf{ID}), (Y, \mathsf{RL}), N)$: Run $\boldsymbol{E}_{\mathsf{abe}} \leftarrow \mathsf{Pair}_{\mathsf{abe}}(X, Y, N)$ and $\boldsymbol{E}_{\mathsf{ibr}} \leftarrow$
$\mathsf{Pair}_{\mathsf{ibr}}(\mathsf{ID}, \mathsf{RL}, N)$. Output $\boldsymbol{E} = \begin{pmatrix} \boldsymbol{E}_{\mathsf{abe}} & O^{m_1^{\mathsf{abe}} \times w_1^{\mathsf{ibr}}} \\ O^{m_1^{\mathsf{ibr}} \times w_1^{\mathsf{abe}}} & \boldsymbol{E}_{\mathsf{ibr}} \end{pmatrix}$

The above pair encoding scheme $\mathcal{PE}$ has correctness due to those of $\mathcal{PE}_{\mathsf{abe}}$ and $\mathcal{PE}_{\mathsf{ibr}}$. Intuitively, when the predicate $\mathsf{P_R}$ is satisfied, we have that $\boldsymbol{k}_{\mathsf{abe}} \boldsymbol{E}_{\mathsf{abe}} \boldsymbol{c}_{\mathsf{abe}}^\top = r's_0$ from correctness of $\mathcal{PE}_{\mathsf{abe}}$, and that $\boldsymbol{k}_{\mathsf{ibr}} \boldsymbol{E}_{\mathsf{ibr}} \boldsymbol{c}_{\mathsf{ibr}}^\top = (\alpha - r')s_0$ from correctness of $\mathcal{PE}_{\mathsf{ibr}}$, and we can get αs_0. The following lemma holds from Theorem 9 in [9].

Lemma 3. *If both* $\mathcal{PE}_{\mathsf{abe}}$ *and* $\mathcal{PE}_{\mathsf{ibr}}$ *are master-key hiding, then the above pair encoding scheme* $\mathcal{PE}$ *for predicate family* $\mathsf{P_R}$ *is also master-key hiding.*

Theorem 1. *If pair encoding schemes* $\mathcal{PE}_{\mathsf{abe}}$ *for predicate family* R *and* $\mathcal{PE}_{\mathsf{ibr}}$ *for predicate family* I *are master-key hiding, then the RABE scheme* $\mathsf{C_1}(\mathcal{ABE}, \mathcal{IBR})$ *is fully secure under the matrix Diffie-Hellman assumption* [16].

Proof. From Lemma 3, if $\mathcal{PE}_{\mathsf{abe}}$ and $\mathcal{PE}_{\mathsf{ibr}}$ are master-key hiding, then the pair encoding scheme $\mathcal{PE}$ for predicate family $\mathsf{P_R}$ is master-key hiding. From Lemma 1, the RABE scheme $\mathsf{C_1}(\mathcal{ABE}, \mathcal{IBR})$ compiled from $\mathcal{PE}$ is fully secure under the matrix Diffie-Hellman assumption [16].

3.2 $\mathsf{C_2}$: RABE Construction from ABE for Boolean Formula

Though the pair encoding framework covers various ABEs, it does not cover some desirable ABEs (e.g., ABE which is secure under the DLIN assumption [24,25]). In this section, we propose our second generic construction $\mathsf{C_2}$ that converts any ABE providing Boolean formulae into RABE. We show that ABE for predicate R, which covers Boolean formulae, implies RABE for predicate R. This construction $\mathsf{C_2}$ can employ ABEs which are currently not described by the pair encoding framework, but the predicate is restricted to what covers Boolean formulae. Therefore a tradeoff exists between our constructions $\mathsf{C_1}$ and $\mathsf{C_2}$.

We employ the CS method [23] where each user identity is associated with a leaf node of a tree. First we recall the CS method.

Complete Subtree Method [23]. Let $\mathcal{T}$ be a full binary tree of depth $\log m$, where m is a maximum number of users. Here we give short description of the algorithm of the CS method. Refer precise description to [23].

$\mathsf{CS.Assign}(\mathcal{T}, \mathsf{ID})$: It takes as input the tree $\mathcal{T}$ and a user identity $\mathsf{ID} \in \mathcal{ID}$ and outputs a node set $\mathcal{V}_{\mathsf{ID}} := \mathsf{Path}(\mathsf{ID})$.

CS.Cover($\mathcal{T}$, RL): It takes as input the tree $\mathcal{T}$ and a revoked user list RL and outputs a covering set $\mathcal{W}_{\mathsf{RL}} := \{v \in \mathbb{L}_{\mathcal{T}} | v \notin \mathcal{X} \wedge \mathsf{Parent}(v) \in \mathcal{X}\}$, where $\mathcal{X} := \bigcup_{w \in \mathcal{S}} \mathsf{Path}(w)$.

When $\mathcal{V}_{\mathsf{ID}} \leftarrow$ CS.Assign($\mathcal{T}$, ID) and $\mathcal{W}_{\mathsf{RL}} \leftarrow$ CS.Cover($\mathcal{T}$, RL), then ID $\notin$ RL $\Leftrightarrow$ $\mathcal{V}_{\mathsf{ID}} \cup \mathcal{W}_{\mathsf{RL}} \neq \emptyset$ holds, where $\emptyset$ denotes the empty set. It is known that $|\mathcal{V}_{\mathsf{ID}}| = \log m + 1$ and $|\mathcal{W}_{\mathsf{RL}}| \leq r \log(m/r)$ where $r = |\mathsf{RL}|$. Refer [23] for details. Figures 1 and 2 are example of CS.Assign and CS.Cover where $m = 8$.

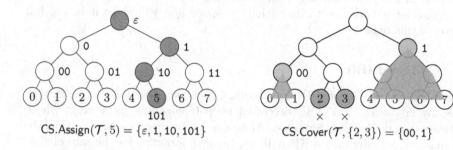

CS.Assign($\mathcal{T}$, 5) = $\{\varepsilon, 1, 10, 101\}$ CS.Cover($\mathcal{T}$, $\{2, 3\}$) = $\{00, 1\}$

Fig. 1. Example of CS.Assign.   **Fig. 2.** Example of CS.Cover.

Although the construction C_2 can employ any ABEs providing Boolean formulae, we consider only a KP-ABE for Boolean formulae for simplicity.

The Construction C_2. Let $\mathcal{ABE}_{\mathsf{Bool}}$ be a KP-ABE scheme for Boolean formula over $\mathcal{U} \cup \mathbb{L}_{\mathcal{T}}$. We construct an RABE scheme $\mathcal{RABE}$ for Boolean formulae over $\mathcal{U}$ by converting its attributes to those of $\mathcal{ABE}_{\mathsf{Bool}}$ as follows:

- **Parameter**: We map $g_{\mathsf{p}}((U, K, S, T), m) = (U + 2m - 1, K + \log m + 1, S + R \log(m/R), T)$. When some parameters are unbounded, the corresponding mapped parameters are also unbounded.
- **Key Attribute**: Consider a Boolean formula f over $\mathcal{U}$ and user identity ID. Run $\mathcal{V}_{\mathsf{ID}} = \{v_1, v_2, \ldots, v_{|\mathcal{V}_{\mathsf{ID}}|}\} \leftarrow$ CS.Assign($\mathcal{T}$, ID), and let $f_{\mathsf{ID}} = v_1 \vee v_2 \vee \cdots \vee v_{|\mathcal{V}_{\mathsf{ID}}|}$. We map $g_{\mathsf{k}}(f, \mathsf{ID}) = f \wedge f_{\mathsf{ID}}$.
- **Ciphertext Attribute**: Consider a set S and a revocation list RL. We map $g_{\mathsf{e}}(S, \mathsf{RL}) = S \cup \mathcal{W}_{\mathsf{RL}}$, where $\mathcal{W}_{\mathsf{RL}} \leftarrow$ CS.Assign($\mathcal{T}$, RL).

Theorem 2. *If an ABE scheme $\mathcal{ABE}_{\mathsf{Bool}}$ is fully secure, then the above RABE scheme $\mathcal{RABE}$ is also fully secure.*

Proof. The following holds and then the theorem follows the embedding lemma.

$$P_{\mathsf{R^{Bool}}}((f, \mathsf{ID}), (S, \mathsf{RL})) = 1 \Leftrightarrow f|_{\{x = \mathsf{true} | x \in S\}} = \mathsf{true} \wedge \mathsf{ID} \notin \mathsf{RL}$$
$$\Leftrightarrow f|_{\{x = \mathsf{true} | x \in S\}} = \mathsf{true} \wedge \mathcal{V}_{\mathsf{ID}} \cap \mathcal{W}_{\mathsf{RL}} \neq \emptyset$$
$$\Leftrightarrow f|_{\{x = \mathsf{true} | x \in S\}} = \mathsf{true} \wedge f_{\mathsf{ID}}|_{\{v = \mathsf{true} | v \in \mathcal{W}_{\mathsf{RL}}\}} = \mathsf{true}$$
$$\Leftrightarrow (f \wedge f_{\mathsf{ID}})|_{x = \mathsf{true} | x \in S \cup \mathcal{W}_{\mathsf{RL}}} \Leftrightarrow \mathsf{R}^{\mathsf{Bool}}(g_{\mathsf{k}}(f, \mathsf{ID}), g_{\mathsf{e}}(S, \mathsf{RL})) = 1.$$

4   IBR Schemes for Construction C_1

In this section, we propose IBR constructions in the pair encoding framework. First, we give a CS-based IBR construction which can be instantiated by employing ABE described by pair encoding framework, whose predicate covers Boolean formulae. Next, we give a SD-based IBR construction which can be instantiated by employing ABE for prefix predicate, which is described by the pair encoding framework. Although we also show that the ALP-IBR scheme [8] can be described in the pair encoding framework with required security, we omit the description of it here due to limitations of space and will show it in the full version of this paper.

4.1   CS-Based IBR

First, we give a CS-based IBR construction. This construction can be instantiated by employing any ABE described by pair encoding framework, whose predicate covers Boolean formulae. Although many predicates cover Boolean formulae, we consider only a KP-ABE for Boolean formulae for the sake of simplicity. We employ CS method which we mentioned in Sect. 3.2.

Our CS-Based IBR. Let $\mathcal{PE}_{\mathsf{Bool}}$ be a pair encoding scheme for predicate family $\mathsf{R}^{\mathsf{Bool}}$. We construct a pair encoding scheme $\mathcal{PE}$ for predicate family I by converting its attributes to those of $\mathcal{PE}_{\mathsf{Bool}}$ as follows:

- **Parameter:** We map $g_\mathsf{p}(m, R) = (2m, \log m, R, 1)$. Here we assume $\mathcal{U} = \{0, 1\}^{\log m}$. When m or R is unbounded, the corresponding mapped parameters are also unbounded.
- **Key Attribute:** Consider an user identity $\mathsf{ID} \in \mathcal{ID}$. Run $\mathcal{V}_{\mathsf{ID}} = \{v_1, v_2, \ldots, v_{|\mathcal{V}_{\mathsf{ID}}|}\} \leftarrow \mathsf{CS.Assign}(\mathcal{T}, \mathsf{ID})$, and let $f_{\mathsf{ID}} = v_1 \vee v_2 \vee \cdots \vee v_{|\mathcal{V}_{\mathsf{ID}}|}$. We map $g_\mathsf{k}(\mathsf{ID}) = f_{\mathsf{ID}}$.
- **Ciphertext Attribute:** Consider a revocation list RL. We map $g_\mathsf{e}(\mathsf{RL}) = \mathcal{W}_{\mathsf{RL}}$, where $\mathcal{W}_{\mathsf{RL}} \leftarrow \mathsf{CS.Assign}(\mathcal{T}, \mathsf{RL})$.

The security of $\mathcal{PE}$ preserves that of $\mathcal{PE}_{\mathsf{Bool}}$. This is followed by the following lemma and the embedding lemma for pair encoding schemes.

Lemma 4. *For all* ID *and* RL, $\mathsf{I}_\kappa(\mathsf{ID}, \mathsf{RL}) = 1 \Leftrightarrow \mathsf{R}^{\mathsf{Bool}}_{g_\mathsf{p}(\kappa)}(g_\mathsf{k}(\mathsf{ID}), g_\mathsf{e}(\mathsf{RL})) = 1$.

Proof. Here we omit the parameters κ and $g_\mathsf{p}(\kappa)$ for the sake of simplicity.

$$\mathsf{I}(\mathsf{ID}, \mathsf{RL}) = 1 \Leftrightarrow \mathsf{ID} \notin \mathsf{RL} \Leftrightarrow \mathcal{V}_{\mathsf{ID}} \cap \mathcal{W}_{\mathsf{RL}} \neq \emptyset$$
$$\Leftrightarrow f_{\mathsf{ID}}|_{\{v = \mathsf{true} | v \in \mathcal{W}_{\mathsf{RL}}\}} = \mathsf{true} \Leftrightarrow \mathsf{R}^{\mathsf{Bool}}(g_\mathsf{k}(\mathsf{ID}), g_\mathsf{e}(\mathsf{RL})) = 1.$$

4.2 SD-Based IBR

Next, we give a SD-based IBR construction which can be instantiated by employing ABE for prefix predicate which described by a pair encoding scheme. In this construction, we employ the SD method [23] where each user identity is associated with a leaf node of a tree.

Subset Difference Method [23]. Let $\mathcal{T}$ be a full binary tree of depth $\log m$, where m is a maximum number of users. Here we give short description of the algorithm of SD method. Refer precise description to [23].

SD.Assign($\mathcal{T}$, ID): It takes as input the tree $\mathcal{T}$ and a user identity ID and outputs a set $\mathcal{V}_{\text{ID}} := \{(v_i, v_j) \in \mathbb{L}_{\mathcal{T}} \times \mathbb{L}_{\mathcal{T}} \mid \text{Sibling}(v_j) \in \text{Path}(\text{ID}) \wedge v_i \in \text{Path}(v_j).\}$.

SD.Cover($\mathcal{T}$, RL): It takes as input the tree $\mathcal{T}$ and a revoked user list RL and outputs a covering set $\mathcal{W}_{\text{RL}} := \{(v_i, v_j) \in \mathbb{L}_{\mathcal{T}} \times \mathbb{L}_{\mathcal{T}} \mid v_i \in \text{Path}(v_j) \wedge \text{Leaves}(v_j) \subset \text{RL} \wedge \text{Leaves}(v_i) \setminus \text{Leaves}(v_j) \subset \mathcal{ID} \setminus \text{RL}\}$

When $\mathcal{V}_{\text{ID}} \leftarrow \text{SD.Assign}(\mathcal{T}, \text{ID})$ and $\mathcal{W}_{\text{RL}} \leftarrow \text{SD.Cover}(\mathcal{T}, \text{RL})$, then ID $\notin$ RL holds iff there exist $v_i, v_j, v_{j'}$ which satisfies both of following two conditions:

1. $(v_i, v_j) \in \mathcal{V}_{\text{ID}}$ and $(v_i, v_{j'}) \in \mathcal{W}_{\text{RL}}$
2. The path from v_i to v_j is a prefix of the path from v_i to $v_{j'}$.

It is known that $|\mathcal{V}_{\text{ID}}| \leq \log^2 m$ and $|\mathcal{W}_{\text{RL}}| \leq 2r - 1$ where $r = |\text{RL}|$. Refer [23] for details. Figures 3 and 4 show examples of SD.Assign and SD.Cover where $m = 16$. As $12 \notin \text{RL}$, we observe that there exists $(1, 10)$ from SD.Assign($\mathcal{T}, 12$) that is a prefix of $(1, 10, 101) = \text{path}(1, 101)$ from SD.Cover($\mathcal{T}, \text{RL}$).

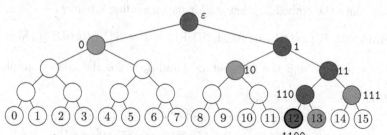

SD.Assign($\mathcal{T}, 12$) $= \{(\varepsilon, 0), (\varepsilon, 1, 10), (\varepsilon, 1, 11, 111), (\varepsilon, 1, 11, 110, 1101), (1, 10), (1, 11, 111),$
$(1, 11, 110, 1101), (11, 111), (11, 110, 1101), (110, 1101)\}$

Fig. 3. Example of SD.Assign.

Our SD-Based IBR. We employ ABE for the prefix predicate which is implied by KP-DSE [2]. See Appendix A for details.

Let $\mathcal{PE}_{\text{prefix}}$ be a pair encoding scheme for prefix predicate R^{prefix}. We construct a pair encoding scheme $\mathcal{PE}$ for predicate I by converting its attributes to those of $\mathcal{PE}_{\text{prefix}}$ as follows. Let $H : \mathbb{L}_{\mathcal{T}} \rightarrow \mathbb{Z}_N$ be a bijective function.[1]

---

[1] A collision-resistant hash also suffices, but Lemma 5 would hold computationally.

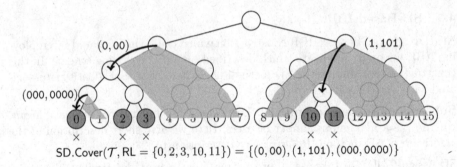

$$\mathsf{SD.Cover}(\mathcal{T}, \mathsf{RL} = \{0, 2, 3, 10, 11\}) = \{(0, 00), (1, 101), (000, 0000)\}$$

Fig. 4. Example of SD.Cover.

- **Parameter**: we map $g_p(m, R) = (N, \log m + 1, \frac{1}{2}(\log^2 m + \log m), 2R - 1)$. When m or R is unbounded, the corresponding mapped parameters are also unbounded.
- **Key Attribute**: Consider a user identity ID. Run $\mathcal{V}_{\mathsf{ID}} \leftarrow \mathsf{SD.Assign}(\mathcal{T}, \mathsf{ID})$, and define $X_{\mathsf{ID}} = \{(H(v_1), \ldots, H(v_k)) \in \mathbb{Z}_N^{\leq \log m} | (v_1, v_k) \in \mathcal{V}_{\mathsf{ID}} \wedge \mathsf{path}(v_1, v_k) = (v_1, \ldots v_k)\}$. We map $g_k(\mathsf{ID}) = X_{\mathsf{ID}}$.
- **Ciphertext Attribute**: Consider a revocation list RL. Run $\mathcal{W}_{\mathsf{RL}} \leftarrow \mathsf{SD.Cover}(\mathcal{T}, \mathsf{RL})$, and define $Y_{\mathsf{RL}} = \{(H(v_1), \ldots, H(v_k)) \in \mathbb{Z}_N^{\leq \log m} | (v_1, v_k) \in \mathcal{W}_{\mathsf{RL}} \wedge \mathsf{path}(v_1, v_k) = (v_1, \ldots v_k)\}$. We map $g_e(\mathsf{RL}) = Y_{\mathsf{RL}}$.

The security of $\mathcal{PE}$ preserves that of $\mathcal{PE}_{\mathsf{prefix}}$. This is followed by the following lemma and the embedding lemma for pair encoding schemes.

Lemma 5. *For all* ID *and* RL, $\mathsf{I}_\kappa(\mathsf{ID}, \mathsf{RL}) = 1 \Leftrightarrow \mathsf{R}_{g_p(\kappa)}^{\mathsf{prefix}}(g_k(\mathsf{ID}), g_e(\mathsf{RL})) = 1$.

Proof. Here we omit the parameters κ and $g_p(\kappa)$ for the sake of simplicity.

$\mathsf{I}(\mathsf{ID}, \mathsf{RL}) = 1 \Leftrightarrow \mathsf{ID} \notin \mathsf{RL}$

$\Leftrightarrow$ There exist v, w and w' such that $(v, w) \in \mathcal{V}_{\mathsf{ID}}$, $(v, w') \in \mathcal{W}_{\mathsf{RL}}$ and the $\mathsf{path}(v, w)$ is a prefix of $\mathsf{path}(v, w')$.

$\Leftrightarrow$ There exist $\boldsymbol{x} \in X_{\mathsf{ID}}$ and $\boldsymbol{y} \in Y_{\mathsf{RL}}$ such that $\boldsymbol{x}$ is a prefix of $\boldsymbol{y}$.

$\Leftrightarrow \mathsf{R}^{\mathsf{prefix}}(X_{\mathsf{ID}}, Y_{\mathsf{RL}}) = 1 \Leftrightarrow \mathsf{R}^{\mathsf{prefix}}(g_k(\mathsf{ID}), g_e(\mathsf{RL})) = 1$.

5   Instantiation and Comparison

In this section, we describe various RABE instantiations obtained by applying our conversions to existing ABE or pair encoding schemes. $\mathsf{C}_1(\mathcal{X}, \mathcal{Y})$ is an RABE scheme for predicate R obtained by applying the C_1 conversion to an ABE scheme $\mathcal{X}$ (for predicate R) and an IBR scheme $\mathcal{Y}$. Any IBR $\mathcal{Y}$ from Sect. 4 can be used. We denote $\mathsf{CS}(\mathcal{A})$ as the CS-based IBR scheme via an ABE scheme $\mathcal{A}$ (see Sect. 4.1) and $\mathsf{SD}(\mathcal{A})$ as the SD-based IBR scheme via ABE for prefix predicate that is then constructed from a KP-DSE scheme $\mathcal{A}$ (see Sect. 4.2 and Appendix A). $C_2(\mathcal{X})$ is an RABE scheme for Boolean formula predicate obtained by applying the C_2 conversion to an ABE $\mathcal{X}$ (for also Boolean formula predicate). Existing schemes will be specified by its reference (*e.g.*, A14 for [2]) and its number in that reference. Note that the schemes in [2] are constructed on composite order groups, but we instantiate those as schemes on prime order groups by employing the pair encoding framework on prime order groups [3].

For $C_1(\mathcal{X}, \mathcal{Y})$, the sizes of keys and ciphertexts will be approximately the sum of those of $\mathcal{X}$ and $\mathcal{Y}$. For $C_2(\mathcal{X})$, key and ciphertext *attribute sizes* increase additively from those of $\mathcal{X}$ approximately by $O(\log m)$ and $O(r \log (m/r))$, respectively, where we recall that m is the size of identity space $\mathcal{ID}$ and r is the size of the revocation list RL. The increase of the corresponding key and ciphertext *sizes* will be different for each scheme (since some scheme admits constant ciphertext *size* even when the ciphertext *attribute size* increases). We list each scheme below; their efficiencies are shown in Table 1.[2, 3]

RABE for Regular Language. We obtain RABE for regular language predicate by applying the C_1 conversion to ABE A14-3 and A14-7 [2] (for regular language), respectively for KP and CP type.[4] Since the original ABEs have constant size public key, when we use IBR with constant size public key, namely, CS(A14-4) and SD(A14-6), the constant-size-public-key property will preserve. If we use IBR with constant size ciphertexts, namely ALP-IBR, no overhead for ciphertext size will be required besides that of the original ABE. We obtain the following KP-RABE (Scheme 1, 1′, 1″) and CP-RABE (Scheme 2, 2′, 2″).

Scheme 1 $C_1(\text{A14-3}, \text{CS}(\text{A14-4}))$	**Scheme 2** $C_1(\text{A14-7}, \text{CS}(\text{A14-4}))$
Scheme 1′ $C_1(\text{A14-3}, \text{SD}(\text{A14-6}))$	**Scheme 2′** $C_1(\text{A14-7}, \text{SD}(\text{A14-6}))$
Scheme 1″ $C_1(\text{A14-3}, \text{ALP-IBR})$	**Scheme 2″** $C_1(\text{A14-7}, \text{ALP-IBR})$

RABE with Constant Size Ciphertexts. We obtain RABE with constant size ciphertexts (for Boolean formula/monotone span program) by applying C_1 and C_2 to ABE with constant size ciphertexts: A14-5 [2], AHY15-CP [4], and AC16 [1]. For C_1, in order to preserve the constant-size-ciphertext property to RABE, we choose IBR with constant size ciphertexts: CS(A14-5), ALP-IBR. We obtain the following KP-RABE (Scheme 3, 3′, 3″), CP-RABE (Scheme 4, 4′, 5).

Scheme 3 $C_1(\text{A14-5}, \text{CS}(\text{A14-5}))$	**Scheme 4** $C_1(\text{AHY15-CP}, \text{CS}(\text{A14-5}))$
Scheme 3′ $C_1(\text{A14-5}, \text{ALP-IBR})$	**Scheme 4′** $C_1(\text{AHY15-CP}, \text{ALP-IBR})$
Scheme 3″ $C_2(\text{A14-5})$	**Scheme 5** $C_2(\text{AC16})$

---

[2] Although we use the big-oh notations in Table 1, we remark that almost all the constants behind them are small. Indeed, one of the largest is the public key size of Scheme 10, 11 and that of DDM16 [14], which is around 100 group elements. Other constants are often less than 10. Most amounts can be inferred from a table in [3].

[3] Our results for Boolean formula predicate can be extended to monotone span program (MSP) straightforwardly; we thus list them as MSP (see Appendix A).

[4] We can also apply C_2 to A14-3 and A14-7, because regular languages cover Boolean formula; however, it would be less efficient compared with construction through C_1.

Table 1. Comparison among fully secure RABE schemes

Scheme	Predicate	Unbounded	$|PK|$	$|SK|$	$|CT|$	Assumption
1	KP-RL	-	$O(1)$	$O(\Sigma + \log m)$	$O(w + r\log(m/r))$	mat-DH, EDHE
$1'$	KP-RL	-	$O(1)$	$O(\Sigma + \log^3 m)$	$O(w + r)$	mat-DH, EDHE
$1''$	KP-RL	-	$O(R)$	$O(\Sigma + R)$	$O(w)$	mat-DH, EDHE
2	CP-RL	-	$O(1)$	$O(w + \log m)$	$O(\Sigma + r\log(m/r))$	mat-DH, EDHE
$2'$	CP-RL	-	$O(1)$	$O(w + \log^3 m)$	$O(\Sigma + r)$	mat-DH, EDHE
$2''$	CP-RL	-	$O(R)$	$O(w + R)$	$O(\Sigma)$	mat-DH, EDHE
3	KP-MSP	No	$O(S + R\log(m/R))$	$O(k + \log m)$	$O(1)$	mat-DH, EDHE
$3'$	KP-MSP	No	$O(S + R)$	$O(k + R)$	$O(1)$	mat-DH, EDHE
$3''$	KP-MSP	No	$O(S + R\log(m/R))$	$O(k + \log m)$	$O(1)$	mat-DH, EDHE
4	CP-MSP	No	$O(K^2S^2u + R\log(m/R))$	$O(K^4S^4u^2 + \log m)$	$O(1)$	mat-DH, EDHE
$4'$	CP-MSP	No	$O(K^2S^2u + R)$	$O(K^4S^4u^2 + R)$	$O(1)$	mat-DH, EDHE
5	CP-MSP	No	$O((K + R\log(m/R)) \cdot (L + S + \log m))$	$O((K + R\log(m/R))^2 (S + \log m) + (K + R\log(m/R))L)$	$O(1)$	mat-DH
6	CP-MSP	No	$O(S + \log m)$	$O(1)$	$O(k + r\log(m/r))$	mat-DH, EDHE
$6'$	CP-MSP	No	$O(S + \log m)$	$O(1)$	$O(k + r\log(m/r))$	mat-DH, EDHE
7	KP-MSP	No	$O(K^2S^2u + \log m)$	$O(1)$	$O(K^4S^4u^2 + r\log(m/r))$	mat-DH, EDHE
8	KP-MSP	Yes	$O(1)$	$O(k + \log m)$	$O(s + r\log(m/r))$	mat-DH, EDHE
$8'$	KP-MSP	Yes	$O(1)$	$O(k + \log m)$	$O(s' + r\log(m/r))$	mat-DH, EDHE
$8''$	KP-MSP	Yes	$O(1)$	$O(k + \log^3 m)$	$O(s + r)$	mat-DH, EDHE
9	CP-MSP	Yes	$O(1)$	$O(s + \log m)$	$O(k + r\log(m/r))$	mat-DH, EDHE
$9'$	CP-MSP	Yes	$O(1)$	$O(s + \log m)$	$O(k + r\log(m/r))$	mat-DH, EDHE
$9''$	CP-MSP	Yes	$O(1)$	$O(s + \log^3 m)$	$O(k + r)$	mat-DH, EDHE
10	KP-MSP	No	$O(1)$	$O(k + \log m)$	$O(sT + r\log(m/r))$	DLIN
11	CP-MSP	No	$O(1)$	$O(sT + \log m)$	$O(k + r\log(m/r))$	DLIN
JX11 [20]	KP-MSP	No	$O(S + R\log(m/R))$	$O(k + \log m)$	$O(sT + r\log(m/r))$	Subgroup Decision
DDM16 [14]	KP-MSP	No	$O(1)$	$O(k + \log^2 m)$	$O(sT + r)$	DLIN

- RL is regular language, and MSP is monotone span programs.
- Let $m := |\mathcal{ID}|$, $r := |\mathsf{RL}|$, $R := \max r$.
- In RL, Σ denotes the number of state transition function of the deterministic finite automaton, and w denotes length of the string.
- In MSP, let 2^u be the size of the attribute space, s be the size of the attribute, and k, l be the size of the policy. Let $S := \max s$, $K := \max k$ and $L := \max l$. T denotes the maximum number of the same attribute in the MSP.
- mat-DH means the matrix Diffie Hellman assumption [16], EDHE means the expanded Diffie-Hellman exponent assumption [2], and DLIN means decisional linear assumption.
- Scheme 5 provides only semi-adaptive security.

RABE with Constant Size Secret Keys. We obtain RABE with constant size secret keys through C_1 and C_2 from ABE with constant size secret keys: AY15-5 [9] and AHY15-KP [4]. For C_1, in order to preserve the constant-size-key property to RABE, we choose IBR with constant size secret keys: CS(AY15-5). We obtain the following KP-RABE (Scheme 6, $6'$) and CP-RABE (Scheme 7).

Scheme 6 C_1(AY15-5, CS(AY15-5))   **Scheme 7** C_1(AHY15-KP, CS(AY15-5))
Scheme $6'$ C_2(AY15-5)

Unbounded RABE. We obtain unbounded RABE schemes through C_1 and C_2 from unbounded ABE schemes A14-4 [2] and AY15-3 [9]. Here, "unbounded" means that attribute size and structure of policy is completely unbounded. In C_1, we employ IBR with constant size public key (and with no bound): CS(A14-4), SD(A14-6). The latter requires smaller ciphertext size via the SD method. We obtain the following KP-RABE (Scheme 8, $8'$, $8''$), CP-RABE (Scheme 9, $9'$, $9''$). Comparing to the best available KP-RABE by [14], our Scheme $8''$ has better ciphertext size and has no bound on the number of allowed attribute multi-use in one policy, T, as required in [14], which inherits this limitation from [25].

Scheme 8 $\mathsf{C}_1(\mathsf{A14\text{-}4}, \mathsf{CS}(\mathsf{A14\text{-}4}))$ **Scheme** 9 $\mathsf{C}_1(\mathsf{AY15\text{-}3}, \mathsf{CS}(\mathsf{A14\text{-}4}))$
Scheme 8′ $\mathsf{C}_2(\mathsf{A14\text{-}4})$ **Scheme** 9′ $\mathsf{C}_2(\mathsf{AY15\text{-}3})$
Scheme 8″ $\mathsf{C}_1(\mathsf{A14\text{-}4}, \mathsf{SD}(\mathsf{A14\text{-}6}))$ **Scheme** 9″ $\mathsf{C}_1(\mathsf{AY15\text{-}3}, \mathsf{SD}(\mathsf{A14\text{-}6}))$

RABE under the DLIN Assumption. We obtain RABE schemes through C_2 from OT12-KP and OT12-CP [25], which are secure under the DLIN assumption. We obtain the following KP-RABE (Scheme 10) and CP-RABE (Scheme 11).

Scheme 10 $\mathsf{C}_2(\mathsf{OT12\text{-}KP})$ **Scheme** 11 $\mathsf{C}_2(\mathsf{OT12\text{-}CP})$

RABE for Other Predicates. Since C_1 is applicable to ABE with arbitrary predicates, we also obtain the RABE for other predicates such as (doubly) spatial encryption, ABE for branching programs, and more [2,3]. To the best of our knowledge, these are also the first such revocable schemes for these predicates.

Acknowledgement. The authors would like to thank members of Shin-Akarui-Angou-Benkyou-Kai for their helpful comments. This work was partially supported by Input Output Hong Kong, I-System, Nomura Research Institute, NTT Secure Platform Laboratories, JST CREST JPMJCR14D6, JST OPERA, and JSPS KAKENHI Grant Numbers JP16K00198, JP16H01705, JP17H01695. This paper is based on results obtained from a project commissioned by the New Energy and Industrial Technology Development Organization (NEDO).

A   Relations Between Predicates

We construct IBR described with the pair encoding framework, from pair encoding schemes for KP-Boolean formulae and for prefix predicate. It it known that KP-Boolean formulae is implied by KP-monotone span programs [18]. Here we show that prefix predicate is implied by key-policy doubly spatial encryption (KP-DSE) [2]. In KP-DSE, policies and attributes are described by affine spaces.

Notion for Affine Spaces. Let $N, d, w \in \mathbb{N}$ where $0 \leq w \leq d$. Let $\boldsymbol{t}^\top$ be a vertical vector in $\mathbb{Z}_N^d$. Let $\boldsymbol{M} \in \mathbb{Z}_N^{d \times w}$ be a matrix whose columns are all linearly independent. An affine space in $\mathbb{Z}_N^d$ specified by a pair $(\boldsymbol{t}, \boldsymbol{M})$ is defined as $\{\boldsymbol{t}^\top + \boldsymbol{M}\boldsymbol{v}^\top | \boldsymbol{v} \in \mathbb{Z}_N^w\}$. $\mathsf{AffSp}(\mathbb{Z}_N^d)$ denotes the set of all affine spaces in $\mathbb{Z}_N^d$.

Key-Policy Doubly Spatial Encryption (KP-DSE) [2]. Briefly, in KP-DSE, a ciphertext can be decrypted by a secret key if the affine space associated with the secret key intersects with the affine space associated with the ciphertext.

- **Parameter**: It is specified by $\kappa = (N, d, K, L, S, T)$, where N and d define the universe $\mathsf{AffSp}(\mathbb{Z}_N^d)$ of the affine space, K and L denotes the maximum size of access policy, S denotes the maximum size of attribute set and T denotes the maximum number of the same attribute in a Boolean formula.
- **Key Attribute**: It is specified by $\mathbb{A} = (A, \rho)$ where A is a matrix in $\mathbb{Z}_N^{m \times k}$ for some $m, k \in \mathbb{N}$, and ρ is a labelling that maps each row in $[1, m]$ to an affine space in $\mathbb{Z}_N^d$.

- **Ciphertext Attribute**: It is specified by a set Y of affine spaces in $\mathbb{Z}_N^d$.
- **Predicate** Let $\mathbb{A}|_Y$ be the set of vectors that takes all the vectors of rows i in A such that there exists an affine space $(t, M) \in Y$ that intersects with the affine space $\rho(i)$. For a set V of vectors, $\mathsf{span}(V)$ denotes the span of V, the set of all linear combinations of vectors in V.

$$\mathsf{R}^{\mathsf{KP\text{-}DSE}}((A, \rho), Y) = \begin{cases} 1 & (1, 0, \dots, 0) \in \mathsf{span}(\mathbb{A}|_Y) \\ 0 & otherwise \end{cases}$$

From KP-DSE to Prefix Predicate. We show that a pair encoding scheme for KP-DSE predicate $\mathsf{R}^{\mathsf{KP\text{-}DSE}}$ implies a pair encoding scheme for prefix predicate $\mathsf{R}^{\mathsf{prefix}}$ by embedding lemma. The conversion is as follows:

- **Parameter**: We map $g_\mathsf{p}(N, \ell, S_1, S_2) = (N, \ell, S_1, 1, S_2, 1)$. When N, ℓ, S_1 or S_2 is unbounded, the corresponding mapped parameters are also unbounded.
- **Key Attribute**: Consider a set $X = \{x_i\}_{i \le |X|}$. We map $g_\mathsf{k}(X) = \mathbb{A} = (A, \rho)$, where $A := (1 \cdots 1)^\top \in \mathbb{Z}_N^{|X| \times 1}$ and $\rho(i) = (t_i, M_i)$, where (t_i, M_i) is defined as follows:

$$t_i = (x_i, 0, \dots, 0) \in \mathbb{Z}_N^{\ell_2}, \qquad M_i = \left(O^{(\ell_2 - |x_i|) \times |x_i|} \ E^{(\ell_2 - |x_i|)} \right) \in \mathbb{Z}_N^{(\ell_2 - |x_i|) \times \ell_2}$$

Note that $\rho(i) = (t_i, M_i)$ is a set of vectors who have x_i as a prefix. Intuitively $\mathbb{A}$ means Boolean formula $\mathsf{P}_1 \vee \mathsf{P}_2 \vee \cdots \vee \mathsf{P}_{|X|}$ where each P_i is true iff $\rho(i)$ intersects with the affine spaces associated with ciphertext.

- **Ciphertext Attribute**: Consider a set $Y = \{y_j\}_{j \le |Y|}$. We map $g_\mathsf{e}(Y) = \{(t'_j, M'_j) \in \mathsf{AffSp}(\mathbb{Z}_N^{\ell_2}) | y_j \in Y\}$, where (t'_j, M'_j) is defined as follows:

$$t'_j = (y_j, 0, \dots, 0), \qquad M'_j = O^{1 \times \ell_2} \in \mathbb{Z}_N^{1 \times \ell_2}.$$

Note that (t'_j, M'_j) is a set who has only $(y_j, 0, \dots, 0)$ as an element.

A pair encoding scheme for KP-DSE predicate $\mathsf{R}^{\mathsf{KP\text{-}DSE}}$ implies a pair encoding scheme for prefix predicate $\mathsf{R}^{\mathsf{prefix}}$. This is followed by the following lemma and the embedding lemma for pair encoding schemes.

Lemma 6. *For all X and Y, $\mathsf{R}^{\mathsf{prefix}}(X, Y) = 1 \Leftrightarrow \mathsf{R}^{\mathsf{KP\text{-}DSE}}(g_\mathsf{k}(X), g_\mathsf{e}(Y)) = 1$.*

Proof. Here we omit the parameters κ and $g_\mathsf{p}(\kappa)$ for the sake of simplicity.

$$\mathsf{R}^{\mathsf{prefix}}(X, Y) = 1 \Leftrightarrow \text{There exist } i \text{ and } j \text{ s.t. } x_i \text{ is a prefix of } y_j.$$
$$\Leftrightarrow \text{There exist } i \text{ and } j \text{ s.t. } (y_j, 0 \dots, 0) \in \rho(i).$$
$$\Leftrightarrow \text{There exist } i \text{ and } j \text{ s.t. the intersectsof}$$
$$\rho(i) = (t_i, M_i) \text{ and } (t'_j, M'_j) \text{ is not empty.}$$
$$\Leftrightarrow \mathsf{P}_1 \vee \mathsf{P}_2 \vee \cdots \vee \mathsf{P}_{|X|} = \mathsf{true}$$
$$\Leftrightarrow \mathsf{R}^{\mathsf{KP\text{-}DSE}}(\mathbb{A}, \{(y_j, 0, \dots, 0) \in \mathbb{Z}_N^{\ell_2} | y_j \in Y\}) = 1$$
$$\Leftrightarrow \mathsf{R}^{\mathsf{KP\text{-}DSE}}(g_\mathsf{k}(X), g_\mathsf{e}(Y)) = 1.$$

References

1. Agrawal, S., Chase, M.: A study of pair encodings: predicate encryption in prime order groups. In: Kushilevitz, E., Malkin, T. (eds.) TCC 2016. LNCS, vol. 9563, pp. 259–288. Springer, Heidelberg (2016). doi:10.1007/978-3-662-49099-0_10
2. Attrapadung, N.: Dual system encryption via doubly selective security: framework, fully secure functional encryption for regular languages, and more. In: Nguyen, P.Q., Oswald, E. (eds.) EUROCRYPT 2014. LNCS, vol. 8441, pp. 557–577. Springer, Heidelberg (2014). doi:10.1007/978-3-642-55220-5_31
3. Attrapadung, N.: Dual system encryption framework in prime-order groups via computational pair encodings. In: Cheon, J.H., Takagi, T. (eds.) ASIACRYPT 2016. LNCS, vol. 10032, pp. 591–623. Springer, Heidelberg (2016). doi:10.1007/978-3-662-53890-6_20
4. Attrapadung, N., Hanaoka, G., Yamada, S.: A framework for identity-based encryption with almost tight security. In: Iwata, T., Cheon, J.H. (eds.) ASIACRYPT 2015. LNCS, vol. 9452, pp. 521–549. Springer, Heidelberg (2015). doi:10.1007/978-3-662-48797-6_22
5. Attrapadung, N., Imai, H.: Attribute-based encryption supporting direct/indirect revocation modes. In: Parker, M.G. (ed.) IMACC 2009. LNCS, vol. 5921, pp. 278–300. Springer, Heidelberg (2009). doi:10.1007/978-3-642-10868-6_17
6. Attrapadung, N., Imai, H.: Conjunctive broadcast and attribute-based encryption. In: Shacham, H., Waters, B. (eds.) Pairing 2009. LNCS, vol. 5671, pp. 248–265. Springer, Heidelberg (2009). doi:10.1007/978-3-642-03298-1_16
7. Attrapadung, N., Libert, B.: Functional encryption for inner product: achieving constant-size ciphertexts with adaptive security or support for negation. In: Nguyen, P.Q., Pointcheval, D. (eds.) PKC 2010. LNCS, vol. 6056, pp. 384–402. Springer, Heidelberg (2010). doi:10.1007/978-3-642-13013-7_23
8. Attrapadung, N., Libert, B., Panafieu, E.: Expressive key-policy attribute-based encryption with constant-size ciphertexts. In: Catalano, D., Fazio, N., Gennaro, R., Nicolosi, A. (eds.) PKC 2011. LNCS, vol. 6571, pp. 90–108. Springer, Heidelberg (2011). doi:10.1007/978-3-642-19379-8_6
9. Attrapadung, N., Yamada, S.: Duality in ABE: converting attribute based encryption for dual predicate and dual policy via computational encodings. In: Nyberg, K. (ed.) CT-RSA 2015. LNCS, vol. 9048, pp. 87–105. Springer, Cham (2015). doi:10.1007/978-3-319-16715-2_5
10. Boldyreva, A., Goyal, V., Kumar, V.: Identity-based encryption with efficient revocation. In: ACM Conference on Computer and Communications Security 2008, pp. 417–426 (2008)
11. Boneh, D., Franklin, M.: Identity-based encryption from the weil pairing. In: Kilian, J. (ed.) CRYPTO 2001. LNCS, vol. 2139, pp. 213–229. Springer, Heidelberg (2001). doi:10.1007/3-540-44647-8_13
12. Boneh, D., Hamburg, M.: Generalized identity based and broadcast encryption schemes. In: Pieprzyk, J. (ed.) ASIACRYPT 2008. LNCS, vol. 5350, pp. 455–470. Springer, Heidelberg (2008). doi:10.1007/978-3-540-89255-7_28
13. Datta, P., Dutta, R., Mukhopadhyay, S.: General circuit realizing compact revocable attribute-based encryption from multilinear maps. In: Lopez, J., Mitchell, C.J. (eds.) ISC 2015. LNCS, vol. 9290, pp. 336–354. Springer, Cham (2015). doi:10.1007/978-3-319-23318-5_19

14. Datta, P., Dutta, R., Mukhopadhyay, S.: Adaptively secure unrestricted attribute-based encryption with subset difference revocation in bilinear groups of prime order. In: Pointcheval, D., Nitaj, A., Rachidi, T. (eds.) AFRICACRYPT 2016. LNCS, vol. 9646, pp. 325–345. Springer, Cham (2016). doi:10.1007/978-3-319-31517-1_17

15. Dodis, Y., Fazio, N.: Public key broadcast encryption for stateless receivers. In: Feigenbaum, J. (ed.) DRM 2002. LNCS, vol. 2696, pp. 61–80. Springer, Heidelberg (2003). doi:10.1007/978-3-540-44993-5_5

16. Escala, A., Herold, G., Kiltz, E., Ràfols, C., Villar, J.: An algebraic framework for diffie-hellman assumptions. In: Canetti, R., Garay, J.A. (eds.) CRYPTO 2013. LNCS, vol. 8043, pp. 129–147. Springer, Heidelberg (2013). doi:10.1007/978-3-642-40084-1_8

17. Gentry, C., Silverberg, A.: Hierarchical ID-based cryptography. In: Zheng, Y. (ed.) ASIACRYPT 2002. LNCS, vol. 2501, pp. 548–566. Springer, Heidelberg (2002). doi:10.1007/3-540-36178-2_34

18. Goyal, V., Pandey, O., Sahai, A., Waters, B.: Attribute-based encryption for fine-grained access control of encrypted data. In: ACM Conference on Computer and Communications Security 2006, pp. 89–98 (2006)

19. Horwitz, J., Lynn, B.: Toward hierarchical identity-based encryption. In: Knudsen, L.R. (ed.) EUROCRYPT 2002. LNCS, vol. 2332, pp. 466–481. Springer, Heidelberg (2002). doi:10.1007/3-540-46035-7_31

20. Jun-Lei, Q., Xiao-Lei, D.: Fully secure revocable attribute-based encryption. J. Shanghai Jiaotong Univ. (Sci.) 16, 490–496 (2011)

21. Lewko, A.B., Sahai, A., Waters, B.: Revocation systems with very small private keys. In: IEEE Symposium on Security and Privacy 2010, pp. 273–285 (2010)

22. Lewko, A., Waters, B.: Unbounded HIBE and attribute-based encryption. In: Paterson, K.G. (ed.) EUROCRYPT 2011. LNCS, vol. 6632, pp. 547–567. Springer, Heidelberg (2011). doi:10.1007/978-3-642-20465-4_30

23. Naor, D., Naor, M., Lotspiech, J.: Revocation and tracing schemes for stateless receivers. In: Kilian, J. (ed.) CRYPTO 2001. LNCS, vol. 2139, pp. 41–62. Springer, Heidelberg (2001). doi:10.1007/3-540-44647-8_3

24. Okamoto, T., Takashima, K.: Fully Secure Functional Encryption with General Relations from the Decisional Linear Assumption. In: Rabin, T. (ed.) CRYPTO 2010. LNCS, vol. 6223, pp. 191–208. Springer, Heidelberg (2010). doi:10.1007/978-3-642-14623-7_11

25. Okamoto, T., Takashima, K.: Fully secure unbounded inner-product and attribute-based encryption. In: Wang, X., Sako, K. (eds.) ASIACRYPT 2012. LNCS, vol. 7658, pp. 349–366. Springer, Heidelberg (2012). doi:10.1007/978-3-642-34961-4_22

26. Rouselakis, Y., Waters, B.: Practical constructions and new proof methods for large universe attribute-based encryption. In: ACM Conference on Computer and Communications Security 2013, pp. 463–474 (2013)

27. Sahai, A., Waters, B.: Fuzzy identity-based encryption. In: Cramer, R. (ed.) EUROCRYPT 2005. LNCS, vol. 3494, pp. 457–473. Springer, Heidelberg (2005). doi:10.1007/11426639_27

28. Seo, J.H., Emura, K.: Revocable identity-based encryption revisited: security model and construction. In: Kurosawa, K., Hanaoka, G. (eds.) PKC 2013. LNCS, vol. 7778, pp. 216–234. Springer, Heidelberg (2013). doi:10.1007/978-3-642-36362-7_14

29. Shamir, A.: Identity-based cryptosystems and signature schemes. In: Blakley, G.R., Chaum, D. (eds.) CRYPTO 1984. LNCS, vol. 196, pp. 47–53. Springer, Heidelberg (1985). doi:10.1007/3-540-39568-7_5

30. Shi, Y., Zheng, Q., Liu, J., Han, Z.: Directly revocable key-policy attribute-based encryption with verifiable ciphertext delegation. Inf. Sci. **295**, 221–231 (2015)

31. Waters, B.: Functional encryption for regular languages. In: Safavi-Naini, R., Canetti, R. (eds.) CRYPTO 2012. LNCS, vol. 7417, pp. 218–235. Springer, Heidelberg (2012). doi:10.1007/978-3-642-32009-5_14

Enforcing Input Correctness via Certification in Garbled Circuit Evaluation

Yihua Zhang[1], Marina Blanton[2(✉)], and Fattaneh Bayatbabolghani[1]

[1] Computer Science and Engineering, University of Notre Dame, Notre Dame, USA
{yzhang16,fbayatba}@nd.edu
[2] Computer Science and Engineering, State University of New York, Buffalo, USA
mblanton@buffalo.edu

Abstract. Secure multi-party computation allows a number of participants to securely evaluate a function on their private inputs and has a growing number of applications. Two standard adversarial models that treat the participants as semi-honest or malicious, respectively, are normally considered for showing security of constructions in this framework. In this work, we go beyond the standard security model in the presence of malicious participants and treat the problem of enforcing correct inputs to be entered into the computation. We achieve this by having a certification authority certify user's information, which is consequently used in secure two-party computation based on garbled circuit evaluation. The focus of this work on enforcing correctness of garbler's inputs via certification, as prior work already allows one to achieve this goal for circuit evaluator's input. Thus, in this work, we put forward a novel approach for certifying user's input and tying certification to garbler's input used during secure function evaluation based on garbled circuits. Our construction achieves notable performance of adding only one (standard) signature verification and $O(n\rho)$ symmetric key/hash operations to the cost of garbled circuit evaluation in the malicious model via cut-and-choose, in which ρ circuits are garbled and n is the length of the garbler's input in bits. Security of our construction is rigorously proved in the standard model.

Keywords: Garbled circuits · Input certification · Input verification · Secure function evaluation

1 Introduction

Secure multi-party computation (SMC) is a mature research area of computer science that has experienced dramatic advances in recent years. A new secure multi-party construction or protocol is expected to be shown secure against a formal security definition specifying the adversarial model. The two most fundamental and now standard security models correspond to modeling the computation participants as semi-honest (or honest-but-curious or passive) or malicious (or active). With semi-honest adversaries, the participants are trusted to follow

© Springer International Publishing AG 2017
S.N. Foley et al. (Eds.): ESORICS 2017, Part II, LNCS 10493, pp. 552–569, 2017.
DOI: 10.1007/978-3-319-66399-9_30

the prescribed computation, while a malicious adversary can instruct the participants under its control to arbitrarily deviate from the computation in the attempt to learn authorized information about the honest parties' inputs. While these definitions are strong and do not tolerate unintended information leakage, the largest limitation of these standard definitions is that they provide no guarantees with respect to inputs of the computation.[1] Thus, a dishonest participant is able to modify its input into the computation, which results in other participants receiving incorrect results, while the dishonest party itself might be able to compute true output based on its knowledge of the original data transformation. This also allows a dishonest participant to set its inputs into the computation in such a way as to learn the maximum amount of information about input of other participant(s) from the output it receives.

The issue with inability of honest participants to control inputs of malicious participants under the current security definitions has been recognized in the literature and various techniques were proposed to mitigate the problem. Examples include employing game-theoretic techniques to incentivize providing truthful inputs into secure multi-party computation (see, e.g., [14,15,28]) and input certification in the context of specific applications such as private set intersection [9,11] and anonymous credentials [8]. More recently, input certification or input validity verification in the form of any function has been added to general secure computation techniques. In particular, Blanton and Bayatbabolghani [3] put forward an efficient construction for server-aided secure two-party computation based on garbled circuit evaluation, where the inputs of the two users are certified and equality of the signed data and inputs into the computation is verified by utilizing signatures with protocols. Katz et al. [16] design an efficient mechanism for adding input verification in the form of an arbitrary function to two-party computation based on garbled circuits so that the computation takes place only if the inputs pass verification (and the computation takes place on the same inputs that were verified). We continue this line of work in this paper.

The focus of this article is on enforcing input correctness in secure computation via input certification. Because signature-based input certification is more amenable to integration with existing malicious-adversary techniques based on homomorphic encryption or secret sharing than garbled circuit evaluation, we would like to tackle the more interesting case of garbled circuit evaluation. To that extent, our starting point was the work of Blanton and Bayatbabolghani [3] for the server-aided two-party setting. We aim to enforce input correctness of both circuit garbler and evaluator in the standard two-party setting using garbled circuit evaluation techniques. Toward this goal, we notice that the mechanism for enforcing input correctness of the user evaluating the circuit in [3] will also work with the regular two-party setup with no changes. In particular, that mechanism requires the circuit evaluator to prove via zero-knowledge proofs of knowledge that the inputs provided into the oblivious transfer (at the time of retrieving garbled labels corresponding to the evaluator's inputs) are consistent with the

---

[1] Note that this does not refer to ill-formed inputs which can be detected in the beginning of the computation, but rather to well-formed incorrect or deceptive inputs.

valued signed by a certification authority. The mechanism for enforcing input correctness of the other user in [3], however, cannot be used for enforcing input correctness of the circuit garbler in the conventional setup. Thus, the focus of this work is on designing an efficient mechanism for enforcing input correctness of the garbler with the help of a certification authority.

Our setup assumes the presence of a certification authority that can certify users' data. For example, in the case of genomic or medical data, the facility performing genome sequencing or running a medical test will issue certification that can later be used with secure two-party computation. Obviously, the use of certification should not reveal any information about the certified values. For example, [3] used signatures with protocols that allows the signature owner to prove statements about signed values in zero-knowledge. Once the certification step is complete, the user will be able to use that information with garbled circuit evaluation to prove correctness of the supplied inputs.

In this work we put forward a novel, non-standard certification construction for use with garbled circuit evaluation that favorably compares with existing signature schemes and other prior work in terms of its performance. The certification authority's work includes only one public-key operation (producing a regular signature) for user's input of any size and the number of symmetric key or hash function operations is $O(n\rho)$, where n is the bitlength of the user's input to be certified and ρ is a statistical security parameter (that determines the number of circuits being garbled). The size of a certificate is $O(n + \rho)$, and the cost of secure function evaluation is only insignificantly higher than that of regular garbled circuit evaluation in the malicious model with no enforcement of input correctness. In particular, the work associated with using garbler's input certification and verification in secure function evaluation based on garbled circuits is only one signature verification and $O(n\rho)$ symmetric key/hash operations when the garbler's input is n bits long. The downside of the approach is that the certification authority's work is linear in the number of times the certificate is to be used in secure computation. That is, in order to use the same input in up to k independent secure function evaluations (with possibly different functions), the user will need to obtain a certificate of size $O(n + \rho k)$ and the certification authority's work increases to $O(n\rho k)$.

2   Related Work

Literature on secure two-party and multi-party computation is extensive and provides different mechanisms for securely evaluating a function on private inputs. Following the seminal work of Yao [30], it has been known that any computable function can be securely evaluated. Consequent work focused on providing stronger security guarantees such as security in the presence of malicious or covert adversaries (see, e.g., [10,21] among many others) or improving performance of existing techniques (see, e.g., [2,5] among others). There is also a large variety of custom constructions optimized for evaluating specific functions with the goal of providing more efficient solutions than their generic counterparts (see, e.g., [4,23] among others).

The original Yao's construction is secure against semi-honest participants, and several solutions for making it resilient to malicious behavior exist. Early examples of constructions secure in the malicious model include [12,13] that utilize zero knowledge proofs of knowledge. An alternative approach to making secure function evaluation based on garbled circuits resilient to malicious behavior is to use cut-and-choose techniques [19,20,24], which we further detail in Sect. 3.

Moving closer to the focus of this work, several publications treat the issue of input consistency or correctness in different settings and using different mechanisms. For example, the issue of input consistency arises in the context of garbled circuit evaluation based on cut-and-choose techniques when multiple circuits need to be evaluated on the same (consistent) inputs and was treated in several publications [20,22,29]. Another work by Kolesnikov et al. [17] proposed a solution for input consistency across multiple user interactions with the help of a semi-honest server at low cost. That is, possibly malicious users engage in executions of secure two-party function evaluation with each other, but the user's input must remain the same for multiple instances of secure computation.

With respect to enforcing input correctness, one line of research applies game theory to function design to incentivize participants to provide their truthful inputs into the computation (see, e.g., [14,15,26–28] among others). These publications typically treat the parties as rational. For instance, Shoham and Tennenholtz [26] studied the question of which boolean functions can be computed by rational agents in a distributed setting and more recent work of Wallrabenstein and Clifton [27,28] revisits game specifications using the specifics of secure multiparty computation setups. In addition, input certification was used with certain types of functionalities to guarantee that computation is run on the same inputs as the inputs previously signed by some certification authority. For example, [9,11] provide solutions for performing private set intersection on certified sets and [8] incorporates certification into anonymous credentials. These techniques, however, are not applicable to general functionalities.

More recently, Blanton and Bayatbabolghani [3] incorporated input certification into general secure function evaluation based on garbled circuits. In particular, the computation takes place between two possibly malicious users who use the help of an untrusted semi-honest server and ensures that the users can only enter inputs that were previously certified into the computation. The construction uses signatures with protocols [6] for this purpose and ties them to the way input is provided into the garbled circuit using zero-knowledge proofs. This paper is used as the starting point for this work. As we mentioned earlier, their mechanism for garbler's input certification applies to regular two-party computation based on garbled circuits, but it is not the case for the circuit garbler and this is why we focus on this task in this work.

Katz et al. [16] proposed a solution to enforce input validity of both garbler and evaluator in secure function evaluation based on garbled circuits. It formulates input validation in the form of two predicates $f_1(\cdot)$ and $f_2(\cdot)$ applied to the input of the first and second participant, respectively. The construction then ensures that the main function $f(\cdot, \cdot)$ is evaluated on the same inputs as those provided during input validation. The underlying techniques include ElGamal-based commitments and a special form of oblivious transfer (OT). Note that the predicates f_1 and f_2 are specified in the form of Boolean circuits and are evaluated using garbled circuits themselves, which means that they could be used to privately verify a private signature on a private input, but the resulting circuit is large. Concurrently with [16], Baum [1] treats a similar problem, but the solution is based on universal hash functions and committed OT. In particular, the predicates $f_1(\cdot)$ and $f_2(\cdot)$ are evaluated by the respective party locally, but the join computation includes evaluation of a hash function on the output of the predicate to verify consistency of the input into the computation. More generally, the techniques of [1] improve performance of secure function evaluation based on garbled circuits when portions of the computation (or sub-circuits) depend only on one party's input.

We note that it is possible to combine the techniques of [1,16] with input certification using signatures with protocols. For example, instead of evaluating predicate f_1 on private input x of the first party P_1, P_1 could prove in zero-knowledge that it possesses a signature on input x and connect it to the evaluation of $f(x, y)$, where y is the input of the second party P_2, in the same way as in [16]. This will serve as an alternative construction to the techniques presented in this paper. Suppose that P_1 is the circuit garbler G and we only consider G's input certification, similar to the construction presented in this work. Then if we take the approach of [16] and combine it with signatures with protocols (such as [6,7]), its performance compared to our approach can be evaluated as follows. Besides the common components such as garbling and checking/evaluation of $O(\rho)$ circuits and executing OT for circuit evaluator's input, the approach based on the techniques of [16] requires $O((n_1 + n_3)\rho)$ public-key operations (modulo exponentiations), where n_1 is the bitlength of G's input and n_3 is the bitlength of the output. In our construction, however, only one signature is verified and the parties perform $O(n_1\rho)$ symmetric key operations (PRF or hash function evaluations) with small constants hidden behind the big-O notation.

If instead of using signatures with protocols we directly compare the approach of [16] to our work, then the number of public key operation in the solution of [16] is still $O((n_1 + n_3)\rho)$ and there is a need to securely verify a private signature on private input using a garbled circuit. This circuit is expected to be large; for example, based on the circuit sizes reported in [18] we can estimate that verification of an RSA signature using a 1024-bit modulus uses over 40 million gates, and the number is obviously several times higher for stronger RSA with a 2048- or 3072-bit modulus (a circuit for producing a signature with RSA-1024 is over 40 billion gates in size).

The techniques of [1] are conceptually similar to those used in [16], but there is no special output handling and public-key operations are used only in the form of commitments and OT. Compared to our construction, the solution of [1] requires invocation of $O((n_1 + \rho)\rho)$ OTs (no OTs or similar operations are used for the garbler's input in our construction), the size of the circuit that needs to be evaluated in the malicious setting is larger due to the need to enforce input consistency using a hash function evaluation, and the predicate in the form of a signature verification needs to be evaluated once using a garbled circuit.

3   Garbled Circuit Evaluation

The use of garbled circuits allows two parties P_1 and P_2 to securely evaluate a Boolean circuit of their choice. Given an arbitrary function $f(x, y)$ that depends on private inputs x and y of P_1 and P_2, respectively, the parties first represent it as a Boolean circuit. One party acts as a circuit generator (or garbler) G and creates a garbled representation of the circuit by associating both values of each binary wire with random labels. The other party acts as a circuit evaluator E and evaluates the circuit in its garbled representation without knowing the meaning of the labels that it handles during the evaluation. The output labels can be mapped to their meaning and revealed to either or both parties.

Once the circuit is garbled, the garbler communicates it (in the form of garbled Boolean gates) to the evaluator together with the labels of the input wires corresponding to the garbler's input bits. The labels of the input wires corresponding to the evaluator's input bits are communicated to the evaluator by means of 1-out-of-2 Oblivious Transfer (OT).

The standard construction used for the semi-honest setting also provides security in the presence of a malicious evaluator (i.e., if the evaluator deviates from the prescribed computation, the evaluation might abort, but the evaluator will not be able to learn unauthorized information). However, to guarantee security in the malicious setting (with either malicious garbler or evaluator) additional techniques need to be employed. A widely used approach to detecting incorrectly garbled circuits is based on cut-and-choose. Given a security parameter ρ, G garbles $O(\rho)$ circuits and sends them to E. The evaluator chooses a number of them to be opened and checks them for correctness. The remaining circuits are evaluated by E, with the algorithm specifying how possible differences in the circuit outputs are to be reconciled (e.g., by using the majority) without disclosing that information to G. This approach allows for the probability of E accepting the output of incorrect circuit evaluation to be at most negligible in ρ.

There are, however, additional attacks that can be mounted at the time of input specification in the attempt to learn additional information about the other party's input and the corresponding countermeasures. First, the utilized approach must enforce that the OT protocol is resilient to malicious behavior. Second, it must enforce that both G and E input consistent bits into all evaluation circuits. This is typically easy to achieve for the evaluator (i.e., the evaluator specifies a single input bit and learns the corresponding labels for all circuits being evaluated), while additional techniques need to be used to enforce G's input consistency. Third, the protocol must be resilient to a selective failure attack, in which G attempts to learn a bit of E's input by providing incorrect information during OT. For example, G could enter an incorrect wire label corresponding to 0 for E's input bit into OT. Then if E's input is 0, it is unable to proceed and aborts and otherwise it succeeds, allowing G to learn one bit of E's input. A solution to this problem is to use ρ input bits into the circuit for each bit of E's input, where all ρ bits are XORed together to result in E's original input bit. Now if G launches a selective-failure attack on a single bit, the leaked bit reveals no information about E's original input. This attack is only successful and results in revealing a bit of E's input when G recovers all ρ corresponding bits of the input, which only has a negligible (in security parameter ρ) probability of success.

Lastly, we need to ensure that authentic output is delivered to both parties after the evaluation. (Note that in general, fairness cannot be achieved in two-party computation, preventing one of the parties from learning the output, but at least we can require that only authentic outputs are accepted.) Various mechanisms for achieving this goal exist and for the purposes of this work any such mechanism will suffice. However, for concreteness of our security analysis, we will assume the following: the meaning of the output wire labels is opened to E. If G is also to learn the (same or different) output, the function is modified as in [20] to compute G's output in a protected form together with the corresponding message authentication tag, which G can verify and recover its output if verification was successful.

We now proceed with defining security of a two-party secure computation protocol in the presence of malicious participants using the standard real-ideal model setting and simulation paradigm. The execution of protocol Π takes place between parties P_1 and P_2 and an adversary $\mathcal{A}$ who can corrupt one of them. Each participant receives its input and security parameters 1^κ and 1^ρ, where κ denotes the computation security parameter and ρ the statistical security parameter. $\mathcal{A}$ receives all information that the party it corrupted has and can also instruct the corresponding corrupted party to behave in a certain way. Let VIEW$_{\Pi,\mathcal{A}}$ denote a tuple consisting of the view of $\mathcal{A}$ at the end of an execution of Π and the output of the honest party.

In the ideal model, all parties interact with a trusted party TP who evaluates function f. The execution begins with each party receiving its inputs and security parameters. Each honest party sends to TP its true input and a malicious party can send an arbitrary value. If TP does not receive input from both parties or if it receives an abort message, it outputs $\perp$ (empty) to the participants. Otherwise, the participants receive f evaluated on submitted inputs. Let VIEW$_{f,S}$ denote a tuple consisting of the output that simulator S with access to the corrupted party's information produces based on its view and the output of the honest party after ideal execution of function f. We obtain the following security definition:

Definition 1. *Let Π be a protocol that computes function $f : \{0,1\}^* \times \{0,1\}^* \rightarrow \{0,1\}^* \times \{0,1\}^*$ with party P_1 contributing input x and party P_2 contributing input y. We say that Π securely evaluates f if for each probabilistic polynomial-time in κ adversary $\mathcal{A}$ in the real model and all $x, y \in \{0,1\}^*$, there exists probabilistic S in the ideal model that run in time polynomial in $\mathcal{A}$'s runtime and IDEAL$_{f,S}(x,y) \cong$ REAL$_{\Pi,A}(x,y)$. Here $\cong$ denotes computational indistinguishability (in the security parameter κ).*

When inputs are certified, the participants have access to certification in the real protocol execution, while in the ideal model the simulator will need to simulate input certification of honest parties (without access to their inputs). Furthermore, if we want to guarantee that the computation takes place on the input equal to the input encoded in the certification, we need to show that a malicious participant is unable to provide an input that differs from the certified input and results in successful completed protocol with more than a negligible probability.

4   Proposed Construction

In our construction we use three independent hash functions h_1, h_2, and h_3 with properties defined below. For the purposes of our security analysis, we need to assume that h_1 and h_2 are universal hash functions, while collision resistance is sufficient for h_3. In addition, we require h_1 to support homomorphic XOR as in $h_1(x \oplus y) = h_1(x) \oplus h_1(y)$. A collection of hash functions $\mathcal{H} = \{h : A \to B\}$ is called universal if for any distinct $x, y \in A$, the probability that a uniformly chosen $h \in \mathcal{H}$ satisfies that $h(x) = h(y)$ is at most $1/|B|$, i.e., its output is uniformly distributed over the function's range. An efficient implementation of a universal hash function with homomorphic XOR can be found in [25]. Collision resilience of a hash function h is defined as inability of an adversary to find two distinct x and y such that $h(x) = h(y)$ with more than a negligible probability in the output size of h. For the purpose of this work, we let the output size of hash functions be governed by the security parameter κ so that the probability of finding collisions is negligible in κ. Collision resilience follows for our universal hash functions h_1 and h_2.

Our construction also relies on a pseudo-random function (PRF) $F : \{0,1\}^\kappa \times \{0,1\}^\kappa \to \{0,1\}^\kappa$, security of which is defined in a standard way. That is, for a randomly chosen key $k \in \{0,1\}^\kappa$, an adversary who can query F_k on different inputs a polynomial number of times is unable to distinguish F_k from a random function f with more than a negligible probability.

The intuition behind our construction is to let the certification authority (CA) associate input bits with random values, which are to be used in circuit generation and evaluation, and generate some "fingerprint" information for enforcing correctness. In this scheme, the CA does not need to perform signing of input bits as in traditional signature schemes, but only performs symmetric key operations and computes one signature independent of the input or circuit size. The evaluator consequently will use the "fingerprint" information to check circuits, and both the garbler and evaluator use information provided by the CA to generate input labels.

In more detail, for each input wire i corresponding to the garbler's input, the CA chooses two random strings s_i^0 and s_i^1 that mean 0 and 1, respectively, and similarly two (pseudo-)random values for each input wire i of each garbled circuit j (denoted by t_{2nj+2i} and $t_{2nj+2i+1}$ in the protocol description where n is the input size). The CA also encodes information that binds all of these random values by their meaning (i.e., all s and t values that correspond to 0 across all input wires and the equivalent values that correspond to 1) and by input wire (i.e., both t values that correspond to a given input wire in a given circuit). These bindings are stored in an encrypted form and are opened to the evaluator for circuits that are to be checked. The CA also releases information related to G's input x as $s_i^{x_i}, s_i^{1-x_i}$ (without revealing the meaning of these strings). These values are used both during circuit checking (for opened circuits to verify their correctness) and circuit evaluation (to compute labels corresponding to garbled input wires using $s_i^{x_i}$'s). In the following, we describe the proposed protocol in detail.

In what follows, x is the input to be signed and sk is the private signing key of the certification authority S. We assume that ρ circuits need to be garbled, where a fraction of them is being checked and the remaining circuits are evaluated.

Input Certification. The input consists of user's input $x = x_0 \ldots x_{n-1}$ to be certified and the signer S holds its private signing key sk (with the corresponding public key pk available to all users).

1. For each input bit $i = 0, \ldots, n-1$, S chooses two random strings $s_i^0, s_i^1 \leftarrow \{0,1\}^\kappa$ representing bits 0 and 1, respectively.
2. S computes $H^0 = h_1(s_0^0 \oplus \cdots \oplus s_{n-1}^0)$ and $H^1 = h_1(s_0^1 \oplus \cdots \oplus s_{n-1}^1)$.
3. S chooses a secret key $k' \leftarrow \{0,1\}^\kappa$ for a PRF F and for $i = 0, \ldots, 2n\rho - 1$ computes a pseudo-random string $t_i = F_{k'}(i)$.
4. For $j = 0, \ldots, \rho - 1$, S computes $P_j^0 = H^0 \oplus h_1(h_2(t_{2nj}) \oplus h_2(t_{2nj+2}) \oplus \cdots \oplus h_2(t_{2nj+2n-2}))$, and $P_j^1 = H^1 \oplus h_1(h_2(t_{2nj+1}) \oplus h_2(t_{2nj+3}) \oplus \cdots \oplus h_2(t_{2nj+2n-1}))$.
5. For each $j = 0, \ldots, \rho - 1$, S computes $V_{0,j} = h_3(h_1(h_2(t_{2nj}) \oplus h_2(t_{2nj+1})))$, $V_{1,j} = h_3(V_{0,j} \| h_1(h_2(t_{2nj+2}) \oplus h_2(t_{2nj+3})))$, $\ldots$, and $V_{n-1,j} = h_3(V_{n-2,j} \| h_1(h_2(t_{2nj+2n-2}) \oplus h_2(t_{2nj+2n-1})))$ and sets $Q_j = V_{n-1,j}$.
6. For each $j = 0, \ldots, \rho - 1$, S chooses a random encryption key $ck_j \leftarrow \{0,1\}^\kappa$ and computes $\mathsf{Enc}_{ck_j}(P_j^0 \| P_j^1 \| Q_j)$.
7. S concatenates $(s_i^{x_i} \| s_i^{1-x_i})_{i=0}^{n-1}$, $(\mathsf{Enc}_{ck_j}(P_j^0 \| P_j^1 \| Q_j))_{j=0}^{\rho-1}$, and stores the resulting string as c. Here each $s_i^{x_i}$ represents input bit x_i and $s_i^{1-x_i}$ its complement. S signs c as $\mathsf{Sign}_{sk}(c)$.
8. S returns $\langle c, \mathsf{Sign}_{sk}(c), (ck_j)_{j=0}^{\rho-1}, k' \rangle$ to the user. Note that information included in c does not reveal whether x_i was 0 or 1.

The above information will be used for producing n garbled label pairs for input wires corresponding to input x into ρ circuits. As described below, each garbled pair for input wire i in circuit j will be formed as $\ell_{i,j}^0 = h_1(s_i^0 \oplus h_2(t_{2n_1j+2i}))$ and $\ell_{i,j}^1 = h_1(s_i^1 \oplus h_2(t_{2n_1j+2i+1}))$. Then the values P_j^0, P_j^1, and Q_j are used to verify correctness and consistency of the garbled circuit j. For each garbled circuit j, these values are opened during the circuit checking phase and are used by E to verify correctness of input labels. The intuition behind the checks is that P_j^0 encodes information about all inputs labels corresponding to input bits equal to 0, while P_j^1 encodes information about all labels corresponding to input bits equal to 1. We refer to checks that use P_j^0 and P_j^1 as "horizontal checks." Additionally, information encoded in Q_j encodes information about each pair of labels $\ell_{i,j}^0, \ell_{i,j}^1$ for each input wire i of the circuit. We refer to this check as the "vertical check".

Secure Function Evaluation with Certified Inputs. Garbler G holds private input $x = x_0 \ldots x_{n_1-1}$, $(ck_j)_{j=0}^{\rho-1}$, k' and supplies public $\langle c, \mathsf{Sign}_{sk}(c) \rangle$, where $c = (s_i^{x_i} || s_i^{1-x_i})_{i=0}^{n_1-1} || (\mathsf{Enc}_{ck_j}(P_j^0 || P_j^1 || Q_j))_{j=0}^{\rho-1}$. Evaluator E holds private input $y = y_0 \ldots y_{n_2-1}$.

0. Initial check: E verifies signature on c using certification authority's public key pk and aborts if verification fails. E stores all components of c.
1. Circuit garbling:
   (a) For each circuit $j = 0, \ldots, \rho$, G generates labels for its own input wires $i = 0, \ldots, n_1 - 1$ as $\ell_{i,j}^0 = h_1(s_i^0 \oplus h_2(t_{2n_1j+2i}))$ and $\ell_{i,j}^1 = h_1(s_i^1 \oplus h_2(t_{2n_1j+2i+1}))$, where each t_i is computed as $F_{k'}(i)$.
   (b) G generates the rest of the circuits in the same way as traditional garbled circuits and sends all circuits to E.
2. Circuit checking:
   (a) E select a predefined number of circuits out of ρ of them at random as checking circuits and asks G to open the selected circuits.
   (b) G reveals each label pair for each wire of each checking circuit and E verified them. If any circuit is malformed, E aborts the computation.
   (c) For each checking circuit with its original index j, G sends to E the key ck_j. E decrypts P_j^0, P_j^1, and Q_j and checks whether P_j^0 is equal to $\ell_{0,j}^0 \oplus \cdots \oplus \ell_{n_1-1,j}^0$ and whether P_j^1 is equal to $\ell_{0,j}^1 \oplus \cdots \oplus \ell_{n_1-1,j}^1$. If any check fails, E aborts the computation.
   (d) For each checking circuit with its original index j, E computes $S_{0,j} = h_3(\ell_{0,j}^0 \oplus \ell_{0,j}^1 \oplus h_1(s_0^{x_0}) \oplus h_1(s_0^{1-x_0}))$, $S_{1,j} = h_3(S_{0,j} || \ell_{1,j}^0 \oplus \ell_{1,j}^1 \oplus h_1(s_1^{x_1}) \oplus h_1(s_1^{1-x_1}))$, $\ldots$, $S_{n_1-1,j} = h_3(S_{n_1-1,j} || \ell_{n_1-1,j}^0 \oplus \ell_{n_1-1,j}^1 \oplus h_1(s_{n_1-1}^{x_{n_1-1}}) \oplus h_1(s_{n_1-1}^{1-x_{n_1-1}}))$. If $S_{n_1-1,j}$ is not equal to Q_j, E aborts.
3. Circuit evaluation:
   (a) The circuits that have not been opened in step 2 are evaluation circuits. For each evaluation circuit with the original index j, G sends to E values $t_{2n_1j+x_0}, \ldots, t_{2n_1j+2n_1-2+x_{n_1-1}}$.
   (b) For each evaluation circuit with its original index j, E computes labels for G's input wires $i = 0, \ldots, n_1 - 1$ as $\ell_{i,j}^{x_i} = h_1(s_i^{x_i} \oplus h_2(t_{2n_1j+2i+x_i}))$.
   (c) G and E engage in OT for E to learn garbled labels corresponding to its input and E evaluates each evaluation circuit and determines the output in the same was as in traditional garbled circuits.

We can see that all circuits garbled by an honest G pass the checks of steps 2(c-d). In particular, for each circuit j, each label $\ell_{i,j}^0$ is constructed as $\ell_{i,j}^0 = h_1(s_i^0 \oplus h_2(t_{2n_1j+2i}))$, so that $\bigoplus_{i=0}^{n_1-1} \ell_{i,j}^0 = h_1\left(\left(\bigoplus_{i=0}^{n_1-1} s_i^0\right) \oplus \left(\bigoplus_{i=0}^{n_1-1} h_2(t_{2n_1j+2i})\right)\right)$.

This is exactly how the value of $P_j^0 = h_1\left(\bigoplus_{i=0}^{n_1-1} s_i^0\right) \oplus h_1\left(\bigoplus_{i=0}^{n_1-1} h_2(t_{2n_1j+2i})\right) = h_1\left(\left(\bigoplus_{i=0}^{n_1-1} s_i^0\right) \oplus \left(\bigoplus_{i=0}^{n_1-1} h_2(t_{2n_1j+2i})\right)\right)$ was constructed by the certification authority. The same applies to checking whether P_j^1 is equal to $\bigoplus_{i=0}^{n_1-1} \ell_{i,j}^1$. As far as the check in step 2(d) does, we see that it will verify if the value of $S_{i,j}$ computed by E for each i is identical to the value $V_{i,j}$ computed by the certification authority in step 5 of input certification. Note that $S_{0,j} = h_3(\ell_{0,j}^0 \oplus \ell_{0,j}^1 \oplus h_1(s_0^{x_0}) \oplus h_1(s_0^{1-x_0})) = h_3(h_1(s_0^0 \oplus h_2(t_{2n_1j})) \oplus h_1(s_0^1 \oplus h_2(t_{2n_1j+1})) \oplus h_1(s_0^{x_0}) \oplus h_1(s_0^{1-x_0})) = h_3(h_1(h_2(t_{2n_1j}) \oplus h_2(t_{2n_1j+1}))) = V_{0,j}$. Similar derivations will apply to other values of i as well, giving us correctness.

5   Security Analysis

We first demonstrate security according to the simulation paradigm in Definition 1 and then proceed with showing that the proposed construction enforces input correctness. We use notation negl to denote a function negligible in its input.

To prove that no information leakage takes place during protocol execution, we rely on the following result:

Lemma 1. *Information* $(s_i^{x_i}, s_i^{1-x_i})_{i=0}^{n-1}, P_j^0, P_j^1, Q_j$ *computed as part of certification for n-bit x for some fixed j together with pairs* $(\ell_{i,j}^0 = h_1(s_i^0 \oplus h_2(t_{2nj+2i})),$ $\ell_{i,j}^1 = h_1(s_i^0 \oplus h_2(t_{2nj+2i+1})))_{i=0}^{n-1}$ *is indistinguishable for any PPT adversary from the same information computed for any n-bit $x' \neq x$.*

Proof. We show that the above values reveal no information about x, from which the claim of the lemma will follow. First, note that the values $s_i^{x_i}, s_i^{1-x_i}$ were chosen uniformly at random and in the absence of other information about x_i, s_i^0's or s_i^1, the ordering reveals no information about x. In other words, the pairs $s_i^{x_i}, s_i^{1-x_i}$ are distributed identically to uniformly chosen random values in the absence of additional information. In what follows, we construct a number of hybrid views and demonstrate that the views are indistinguishable from each other.

Hybrid 0: The same as the original set of values consisting of $s_i^{x_i}$'s, $s_i^{1-x_i}$'s, P_j^0, P_j^1, Q_j, $\ell_{i,j}^0$'s, and $\ell_{i,j}^1$'s for a fixed j and $i = 0, \ldots, n-1$.

Hybrid 1: In this view, we replace each $h_2(t_{2nj+2i})$ and $h_2(t_{2nj+2i+1})$ used in the creation of P_j^0, P_j^1, Q_j, and each $\ell_{i,j}^0$ and $\ell_{i,j}^1$, with strings $r_{i,j,0}$ and $r_{i,j,1}$, respectively, chosen uniformly at random over h_2' range. Because we are modifying all values constituently, any relationships between them (such as $P_j^0 = \bigoplus_{i=0}^{n-1} \ell_{i,j}^0$, etc.) will still hold. These values are indistinguishable from the values in Hybrid 0 because h_2 is a universal hash function. In particular, inputs t_{2nj+2i} and $t_{2nj+2i+1}$ into the hash function are pseudo-random and satisfy the min-entropy requirements for the output of h_2 to be treated as pseudo-random [25].

Hybrid 2: In this view, we replace $s_i^0 \oplus r_{i,j,0}$ and $s_i^1 \oplus r_{i,j,1}$ with uniformly chosen random strings $r'_{i,j,0}$ and $r'_{i,j,1}$, respectively, of the same length (or, equivalently, we replace $h_1(s_i^b \oplus r_{i,j,b}) = h_1(s_i^b) \oplus h_1(r_{i,j,b})$ with $h_1(r'_{i,j,b})$ for $b = \{0,1\}$) in the creation of P_j^0, P_j^1, and each $\ell_{i,j}^0$ and $\ell_{i,j}^1$. This view is distributed identically to Hybrid 1 because XOR of a uniformly chosen string with any value produces a uniformly chosen string.

Now we arrive at a view where all s_i^0's and s_i^1's have been completely eliminated. The remaining information is the pairs $s_i^{x_i}, s_i^{1-x_i}$ and values derived from random $r_{i,j,b}$ and $r_{i,j,b}'$. It is clear that no information about x is revealed to a computationally bounded adversary and the claim of this lemma follows.   □

Now we are ready to proceed with showing that the construction complies with the security requirements for secure two-party function evaluation in the presence of malicious adversaries. In our result and its proof below, we assume a secure realization of the OT protocol secure in the presence of malicious parties is available to the participants, which they can call as a sub-protocol. Similarly, we rely on a secure realization of garbled circuit evaluation (in the presence of a semi-honest garbler).

Theorem 1. *Given an OT protocol secure against malicious participants and a circuit garbling and evaluation scheme secure against a semi-honest garbler and malicious evaluator, the proposed construction for secure function evaluation with certified inputs is secure according to Definition 1.*

Proof. First, suppose G is malicious and we denote the corresponding adversary as A_G. In the ideal world, simulator S_G resides between A_G and the trusted party and simulates G's view during the protocol execution as follows:

1. S_G invokes A_G on its input.
2. At the initial check step, S_G acts as honest E and verifies the signature on c. If verification fails, S_G aborts the execution.
3. S_G continues to act as an honest E would in steps 1 and 2, i.e., it receives the circuits, asks a predefined fraction of them at randomly chosen indices to be opened, and checks the opened circuits. If any of the checks fail, S_G aborts the execution.
4. In step 3(a), S_G simulates the OT with A_G. If any malicious behavior is detected, S_G aborts the execution and otherwise receives $t_{2n_1j+x_0}$, ..., $t_{2n_1j+2n_1-2+x_{n_1-1}}$ from A_G for each evaluation circuit j.
5. S_G obtains $f(x, y)$ from TP and communicates G's output according to the protocol to A_G.

We now need to analyze the differences in the real and simulated views. The first difference comes from the fact that S_G simulates the OT in step 4 as it does not possess E's real input. A_G, however, has a negligible chance in observing any differences because of the security of the underlying OT protocol (i.e., its simulation is indistinguishable from real execution). The second difference comes from the fact that in real execution E might fail to output the correct output because the circuits that it evaluated were incorrect. This, however, can happen only with probability $\mathsf{negl}(\rho)$. We therefore obtain that A_G is unable to distinguish the views with more than a negligible probability and they are indistinguishable.

Now suppose E is malicious. In the ideal world, simulator S_E resides between E and TP and simulates E's view during the protocol execution as follows:

1. S_E obtains certification $\langle c, \mathsf{Sign}_{sk}(c), (ck_j)_{j=0}^{\rho-1}, k' \rangle$ from the certification authority for some input $x' = x'_0 \ldots x'_{n_1-1}$ of its choice.
2. S_E invokes A_E on its input.
3. S_E extracts A_E's choices j for which circuits are to be opened during circuit checking and constructs those circuits correctly as an honest G would using information from c and the corresponding strings t_i's derived using k'.
4. To construct evaluation circuits, S_E creates G's input labels as an honest G would using certification information obtained for input x'. S_E then receives $f(x,y)$ from TP and construct the remaining portion of the garbled circuits so that they always output $f(x,y)$ (i.e., the circuits are input-insensitive).
5. S_E sends all circuits to A_E and opens the checking circuits upon A_E's request as an honest G would.
6. During circuit evaluation, S_E executes the OT with A_E as an honest G would. If any malicious behavior is detected, S_E aborts the execution and otherwise it sends $t_{2n_1j+x'_0}, \ldots, t_{2n_1j+2n_1-2+x'_{n_1-1}}$ generated using k' to A_E for each evaluation circuit j.
7. S_E continues as an honest G would.

With this simulation, we have two sources of potential differences between the real and simulated views. The first comes from modifying the way the evaluation circuits are constructed in step 4 to output a fixed value. This change has been shown in [20] to be indistinguishable to an adversary who has only a single set of labels corresponding to the inputs. That is, evaluation of modified circuits on arbitrary inputs is indistinguishable from evaluation of correct circuits on inputs x and y.

The second difference is that the certification corresponds to a randomly chosen x' instead of actual G's input x, which we need to analyze in more detail. In particular, c that A_E observes includes the pair $s_i^{x'_i}, s_i^{1-x'_i}$ for each input bit x'_i of x'. Because the certification authority chooses these strings uniformly at random for any possible input, the pairs $s_i^{x_i}, s_i^{1-x_i}$ and $s_i^{x'_i}, s_i^{1-x'_i}$ are distributed identically in the real and simulated views. For each opened (checking) circuit j, A_E also learns the values of P_j^0, P_j^1, Q_j, as well as G's input wire label pairs $\ell_{i,j}^0, \ell_{i,j}^1$ for each input wire i. From Lemma 1 we learn that these values are indistinguishable for inputs x and x' as well.

Lastly, for each evaluation circuit j, A_E only sees values $s_i^{x'_i}, s_i^{1-x'_i}, t_{2n_1j+2i+x'_i}, \mathsf{Enc}_{ck_j}(P_j^0 || P_j^1 || Q_j)$. Assuming CPA-security of the underlying encryption scheme, there is only a negligible chance that ciphertexts $\mathsf{Enc}_{ck_j}(P_j^0 || P_j^1 || Q_j)$ reveal any information to A_E. Lastly, in the absence of other relevant information, triples $s_i^{x'_i}, s_i^{1-x'_i}, t_{2n_1j+2i+x'_i}$ and $s_i^{x_i}, s_i^{1-x_i}, t_{2n_1j+2i+x_i}$ are identically distributed, giving A_E no information about the input bit to which the triple corresponds. Thus, the views in ideal and real executions are indistinguishable as well.

We obtain that the real and simulated views are indistinguishable when either G or E is corrupt, which concludes the proof. □

Recall that we rely on current countermeasures for defeating G's incorrect behavior such as cut-and-choose that instructs garbling of $O(\rho)$ circuits, checking a fraction of them, and evaluating the rest. Then according to the previously showed results, we obtain that any property verified at the circuit checking time will hold in the computed result with probability $1 - \mathsf{negl}(\rho)$. Our input correctness result for the garbler is as follows:

Theorem 2. *If all checking circuits pass all tests at the checking phase, the function is evaluated using garbler's inputs certified by the certification authority with probability $1 - \mathsf{negl}(\kappa) - \mathsf{negl}(\rho)$.*

In order to show this, we first prove a supplementary result.

Lemma 2. *If the checks of steps 2(c) and 2(d) hold for a garbled circuit and E can successfully evaluate the circuit (i.e., evaluation does not abort), the circuit used correct label pairs (ℓ_i^0, ℓ_i^1) generated by the certification authority for each of G's input wire i with probability $1 - \mathsf{negl}(\kappa)$.*

Proof. For simplicity of presentation, in this proof we omit notation j corresponding to the jth garbled circuit. Recall that we refer to the tests of step 2(c) as the "horizontal check," i.e., a consistency check performed over all inputs with the same value (such as zero bits and one bits) across all input bits, and the tests of step 2(d) as the "vertical check," i.e., a consistency check performed over both inputs of each input bit.

Recall that E evaluates a garbled circuit on labels $\ell_i^{x_i}$ computed as $h_1(s_i^{x_i} \oplus h_2(t_{2i+x_i}))$, where each $s_i^{x_i}$ comes from the certification authority. Thus, the goal of a corrupt G is to create a garbled circuit in such a way that E will compute a valid label for bit $1 - x_i$ using $s_i^{x_i}$ supplied by the certification authority. This could involve providing E with an incorrect value of t_{2i+x_i} or simply using $\ell_i^{x_i}$ to represent bit $1 - x_i$ for the ith input wire in the circuit. As we show below, the probability that the adversary is successful in carrying out either of this attacks is negligible in the security parameter κ.

Suppose that malicious G selects one specific input wire i for which it wants to corrupt labels. In what follows, we analyze two cases: (1) the adversary supplies the correct t_{2i+x_i} value to E, sets $\hat{\ell}_i^{1-x_i} = h_1(s_i^{x_i} \oplus h_2(t_{2i+x_i}))$ in the circuit, and adjusts other values accordingly and (2) the adversary supplies an incorrect $\hat{t}_{2i+x_i}$ to E, sets $\hat{\ell}_i^{1-x_i} = h_1(s_i^{x_i} \oplus h_2(\hat{t}_{2i+x_i}))$ in the circuit, and adjusts other values as needed. Recall that it is given that the circuit passes the checks of steps 2(c) and 2(d) and that the circuit could be successfully evaluated (i.e., the gates are correctly formed and use the labels that E computes). In what follows, we refer to the adversary and G interchangeably.

1. In this case, G communicates t_{2i+x_i} to E who will compute the value $h_1(s_i^{x_i} \oplus h_2(t_{2i+x_i}))$ at circuit evaluation time, while G's intent is to set $\hat{\ell}_i^{1-x_i} = \ell_i^{x_i} =$

$h_1(s_i^{x_i} \oplus h_2(t_{2i+x_i}))$ instead of the original $\ell_i^{1-x_i}$ during circuit garbling. Then if G sets $\hat{\ell}_i^{1-x_i} = \ell_i^{x_i}$, it will need to set $\hat{\ell}_i^{x_i} = \ell_i^{1-x_i}$ to be able to pass the vertical check (or break collision resistance of h_3 which only has a negligible probability of success). Now because the labels for both input bits of the ith input wire are modified from their expected values, the adversary needs to use other input labels to compensate for the difference to be able to pass the horizontal check. In particular, P^0 and P^1 values computed in step 2(c) of the protocol will be different by $\ell_i^{x_i} \oplus \ell_i^{1-x_i}$ from its expected value and G might use labels from $k \geq 1$ other input wires to compensate for the difference.

Now note that because h_1 is a universal hash function and its output is distributed uniformly over the entire space, $\ell_i^{x_i} \oplus \ell_i^{1-x_i}$ will also be uniformly distributed over the output space. Thus, if the adversary attempts to swap the input labels for any number of other input wires, it has only a negligible chance of matching the difference exactly. That is, for every new combination of input wires with swapped labels there is only a negligible probability of eliminating the difference and the adversary is limited to trying a polynomial number of such combinations.

If the adversary employs some strategy other than swapping input labels to compensate for the difference, it will be equivalent to solving case 2 below.

2. In this case, G sets $\hat{\ell}_i^{1-x_i} = h_1(s_i^{x_i} \oplus h_2(\hat{t}_{2i+x_i}))$ for some $\hat{t}_{2i+x_i} \neq t_{2i+x_i}$ instead of the original $\ell_i^{1-x_i}$ during circuit garbling. We can further sub-divide this into two cases:

   (a) The adversary was able to produce $\hat{\ell}_i^{1-x_i} = h_1(s_i^{x_i} \oplus h_2(\hat{t}_{2i+x_i}))$ to have the same value as the expected label $\ell_i^{1-x_i} = h_1(s_i^{1-x_i} \oplus h_2(t_{2i+x_i}))$. Then if $s_i^{x_i} \oplus h_2(\hat{t}_{2i+x_i}) = s_i^{1-x_i} \oplus h_2(t_{2i+x_i})$ and consequently $h_2(\hat{t}_{2i+x_i}) = s_i^{x_i} \oplus s_i^{1-x_i} \oplus h_2(t_{2i+x_i})$, the adversary has to break the one-way property of hash function h_2 to succeed in determining $\hat{t}_{2i+x_i}$, which it has to provide to E. This has only a negligible probability of success. Otherwise, $s_i^{x_i} \oplus h_2(\hat{t}_{2i+x_i}) \neq s_i^{1-x_i} \oplus h_2(t_{2i+x_i})$ and the adversary has to break the collision resistance property of h_2 to succeed, which also has only a negligible probability of success.

   (b) The adversary produces label $\hat{\ell}_i^{1-x_i} = h_1(s_i^{x_i} \oplus h_2(\hat{t}_{2i+x_i}))$ that differs from the expected label $\ell_i^{1-x_i}$. Then in order to pass the vertical check, the adversary will need to compute $\hat{\ell}_i^{x_i}$ such that $\hat{\ell}_i^{x_i} \oplus \hat{\ell}_i^{1-x_i} = \ell_i^{x_i} \oplus \ell_i^{1-x_i}$ or break the collision resilience property of hash function h_3. The probability of success in the latter case is negligible in the security parameter, while the former case can be analyzed as follows.

   Suppose G computes $\hat{\ell}_i^{x_i} = \hat{\ell}_i^{1-x_i} \oplus \ell_i^{x_i} \oplus \ell_i^{1-x_i} \neq \ell_i^{x_i}$. Then the use of $\hat{\ell}_i^{x_i}$ will fail the horizontal check if other labels are not modified. Consequently, the adversary might attempt to modify other labels to pass the check. Suppose the adversary chooses other $k \geq 1$ input wires $i_1, \ldots, i_k$ for which it will modify labels $\ell_{i_j}^{x_i}$ in the attempt to pass the horizontal check. That is, G is to compute $\hat{\ell}_{i_1}^{x_i}, \ldots, \hat{\ell}_{i_k}^{x_i}$, where $\bigoplus_{j=1}^{k} \hat{\ell}_{i_j}^{x_i}$ equals a specific value. First, suppose that $k = 1$. This means that G is to compute $\hat{\ell}_{i_1}^{x_i}$ that simultaneously satisfies $\hat{\ell}_i^{x_i} \oplus \hat{\ell}_{i_1}^{x_i} = t_1$ and $\hat{\ell}_{i_1}^{x_i} \oplus \ell_{i_1}^{1-x_i} = t_2$ for some fixed values t_1 and t_2 to pass the horizontal check using P^{x_i} and the vertical check for input wire i_1. Because $\hat{\ell}_i^{x_i}$ and $\ell_{i_1}^{1-x_i}$ are produced using hash function h_1, their values are uniformly distributed over the hash function's output space. This means that $\hat{\ell}_{i_1}^{x_i}$ can meet both of these requirements only with a negligible probability if $\ell_{i_1}^{1-x_i}$ remains unchanged. Thus, G could also change both labels for input wire i_1 (i.e., it sets $\hat{\ell}_{i_1}^{x_1} = t_1 \oplus \hat{\ell}_i^{x_i}$ and $\hat{\ell}_{i_1}^{1-x_1} = t_2 \oplus \hat{\ell}_{i_1}^{x_i}$). This, however, will require G to supply a consistent $\hat{t}_{2i_1+x_{i_1}}$ to E (for bit x_{i_1} which is equal to either x_i or $1-x_i$) to produce $\hat{\ell}_{i_1}^{x_{i_1}}$ using authentic $s_{i_1}^{x_{i_1}}$, which in turn can be done only if G inverts h_2. Now if we generalize the analysis to $k > 1$, we will still run into the case that there are more contradicting constraints on the values of $\hat{\ell}_{i_j}^{x_i}$ than the number of labels that G needs to set resulting in inability of the adversary to meet all of the constraints simultaneously or G will be required to invert h_2 at least for one input wire i_j.

Thus, we obtain that the adversary can succeed in modifying its input with probability at most negligible in κ in every possible case, which concludes the proof. □

We can now return to proving our main input correctness result.

Proof (Theorem 2). Recall that based on prior results, all properties verified during the circuit checking phase will hold for the computed result with probability $1 - \mathsf{negl}(\rho)$. This means that the conditions of Lemma 2 will also be satisfied with probability $p_1 = 1 - \mathsf{negl}(\rho)$. Furthermore, the result of Theorem 2 guarantees garbler's input correctness with probability $p_2 = 1 - \mathsf{negl}(\kappa)$, and input correctness will hold when both conditions are true. This happens with probability $p_1 \cdot p_2$ giving us probability of input correctness $1 - \mathsf{negl}(\kappa) - \mathsf{negl}(\rho)$ as desired. □

6   Conclusions

In this work, we treat the problem of strengthening the security guarantees of traditional formulations of secure multi-party computation. This is achieved by enforcing input correctness through input certification and tying certification to instances of secure function evaluation. The focus of this work is specifically on enforcing correctness of the garbler's input in secure two-party computation based on garbled circuit evaluation in the malicious model. We put forward a new certification mechanism specifically designed to be used with garbled circuit evaluation and show how to integrate certificates into secure computation to guarantee correctness of garbler's input. Our construction incurs minimal overhead and adds only one signature verification and $O(n\rho)$ symmetric key/hash operations to conventional garbled circuit evaluation using cut-and-choose in the malicious model that consist of garbling ρ circuits and where n is the size of the garbler's input in bits. We formally prove security of our construction.

Acknowledgments. This work was supported in part by grants 1223699 and 1319090 from the National Science Foundation and FA9550-13-1-0066 from the Air Force Office of Scientific Research. Any opinions, findings, and conclusions or recommendations expressed in this publication are those of the authors and do not necessarily reflect the views of the funding agencies.

References

1. Baum, C.: On garbling schemes with and without privacy. In: Zikas, V., Prisco, R. (eds.) SCN 2016. LNCS, vol. 9841, pp. 468–485. Springer, Cham (2016). doi:10. 1007/978-3-319-44618-9_25
2. Bellare, M., Hoang, V., Keelveedhi, S., Rogaway, P.: Efficient garbling from a fixed-key blockcipher. In: IEEE Symposium on Security and Privacy (SP), pp. 478–492 (2013)
3. Blanton, M., Bayatbabolghani, F.: Efficient server-aided secure two-party function evaluation with applications to genomic computation. Proc. Priv. Enhanc. Technol. (PoPET) **4**, 1–22 (2016)
4. Blanton, M., Gasti, P.: Secure and efficient protocols for iris and fingerprint identification. In: Atluri, V., Diaz, C. (eds.) ESORICS 2011. LNCS, vol. 6879, pp. 190–209. Springer, Heidelberg (2011). doi:10.1007/978-3-642-23822-2_11
5. Bogdanov, D., Laur, S., Willemson, J.: Sharemind: a framework for fast privacy-preserving computations. In: Jajodia, S., Lopez, J. (eds.) ESORICS 2008. LNCS, vol. 5283, pp. 192–206. Springer, Heidelberg (2008). doi:10.1007/ 978-3-540-88313-5_13
6. Camenisch, J., Lysyanskaya, A.: A signature scheme with efficient protocols. In: Cimato, S., Persiano, G., Galdi, C. (eds.) SCN 2002. LNCS, vol. 2576, pp. 268–289. Springer, Heidelberg (2003). doi:10.1007/3-540-36413-7_20
7. Camenisch, J., Lysyanskaya, A.: Signature schemes and anonymous credentials from bilinear maps. In: Franklin, M. (ed.) CRYPTO 2004. LNCS, vol. 3152, pp. 56–72. Springer, Heidelberg (2004). doi:10.1007/978-3-540-28628-8_4
8. Camenisch, J., Sommer, D., Zimmermann, R.: A general certification framework with applications to privacy-enhancing certificate infrastructures. In: Fischer-Hübner, S., Rannenberg, K., Yngström, L., Lindskog, S. (eds.) SEC 2006. IIFIP, vol. 201, pp. 25–37. Springer, Boston, MA (2006). doi:10.1007/ 0-387-33406-8_3
9. Camenisch, J., Zaverucha, G.M.: Private intersection of certified sets. In: Dingledine, R., Golle, P. (eds.) FC 2009. LNCS, vol. 5628, pp. 108–127. Springer, Heidelberg (2009). doi:10.1007/978-3-642-03549-4_7
10. Damgård, I., Pastro, V., Smart, N., Zakarias, S.: Multiparty computation from somewhat homomorphic encryption. In: Safavi-Naini, R., Canetti, R. (eds.) CRYPTO 2012. LNCS, vol. 7417, pp. 643–662. Springer, Heidelberg (2012). doi:10. 1007/978-3-642-32009-5_38
11. Cristofaro, E., Tsudik, G.: Practical private set intersection protocols with linear complexity. In: Sion, R. (ed.) FC 2010. LNCS, vol. 6052, pp. 143–159. Springer, Heidelberg (2010). doi:10.1007/978-3-642-14577-3_13
12. Goldreich, O., Micali, S., Wigderson, A.: Proofs that yield nothing but their validity or all languages in NP have zero-knowledge proof systems. J. ACM **38**(3), 690–728 (1991)

13. Goldwasser, S., Micali, S., Wigderson, A.: How to play any mental game, or a completeness theorem for protocols with an honest majority. In: ACM Symposium on the Theory of Computing (STOC), pp. 218–229 (1987)
14. Halpern, J., Teague, V.: Rational secret sharing and multiparty computation. In: ACM Symposium on Theory of Computing (STOC), pp. 623–632 (2004)
15. Kantarcioglu, M., Nix, R.: Incentive compatible distributed data mining. In: IEEE International Conference on Privacy, Security, Risk and Trust (PASSAT) (2010)
16. Katz, J., Malozemoff, A.J., Wang, X.: Efficiently enforcing input validity in secure two-party computation. IACR Cryptology ePrint Archive Report 2016/184 (2016)
17. Kolesnikov, V., Kumaresan, R., Shikfa, A.: Efficient verification of input consistency in server-assisted secure function evaluation. In: Pieprzyk, J., Sadeghi, A.-R., Manulis, M. (eds.) CANS 2012. LNCS, vol. 7712, pp. 201–217. Springer, Heidelberg (2012). doi:10.1007/978-3-642-35404-5_16
18. Kreuter, B., Shelat, A., Mood, B., Butler, K.: PCF: a portable circuit format for scalable two-party secure computation. In: USENIX Security Symposium (2013)
19. Lindell, Y.: Fast cut-and-choose based protocols for malicious and covert adversaries. In: Canetti, R., Garay, J.A. (eds.) CRYPTO 2013. LNCS, vol. 8043, pp. 1–17. Springer, Heidelberg (2013). doi:10.1007/978-3-642-40084-1_1
20. Lindell, Y., Pinkas, B.: An efficient protocol for secure two-party computation in the presence of malicious adversaries. In: Naor, M. (ed.) EUROCRYPT 2007. LNCS, vol. 4515, pp. 52–78. Springer, Heidelberg (2007). doi:10.1007/978-3-540-72540-4_4
21. Lindell, Y., Pinkas, B.: A proof of security of Yao's protocol for two-party computation. J. Cryptol. **22**(2), 161–188 (2009)
22. Mohassel, P., Franklin, M.: Efficiency tradeoffs for malicious two-party computation. In: Yung, M., Dodis, Y., Kiayias, A., Malkin, T. (eds.) PKC 2006. LNCS, vol. 3958, pp. 458–473. Springer, Heidelberg (2006). doi:10.1007/11745853_30
23. Sadeghi, A.-R., Schneider, T., Wehrenberg, I.: Efficient privacy-preserving face recognition. In: Lee, D., Hong, S. (eds.) ICISC 2009. LNCS, vol. 5984, pp. 229–244. Springer, Heidelberg (2010). doi:10.1007/978-3-642-14423-3_16
24. Shelat, A., Shen, C.: Two-output secure computation with malicious adversaries. In: Paterson, K.G. (ed.) EUROCRYPT 2011. LNCS, vol. 6632, pp. 386–405. Springer, Heidelberg (2011). doi:10.1007/978-3-642-20465-4_22
25. Shelat, A., Shen, C.H.: Fast two-party secure computation with minimal assumptions. In: ACM Conference on Computer and Communications Security (CCS), pp. 523–534 (2013)
26. Shoham, Y., Tennenholtz, M.: Non-cooperative computation: boolean functions with correctness and exclusivity. Theor. Comput. Sci. (TCS) **343**(1), 97–113 (2005)
27. Wallrabenstein, J.R., Clifton, C.: Equilibrium concepts for rational multiparty computation. In: Das, S.K., Nita-Rotaru, C., Kantarcioglu, M. (eds.) GameSec 2013. LNCS, vol. 8252, pp. 226–245. Springer, Cham (2013). doi:10.1007/978-3-319-02786-9_14
28. Wallrabenstein, J.R., Clifton, C.: Realizable rational multiparty cryptographic protocols. In: Poovendran, R., Saad, W. (eds.) GameSec 2014. LNCS, vol. 8840, pp. 134–154. Springer, Cham (2014). doi:10.1007/978-3-319-12601-2_8
29. Woodruff, D.P.: Revisiting the efficiency of malicious two-party computation. In: Naor, M. (ed.) EUROCRYPT 2007. LNCS, vol. 4515, pp. 79–96. Springer, Heidelberg (2007). doi:10.1007/978-3-540-72540-4_5
30. Yao, A.C.: How to generate and exchange secrets. In: IEEE Symposium on Foundations of Computer Science (FOCS), pp. 162–167 (1986)

Author Index